Marriage and Family Interaction

THE DORSEY SERIES IN SOCIOLOGY

Editor

Robin M. Williams, Jr.　*Cornell University*

FOURTH EDITION

Marriage and Family Interaction

ROBERT R. BELL
Temple University

 **1975**

THE DORSEY PRESS   *Homewood, Illinois   60430*
Irwin-Dorsey International   London, England   WC2H 9NJ
Irwin-Dorsey Limited   Georgetown, Ontario   L7G 4B3

Fourth Edition

First Printing, February 1975

ISBN 0-256-01631-3
Library of Congress Catalog Card No. 74–24457
Printed in the United States of America

To my wife,
PHYLLIS
and our daughters,
MARTA LEE and ROBIN ANN

Preface

In planning the fourth edition of this text I considered the possible inclusion of a number of new topics, as well as the possibility of alternative ways of presenting and interpreting data. But it seemed that any major shift in orientation would result in a book quite different from the first three editions. Therefore, in deciding what approach to take toward the revisions, I held to the definition presented in the Preface of the first edition: this book "is primarily a functional text for marriage and family courses, but the orientation is not functional in the 'how-to-do-it' sense." I continue to believe that any contribution I might make to the student is as a sociologist of the family and not as a prescriber of behavior.

In this fourth edition the number of chapters has been expanded from 21 to 24 by the addition of three new chapters (Chapters 7, 13, and 24). I have pruned from many chapters material that no longer appeared appropriate. Most chapters have been modified on the basis of new materials and ideas since the previous edition. As a result some of the chapters have been changed very little and others very much.

As always I am most indebted to my wife for her interest and for the professional contribution she makes to my work.

January 1975

Robert R. Bell

Contents

Part Three
Marriage, Parenthood, and Other Adult Roles

Part Four
Marriage Breakdown and Alteration

Part One

Background

Chapter 1

The Study of Marriage and the Family

With few exceptions, all who read this book have had the experience of being a member of a family. As a matter of fact, most Americans will be members of three different, but related, families: the family of *orientation,* in which the role is that of the child, and the primary relationships are to parents and siblings; the family of *procreation,* in which the role is that of husband or wife, and the primary relationships are to the spouse and children; and the *in-law* family, in which the role is that of an in-law, and the primary relationships are to parents-in-law and siblings-in-law. Because of these common, personal experiences, the individual often sees himself as an authority on the family—and he is, as regards his own, personal family relationships.

The individual moving through his own families of orientation and procreation develops the characteristics of becoming social, and the acquisition of these social skills enables him to contribute to the perpetuation of society. As Arensberg has pointed out, the families of orientation and procreation are two families in "a repetitive succession of like social organisms, families, endlessly transmitting cultural and social experience."[1] That is, they are constantly making the individual social and—by doing so—they are at the same time perpetuating society.

---

[1] Conrad M. Arensberg, "The American Family in the Perspective of Other Cultures," in Eli Ginzberg, ed., *The Nation's Children* (New York: Columbia University Press, 1960), p. 54.

This book will attempt to move its readers from their personal understanding of the family to a broader, more generalized understanding of marriage and family relationships in contemporary America. An individual may react to portions of the discussion with, "I know that from my own experience." Certainly much that will be said about the family will correspond to everyone's experience, because of cultural patterns common to American society. However, the social scientist often studies what people *think* they already know in order to provide evidence about the accuracy of those assumptions. And sometimes the results of such studies indicate that what we "know" is not, in fact, true.

This book is based on the belief that disciplined thought and controlled research are the best means of providing knowledge and understanding of marriage and family relationship. This is not to say that an individual, with skillful uses of his senses and intelligence, cannot give an insightful picture of marriage and the family. He can, and does—as, for example, the able novelist does—but he is restricted for the most part to his own, always limited observations. The social scientist, on the other hand, draws upon the disciplined analysis of many observers to provide a general picture of marriage and the family.

STUDYING AMERICAN MARRIAGE AND FAMILY

A number of different approaches to an academic analysis of marriage and family relationships exist. No one approach can—or at least it rarely does—claim absolute jurisdiction, but each sees the family within the confines of its specific orientation. A single text cannot possibly incorporate, in a meaningful way, the orientations and findings of all the many different approaches that are concerned with marriage and the family. For example, the various "personality" approaches (for the most part ignored in this book) study and treat the individual and his family experiences from or "through" the individual personality. But while "personality" findings are of great significance, they do not always lend themselves to analysis within the *social* framework of a book such as this.

The study of the family in this book centers around a sociological and a social-psychological approach. These two interrelated approaches are the theoretical orientations followed by many sociologists in studying marriage and the family. Social scientists usually focus on any one, or combinations of four interrelated sets of family characteristics: first, the formal nature of family relationships, such as kinship ties; second, the demographic or population factors related to the family; third, the cultural approach, which looks at the family in relationship to the specific culture of which it is a part; and fourth, the social-psychological relationships[2] of which the family is a part. All of these points of emphasis will be used to some extent in discussing marriage and family relationships; however, this book primarily follows the social-psychological approach.

The following definition of the family, taken from Burgess and Locke, indicates the basic conception of the family used in this book:

> The family is a unit of interacting and intercommunicating persons enacting the social roles of husband and wife, mother and father, son and daughter, brother and sister. The roles are defined by the community, but in each family they are powerfully reinforced by sentiments, partly traditional and partly emotional, arising out of experience.[3]

The family as a concept is an abstraction. It serves as a guide to what societies define as appropriate. For example, the ideal family, as an abstraction, consists of a husband and wife and their dependent children, living in a household of their own, provided for by the husband's earnings as the main breadwinner, and emotionally united by the wife's exclusive concentration on the home. This is an ideal rather than an absolute reality because "probably no more than one third of all families at a particular moment in time, and chiefly in the middle and would-be middle classes, actually live up to this image."[4]

Later in this chapter, more will be said about the theoretical approach to be taken, but at this point it is more germane to discuss the nature of research in the marriage and family area. Social scientists accept the need for empirical research as a basic tenet of their discipline. In studying marriage and the family, particular research problems emerge because of the nature of the subject matter. While individuals frequently react with little personal emotion to an economist studying consumer behavior or a political scientist analyzing voting behavior, they will often react strongly to the sociologist studying an area of marriage and family that is of interest and importance to his discipline. For example, the study of sexual behavior is one of the most important areas for sociological research—yet it has been, at the same time, probably the most sensitive study area as far as the general public is concerned. It is also a substantive area that has been of limited research interest to sociologists.

Research Problems

Behavioral studies of premarital sex have had the effect of forcing many adults to recognize that the behavior of the young unmarried

---

[2] Ernest W. Burgess and Harvey Locke, *The Family* (New York: American Book Co., 1953), p. 7.

[3] Ibid., p. 6.

[4] Suzanne Keller, "Does the Family Have a Future?" *A Warner Modular Publication,* reprint 64 (1973), p. 4.

population does not correspond to society's values. Because their personal assumptions are thus questioned, many Americans feel threatened by these behavioral studies; as a result, many react to them with great moral indignation, thereby implying that human sexual behavior would be better left unstudied. Disbelief is another common reaction when people are faced with behavioral information that indicates not everyone behaves in a prescribed manner. People prefer to cling to an idealized, nonfactual interpretation of human behavior, rather than accept the unidealized, documented version presented by the social scientist. Sometimes a person will react by saying, "Maybe the rest of the world is that way, but not the part I live in." The rest of the world may be perceived as different without discomfort, but not the part identified with by the individual himself.

Further, because the human being functions in a social setting, he often feels that he knows as much about general human behavior as the social scientist. Yet the social scientist, with all the limitations and problems he encounters as a result of the complexity of his data, presents a far more accurate picture of human behavior than does the untrained individual. Some of the assumptions and controls followed by the sociologist illustrate this greater reliability. First, he believes that all areas of human behavior can be made the focus of study, though he recognizes that some areas are much more complex and difficult to study than others. "There is an honesty in science which refuses to accept the idea that there are aspects of the material universe that are better not investigated, or better not known, or the knowledge of which should not be made available to the common man."[5]

Second, a basic tenet of all science is that scientific knowledge is open to all, rather than reserved for a select few. Thus, in a democracy, the individual has the right of access to knowledge and the choice of its use, within the limits of legal and social sanctions. In a totalitarian society, on the other hand, few such rights exist, and little or no social science exists because human behavior is determined and explained by political dogma. People in a democracy do not assume a single dogmatic explanation of human behavior; rather, they recognize a pluralistic explanation. For example, the scientific, the religious, the artistic, and the philosophical points of view all have an equal right to be heard and evaluated.

Third, the scientist makes every possible attempt to control biases in his investigations. The greater the degree of control over biases, the closer research findings will be to the scientific ideal of objectivity. Because scientific research seeks unbiased, empirical evidence, the results of scientific inquiry may go counter to accepted social beliefs. Hence,

---

[5] Alfred C. Kinsey et al., *Sexual Behavior in the Human Female* (Philadelphia: W. B. Saunders, 1953), p. 9.

the scientist must be constantly aware of the dangers of bias or vested interest. No study can be called scientific if the results have not been arrived at objectively, or if the results are altered to fit some predetermined value assumptions.

Fourth, a distinction must be made between a moral and a scientific interest in right and wrong. The moralist believes certain human behavior to be right; evidence showing that many people do not function accordingly does not repudiate his moral definition. He continues to believe that certain behavior is right and that this is a prescription for human action, even if it is not a description of actual behavior. The scientist, then, views right and wrong only as values and attitudes to be studied and considered in his investigations. His findings attempt to describe and explain behavior as he finds it, not according to what he thinks it should be. It is important to keep in mind that science cannot provide a system of morality, not even a rational morality, because "moral values cannot be scientifically proven; they must be chosen."[6]

Even without such problems, however, the researcher interested in the family in America does not study all areas of marriage and family, nor is the amount of his research always determined by some measurement of significance. In general, family research has been most concentrated on dating and courtship, sexual behavior, and the socialization of the child. By contrast, much less has been done on various aspects of marriage relationships, and particularly on the older person in marriage and family relationships.[7]

The focus of research so far has been influenced partly by the researcher's particular interests, and often by the high cost of many types of research. Costs not only influence what will be studied, but often the method of study and the particular populations studied. The most extensive, and usually the methodologically most sophisticated, studies have been done when large grants were available and "team research" was possible. The comprehensive studies on sexual behavior and family fertility are illustrations.[8]

Many marriage and family research studies have used samples of only several hundred; extending the findings to larger populations must be done with caution. For example, the family researcher is often accused

---

[6] Ira L. Reiss, "Personal Values and the Scientific Study of Sex," in *Advances in Sex Research* (New York: Harper & Row, 1963), p. 8.

[7] Nelson N. Foote, "New Roles for Men and Women," *Marriage and Family Living*, November 1961, pp. 325–29.

[8] See Kinsey et al., *Female*, Ronald Freedman, Pascal K. Whelpton, and Arthur A. Campbell, *Family Planning, Sterility, and Population Growth* (New York: McGraw-Hill Book Co., 1959); Charles F. Westoff et al., *Family Growth in Metropolitan America* (Princeton, New Jersey: Princeton University Press, 1961); and Charles F. Westoff and Norman B. Ryder, "United States: Methods of Fertility Control, 1955, 1960, and 1965," *Studies in Family Planning*, no. 17 (1967).

of studying the "college sophomore." The charge contains a great deal of truth, and implies that he should be studying some larger and more representative population sample. The researcher would agree, except that often his choice is to study the small group, or none at all. Even the small groups studied provide at least some empirical evidence for an understanding of marriage and the family. In this book, many such small studies will be quoted. The tentative and restricted nature of the findings should always be kept in mind; but the findings should be recognized as providing at least some empirical evidence more reliable than individual experiences or nonempirical armchair speculation.

AMERICAN MARRIAGE AND FAMILY

Man, with his specialized ability to use symbols, has the ability to create a vast variety of complex and often different social systems. "Marriage and the family in human society are what they are because man, although biologically conditioned, yet has a capacity for creativity so that repeatedly he invents something new and unexpected."[9] Uniformities, as well as many cultural variations, are usually found in families of different societies. Furthermore, a function performed by the family at one point in time may, at another point, be taken over by other agencies of society. Some functions performed by the family are often interpreted as being functions that can *only* be performed by the family. Yet, given different cultures or variations within any one culture, probably all functions that are traditionally the family's have been performed on some occasions by other social agencies. For example, Reiss suggests that the family institution is a small, kinship-structured group that *generally* performs the key function of nurturance. This is usually provided by the parents, although there is nothing inherent in the function itself that requires that it be done by the biological parents, or even by a female or an adult.[10] The *only* requirement is that the nurturant function be performed by some socially functioning individual.

It appears that the small family unit, made up of parents and children, and referred to as the nuclear or conjugal family is not only common to the United States but also to most countries of the world today. Burch found in his analysis of population data from many countries that none had a national average family size greater than 6.5 persons. He goes on to observe that in every country except India, "the nuclear family comprises 80 percent or more of the total family group (all related persons living in the household). Looked at differently, less than one quarter of

---

[9] Arnold S. Nash, "Ancient Past and Living Present," in Howard Becker and Reuben Hill, *Family, Marriage and Parenthood* (Boston: D. C. Heath & Co., 1955), p. 85.

[10] Ira L. Reiss, "The Universality of the Family: A Conceptual Analysis," *Journal of Marriage and the Family,* November 1965, p. 449.

the members of families see persons other than the head, his spouse and own children, that is, other relatives."[11]

The belief in the conjugal family asserts the right of the person to choose his own partner in marriage, where they want to live, and even what kinship ties they want to accept. "It asserts the worth of the *individual* as against the inherited elements of wealth or ethnic groups. The *individual* is to be evaluated, not his lineage."[12]

The American family has been historically characterized by change and the loss of many traditional functions. As a result, the family "has become a more specialized agency than before, probably more specialized than it has been in any previously known society."[13] For example, the American family has partly relinquished to other social agencies such functions as: economic unit of production, formal teaching of offspring, protection, care of the aged, and recreation. The result, of course, as Dager suggests, is that however functional these changes may be for the larger society, they are becoming increasingly nonfunctional for individuals. "Symbolic of this nonfunction is the increasing reliance by families upon many secondary agencies: social security, industrial retirement programs, care of the aged, a plethora of welfare agencies, care for the young in the form of day nurseries, play schools, nursery schools, pre-kindergartens, and baby-sitting, fringe benefits, and so on."[14]

Parsons and Bales have pointed out that, as a result of these changes, the American family now has only two basic functions: "first, the primary socialization of children so that they can truly become members of the society into which they have been born; second, the stabilization of the adult personalities of the population of the society."[15] But even though these two functions are primarily assigned to the family, other agencies of society are also involved. For example, the extending of formal education in nursery schools down to younger ages means that the educational institution is entering the socialization of the child at an earlier age than ever before. The nonfamily influences on adult personalities are recognized by Parsons and Bales when they write that "adult members must have roles other than their familial roles which occupy strategically important places in their own personalities."[16]

In line with the two functions suggested by Parsons and Bales, an-

---

[11] Thomas K. Burch, "The Size and Structure of Families: A Comparative Analysis of Census Data," *American Sociological Review*, June 1967, p. 358.

[12] William Goode, *World Revolution and Family Patterns* (New York: The Free Press of Glencoe, 1963), p. 19.

[13] Talcott Parsons and Robert F. Bales, *Family, Socialization and Interaction Process* (Glencoe, Illinois: The Free Press, 1955), p. 9.

[14] Edward Z. Dager, "Socialization and Personality Development in the Child," in Harold T. Christensen, ed., *Handbook of Marriage and the Family* (Chicago: Rand McNally & Co., 1964), p. 776.

[15] Parsons and Bales, *Interaction Process*, pp. 16–17.

[16] Ibid., p. 19.

other primary basic function, especially in the middle class, centers around the satisfaction of ego-needs through marriage and family relationships. By *ego-needs* is meant the desire of the individual to achieve emotional satisfaction from the giving and receiving of meaning and importance in interaction with another person. Ego-needs extend to many social relationships outside of the marriage and family setting. However, our main interest is in the family, where the basic ego-needs center in the emotional give and take between husband and wife, parents and children, and siblings.

The American family continues to be for most individuals the setting for satisfying their basic ego-needs. However, more individuals are looking outside the traditional family setting to have their ego-needs met. To some extent it appears that the family is less overwhelming in meeting ego-needs of as many persons as it was in the past.

The high divorce rate in the United States offers further support as to the importance of ego-need satisfaction. Many individuals get a divorce because they failed to find satisfaction with the person they had married. Apparently, however, they were not disillusioned with marriage in general, but rather with a specific marriage, as attested by the very high remarriage rates of the divorced. Often the divorcee enters the second marriage hoping to find a satisfying ego-need relationship that did not exist in the first marriage.

The ego-need factor in marriage and family relationships is one of the major themes of this book. The reader may assess the validity of the argument after he reads the book; that is, after evidence supporting the theme has been analyzed throughout discussion of the various facets of marriage and family interaction.

One other general characteristic of the American family should also be kept in mind: In at least one important respect the family as a social institution is very different from other social institutions; it is in the family setting that the individual usually spends the greatest number of years in his most pervasive interpersonal relationships. Because the individual often has a strong emotional commitment to certain family roles and role relationships, he may be "used" in his family roles to meet the needs of other social institutions. This point can be illustrated by the example of the relationship of family roles to illness as it is controlled by medical institutions.

Often the family's responsibility in taking care of its sick members is seen as primarily meeting the needs of medical institutions, and only in a secondary way is there any concern with how the family's care of its sick members may affect the family itself. For example, the home-care movement in the United States is supported by funds from agencies with an interest in increasingly facilitating their own beliefs about the care of the ill. Some of these home-care agencies' assumptions about the family's role are illustrated by their hope to return mentally ill persons to their families. Vincent writes that "the family is expected to adapt to the return of its mentally ill or emotionally disturbed members, just as it was expected to adapt to the return of the parolee member of the family several decades ago. The family will also be expected to adapt to the intrusion of the mental health personnel concerned with the rehabilitation of the patient, just as it has adapted to the intrusion of the parole and probation officers, the judge of the juvenile court and the social worker."[17] Given the emotional involvement of family members with one another, it is not difficult to persuade them of their "responsibility." As Vincent puts it: "Given the mores of our society, how could the family maintain its ideological image if it refused to accept one of its members convalescing from mental illness or rehabilitating from crime or delinquency."[18]

There are institutions besides those of health care that may use the emotional commitment of family members to one another. For example, institutions of education, or of government, or of religion. This is not to say that the "use" of the family is necessarily undesirable, but simply to point out that the special emotional nature of the family makes it susceptible to being persuaded that it is serving its members, while in fact it is at the same time meeting the needs of another social institution.

SOCIAL CLASS

The complexity of marriage and family relationships in the United States today is great. To talk about "American marriage and the family" is to state a generality that stresses common patterns. However, anyone who studies the family quickly realizes that, within American marriage and family, many significant variations exist. For example, there are significant differences by social class, religion, ethnic, and racial background. The decision to concentrate in this book primarily on modern middle-class marriage and family relationships was made for several reasons. First, the middle class is increasing in size and significance in the American society. If any marriage and family pattern is emerging as typical of American society, it is that of the middle class. Second, the great bulk of empirical research has been done with middle-class subjects. Therefore, middle-class orientation provides the best opportunity for showing what is known through research. Third, the vast majority of readers of this book either are in or will be in the middle class. An academic analysis may contribute to a greater understanding of the nature of middle-class marriage and family, allowing the reader to better "see"

---

[17] Clarke E. Vincent, "Familia Spongia: The Adaptive Function," *National Council on Family Relations,* Toronto, Canada, October 1965, p. 13.

[18] Ibid., p. 13.

the family relationships he has experienced and will experience at various stages of marriage and family interaction.

Meaning

Social class, as a variable of social analysis, is of great significance in describing, explaining, and predicting many facets of social thought and behavior. Lloyd Warner, one of the pioneers in the sociology of social classes, writes "recent scientific studies of social class in the several regions of the United States demonstrated that it is a major determinate of individual decisions and social action; that every major area of American life is directly and indirectly influenced by our class order; and that the major decisions of most individuals are partly controlled by it."[19] This statement does not suggest that social class is an absolute variable, but rather that it is more reliable than many other variables in distinguishing significant variations in social thought and behavior.

One problem, still far from being resolved in the study of social class, is determining the number of different classes in the United States. The number has been estimated at anywhere from two to twelve. However, six class levels will be used here. As Bergel suggests, "on a nationwide basis the six categories are preferable—scale provides an excellent working proposition ('statistical' classes) and fairly depicts the actual situation ('social' classes)."[20]

The six classes are:

Upper-upper class	Lower-middle class
Lower-upper class	Upper-lower class
Upper-middle class	Lower-lower class

Differing social classes should be considered as a conception of "ideal types," or models that describe hypothetical social class positions. A hierarchy of "ideal types" makes it possible to relate, order, and compare the fit of social reality. Persons or families might be placed, for example, in the upper-middle class because they more closely approximate that "ideal type" than any of the others; but few will "fit" exactly. The use of "ideal-type" social classes is essentially the same as the method used in medicine to diagnose a health problem. The physician catalogs as many of the patient's determinable variables as possible, and then "names" the patient's medical problem as that which most closely approximates one of his medical "ideal types." Analogously, in the study of social class one can rarely be absolutely sure of diagnoses because

[19] W. Lloyd Warner, Marchia Meeker, and Kenneth Eells, *Social Class in America* (New York: Harper Torchbooks, 1960), p. 6.

[20] Egan E. Bergel, *Social Stratification* (New York: McGraw-Hill Book Co., 1962), p. 259.

cases rarely fit the "ideal type," and because "ideal types" are never complete or absolute empirical models.

How Social Classes Differ. Most Americans can and do make crude distinctions between themselves and others on the basis of social class, whether they are aware they do or not. Such frequently heard expressions as "We have nothing in common," "They live differently," or "They are not our kind" often imply social class distinctions. However, the characteristics which show social class differences are more numerous and complex than the casual observer generally recognizes.

Social scientists have used several approaches to distinguish social classes.[21] By what may be called the *subjective* approach, individuals rate themselves or rate others in their community. Self-ratings often produce great distortion; for example, as many as nine out of ten Americans identify themselves as middle class.[22] Ratings of individuals by other individuals are more reliable but require a community where many individuals are known to each other.[23] In a second approach, which may be called the *objective,* ratings according to certain variables (education, income, etc.) are made either singly or through the use of multiple correlation scales. In general, the objective approach is more reliable than the subjective.

Individuals in a given social class share both the same general degree of a certain variable and common values. Social-class value orientations "usually combine aspects of *ought* (value) and aspects of *is* (existential beliefs about reality)."[24] The sharing of social-class values is related to differential social interaction; that is, because most significant relationships occur between individuals of the same social-class level, at least some values, qualities, and skills common to the particular social class are inculcated and cultivated.

The family is the most important agency, at least initially, in determining the differential social-class associations of the individual. The family is important because the children of a family, at least until they grow up, have the social-class position of their parents. Norms and values differ from one social class to another, but whatever they are, they help guide social interaction and provide some of the standards an individual uses in making evaluations. The family initially provides the norms and values which must be socially acquired. Because various values related to social-class position are acquired during the formative years, they often

---

[21] For a good discussion of the various theories and methods used in the study of social class, see Leonard Reissman, *Class in American Society* (Glencoe, Ill.: The Free Press, 1959).

[22] Bergel, *Stratification,* p. 260.

[23] Warner, *Social Class,* p. 6.

[24] Joseph A. Kahl, *The American Class Structure* (New York: Rinehart & Co., Inc., 1957), p. 185.

seem "natural" to the individual. Furthermore, these values are often re-inforced by nonfamily associates, since the individual usually interacts with persons of similar social-class background. The very fact that the person feels at ease and has a sense of naturalness with others like himself tends to drive a wedge between his "world" and those in different social-class "worlds."

The fact that the family is the unit for measuring social stratification has some limiting factors. For example, in 1970 about 11 percent of the population over age 18 were defined as unattached individuals. They would not be examined or studied under the family unit measurement of stratification. Furthermore, because the social position of the family is determined by the status of the male head of household, the status of women is determined by the males to whom they are attached.[25] It is wise to keep these limitations in mind in the later discussions of social-class differences.

The lines between the different social classes cannot be sharply drawn or held to be absolute. Some families will fall between two adjoining social classes and not fit one more than the other. American society is complex and contains a variety of hierarchies of social values and variables. Therefore, an individual may fall into one social class according to a number of different criteria, but into a different class according to other criteria, making his overall social-class position difficult to determine. But, even recognizing the problems of classification, significant general differences between the social classes may still be observed. The various classes should be seen as having average, but not absolute, differences.

The Middle Class

The old middle class in the United States represented the rather small percentage of the population that had its economic base in the ownership of small, independent property. Since about the time of the Civil War, however, a new and much extended middle-class, occupationally centered around technical-managerial, professional, and clerical employees, has emerged.

The percentage of the American population in the middle class cannot be estimated accurately, but Bergel's estimate of about 40 percent of the population will suffice for our purposes. Of this estimate, about 15 per-cent are in the upper-middle class and the other 25 percent in the lower-middle class. By occupation, clerical and sales workers constitute the bulk of the lower-middle class, while professionals, proprietors, and man-

---

[25] Joan Acker, "Women and Social Stratification: A Case of Intellectual Sexism," in Joan Huber, *Changing Women in a Changing Society* (Chicago: University of Chicago Press, 1973), p. 175.

agers characterize the upper-middle class.[26] By education, the lower-middle class usually has no more than a high school education, while the upper-middle class has at least some college. The variables used to distinguish the two middle classes are admittedly crude, but provide a general picture. While the broad middle class will often be discussed, the *upper*-middle class is the more common focus in this book.

The three values briefly discussed next provide a broad framework for understanding some areas of middle-class marriage and the family. These values often overlap, of course, and have varying influences on each other.

Social Mobility. A common belief, handed down as part of the American democratic tradition, has supported the idea of the "rugged individualist" who could attain upward social mobility by hard work and perseverance. In part, this belief still prevails, but upward mobility is more often believed to be best achieved today by proper preparation, particularly through the use of extended formal education.

An outstanding characteristic of contemporary mobility aspirations is that the values are instilled by the parents early in the child's life. Middle-class parents feel that they must at least help their children solidify their social-class position and, if possible, improve it; thus, one common middle-class value is the parents' conscious concern for their children's social mobility.

That upward social mobility is possible is shown by the fact that individuals do move up from their parents' social class. However, social mobility as a value often leads to problems. For example, what happens to the individual taught to be socially mobile, but who is unsuccessful? While some individuals reassess their mobility aspirations in light of their experience, many who have accepted the values probably feel at least some sense of frustration. Myers and Roberts found mobility frustration highly correlated with mental health problems. The patients they studied were under constant tension because of their mobility efforts and felt extremely frustrated by their lack of success.[27]

Even those who are successful may have problems. Ironically, parents who help their children move up in the social-class hierarchy often find that their children's new values and way of life make strangers of them. Successfully mobile children may also be insecure in their new position and have to make a constant effort to present a correct "front." Goffman writes, "commonly we find that upward mobility involves the presentation of proper performances and that efforts to move upward and efforts to keep from moving downward are expressed in terms of sacrifices made

---

[26] Bergel, *Stratification*, p. 272.

[27] Jerome K. Myers and Bertram H. Roberts, *Family and Class Dynamics in Mental Illness* (New York: John Wiley & Sons, Inc., 1959), p. 252.

for the maintenance of front."[28] Max Lerner vividly illustrates the nature of mobility anxiety when he writes: "They (the middle class) form a loose collection of occupational strata, probably more anxiety-ridden than the rest of the culture, dominated by the drive to distinguish them- selves from the working class, uncohesive, held together by no common bond except the fact that they are caught in a kind of Purgatory between the Hell of the poor and weak and the Heaven of the rich and powerful."[29]

Success. Closely related to the belief in social mobility is the belief in success; but success, like mobility, has a different meaning today than it had in the past. In theory, the sky was the limit for personal success in the past; today, the kind and degree of success is stressed. "Not economic security alone but a whole psychic security syndrome is involved"[30] in middle-class success. Many times the successful young man is one who enters an occupation that provides only a limited possibility for individual achievement but gives him the security of having a place, of belonging.

Thus in the middle class, success and security have become inter- related. The individual sees himself in competition with an amorphous "they"—those he wants to move away from through social mobility. On the other hand, he sees his social-class peers in much less of a competi- tive sense because he doesn't want to *compete* with them, but rather *be* one of them. Therefore, security becomes an important criteria of individ- ual success. In effect, middle-class "success" is often the movement from one group to another, where the measurement of personal achievement is acceptance in and a sense of belonging to the achieved group.

Happiness. Both mobility and success are also closely related to what may be the main goal in life for the middle class—the seeking of happi- ness. Happiness is reflected in the seeking of ego-need satisfaction by many individuals; if their ego-needs are met, they feel "happy." Not only is it believed that happiness can be achieved by all, but also that every person has a natural right to happiness. Because of the importance of ego needs, happiness is defined as being accepted by others as a signifi- cant person. Acceptance is sought in the close relationship of marriage, and also in work and leisure-time associations. Thus, social success is often determined by being accepted by those held to be significant, which in turn gives to the individual his belongingness—his happiness.

A great concern with being liked and accepted is an important part of the socialization process of the middle-class child. He is often reared un- der a reward-and-punishment system based on parents giving and with- holding love and approval for his behavior. When he conforms, he is

---

[28] Erving Goffman, *The Presentation of Self in Everyday Life* (New York: Double- day Anchor Books, 1959), p. 36.

[29] Max Lerner, *America As a Civilization* (New York: Simon & Schuster, 1957), p. 488.

[30] Ibid., p. 692.

often loved, but when he deviates he may find the love withdrawn. Thus, there is a close relationship between love and approval—of having others show through approval that they love you or like you.

A popular belief is that one achieves happiness when he is accepted, and acceptance is defined as belonging. Therefore, a personality cult emerges, revolving around a mutual admiration society in which the group members approve of each other because they are essentially alike; by approving of the others, each thereby approves of himself. Whether this is really happiness is left to the philosopher to determine, but the fact that many in the middle class believe it is happiness tends to determine behavior and perpetuate the belief.

These general values of mobility, success, and happiness permeate many middle-class thoughts and patterns regarding marriage and the family. However, these same values, since they are not clearly defined and are often contradictory, contribute to some of the problems and frustrations of middle-class life. The interest of this book is not in the "right" or "wrong" of these values, but rather in how they are reflected in middle-class courtship, marriage, and parent-child interaction.

THE INTERACTIONIST APPROACH

One last introductory area remains to be discussed—the theoretical approach that will be followed in the analysis of marriage and the family. Theory provides a framework for giving order and relationship to what otherwise may seem a series of unrelated areas. Theory also guides research, gives it direction, and attempts to provide some logical consistency. A theory or consistent approach need not be developed in extensive detail in a book that is primarily "functional" in approach, as this book is. But the theoretical assumptions made by the writer, as well as some explanation of the concepts that will be used, do need to be stated.

The approach in this book is that of symbolic interactionalism, which has its historical roots with John Dewey, Charles Cooley, Robert Park, and, particularly, George Herbert Mead. Its modern development and application can be read in the texts of Coutu, Lindesmith and Strauss, Rose, and Shibutani.[31] The interactionist approach is a social-psychological theory that centers around two major problems: "The first is that

---

[31] See: Walter Coutu, *Emergent Human Nature* (New York: Alfred A. Knopf, Inc., 1949); Alfred R. Lindesmith and Anselm L. Strauss, *Social Psychology* (New York: The Dryden Press, 1956); Arnold M. Rose, *Human Behavior and Social Processes* (Boston: Houghton Mifflin Co., 1962); and Tamotsu Shibutani, *Society and Personality* (Englewood Cliffs, N.J.: Prentice-Hall, Inc., 1961). For a discussion of symbolic interaction related to the study of the family, see Sheldon Stryker, "Symbolic Interaction as an Approach to Family Research," *Marriage and Family Living*, May 1959, pp. 111–19.

of socialization: how the human organism acquires the ways of behaving, the values, norms and attitudes of the social units of which he is a part. The focus here is on development—that which happens over time in the human neophyte. The twin of the problem of socialization is that of personality: the organization of persistent behavior patterns."[32]

Certain basic assumptions made by symbolic interactionists must be clearly understood in order to understand the direction and emphasis of the theoretical approach. First is the belief that man is unique and must be studied not merely by comparing him to other forms of life, but on his own level; therefore, the position is antireductionist. Second, the belief is that one can better understand the social behavior of individuals by studying society. Third, the belief is that the newborn infant is asocial but has the potentialities for social development. The final assumption is that the human being is an actor as well as a reactor and does not simply respond to stimuli occurring outside himself.[33]

The basic unit in social interaction, the *social act*, refers to the relationship between two people. The action is social because when one individual acts, the other reacts with reference to the first actor. "Thus every social act implicates at least two individuals, each of whom takes the other into account in the processes of satisfying impulses."[34] The life of the social being is made up of an unlimited number and variety of social acts. Because new social acts influence the individual's social life, it is constantly in process and never in equilibrium; therefore, the individual is constantly adapting and functioning in a world of ever-changing social relationship.[35] Stryker suggests that by using the concept of *social act* as the starting point of analysis in symbolic interaction "an articulation between sociology and social psychology [is permitted] which alternate frameworks can forge, if at all, only with great difficulty."[36]

Of basic importance to the interactionist approach is man's ability to use symbols. Man's social world achieves its meaning because of man's use of symbols. Symbols refer to all conventional signs of human symbolic activity, and language is *more* than merely a system of symbols because it is "the activity of using and interpreting symbols."[37] So, in order for man to react socially to his environment, his use of symbols must always be involved. Even a physical gesture or expression has no meaning for the individual, unless he interprets it through language. For example, a

---

[32] Stryker, "Symbolic Interaction," pp. 111–12.

[33] Ibid., p. 112.

[34] Ibid., p. 113.

[35] Rose, *Social Processes*, p. ix.

[36] Sheldon Stryker, "The Interactional and Situational Approaches," in Harold T. Christensen, ed., *Handbook of Marriage and the Family* (Chicago: Rand McNally & Co., 1964), p. 135.

[37] Lindesmith and Strauss, *Social Psychology*, pp. 56–57.

husband arrives home at the end of the day and before he says a word, his wife knows he has had a bad day. She can "read" her husband—she knows from past experiences how to symbolically interpret his facial expressions, his walk, his bearing.

Interpretation through language always occurs between the stimulus and response in human behavior.[38] The symbolic nature of man means that he lives in a symbolic world and can be stimulated to act by symbols.[39] When a man says "I love you" to a woman, the words convey a vast variety of meaning and very often drastically influence her future behavior. The importance of the symbol becomes obvious if we imagine the reaction of a woman who had never before heard the word "love." The word itself is not important, but rather the meaning attached to it by individuals who share in their general agreement of symbolic meaning. Hence, the social world of the individual is circumscribed by the limits of effective communication.[40] For example, the lower-lower class has a more restricted world of communication because the development of language is often much more limited than in the middle class.

Symbolic interaction implies both action and reaction. For instance, through the use of language one person says something that is meaningful to a second person, who—in turn—is often stimulated by the other's verbal action to respond with a verbal reaction. Furthermore, the patterns of interaction frequently follow a predictable pattern, not usually in a long-range sense, but in some accurate anticipation of how the other person will react. If one uses the symbols of friendship, he does not expect the symbols of hostility in return.

Symbolic interaction does sometimes involve anxiety, however, when a person is unable to or insecure in predicting responses. For example, a child may be "anxious" in asking his parents' permission because he knows the reaction he wants, but is not sure exactly what he is going to get. But, most symbolic interaction involves a generally accurate prediction of action-reaction. Exchange has a routine of standardized quality.

Role is another concept of basic importance to the interactionist approach. The concept of *role* refers to the expected behavior attached to a social position.

> These expectations are social in the same sense symbolic behavior is always social: the ultimate meaning of the positions to which these expectations apply is shared behavior. They are social in another and most important sense, namely, that it is impossible to talk about *a* position without reference to some context of *other* positions: one cannot talk

[38] Herbert Blumer, "Society as Symbolic Interaction," in Rose, *Social Processes*, p. 180.

[39] Rose, *Social Processes*, p. 5.

[40] Tamotsu Shibutani, "Reference Groups and Social Control," in Rose, *Social Processes*, p. 136.

about the behavior of father except with reference to the positions of mother, child, and so on. Thus every position assumes some counter-position, and every role presumes some counter-role. To use the term 'role' is necessarily to refer to an interpersonal relation.[41]

To say that a role refers to expected social behavior does not mean that it is rigid or that the individual has no flexibility in filling the role. A role carries general rights and obligations; so long as the individual stays within the limits of the socially defined role expectation, he is adequately filling it. For example, a man in the role of father has a number of approved alternatives in dealing with the discipline of his child; however, he cannot go beyond a certain point without being socially punished.

The fact that roles have meaning only in relation to other roles gives order and some predictability to many social relationships. In addition to general knowledge, part of a young woman's knowledge of how to fill her new role as wife is based on predicting how the man she marries will fill the counter role of husband. The individual is often confused when he enters a new role and is unsure of his, and the related, role requirements. For example, someone not used to handling children but put into a role of supervising their activities may not be sure of how he should act or of how the children will act or react.

Role performance involves a number of possible sources of conflict. First, the individual may find that the demands of the role conflict with his self-interests. An example would be the father who is expected to provide for his children but doesn't want that responsibility. Second, the individual may define his role differently than someone in a related role defines it: the husband may want to make all the decisions in a marriage, while his wife thinks he should consult her. This points out the interrelationship of related roles: each individual involved must define not only his own, but also the related role. Third, different role demands being filled by the same individual may conflict. For example, a working mother may on occasion find the demands of her role as mother and her role as employee occur at the same time so that it is impossible to satisfy both. Fourth, a role definition may be confused—what is expected is not clear. Many modern women are faced with a wife-mother role different from the traditional role; this lack of clarity in social definition results in role confusion.

The extent to which the sources of conflict are minimized determines the efficiency of role relationships in various social settings. Therefore, an important question in analyzing roles "becomes one of the congruence of definitions, situation, role and self, of the interacting persons. Congruence permits efficient, organized behavior."[42]

[41] Stryker, "Symbolic Interaction," p. 114.
[42] Ibid., p. 117.

The importance of role learning can be seen in the process of socialization. "The child becomes socialized when he has acquired the ability to communicate with others and to influence and be influenced by them through use of speech."[43] The newborn infant starts life with the capacity for social development, but for a time remains unsocialized because his elders' symbols as such have no influence on him. As the infant's awareness of language, self, and others increases, his social world develops.

The development of the *self* in the youngster means a development of social self-awareness. With time, he learns to respond to himself as he responds to other people, "by naming, defining, classifying himself."[44] The self is "defined in terms of socially recognized categories and their corresponding roles. Since these roles necessarily imply relationships to others, the self necessarily implies such relations. One's self is the way one describes to himself his relationships to others in a social process."[45] The development of the self in the child is a slow and continual process; with time, the self becomes more complex as the child finds himself in more social relationships. The child is increasingly called upon to relate himself to a variety of different role situations. The child moves from the relatively limited relationships of the parental home into expanded relationships with other adults and other children, and he does this within the different social settings where those relationships occur.

An important part of the "self" development in socialization is determined by *role taking*. Role taking "refers to anticipating the responses of others associated with one in some social act."[46] For instance, from previous parental discipline the child often disciplines himself through role-taking. He decides on an action by taking his mother's role and anticipating her reaction to the possible behavior. If he anticipates that the behavior will make her angry, he may then decide against it. While role taking may involve anticipating the reactions of a specific "other," it frequently involves "the anticipation of response of what Mead called the 'generalized other.'"[47] *Generalized other* means that "one is taking the related roles of all the other participants rather than the role of just one other person."[48] This does not refer to an actual group of people but rather an abstract "they," and may represent the individual's conception of abstract moral standards.[49]

Role taking also has an important dimension in planning and learning of future roles. By imaginative participation in the behavior of others, the youngster lays the foundation within himself for playing these roles

[43] Lindesmith and Strauss, *Social Psychology*, p. 160.
[44] Stryker, "Symbolic Interaction," p. 114.
[45] Ibid., p. 115.
[46] Ibid., p. 115.
[47] Ibid., p. 115.
[48] Lindesmith and Strauss, *Social Psychology*, p. 394.
[49] Ibid., p. 394.

later in life. The play world of the child is a good illustration of role playing related to future roles. The little girl playing house is playing the role of the mother and imitating many of the traits of the woman's role in the home as she has observed them in her own mother. When she reaches the age of marriage, she will have partially learned through role playing the role she is entering. Role taking may also serve as a powerful force in striving to achieve a role. Through a positive identification with some future role behavior, an individual may work with great energy and effort in the process of achieving the role.

Of course not all "others" will be of equal influence on the individual as role models. Symbolic interactionists refer to the role models the individual considers important as *"significant others,"* because "others" are differentially viewed by the individual as having significance for his thoughts and behavior. For example, the eight-year-old boy may view the ten-year-old as a "significant other" and desire to act like him and be accepted by him as an equal; but compared to another boy twelve years old, the ten-year-old becomes less significant. In this way the perceiver may rank order or place "significant others" on a continuum, which will vary with time and social setting.[50]

The use of the terms *role* and *role taking* are sometimes falsely interpreted to connote some kind of artificial behavior. On the contrary, roles are usually behavior patterns which the individual accepts and which meaningfully influence his behavior. But role-playing by the individual often does have a "theatrical" quality, which may arise from the "taking the role of the other." That is, the individual does not always act publicly as he wants or feels, but as he thinks others want him to act.

Goffman points out that "there is hardly a legitimate everyday vocation or relationship whose performers do not engage in concealed practices which are incompatible with fostered impressions."[51] So role playing often involves the element of *front,* the concern with giving an impression to the audience that may or may not accurately reflect the role player. In dating, "front" is very common. Because neither the boy nor the girl has a commitment from the other both will often try to mask their "true" selves. Young people are often aware of the use of "fronts" in dating, and therefore enter and continue the relationship with caution and, sometimes, suspicion.

Because "front" has a contrived nature, the individual must constantly be alert. Frequently in dating and courtship, a person becomes upset when the other's behavior seems inconsistent. Inconsistency can occur either when the actor lets his "true self" show through or the other person defines as inconsistent what the actor feels is consistent role playing.

---

[50] Stryker, "Symbolic Interaction," p. 115.
[51] Goffman, *Self in Everyday Life,* p. 64.

For instance, the male, who has been putting on a "front" of great consideration for the desires of the female, may do something she defines as inconsiderate. His action may actually be a revealing slip on his part, or may only be defined by the female as inconsistent with his "front."

The intent of this discussion has not been to develop the symbolic interactionist theories comprehensively, but rather to provide some useful concepts for studying marriage and the family. The reader should keep in mind the suggested concepts, as well as the assumption that many middle-class family relationships have an ego-need focus, for these are the basic conceptual orientations used in this book's study of marriage and family interaction.

Chapters 2 and 3 constitute the rest of the introductory section. Chapter 2 provides a historical contrast to the contemporary middle-class family, and Chapter 3 shows some family variations within today's American society. Marriage and family relationships are ongoing processes; in the aggregate, individuals are at all points in the process at a given point in time. Chapter 4 begins the common procedure of entering the process at the dating-courtship stage. Succeeding chapters follow the life cycle of marriage and family interaction until they have been discussed at all stages.

SELECTED BIBLIOGRAPHY

Acker, Joan "Women and Social Stratification: A Case of Intellectual Sexism," in Joan Huber, *Changing Women in a Changing Society*. Chicago: University of Chicago Press, 1973, pp. 174–83.

Bergel, Egan E. *Social Stratification*. New York: McGraw-Hill Book Co., 1962.

Burr, Wesley R. *Theory Construction and the Sociology of the Family*. New York: John Wiley and Sons, 1973.

Coutu, Walter *Emergent Human Nature*. New York: Alfred A. Knopf, Inc., 1949.

Goffman, Erving *The Presentation of Self in Everyday Life*. New York: Doubleday Anchor Books, 1959.

Kahl, Joseph A. *The American Class Structure*. New York: Rinehart & Co., Inc., 1957.

Keller, Suzanne "Does the Family Have a Future?" *A Warner Modular Publication*, reprint 64, 1973, pp. 1–14.

Lerner, Max *America As a Civilization*. New York: Simon & Schuster, Inc., 1957.

Lindesmith, Alfred R., and **Strauss, Anselm L.** *Social Psychology*. New York: The Dryden Press, 1956.

Mead, George H. *Mind, Self and Society*. Chicago: The University of Chicago Press, 1934.

Parsons, Talcott, and **Bales, Robert F.** *Family, Socialization and Interaction Process*. Glencoe, Illinois: The Free Press, 1955.

Reiss, Ira L. "The Universality of the Family: A Conceptual Analysis." *Journal of Marriage and the Family,* November 1965, pp. 443–53.

Reissman, Leonard *Class in American Society.* Glencoe, Illinois: The Free Press, 1959.

Rose, Arnold M. *Human Behavior and Social Processes.* Boston: Houghton Mifflin Co., 1962.

Shibutani, Tamotsu *Society and Personality.* Englewood Cliffs, N.J.: Prentice-Hall, Inc., 1961.

Stryker, Sheldon "Symbolic Interaction as an Approach to Family Research." *Marriage and Family Living,* May 1959, pp. 111–19.

———— "The Interactional and Situational Approaches," in Harold T. Christensen, ed., *Handbook of Marriage and the Family.* Chicago: Rand McNally & Co., 1964, pp. 125–70.

Warner, W. Lloyd, Meeker, Marchia, and **Eells, Kenneth** *Social Class in America.* New York: Harper Torchbooks, 1960.

Chapter 2

The Puritan Family

The roots of today's American family go back to many cultural influences—particularly, in the Western World, to the early Hebrew, Greek, and Roman families. From those early family systems came many of the patterns and values found in marriage and family interaction today.[1] The focus in this chapter is not on the entire historical development leading to the modern American family, however, but rather on one specific early American family system—the Puritan family.

Historically, the American family extends back to about the start of the 17th century, and therefore is less than 400 years old. The early American colonists brought with them to America the family systems of the cultures within which they had been reared, but the American colonial family that emerged was not simply a European institution transplanted to the new continent; it had many new and original developments, though these were usually within the framework of the old country family system.

The old system was altered in part by the need to cope with the environment of the New World. Furthermore, because of distance and restricted transportation, as well as limited communication with the old

---

[1] See Willystine Goodsell, *A History of the Family as a Social and Educational Institution* (New York: The Macmillan Co., 1919); and Edward Westermarck, *The History of Human Marriage* (New York: The Allerton Book Co., 1922).

culture, the influence and reinforcement important to the maintenance of the old-country values in the New World was limited. While originally the colonists may have desired to transplant the old-country family system complete, its maintenance became impossible, and so with time it was gradually altered in the various colonies.

Because the early colonists came from different cultures and settled in different locations with different environmental demands, the family systems varied in the different colonies. For example, the problems of acquiring food in New England were more difficult than those in the Southern colonies. With communication and contact between the early seaboard colonies very restricted, exchange between them was also limited, resulting in some degree of autonomy for each. Exchange was further restricted by the tendency of individuals in one colony to view individuals in other colonies as culturally different and as "foreign" in their behavior patterns, even though all were settlers in the New World.

Traditionally the early colonies have been divided into three geographical groups: New England, from Maine to New York; the Middle States, from New York to Maryland; and the South, from Maryland to Georgia. While the family systems of the three geographical regions had many similarities, they also had many differences.[2] Finally, the fact that "the United States was settled by isolated farm families rather than by village communities as in Europe determined in great measure the distinctive characteristics of American family tradition."[3]

The description in this chapter of the early New England Puritans and their family system is included to provide the reader with some understanding of *one* early American family system that may, by contrast, make clearer some areas of family change that have developed over time in the United States. Often, the individual is so much a product of his culture that he is unable to realize that what seems natural to him has not always been the "normal" way of doing things. An historical contrast, and some variations in the modern family (as discussed in Chapter 3), may also serve to remove the reader from his middle-class orientation to a more objective view of that family system.

The Puritan family was selected, rather than another early colonial family system, because "the culture of Puritan New England had more to do with the shaping of our national culture than did that of any other colonial region or that of any subsequent immigrant group."[4] Many val-

---

[2] See Arthur W. Calhoun, *A Social History of the American Family: Colonial Period*, vol. 1 (New York: Barnes & Noble, Inc., 1960).

[3] Bernhard J. Stern, *The Family Past and Present* (New York: Appleton-Century-Crofts, Inc., 1938), p. 186.

[4] Manford H. Kuhn, "American Families Today: Development and Differentiation of Types," in Howard Becker and Reuben Hill, *Family, Marriage and Parenthood* (Boston: D. C. Heath & Co., 1955), p. 134.

ues felt to be basic to contemporary American society have their origins with the New England Puritans. For example, the Puritan beliefs in thrift and hard work continue to be values highly respected in theory, if not always in practice. The term "puritanical," which is frequently used as a synonym for prudery, refers to behavior often attributed to the early American Puritans. Social historians disagree on what the Puritans were *really* like, but more important than these academic disagreements is the fact that values attributed to the Puritans continue to be influential in the American middle class.

PURITANISM

Historically, Puritanism developed out of a desire for liturgical reform and as a corrective movement aimed at "purifying" the established church from "popery." It emerged as a hard-headed and sometimes frightening religion built upon the theological assumptions of human depravity and predestination. "Eternal damnation was certain for many, and thus fear of the hereafter, coupled with a sense of personal guilt before God, became a constant element within the Puritan conscience. Mundane pleasures, though good and right as far as they went, were suspect. Health, beauty, and the natural body appetites were to be enjoyed—but here was the snare—only provided that they were no encroachment upon the supreme good and were kept always subordinate. The very fact that man desired such pleasures made them suspect."[5] Therefore, the "good" Puritan often rejected sensate pleasures in order to give proof that he was good. The same logic applied to Puritan thinking about punishment and justice. "If an accused person standing before the court is scheduled to spend eternity in hell, it does not matter very much how severely the judges treat him, because all the hardships and sufferings in this world will be no more than a faint hint of the torments awaiting him in the hereafter."[6]

Puritanism meant the belief in the supreme sovereignty of God and, since the fall of Adam, the totally sinful and corrupt nature of man; this basic human depravity was believed to extend even to the newborn infant. The Puritan was caught in a personal trap in reference to predestination for himself. If he lived an exemplary life on earth it might be an indication that he was one of the "chosen"—but it was no guarantee. So he might give up all of the pleasures of life on earth for the next life and yet never be sure that he was going to be one of the "chosen."

One of the best ways for a person to try to convince others (and pos-

---

[5] Eric J. Dingwell, *The American Woman* (New York: Signet Books, 1957), p. 32.

[6] Kai T. Erickson, *Wayward Puritans* (New York: John Wiley & Sons, Inc., 1966), p. 190.

sibly himself) that he was truly saved was to become totally devoted to the church and completely loyal to the state. Erickson points out that the Puritan ministers were not suggesting that outer conformity was necessary to "*earn* salvation, but they seemed to be saying that outer conformity was a convenient way to *prove* salvation."[7]

The churches in Plymouth Colony made a fundamental distinction between persons who had been "converted" and those who had not. Only the converted were eligible for membership in the church. But Demos says these standards were applied liberally. As a result, individuals were asked to make some profession as to their inner experience of God's grace; but they were not submitted to detailed cross-examination. "Thus in practice a considerable part of the adult population would sooner or later become church members."[8]

The Puritans in England were subjected to severe religious persecution, and one of their chief motives in coming to America was their search for religious liberty. However, the fact that the Puritan colonists came seeking religious freedom did not mean that they were tolerant or accepting of other religious faiths. By the very nature of their religion the Puritans *knew* they were right, and those who believed differently were wrong. Thus, the Puritans left the old country where they had suffered religious persecution, and came to the New World where, in many cases, they then became the persecutors of those who would not accept Puritanism.

The Puritans who colonized America were a selected group with strong clerical leadership. Their initial purpose was not primarily to develop the New World, but rather to accomplish what they had been prevented from accomplishing at home, a Puritan society.[9] Their colony was planned as a legal extension of the old country, one where all the wrongs that existed at home would be corrected. "It was to be a 'heavenly translation' of Puritan theory into a living community of saints, a blueprint for the City of God."[10] The Puritan colonist was completely dedicated to his religion. He was characterized by an intense zeal to reform and to order everything in light of God's demand upon him.[11] The all-encompassing nature of the Puritan religion must be kept in mind in looking at the Puritan family. The great importance and control of the church is shown by the fact that "in 1635 a law was passed in Massachusetts making

---

[7] Ibid., p. 86.

[8] John Demos, *A Little Commonwealth: Family Life in Plymouth Colony* (New York: Oxford University Press, 1970), p. 8.

[9] *Encyclopaedia Britannica*, s.v. "Puritanism."

[10] Erickson, *Wayward Puritans*, p. 43.

[11] *Encyclopaedia Britannica*, s.v. "Puritanism."

church attendance compulsory, and in 1638 every resident was taxed for the ministry, whether church member or not."[12]

Puritan values prevailed for almost three quarters of a century in New England and during that time were, in effect, the laws of the land. The period of greatest Puritan strength and influence ran from the first settlement in Massachusetts established in 1630 to the loss of the old charter in 1691. Erikson suggests that the end of the Puritan experiment in Massachusetts in 1692 resulted from more than the original charter being revoked and a royal governor being appointed by the king. The Puritan experiment ended in 1692 "because the sense of mission which had sustained it from the beginning no longer existed in any recognizable form, and thus the people of the Bay were left with few stable points of reference to help them remember who they were."[13] Under the leadership of Jonathan Edwards in the 1730s, an attempt was made to reconstitute the old Puritan order on a new basis, but it was generally not successful.[14]

The relatively long period of Puritan success in New England was due in great degree to their success in maintaining nearly absolute control of their religious ideals. But as the number of colonists with different religious backgrounds increased, the Puritans began to have difficulty controlling not only the other religions, but also their own younger generations. A strong economic force also contributed to a weakening of Puritan control. Schneider writes, "The Puritans of their own strength might have kept New England holy, but in order to keep it at all, and to give it the necessary footing, they were compelled to invite outsiders by adopting a new liberal land policy."[15]

Lastly, changes in the demands of life eased the strength of Puritanism. "Social life became freer and more pleasure-loving throughout the colonies. The severest phases of the struggle for existence in the new land were past and even in New England the harsh Puritan spirit was gradually becoming softened."[16]

The discussion that follows is limited to the time when the Puritans were a dominant force and exerted strong controls over their family life. Over time, the Puritan values have been diffused, but they have never been completely eliminated. Therefore, a description of the Puritan family during its period of greatest strength provides a contrast with the modern American middle-class family, indicating both differences and some of the Puritan values that continue to operate. The areas of mar-

---

[12] Herbert W. Schneider, *The Puritan Mind* (New York: Henry Holt & Co., 1930). p. 75.

[13] Erikson, *Wayward Puritans,* p. 155.

[14] *Encyclopaedia Britannica,* s.v. "Puritanism."

[15] Schneider, *Puritan Mind,* p. 79.

[16] Goodsell, *Family as Institution,* pp. 363–64.

riage and family interaction are discussed in the same order for the Puritans as they are in the rest of this book for the contemporary middle-class family.

COURTSHIP

The Puritan family was patriarchal, with the male's authority derived from the patriarchal values of the religion. In mate selection, as is almost always the patriarchal case, the parents, and particularly the father, played a dominant role in arranging their children's marriages. The Puritan father, even if he did not actually select the mate, made the ultimate decision as to marriageability. Because an important value in the patriarchal system was the strong obedience of children, Puritan offspring generally accepted the decision of the father without question. To go against him was rebellion against the family and, even more important, against the accepted religious beliefs.

While the parents exerted strong control over mate selection, the young person did have a degree of freedom. Calhoun argues that some freedom was given to the young because in a "new country, needing population, it was natural that pious authorities should frown upon any discouragement of legitimate increase. The interests of the community took precedence over the private interests of parents, guardians, and masters."[17] Many social factors that later served as barriers to marriage in the United States did not exist in the early Puritan colonies. Because the early Puritans were alike in many of their social characteristics, the likelihood of choosing a partner who was significantly different was minimized. With time, the economic factor became increasingly important, and as a result, courtship was increasingly permeated by economic considerations.[18] Thus, even when the marriage was successful, "happy husbands were ready to sue their father-in-law if he proved too tardy or remiss in the matter of the bridal portion."[19]

Courtship interaction between the young couple was very limited because of several factors. First, discovering the personality of the future mate was not important, and even if it were considered, discovery would come after marriage. The Puritans believed that one did not marry for love, but that love was found in all good Puritan marriages. Married love did not mean to the Puritans what it means to us today; the Puritans believed that it was God's will that a husband and wife love each other. Therefore by definition, if one were a good Puritan, one loved his spouse. Second, there was little time for courtship; survival and material attain-

---

[17] Calhoun, *Family: Colonial Period,* p. 55.

[18] Ibid., p. 59.

[19] Ibid., p. 59.

ment demanded excessively long hours of work for all able-bodied Puritans. Furthermore, where distance separated the colonists, the opportunities for the social interaction of extended courtship were limited by the restricted means of transportation. Therefore, young people often had neither the time nor the energy to pursue an extended courtship. Third, the pleasurable aspects of courtship, as we know them today, rarely existed for the Puritans. The sharing of recreation and pleasure would have violated the Puritan ban on such activities. Modern courtship also implies some degree of privacy for the couple, but the Puritans—believing that man must constantly fight against his basic depravity—would have viewed privacy for a young unmarried couple as playing into the hands of the devil. (A Puritan could be suspect not only in action, but also in thought; unmarried privacy would certainly be highly tempting to immoral thoughts, if not actions.)

These courtship restrictions are suggested as general norms governing the behavior of the Puritans. However, it is questionable whether any society, even with a system of severe punishments, can achieve complete control over the personal behavior of all individuals. Many historical reports indicate some degree of deviancy from the Puritan norms; the strength of the norms may, therefore, be more accurately assessed in terms of relative, rather than absolute, control. For example, it cannot be assumed that romantic love was never found among the Puritans. "But it was obviously hampered by the habit of driving hard bargains which, in turn, were traceable partly to the narrow margin of survival and partly to the stern code of Puritanism."[20] In other areas of deviation from the norms, Hunt points out that "the court and church records of early New England are filled with case histories of men and women who gamed, swore, fought, and got drunk—but who were Puritans."[21] Some of the Puritans must be recognized as individualists for going against norms which carried such severe punishment for those who were caught. The internal controls of the Puritan conscience did not always seem to work either, because some of the Puritan deviants do not seem to have been greatly bothered by feelings of guilt.

PREMARITAL SEXUAL BEHAVIOR

Unlike those adherents of many other patriarchal systems, the Puritans believed in the premarital chastity of both male and female. Calhoun writes that "the Puritan emphasis on sexual restraint was of a piece with the general gospel of frugality so appropriate among a class of peo-

---

[20] Stuart A. Queen, Robert W. Habenstein, and John B. Adams, *The Family in Various Cultures* (Philadelphia: J. B. Lippincott Co., 1961), p. 278.

[21] Morton M. Hunt, *The Natural History of Love* (New York: Alfred A. Knopf, Inc., 1959), p. 232.

ple trying to accumulate capital in an age of deficit. Urgent economic interests furthered the novel virtue of male chastity. The necessity of accumulation led the Puritan to reprobate all unprofitable forms of sin including licentiousness, that prodigal waster."[22] For those strongly influenced by Puritan theology, premarital sexual behavior was interpreted as succumbing to the temptations of the flesh—behavior not found among the "chosen." Thus, the strength of the premarital chastity norms was derived from both economic and religious beliefs. However, the high value set by the Puritans on premarital chastity was not the same as that placed on virginity by the Roman Catholic church. The Catholic church had set up the ideal of virginity and it forbade the marriage of its priests. But the Puritans had no ideal of virginity as such; they encouraged marriage at an early age, and their ministers usually married.[23]

Yet, even with their strongly supported norms against premarital sexual experience, a number of Puritans clearly deviated. The church records suggest a degree of deviancy from the norms that seems very alien to the traditional picture of Puritanism. The records of the Groton church show that of 200 persons owning the baptismal covenant there from 1760 to 1775, 66 confessed to fornication before marriage.[24] In all types of disciplinary cases mentioned in the records of Massachusetts churches, a plurality of them concerned fornication. "It was, in other words, the most prevalent and most popular sin in Puritan New England."[25]

Several explanations may be suggested. First, the barrenness and economic dearth that oppressed the first settlers helped to reduce life to elemental levels.[26] Even with stern religious restrictions on pleasures, the early Puritans' lives were so restricted that sexual encounters were sought partly because there were so few other opportunities for "pleasure." Second, where wealth was scant, questions of legitimacy and inheritance were less urgent.[27] Therefore, premarital chastity norms were not always given strong support by economic values. Third, Calhoun suggests that deviations may partly have been due to a morality that did not allow for a class of recognized prostitutes.[28] When sexual deviancy occurred, one of the Puritan women had to be the partner in the act. In contrast, many patriarchal societies protect the sexual purity of their women by providing a group of prostitutes to meet the sexual needs of a large number of men. The pattern of premarital sex for the Puritan and

---

[22] Calhoun, *Family: Colonial Period*, p. 39.

[23] George R. Stewart, *American Ways of Life* (New York: Dolphin, 1964), p. 164.

[24] Ibid., p. 133.

[25] Hunt, *History of Love*, p. 235.

[26] Calhoun, *Family: Colonial Period*, p. 134.

[27] Ibid., p. 134.

[28] Ibid., p. 135.

today's middle-class female may be similar. That is, few women today are sexually promiscuous, but a number may have sexual experience with only one male, resulting in a large number having premarital sexual experience—since a large number do have such experience.

For the Puritan, the risks of engaging in premarital intercourse were great, especially for the female. "The matter of fornication before marriage was given shameful notoriety. Groton church records show that until 1803 whenever a child was born less than seven months after marriage a public confession had to be made before the whole congregation."[29] Hunt points out that the Puritans punished more sex sinners than the courts and "employed a public form of confession far more painful than the Catholic confessional they had repudiated."[30]

Puritan repression of pleasures in general, and of sexual pleasure in particular, has been offered as a causal explanation of many personal and social characteristics of the Puritans. Hunt writes that sexual repression "undoubtedly played a part in the two outbreaks of witchcraft hysteria in New England; the earlier one began in 1647 and resulted in the execution of fourteen witches in Massachusetts and Connecticut, while the Salem frenzy in 1692 brought about the execution of twenty persons and two dogs."[31] In light of present psychological knowledge, such strong sex repression along with other restrictions of pleasure must clearly have had a strong influence on the Puritan personality. One can also speculate that personal guilt and trauma must have been very great for those who sexually deviated but were otherwise strong Puritans.

Bundling. Historically, bundling was a means of courtship utilized on the American frontier, but it was also found at an earlier date in New York, Pennsylvania, and some of the New England colonies. Bundling, according to Calhoun, prevailed to a very great extent in New England from a very early time. *Bundling* refers to the practice of allowing a young couple to get into bed together so they could talk in privacy without using the candles that would be necessary if they stayed up. The couple were not completely trusted: They often entered the bed fully clothed and, in some cases, a wooden bar was put on top of the coverings to make sure they stayed apart.

In some situations bundling had nothing to do with courtship. Many of the early dwellings consisted of only one or two rooms, and members of the family occupied all available beds. However, a friendly wayfarer had to be accommodated, if only with half a bed.[32] When this happened, there seems little evidence that the husband moved his wife out of his

---

[29] Ibid., p. 132.
[30] Hunt, *History of Love,* p. 234.
[31] Ibid., p. 230.
[32] Calhoun, *Family: Colonial Period,* p. 129.

bed and shared it with the male stranger. Either he had confidence in another female family member as a bed partner for the stranger, or simply was not willing to disturb his routine of sharing a bed with his wife.

The practice of bundling was found among the Puritans, but it provoked a great deal of controversy. Over a period of time, the practice was extended beyond its original intent and, at last, was viewed as such a scandal that the church felt forced to suppress it. "Jonathan Edwards attacked it on the pulpit and other ministers, who had allowed it to go unnoticed, joined in its suppression."[33] By 1800 the practice survived only in very few places, although in 1804 the New York Supreme Court ruled, in a seduction case, that since the girl's parents had permitted her to bundle they had no right to complain of the consequences which "naturally followed. . . ."[34]

MARRIAGE

For the Puritans, marriage was a very important relationship based upon religious, social, and economic values. A man needed a wife and children so as to survive and to prosper. Today, children are often an economic liability because they contribute little or nothing to the family's economic worth, but in the Puritan society, children even at very young ages were an economic asset.

As is almost always the case in a patriarchal society, the woman had little choice of adult role other than that of wife-mother. The inevitability of the Puritan girl's marriage was supported by her upbringing and by the religious values that saw the woman's natural adult state as that of wife-mother. A few women chose an adult role other than marriage, though they were often widows or women unable to acquire a marriage mate. For the vast majority, marriage was the only adult status.

The male had equally strong motivations to marry. "Each man urgently needed a wife to satisfy imperative needs—clothing, food, medical care, companionship, sex, and, not least of all, status."[35] Religious values also made marriage a highly desired state for the Puritan male. Patriarchally oriented, he needed a wife to provide him with economically important children. Given the great importance attached to marriage, "it was common for a man to meet a girl, appraise her, propose to her, and publish the bans all within a few weeks or less."[36]

Marriage, once accomplished, was not treated lightly by the Puritans.

---

[33] Ibid., p. 131.

[34] Ray E. Baber, *Marriage and the Family* (New York: McGraw-Hill Book Co., 1953), p. 32.

[35] Hunt, *History of Love*, p. 238.

[36] Ibid., p. 239.

Both husband and wife had a moral obligation to function as completely as possible according to the religious and social expectations for marriage. Calhoun writes that "so important was proper family relations that persons living apart from their spouses were sometimes ordered to get their partners or clear out. The well-being of the community was conceived to depend on rigid family discipline and if a man had no family he must find one."[37] Today's concern with happiness in marriage was not of great importance to the Puritans, particularly if the stability of the marriage was threatened. But, since individuals did not go into marriage expecting great personal happiness, they therefore had no such expectations with which to compare reality.

The Puritan definition of marriage as secular contradicts their strong religious values until it is viewed against their rebellion against the Catholic church. The Puritans, and others in New England, called a halt to the growing tendency to make marriage an ecclesiastical function. "Marriage was declared to be a civil contract, not a sacrament, and to require no priestly intervention."[38] Over the years, the Puritan contention has prevailed, and marriage in the United States has been secularized and brought under the control of civil law. Even today, a minister performing the marriage ceremony is legally acting as an agent of the state and not in his religious capacity. The Puritans had no prescribed marriage ritual; any appropriate words might be used. And in the earliest years, marriages were not performed in the church but, customarily, took place at the bride's home. In line with Puritan thought, marriage was viewed with seriousness and there was little festivity or celebration.[39]

Because the Puritans took a matter-of-fact view of marriage, and because the courtship period was of little importance, the early Puritans entered marriage at young ages. Girls often married at 16 or under, but there is no evidence that the child marriages, so common in England at that time, were ever permitted in America. However, there is some evidence that the average age of marriage was older than generally assumed. For men the age ranged downward from about 27 at the time of settlement to a little under 25 at the end of the Old Colony period. "For women the average age was just over 20 at the start, and rose during the same span to about 22."[40]

Social and religious values for marriage were so strong that old maids were ridiculed or even despised. "A woman became an 'ancient maid' at 25. Bachelors were rare and were viewed with disapproval. They were almost in the class of suspected criminals. In Hartford solitary men were

---

[37] Calhoun, *Family: Colonial Period*, p. 71.

[38] Ibid., p. 60.

[39] Queen, Habenstein, and Adams, *Various Cultures*, p. 279.

[40] Demos, *Plymouth Colony*, p. 151.

taxed twenty shillings a week."[41] Because failure to marry was counter to the norms supported by both religious and social values, a person refusing to marry was seen not only as defying the values of his religion, but also as an economic threat.

The demands of the New World and Puritan theology made colonial New England a man's world. "Life conditions allowed a type of patriarchism that found affinity in the Old Testament regime. The Puritan views, as expressed and followed by the men, as to proper relations between husband and wife, parent and child, or between man and maid before marriage, came directly from the scriptures."[42] The father's authority could not be openly questioned without implying a questioning of basic religious tenets.

Male dominance was an accepted principle all over the Western World at this time. The basic Puritan sentiment was expressed by Milton in the famous line in *Paradise Lost:* "He for God only, she for God in him." In Plymouth there was a suspicion of women solely based on their sex. Some basic taint of corruption was thought to be inherent in the female constitution—"a belief rationalized, of course, by the study of Eve's initial treachery in the Garden of Eden."[43]

The father's roles within the family and within the church were often closely interwoven; frequently, the requirements of the church took precedence over the requirements of the family. The fathers adopted the maxim that "families are the nurseries of the church and the commonwealth; ruin families and you ruin all."[44] The maintenance of family religion was universally recognized in early New England as a duty and was seriously attended to in most families. The scriptures were read and worship was offered to God daily.[45]

While the husband had nearly absolute authority over his wife and children, some restrictions were placed on him. Since the wife and children were expected to be obedient, he could punish them for disobedience; but he was expected to act within reason. His reasonableness arose from practicality: Every last individual was needed to cope with the harsh environment of the New World. To be too severe in the physical punishment of a family member would have been to deprive himself and the community of the individual's contributions. The father was also expected to take care of his family according to his financial ability. Goodsell writes, "The husband must maintain his wife in accordance with his means, whether or not she brought him property at marriage."[46] Further-

[41] Calhoun, *Family: Colonial Period,* pp. 67–68.

[42] Ibid., p. 83.

[43] Demos, *Plymouth Colony,* pp. 82–83.

[44] Ibid., p. 75.

[45] Ibid., p. 76.

[46] Goodsell, *Family as Institution,* p. 347.

more, the man was not expected to add to his prosperity by depriving his family members of their rightful due.

There is some evidence that the woman's subordinate role under the Puritan patriarchy was somewhat different from that under earlier patriarchal systems. While still subordinate to her husband, the wife often had a relationship with him which drew upon her as an individual personality, and not just as a worker and bearer of children. In general, Puritan women were supposed to be good companions to their husbands. "Puritan writers stressed the importance of emotional harmony between man and wife."[47] The Puritan wife role seems to fall somewhere between that found in traditional patriarchal societies and that of the modern middle-class family with its emphasis on husband-wife companionship.

The Puritan woman also made some gains over her old-country counterpart in the area of legal rights. For example, women began to receive some legal protection over their property interests. "In 1646 the consent of the wife was made necessary to the sale of houses or lands. Massachusetts (1647) allowed the widow one third of her husband's estate as dowry."[48] As a further example, "In Puritan New England a woman whose husband beat her could win legal separation and sometimes divorce; in the Southern colonies, where the influence was Anglican and Cavalier, the law made no such provision."[49] While the woman attained some rights, she continued for the most part to be controlled, both in person and in property, by her husband whom she was bound to serve and obey under the English private law which became the "common law" of the colonies.[50] However, the oft-described "rigidity" of the Puritans should be recognized as an easing of traditional values, for in some practical ways, woman's status was improved under the Puritans.

A universally severe problem faced by woman in all societies, including the Puritan, was the burden of interminable childbearing. Among the Puritans, large families were the rule. Families with eight or nine children were common. The household of a man of 45 might contain a full-grown son about to marry and start his own farm, all the way to an infant, with all ages of children in between.[51] Puritan social and religious values placed importance on large families, and even if individuals had desired to limit the number of their offspring, the knowledge of how to do so was very restricted.

Continuous childbearing took a heavy toll of Puritan wives. Great numbers died at childbirth, and the number and close spacing of births, plus the harsh nature of the environment during the early days of settle-

---

[47] Hunt, *History of Love*, p. 236.
[48] Calhoun, *Family: Colonial Period*, p. 95.
[49] Hunt, *History of Love*, pp. 251–52.
[50] Goodsell, *Family as Institution*, p. 345.
[51] Demos, *Plymouth Colony*, p. 69.

ment, brought about old age and death long before it was chronologically due. There were also dangers of maternal mortality. Demos estimates about 20 percent of the deaths among adult women were due to factors related to childbirth. Something like one birth in 30 resulted in the death of the mother.[52] The mother also had to live with the expectation of losing a number of her children. "With freezing homes, bad diet, and Spartan treatment it does not seem strange that a large proportion of 17th century children died in infancy. This was the case even in the most favored families; thus of Cotton Mather's 15 children only 2 survived him and of Judge Sewall's 14 only 3 outlived the father."[53]

The life of the Puritan wife-mother was highly restricted and almost wholly bounded by the interests of maintaining the home. Her social life was often no more than a weekly visit to church on Sunday and a religious "lecture" on Thursday.[54] During the earliest period, demands on the woman were great, but they eased off over time, particularly in the more economically successful families. Calhoun writes:

> But the impression that the colonial dame performed Herculean labors is a myth. These *tours de force* were rarely performed by a one-woman household. The wife bore and reared children and superintended the house; but she did not do the heavy work if there was need of her services in other lines. Some families had numerous trained and capable servants. In the country daughters not needed at home worked in neighbor's households until married. Many families in town and country took bound children to raise for the return of their labor. . . . The commonest helpers were the unmarried sisters of husband or wife. Moreover, most of the large families of earlier times were the offspring of at least two mothers, and the later wives had fewer children. The first wife would get quickly six or seven children and die exhausted by maternity and labor. The next wife, young and sturdy, would take hold and bring up the family, some of whom were likely old enough to be of help. She would have three or four children, perhaps at longer intervals.[55]

Formerly it was believed that the common pattern among the Puritans was some kind of extended family where a number of persons of different generations and of various kinship lived under a common roof. However, the early families were often restricted or nuclear units similar to our present family units. "The various deeds of gifts and inheritance speak more directly to the same point. They show beyond any possibility of reasonable doubt that one married couple and their children always formed the core of the family—and often comprised its entire extent."[56]

What little personal life the Puritan wife achieved was often in her

---

[52] Ibid., pp. 65–66.
[53] Calhoun, *Family: Colonial Period,* p. 106.
[54] Goodsell, *Family as Institution,* p. 352.
[55] Calhoun, *Family: Colonial Period,* pp. 97–98.
[56] Demos, *Plymouth Colony,* pp. 62–63.

relationship to her husband. While he was in theory the unquestioned authority, no doubt a number of Puritan wives were able to make their feelings felt, and influence or even manipulate their husbands. For even with the unemotional nature of courtship and marriage, real affection probably existed between many Puritan husbands and wives. But demonstrations of such affection had to be very private; it was not prudent for the Puritan to be publicly demonstrative. Calhoun relates that "Captain Kemble of Boston sat two hours in the public stocks for his 'lewd and unseemly behavior' in kissing his wife 'publicquely' on the Sabbath upon his doorstep when he had just returned from a voyage of three years."[57]

Even though the Puritan woman had the generally low status common to women in patriarchal societies, she nevertheless played a significant part in the history of the New England Puritan era. Erikson, in his recent study of deviancy in Puritan society, traces three major "crime waves." Of particular interest is that in all three women played major roles. The first, in 1636, was a theological argument involving Mrs. Anne Hutchinson. The fact that one of the disputants was a woman must have added to the elders' sense of irritation.[58] The Puritan view as to the intellectual capacities of women is reflected in a statement by John Winthrop "that a woman of his acquaintance had been mentally ill as a result of reading too many books."[59] The second "crime wave" was the Quaker persecutions of 1656 to 1665, and the first open indication of this trouble was when two Quaker housewives were arrested on ship in Boston Bay. They were taken to jail, stripped of their clothing, and searched for markings of witchcraft.[60] The third Puritan "crime wave" was the Salem Witchcraft outbreak of 1692. In the period that followed, a number of girls and women were accused, tried, and found guilty of witchcraft.[61] In all three of these major historical events women made their presence strongly felt in the Puritan community.

One common stereotype is that the Puritans were against sex. However, for all their emphasis on the sinfulness of fornication and adultery, the early Puritans cannot be said to have been against sex as such. "Not only did they breed large families and take pride in so doing, but their spiritual leaders praised married sex and roundly condemned the 'Popish conceit of the excellency of virginity.' "[62] An example of the value placed on marital sex is given in an account by Hunt:

> At the First Church of Boston, the congregation considered action against one James Mattock for several offenses, one of them being, of all things, sexual abstinence. Mattock, it appeared, had denied his wife conjugal

---

[57] Ibid., p. 92.

[58] Erikson, *Wayward Puritans*, p. 82.

[59] Ibid., p. 82.

[60] Ibid., p. 115.

[61] Ibid., pp. 141–53.

[62] Hunt, *History of Love*, p. 234.

relations for two years on the grounds that he was punishing himself for his sins; the congregation voted this was unnatural and unchristian, and expelled him from membership in the church.[63]

The evidence indicates that the Puritans were not so totally against sex —at least in marriage—as many have believed. However, they may have suffered a severe conflict because sexual satisfaction, even in marriage, might indicate a weakness to "things of the flesh"—negative evidence of the possibility of being one of the "chosen."

Sexual relationships outside of marriage *were* severely condemned. Adultery was seen as the most serious distortion of marriage. John Robinson called it "that most foul and filthy sin . . . the disease of marriage," and concluded that divorce was its necessary "medicine."[64]

No distinctions were made in the Puritan laws between men and women concerning adultery, and both were supposed to suffer the same consequences. As it happened, however, female offenders were generally more severely punished than male offenders.[65] In 1707, in Plymouth, a couple were tried for adultery and the woman was sentenced to be set on the gallows, receive thirty stripes upon her naked back, and forever after to wear the Capital A (for *adultery;* cf. Hawthorne's *The Scarlet Letter*). The man was acquitted with no assignment of reason.[66] The adultery of the wife was treated as a violation of her marriage and therefore grounds for divorce *and* an offense against the community and cause for legal prosecution. But for comparable behavior by husbands only the first consideration applied.[67] Yet not all Puritan men escaped punishment. For example, in 1661, the first civil divorce case occurred under the colonial legislature, and the court "granted a divorce to Elizabeth Burge on the ground of her husband Thomas's adultery—a crime of which he was sentenced to be severely whipped."[68] Adultery not only countered religious values, but was also seen as threatening to family and community beliefs.

CHILDREN

Calhoun writes that "colonial childhood is largely hidden in obscurity."[69] The letters and diaries that provide records of the Puritan's life

---

[63] Ibid., p. 234.

[64] Demos, *Plymouth Colony*, p. 96.

[65] Hunt, *History of Love*, p. 234.

[66] Calhoun, *Family: Colonial Period*, p. 138.

[67] Demos, *Plymouth Colony*, p. 97.

[68] Nelson M. Blake, *The Road to Reno* (New York: The Macmillan Co., 1962), p. 35.

[69] Ibid., p. 105.

rarely mention children except for the records of their births, illnesses, and deaths. "Children were 'to be seen not heard,' and not seen too much either."[70] Children had no legal rights, and the father was the sole guardian of the offspring of his marriage. He alone could determine important questions concerning the education, religious training, preparation for life-work, and marriage of his children.[71]

Subservience

Children were expected to obey the will of their parents without question; in some cases of disobedience, punishment permissible under the laws was unbelievably severe. The Piscataqua Colony had the following law: "If any child or children above 16 years old of competent understanding, shall curse or smite their natural father or mother, he or they shall be put to death unless it can be sufficiently testified that the parents have been very unchristianly negligent of the education of such child . . . if any man have a rebellious or stubborne son of sufficient years and understanding, that is to say, 16 years of age or upwards, which shall not obey the voice of his father or the voice of his mother, yet when they have chastened him will not harken unto them . . . such son shall be put to death, or otherwise severely punished."[72] Even in day-to-day activities, the discipline of children, by today's standards, was very severe. In some households the children were made to stand through meals, eating whatever was handed to them. They were taught that it was sinful to complain about food, clothing, or their lot in life. The parents, particularly the father, insisted upon courtesy of a very formal and subservient nature.[73]

The children were treated as miniatures of their parents. There was no notion that each generation should have separate spheres of activities. "Children learned the behavior appropriate to their sex and station by sharing the activities of their parents."[74] The colonists knew no other way of training the young than through control by the parents. They taught the children to accept the conventions that held the community together and to obey the laws of God and man. Fathers and mothers passed on to their children the skills with which to earn a living, find shelter against the elements, and guard against the daily perils of life.[75]

---

[70] Ibid., p. 105.

[71] Goodsell, *Family as Institution*, p. 346.

[72] Calhoun, *Family: Colonial Period*, p. 121.

[73] Queen, Habenstein, and Adams, *Various Cultures*, p. 280.

[74] Demos, *Plymouth Colony*, pp. 139–40.

[75] Oscar Handlin and Mary F. Handlin, *Family Life: Youth and the Family in American History* (Boston: Little, Brown & Co., 1971), p. 14.

Industry

Puritan children were not given personal freedom or allowed a "childhood world." They had to work from an early age. In Puritan ethics, idleness was a serious sin, and the child with no work to do was highly susceptible to temptation. In addition, the economic factor was important; Puritan child labor was "fundamentally a response to a condition rather than to a theory. It was a compliance with the exigencies of the case. The rigor of the struggle for existence in early New England made impossible the prolongation of infancy that marks high civilization."[76]

Religion

Children were in no way exempted from or given special privileges easing the harshness and pervasiveness of Puritan religious dogma. Because of the depravity of human nature, it was necessary to seek infantile conversion. Starting in the earliest years, children were constantly confronted with the terrors of hell and told that they could only escape by following what they were being taught about religion and by rejecting almost everything they might naturally as children want to do.

Cotton Mather wrote:

> "I took my little daughter Katy (aged four) into my study and there told my child that I am to die shortly and she must, when I am dead, remember everything I now said unto her. I set before her the sinful condition of her nature and charged her to pray in secret places every day. That God for the sake of Jesus Christ would give her a new heart. . . . I gave her to understand that when I am taken from her she must look to meet with more humbling afflictions than she does now she has a tender father to provide for her." (This was 30 years before he died.)[77]

The excessive nature of the fears of hell and damnation directed at children must have greatly disturbed the personality balance of many youngsters.

The lot of Puritan children was obviously not an easy one. It contrasts sharply with the benevolent treatment of children common today. Within the limits of the Puritan value system, the children who managed to survive infancy were probably loved as much by their parents as children are today, but "they were denied all the normal sources of joy and happiness."[78] Because a set pattern for all children was accepted, "a pert child was generally thought to be delirious or bewitched."[79] The give-and-take

---

[76] Calhoun, *Family: Colonial Period*, p. 122.

[77] Ibid., p. 108.

[78] Ibid., p. 111.

[79] Ibid., p. 111.

companionship of parents and children often found in today's middle-class family was almost totally absent among the Puritans. It is hard to imagine any parent-child "democracy" among the Puritans, when children's manners were so formal that parents were often addressed as "esteemed parent" or "honored sir and madam."[80]

DIVORCE AND REMARRIAGE

When the Puritans came to the New World, they brought English law with them; but they parted from it in respect to divorce by adopting, as they thought, the Rules of the New Testament. According to Calhoun, "By following what they construed to be the spirit of the book, rather than the letter, they spread out from adultery and desertion as the only causes of divorce. Dissolution of the marriage bond was freely granted for a variety of causes, such as desertion, cruelty, or breach of vow. Generally, though not always, husband and wife received equal treatment at the hands of the law."[81] However, Goodsell states that "Although far more generous treatment was accorded wives, in respect to divorce or separation than was conceded in the other colonies, discrimination in favor of men very generally existed."[82] (For example, the husband could and did obtain divorce on the single ground of adultery, whereas in the vast majority of cases the wife could not.) In the new colonies, it was the "Puritans who took the lead in developing a liberal civil divorce policy. About 40 Massachusetts divorce cases have been discovered for the years up to 1692; there may have been more; the records are incomplete. Ignoring ecclesiastical law, the Massachusetts magistrates granted either absolute divorce or none at all."[83] Two important factors contributed to the liberality of divorce views in New England. First, the Puritans were openly rejecting the sacramental theory by making marriage secular, and following logically from this came their liberal, secular views about divorce. Second, in many cases, wives had been left in the old country and could or would not come to the colonies. Because the new life was very difficult without a wife, and because population increase and family life were felt to be so important, it was necessary to allow the acquisition of new spouses. The more liberal attitudes of New England were not found in the colonies of the Middle States or the South, the primary reason being that the New England colonists did not hesitate to go counter to English law and practice in regard to the dissolution of marriage, while the other colonists did.

In the case of the death of a husband or wife, remarriage among the

---

[80] Ibid., p. 111.

[81] Ibid., p. 146.

[82] Goodsell, *Family as Institution*, p. 379.

[83] Blake, *Road to Reno*, p. 36.

Puritans was often very quick. "The first marriage in Plymouth Colony was that of Edward Winslow, who had been a widower only seven weeks, to Susanna White, who had been a widow not twelve weeks."[84] One particular case vividly illustrates the amount of remarriage in one family. "Peter Sargent, a rich Boston merchant, had three wives. His second had had previously, two husbands, who had three wives. His father had four, the last three of whom were widows."[85] Widows were obviously of great value on the marriage market, often much more so than the younger single woman. Calhoun suggests that the principal reason was that the widow often had some wealth from her previous marriage to take into the remarriage.[86]

Life was full of dangers, and the chances of early death were great among the colonists. A man's life was constantly endangered by his day-to-day dealings with the environment, a woman's by extensive childbearing, and both men's and women's by the limited control over disease and the primitive state of medical knowledge. These factors, combined with the strong social and religious values placed on marriage, usually moved individuals into a new marriage as soon as possible.

SIGNIFICANCE OF THE PURITAN FAMILY FOR TODAY

As we said at the beginning of this chapter, the purpose in discussing the Puritan family is twofold: First, the Puritan family system is enough different from today's middle-class family to provide a better understanding of what *is* as contrasted with what *was;* second, enough Puritan values continue to prevail to make the Puritan family historically significant.

It is true that many areas of Puritan family activity were quite different from what is held to be right and proper for middle-class marriage and family interaction today. Little interpersonal interaction occurred between a Puritan couple prior to marriage. Marriage was entered into not because the couple were in love, but because it was the religious and economical thing to do. Furthermore, the personal demands of courtship were few because in most cases the parents did the important arranging. When the Puritan couple entered into marriage, they entered a formal status relationship. The success or failure of the marriage was not usually determined by the personal ego-satisfactions achieved from the marriage, but rather by how the marriage conformed to the well-defined expectations of the Puritan community. Thus, the frustration of personal expectations often found in today's marriages was not apt to be found

---

[84] Calhoun, *Family: Colonial Period*, p. 69.
[85] Ibid., p. 70.
[86] Ibid., p. 70.

in the Puritan marriage. The greatest contrast between the Puritan and today's middle-class family, however, is probably in the relationship of parent and child; complete subservience and obedience of children is a concept almost totally alien to most modern middle-class thinking.

On the other hand, there are some close similarities between the Puritan family and the middle-class family of today. For example, the Puritan concept of the wife being a companion to her husband has a very modern sound. And the acceptance of the rights of marital sex for both the husband and the wife, while probably not a common norm, seems to have existed in some Puritan thinking. Another similarity is the acceptance and encouragement of remarriage, although today that involves more divorced than widowed persons, since there are more divorces and fewer widows than in the past.

Without question, many Puritan values have been transmitted to today's society. However, the values have altered since their origin several centuries ago. To attribute to the Puritans all of the qualities found under the popular heading of "puritanical" is not historically accurate. Daniel Bell argues that there has long been a *legend* in the United States about the "puritan" culture. Bell suggests that this legend has arisen out of a mistaken identification of the protestant ethic with the Puritan code. "Puritanism and the 'New England mind' have played a large intellectual role in American life. But in the habits and mores of the masses of the people, the peculiar evangelicism of Methodism and Baptism, with its high emotionalism, its fervor, enthusiasm, and excitement, its revivalism, its excesses of sinning and of high-voltage confessing, has played a much more important role."[87] The "puritanism" that has been handed down is, thus, in many cases the product of influences developed much later in American history. The Puritans were no doubt strict and harsh in many areas of family life, but they are certainly not "guilty" of all they have been accused of.

SELECTED BIBLIOGRAPHY

Calhoun, Arthur W.   *A Social History of the American Family: Colonial Period*, vol. I. New York: Barnes & Noble, Inc., 1960.

Demos, John   *A Little Commonwealth: Family Life in Plymouth Colony.* New York: Oxford University Press, 1970.

Encyclopaedia Britannica   "Puritanism," Vol. XVIII, pp. 777–80, s.v. "Puritanism."

Erickson, Kai T.   *Wayward Puritans.* New York: John Wiley & Sons, Inc., 1966.

Goodsell, Willystine   *A History of the Family as a Social and Educational Institution*, chap. x. New York: The Macmillan Co., 1919.

---

[87] Daniel Bell, *The End of Ideology* (New York: Collier Books, 1961), p. 113.

Hunt, Morton M.   *The Natural History of Love,* chap. vii. New York: Alfred A. Knopf, Inc., 1959.

Queen, Stuart A., Habenstein, Robert W., and Adams, John B.   *The Family in Various Cultures,* chap. xiii. Philadelphia: J. B. Lippincott Co., 1961.

Schneider, Herbert W.   *The Puritan Mind.* New York: Henry Holt & Co., 1930.

Stern, Bernhard J.   *The Family Past and Present,* chap. vi. New York: Appleton-Century-Crofts, Inc., 1938.

Stiles, Henry Reed   *Bundling.* New York: Book Collectors Association, Inc., 1934.

Westermarck, Edward   *The History of Human Marriage.* New York: The Allerton Book Co., 1922.

Wright, Louis B.   *The Cultural Life of the American Colonies.* New York: Harper Torchbooks, 1962.

Chapter *3*

Social Class Variations in Marriage and the Family

As stated in Chapter 1, this book's focus is the contemporary middle-class family in the United States. The Puritan family discussed in the previous chapter provides both contrast and background for an analysis of the modern middle-class family. In this chapter, the upper and lower social-class levels are analyzed to provide contemporary contrasts with the middle-class family.

A number of other contemporary family types with particular social characteristics—based, for example, on religious, racial, or ethnic variations—could also be used to provide contrast with or show variations within the middle class. Our choice was made for several reasons. First, the analysis of various other social-class families is consistent with this book's focus, the middle-class family. Second, social class as an analytic tool for studying variations in social behavior is one of the most fruitful and important approaches available to the social scientist. Third, many Americans are increasingly aware of, and interested in, social class, as illustrated by the common use of a social-class focus in various areas of mass communication. Finally, some insight into social-class variations may give the reader a greater understanding of the marriage and family characteristics of his own social class, and of the relativeness of certain family characteristics he may have formerly assumed were universal in the American culture.

THE LOWER-CLASS FAMILY

Lower class as used here is often referred to as the lower-lower class, to distinguish it from the upper-lower class which has more of the traits and values of the middle class. The lower class to be discussed includes roughly 5 to 10 percent of the total American population. For purposes of discussion, certain arbitrary decisions have been made in defining this lower class. To go into all of the variations of lower-class life, as related to rural-urban, geographical, migrant-nonmigrant, racial, and ethnic factors, would demand a number of chapters or possibly another book. Therefore, the description of the lower class that follows refers for the most part to *a* white, urban lower class.

Some common social characteristics of this lower class are as follows. (1) The level of formal education is eight years or less. (2) The male's occupation is almost always semiskilled or unskilled, and his work pattern is often sporadic, with long periods of unemployment. There is also a strong probability that the woman works in unskilled or service occupations. (3) The total income of the male is rarely over four or five thousand dollars a year, and the families make up a large number of those on the public assistance rolls. (4) Their place of residence is found in the slum areas of the city, often in old homes and buildings converted into small apartments. The ratio of persons per room is often three or four to one, and frequently as many as 20 people share the use of a single toilet.

In looking at the values and behavior patterns of the lower class, we must be careful to avoid imposing middle-class evaluations. The language used to describe lower-class patterns can convey to the reader an interpretation. It should not. Rodman writes, "It is little wonder that if we describe the lower-class family in terms of 'promiscuous' sexual relationships, 'illegitimate' children, 'deserting' men, and 'unmarried' mothers, we are going to see the situation as disorganized and chock-full of problems."[1] Such words as "promiscuous" and "illegitimacy" are often evaluations made by middle-class observers and are frequently not a functional part of the language used by the lower class for describing and assessing its own behavior. (The very term "lower class" itself may sound interpretive.)

Some middle-class people believe that because the lower class has a low commitment to many middle-class values, this suggests a lower-class tolerance for different values and behavior patterns. However, studies have found that while the lower-middle class was at least forgiving of "conventional morality—that is, heterosexual misconduct, drunkenness,

---

[1] Hyman Rodman, *Marriage, Family and Society* (New York: Random House, 1965), p. 223.

and swearing," it was "most harsh in condemnation of other sorts of deviants; the atheist, the homosexual, the 'un-American,' the radical, the artist-intellectual."[2]

Related to lower-class conservatism toward deviant behavior is the conservatism of their views of roles they feel most at ease with. Cohen and Hodges write that "one of the clearest outcomes of this study is an image of the lower-lower class as one reluctant to meet new people and new situations, to form new social relationships, and above all to initiate interactions with strangers. On the contrary, he values and seeks out, more than anybody else, the routine, the familiar, the predictable."[3] Within the same context, and for the same general reasons, Cohen and Hodges also found that "role relationships are more likely for the lower-lower class to be defined in terms of somebody responsible for carrying them out."[4] Such research suggests that when the lower class are compared with the middle class they prefer fewer role involvements and they want their role-sets to be clearly defined in terms of power.

The lower-class philosophy of life is also reflected in the following beliefs or ways of seeing the world around them. *Luck:* What happens in the world is determined primarily through forces external to the individual. "One may be spared unpleasantness by good fortune, one may be 'lucky,' but one cannot be personally successful against difficulty."[5] Luck is closely related to lower-class *fatalism.* Lower-class individuals often see the world around them as confusing and chaotic; they do not feel that they understand it, and they feel that what goes on is essentially unpredictable—up to fate. Many attempt to explain or rationalize the chaos and lack of control over their own destiny by blaming it on an abstract "they," a scapegoat which often materializes as individuals seen as "powers"—the police, employers, city hall, and so forth. And because lower-class life tends to focus on the present, the time dimension in life is *the present,* with a tendency to forget the past and ignore the future. Because the problems of the present often seem overwhelming, lower-class individuals view the future as beyond their control and, in consequence, rarely plan ahead.

Another important influence on lower-class life patterns is the constant fear of "getting into *trouble*," a major concern of male and female, adults and children. Miller writes, "For men, 'trouble' frequently involves fighting or sexual adventures while drinking; for women, sexual involvement

---

[2] Albert K. Cohen and Harold M. Hodges, Jr., "Characteristics of the Lower-Blue-Collar Class," *Social Problems,* Spring 1963, p. 321.

[3] Ibid., p. 316.

[4] Ibid., p. 320.

[5] Lee Rainwater, *And the Poor Get Children* (Chicago: Quadrangle Books, 1960), p. 52.

with disadvantageous consequences."[6] "Trouble" is not a concern over the moral or legal implications of behavior, but rather over the possible consequences.

The concept of *fun* is also important to many lower-class individuals. Many middle-class "satisfactions with achievement" are not available or are of little interest to the lower class. The stress on the present, rather than the future, implies a seeking out of immediate pleasures. This interest in fun is also related to the fear of trouble, because trouble implies the pressure of forces that will curtail the amount of fun. Fun also implies some personal modification of the fatalistic attitude in that the individual can seek out the pleasurable and thereby he can determine some aspects of his own life.

Family relationships are often important to lower-class individuals because they are not "joiners," and, being suspicious of formal agencies, will turn to relatives or a few friends when help is needed. A study of lower-class migrants found that "family, kin, and close friendship have much deeper personal roots for migrants into the urban community than might have been anticipated. This seems to be true for both recent migrants and for those who were older and more settled."[7] When the world around is viewed as hostile and confusing, it becomes natural to seek out those who live in the "same world" with the same kinds of problems. Another reason that the lower class often turn to relatives for help is that they frequently have relatives handy to them. One study of the lower class found that about half, as compared to about one tenth of a middle-class sample, had close relatives within a four-block radius.[8]

These general values of the lower class will serve as a background for a discussion of some of the characteristics and values found in courtship, marriage, and the family. A few comments on the world of the lower-class adolescent precede this discussion. Miller points out that the worlds of both boys and girls are the *one-sex peer unit* rather than the two-parent family unit.[9] Because lower-class home life is often limited by absent parents and crowding, children at very young ages move out onto the streets. There, they usually interact and identify with their age-sex groups. The interaction across sex lines is often limited, in contrast to middle-class interaction, because the lower-class adolescent generally

---

[6] Walter B. Miller, "Lower Class Culture as a Generating Milieu of Gang Delinquency," in Marvin E. Wolfgang, Leonard Savitz, and Norman Johnson, *The Sociology of Crime and Delinquency* (New York: John Wiley & Sons, Inc., 1962), p. 268.

[7] Leonard Blumberg and Robert R. Bell, "Urban Migration and Kinship Ties," *Social Problems*, Spring 1959, p. 331.

[8] Cohen and Hodges, "Lower-Blue-Collar Class," p. 310; and Russell L. Curtis, Jr. and Louis A. Zurcher, Jr., "Voluntary Associations and the Social Integration of the Poor," *Social Problems*, Winter 1971, pp. 339–57.

[9] Miller, "Gang Delinquency," p. 273.

lacks the verbal skills needed for extended boy-girl social interaction. Also his age-sex peers provide him with what sense of identification he has, and they frequently act as a one-sex group or gang.

The importance of the age-sex peer group, particularly for the adolescent boy, is illustrated by the following description of what it is like for a boy to grow up in the lower-class culture.

> A boy spends the major part of the first 12 years in the company of and under the domination of women. He learns during that time that women are the people who count, that men are despicable, dangerous, and desirable. He also learns that a 'real man' is hated for his irresponsibility but is considered very attractive on Saturday night. He learns, too, that if he really loves his mother, he will not grow up to be "just like all men," but that despite her best efforts, his mother's pride and joy will very likely turn out to be as much a "rogue male" as the rest. In short, he has sex-role problems.[10]

The boy's adolescent associations with his age-sex peers is the process whereby he attains his independence and masculinity, and acquires all of the characteristics his mother had told him were undesirable about men.

The values the lower-class boy accepts and the roles he tries to fill center around activity defined as masculine; his focal concerns are trouble, toughness, smartness, excitement, fate, and autonomy. Miller suggests that "the genesis of the intense concern over 'toughness' in the lower class culture is probably related to the fact that a significant proportion of the lower class males are reared in a predominantly female household, and lack a consistently present male figure with whom to identify and from whom to learn essential components of a 'male' role."[11] In one respect the lower-class boy is effectively socialized by the lower-class man—the boy imitates the man's rejection of the home as well as his high involvement in all-male groups.

Lower-class adolescent girls value being attractive to the males, even though they are reared by the same mothers as the boys and have been told the same negative things about men. That men are irresponsible and frequently mean, the girls have often observed for themselves in their own fathers and other men. Regardless of what they have been told and have seen, the girls often see relationships with boys as adventurous and romantic, especially in contrast to the life they are leading. Many of them are quite romantic in their thinking and tend to believe what they have heard and seen is true for men in *general*, but not for the *particular* man they will find for themselves.

---

[10] David J. Bordua, "Delinquent Subculture: Sociological Interpretation of Gang Delinquency," *The Annals*, November 1961, p. 129.

[11] Miller, "Gang Delinquency," p. 220.

Dating and Courtship

In most cases, lower-class adolescents follow a pattern of early and steady dating. A "significant other" is often needed and may be acquired through the agreement of "going steady." This, in addition, partially protects the girl, because if she dates randomly, she is not identified with any one boy and may, therefore, be subject to strong sexual pressures. Probably, too, the lower-class youngster so desperately seeks adult status that the semipermanent relationship of "going steady" gives him the illusion of engaging in adult behavior. This early, steady dating pattern often results in sexual laxities, unplanned pregnancies, and early marriages.

Lower-class adolescents do very little shopping around through random dating for the eventual marriage partner. Rainwater writes that "many in the lower class give the impression of having just drifted together—they do not seem to have regarded themselves as active choosers of a mate but are inclined to think simply that it was about time to get married."[12] Drifting together reflects the lower-class value of stressing the present not the future. The pattern of thinking and planning needed in seeking out the best mate and planning marriage is often alien to the lower class. Rainwater goes on to point out that members of the lower class rarely show enterprise in seeking or choosing marriage partners. "Rarely do they express strong feelings about the decision to marry. Resignation, a feeling that fate is dictating what is happening, and a lack of much elaboration in conscious planning and consideration are frequently reflected in the use of such phrases as 'it was just time,' 'somehow it was settled' or 'we just did it.' "[13]

When compared with the middle-class, dating and "going steady" in the lower class are different relationships, characterized by a lack of planning and, often, a desire to escape from role frustrations rather than enter new roles through anticipation. Stress on immediate satisfactions and time restriction to the present often make dating and courtship in the lower class less of a process leading to marriage and more of a series of day-to-day events frequently having little logic or pattern to provide overall continuity. As a result, when marriage does occur, it just happens; it is not seen as the meaningful end result of a dating-courtship process, as it often is in the middle class.

Premarital Sex. Attitudes about premarital coitus are more commonly permissive in the lower than in the middle class. It should not be assumed, however, that lower-class attitudes toward sex in general are more liberal. While premarital intercourse is often viewed as normal, and visiting prostitutes is acceptable, such sexual expression as heavy and ex-

---

[12] Rainwater, *And the Poor Get Children,* p. 62.
[13] Ibid., p. 63.

tended petting and masturbation are strongly condemned and often viewed as perversions. What is accepted is the sexual act as related to actual coitus with little foreplay or variations in technique and procedure.

Permissiveness about premarital coitus is reflected in the lower-class male's preoccupation with sex. The male sees sexual conquest as a strong sign of his masculinity, and in a world where other signs are often unavailable, the sex sign takes on great significance. By seeing sex as conquest, he gains a sense of personal achievement. Restricting sex to the act, without frills, also means that the sexual act is to satisfy only the male, thereby providing him with an activity considered exclusively male. Even when the female achieves satisfaction from sexual relations, the male interprets that as a sign of *his* sexual ability.

Miller suggests that "a concern over homosexuality runs like a persistent thread through lower class culture."[14] This may be due to the early female dominance in the boy's life and because of the few achieved activities that give him a sense of his masculinity. Any indication of homosexuality is threatening to his sexual prowess with girls, which is so important to his sense of masculinity. Middle-class boys will kiddingly call one another "queer," but in the lower class this is taboo.

The male has no respect or concern for the promiscuous girl because she only functions as a sex outlet, while the "one-man" girl not only provides a sexual outlet, but also can satisfy his ego-need for masculinity through personal conquest and sexual exclusiveness. Because of respect, many of the "one-man" girls are married by the boy if they get pregnant. This appears to be common because the number of lower-class girls pregnant at the time of marriage is high. When all unmarried pregnancies are taken into account, probably over half of all lower-class women are pregnant at some time prior to marriage. However, the pregnant girl does not necessarily have either the inclination or the ability to get the father to marry her.

"One-man" girls probably provide only a small part of the total premarital sexual experience of the lower-class male. The much higher frequency of premarital experiences for the male than for the female suggests that prostitutes and "promiscuous" girls account for a large majority of his premarital sexual experiences. Kinsey found that in the 16- to 20-year-old group with an eighth-grade education or less, the frequency per week of premarital coitus for the male was 1.6 times as contrasted with 0.3 times for the female. In contrast, among the college population coital frequency for the male was 0.2 per week and the female 0.1.[15] By educational level, the differences among the females was not great, but among the males it was very great. It may also be noted that

---

[14] Miller, "Gang Delinquency," p. 270.

[15] Alfred C. Kinsey, et al., *Sexual Behavior in the Human Female* (Philadelphia: W. B. Saunders, 1953), p. 78.

the less educated female has a slightly higher frequency of premarital coitus per week than does the college-level male.

The lower-class girl's decision as to premarital coitus is obviously difficult. She may feel that virginity is one of her strongest weapons in acquiring a husband. Yet because of the male's great desire for sexual conquest, he may not be willing to continue a relationship with her without sexual relations. In many cases, rather than lose him the girl will engage in premarital coitus. However, if she does this with more than one or two boys, she may find herself defined as "promiscuous" and have her chances of marriage greatly reduced. If the girl gets pregnant, no great personal or social pressure is put on the boy to marry her, and she may find herself an unmarried mother, with marriage even more difficult because of the baby.

Thus, in the lower class, premarital sex frequently centers around "exploitation." The boy seeks sexual conquests without personal commitment as an expression of his masculinity, while the girl tries to use sex to move the male into marriage. In the lower class, neither the male nor the female generally believes that sex has any great personal satisfaction for the female. Therefore, to say that the lower-class female "uses sex" is accurate in the sense that she frequently gets no personal satisfaction from it. Then, too, when a girl has premarital coitus and gets pregnant, she often says it is really not her fault, but the fault of the man. The view is that men, because of their sexual insistence, are responsible for the pregnancy, but that the girl must "pay" for the man's sexual desires.

Marriage.   To say that a lower-class couple are married does not always imply the same thing it does in the middle class. Lower-class "marriage" may mean simply that a couple are living together; whether they are legally married may be of little importance. A woman may be "married" a dozen times in her lifetime and have children from a number of different "husbands" in that in any given relationship the woman may define herself as being "married." The temporary nature of numerous "marriages" does not usually stop the woman from entering new "marriages." In part this reflects the fact that the lower-class woman expects little from a "husband." Rainwater points out that the lower-class woman is often quite willing to settle for some permanence in a not-too-happy relationship because she feels nothing better is to be gained from a man; indeed, she feels lucky if he will just stay around.[16] Marriage may offer little to the lower-class woman, but she nevertheless sees it as better than nothing.

Women in the lower class frequently enter marriage at a young age because they feel somewhat lost when they outgrow the status of daughter, and they look forward to establishing themselves in what often seems the clear-cut status of wife and mother. As officially recorded, the average age

---

[16] Rainwater, *Poor Get Children*, pp. 72–73.

for first marriage of lower-class women cannot be reliably used because the records do not include the many who enter a "marriage" relationship without being legally married. Eighteen years of age would seem a reasonable average for the lower-class woman's first marriage.

Studies show that the age difference between husband and wife is greater in the lower than in the middle-class. The age differential may be due to the male resisting marriage and the female seeing the older male as a somewhat better marriage partner.

Entering into marriage for the lower class calls for little celebration and often little significant change in role behavior. Life continues after marriage as it did before, except that the couple define themselves as married. Marriage may mean little more for the male than complete sexual rights, and for the female than that the husband probably will contribute something to their living expenses. At the start of marriage, the lower-class couple often do not set up any kind of home of their own.

The values of companionship and sharing so important in middle-class marriages are often absent from the marital interaction of lower-class couples. A necessary condition for effective husband-wife interaction is that both have the ability and the motivation to communicate with each other. Komarovsky found in her sample that while little marital communication was characteristic of only 12 percent of the high-school educated wives she studied, it was descriptive of 41 percent of the less educated women.[17] However, it may be that many in the lower class *expect* little communication between husband and wife and, therefore, don't find its absence too important. This appears to be the case in the Komarovsky study, where 59 percent of the high-school educated spouses believed that a lack of conversation in marriage was a genuine problem, but only 26 percent of the lower educated spouses gave the same assessment.[18]

Leisure time is usually not pursued by the lower-class husband and wife in a paired relationship. This is reflected by their having few friendships as a couple with other couples, and also because they seldom go out as a couple for an evening's entertainment. Komarovsky found that "about one fifth of the couples never visit with another couple apart from relatives. An additional 16 percent do so only infrequently, a few times a year."[19] When the lower-class male is at home, he usually wants to be let alone—not bothered with family demands. When he goes out, he generally goes with other men and his destination is often neighborhood bars that are for the most part all-male hangouts. Yet there is some evidence that while many lower-class men function as a part of all-male groups, they do not develop close friendships with any one man. The male's low

---

[17] Mirra Komarovsky, *Blue-Collar Marriage* (New York: Random House, 1962), p. 144.

[18] Ibid., p. 119.

[19] Ibid., p. 311.

interpersonal involvement, when compared to that of the woman, seems to hold true both in and out of lower-class family relationships. For example, Komarovsky found that while about 60 percent of the wives had close friendships outside the family, only about 20 percent of the husbands did.[20] But even though the lower-class male has few close friends, his all-male social groups are important to him because that masculine world contributes to his personal sense of masculinity.

Other studies have also shown that the experiences of working-class women are more localized and circumscribed than for their male counterparts. Working-class women have minimal experiences in the outside world and tend to view it fearfully. Often when they can move to better areas they regret the move, despite better living conditions, because of the disruption of the kinship and friendship network.

The wife's social life often centers around relatives or friends of the same sex. The husbands of these friends are absent for the same reasons as her own is. With her husband often not functioning in a close role relationship, the lower-class wife frequently turns to others for a significant role relationship. Komarovsky found that "two thirds of the wives have at least one person apart from their husbands in whom they confide deeply personal experiences. In 35 percent of the cases the wife not only enjoys such intimate friendships but shares some significant segment of her life *more fully* with her confidants than with her husband."[21]

The generally low family involvement of the lower-class male often means there is no great difference in his behavior patterns before and after marriage. If he gives some of his earnings to his wife, he often defines himself as being a good husband. Since neither his marriage nor his job contribute very much to his sense of masculinity, the maintained interaction with his sex peers therefore continues to be important. Unlike many middle-class males, he rarely has any positive identification with his occupation. In fact, in the lower class, the aim is often to escape from thinking of the job. In his perceptive article "The Myth of the Happy Worker," Harvey Swados writes, "The worker's attitude towards his work is generally compounded of hatred, shame, and resignation," and adds that the kind of work done is degrading "to any man who ever dreams of doing something with his life."[22] Thus, to gain at least some assurance of significance, the male turns to the world of other males like himself, putting aside home demands and the demanding nature of his job.

---

[20] Ibid., p. 215.

[21] Ibid., p. 208.

[22] Harvey Swados, "The Myth of the Happy Worker," in Maurice R. Stein, Arthur J. Vidich, and David M. White, *Identity and Anxiety* (Glencoe, Ill.: The Free Press, 1960), pp. 199, 202. Also see H. Roy Kaplan and Curt Tausky, "Work and the Welfare Cadillac: The Function of and Commitment to Work among the Hard-Core Unemployed," *Social Problems,* Spring 1972, pp. 469–83; and Leonard Goodwin, "How Suburban Families View the Work Orientations of the Welfare Poor," *Social Problems,* Winter 1972, pp. 337–48.

Some disagreement exists between the lower-class man and woman as to what constitutes a "good husband." Rainwater writes, "Men tend to give first importance to being a good father, but few women do. Instead, women are more likely to want their husbands first of all to be either good providers or good lovers. Three fifths of the lower class women in our sample ranked being a good lover first or second in importance for a good husband, yet less than 5 percent of the lower class husbands ranked this role as high, and three fifths of them put it in the 'least important' category."[23] Many lower-class women see a "good lover" as extending far beyond sexual relations to the much broader desire for some consideration of them by their husband. On the other hand, the husband probably ranks "good lover" low because he also sees it as meaning he should give his wife emotional consideration, which he is often not willing to give because it is not "masculine" behavior.

There is some argument that the performance of the mother role tends to be standardized across social class lines. While by contrast, father roles change more notably as class and education attainment varies. This would suggest that mothers are similar in how they fill their roles because what they can and must do as mothers is relatively fixed. Certainly for mothers there are fewer options available than there are for men in filling the father role.[24]

The primary role of the woman centers around her being a mother, rather than a wife. She often has the responsibility not only of caring for the children, but also of meeting the day-to-day needs of the family. A study by Olsen found that "responsibility taken by husbands—both alone and jointly with their wives—is greatest in middle-status families and less in high- and low-status homes."[25] Rainwater found that lower-class men "sharply restrict the definition of a good wife to the mother-housekeeper components."[26] For many middle-class women there is often a strong personal desire to fill roles besides the traditional ones of wife and mother. But for lower-class women there appears to be little personal frustration related to any low evaluation of the traditional roles of wife, mother, and housekeeper. Komarovsky found there was hardly a trace of any feeling of low prestige attached to being housewives by working-class or lower-class wives.[27]

Very often the lower-class woman is the head of her household. Female-head households account for almost 40 percent of those below the

---

[23] Rainwater, *Poor Get Children*, p. 67.

[24] Cora A. Martin and Leonard Benson, "Parental Perceptions of the Role of Television in Parent-Child Interaction," *Journal of Marriage and the Family*, August 1970, p. 414.

[25] Marvin E. Olson, "Distribution of Family Responsibilities and Social Stratification," *Marriage and Family Living*, February 1960, p. 65.

[26] Rainwater, *Poor Get Children*, p. 67.

[27] Komarovsky, *Blue-Collar Marriage*, p. 49.

poverty line. This suggests that the economic and social disadvantages of being female may have an impact on class differentials in family structure. Joan Acker points out that when stratification theorists talk about some classes, they are really talking about women to a great extent. "It is possible that some of the differences they discuss are sex rather than class differences."[28] This is an aspect of analyzing the lower class that needs much more research.

Marital Coitus.   Many of the middle-class values regarding marriage interaction are either totally absent or modified in the lower class. The lower-class marriage is of a patriarchal nature when there is a husband present. The male tends to be patriarchal in his assumed rights of authority, but not usually in his obligations. The patriarchal pattern is limited because most of the time the male's world centers around other men; therefore, such values as sharing and mutual ego-satisfaction common to middle-class marriages are often totally absent from lower-class marriages.

The absence of "sharing" is further illustrated by lower-class attitudes about marital sex. While marital sex is an important part of lower-class life, particularly for the husband, actual knowledge about sex is restricted. "The typical lower class pattern among men includes at most the knowledge that men and women have sexual intercourse, and that contraception can be effected with a condom." Rainwater goes on to point out that lower-class women generally have even less information about sex and methods of birth control than do men.[29] Thus, in the lower class, sexual satisfaction is basically for the male. "Both husbands and wives feel that sexual gratification for the wife is much less important, so that, consciously at least, wives seem generally content if intercourse results in the husband's pleasure even if not their own."[30] Sexually satisfying her husband indicates to the wife that she continues to have the sex "weapon" in dealing with him. The fact that marital sex may be so viewed is reflected in the male view that marital coitus is a "getting-on-getting-off" experience. "It is a good idea to get away from the woman as quickly as possible—to run or to retreat into oneself—in order to avoid consequences and possible demands."[31] Marital sex is often, therefore, a constant battle, with the male "getting" but trying not to give, and the wife "giving" and hoping to get something in return.

A number of studies have indicated a positive relationship between sexual satisfaction and overall adjustment in marriage. But Komarovsky points out that this relationship may vary with social class. She writes,

[28] Joan Acker, "Women and Social Stratification: A Case of Intellectual Sexism," in Joan Huber, *Changing Women in a Changing Society* (Chicago: University of Chicago Press, 1973), pp. 177–78.

[29] Rainwater, *Poor Get Children,* p. 64.

[30] Ibid., p. 94.

[31] Ibid., p. 81.

"Because some of our less-educated women expect little psychological intimacy in marriage, and their standards of personal relationships are not demanding, they were able to dissociate the sexual response from the total relationship."[32] This also suggests that marital sex is less apt to be a part of a broader interpersonal intimacy in the lower class than it often is in the middle class.

The lack of importance attached to marital sex by the lower-class wife is reflected in the lack of sexual satisfaction she achieves. Rainwater found in his sample that only about 25 percent of the lower-class women indicated some measure of personal enjoyment in sexual relations, and "about 40 percent of the lower-lower class women indicate a real rejection of sexuality."[33] Further evidence is found in the Kinsey study of the female, by education, and achievement of orgasm in marital coitus. For example, for those females with eight years of education or less, 28 percent had never achieved orgasm even after five years of marriage, as contrasted with 17 percent with "some high school" and 15 percent with "some college."[34] Generally, a "good" wife in the lower class is not expected to show any great interest in, or satisfaction with, marital sex. Being interested in sex, even with her husband, may raise questions about her "goodness." This is reflected in the belief that "good women stay at home and are not too interested in what goes on in the outside world. Bad women, of course, are mainly interested in sex, and are to be found mostly in bars and hotel rooms."[35]

So the lower class is characterized by a minimum concern for the sexual needs of the wife—even when it is recognized that she has such needs. To illustrate, Masters and Johnson found that the lowest-educated males rarely seek help for premature ejaculation. In fact in the lower class this may not even be considered a problem and may provide welcome relief for the woman "accepting and fulfilling a role as a sexual object without exposure to or personal belief in the concept of parity between the sexes in the privileges and the pleasures of sexual functioning. Rapid release from sexual service frequently is accepted as a blessing by women living in the restrictive levels of this subculture's inherent subculture."[36]

It logically follows from the attitudes of the lower class that extramarital relations are acceptable for the male but severely condemned for the female. The wife is expected to be completely faithful. But for the male, extramarital adventure is not barred, though he may try to keep it separate from his married life. In most respects, the married man sees his

---

[32] Komarovsky, *Blue-Collar Marriage,* p. 349.

[33] Rainwater, *Poor Get Children,* p. 121.

[34] Kinsey, et al., *Female,* p. 401.

[35] Rainwater, *Poor Get Children,* pp. 79–80.

[36] William H. Masters and Virginia E. Johnson, *Human Sexual Inadequacy* (Boston: Little, Brown & Co., 1970), p. 93.

potential world of sexual outlet in the same way as he did when he was single. A common rationalization is used by both men and women to explain the husband's philandering—"that's the way men are." The greatest threat to the lower-class wife from her husband's philandering is often not her "ego" loss, but the implied loss of the use of marital coitus as a means of control or influence over her husband.

Children. The attitudes and behavior patterns of the lower class in regard to sex are closely related to some of the attitudes about having children. The woman who both desires and has children is strongly approved in the lower class because having children is seen as the woman's primary reason for being. Rainwater says: "The woman who wants only one child is condemned . . . emphatically for being a bad person, for going against her nature—and the woman who wants no children is beyond the pale, she should not have married at all."[37] The lower-class woman who accepts these values not only wants children, but wants a number of them. Her own experience of growing up in a large family with poverty around her does not deter her from moving into the same situation. In part, this reflects her inability to relate past experience to the present in realistically anticipating the future. The male's interest in children often centers around his own ego-needs, rather than around interest in the children. "Since they (the males) tend to feel ineffective and weak in relation to their world, fathering a string of children comes to represent a kind of defiant demonstration that they are real men."[38] They are getting their wife pregnant as one of the few signs of their masculine effectiveness.

Given the woman's strong desire for children, and the man's view of his wife's pregnancies as a sign of his masculinity, attempts to control pregnancy are obviously often limited and ineffective. Even when there is a feeling of having enough children, wishfulness often substitutes for action; that is, lower-class limitation of family size is often "a subject for fantasy and tentative goals, but not one in which concerted effort is devoted."[39] As a result of lack of interest or ability in controlling family size, the lower-class wife expects to have a large number of children and, in general, is more likely at any age to become pregnant. Couples in the middle class who exert increasingly efficient rational control over pregnancy sometimes find it hard to understand the frequency with which lower-class couples have large numbers of children. A partial explanation is the "fatalistic" attitudes toward pregnancy that restrict motivation toward, or any interest in, contraception.

Often, even when the lower-class woman wants to practice contraception, she gets little help or understanding from her husband. In Rain-

---

[37] Rainwater, *Poor Get Children*, p. 55.

[38] Ibid., p. 85.

[39] Ibid., p. 59.

water's study, 65 percent of the women claimed that contraception was noneffective for them because the husband was impatient and demanding. "Such men feel that having sexual relations is their central right in marriage and that their wives are duty-bound to make themselves available on demand. The husbands are therefore highly impatient with the interferences which contraception represents."[40]

Another attitude among lower-class women that limits the effectiveness of contraception is stated as, "He's the one that always wants it, let him worry about the protection."[41] Thus, the woman leaves it to the male to take the responsibility by using a condom. But the male is not often willing to take responsibility because contraception interferes with his sexual rights. The title of Rainwater's book accurately describes the result of these attitudes: *And the Poor Get Children.*

The lower-class mother is characterized by a large number of children and by having her first pregnancy at a young age. In a recent study in New York City it was found that about 40 percent of the mothers on welfare had five or more children. The same study found that a quarter of the mothers first became pregnant when they were 16 years of age or less, and half were pregnant at age 18 or younger. The fact that many of them had far more children than they wanted is reflected in the finding that almost 60 percent said if they could start over again they would have two children or less.[42]

An interest in contraception does not usually develop, if it ever does, until after the lower-class woman has had several children. Initially the woman sees children as her primary means of attaining personal significance. So long as the children do not interfere with the husband's "rights," the mother controls the children's lives—the notion of shared parental roles being largely absent in lower-class families. The mother sees the children as her property and her responsibility, "and it is through them that she expects to fulfill herself and her potentialities; if her children love her now and in the future, she feels she has gained the only really important gratification which her world allows her."[43] However, as indicated by the son breaking away from her in his early adolescence and the daughter entering marriage in her late teens, the mother does not, for long, maintain importance for her children.

The father's role is often sporadic and may last only a short period of time. The father's reaction to his children—when he is around them—is generally determined by his mood. He can be indulgent if he feels like it, because he does not concern himself with the rearing of the child. When

---

[40] Rainwater, *Poor Get Children*, p. 240.

[41] Ibid., p. 241.

[42] Laurence Podell, *Families on Welfare in New York City* (The City University of New York, 1968), pp. xx–xxi.

[43] Rainwater, *Poor Get Children*, p. 86.

the father is home, the home is often father-centered, not child-centered as is often the case in the middle class. Because the father has a strong sense of his "rights" in the home, he is not apt to brook violation and interference from either the wife or the children. With physical punishment and even violence common in the lower class, the male can and does make sure of his "rights" through his greater physical strength. The depressed nature of the home setting often spurs on the male's feelings of frustration and suspicions of self-inadequacy, so that he is apt to strike out in any direction at what may seem slight provocation by his wife or children. If his negative feelings become strong enough, he may walk out and disappear.

It appears that many lower-class males want to be *seen* as being influential and possessing power with regard to their families, but not necessarily to *function* accordingly. The male may judge the respect given to him in his husband and father roles on the basis of the amount of compliance by his wife and children to his wishes, but this does not mean he will attempt to run the household; he will leave that to his wife. Rainwater points out that the lower-class husband's being tangential to family functioning is also often what the wife prefers. "That is, in spite of the worrying she may do about the possibility of her husband straying away from home and thus depriving the family of its source of support and measure of respectability, the lower-lower class wife seems to find handling the family on her own to her liking, or at least consistent with what she has learned to expect from living in her particular social world."[44]

Childrearing practices in the lower class, as followed by the mother, often show a mixture of permissiveness and authoritarianism. For example, lower-class mothers, often more permissive in feeding, weaning, and toilet training their children than are middle-class mothers, lack the compulsiveness to "move the child along," possibly for several reasons. The mother does not concern herself with the future, and therefore has no great interests in leading the child into anticipated stages of development; time and order have less importance in the thinking of the lower class than the middle class, and it does not matter if something is done now or later; and finally, there is not the middle-class stress on neatness and cleanliness and, therefore, the need for such learning as toilet training does not loom as important. In other areas, the mother may be very authoritarian and arbitrary and punish the child with little rhyme or reason. This may be due to the acceptance of physical expression, the inability to verbalize, the sense of personal frustration, and the lone-parent responsibility of the lower-class mother.

As previously mentioned, there is evidence to suggest that children are

---

[44] Lee Rainwater, *Family Design* (Chicago: Aldine Publishing Co., 1965), pp. 59–60.

very important to the lower-class woman because she has few other adult roles that give her personal satisfaction. Yet the problems of rearing a child in the lower class may cut down on the satisfactions she can achieve through the mother role. One study found that about one fifth of the low-social-class parents studied said their children gave them more trouble than pleasure and this was about five times the rate found for the high social class respondents. This finding "seems a direct contradiction of the popular statement that the pleasure of the poor is in their children, that this is their form of 'wealth.' "[45]

As mentioned in Chapter 1, a high aspiration level for her children is an important value to the middle-class mother. The lower-class mother, on the other hand, because of the reality of the world and the feeling of inability to influence the future, often has very limited expectations for her children. Continued education seems both hopeless and useless.[46] The lower-class mother may hope for nothing more than that her children will stay out of trouble and be decent to her in the future. Hoping that the child will be able to move out of the lower class is completely outside the frame of reference—the realm of possibility—of lower-class thinking. When the mother does have expectations for the child's upward social mobility, it generally means that she has a membership in the lower class, but has taken on at least some middle-class values as her reference. Such a mother is in, but not of, the lower class.

Marriage Instability. By social-class level, divorce and desertion rates are highest in the lower classes. But the official records say little about the many relationships that are named as "marriages" by the couple and then end after a period of time. A rough overall estimate would suggest that probably no more than one third of the number of marriages in the lower class are permanent. When contrasted with other social classes, a lower-class marriage is much more apt to end through desertion or divorce than death.

Many lower-class women who have been married have a low level of expectation about their husbands and their marriages and see little future for themselves in permanent relationships. For example, in the New York study "most formerly married women did not expect to reconcile or remarry in the next few years; most of them said that they were unconcerned about being without husbands."[47] And when many do move into new relationships the expectations are not very high.

After one marriage relationship ends, the individuals often move into new marriage relationships, either legally or illegally. For example, legal

---

[45] Thomas S. Langner and Stanley T. Michael, *Life Stress and Mental Health* (New York: The Free Press of Glencoe, 1963), p. 341.

[46] See Christopher Jencks, *Inequality: A Reassessment of the Effect of Family and Schooling in America* (New York: Harper, 1972).

[47] Podell, *Families on Welfare,* p. xvii.

records show that "a fourth of the recently married persons with no high school education had been married twice or more, whereas only a tenth of the college graduates had been remarried."[48] When unofficial marriages are added to official marriages, then the "serial marriage" of the lower class is very frequent. The social pattern of "remarriage" seems to be about the same as first marriage in that the male expects exclusive sex rights, expects the woman to cook for him, and expects "to be let alone." The female wants some financial help and some indication that the husband cares for her. Because the partners' sets of expectations are seen as contradictory, the relationship is often ripe for ending almost as soon as it is started.

Out of the series of "marriages" comes a large number of children, and with the large number of broken marriages and remarriages, lower-class children often experience marriage breakup and step-parents, almost always a stepfather. Mayer estimates that at the lower-class level, 50 to 60 percent of the families with adolescent children have been broken, often more than once.[49] Since parents are important role models for marriage, many lower-class children obviously grow up seeing marriage as a series of transitory relationships with a variety of partners.

Although some writers romanticize the lower class, the actual situation in regard to their family life does not justify it. The picture of the lower lower-class family presented here is a dismal one, both from a social and personal point of view. However, the picture presented has been a general one, and there are of course exceptions to all that has been said about lower-class attitudes and behavior.

THE UPPER-CLASS FAMILY

Compared to the many studies done on the middle class, the discussion of the lower-class family drew upon a limited body of empirical research. Empirical research on the upper class is even more limited. The works of Baltzell and Hollingshead are the main sources in the discussion that follows.[50]

Upper class as used in this discussion refers to the social-class level that

---

[48] Paul C. Glick and Hugh Carter, "Marriage Patterns and Educational Level," *American Sociological Review*, June 1958, p. 296.

[49] Kurt B. Mayer, *Class and Society* (New York: Doubleday and Co., Inc., 1955), p. 51.

[50] E. Digby Baltzell, *Philadelphia Gentlemen* (Glencoe, Illinois: The Free Press, 1958); and August B. Hollingshead and Frederick C. Redlich, *Social Class and Mental Illness* (New York: John Wiley & Sons, Inc., 1958). The writer is greatly indebted to E. Digby Baltzell for providing many insights into the upper-class family through private conversations, as well as through speaking to the writer's Marriage and Family classes on the upper-class family.

has sometimes been referred to as the upper-upper class. Two variables are important in defining the upper-upper class: First, the family has money. How much money is difficult to say, but the amount must at least be adequate for maintaining an upper-class style of life. Second, the family must have had its money for at least two generations, and very frequently for three or more generations. This second point distinguishes the upper-upper class from the lower-upper class (or *elites*, in Baltzell's terminology). In many cases, the lower-uppers may have more money than the upper-upper class, but they do not qualify as upper-uppers because their money is first generation.

Of all social-class levels, the upper class is by far the smallest, probably including less than 1 percent of the total American population; however, in wealth, power, and influence, members of this class are an extremely significant part of the population. To the rest of the social-class hierarchy the upper class may be unknown, vaguely recognized, held to be a "different world," or, for the upper-middle or the lower-upper, represent the class level for mobility aspirations that will rarely be reached.

Having had wealth for at least two generations is important because of what it has meant in the socialization of the upper-class individual. Growing up without financial problems produces a socialization process different from one in which money problems are serious considerations. When money is not a problem, one grows to accept that which is presented to him; the fact of the money itself is of little significance. For example, the youngster in the upper class is provided with the care, education, and privileges that money will provide, with little conscious awareness that money is involved. This is in contrast to the mobility-oriented middle class where the child grows up with aspirations for things that must be achieved. In the upper class, the child is reared in a family with no sense of social striving because they are already at the top. He is taught the values of a social position he acquired at birth, and social anxiety is not a part of his socialization process.

The values and way of life in the upper class are based upon the family *not* striving; the symbols of class position are not important because they do not *have* to be shown. The fact that they are there is known by those who matter, their fellow members of the upper class; recognition by the lower social classes is generally of no importance. The upper class believes in being inconspicuous; the compulsion to show material wealth in conspicuous ways often gives away the elite (lower-upper) class.

Clearly, the family is the basic unit in the upper class, and various families through interaction with one another define upper-class attitudes and behavior. Baltzell writes, "These families are at the top of the social class hierarchy; they are brought up together, are friends, and are intermarried with one another; and finally, they maintain a distinctive style of life and a kind of primary group solidarity which sets them apart from the rest of the population."[51] The distinctive style is illustrated by Baltzell by the speech of the upper class. The following illustrates upper-class as contrasted with middle-class usage: "The upper class *live* in a *house, employ servants* to *wash* the *curtains* and clean the *furniture,* including a *sofa;* they use the *toilet,* the *porch, library,* or *playroom.* The middle classes *reside* in a *home, hire help* or *domestics* to *launder* the *drapes* and clean the *house furnishings* which include a bedroom *suite* (like suit) and a *davenport;* they use the *lavoratory,* the *veranda, den,* or *rumpus room.*"[52]

To summarize, the basic values of the upper class are: one, respect for familism and lineage; two, a belief that money is important, but *only* as a means to achieve ends; three, contempt for pretense, striving, and conspicuous consumption. It will be seen that these values are reflected in a number of ways in the upper-class marriage and family patterns.

Dating and Courtship

The world of the upper-class adolescent is tightly circumscribed by his social class because many of his activities are determined by the family or by peer groups that tend to reflect upper-class parental values. Upper-class adolescent life is usually much more formalized than that of the middle class because the basic values of formality, important both for the present and the future, are being transmitted. The very fact that almost all of the important social activities of the adolescent are with the family or with the children of other upper-class families provides a situation where strong homogeneous values can be transmitted and reinforced. The upper-class adolescent follows a way of life which stresses what he is and will continue to be by virtue of his birth. By contrast, the middle-class adolescent is being prepared for a somewhat unknown future that he is to achieve.

Dating in the upper class, especially for girls, is restricted to persons within the same class level. For most upper-class girls, dating outside the social class is limited simply because they do not come into contact with boys in other social classes. Upper-class girls' contacts with boys are more closely watched than are those of middle-class girls; furthermore, they are often going through a finishing-school process preparing them for their adult roles. Reflecting the patriarchal tradition which continues to prevail in the upper class, the girl is carefully watched and protected. At home the family is in control; and in school the authorities are usually very restrictive. Protection is not usually through force, but rather through

---

[51] Baltzell, *Philadelphia Gentlemen*, p. 7.
[52] Ibid., p. 51.

socialization where little contact with males from other social classes makes the girl's class-limited relationships seem perfectly normal. However, the woman is not expected to deviate from the upper-upper class values, and if she does, she may be severely punished.

The upper-class boy is also socially controlled, but not to the same degree as the girl. A patriarchal tradition implies that males will have more freedom, and while boys may be allowed to interact with girls on a different social-class level, it is expected that the relationships will be casual. If the boy gets too serious with a girl from the lower social classes, the family can and does exert strong social pressure to bring him back into line. Although the family may not always be successful, their success rate far exceeds their failure rate.

During early adolescence, many boy-girl relationships are encouraged because of the need for both sexes to be taught approved patterns of upper-class behavior, such as the acquisition of social graces. As the children grow older, and nearer the age of mate selection, the family exerts many kinds of pressures to move mate selection into the proper channels. This does not mean that romance is absent from the upper class, but as Baltzell points out, "Where romantic love is a reason for marriage it is deftly channeled within a relatively coherent subcultural circle, and the informal sanctions of relatives and friends are strong."[53] Rarely is correct behavior forced on the young people, but rather its acquisition reflects an effective socialization process.

It has generally been assumed by family sociologists that mate selection in the upper class is tightly controlled, resulting in few young people marrying outside. Recently Rosen and Bell undertook a study using the Philadelphia *Social Register* for 1940 and 1961 to determine how many marriages in those years were between upper-class individuals. In their study, the upper class was limited to those listed in the *Social Register* (the method used by Baltzell). They found that in 1940 in only 31 percent of the marriages were *both* spouses listed in the *Register*, in 29 percent only the groom was listed, and in 40 percent only the bride. In 1961, in only 21 percent of the marriages were *both* the bride and groom listed in the *Social Register*, in 39 percent only the groom was listed, and in 40 percent only the bride was listed.[54] On the basis of this study, upper-class rates of homogamy were not high.

However, Rosen and Bell suggest that the potential marriage market for upper-class individuals may be thought of as consisting not only of those listed in the *Social Register*, which constitutes a small group (A), but also a larger group (B) consisting of a contiguous white Anglo-Saxon Protestant population, and, last of all, (C) the great majority of the

---

[53] Ibid., p. 161.

[54] Laurence Rosen and Robert R. Bell, "Mate Selection in the Upper Class," *Sociological Quarterly*, Spring 1966, p. 162.

American population. Ideally, the upper class is encouraged to marry a partner from (A), or from (B) where the outside individual can through his marriage be easily absorbed into the upper class. It appears uncommon for the upper-class individual to marry into (C), and when one does he may drop or be dropped from the upper class (the *Social Register*).[55]

Premarital Sex. Empirical information on the premarital sexual behavior of the upper class is completely absent. The stated attitudes for the most part reflect the patriarchal tradition. A girl is expected to be a virgin at the time of marriage, but the male is often assumed to have had some sexual experiences. (In acquiring sexual experiences, the male is expected to be very discreet so that no scandal will occur to damage the family.) The actual sexual experiences of the upper-class female are difficult to assess. The upper-class social group is almost impossible to study, and impressions given in the mass media are unreliable because of the power of the upper class to keep information about its personal behavior from becoming public.

Marriage

Upper-class marriage extends the family line and binds together upper-class families, in contrast to the middle-class marriage that centers around the ego-needs of the individual. Because of the effectiveness of the upper-class socialization process, it seems likely that most young people accept the value of family importance in mate selection and do not enter marriage primarily for ego satisfaction. This is not to say that upper-class marriages do not provide personal satisfactions, but rather that they are achieved within the context of a family, rather than a personal, orientation to marriage.

The great importance of marriage is reflected in Baltzell's findings that upper-upper class women are almost twice as likely to be married (64 percent) as the elites (37 percent).[56] The high percentage married is due to a very low divorce rate, and to the fact that very few upper-class women reject marriage for a career.[57] The high marriage rate reflects upper-class patriarchal values, which continue to give the highest recognition and status to the woman in the wife-mother role.

Marriage in the upper class does not imply the creation of a new and autonomous conjugal family, but rather an addition to the extended family relationships of the past and the present. While each new family created through marriage usually maintains a separate household, they do

---

[55] Ibid., pp. 165–66.

[56] Baltzell, *Philadelphia Gentlemen*, p. 161.

[57] Ibid., p. 162.

not conceive of themselves as a unit apart from the larger kin group.[58] Obligations to the extended family almost always take precedence over nonfamily social demands, and this importance is reinforced through continued close interaction with the extended family.

Acceptance of the extended family by the new conjugal marriage unit has a practical economic side. The upper-class way of life, to which the couple has been completely socialized, is often dependent, at least for some time after marriage, on the extended family. Hollingshead writes, "Usually a number of different nuclear families within a kin group are supported, in part at least, by income from a family estate held in trust."[59] This may be true of both the husband and wife's families. "Because of the practice of intermarriage it is not unusual for a family to be beneficiary of two or more estates held in trust."[60] Thus, the internal forces of the upper class have great power through socialization, economic control, and intermarriage.

The role of the husband is in part determined by the values of a patriarchal system. Baltzell points out that the "patriarchal nature of the upper-class family is shown by the fact that the college attended by the wife (if any) is *never* listed in the *Social Register*."[61] Formal education has no prestige significance for the upper-class woman; the males are the ultimate arbiters of acceptability and of membership definition in the upper class. For example, in Philadelphia, "an annual invitation to the hallowed Assembly Balls is still the best index of first-family status in the city. Unlike many such affairs held elsewhere in America, which are usually dominated by women, the Philadelphia Assembly has always been run by men."[62]

The upper-class male's occupation does not have the same ego significance as it does for the middle-class male, because he chooses his occupation according to his own or his family's feelings about how he will occupy himself in his adult years. A large number of upper-class men enter the world of finance because of the need to handle and, if possible, add to the family wealth. Many upper-class men are able to choose an occupation because it interests them, or even to pursue *no* occupation other than leading a "gentlemanly" life. Except for personal satisfaction, the male is usually not occupationally seeking or striving in the middle-

---

[58] August B. Hollingshead, "Class Differences in Family Stability," in Reinhard Bendix and Seymour M. Lipset, *Class, Status and Power* (Glencoe, Ill.: The Free Press, 1953), p. 286.

[59] Ibid., p. 286.

[60] Ibid., p. 286.

[61] Baltzell, *Philadelphia Gentlemen*, p. 27.

[62] Ibid., p. 163.

class sense; the upper-class male often *enters* an occupation; he does not *pursue* one.

The primary role of the woman centers around having children, running the household, and participating in a variety of social activities. Generally the mother does not devote a great deal of time to rearing her children because others handle their day-to-day care. This allows her to enter the many social activities important to the upper class.

The husband-wife relationship in the upper class of course varies a great deal with different couples. The very fact that the great stress on ego-needs that is found in the middle class is usually absent makes it probable that upper-class individuals demand and expect less of each other in marriage. Also, because family lines are of great importance, the personal nature of marriage is somewhat less important. The upper class has the money and the knowledge of many areas of interest to enable them to pursue a way of life that makes them less dependent on the marriage relationship. In the middle class, one's spouse is usually the most important "significant other," while in the upper class, the partners may have a number of other "significant others."

Only speculations can be offered as to the sexual nature of the upper-class marriage. Because less importance is attached to ego-need satisfaction in marriage, the upper-class couple may be less apt than the middle-class couple to seek personal reassurance through their sexual relationships. This is not to say that being significant as a sexual partner is unimportant, but rather that significance lies within a less extended psychological context. Second, the possession of money and power means that with a minimum of difficulty some in the upper class can and do seek sexual satisfaction outside of marriage.

An extramarital relationship, carried out with discretion, is not usually a reason for ending an upper-class marriage because the exclusiveness of the marriage relationship was not the prime reason for entering or maintaining the marriage.

Children.   That children are important follows from upper-class patriarchal values. Family lines perpetuate themselves through the children and, thus, having a son is of particular importance. Baltzell found that the upper-upper class family had more children (2.66) than the elite family (1.62).[63] Conditions are favorable for having larger families because upper-class women can have the best in medical care and relief from the demanding burdens of child rearing.

To say children are important to the upper class does not mean that the family is child centered. The upper-class home tends to center around adult living; the children live within the adult world, their activities often restricted to their segregated section of the home or to peer associations

---

[63] Ibid., p. 162.

outside the home. The adult world of the home is important to the socialization of the children because they are expected to learn to interact according to adult standards in dress, manners, and behavior patterns. They participate in adult activities as "young adults," not as children. One implication of this type of socialization is pointed out by Mills when he writes, "Adolescent boys and girls are exposed to the table conversations of decision makers, and thus have bred into them the informal skills and pretensions of decision makers. Without conscious effort, they absorb the aspiration to be—if not the conviction they are—the Ones Who Decide."[64]

In the upper class, many values and patterns of behavior are taught by highly specialized agencies. Baltzell says that the private school and college are a kind of surrogate family.[65] "The private education institutions serve the latent function of acculturating the members of the young generation."[66] Attendance at the right private school is so important that Baltzell says it "is the best index of ascribed upper-class position, even more indicative than neighborhood, religion, or social register affiliation."[67] As it becomes more difficult for the family to maintain direct control over the children, the school is used more and more as the means of "correct" socialization.[68]

Divorce. Because of the minimum importance of ego-need satisfaction in marriage and because of the great importance of the extended family the upper class has a low divorce rate. In general, divorce is to be avoided if at all possible. And because they often have the money to live together and practice "avoidance" means that they can often easier adjust to their difficulties than can the less affluent, middle-class couples.

The dominant values of the upper class regarding marriage and family relationships may be summarized as wealth, the importance of the family, and the patriarchal nature of family relationships. The socialization of the children into the upper class is the key factor in understanding how the upper class maintains itself. As long as socialization is controlled, the upper class can maintain itself and determine the admission of new members.

The discussion of the lower and upper classes in this chapter provides contrasts with middle-class marriage and family relationships. The lower and upper classes, though at the opposite ends of the social-class hierarchy, *share* certain values in regard to marriage and the family that are not usually a part of the middle-class family's values. Both lower and

---

[64] C. Wright Mills, *The Power Elite* (New York: Oxford University Press, 1956), p. 69.

[65] Baltzell, *Philadelphia Gentlemen*, p. 293.

[66] Ibid., p. 293.

[67] Ibid., p. 295.

[68] Ibid., p. 293.

upper class lack, for example, the mobility interests which are so common in the middle class. The lower class tends to see social mobility as beyond them; the upper class is already at the top.

The similarities, as well as the differences, between the lower and upper class should be kept in mind in the chapters that follow, in order to distinguish many areas in marriage and family relationships peculiar to the middle class. The differences to be shown between social-class levels do not indicate the superiority of any one set of values over another, but rather that many of the values accepted as natural must be seen within the context of a particular socialization experience.

SELECTED BIBLIOGRAPHY

Acker, Joan   "Women and Social Stratification: A Case of Intellectual Sexism," in Joan Huber, *Changing Women in a Changing Society* (Chicago: University of Chicago Press, 1973), pp. 174–83.

Baltzell, E. Digby   *Philadelphia Gentlemen.* Glencoe, Ill.: The Free Press, 1958.

Blumberg, Leonard, and Bell, Robert R.   "Urban Migration and Kinship Ties," *Social Problems,* Spring 1959, pp. 328–33.

Bordua, David J.   "Delinquent Subculture: Sociological Interpretation of Gang Delinquency." *The Annals,* November 1961, pp. 119–36.

Cohen, Albert K., and Hodges, Harold M., Jr.   "Characteristics of the Lower-Blue-Collar-Class." *Social Problems,* Spring 1963, pp. 303–34.

Jencks, Christopher   *Inequality: A Reassessment of the Effect of Family and Schooling in America.* New York: Harper, 1972.

Kahl, Joseph A.   *The American Class Structure.* New York: Rinehart & Co., Inc., 1957.

Kohn, Melvin L.   "Social Class and Exercise of Parental Authority." *American Sociological Review,* June 1959, pp. 352–66.

Komarovsky, Mirra.   *Blue-Collar Marriage.* New York: Random House, 1962.

Mayer, Kurt B.   *Class and Society.* New York: Doubleday & Co., Inc., 1955.

Olsen, Marvin E.   "Distribution of Family Responsibilities and Social Stratification." *Marriage and Family Living,* February 1960, pp. 60–65.

Rainwater, Lee   *And The Poor Get Children.* Chicago: Quadrangle Books, 1960.

Rosen, Laurence, and Bell, Robert R.   "Mate Selection in the Upper Class." *Sociological Quarterly,* Spring 1966, pp. 157–66.

Warner, Lloyd W., Meeker, Marchia, and Eells, Kenneth   *Social Class in America.* New York: Harper Torchbooks, 1960.

Part Two

Dating–Courtship

Chapter 4

The Dating–Courtship Process

In contemporary American society it is expected that adolescent boys and girls will interact in a variety of social settings. The trend is for less segregation of the sexes, and often the relationships between boys and girls are approved and encouraged by middle-class adults. This is true for two reasons: (1) Dating and some aspects of courtship are a part of the social and personal patterns of behavior associated with adolescent entertainment and recreation; (2) dating and courtship are ultimately related to the important business of selecting a marriage mate.

Dating and courtship may be thought of as a process made up of stages—with transitions from one stage to the next. For many individuals the process is through the stage of dating, to the stage of going steady, to the stage of engagement, to marriage. Each of the stages is dynamic for the individuals involved. For example, in going steady the relationship is altered as the two individuals develop their own common experiences. The relationship of two individuals starting to go steady is not the same as the relationship between them after having gone steady for a period of time. The stages do not necessarily mean the same thing for all people going through them or even for the individuals in any given pair. For some individuals, going steady may be a more serious commitment than it is for others. It is possible that these stages have become more blurred in recent years and moving from one to another has less meaning than it did previously. Certainly for many young people these stages appear to have less significance than they did a decade ago.

Experience with at least some aspects of dating and courtship is common to almost all middle-class Americans. The experiences range from a single date with a person to the mutual exclusiveness and commitments of formal engagement. The discussion that follows moves from the primarily ego-centered stage of dating, through going steady, to the paired commitment stage of engagement. The emphasis in this chapter is on some patterns common to dating-courtship in the American middle class.

DATING

Emergence of Dating

In the past, in most cultures—including the American—the relationships between the unmarried boy and girl were carefully circumscribed. Traditionally, during adolescence—the period primarily associated with dating—social relationships between the sexes were limited. This was true for several reasons: (1) Sex roles were more clearly differentiated than they are today. As adulthood was approached the individual learned a sex role primarily related to his future adult role. This was usually taught to him by older members of his own sex. The young man was prepared for his future occupational role by his father or other male adults; the young woman was taught her future occupational role of wife-mother-housekeeper by her mother or other female adults. (2) There was less leisure time than today, and, when it did exist, it was often pursued within one's sex group or within the family setting. (3) The selection of a marriage partner was not achieved through extended emotional interaction between two individuals but was often arranged by parents or other adults in the society.

From such a system of limited premarital social interaction for young people, the American society developed a system at almost the opposite extreme. There are few other societies where the kind of adolescent–young adult cross-sex interaction has developed to the degree that it has in the United States. (There is, however, some evidence that the American system is beginning to influence that of other countries of the world.[1])

In most societies the needs of the individual were achieved as part of the overall needs of the family unit. When a young person reached the age of marriage the selection of a mate was primarily determined by factors important to the family, and the values stressed were often economic.

---

[1] See David Mace and Vera Mace, *Marriage East and West* (Garden City, New York: Doubleday & Company, Inc., 1960).

In contrast, today in the United States the needs of the individual are believed to be the crucial elements in mate selection. Whether the person will achieve happiness and need-satisfaction in the person he chooses as a mate is often *the* crucial question. This change is in part due to the shift of the American family from a rural setting with extended patriarchal values to an urban one with conjugal democratic values. As the value stress moved from the family to the individual, a decrease in parental control was inevitable. The individual was increasingly oriented to make a marriage choice that would meet his own psychological needs, the assumption being that this would lead to greater personal happiness. Thus, the emphasis was placed on emotional factors of need-satisfaction rather than the more practical factors related to the broader needs of the family unit. This transition from parental control to individual decision-making in mate selection is not absolute, however, because the parents, in varying degrees, continue to influence their children.

Along with the shift away from family control over mate selection, an increasing amount of time spent in premarital social relationships also emerged. For the young adolescent, dating may have only an indirect relationship to future mate selection, but the relative privacy it affords is important because it contributes to the belief that mate selection is a private decision.

The increasing privacy of the paired relationship was influenced by the movement out of the home to satisfy leisure-time recreational needs. In the past, recreation centered around the family unit either in the home or in the family's participating together away from home. But commercial recreation has developed to such an extent that the amount of entertainment centered around the home is minimal for most young people. Furthermore, commercial recreation has developed around specialized appeals to specific age groups. Even when young people pursue recreation at home it often centers around friends of their own age and activities focused around their own age interests.

Another contributing factor, along with freedom from the parents, has been the increasing freedom of the American female. The stress on individuality in dating and courtship could not have been achieved if freedom had been given only to the male. As women acquired the right to enter more occupations, to extend their education, to attain greater legal equality with the male, and to have more freedom in social relationships, a demand for greater freedom in premarital activities also occurred. In many areas of life the female still has only second-class citizenship, but in dating and courtship she has achieved near equality with the male; she has basically the same rights as the male in seeking satisfaction from dating and in making the important decision of mate selection. This is not to say that the girl is no longer affected by special role requirements of being a female. The rights and obligations for the roles of male and female are different, but the opportunities to pursue sex roles of near equality in dating and courtship are available to both.

None of the influences of the past have completely disappeared, however. The parents still exert some influence; the family unit is still viewed as having some importance; the female is not completely equal in rights to the male; and, all leisure time is not spent completely beyond the influence of parents. The transition has not been complete, but the direction of change has been consistent—moving in the direction of individual need-satisfaction.

A *date* is an end in itself, with no further commitment. (In this discussion we will use "date" to refer to the event, the person one goes out with as the "person dated.") A date is viewed primarily as recreational and it lasts for a short period of time. When a boy picks up a girl at her home at eight o'clock on a Saturday night, their commitment to one another starts; it ends when he leaves her at her home at the end of the evening. Even if he makes another date with her for the following Saturday night, there is no commitment on either of their parts between the end of the first date and the start of the second. If there is a commitment (for example, an agreement not to go out with any other person), they are no longer dating but have moved into a new relationship. *Lack of commitment* is the crucial element in defining dating, whether it be the first or the tenth time the two individuals have gone out together.

Some Functions of Dating

Through the process of dating, certain functions are performed for society as well as for the individual. Dating serves recreational ends at the same time that it provides the means through which a mutual commitment to marriage may arise. Whether or not it is the most effective means for both goals, it is the procedure followed by most Americans. A discussion of some main functions of dating in the United States follows.

Learning of Sex Roles. For the first few years of life, generally not much attention is directed at sex differences among children. A young boy is just as apt to choose a little girl as a best friend as to choose another boy. However, from age four to eight a sharp awareness of the sex differences between the boy and the girl usually develops. This age period may be seen as one of strong sex identification, particularly on the part of the boy. Then, from the ages of ten to twelve, there is usually a tentative movement back in the direction of the opposite sex. From this point on, the stress in the middle class is increasingly on the paired nature of sex roles in a vast variety of social activities.

From the initial tentative movements of interest in the opposite sex on through adolescence, the facility for filling one's sex role and relating it to the opposite sex generally improves. Initially the contacts are awkward and the youngsters are often unsure of how to interact. For example, the preadolescent boy may treat a girl in about the same way he treats a boy of the same age. He may punch her on the arm or throw snowballs at her. While his behavior may seem inappropriate, it does represent a change from when he was a year or two younger and simply ignored girls. For the preadolescent girl, the relationship may not be quite as awkward because she has probably not rejected boys to the same extent. She can also focus her interest on a boy a year or two older than herself, one who has started to move out of the fumbling, awkward stage of the exclusive male world.

Many times the initial adolescent social relationships with the opposite sex are made a little easier through group dating. In this situation the youngsters support and fortify one another in the new and tenuous dating relationship, but as some degree of sophistication and confidence is achieved the tendency is to move in the direction of the paired relationship. But it appears that in many parts of the United States the young develop their paired relationships within their peer-group setting. That is, they don't go out alone as a couple but only meet each other in the company of their age peers.

From the hit-or-miss, trial-and-error initial relationships, important role learning takes place. An increasing awareness of the self as a boy or girl emerges and the significance of the role played by the individual is greatly determined by the related role played by an age peer of the opposite sex. That is, one important aspect of adolescence is dating—and dating means a pair relationship. This is the start of a relationship that most individuals will participate in for the rest of their lives—the close role-relationship to a member of the opposite sex. Role learning also provides an opportunity to develop one's personality, and to see more clearly some of the facets of role playing in relationship to a "significant other." Dating provides an understanding of self-role and significant-other role that is basic for socialization to adult roles. The adolescent through dating is extending his world of "significant others" and having his attitudes and behavior shaped by their influence.

Pleasure and Recreation. When adolescents go out on a date, it is usually to engage in behavior of a pleasurable nature. It should be remembered that in most cases adolescents decide what they are going to do on a date. So, within limits, they will choose doing what they find enjoyable. In this sense dating is quite different from more serious relationships, because, in dating, the realities of life can often be ignored. This may explain why many older people look back with nostalgia to their dating days—days of relative irresponsibility. Pleasure is also involved in the satisfaction achieved by the girl in being chosen for a date and by the boy in being accepted. Success in dating also implies success in the peer-group value system.

For many adolescents the actual time spent on dates may be only a few hours a week, but its influence on their interest may take up many hours of the week. There may be daydreaming and anticipation about the date already arranged and time-consuming recollections of the date after it has occurred. Because middle-class adolescents tend to be highly vocal about their dating interests, they do not have to restrict their thinking to themselves. They have friends more than willing to discuss dates, both past and present, their own, and the friends'.

Prestige.   Related to the recreational function of dating is that of receiving prestige. To be successful in dating is to meet the standards of the peer group. For many youngsters it is not just meeting the standards, but also of competing with one another. Sometimes prestige is achieved by the sheer frequency of dating different individuals. This may be seen as popularity of a quantitative dimension. There may also be a qualitative dimension where prestige is determined not by numbers but by the prestige of the individuals dated. One person may have far fewer dates than another but be given higher prestige by the peer group. In high school, a date with the captain of the football team may be worth five dates with boys having no particular prestige qualities. But once again it appears that these status factors are of somewhat less importance than they were a decade ago.

The prestige element in dating is not limited to the young adolescent. A number of dating studies of college students have been made since the classic dating-rating study of Waller, and one such study indicates that prestige is not limited just to *dating* for college students, but is found at all stages of the courtship process.[2] While the prestige stressed varies in different types of colleges, there seems little question that it is an important factor. For college students, it may be related to desirable values in a future marriage partner. In the writer's university, coeds place much higher prestige on dating young men from the professional schools than those from the undergraduate schools. This is not simply a question of age differences between the two possible dating groups; it is attributable to the higher prestige of the male continuing his education beyond the undergraduate degree. (However, this is not true of all graduate training—for example, there is much less prestige in dating a young man going into academic than there is in dating a young man training for the highest prestige profession, medicine.)

Mate Selection.   That dating during the younger years has, at the least, an indirect relationship to future mate selection is important enough to restate. As the individual enters late adolescence and the early adult

---

[2] Everett M. Rogers and Eugene A. Havens, "Prestige Rating and Mate Selection on a College Campus," *Marriage and Family Living,* February 1960, p. 59.

years, dating becomes more directly related to mate selection. With time, dating provides the opportunity for developing an awareness of one's own needs and how they are related to the needs of others. Even the blind date that turns out to be a complete flop may have some value as a learning experience, indicating as it does the lack of desire for a relationship to develop between the two individuals.

As dating occurs for the older person, it becomes increasingly important. In American society almost the only way to reach the more committed stages of courtship leading to marriage is through the initial experience of the date. The individual realizes that to go beyond dating he must continue to date until he finds a person to move on with to succeeding stages. College students, particularly upperclassmen, increase the number of dates they have with different individuals. As marriage becomes more important, college students are inclined to spend less time checking out one individual by dating the one a number of times. Rather, they tend to make faster assessments and move on to the next individual.

Ultimately the proof of dating success lies in whether the individual feels it has been adequate for finding the kind of mate he wanted. While the opportunities for dating vary greatly for different groups of individuals, it seems to be successful for the majority. However, the high marriage rates of Americans should not be taken as complete evidence that the dating system provides sufficient contacts. It would seem adequate in at least providing the opportunities to find a person to marry, but we have no way of knowing whether the person chosen was a limited, "forced" choice or a "free" choice selected from a large market. This is a hypothetical point because even the person who has dated many different individuals might have selected someone else if they had dated a few more. It may be suggested that the fewer individuals dated, the greater the probability of "forced" choice in mate selection.

The functions of dating may work together or separately for a given individual at different points in time. That is, an individual's main motivations in dating can be placed along a continuum from where dating is totally expressive (an end in itself) to totally instrumental (as a means to a greater goal). At the same time the person's emotional involvement may fall along a continuum of no emotional involvement to high emotional feelings. In general, the closer to expressive commitment in dating, the higher the emotional commitment. Skipper and Nass go on to suggest several logical interpretations based on the person's positions along the continuums of commitment and emotional involvement. First, an individual whose main interest in dating is to find a mate is apt to have a high instrumental orientation along with a strong emotional involvement. Second, a person whose primary concern in dating is either socialization or status seeking is apt to have both low instrumental and low emotional involvement. Third, a person whose primary motive is to date for recreational purposes is likely to have a strong expressive orientation and a low emotional involvement.[3]

Some Elements of Dating

The previous discussion centered around the functions or purposes of dating. In this section we will discuss some of the elements that shape dating behavior in the American middle class.

Role of the Parents. We have suggested that over the years the influence of parents upon the premarital behavior of young people has decreased. Yet, parents maintain a strong interest in the dating of their youngsters and continue to influence them both directly and indirectly. Parents are interested because of their emotional involvement with their children and their desire for them to be successful as adolescents and adults. Parents know that a part of success centers around their children's ability to date. However, parents realize that the values of dating they believe to be important are not necessarily the ones their children accept and they sometimes find their own values about dating in conflict with the peer-group values accepted by their children.

Parents can exert various kinds of influences on dating. They can set the time and frequency. They can often give or withhold the financial assistance important for successful dating—children's allowances, buying of the clothes they want, providing an automobile, and so on. Most parents probably do not use this kind of direct control over dating if they can avoid it. Even if this kind of control is used, it becomes less effective as the young person grows older and has the means of achieving his own financial base for dating.

A more important parental influence on dating, as well as on eventual mate selection, is indirect. The parents have reared the child and have had the opportunity of instilling in him certain values they as parents feel are important. When their child reaches dating age his selection of a person to date and his behavior during the date will be a reflection of the values his parents have passed on to him. Yet, the ultimate effectiveness of the parents' training will be to a great degree influenced by the values of the peer group.

Peer Group. The age-peers the adolescent associates with quite often constitute his most important reference group. His identification with the peer group makes him highly susceptible to their reward and punishment system. In many situations the values of the family and of the peer group

---

[3] James K. Skipper and Gilbert Nass, "Dating Behavior: A Framework for Analysis and an Illustration," *Journal of Marriage and the Family*, November 1966, p. 413.

are in essential agreement and tend to reinforce one another, thereby minimizing the possibility of conflict between the youngster and his parents. However, in other cases values may differ significantly and the youngster may find himself in a position of role conflict. In order to satisfy his role expectations as a son, he may not, at the same time, be able to meet the role expectations of his peer group. And if he chooses the expectations of his peer group, he is not able to meet the expectations held by his parents. Many times the youngster evades a role conflict by keeping his role in the peer group separate from his role of son and not allowing his parents to see his different behavior in the peer group. While this happens in many areas, it is of particular relevance in dating behavior. Many youngsters allow their parents to believe the parents' role definition is accepted, but in actuality they perform according to peer-group definitions. As a consequence, many aspects of dating behavior are determined by the peer group—individuals to be dated, where to go and what to do on a date, degrees of intimacy, and styles of dress. Dating behavior in the peer group context is very important to the adolescent because it is often symbolic of adult behavior and therefore provides one of the initial footholds in the climb to adult status.

Exploitation.   One other element important to dating is the possibility of exploitation. Dating is ego-centered, rather than pair-centered, and the individual has a minimum of responsibility to the person dated. For many individuals the selection of the person to go out with is determined by an estimate of what the person dated can contribute to his need-gratification. This may center around prestige, or it may be more psychologically oriented in the direction of ego-fulfillment.

Whatever factor is uppermost, the individual tends to ignore the needs of the person dated. Oftentimes this leads to exploitation; but the exploitation is not always one way. Frequently the two on a date will contest which one is going to exploit the other. This is of course well illustrated in the area of sexual behavior. The boy may try to enhance his self-esteem as a male by pushing the sexual relationship as far as possible. The girl, on the other hand, may be less interested in the sexual aspect and more interested in getting an emotional commitment from the boy which can provide her with control over the situation and enhance her self-esteem as a love object. Because the two sets of needs are often incompatible, exploitation frequently *results* if one scores a decisive victory.

One factor that may influence possible exploitation results from the feelings of the individuals toward the other at the end of their first date. During adolescence girls may become more involved than boys at the end of a first date, but as girls move into the early adult years they may become more critical of their dates than do boys. Older girls are more marriage-oriented and therefore less inclined to want to spend their time in casual dating. Coombs and Kenkel found that after a first dating situation men "were more prone to be satisfied with her personality, physical appearance, and popularity standing and to think it possible to be happily married to such a person."[4] By contrast, the women were more critical and rejecting of the men dated. They would therefore, with less commitment, appear to be less prone to exploitation than the men.

Whatever the specific situation may be, exploitation is always of potential significance in dating because of the lack of commitment to the other person. This is not to say that all dating is a constant and conscious struggle for personal gain. The struggle may not emerge unless there is some significant need difference between the two individuals; when there is, the wants of the individual usually take precedence because the individual cares directly about himself and often only indirectly about the other.

Ability to Date

Given the importance of dating as both a recreational end and as a means of eventual mate selection, the opportunities and abilities for dating take on great significance. Because dating ability varies a great deal among young people, it is necessary to look at some of the factors which affect success in dating.

Age. The phenomena of dating had hardly begun to be common to college students in the 1920s when it slowly began to reach down into younger age groups. Burchinal suggests that it was during the late 1930s and the 1940s that dating moved to the high-school level.[5] Several studies provide information as to the age at which young people start dating. A study done in the 1940s found that during "the thirteenth year, 20 percent of the girls and 15 percent of the boys had their first date."[6] Another study carried out in 1968 found the mean age of the first date for 207 coeds was 13.2 years.[7] Another study of adolescents

---

[4] Robert H. Coombs and William F. Kenkel, "Sex Differences in Dating Aspirations and Satisfaction With Computer-Selected Partners," *Journal of Marriage and the Family,* February 1966, p. 66.

[5] Lee G. Burchinal, "The Premarital Dyad and Love Involvement," in Harold T. Christensen, ed., *Handbook of Marriage and the Family* (Chicago: Rand McNally & Co., 1964), p. 624.

[6] Ernest W. Burgess and Paul Wallin, *Engagement and Marriage* (Philadelphia: J. B. Lippincott Co., 1953), p. 106.

[7] Robert R. Bell and Jay B. Chaskas, "Premarital Sexual Experience among Coeds, 1958 and 1968," *Journal of Marriage and the Family,* February 1970, p. 82.

found that they started dating at young ages with "45 percent of the boys and 36 percent of the girls saying they began dating in the fifth grade or at ages ten and eleven."[8] The available evidence indicates that over the last few decades the trend has been to start dating at younger and younger ages.

The evidence also suggests that girls start dating at slightly younger ages than boys. This is due to the age differential of the male-female relationship that shows itself even at very young ages. We also know that romantic interests appear at younger ages for girls than for boys. In a study of youngsters in the age range 10 to 13 it was found that "girls were far more romantically oriented than boys although they were at about the same level in terms of actual heterosexual interaction."[9]

Many of the dates of the young adolescent are probably lacking in the privacy and emotional involvement that goes with somewhat older-age dating. The early period may represent an initial transition to an emotional commitment to a member of the opposite sex that will not reach a high degree of involvement until late in adolescence. "It is significant that children under 16 seldom name another boy or girl as the one they love best. Their attachments to their parents are still the strongest of all."[10]

There is also evidence that starting to date at younger ages than their age peers may have some implications for girls in their future dating, courtship, and marriage behavior. Burchinal found "that girls who married while still in high school had begun dating earlier, dated more frequently, dated more boys, had gone steady earlier, and felt that they had been in love with a greater number of boys than [had] a control group of girls."[11] Lowrie found "no significant relationship between the age at which brides had their first dates and premarital pregnancy."[12]

In a later study Lowrie came to several conclusions about dating in terms of family background factors. He found, first, that girls from the more thoroughly assimilated parts of the population began to date at younger ages than did girls of more recent foreign origins. It was also found that children of higher educated parents start to date at younger ages than girls of lower educated parents. Also, girls from small families start dating younger than girls from large families. He also found that

---

[8] Carlfred B. Broderick and Stanley E. Fowler, "New Patterns of Relationships Between the Sexes Among Preadolescents," *Marriage and Family Living*, February 1961, p. 28.

[9] Carlfred B. Broderick, "Social Heterosexual Development among Urban Negroes and Whites," *Journal of Marriage and the Family*, May 1965, p. 203.

[10] Burgess and Wallin, *Engagement and Marriage*, p. 113.

[11] Burchinal, "Premarital Dyad," p. 630.

[12] Samuel H. Lowrie, "Early Marriage: Premarital Pregnancy and Associated Factors," *Journal of Marriage and the Family*, February 1965, p. 52.

"the age of dating seemingly varies from region to region; particularly does dating in the South begin earlier than in either of the other areas."[13]

There is also some evidence that starting to date late in adolescence may have some consequences for the marriage future of the individual. Lowrie found that "the evidence suggests that late daters are likely to rush into marriage with persons they do not know well enough to judge or size up as mates."[14] Another study of almost 38,000 individuals found a weak relationship between early dating and early marriage. That study found that "age at the beginning of dating did not seem crucial to marital well-being but that length of the dating experience prior to marriage was important."[15]

Frequency. Not only do girls start dating at a younger age than boys, but when age is held constant they have dated more frequently and more different individuals.[16] The writer found the estimated number of different individuals dated by college women and men with a mean age of 20 years was 53 and 43, respectively. In a study in which respondents kept records over a 28-day period, the average girl went out on dates seven times and the boy five times. During the same period the number of different individuals dated was 3.3 for the girls and 2.5 for the boys.[17] These figures indicate that for many college students the frequency of dating is high.

In a study comparing dating behavior of coeds in the same university over a ten-year period some differences in the number of different individuals dated were noted. In 1958 the mean number of different individuals ever dated was 53, while in 1968 it was only 25. In 1968 the coeds went out on dates just as often but went out more often with the same individuals in a dating relationship than did the coeds in 1958.[18]

In 1968 Richard Klemer followed up a sample of coeds from 1956 to examine relationships between their college dating behavior and their later marriages. He found that those women who had dated the most often were the most likely to have married the earliest. He also found that high self-esteem women were not much different from their peers in terms of the proportion which had married early. But the group who had shown high self-esteem during their college days had more divorces,

---

[13] Samuel H. Lowrie, "Early and Late Dating: Some Conditions Associated with Them," in Bernard Farber, *Kinship and Family Organization* (New York: John Wiley and Sons, Inc., 1966), p. 185.

[14] Ibid., p. 188.

[15] Alan E. Bayer, "Early Dating and Early Marriage," *Journal of Marriage and the Family*, November 1968, p. 630.

[16] Robert R. Bell, "Some Dating Characteristics of Students in a Large Urban University," unpublished.

[17] Ibid.

[18] Bell and Chaskes, "Experience among Coeds," p. 82.

and there were more among them who had not married.[19] This would suggest that high self-esteem has some relationship to options other than marriage.

Because the getting of dates is a problem to be solved by the young person, certain institutionalized procedures have developed. The young person is highly dependent on the peer group for the getting of dates and tends to get dates within the peer-group system, either through personal contacts or through peer-group friends. Table 4–1 shows that in one study,

TABLE 4–1

How Students in a College Sample Met Dates, by Sex* (percent)

	Male	Female
Blind date	28	35
Through friend	15	19
At college	16	15
Party or dance	16	12
In high school	10	6
Other sources	15	13
	100	100

* Bell, Robert R., "Some Dating Characteristics in a Large Urban University," unpublished.

the getting of dates through a friend or through a "blind date" accounted for 43 percent of the college boys' and 54 percent of the college girls' dates. It is of interest to note that the help of the family in arranging dates was found to be numerically insignificant. With friends so important in arranging dates, the peer group can exert strong control over dating behavior. Thus, the peer group not only contributes a great deal to the desire for dating and provides the "contacts" that influence who is dated, but it also affects dating patterns.

The sex-role patterns for the attainment of dates are generally clearly defined. With few exceptions the girl is expected to wait until she is asked by the boy. This places different ego demands on the two sexes. The choice rests with the boy as to whether the initial step will occur. The girl cannot usually initiate directly the request for a date, although there are methods of letting the boy know she is interested in going out with him. The girl must usually wait for the phone call—that may or may not come. She does have some advantage in the contest of relative commitment, however, because the boy shows his interest in her by asking for the date. This initial one-way commitment of interest makes

---

[19] Richard H. Klemer, "Self-Esteem and College Dating Experience as Factors in Mate Selection and Marital Happiness: A Longitudinal Study," *Journal of Marriage and the Family*, February 1971, p. 185.

it difficult for some boys to ask for a date because of the possibility of being rejected. This may in part explain the popularity of the "blind" date where both individuals start with an equal *non*commitment. It might be speculated that boys sensitive to the ego-commitment of asking for a date would be most satisfied with "blind" dates and girls most desiring ego-commitments by the boy least satisfied with "blind" dates.

There does appear to be among many young people an increasing acceptance of girls asking boys to go out with them. Certainly the set routines of the past are being altered. One can predict that as greater sexual equality develops the pattern of girls asking boys out will increase.

Dating Problems. We have suggested that a crucial dating problem centers around the ability and opportunity to date. As a person grows older, and nears the age of mate selection, dating becomes increasingly important. Studies agree that age is the most important variable influencing the frequency of dating, with frequency of dating increasing with increased age.[20]

Given the great importance of dating, both as an end in itself and as the means for entering the courtship process, one potentially important problem centers around the individual's ability to enter and participate in dating. It seems clear that a strong majority of middle-class young people initially begin dating while in high school. Yet Reiss has estimated that for the high-school age group about one third of the boys and one fifth of the girls are *not* involved in dating.[21] Even those who are dating may be dissatisfied with the frequency of their dating or with the individuals they are able to date.

Problems related to the ability to date have both personal and social implications for the individual. Burgess and Wallin point out that "the evidence from personality tests given to college youths shows that those who do not date are disposed to be socially retiring but with only a slight tendency toward emotional maladjustment. Evidently the majority have found more or less satisfactory compensation for their lack of association with the other sex."[22] Inability to date or inadequacy of dating may have more serious consequences for the individual as he nears the age of marriage. As mentioned, limitations on the individual often have the ultimate effect of narrowing the market of mate selection. Some may have to make a "forced" choice because, when marriage becomes of increasing importance, the desire to find a mate intensifies. This may mean that a particular choice might not have been made if more dating opportunities had been available. The choice may be determined by a

---

[20] Burchinal, "Premarital Dyad," p. 629.

[21] Ira L. Reiss, "Sexual Codes in Teen Age Culture," *The Annals*, November 1961, p. 60.

[22] Burgess and Wallin, *Engagement and Marriage*, p. 125.

strong desire to marry rather than through the impact of a specific individual.

It has long been recognized that there may be social-class differences in how males and females perceive the meaning of dating. For example, the middle-class boy dating the lower-class girl may see the relationship as sexual and she may see it as hopefully a serious emotional relationship. But it has not been generally recognized that such differences in dating definitions may also be found within the middle class. Skipper and Nass have shown that differences are often found in the dating experiences of student nurses. The boy dating the nurse often sees her as "knowing the score" about sexual matters and in addition the "knowing" is transformed into "she likes it." "From the typical college boy's definition of the situation, these are girls to have fun with but not the type one takes home to mother. In this respect the student nurse and the divorcee may have comparable problems which tend to obstruct the attainment of a courtship relation."[23] This often leads to strong differences in dating motivation for the nurse and the young men who date her. The nurse's courtship motivation involves a high degree of instrumental and emotional involvement while the male is much more recreationally oriented. These differences often lead to conflict in the dating encounters. "The male controlled the relationship in large part because he had less to lose if it was discontinued. He was not emotionally involved with *the* student nurse and could easily find another for purposes of recreation."[24]

The nature of the college world generally provides students with extended opportunities for meeting a variety of different individuals for dating. However, this is not always true for the many individuals of the same age who are not in college. Since very few approved agencies exist in the United States through which young people can meet, they are often left to their own devices, which may be inadequate. The person with limited dating contacts may suffer severe frustration. For some, so few dates may come along that any person who seems reasonably satisfactory will continue to be dated. While dating is a basic requirement for mate selection, the social opportunities out of college for meeting a variety of potential mates are often inadequate.

Although dating patterns in contemporary middle-class America present many problems as related to the overall courtship process, they are still functionally related to our present marriage system. Furthermore, the major values of dating and courtship have remained relatively consistent over the past few decades. Burchinal argues that changes "that have occurred over the long run have strengthened those aspects of the dating

---

[23] Skipper and Nass, "Dating Behavior," p. 417.
[24] Ibid., p. 420.

and courtship system which should contribute to increased competency in marriage. Modern youth, it seems, acquire more experience in heterosexual association before engagement and marriage than was true for youth several generations ago."[25]

GOING STEADY

Almost all Americans eventually make the move from the non-committed and ego-centered relationship of dating into a premarital relationship of some commitment to another person. This may be either through going steady or engagement. Going steady may be defined as an agreement between two people that they will not date any other individual. In our discussion of going steady a distinction will be made between the older and the younger age groups. The older refers to late adolescence and the early adult years and the younger to under 16 or 17 years of age.

Older. Going steady for individuals entering and in the marriageable ages has been a part of the American dating-courtship system for some time. Generally, if the relationship lasts over a period of time, it will move into the greater commitment of engagement or marriage.

During adolescence there is often a great deal of pleasure in the adventurous qualities of dating—that is, the sense of excitement associated with the anticipation of each new date. But with increasing age the sense of adventure with regard to random dating decreases. Burchinal found that "students gradually become disenchanted with the competitive dating world of the first several years of college and replaced this 'whirl' with more individualized pair activities."[26]

Studies of going steady for college students give some evidence as to the age and frequency of going steady among the older group. One study of college students with an average age of 19 years showed that 68 percent of the females and 72 percent of the males had gone steady at least once.[27] Another study of a similar age group found 69 percent of its respondents had gone steady.[28] In the former study, of those college students who had gone steady the males had gone steady 2.2 times, the females 1.6 times.[29] In the latter study, where no distinction was made by sex, 45 percent of the respondents had gone steady one or two times and 24 percent three or more times.[30]

---

[25] Burchinal, "Premarital Dyad," p. 635.

[26] Ibid., p. 634.

[27] Robert R. Bell and Leonard Blumberg, "Courtship Intimacy and Religious Background," *Marriage and Family Living*, November 1959, p. 358.

[28] Burgess and Wallin, *Engagement and Marriage*, p. 127.

[29] Bell and Blumberg, "Courtship Intimacy," p. 358.

[30] Burgess and Wallin, *Engagement and Marriage*, p. 127.

Lowrie found a relationship between age at first date and going steady. He found that dating at an early age was associated with dating a number of different individuals, with going steady after extended experience in dating, and, after ending a going steady relationship, returning to play the field. "In contrast, beginning to date at a relatively late age usually involves beginning to go steady without dating long, presumably with few individuals, and, by implication, becoming emotionally involved."[31]

In the Bell and Blumberg study, of those who had gone steady, the average age of first going steady was 17 years for the females and 17.2 for the males.[32] In the Burgess and Wallin study, of those who had gone steady, 67 percent of the males and 87 percent of the females had gone steady for the first time before they were 18 years of age.[33] The two studies indicate that by the time the young person has reached college age he has had, in the majority of cases, at least one experience with going steady.

Younger. Going steady in the lower age groups is probably an American phenomenon which has developed since the end of World War II. For the younger groups, going steady has only a limited and indirect relationship to marriage. The middle-class 16-year-old going steady does not usually perceive the relationship as one that will move into marriage in the near future. In one study of high school students, two types of going steady were distinguished. "One was marriage-oriented, and the dating of students with this view represented courtship. The other type implied no thought of marriage and represented a relationship maintained for recreation, fun, education, or other reasons."[34] The frequency of going steady in the younger ages is difficult to estimate. The Burgess and Wallin data show that of those who had gone steady, 30 percent of the boys and 46 percent of the girls had gone steady before they were 16 years of age.[35] In the middle class, going steady is probably an experience for at least half before they reach 17.

We defined going steady as an agreement between two people that they will not date any other individual. For many young people their peers put pressure on them to "go with" someone so that in their peer group the names can be linked together in pairs. But often this means that they are together as a couple when with their peers or when they call each other on the telephone. However, they generally do not spend much time privately together as a couple. The going together often appears to be more symbolic than interpersonal.

---

[31] Lowrie, "Early and Late Dating," p. 187.

[32] Bell and Blumberg, "Courtship Intimacy," p. 358.

[33] Burgess and Wallin, *Engagement and Marriage*, p. 127.

[34] R. D. Herman, "The Going Steady Complex: A Re-Examination," *Marriage and Family Living*, vol. 17 (1955), p. 38.

[35] Burgess and Wallin, *Engagement and Marriage*, p. 120.

The discussion that follows focuses on some of the reasons for, and problems related to, going steady in the younger age groups. Special notice is given the younger age groups because early going steady seems to be the most significant recent development in the dating-courtship process. The younger age groups have taken over a behavioral relationship from the older groups and emerged with a relationship that is in some ways quite different.

Some Reasons for Going Steady

The increase in going steady for the younger adolescent has many causes, and the following sections will suggest some of the pressures that are being exerted. It should, however, be recognized that adolescent behavior varies in different parts of the United States and by social class. The suggestions made here are for the urban middle-class youngster.

Security. Sociological literature is full of empirical material illustrating the modern American stress on security. In the adult world, particularly since the depression of the 1930s, strong emphasis has been placed on the achievement of psychological, social, and economic security. The values of the adult world permeate the adolescent world and may be taken up in totality or with various modifications.

For many youngsters, going steady provides a form of security. In the discussion on dating, some insecurity aspects for the individuals who must compete in getting dates in sufficient number and adequate prestige were suggested. The young person going steady is assured of a date for "important" occasions and does not have to compete openly, with the consequent possibility of being rejected or of not being asked.

A concern with security in the boy-girl relationship seems to have emerged since World War II. In the period between the two world wars, dating popularity was based on having as many different partners as possible. Ehrmann points out that that popularity trend "was manifested even at dances with the stag lines and the custom of 'breaking in,' whereby success and failure were measured by the frequency of changes of partners during a single dance and in the course of an evening."[36] The values of dating competitiveness are different from the values of going steady frequently found today. Henry argues that for American boys and girls today the "steady" is the answer "to the instability, emptiness, and anxiety inherent in other types of boy-girl relationships, and becoming 'steadies' sometimes gives the boy-girl relationship solemnity, dignity, and meaning."[37] Yet, the security provided by going steady may in the

---

[36] Winston Ehrmann, "Marital and Nonmarital Sexual Behavior," in Harold T. Christensen, ed., *Handbook of Marriage and the Family* (Chicago: Rand McNally & Co., 1964), p. 594.

[37] Jules Henry, *Culture against Man* (New York: Random House, 1963), p. 154.

long run be dysfunctional because it removes the adolescent from learning experiences easier assimilated during adolescence than during adulthood.

The increase in going steady may also be related to the rise in the status of the female. With dating often having highly exploitative qualities, the girl may feel less inclined than in the past to stay with noncommitted dating and instead to seek out the more emotionally satisfying relationship of going steady. If other dating opportunities are available, she realizes that at any time she may break a relationship that does not meet all her needs and can move on until she finds one that does.

Insecurity.   The possibility of insecurity resulting from going steady can occur in several ways. First, the adolescent is in a transitional role between that of child and adult. He often places great importance on the peer group and gains acceptance by living up to its norms and values; therefore, he is anxious to do what will make him acceptable. If the values of the peer group stress going steady, going steady becomes important in gaining group acceptance. A premium is placed on the ability of the individual to meet the expectations of the peer group; inability to do so may lead to individual frustration.

Second, the transitional nature of adolescence may have an influence in another way. Many times the adolescent is anxiously striving for adult status, and this striving intensifies the importance of what he defines as the symbols of adulthood. Going steady may appeal to many adolescents because it implies an adult relationship and achievement of some adult status. Very often, adults fail to recognize the great significance of adult symbols for the adolescent. Adults simply do not see the role insecurity of the adolescent resulting from being neither an adult nor a child and not having a well-defined adolescent role.

There is also some evidence that going steady contributes to the adolescent's emancipation from his parents. Going steady provides a highly important "significant other" and often serves to shift away from the parents some of the adolescent's emotional commitment and involvement. One study found that serious dating was more significant for males than for females in their emancipation from parents.[38]

Parents' Influence.   Many parents have strong objections to youngsters going steady. But many times they find themselves almost powerless to do anything about it because they are in opposition to the adolescent reference group. Parents then find themselves in a dilemma. They want their children to be successful and popular but this may mean the youngster feels he must go steady or be unpopular. So the parents may accept what they feel to be the lesser of the two evils—going steady.

---

[38] Charles W. Hobart, "Emancipation from Parents and Courtship in Adolescence," *Pacific Sociological Review*, vol. 6 (1958), pp. 25–29.

Research on the relationship between the young person going steady and his parents would be valuable. Many adolescents may seek an emotional satisfaction through going steady that they do not have with their parents. Almost all human beings at all ages need to be significant to some "other." If the young person feels that he is not significant to his parents, the emotional relationship of going steady may be felt to meet this need.

Problems of Youthful Going Steady

It is difficult to make a positive case for going steady during early adolescence. A discussion of some of the problems should illustrate why this is so. To begin with, a psychological examination of those who go steady would probably find some basic personality problems for at least some of the individuals. Going steady excessively may in some cases be symptomatic of important personality problems.

Limited Dating Experience. The longer an adolescent spends in going steady, the less time he has to date different individuals. The young person going steady is not acquiring a variety of experiences with different individuals. If we assume that a variety of dating experiences allow the adolescent to learn more about himself and how his needs are related to others, then frequent going steady limits the variety of experiences important to mate selection.

It might be argued that instead of having superficial experiences with a variety of different individuals he will have had extensive experience with a few, and this will enable him to have interpersonal experience in greater depth. However, it may well be that it is more valuable to learn something about a broader variety of personalities before moving into a depth relationship with one person. Early emotional relationship may be moving the young person into an intense involvement before he is familiar with the variety and choices of possible relationships.

In the American society, where ultimate mate selection rests primarily in the hands of the young person, any social mechanism that restricts the opportunity for the best preparation possible may contribute to later problems. Therefore, extended dating with a variety of different individuals is generally needed if the system of mate selection is to function most efficiently.

Making Adult Decisions. The adolescent is in the process of reaching adult status. Generally, the younger the adolescent, the less apt he is to be an adult physically, psychologically, and socially. While some older adolescents are coming close to adequate fulfillment of adult roles, the younger adolescents are not. And going steady often places the younger adolescents in a role position that in many ways has adult dimensions.

The young adolescent may be required to make adult decisions about the closeness of a relationship that he is not as yet equipped to make. The area of sexual behavior provides probably the most vivid illustration. The young adolescent is physically capable of indulging in adult sexual behavior, but not necessarily psychologically or socially mature enough to make an adult decision about a sexual relationship. A person of 15 is about as sexually capable as he will be at 20, but he is not socially ready to make decisions that he should be adult enough to make at age 20. Thus, going steady may force adult decision making on the individual before he is ready.

Premature adult decision making can also be a problem in other areas of the going-steady relationship. The nature and the degree of the emotional commitment, for example. Many of the feelings that develop are adult in nature but unadult in their application. The young person may behave irrationally because he has not developed the ability and lacks the experience necessary to function in a fashion defined as socially mature.

Many of these criticisms of social immaturity may also be directed at the older adolescent or even the adult; however, it seems logical that the younger the age, the greater the probability of immaturity. Therein lies what is probably the most crucial problem of youthful going steady.

Going steady a number of times at various ages may have significance for future adult behavior. Since going steady is generally not a permanent commitment and often involves a series of "steadies," the individual must learn to get over the "old" and move into the "new" relationships. From such learning may emerge an awareness that one may be in love a number of times. The phenomenon of going steady a number of times may also help socialize the individual to the possibility of future divorce and remarriage.

ENGAGEMENT

The final stage in the process of dating and courtship for a majority of middle-class Americans is engagement. When compared with going steady, engagement is a more serious paired commitment. It has the explicit end of moving into marriage, and may be viewed as the most exclusive pair commitment outside of marriage in the United States. But, when compared with marriage, engagement does not carry the same rights and obligations.

Engagement is a social ritual developed and utilized by almost all societies. Waller and Hill have pointed out that the common usage of engagement by societies is due to at least two common human needs: the need for facilitating the transition from the adolescent to the adult status of marriage and parenthood—the transfer from single irresponsibility to married responsibility; and, because the transition is important, the need for socially developed group sanctions related to the roles that go along with the assumption of mature adult responsibility.[39] Therefore, engagement is important both to the individuals involved and to the society.

Engagement Characteristics

Engagement is highly developed in the American middle class and is often felt to be a necessary prelude to marriage. With the lowering of age at marriage for Americans and the increased number going on to college, both engagement and marriage are now common occurrences for college students. One study of college students found that the average age of first engagement was 19.1 years for females and 21.7 years for males.[40]

Symbols of the Engagement. Two symbols of engagement with a long historical heritage are still found in the American middle-class: the engagement announcement and the engagement ring. Historically, the function of the announcement is to inform the community that the couple are to be married. The anouncement is made because marriage of individual members is of importance to society. But as the American culture developed in size and complexity, the announcement lost its importance as a statement of marriage intent to a responsive community, and probably its most important aspect today is the prestige it may give to the individuals involved. Such prestige may be secured through the engagement party to which friends and relatives are invited and at which the engagement is announced, or through an announcement carried in local newspapers. Society-page editors usually determine the amount of space given to an engagement announcement on the basis of the news value it is assumed to have. A girl coming from a prominent family will be given more space for both story and picture than a girl coming from a less socially important family. This stress on prestige aspects is also shown by the information presented in the engagement story. The social prominence of either set of parents, as well as membership in organizations and the schools attended by the engaged pair, will be mentioned. Very often a chief concern of the engaged couple and their families is the amount of space given the announcement.

The ring is a symbol for all who care to observe that the girl is "chosen," and in many cases the ring is also a prestige symbol. The engagement ring is generally a diamond and often the belief is: the bigger the better. The size (cost) of the diamond indicates that the girl has not only been successful in being chosen, but that she has been successful in

---

[39] Willard Waller and Reuben Hill, *The Family* (New York: The Dryden Press, 1951), p. 143.

[40] Bell and Blumberg, "Courtship Intimacy," p. 359.

being chosen by an affluent male. But the ring appears to be of less importance to many young women. This may be because many see it as symbolic of an implied subservient relationship to the male. So while the parents often think the engagement ring is very important, the young couple may reject it as uneconomical and symbolically undesirable.

The Importance of the Female. For a large number of American women, the period of highest personal prestige is during engagement, reaching its peak on the wedding day. This is not to suggest that it *should* be that way but rather that it *is* that way. The engaged girl in the United States is often a symbol of happiness and beauty. (Not long after she marries, her personal glamor leaves her and she enters the unromantic ranks of married women.) While engagement is a period of high prestige for the girl, it is not equally prestigeful for the male. The girl has the symbol of engagement—the ring. There is no observable symbol for telling the world that the young man is engaged. Second, most engagement parties are for the girl. She has showers given for her and she participates in the planning of the wedding to a far greater extent than the male. Many times the prime duty of the male seems to be to serve as a chauffeur for his fiancée—and her mother. In fact, during engagement and at the wedding the girl's mother may be the second most important figure. (Some young engaged women have suggested she is *the* most important figure.) Generally, the girl and her mother share in most of the activities of engagement and planning the wedding; the engaged male's role is much, much less significant.

The Process of Engagement

Falling in love is a prerequisite to engagement for most Americans. Once the couple decide they are in love, then the natural development is to become engaged, with marriage in the near future. The development of love is discussed in Chapter 5, but it should be pointed out here that the dating and going-steady relationships move (with possible ups and downs) toward the awareness of love. The forces and processes that draw the couple together are many and varied, but they must usually occur before love and engagement develop for the individuals.

Pair Identification. The process of dating and courtship is one of moving from ego-centered interests to increasingly pair-oriented involvement. Many of the factors of pair-identification occur prior to engagement and are important contributing factors to engagement. Waller and Hill describe the pair development as follows:

> A boy and girl have a date and they hear some particular song, or sing it, and that is their song from then on. They soon develop a special language, their own idioms, pet names, and jokes; as a pair they have a

history and a separate culture. They exchange rings or some other articles as soon as possible, striving to make tangible and fixed that elusive something between them.[41]

Through the social mechanism of pair-identification, the two individuals see their relationship as being of such a special nature to them that it becomes important to further solidify it—through engagement and marriage.

The result of pair-identification is a sense of exclusiveness. If the relationship is to continue, the individuality of the two members must, to a certain degree, be subordinated.[42] The degree of subordination may be taken as a rough measure of the exclusive paired nature of the relationship. If the individuals function primarily in response to their own personal needs, the relationship is less an exclusive bond than a working partnership for the ego-satisfaction of individual desires. That is to say, the exclusiveness of engagement demands a minimizing of individuality, at least on many occasions.

The exclusiveness found in the paired relationship of engagement may lead to trouble. "The obvious fact that the dyad is composed of two and only two individuals limits the placement of blame and responsibility for errors and mistakes."[43] Any trouble that arises within the relationship must be resolved within it. In more extended relationships, praise and blame can be spread out; but in engagement, where the couple has cut itself off from the rest of society, there is no available third party on whom to displace hostility and blame.[44] Under such circumstances, one technique is to use individuals outside the pair relationship as scapegoats even though they had little or nothing to do with the problem. Transference of blame allows the couple through rationalization to maintain the purity of their relationship.

For many engaged couples, the experience of an intense pair-relationship probably leads to rational and honest understanding. The awareness of one another and satisfaction with the privacy of the relationship exists in a world where the dyad is recognized as only one small part. It seems reasonable to assume that this understanding develops in those engagements and marriages that achieve some degree of success. The very fact of achieving some degree of success would indicate the integration of the private paired world with the large public world of which it is a part. Burgess and Wallin felt that in the population of engaged couples they studied there was good evidence for the assumption that excessive idealization in courtship or marriage was not widespread.[45] No doubt, the

---

[41] Waller and Hill, *Family,* p. 189.

[42] Ibid., p. 239.

[43] Ibid., p. 232.

[44] Ibid., p. 232.

[45] Burgess and Wallin, *Engagement and Marriage,* p. 237.

degree and the duration of exclusiveness in the love relationship varies with different couples, but it probably rarely extends at a high pitch very long into the marriage relationship.

Expression of Love. Closely related to the pair-identification aspect is the importance of engagement as a period of time for expressing and receiving love. The giving and receiving of love is a socially conditioned need that reaches a high level of expectation during engagement. While many individuals have been in love before engagement, the notion of love takes on greater importance during engagement because it is love for the person to be married. Therefore, this love is seen as mature adult love and the individual often approaches it with seriousness and possible apprehension.

The means of expression and the intensity of love demonstration some-times lead to disagreement by the couple. The expression of love as re-lated to sexual involvement is discussed in Chapter 12; the concern here is with the broad demonstration of love. Psychological and sociological factors both contribute to different attitudes about the demonstration of love. The psychological factors refer to the differences of various per-sonalities in their need to give and receive love. The sociological factors refer to the differences by sex in the giving and receiving of love. In the American culture the female is more apt to be inhibited. While engage-ment provides a socially approved setting for some display of affection, there may be significant differences in what is seen as acceptable by the female as contrasted with the male.

Burgess and Wallin found among the engaged couples they studied that almost half of the men and women did not always agree on display of their love. They found the most common disagreement resulted from one desiring more than the other was willing to give.[46] This reaction is not surprising when it is realized that during engagement love is very tenuous and one or both of the individuals may desire frequent reassur-ance of the love of the other. The insecurity of engagement is vividly illustrated by the Burgess and Wallin findings of the engaged couples' feelings about the future marriage. They found that 41 percent of the males and 48 percent of the females felt some hesitation about marrying their betrothed.[47]

Engagement also tends to make many individuals more realistic about themselves and their future mates. One study found that persons in the engaged status tended to be more realistic in their attitudes toward love than those persons who were not engaged. In fact the engaged tended to be more conjugal than they were romantic.[48]

Final Testing. Under the assumption that a broken engagement is less

---

[46] Ibid., p. 249.

[47] Ibid., p. 180.

[48] David H. Knox, Jr., and Michael J. Sporakowski, "Attitudes of College Students toward Love," *Journal of Marriage and the Family*, November 1968, p. 641.

personally and socially disruptive than a broken marriage, engagement is often seen as a final testing period prior to marriage. This reflects the belief that engagement allows the couple to become closer and to gain more insight each other and thereby discover some problem areas that might make marriage difficult. While some severe problems may emerge that end an engagement, it cannot be assumed that the only alternative is the feeling that the relationship is perfect. In most engagements there is probably some feeling of insecurity because of the highly emotional nature of the relationship.

Some Engagement Problems

An important part of a successful engagement is the meeting and handling of problems that arise.

Pair Disagreements.   The very nature of their close new role relationships means that the engaged couple must develop an understanding and working agreement around areas of importance. It is unrealistic to assume that engaged couples agree on everything; in fact, it can be argued that some disagreement is basic to a better understanding of the self and the "significant other." One set of empirical findings indicates that nearly four fifths of the engaged couples studied report disagreements in one or more areas. Only 1.7 percent state they "always agree" on all areas.[49]

While disagreements are common and sometimes contribute positively to the relationship, there may be danger if the disagreement is extended in intensity and scope beyond the specific areas of difference. There may also be danger when the couple argue for the sake of arguing. Unless the two individuals differ in an area that has significance for both of them, argument can probably be eliminated or held down. This seems to be a tendency in successful engagements.

One area that often has high emotional impact for many engaged couples is any discussion of old boy friends or girl friends. The mention of a past love may threaten the security of one member of the couple as to the exclusive personal commitment of the other in the present love relationship. This sensitivity may be a little greater for the male than for the female because of his somewhat greater possessive feeling.

Parents.   One very common source of difficulty for the engaged couple centers around the parents' reactions to the fiancé(e). The conflict may center around incongruity in defining the young person's role—the engaged person feeling that mate selection is his own choice, with his parents having little to do with it, and the parents feeling they should play an important part in their offspring's selection of a mate. The conflict may also revolve around the idealistic romantic beliefs of the young

---

[49] Ibid., p. 247.

person and the more realistic values of the parent. It is probable that girls, because of close ties to their mothers, are more willing to listen to their parents and to be influenced by the parents' wishes.

Even though young people want to think that engagement is almost entirely their own concern, their parents may influence them either directly in ending the relationship, or indirectly contribute to its end by pointing out the faults and dangers of the relationship.

Broken Engagements. All individuals who have any experience in the dating-courtship process have had the experience of ending a relationship. When a person dates an individual on only one occasion, the emotional commitment is not great and the ending of the relationship rarely carries any great difficulties. However, as the stages of courtship are entered into, the emotional commitment increases and it becomes more difficult to deal with and adjust to the ending of the relationship. More personal pain will probably be associated with a broken engagement than with the ending of going steady, and more pain over a broken marriage than a broken engagement. Regardless of the emotional pain involved, the broken engagement is relatively common in American culture. While we have indicated that parents may play a part in breaking engagements, the more important fact is that individuals select their love objects with a strong desire for happiness and ego-satisfaction. An engagement lacking these qualities is a prime candidate for dissolution.

Because of the high emotional involvement, adjustment to a broken engagement often takes time and an emotional toll. Many persons become "gun-shy" after a broken engagement and are in no hurry to enter into a new relationship. Often it is more difficult for the girl to get back into dating circulation than it is for the boy. The boy can reenter the dating-courtship process by actively seeking out dates, while the girl must usually wait until word gets around that she is again in circulation. In addition, the girl is not perceived as datable for some time because she often goes through a period of "mourning." Girls probably take longer to recover from a broken engagement than boys because of the greater significance the female attaches to love. Because there is a common belief that love is more deeply felt by the girl, boys may be hesitant to ask the ex-engaged girl for a date because of the fear that she is still in love. A girl seems to accept a date from the ex-engaged boy with less fear.

Given human recuperative powers, individuals recover from the broken engagement and eventually almost all move back into the dating-courtship process. Going back and starting all over again with dating may be difficult for many, but go back they do—often wiser and more careful. With love and marriage so important to most Americans, the period of remorse and mourning tends to be intense, but short. Because love and marriage are so personally and socially important, the individual must recover from the broken engagement and start again the forward march through the dating-courtship process.

The dating-courtship process provides for many young people in the middle class the socialization necessary for moving into the marriage relationship as well as other adult relationships. Dating and courtship contribute to a familiarity and ability to enter the "paired world" of the adult man and woman. The behavior of adult models is often supported by peer group values that give great importance to cross-sex interaction. The individual is thus socialized to the skills of "relating" and "belonging" which are so important to the middle class in a wide variety of social settings.

Living Together.   Before ending this chapter it is necessary to say something about what appears to be a new premarital relationship.[50] This is where young couples, usually of college age, choose to live together. They often do not define themselves as engaged and may have no commitment to marry at some future time. They frequently live together with a high level of interpersonal commitment to one another and are generally sexually monagamous. It may not be that living together is a rejection of marriage in general, but rather a rejection of the commitments and responsibilities of marriage at that point in their lives. The relationship also recognizes that people may feel very close to one another but still feel that closeness may not last or that even if it continues there is no need for the formal commitment of marriage. There is no reliable data on how many young couples live together. But certainly in the middle class, and especially in college and university environments, it appears to be relatively common. But what may be most important is that it is seen as an alternative to the formal relationships of engagement and marriage that have prevailed in the past. We need studies to learn more about its frequency as well as its successes and failures.

SELECTED BIBLIOGRAPHY

Bayer, Alan E.   "Early Dating and Early Marriage" *Journal of Marriage and the Family,* November 1968, pp. 625–35.

Bell, Robert R., and **Blumberg, Leonard**   "Courtship Intimacy and Religious Background." *Marriage and Family Living,* November 1959, pp. 356–60.

Broderick, Carlfred B., and **Fowler, Stanley E.**   "New Patterns of Relationships Between the Sexes Among Preadolescents." *Marriage and Family Living,* February 1961, pp. 27–30.

Burchinal, Lee G.   "The Premarital Dyad and Love Involvement," in Harold

---

[50] See Joann S. Delora and Jack R. Delora, *Intimate Life Styles: Marriage and Its Alternatives* (Pacific Palisades, Calif.: Goodyear Publishing Co., 1972); and Nena O'Neill and George O'Neill, *Open Marriage: A New Life Style for Couples* (New York: Avon Books, 1973).

T. Christensen, ed., *Handbook of Marriage and the Family*. Chicago: Rand McNally & Co., 1964, pp. 623–74.

Delora, Joann S., and **Delora, Jack R.**   *Intimate Life Styles: Marriage and Its Alternatives*. Pacific Palisades, Calif.: Goodyear Publishing Co., 1972.

Kephart, William M.   *The Family, Society and the Individual*. Boston: Houghton Mifflin Co., 1961, chap. x.

Klemer, Richard H.   Self-Esteem and College Dating Experience as Factors in Mate Selection and Marital Happiness: A Longitudinal Study." *Journal of Marriage and the Family*, February 1971, pp. 183–87.

Rogers, Everett M., and **Havens, Eugene A.**   "Prestige Rating and Mate Selection on a College Campus." *Marriage and Family Living*, February 1960, pp. 55–59.

Skipper, James K., and **Nass, Gilbert**   "Dating Behavior: A Framework for Analysis and An Illustration." *Journal of Marriage and the Family*, November 1966, pp. 412–20

Chapter 5

Love

The interest here is with the love of men and women leading to and resulting from marriage. This focus on love shall be called conjugal love and it may be defined as a strong emotion directed at a person of the opposite sex and involving feelings of sexual attraction, tenderness, and some commitment to the other's ego-needs. In the American middle class, conjugal love places a great stress on each individual's varied ego-needs being satisfied by the other. In this chapter we look at various facets of love, including the influence of romantic love, the psychological and cultural nature of love, and some theories about love.

Conjugal love, with its stress on ego-needs, is probably more important and more basic to the American culture than to almost any other culture of the world. To be unloved in the United States is to be more than unwanted; it is to lack importance in the eyes of a "significant other"—it is to be unchosen. This is often extremely upsetting in a culture in which being chosen is often equated with having social worth as a human being. Furthermore, love is important both as a condition for marriage and for marriage satisfaction.

One important historical influence which has been handed down over the centuries in the Western world, and which has contributed to contemporary American beliefs about love, has been the notion of romantic love. A brief historical description of the origins of romantic love and how it has been altered over time and ultimately incorporated into the values of American society follows.

ROMANTIC LOVE

The Greeks developed two concepts of adult love: *eros*, which was a carnal love associated with the sensual, physical, and sexual; and *agape*, a spiritual love associated with the more "pure" human emotions. Originally neither of these types of love had anything to do with marriage, because love was not related to mate selection or the relationships of husband and wife. The main reason for marriage was reproduction; having children, particularly sons, was of great importance to the Greek man, but love between husband and wife was usually not.

Love among the Greeks stressed physical beauty, but the Greek male did not often feel that beauty could be found in the female, and certainly not in a wife. Actually the status of the female was so low that she was often felt to be unworthy of idealistic love; furthermore, as a female she was incapable of returning the love. The ideal Greek love tended to be homosexual, between an older man and a younger boy. It was based on the belief that the essence of beauty and therefore the realization of love could be found by the male in the male. It is an ironical historical fact that love as it is viewed today, with the exchange of deep emotional commitment between members of the opposite sex, had partial roots in male homosexuality.[1]

The next great historical influence on romantic love was early Christianity. The Church began a strong fight against the temptations of the flesh and, as often happens with social reaction, its objection took a position at the extreme. For the early Christians, the highest achievement of man was as complete a rejection of his body as possible while still retaining life. The priesthood represented the highest level of achievement because it resisted as completely as possible all things sensual. Because priesthood could not be the state for many, marriage was tolerated, but even here the highest form of marriage was one of physical continence.

At the root of all evil were women. Women were believed, simply because they were women, to possess evilness and therefore were to be distrusted, watched, and controlled. The highest state for the woman was in the glory of everlasting virginity. "Reasoning ran something like this—in Paradise, Eve was a virgin. Virginity, therefore, is natural; hence wedlock only follows guilt."[2] This historical period was characterized by severe ascetic attacks against the inherent evilness and implied witchery of

---

[1] Morton M. Hunt, *The Natural History of Love* (New York: Alfred A. Knopf, Inc., 1959), p. 8.

[2] Isabel Drummond, *The Sex Paradox* (New York: G. P. Putnam's Sons, 1953), p. 8.

women. The following passage, written by Saint John Chrysostom in
A.D. 370 to a friend who had said he was in love with a young woman
and wanted to marry her, provides a vivid picture of the woman:

> The groundwork of this corporeal beauty is nothing else but phlegm
> and blood and humor and bile, and the fluid of masticated food . . .:
> If you consider what is stored up inside those beautiful eyes, and that
> straight nose, and the mouth and cheeks, you will affirm the well-shaped
> body to be nothing else than a whited sepulchre: . . . Moreover, when
> you see a rag with any of these things on it, such as phlegm, or spittle,
> you cannot bear to touch it even with the tips of your fingers, nay you
> cannot endur' looking at it; are you then in a flutter of excitement about
> the store houses and repositories of these things?[3]

During the rise of Christianity, the Church struggled constantly against
the sensate behavior of the people. As a revolt against the rigid dictates of
the Church, a movement based on the Romantic Ideal emerged in Europe. This movement had its origins in southern France near the end of
the 11th century; it emerged from, and for the most part stayed with, that
group with enough power to oppose the Church—the upper class of
noblemen. Some contradiction and disagreement exists among historians
as to the degree of sexual behavior in the romantic movement. Probably,
the early romantic movement was clandestine and idealistic, and involved
a great deal of sexual frustration because it was often pursued in a highly
erotic setting, but presumably with no sexual intercourse. Knights and
their ladies were sometimes put nude into bed together and making love
was expected so long as intercourse did not occur.

This was a kind of "adventure" and "courage was associated with love
of adventure and the glorification of war. Their [the knights'] religion was
apt to be a mere formality. Their courtesy was for the ladies of the
castle, not the women of the cottages."[4]

A large part of court behavior developed to mock both religion and the
prevailing system of marriage. Love practiced by the troubadours was devotion to little more than an inanimate object; "the lady was an inert,
icon-like figure."[5] It must be stressed that courtly love had nothing to do
with mate selection, because marriages were arranged and the basis for
arrangement was usually economic. The ideal of chivalry and its particular definition of love was more important than marriage or reproduction. Marriage was one point on which romantics and the ecclesiastical
were in agreement—it was a duty rather than a pleasure.[6]

The long historical period from the rise of Christianity, through the
age of Chivalry, and into the Renaissance was generally one of hatred and

---

[3] Ibid., p. 110.

[4] Stuart A. Queen, John B. Adams, and Robert W. Habenstein, *The Family in
Various Cultures* (Philadelphia: J. B. Lippincott Co., 1961), p. 232.

[5] Hunt, *History of Love*, p. 151.

[6] Queen, Adams, and Habenstein, *Various Cultures*, p. 237.

contempt of women. Drummond points out that it was during the "dark age" of woman that the doctrine of the immaculate conception arose.[7] To compare the status of women during that "dark age" with their status in modern American society is to illustrate a great and significant social change.

Over the centuries, the influence of romantic love varied greatly. Morton Hunt argues that three general influences emerged: (1) a greater emotional relationship between men and women, which meant an uplifting in a part of the woman's status; (2) sexual fidelity to a single partner (even though, during the early period this meant fidelity within the framework of adultery); (3) the idea that love must be mutual, which also contributed a great deal to improving the status of women."[8] The adulterous flirtation and illicit infatuation of the Middle Ages were the very instrument that began to enhance woman's status and, hence, eventually to alter marriage."[9]

Over time, many influences and changes developed around the concept of romantic love. Today it has a variety of meanings and must be viewed as a loose collection of beliefs and customs. Hunt writes that "as it passed down the centuries, some [ideas and customs] were continually sluffed off and others added; it is something like the philosopher's much darned socks, the fabric of which was eventually altogether changed, but which never lost their identity as a specific pair of socks."[10] Hunt further points out that "it is therefore a paradox of no mean order that modern love began with Greek love and owes so much to it, although the forms and ideals of Greek love are considered immoral and, to a large extent, illegal in modern society."[11]

Over the centuries when the notion of love was being altered and assimilated in the Western world, no equivalent process occurred in most Eastern countries. The Maces[12] point out that "it is a rigid principle of Eastern life that the stability of the family and the maintenance of the social order always come before the happiness of the individual. Romantic love is an unruly emotion, which out of control can do as much damage as uncontrolled anger."[13] But in many countries of the Eastern world the traditional patterns are now beginning to break down and romantic love is being accepted by the younger generation primarily because of the increasing infiltration of Western ideas. However, there is some evidence that a romantic approach to marriage is not being quickly assimilated. A

---

[7] Drummond, *Sex Paradox*, p. 8.

[8] Hunt, *History of Love*, p. 171.

[9] Ibid., pp. 171–73.

[10] Ibid., p. 299.

[11] Ibid., p. 16.

[12] David Mace and Vera Mace, *Marriage East and West* (Garden City, N.Y. Doubleday and Company, Inc., 1960), p. 121.

[13] Ibid., p. 124.

study using Indian, Burmese, and Singapore Chinese respondents found that although they were from the segment of their societies most subject to Western influences; they did not show an acceptance of the American-type romantic orientation to marriage.[14] Nevertheless, the influence of romantic love is of a far-reaching nature and must be assessed as having worldwide implications.

From the rich and often contradictory historical tradition of romantic love, some ingredients may be found in American society today. Although no list could be complete, certain elements may be suggested as important to many Americans when they think of romantic love.

Idealization—the placing of the love object on a pedestal, untouched by the commonness and coarseness of the everyday world. A high degree of selective perception on the part of the lover is often involved. He sees only what he wants to see—often in an exaggerated fashion—and ignores the love object's human frailties. Generally, this idealization has a strong positive influence on the loved one because most of us thrive on esteem and cannot help being responsive to the one who esteems us.[15]

Fantasy—the tendency to withdraw into a world of make-believe and to create images of what should be in a most perfect-of-all-worlds with the most perfect-of-all-individuals. As with idealization, fantasy suggests ignoring what may go counter to the imagined.

Highly Emotional—the wish to "feel rather than think." This ideal is often held to be so strong that it defies rational understanding or analysis; in fact, to attempt either would be to destroy it.

Exclusiveness—the stress on the privacy and singular nature of the love experience. The belief is that in true romantic love neither person can really care about anything or anyone else. The couple live in a world of their own, and when it is necessary to move out and deal with the world at large, the overriding desire is to return to the exclusiveness of the private world as soon as possible.

The above ingredients are not found in all love relationships of a romantic nature, nor necessarily in quite the fashion described. Rather, they describe a few beliefs that exist and affect some people. What might be called the American folklore of romantic love, which is often found in mass-media productions and is frequently presented as being necessary to "real or true love," further illustrates the influence of romantic love in today's society.

ıre

he belief in a soulmate is that in this great wide world ı, and only one, meant for each of us. This belief is very

heodorson, "Romanticism and Motivation to Marry in the United Burma and India," *Social Forces*, September 1965, p. 27.

y of Love, p. 98.

ego-satisfying because it suggests that each of us is so special that only one person can meet our needs, and that one person has been created especially to do so. It also implies an adventurous quality, because adolescence and the early adult years can be devoted to a search for the soulmate.

While many young people may say they do not believe in a soulmate, their actions often indicate they do. Many find it psychologically difficult to accept the idea that they could fall in love with any one of many different individuals, particularly when *they* define themselves as being in love, because it seems to them impossible to imagine loving someone else. Being in love, therefore, often reinforces the soulmate idea because once a loved one has been found it is psychologically reassuring to believe that there are no other possibilities.

A person frequently enters the romantic maze and, after many a false start and dead end, finds his way to the "bait" at the exit. But because of the exclusive nature of the "bait" he mistakenly thinks it was the only "bait" at the only exit of the maze. He has no way of knowing what other exits with their various "baits" he might have reached.

Love-at-first-sight. This love is found "across the crowded room"— their eyes meet and they know they are meant for each other. When love at first sight occurs, it can be based on little more than physical attraction. Like the belief in a soulmate, it too has an adventurous quality. Part of the belief is that when the couple meet they will really *know* it: something dramatic and earth shaking—an exchange laden with cosmic meaning—will occur between them. All other individuals will become only vague shadows in the background of the newly discovered exclusive world. And the clincher will be the first kiss—an event during which some believe the world observes 30 seconds of silence.

A measurement of when love-at-first-sight actually happens would be useful in checking the belief. People telling when they fell in love are usually describing something that *has* happened, not what *is* happening, which may influence their willingness to believe in love-at-first-sight. A favorite argument between young lovers is which one knew he loved the other one first. When remembering, however, each tends to move back the time when he said to himself he was in love. Unable to remove himself from the intervening experiences and emotions, he sees the past event not as it was, but in the light of what he has experienced since.

Some dangers are involved for the individual who believes in love-at-first-sight. The highly significant first meeting may never occur; love doesn't always follow the folklore script. Thus, he may never experience "real" love or may feel frustrated in a love relationship which develops over time, because the first meeting lacked a dramatic quality.

Overcoming Frustration. An important component of the American folklore of true love is that it should be put to a test. If it passes the test, it is true love; if it doesn't, then it may not be "real" love after all. Many popular mass-media magazine stories have as their theme a couple over-coming the frustrations confronting their love: Boy meets girl, obstacle enters, and when they surmount the obstacle, they live happily ever after. Only the nature of the obstacle ever seems to vary. Typically, the girl wants a career instead of marriage, the boy thinks he is in love with some-one else, or the parents have strong objections. If the story has a happy ending, as it generally does, the great love which has resolved the prob-lem is proved "real."

For young people who have been reared with the belief that "true love never runs smooth," problems may arise in their own love affairs. They may search for obstacles to be conquered and for an opportunity for the virtue of love to win out over the evil of obstruction. Some may exagger-ate a situation into an obstacle, or even dream up an obstacle. Others who face no obstacles may feel that something is lacking, that their love has not been put to a true test, and so they cannot be sure it "really" is love.

Love Conquers All.   With love conquering all, romantic love becomes paramount—with it nothing in the world is unattainable. This belief may cause several reactions. Individuals may put aside the realities of life and retreat into the protective cocoon of love. They need not, then, worry about such mundane, unromantic problems as housing or food, because love will find a way. When they discover all the world doesn't really love the lover, the romantic pair may be somewhat jolted.

Cues of possible interactional difficulty in the relationship may also be ignored. Idealization often means ignoring certain qualities in the other person that may lead to future difficulty. What may be even more danger-ous is to recognize faults, but believe that love can overcome them. The writer once talked to a woman who had just divorced her alcoholic hus-band. Her husband had previously been divorced for the same reason. When asked if she knew he was an alcoholic when she married him she replied, "Yes, but I believed that my love would straighten him out."

In one respect, a belief in love helping to conquer many difficulties has some truth. Many newly married young couples, facing rather severe role adjustments and often with limited financial support, find their love in-volvement helps them over rough spots and may even make enjoyable what without love would be unpleasant. When this happens, love is not a replacement for reality, but rather a positive force in helping to deal with it.

Assessment of Romantic Love

The reader may feel that the preceding picture of contemporary Ameri-can romantic love is unfair and exaggerated. If the description of romantic love has been extreme, consider it as one end of a continuum. The other end might be called "rational mate selection." A picture of the opposite end of the continuum will describe the selection of a mate on extremely rational or objective grounds.

Imagine that a girl looking for a husband wants to use objective, rational criteria for making her final choice. She will try to control emotional influences—other than possibly some feeling of physical attraction, which would have some significance for her future sexual adjustment. She meets a physically attractive young man and must decide if he is the man to marry. To be purely rational and objective, what could she theoretically do? First, she could turn him over to a board of psychologists and psychiatrists. They could probe his psychological makeup, and measure his intelligence, motivation, aspirations, and the overall strengths and weaknesses of his personality. His potential as a husband and father and provider, his mental health and stability might also be assessed. Second, she could turn him over to a group of biologists and medical experts. His family background could be thoroughly examined to determine possible genetic skeletons in his family closet and possible positive genetic contributions he might make to their children. The state of his physical health and some estimate of possible life expectancy might also be established. A third test would subject him to a variety of new social experiences, with the results used to analyze his ability to adapt and adjust adequately. As a final test, he might be followed day and night for at least six months by a competent private detective agency.

This purely rational, objective approach is the extreme at the other end of the continuum. In life, very few individuals make their choice at either extreme on the continuum (romantic or rational), but rather at points in between.

Since romantic love is an important part of the social fabric, to exclude it completely from the love relationship is to ignore social reality. Most individuals in love probably find a satisfactory middle ground between the romantic and the rational. The romantic emphasis may be stronger during courtship and the early stages of marriage because of the newness of the experience and because emotional ties are the primary bases for the new relationship. But through the common experiences of living together, a new relationship often emerges, one that replaces some of the romantic emotionality of the earlier relationship. We will have more to say on the changing nature of love later in the chapter.

LOVE IN CONTEMPORARY AMERICAN SOCIETY

While romantic love is an important and dramatic part of the American love ethos, it is not all of it. A marital love pattern can be distinguished from the romantic love complex. Goode suggests that under the love pattern "love is a permissible, expected prelude to marriage, and a usual element of courtship. There is also the ideological prescription that falling in love is a highly desirable basis of courtship and marriage and love is strongly institutionalized."[16] These aspects of the conjugal love pattern have been borrowed from the romantic love complex, but should not be viewed as synonymous with it.

For the vast majority of Americans, love and marriage go together; an important, and recent, social invention is that love is the reason for marriage. This change is closely related to the shift of emphasis from the family members as a group to the family member as an individual. When the family group had greater control in choosing the marriage partner, premarital love was not usually important. The predominant values stressed in the selection of a mate satisfied the needs of the family unit, not the ego-needs of the individual getting married. But with mate selection increasingly determined by the person getting married, love came to be the important factor in choosing a mate. Loving and being loved satisfied the ego-needs of the two individuals involved. The anthropologist Stephens suggests that the *notion* of romantic love, used as a rationale for marriage, emerged to fill an ideological vacuum caused by the disappearance of arranged marriage.[17]

For many individuals in the American middle class love serves as a reward motive that leads them into the socially important positions of wife-mother and husband-father. Greenfield suggests that the function of romantic love in the United States seems to be to motivate persons—where there is no other means of motivating them—to occupy the positions that form nuclear families that are basic to the maintenance of society.[18] In other words, he is arguing that romantic love is the instrumental means that bring people together into new families of procreation which are the basic social units of society.

Most Americans not only believe that marriage must be preceded by love but also that the only satisfactory consequence of being in love is to marry. If two people in love cannot marry for some reason, it is generally viewed as a tragedy by the individuals and as unfortunate by society at large. American literature is full of stories of individuals who have led a life of misery and unhappiness because they could not marry their beloved. The reaction of society to unfulfilled love varies according to the reason marriage did not occur. If a woman chooses against love and marriage and pursues a career, she receives little sympathy from society, and her basic "womanliness" is often subject to question. However, if she

[16] William J. Goode, "The Theoretical Importance of Love," *American Sociological Review,* February 1959, p. 42.

[17] William N. Stephens, *The Family in Cross-Cultural Perspective* (New York: Holt, Rinehart & Winston, Inc., 1963), p. 206.

[18] Sidney M. Greenfield, "Love and Marriage in Modern America: A Functional Analysis," in Jeffrey K. Hadden and Marie L. Borgatta, *Marriage and Family* (Itasca, Ill.: F. E. Peacock, 1969), p. 253.

does not experience love because she must care for an ailing or aging parent, she is usually treated with respect and sympathy.

SOME THEORIES OF LOVE

In American society there is no shortage of theories or definitions of love. Ranging from the simple to the complex, theories have been developed by social observers of various types and interests. One of the briefest definitions of love was made by H. L. Mencken when he called it "a state of perpetual anesthesia."[19] After extensive study of the various theories of love, Morton Hunt came to the conclusion that "most of the learned people who write about love seem to equip themselves in advance with a special theory; with this as a kind of butterfly net, they then sally forth and attempt to capture cases to prove or exemplify their point."[20]

Most definitions suggest that love is a strong emotion between two individuals which involves and satisfies the need of giving and receiving. This implies either the reality or the expectation of emotional, physical, and intellectual exchange. Based on this general statement, the following sections will examine some common love components, as well as love as a process.

Love Components

The ingredients to be suggested should not be seen as a checklist for determining whether or not love exists. Rather they are characteristics, without set manner or degree, that are often, but not always, associated with love. As with romantic love, *idealization* contributes to the extent that the loved one is seen as having some special qualities for the lover. Often a somewhat exaggerated notion of qualities felt highly desirable compensate for those qualities not so highly prized. This is often idealization within rational limits. *Respect* for the loved one as an individual, in what he does and how he thinks and feels, is also an important quality. The individuality of the two is never completely destroyed by the paired relationship. *Sexual attraction* enters when the other person is a meaningful and satisfying physical counterpart. Although almost everyone needs physical satisfaction, the need varies greatly among different individuals. Particularly for the female, the sexual act becomes meaningful through love and often only with the loved one. *Companionship* indicates that the couple find satisfaction in being and doing together, but not to the complete exclusion of others or the destruction of the identity of each in the relationship. Rather, some experiences are shared, with the amount depending on the changing needs of the individuals.

---

[19] Hunt, *History of Love,* p. 5.
[20] Ibid., p. 8.

Selflessness suggests that the individual can move outside himself and attempt to meet the other's needs. Sometimes personal preferences and desires are put aside for the fulfillment of the other person, and this is often reciprocated. Selflessness recognizes that on some occasions individuality may temporarily have to give way to the basically interdependent nature of the pair relationship. A final ingredient, *maturity*, refers to the ability and motivation to accept adult rights and obligations in a variety of adult role relationships. Adult responsibility entails attempting, as sincerely as possible, to deal with all contingencies. For example, the young wife who turns to her mother for support after an argument with the husband is not socially mature in her adult fulfillment of the wife role.

Love Process

Love is not generally assumed to be there today and gone tomorrow, but to last over time. American cultural values generally suggest that love should be retained through periods of strain and not disappear without just and sufficient cause. While the ideal is that love will continue for the rest of the individual's life, many love relationships probably do not realize this ideal.

Some writers like to characterize love as growing, but it may be more accurately described as changing. Growing implies maintaining what has existed and adding to it. But elements important early in love relationships may, over time, be discarded and replaced by new ones. For example, early idealization may be replaced by a feeling of interdependability based upon the cumulative experience of the pair relationship.

No discussion of the ingredients and process of love should be considered final or authoritative. Love affairs differ in the strength of each ingredient. For example, some individuals feel that sexual attraction is of great significance, but others may limit its importance. One writer argues that only one thing really matters: No element should be missing.[21] This argument, that love is not really love if some ingredients are absent, seems arbitrary and questionable. The best that can be said is that many love relationships contain these ingredients. A related point is that not any list of ingredients should ever be viewed as complete. The elements of human emotions, the variety of individual responses, and the differential impact of cultural values are not well enough understood to make arbitrary decisions on exactly what constitutes real love. That is why mass magazines that provide checklists for determining *whether your husband really loves you* are misleading, dishonest, and sometimes dangerous. Some professional social scientists contribute to the illusion that

---

[21] Robert O. Blood, *Anticipating Your Marriage* (Glencoe, Ill.: The Free Press, 1955), p. 100.

love is exact. One writer tells her readers that "seven qualities give strength to love that is good enough for marriage."[22] While that kind of authoritarianism may be reassuring to some readers, it is nevertheless misleading. Such writers rarely provide any empirical research to substantiate the ingredients they are selling as "real" love.

Infatuation versus Love

Many family writers like to distinguish between love and infatuation. Most believe the two emotions are different, but no one is quite sure in what way. Infatuation is generally viewed with suspicion—a kind of ersatz love that will lead the follower down the path of disillusionment. Infatuation is often described as being on a lower level than love and unworthy of marriage.[23] Rarely, however, does the individual involved define a current emotional experience as infatuation. Kephart points out that "whenever individuals speak of their infatuation it is nearly always in past tense. Very few individuals report themselves as being currently infatuated, yet at a given time a fair number considered themselves to be in love."[24]

Apparently, when individuals are going through the emotional relationship, they call it love; when it is over, they often call it infatuation. By calling past love affairs infatuations, the individual maintains the uniqueness of love, so that when he falls in love at some future time, the term *love* will refer to the new, not the used. Many individuals, however, will admit to having been in love on several occasions. The concept of infatuation seems to be of little analytical value for anyone trying to understand love. Because of its *ex post facto* nature, it is useful only for categorizing past love relationships, not for understanding present or future ones.

The evidence also indicates that previous romantic involvements are more admitted to by females than by males. Kephart found that age, for age, "the romantic experience figure for females is greater than that for males, although by age 23–24 the difference virtually disappears."[25] Kephart also found that the romantic displacement is a function not simply of the female's age, but of her closeness to marriage. The closer she gets to marriage the less important are previous involvements for her. It is possible that years after she gets married she may remember some of the

---

[22] Ruth S. Cavan, *The American Family* (New York: Thomas Y. Crowell Co., 1953), p. 117.

[23] Ibid., p. 117.

[24] William Kephart, *The Family, Society and the Individual* (New York: Houghton Mifflin Co., 1961), p. 322.

[25] William M. Kephart, "Some Correlates of Romantic Love," *Journal of Marriage and the Family*, August 1967, p. 471.

romantic involvements she has forgotten. This might be true because she is secure in the love of the marriage and can recall previous experiences and they are not threatening to her marital love. Or it may be that she wants to romanticize her youth and recalls love affairs as evidence of her past popularity. That might also be a compensation for a marriage where the love relationship is no longer adequate and she remembers what might have been.

This section has suggested a list of ingredients often found in love. That the ingredients should not be taken as absolute, either in conclusiveness or degree of existence, has been stressed. Furthermore, little is known about the interrelationship of ingredients other than they operate as part of a total package, no doubt affecting and being affected by each other. As examples, idealization may be minimized by strong sexual attraction; different personalities will relate to the ingredients of love in different ways; or two self-sufficient personalities in marriage may have less need for companionship than a couple who both need personality reassurance.

CULTURAL INFLUENCES ON LOVE

The previous section concentrated primarily on the psychological elements of love for the individual and in his relationship with a loved one. This section will consider cultural factors. Ego-need love is not a universal found in all cultures at all times. While it prevails for most members of the American culture today, it is not the common pattern in many other cultures of the world nor was it the common pattern in the American society of the past.

Love is clearly a learned behavior. People are born with the capacity for all kinds of social learning, including the capacity for love, but they must learn to love as they must learn, for example, to hate. This section is concerned with the cultural factors that contribute to the individual's learning a love that is meaningful to himself and in his relation to a "significant other."

The American culture regards some form of love relationship as an ideal for all periods of a person's lifetime. The newborn infant will, with socialization, presumably enter into a love relationship with, at least, his parents. Most social scientists believe the effectiveness of this love is crucial to the child's emerging personality. Since the socialization of the child affects his preparation for future adult love relationships, early participation in, and learning of, love becomes a significant cultural factor. If young children are conditioned to marriage as a future adult expectation before they learn of love as the prerequisite to marriage, it may be because marriage and marriage roles are easier to identify with and grasp than the more abstract concept of love. Children often perceive love and marriage as a basic characteristic of adult status. They learn to believe that these values are as natural to their future as growing to adult height.

As children enter adolescence, the part that love plays in their lives increases. They hear others telling about their love experiences (often imaginary) and begin to anticipate the experience for themselves. Because love is thought of as "grown-up" and because adolescence is a period of age-role insecurity, love is yearned for as proof of attaining adult status. Indicating these pressures, Kirkpatrick writes: "Young persons of dating age fully expect that sooner or later they will be caught in the magic spell of love and experience the pangs and delights which seem as inevitable as growing older or being mortal. It is well known that cultural expectations produce real results."[26]

To what extent adolescents seek out love for its own sake, and to what extent for its symbolic adult attributes, is hard to say, but no doubt both influences are operating. Another pressure is added if the mode of the peer group is to fall in love. Few other groups in American society demand as much conformity as the adolescent subgroup. Thus, the adolescent is simultaneously reaching for and being pushed into a new role. Oftentimes when the adolescent feels he has found love, his new self-image becomes very important to himself and to others who care to observe it. As Morton Hunt puts it, the "jaunty step, new-minted optimism, and smug contentment of the adolescent in love means that he has found two things to be of great value—his beloved, and himself."[27] He has attained that which society has taught him to seek and attain.

Cultural conditioning is often so effective and efficient that the adolescent, and many times the adult, believes that when he has fallen in love he has discovered something distinctly unique, discovered by few others, past or present. When the individual who has fallen in love thinks his experience is unique, mysterious, and without precedent, his culture has usually taught him to so think. He has so well internalized external cultural values that he has come to believe they originated within himself.

As the young person reaches late adolescence and enters the early adult years, various pressures that help propel his internalized value of finding love increase. Because marriage is of great importance in the American society—especially for the girl—love must be encouraged to develop so that marriage can and will occur during the accepted age period. Goode argues that because love, as related to marriage, is so important to society, it must be controlled before it appears.[28] Therefore, the constant early emphasis on love values is closely related to future marital choice.

---

[26] Clifford Kirkpatrick, *The Family As Process and Institution* (New York: The Ronald Press Co., 1955), p. 273.

[27] Hunt, *History of Love,* p. 374.

[28] Goode, "Importance of Love," p. 43.

Parents often increasingly pressure the young person to fall in love; more specifically, they try to direct their children to fall in love with the "right kind of person." When parental pressure starts early in adolescence, parents are often able to control the children's choice of a love partner. Parents "threaten, cajole, wheedle, bribe, and persuade their children to go 'with the right person,' during both the early love play and later during courtship phases."[29]

The peer group can support or undercut parental influence, depending on whether the general values of parents and peer groups are alike or different. When the values are essentially the same, the individual will, presumably, suffer only minimal conflict finding a proper kind of love partner. But when parents and peers differ, the potential for conflict is great, depending upon the influence and meaningfulness of each of the pressure groups for the individual.

Pressures intensify during the age period when increasing numbers of the individual's age peers are finding love and marriage. The peer group splits sharply between the "chosen" and the "unchosen." Increasingly concerned with a negative, "unchosen" status, both the individual and his parents may actively try to wipe out the stigma.

At this age stage rather sharp differences occur, determined by the sex of the young person. Girls are generally much more preoccupied with thoughts of marriage than boys of the same age because love and marriage usually mean more for the future adult roles of the girl than of the boy. This probably continues to be true even though many young women are choosing occupational roles over marriage and family roles. But this trend is still only for a minority of young women. It is our contention that the most important adult role for most American girls is still that of wife-mother; and to achieve this role she must first fall in love. For the boy, the most important adult role is probably his occupation, the achievement of which is not dependent on love. In fact, the boy may view love as a threat to occupational achievement, fearing that marriage and parenthood may restrict his occupational education or the chance of directing his full energies toward successful job fulfillment. Thus, girls and boys, especially those in college, often view marriage differently: The former see it as something to be achieved as soon as possible, the latter as something that should be at least temporarily postponed. A college boy will frequently explain that his break-up with a girl was due to her "getting too serious." On the other hand, resistance to marriage is obviously not true for a large number of young college men. Largely because college and marriage were combined by the GIs of World War II, a pattern of college marriage has continued to prevail. This trend has been strengthened by parental encouragement and finan-

---

[29] Ibid., p. 45.

cial aid. In view of the girl's stronger marital interest, it would be interesting to discover whether financial aid comes most often from the
girl's parents.

Male-Female Differences

As already indicated there are some differences between how males
and females respond to and define being in love. Several studies have
indicated that females tend to be more realistic in their attitudes toward
love than do males. Conversely, males view love more romantically than
females. In part this may be a reflection of the fact that love has a
greater instrumental importance for females than for males. That is, the
female relates love to marriage and her future more than does the man
and must therefore be at least somewhat realistic.

There are some patterns of difference in how males and females
interact with each other. For example, there is some evidence that
American women find it easier to empathize with males than the American male has found it to empathize with females. "This may help to
explain why she seems to understand her men better than her men seem
to understand her."[30]

We must also recognize that maleness and femaleness are defined in
their relationship to one another. It appears that men who are secure
in their maleness and who can enjoy being with women are probably
more manly than those who feel themselves to be real men only when
they are away from women. Furthermore, women who are uncomfortable with men or who resent them are less secure in their own
femininity than women who enjoy men." In fact, it is possible for the
sexes to enjoy each other socially only when both are so secure in their
sexual identity that the other is neither threatening nor invidious."[31]

Kanin also finds some evidence for the argument that males are sometimes more romantic than females. Kanin found that about twice as
many males as females indicated that it was easy to become attracted
to persons of the opposite sex. They further found that males rather than
females were more likely to show interest in their partners at the time
of initial encounter. The males also scored higher than females on romanticism scales and were significantly more likely to recognize love
earlier than were females.[32] It was also found that females appear to

---

[30] Wainwright Churchill, *Homosexual Behavior among Males* (New York: Hawthorne Books, 1967), p. 165.

[31] Jessie Bernard, "Women, Marriage and the Future," in Constantina Safilios-
Rothschild, *Toward a Sociology of Women* (Lexington, Mass.: Xerox College Publishing, 1972), pp. 324–25.

[32] Eugene J. Kanin, Karen R. Davidson, and Sonia R. Scheck, "A Research Note
on Male-Female Differentials in the Experience of Heterosexual Love," *The Journal
of Sex Research*, February 1970, p. 64.

demonstrate their more romantic behavior in a more judicious and rational fashion than did the men. "She chooses and commits herself more slowly than the male, but, once in love, she engages more extravagantly in the euphoric and idealization dimensions of loving."[33] In other words, the male commits his feelings and engages in the related expressions of love faster than the female. She wants to be sure and when she is she may then express her love in a more intense and complex way than does the male. This difference would appear to reflect the differential socialization of the two sexes, with the female generally being taught to control her expressions more in romantic relationships because she is usually believed to have more invested, with a greater potential profit or loss. Kanin and his colleagues indicate that the female's more pronounced ability to idealize and experience the euphoria of love may be the consequence of two factors. "First, it is quite apparent that she is socialized to a highly romanticized anticipatory socialization for love and marriage that began in early childhood. Secondly, the status and role consequences of marriage for females makes the selection of a love object a more crucial experience."[34]

There is also evidence that feelings of love vary for males and females at different stages of courtship. For example, idealization appears to be greater for both sexes at the casual dating stage than at either moderate or serious stages. Pollis has suggested that it might be that the high idealization at the casual dating level is a result of anxieties and inadequacies that are experienced in attempting to anticipate and meet expectations of dating partners. "Lacking the perspective and support of expectations that emerge with prolonged interaction, casual daters may have a tendency initially to overvalue many of their dating partners. With the development of moderate involvement in a dating partner, an individual's judgments about the characteristics of his or her dating partner come to coincide more closely, than at the casual stage, with those made by his best friends concerning his partner."[35]

The Pollis study further found that idealization among the persons seriously involved was less for males than for females. There are two probable reasons as to why that is true. First, many men are career oriented around future occupational roles. Because of that kind of role involvement they have less time and involvement for high idealization of their mate. "A second explanation could be that the role of sexual frustration, particularly on the part of the male, has only minimal influence on the tendency toward idealization and, to the extent that it does

---

[33] Ibid., p. 70.

[34] Ibid., p. 71.

[35] Carol A. Pollis, "Dating Involvement and Patterns of Idealization: A Test of Waller's Hypothesis," *Journal of Marriage and the Family*, November 1969, p. 770.

operate, is greater initially than at later stages in the dating process."[36]
But all of the evidence indicates the greater involvement in love for the
female especially as the relationship moves toward marriage.

LOVE AS A NAMING STAGE

The process nature of love has been suggested—each individual must
be taught to love, prepared for love, and then given the chance for it to
occur. As the male-female relationship develops an emotional awareness
of the self and the "significant other," each of the individuals reaches a
point when he defines himself as being in love with the other person. Until the naming occurs, love does not exist for the individual, either as a
conscious self-awareness or as a determinant of action. The process and
the ingredients contributing to a conscious awareness of love will vary
with different individuals. Awareness may come as a gradually emerging
consciousness for some, but may just happen, without any emerging
consciousness, for others. But the consequence is the same—the individual honestly and consciously believes himself to be in love.

To argue that people can say they are in love but are clearly not is to
imply that the evaluator knows what love is and the person being evaluated doesn't. However, an axiom of sociological research is that if a man
defines situations as real, they are real in their consequences. Hence, if
a person believes he is in love, insofar as this belief contributes meaningfully to his behavior, he is. Therefore, love as a naming stage has two
aspects: (1) the self-definition of being in love and (2) the consequent
action resulting from that self-definition. For example, since love is a
prerequisite to marriage, the person defining himself as in love will commonly move in the direction of marriage.

Some observers mistakenly assume that the existence of love can be
determined by actions. Actions may occasionally, but cannot universally,
be applied as determinants. On the one hand, a valid determination pre-
supposes knowledge of action patterns related to love and lack of love
applicable to all individuals. For example, one might say, "He doesn't
show her respect, therefore he doesn't love her." But the individuals in
a particular relationship may not perceive respect in the same way as the
viewer. On the other hand, the needs of love vary for different individuals
and different couples. If the needs of the individuals in a pair-relationship
differ drastically, problems may emerge. However, the couple may work
out a compromise that to an outsider seems inadequate, but to them is
quite adequate. Thus, any attempt to assess or predict actions for all
people in love is highly questionable.

In most cases of love, many of the ingredients will be found and they

---

[36] Ibid., pp. 770–71.

will develop, through an emergent process, to the naming stage. Kirkpatrick's "component-package" theory amplifies this statement.[37] Kirkpatrick's theory simply suggests that different ingredients, in different degrees, operate for different individuals who define themselves as being in love. His theory further indicates that the statement that love changes for the individual over time means that the person continues to define himself as in love, but that the component parts of his love may be altered, reshuffled, or changed.

The naming stage can also be applied to falling out of love. When a person consciously ceases to define himself as being in love, he ceases to be in love. When the individual no longer perceives the object as a loved one, his actions are usually influenced. Even if his actions do not greatly change, his emotional involvement with the person is bound to be affected. The married individual who no longer defines his feelings as love may continue to treat his partner in essentially the same way as before, because of other important relationship values, but his emotional attachment will have been altered.

FREQUENCY OF LOVE

For a large number of Americans, the romantic notion of a single, everlasting love is not a reality. Many people fall in and out of love on a number of occasions, as a number of empirical studies have shown.

Of the college students who had experienced love, many had experienced it more than once. In fact, a large number of college students experienced love before they entered college. Burgess and Wallin report that 84 percent of the college girls in their sample had been infatuated or in love between the ages of 12 and 20; and that 50 percent had been infatuated or in love five or more times between ages 12 and 18.[38] A study by the writer found that for those coeds who had been in love, with a median age of 19 years, 53 percent had been in love on two or more occasions.[39] Based on a large sampling of college students, Kephart speculates that the average college student has somewhere between six and ten romantic experiences prior to marriage.[40] Although the findings of these studies differ widely, and although many of the relationships were not defined as love, the evidence clearly indicates that love relationships are common among college students and that a majority experience love more than once.

---

[37] Kirkpatrick, *Family as Institution,* pp. 275–76.

[38] Ernest W. Burgess and Paul Wallin, *Engagement and Marriage* (Philadelphia: J. B. Lippincott Co., 1953), p. 120.

[39] Robert R. Bell, "Some Factors Related to Coed Marital Aspirations," *The Family Life Coordinator,* October, 1962, p. 91.

[40] Kephart, *Individual,* p. 323.

The various romantic experiences that young people have during the process of dating contribute later to the love that ends in marriage. Yet terminal love affairs have many of the same characteristics as those that move into marriage. "The action tendencies generated in early love affairs are of the same kind as those which later lead to mating, but they fail because they are counter-poised by other attitudes."[41] When an individual has been in love before, he probably recognizes and contrasts a new love relationship with previous ones—and may think of marriage after a relatively short courtship. Burgess and Wallin suggest that "couples who fall in love and decide they wish to marry tend to achieve this stage with moderate rapidity, in an interval ranging from about six months to a year after they first begin to date."[42]

Platonic Relationships

A complete discussion of cross-sex interaction must consider the possible kinds of love relationships that are free from sexual desire. A platonic relationship between a male and a female involves neither romance nor sex. The writer has found that a majority of college students believe platonic relationships can exist, but when they are asked to describe the nature of the relationship, their illustrations almost always fall into specific categories such as the following:

Dating rejects—The individual was dated at one time but is no longer viewed as datable for various reasons.

Pseudo-family—The individual has grown up with the person in a close, "brother-sister" type relationship.

The committed—The friend is going steady, is engaged or married, and is therefore not a dating possibility.

The different—The person is of a different race, religion, age, etc.

These categories are essentially *safe* relationships in which the platonic friend is not perceived in the role of a possible love interest. It is always possible that the safe factor may be destroyed if the individual starts to define the friend in a romantic light. But essentially, the friend is usually defined as platonic because it is believed that he can't be a romantic figure.

"Safe" platonic relationships are probably common among students only when the institutional framework permits them. It is much more difficult to have even a "safe" friendship in other institutional settings. Furthermore, with few exceptions, close paired friendships are restricted to the unmarried person. Once a person is married, friendships are either

---

[41] Willard Waller and Reuben Hill, *The Family* (New York: The Dryden Press, 1951), p. 128.

[42] Burgess and Wallin, *Engagement and Marriage*, p. 169.

between members of the same sex or between married couples. In American society, a close friendship between a married man and a married woman is viewed with suspicion. What the couple may view as a platonic friendship will often be viewed as romantic or sexual by others. The implications are twofold: By the early adult years, the person must, in most cases, exclude members of the opposite sex from close personal paired friendship; the importance of the loved one intensifies because he must satisfy most of the needs of the other for cross-sex involvement.

LOVE AND MARRIAGE

The importance of marital love to roles and role relationships in marriage will be discussed in a later chapter. However, a few comments on marital love are necessary here for a logical development of premarital love. As mentioned earlier, romantic love is probably most emphasized during courtship and the first year or two of marriage. Later in marriage, the relationship increasingly depends on the realities of the partners' accumulated shared experiences.

Some brief suggestions on ingredients commonly found in enduring marital love follow.[43]

Physiological—All kinds of bodily and sexual attractions. Courtship love differs from conjugal love: In the former, physical interest is often based on the unknown and the mysterious elements of the other as a sex object; after marriage the satisfactions often come from what is known and learned through marital interaction.

Psychological—Various sentimental and affectional feelings. The psychological satisfactions result from the emotional interaction between the two personalities in the marriage.

Sociological—The many adjustments which make the man and woman companionable and interdependent upon each other. Role-playing abilities, as well as the relating of the various facets of marriage roles, are developed.

An important part of marriage and love is the changing nature of love from the premarriage through the marriage period, but one must be careful in measuring love over time as if it were a quantifiable item. As Folsom has suggested, there is no constant quantity of love in general. So far as we know, love does not have its own special budget of bodily or mental energy.

There is good reason to believe that those satisfied with their marriages have the insight and ability to perceive the changes in their relationship and to assess their love within the context of change. What they currently have in their marriage they often feel to be more important than

---

[43] Harold T. Christensen, *Marriage Analysis* (New York: The Ronald Press Co., 1958), p. 225.

what took them into the marriage. In many marriages characterized by disillusionment and unhappiness, the partners probably tend to look back on the ego-exciting elements of courtship and the early stages of marriage and feel deprived because those elements are gone. If nothing has developed to replace the old excitement, then the marriage is in trouble.

A study by the writer attempted to get at some views of love by the college-educated wife.[44] The average length of marriage for the wives studied was five years. Eighty-three percent were satisfied with their husbands' romantic treatment and 14 percent were dissatisfied; 3 percent said it was unimportant. When asked to compare the husband's romantic treatment now with that when they were first married, 35 percent said it was greater, 47 percent said it was about the same, and 18 percent said it was less. The wives were probably defining romantic love differently than they did when they were first married, but the findings indicate that the majority of college-educated wives studied were generally satisfied with the romantic aspect of their marriages.

The wives were also asked to contrast other respects of their love now to that when they were first married. When they were asked to compare their love for their husbands now and when they were first married, 67 percent said they now loved their husbands more, 28 percent said "about the same," and 5 percent said "less." Asked to evaluate the love of their husbands for them now with that when they were first married, 62 percent of the wives felt their husbands now loved them more, 32 percent said, "about the same," and 6 percent said "less." The findings suggest that over 90 percent of the wives studied felt no decrease in love either by their husbands or by themselves.

Since love is a prerequisite to marriage for most Americans, it follows that the failure of love in the marriage raises serious questions about continuing the marriage. When one or both of the married pair no longer define themselves as in love, the marriage becomes difficult, if not intolerable. But while many couples may no longer define themselves as in love, they often continue their marriage for a variety of reasons. Many times the reasons are seen in a negative rather than a positive sense: for example, concern with what ending the marriage will do to children, relatives, and friends; the fear of social criticism; financial difficulties; and so forth. Therefore, many marriages continue even though the love doesn't. Yet the common ideal is that when love ceases so should the marriage.

MASS MEDIA AND LOVE

The impact of mass communications on beliefs about love is difficult to assess, but it cannot be denied that the images presented are important

---

[44] Robert R. Bell, unpublished research.

indications of what is believed, or assumed to be believed, about love in the American society. The mass media teach or support many people's attitudes toward love, and because of the increasingly strong role they play in the ongoing socialization of the individual, it is important to recognize this influence. Mass media include radio, television, movies, popular novels, and mass circulation magazines and newspapers.

Here are some images about love which are implied in many mass media presentations:

1. *Romantic love belongs to the young.* The general picture of romantic love is associated with the young and the immature. While older people may love one another, their love is expected to be sedate, private, and unromantic. While all the world may love a lover, it is the young lover they love, and if an older person behaves as do the young, he is criticized for being in his second childhood. With an increasing percentage of the population in the older age groups, and with increasing rates of remarriage, the emphasis on youth as a prerequisite to love and marriage is partially unrealistic for today's American society.

2. *The female "understanding" of love.* As popularly pictured, the male is *allowed* to believe he is the aggressor, while in reality he is being manipulated by the shrewd female. Women are assumed to know more about love and to be best qualified to deal with questions of the heart. In matters of love, it is implied that women really know what is best for the man and because right must win out, they bring the man around to their way of thinking.

3. *Love conquers all.* There is no problem or situation that true love can't conquer. If love isn't the panacea for all social ills, it will do until something better comes along.

4. *The female as the romantic sex.* A common picture is the never-ending battle between the sexes, resulting from the woman's lofty, idealistic notion of love and the male's predatory, sexual lust. The woman always wins and "tames the beast" because her understanding of true love—which always emerges victorious—is correct.

5. *The pathetic loveless.* Without love, the male becomes an unhappy, cynical bachelor and the female a sour, frustrated spinster. Without the experience of romantic love, individuals are considered lacking as basic human beings, and their lives are perceived as incomplete and empty.

Mass media images probably present some truth, but their tendency to exaggerate is dangerous. The ultimate balance that seems to be important in love lies somewhere between the idealistic and the realistic. When a balance can be achieved, the individual may be able to relate the pleasures of emotion with the satisfactions of reality and achieve a level of happiness satisfying to the self and the loved one.

SELECTED BIBLIOGRAPHY

Burgess, Ernest W., and Wallin, Paul *Engagement and Marriage.* Philadelphia: J. B. Lippincott Co., 1953, chap. 4, 5, and 13.

Chafetz, Janet Saltzman *Masculine/Feminine or Human?* Itasca, Ill.: F. E. Peacock Pub., 1974.

Figes, Eva *Patriarchal Attitudes.* Great Britain: Panther Books, 1972.

Friedan, Betty *The Feminine Mystique.* New York: W. W. Norton & Company, Inc., 1963, chap. 2 and 10.

Goode, William J. "The Theoretical Importance of Love." *American Sociological Review,* vol. 24, no. 1 (February 1959), pp. 38–47.

Greenfield, Sidney M. "Love and Marriage in Modern America: A Functional Analysis." *The Sociological Quarterly,* vol. 6 (1965), pp. 361–77.

Hunt, Morton M. *The Natural History of Love.* New York: Alfred A. Knopf, Inc., 1959.

————*Her Infinite Variety.* New York: Harper and Row, Publishers, 1962, chap. 3 and 4.

Kanin, Eugene J., Davidson, Karen R., and Scheck, Sonia R. "A Research Note on Male-Female Differentials in the Experience of Heterosexual Love." *The Journal of Sex Research,* February 1970, pp. 64–72.

Kephart, William M. "Some Correlates of Romantic Love." *Journal of Marriage and the Family,* August 1967, pp. 470–74.

Lewensohn, Richard *A History of Sexual Customs.* New York: Harper & Brothers, 1958.

Queen, Stuart A., Adams, John B., and Habenstein, Robert W. *The Family in Various Cultures.* Philadelphia: J. B. Lippincott Co., 1961, chap. 12.

Taylor, G. Rattnay *Sex in History.* New York: The Vanguard Press, 1954.

Theodorson, George A. "Romanticism and Motivation to Marry in the United States, Singapore, Burma, and India." *Social Forces,* September 1965, pp. 17–27.

Chapter 6

Mate Selection

M ost human beings reach a point in adolescence or in their adult years when they move into a marriage relationship. In all cultures, a number of persons of the opposite sex are theoretical marriage mates, yet in no culture is the selection of the marriage partner one of random choice. There are always restrictions that limit the final choice. All cultures have social restrictions and most cultures also have personal restrictions. The social restrictions can be such factors as the person being of the proper age, not already married, not too closely related to the chosen partner, and so forth. The personal factors involve the individual's satisfaction of his ego-needs—as in the United States where reciprocal love is of great importance.

In most cultures, the selection of a mate has not rested as much with the young people entering marriage as it does in the United States today. In a comparative study of 39 societies, Stephens found only 5 societies besides our own in which free choices were customarily permitted.[1] In most societies the possible mates are determined by the parents, usually the father, or other elder males connected with the family. Parents in other societies have limited the choice of a marriage mate for several reasons: (1) In the patriarchal society the father made most of the im-

[1] William N. Stephens, *The Family in Cross-Cultural Perspective* (New York: Holt, Rinehart & Winston, Inc., 1963), p. 198.

128

portant decisions. (2) The choice of marriage partner was often related to economic factors important to the family. Through the use of bride price and a dowry system, marriage relationships were based in part on economic alignments between families. (3) When the young person selected a mate, limits of choice had usually already been set by the father. However, the final choice of a specific mate was, at least in part, that of the young person.

The courtship systems of all societies are in effect one form or another of a market or exchange system. They are different from each other with regard to *who* does the buying and selling, what characteristics are valuable in that market, and how open the bargaining actually is. "In a conjugal family system mutual attraction in both courtship and marriage acquires a higher value. Nevertheless, the elders do not entirely lose control."[2]

On the broadest cross-cultural level the common and traditional pattern for selecting a mate has been characterized by bargaining between the kin groups of the parents of the two young people involved. "Eligibility was not *bargained* about; instead, exchange terms were set in much the same way that prices in American stores are set."[3] However, this pattern has never been common in the United States. In the modern arrangement the two young people make their decision to marry and announce their intentions to both sets of parents. So, from the traditional setting in which only the kin groups participated, the change has been through an intermediate stage where both sets of parents participated along with the young couple to a system which does not include the participation of either set of parents as participating bargaining agents.[4]

The shift from kin selection of mates to that of individual choice has also drastically altered the potential marriage market for the individual. In the present system, theoretically, every person with whom one comes into contact of the opposite sex and within the acceptable age range is a possible mate regardless of marital status, race, religion, social class, and so forth. The fact that these mates can be chosen does not mean that they will be. But what is different is that in the past they would not have been chosen under any circumstances, while today there are circumstances that make it possible.

Mate selection in American society is a gradual process that starts with dating and moves through the courtship process. It does not happen to an individual "all of a sudden," but rather it is the culmination of the

---

[2] William J. Goode, *World Revolution and Family Patterns* (New York: The Free Press of Glencoe, 1963), p. 8.

[3] Michael M. McCall, "Courtship as Social Exchange: Some Historical Comparisons," in Bernard Farber, *Kinship and Family Organization* (New York: John Wiley and Sons, Inc., 1966), p. 194.

[4] Ibid., p. 197.

young person's preparation over a number of years. Determined by his previous experiences and ego-needs, a person reaching the age of marriage starts to focus on a particular individual. His values have been pretty well established by the age of marriage, and the general type of person he will marry has, within reasonable limits, already been determined.

The experiences leading up to mate selection, and the values involved, combine emotional with rational factors. As Waller and Hill write, "A man does not select the type of woman who will make a good wife, all things considered; he almost necessarily selects the sort of woman with whom he can fall in love, and women likewise select husbands on the same gloriously irrelevant basis."[5] Anthropological evidence indicates that when people are free to choose their own mates, individual and personal motives come into play. Some of these are "romantic love, sexual desire, loneliness, desire for children and full adult status, or more exotic motives. (One personal, "exotic" motive among the Siwai is the desire to raise one's own pigs.)"[6] The direction of choice, whether romantic or rational, will vary with different individuals. But regardless of variations by different individuals, the young person selecting his own mate today places far greater importance on the personal and emotional than did the parents of the past when they more actively helped select mates for their offspring.

Two general social changes in mate selection and marriage have developed over time in the United States: The percentage of Americans that marry has increased, and the age of marriage has lowered. About 95 percent of the population will be married at least once during their lifetime. Glick estimates that of all young adults in 1960, probably all but three or four percent will eventually marry. "This is only about one-third the corresponding level of those who reached adulthood one generation earlier."[7] At the present time, the population of single persons is at its lowest point since 1890.[8] In 1963, 71 percent of all males and 68 percent of all females at age 14 and over were married.[9] The state of marriage has achieved a high popularity in the United States, and increasingly with younger people. In 1960 the median age for marriage in America was 22.8 years for males and 20.3 years for females, contrasted with the 1890 median age of 26.1 years for males and 22.0 years for females. This

---

[5] Willard Waller and Reuben Hill, *The Family* (New York: The Dryden Press, 1951), p. 195.

[6] Stephens, *Family in Perspective*, p. 187.

[7] Paul C. Glick, "Bachelors and Spinsters," in Jeffrey K. Hadden and Marie L. Borgatta, *Marriage and the Family* (Itasca, Ill.: F. E. Peacock, 1969), p. 71.

[8] Hyman Rodman, *Marriage, Family and Society* (New York: Random House, 1965), p. 290.

[9] Ibid., p. 290.

shows that over the 70-year period from 1890 to 1960, the median age at marriage for the male decreased by 3.3 years and for the female by 1.7 years.[10] (The greater decrease for the male reflects the tendency in the past for the male to postpone marriage until he had achieved some adult economic security. Today, many young men marry when they are just starting their occupational careers or while still in school.) However, there is some indication during the early 1970s of a slight move away from the very high rates of marriage. But it is still too early to predict a significant counter-trend against marriage.

The sex ratio in a society also has an influence on mate selection. In 1950 the sex ratio (males to females) was 104.2 and in 1970 it was 97.0. This meant a slight surplus of men in 1950 and a slight scarcity in 1970. The slight increase in age at marriage in 1970 for females probably reflects the increased difficulty for females to find marital partners because of the scarcity of marriageable males.[11]

The discussion thus far has indicated some of the general marriage characteristics in the United States. Given the interest in marriage as reflected in our high national marriage rates, it is important to look at some of the variables that contribute to mate selection. The following discussion indicates the more important factors that help narrow the range of marital possibilities for the individual.

ENDOGAMY

Endogamy refers to the general norms of preferred or required mate selection within a particular group. It is used here to refer to the selection of a mate similar to the individual, in that they are both members of the same broad social grouping influenced by the same general norms.

Endogamy Factors

Propinquity. Propinquity means nearness. In its broadest sense it states the obvious—that people must meet if they are to select one another as mates. In family research, however, propinquity also refers to certain social variables of similarity that tend to encourage the individuals to select each other for marriage. The most common of these are residential propinquity and occupational propinquity.

Strictly speaking, propinquity is not a category of endogamy. Propinquity often affects endogamy, but no "within-group" connotation is at-

---

[10] Bureau of the Census, "Population Characteristics," *Current Population Reports,* series P-20, no. 105, November 2, 1960, p. 3.

[11] Jeanne Clare Ripley, "The Effects of Population Change on the Roles and Status of Women," in Constantina Safilios-Rothschild, *Toward a Sociology of Women* (Lexington, Mass.: Xerox College Publishing, 1972), p. 378.

tached to it. Thus, propinquity does not imply norms or values, but it is included at this point because—just as endogamy does—it refers to "like marrying like."

Residential propinquity is a factor, of course, because two people who live close to each other have a better chance of meeting and deciding on marriage than if they live some distance apart. A study done in Duluth, Minnesota, in 1952 found that residential propinquity was a decisive factor. Marches and Turbeville found that 21 percent of the married couples they studied in Duluth had lived within 5 blocks of each other and 43 percent within 20 blocks.[12] These findings indicate that segments of the population find their mates through or because of residential propinquity—nearness.

However, to say that people tend to marry those who live near them does not tell the whole story. In many cases, close residency is a reflection of other, more important endogamous factors. Residential areas in and around cities tend to be homogeneous. The people that live in such areas are often alike in race, religion, ethnic background, and general socioeconomic status. It is possible that if neighborhoods were more heterogeneous, high rates of residential propinquity in mate selection would be greatly reduced.

Occupational propinquity refers to the tendency of people working in the same occupational areas to marry one another; in other words—again to state the obvious—they are very apt to meet each other. But occupational propinquity is also influenced by other important social variables, particularly education. There is evidence that the higher the social class, the greater the degree of occupational propinquity, a link that can be explained by the importance attached to educational similarity in the higher social classes. Further, in occupational propinquity, prospective mates are often in different but related occupations, with the male's educational level and prestige being higher than the female's: the physician and nurse, or the dentist and dental technician, for example.

Race. Of all the factors of endogamy, race exerts the strongest influence. The mores against interracial marriage are extremely strong in the United States. The social pressures are so strong that the actual rate of interracial marriage is very low. It was estimated in the 1960 Census that 0.12 of 1 percent of all married couples were black-white.[13]

It has been stated that the city of Los Angeles may have had the highest rates of interracial marriage of any city in the continental United States. In Los Angeles, the estimate for 1959 was that during that year

---

[12] Joseph R. Marches and Gus Turbeville, "The Effect of Residential Propinquity on Marriage Selection," *American Journal of Sociology*, May 1953, p. 594.

[13] Hugh Carter and Paul C. Glick, *Marriage and Divorce: A Social and Economic Study* (Cambridge, Mass.: Harvard University Press, 1970) p. 117.

interracial marriages made up about 1.6 percent of all marriages occur-ing.[14] The overwhelming tendency for Americans, then, is to select a mate racially like themselves, and the available evidence indicates that race will probably continue to be the strongest type of endogamy practiced in the United States for many years in the future.[15]

In presenting data from various studies on interracial and interfaith marriages, sometimes rates of *marriage* are given, referring to the per-centage of all marriages that are mixed according to some specific social category, and sometimes rates of *individuals* in mixed marriages are given, referring to the percentage of all married individuals according to some specific social category.[16] How these two differently based marriage rates can confuse may be illustrated as follows: Suppose that of 10 mar-riages there are 6 where both partners are Catholics and 4 where one partner is Catholic and his spouse is a Protestant. We could say that 40 percent of the *marriages* are religiously mixed. However, of the 20 in-dividuals involved in the 10 marriages, 16 are Catholics and 4 are Protestants. Therefore, if our interest is in the number of non-Catholics in the 10 marriages, we have only 4 out of the 20 *individuals,* or 20 per-cent, half of the first percentage. It is useful to keep this distinction in mind when comparing different marriage rates.[17]

Religion.   Most Americans select mates of the same religious back-ground. No laws prohibit marriage across religious lines, but few, if any, religions encourage marriage outside the religion, particularly if the person marrying, or his children, are lost to the religious group. The belief in the norm of marrying within one's religion is reflected in the dating patterns of young people, for the evidence indicates that dating within the religion is the preferred pattern of behavior. This appears to be true, even though there is often a discrepancy between liberal views stated and the actual behavior followed.

A recent study on a midwestern campus asked, "How important is it to you that your date be a member of the same religion?" The response given by 25 percent of the females and 42 percent of the males was, "It makes little difference."[18] A similar, recent, nationwide study of adoles-

---

[14] George E. Simpson and J. Milton Yinger, *Racial and Cultural Minorities* (New York: Harper & Brothers, 1958), p. 559.

[15] See Lee G. Burchinal, "The Premarital Dyad and Love Involvement," in Harold T. Christensen, ed., *Handbook of Marriage and The Family* (Chicago: Rand McNally & Co., 1964), pp. 646–47.

[16] Simpson and Yinger, *Minorities,* pp. 558–59.

[17] Hyman Rodman, "Technical Note on Two Rates of Mixed Marriage," *American Sociological Review,* October 1965, pp. 776–78.

[18] Robert H. Coombs and William F. Kenkel, "Sex Differences in Dating Aspira-tions and Satisfaction with Computer-Selected Partners," *Journal of Marriage and the Family,* February 1966, p. 63.

cents found that only 35 percent said they thought it very important to marry someone of the same religious belief.[19] (The studies also indicate that boys are more liberal in their stated attitudes than girls.) But it seems that even after college students state these liberal values they behaviorally tend to stay within their religion, because of the possibility that the dating relationship will move to a more serious relationship. By not dating outside their religion, they do not allow this possibility.

Because there is no central agency for the uniform collection of data on religious endogamy, we are dependent upon the educated estimates provided by experts. It is estimated that the percentage of individuals entering an interfaith marriage is at least 24 percent for Catholics, 9 percent for Protestants, and 7 percent for Jews.[20] But it is clear that Protestants, Catholics, and Jews marry one another to a much greater degree than they did two generations ago. An increasing egalitarianism plays a role in the traditional breakdown of the barriers between marriage markets.

A similarity of religious background means a similarity in many beliefs and patterns of life. Therefore, to say that people come from the same religious background implies more than a similarity of religious beliefs. Yet, even though the religious affiliation is the same, the religious involvement of individuals can vary greatly. Individuals in all major religious groups range from the highly devout to the nominally religious; therefore, religious intensity may be a factor of similarity or difference in mate selection. Wide differences in intensity of religion may indicate an area of conflict for the two individuals. Though a quantitative comparison is impossible, one could argue that the difference in religious intensity between an Orthodox Jew and a Reformed Jew is greater than the difference between a Reformed Jew and a Unitarian. However, social beliefs of religious prejudice and discrimination cloud the issue and often make the influence of religion more than one of theological differences.

Age. Age at marriage varies for the American population. For example, the lower educated and lower social-class levels marry at younger ages. There is also evidence of differences for age at marriage by religious background. Jews marry at later ages than do Protestants or Catholics. One study found that the median age at first marriage for Jewish males was 26.0 compared to 22.8 for the total male population. "The later age at marriage of Jews may be a consequence of their concentration in social groupings—particularly in high educational and occupational categories—which have traditionally been associated with deferred and delayed marriages."[21]

Burchinal has done a great deal of research on young marriages.

[19] *Newsweek,* "The Teenagers," March 21, 1966, p. 57.

[20] Rodman, *Marriage, Family, Society,* p. 58.

[21] Calvin Goldscheider and Sidney Goldstein, "Generational Changes In Jewish Family Structure," *Journal of Marriage and the Family,* May 1967, p. 270.

Young marriages are arbitrarily defined as those entered at under 19 years of age. "Youthful marriage rates among the white population are greater than pre–World War II, but have probably remained relatively stable during the past decade."[22] Individuals who select a mate in the younger age groups have certain characteristics that distinguish them from the older group. Burchinal found that early marriages:

1. Usually involve young girls and their slightly older husbands.
2. Involve premarital pregnancies in between approximately one third to one half of all cases.
3. Disproportionately involve persons with lower- or working-class backgrounds.[23]

Another study of young marriages indicates that girls who marry young are emotionally less stable than those who marry later, and they have less satisfactory relationships with their parental families.[24]

Burchinal suggests that the rates of young marriages may go down in the near future. He thinks it possible that the increasingly greater value attached to extending education will have an impact on young marriages: "Increased school and post-high-school attendance should be associated with a reduction in young marriage rates. Among 17-year-olds, school dropout rates declined from 32 percent in 1950 to 24 percent in 1960."[25] But while marriage frequently leads to ending formal education if the individuals are in high school, it is much less apt to have the same negative effect when the couple are older and in college. There is some evidence to support Burchinal's contention. Parke and Glick show that 23 percent of all the women who were 30 to 34 years of age had married before age 18. "The rate of early teen-age marriages is successively smaller for each younger group of women. Only 15 percent of all the women who are currently 18 and 19 years old married before age 18."[26]

Those who marry at older ages, because they have lived as single adults for a long period, may find it difficult to adjust to the demands of the paired relationship of marriage. The fact that they have postponed marriage beyond the ordinary marriage period would indicate that they are different in some respects; possibly many had low marriage motiva-

---

[22] Lee G. Burchinal, "Research on Young Marriages: Implications for Family Life Education," *Family Life Coordinator*, September–December 1960, p. 7.

[23] Ibid., p. 11.

[24] J. J. Moss and Rudy Gingles, "The Relationship of Personality to the Incidence of Early Marriage," *Marriage and Family Living*, November 1959, p. 377.

[25] Lee G. Burchinal, "Trends and Prospects for Young Marriages in the United States, *Journal of Marriage and the Family*, May 1965, p. 247.

[26] Robert Parke, Jr., and Paul C. Glick, "Prospective Changes in Marriage and the Family," *Journal of Marriage and the Family*, May 1967, p. 251.

tion. Glick suggests that marriages contracted at unusually advanced ages are of relatively short duration.[27]

Age endogamy is specifically, then, the selection of a mate within an age range close to the individual. Among couples who married between 1947 and 1954, the median difference in ages of the spouses was three years,[28] and the pattern in the United States is for the man to select a woman from a slightly younger age group than his own. The longer the man postpones marriage, the greater is his tendency to marry a woman in an extended younger age group. In other words, the older the man when he first marries, the greater the age difference between bride and groom. When the groom is 20 years old, the bride is only a year younger; when the groom is 26, the bride is 3.8 years younger; when the groom is 34, the bride is 6.5 years younger.[29]

There is some evidence that the age difference of mates is becoming less among the younger generation. For example, in 1960 husbands over 55 years of age were on the average 3.6 years older than their wives. By contrast, husbands under 35 were only 1.9 years older on the average. "Forty-two percent of the older husbands were at least five years older than their wives as compared with only 17 percent of the younger husbands."[30] This decreasing age difference between spouses has implications for their marital futures. Most important is that the lessening of age differences means a significantly improved chance of joint survival of the married couple. In 1965, 64 percent of all women 55 to 64 years of age were married and living with husbands. However, experimental projections suggest that by 1985 the rate may be up to 72 percent.[31]

The increasing age difference with older age at marriage has important consequences. It means that the older male desiring to marry—because he can marry down in age—has a wide market out of which to select a mate, while the older woman—because she must generally marry up in age—has a narrow market. Thus, while it is true that the longer each sex postpones marriage the less chance each has for marriage, the decrease of marriage probability with increased age is greater for the female than for the male.

Education.   In the discussion thus far, the endogamous factors of mate selection have been treated independently. This approach should be recognized as an analytical device. In reality, of course, none of the variables remain or operate unaffected by the others. Thus, although the present section deals with educational levels, it is also necessary to relate a part of it to age factors.

---

[27] Glick, "Bachelors and Spinsters," p. 111.

[28] Ibid., p. 125.

[29] Ibid., p. 123.

[30] Parke and Glick, "Prospective Changes," p. 250.

[31] Ibid., p. 250.

Most Americans usually select a mate from the same general educational level. As a rule, men marry women of the same or a lower level of education, and women marry men of the same or a higher educational level. This is more likely to be true among the more highly educated. In the lower social classes, formal education is less important in separating the male from the female in mate selection. But, the higher the educational level, the greater the importance attached to education by both men and women and, therefore, at the higher levels, the greater importance attached to men having the same or higher levels of education than women.

For the total American population, Glick found that on the average, among every 100 first marriages, the husbands and wives in 45 were in the same broad educational level; in 28, the wives were in a higher educational level; and in 27, the husbands were in a higher educational level.[32]

For the male, educational level makes little difference in the percentage married. By years of education, the percentage of white males married, who are between 30 and 34 years of age is: eight years or less, 83 percent; high school graduates, 85.9 percent; and college graduates, 84.9 percent. Some variations exist in the percentage of married white women between the ages of 30 and 34 by education: eight years or less, 77.5 percent; high school graduates, 86.9 percent; and college graduates, 77.7 percent.[33] The statistics indicate a greater probability of being married for high-school-educated females than for the other two educational groups. For the college-educated woman, the chances of marriage have increased; in 1940, only 62.9 percent between the ages of 30 and 34 were married, but by 1950 the number increased by 14.8 percent to reach 77.7 percent.[34]

The pattern in the past was one of postponing marriage with increased education, and, while this tendency has been reduced, the college educated continue to marry at somewhat older ages than the rest of the population. Age at first marriage for those with eight or fewer years of education is 21.5 years; high school graduates, 21.1 years; and college graduates, 23.9 years.[35] A trend to a lower marriage age for the college educated reflects attitudes about combining marriage and education which were probably influenced by the high marriage rate of GIs attending college after World War II.

Level of education has limited effect on age differences between husbands and wives. The husband with eight years of education or less

---

[32] Glick, "Bachelors and Spinsters," p. 117.

[33] Ibid., p. 107.

[34] Ibid., p. 107.

[35] Ibid., p. 116.

marries a wife 3.7 years younger; the high-school graduate male marries a wife 2.8 years younger; and the college-graduate male, a wife 3.1 years younger.[36] The higher the male's level of education, the older his and his bride's ages will be when they marry.

Educational level may have important implications for the woman who extends her formal education, particularly beyond the undergraduate degree. For the woman, extended education and increased age places her in a marriage market in which the number of available males meeting the requirements of as much or more education and an older age are very limited. In addition, the man can marry down both in age and education, which means increased competition by younger and less educated women for the available unmarried men. The unmarried male with a high level of education is in an optimum position for mate selection.

There are other factors of education related to marriage. For example, the more academically successful the student, the less likely he or she is to marry early. It has been found that attendance at a co-educational institution does not increase the probability of a student getting married, nor does attendance at a single-sex institution decrease it. The item that best predicted a woman's being single in the follow-up after she finished college was her stated intention when she was a freshman to getting a master's degree.[37]

Social Class.   Most of the variables already discussed are determinants of social-class position. In social-class analysis, education, occupation, and income are generally considered to be the most important variables. Therefore, social class may be considered a broad category of endogamy in mate selection. Because similarity of class often implies similarity of values and attitudes, social class factors are of prime importance in mate selection. For example, two middle-class individuals may share values about marriage roles, the having of children, adult ambitions, and so forth that make them alike in a very personal way.

In recent years, however, formal education has contributed to marriage between individuals of somewhat different social-class backgrounds. This often implies upward social mobility through education for the individual coming from the lower social-class background. The mate selection of individuals of different social-class backgrounds has, to a great extent, developed since the end of World War II and has centered on males moving up in the social system through education and marrying females from higher social-class backgrounds.

On many college campuses, the coeds come from a higher social-class background than do the men. Formal education is considered more important for men because of its direct relationship to the male's im-

---

[36] Ibid., p. 128.

[37] Alan E. Bayer, "Early Dating and Early Marriage," *Journal of Marriage and the Family,* November 1968, p. 604.

portant adult occupational role. Therefore, males are often more personally motivated and socially encouraged to go to college if they have ambition of upward mobility. Women are more apt to be sent to college because it is socially the thing to do, rather than for occupational preparation or intellectual development. If a family has limited economic means for assisting the college education of its offspring, the son will usually be given preference over the daughter. (Also, after World War II, the GI Bill sent many men to college who would not have otherwise attended and, moreover, sent them to schools they would not have been able to afford, even if they had gone on to college. It is possible that World War II veterans who went on to college had a high rate of marriage with females coming from a higher social class.)

Marriage of individuals from different social classes among college students is often seen more realistically by the young people than by their parents. The young person tends to place less emphasis on background and more on the assets of the other person, while the parents, who know less about the other person, place greater emphasis on his background. With the increase in the number of individuals going on to college, it seems safe to predict that college will continue to provide a setting for the mate selection of individuals from somewhat different social-class backgrounds.

If a male does not marry while he is in college, his education provides him with an upward mobility into an occupational grouping that predisposes him to select a mate from his achieved social-class level. His new social-class level places his personal interests and behavior in a setting and market out of which usually comes his eventual selection of a mate.

In a study by Cutright it was found that income had a more powerful direct effect on the probability of marriage than did either educational or occupational status. "The effects of education and occupation are predominately indirect and operate only through their rather modest influence in determining the man's level of income."[38]

Endogamy Deviations

None of the endogamy factors in mate selection are absolute. Some individuals marry persons from different residential or occupational areas, of different race or religion, or different age or education, or from different social class levels. In American society the two areas of endogamous deviation of greatest interest are interracial and interfaith mate selection.

Interracial Mate Selection. The American society's concern over mate

[38] Phillips Cutright, "Income and Family Events: Getting Married," *Journal of Marriage and the Family*, November 1970, p. 636.

selection across racial lines is often provoked by attitudes of prejudice and discrimination, rather than by the actual frequency of the event. The number of interracial marriages in the United States is not great. And there is no evidence that racial intermarriage is greatly increasing in the United States. Heer observes that "it is hard to imagine a set of conditions under which Negro-white marriage rates would increase so rapidly as to achieve any large intermingling within the next 100 years."[39] (The discussion in this section refers to the most commonly prohibited interracial marriage: black-white marriages, where the black background is known or openly presented.)

There is some evidence that when interracial marriage does occur, the tendency is greater for the black male to marry outside the racial group. A California study of interracial marriages indicates that in 78 percent of the instances it was the black male who married the white female.[40] There is also evidence that people who enter interracial marriages are somewhat older at the time of their marriages than those who marry within their race.[41] A study of 16,532 marriages performed in Hawaii found that in racially unmixed marriages the couples were usually about the same age or the groom was slightly older, while in interracial marriages the groom was often much older than his bride—although sometimes he was several years her junior.[42]

While feelings of racial prejudice probably account for a majority of individuals not marrying outside the racial group, other factors also operate. Because racial groups strongly circumscribe the social relationships of the individual, many persons have little or no contact with members of other races. When social interaction does occur, the relationship is often formalized and does not lead to the kinds of interpersonal involvement related to mate selection.

When individuals cross the lines of race in mate selection, they often encounter extreme difficulties in developing a satisfactory marriage relationship. Many times the individuals find themselves rejected by relatives and friends on both sides. The couple are often forced through social rejection into marginal groups. Many times they receive reassurance and support only if they seek out and interact with other couples like themselves. The individual from the majority group also undergoes a drastic role change if and when he is treated with prejudice for the first time. Because of his love for his spouse, the prejudiced treatment

---

[39] David M. Heer, "Negro-White Marriage in the United States," *Journal of Marriage and the Family,* August 1966, p. 273.

[40] Larry D. Barnett, "Interracial Marriage in California," *Marriage and Family Living,* November 1963, p. 626.

[41] Quoted in Burchinal, "Premarital Dyad," p. 647.

[42] Robert C. Schmitt, "Age Differences in Marriage in Hawaii," *Journal of Marriage and the Family,* February 1966, pp. 59–60.

directed at them individually and together is often very painful because the loved one is the "cause" of the attack. The individual from the majority group has not been socialized to the nature of prejudice, either for himself or for his loved ones.

Very little is known about the "social types" who racially intermarry. A study in Chicago found that most of the intermarried couples fell into four broad groups: "(1) the intellectuals and 'Bohemians,' (2) the religious and political radicals, (3) the 'sporting' world, and (4) the stable middle class. If the white spouse in a Negro-white marriage does not belong to one of these groups, that spouse is likely to be a foreign-born person who is incompletely assimilated into American life and does not fully realize what intermarriage means, or did not at the time of marriage."[43]

Together with evidence that it is more often the black male who marries the white female than it is the black female marrying the white male, there is some evidence that the first type of intermarriage is less characterized by divorce than the second type. That is, divorces of white husbands married to nonwhite wives are more numerous than are divorces of nonwhite husbands married to white wives.[44] Monahan found in his studies of black-white marriages in Kansas and Iowa no evidence of any proclivity to divorce, but rather somewhat more stability than found in marriages where both partners were black.[45]

There may also be social-class factors related to whether it is a white man or a white woman who enters an interracial marriage. The evidence suggests that white men entering interracial marriages tend to marry down more often than up by education. But that tendency does not appear to be true of white women who enter interracial marriages. But in general, racial intermarriages seem to be as homogeneous educationally as marriages between black men and women. "The wives of Negro men —whether white or Negro—tended to average more schooling than their husbands, reflecting the generally lower level of schooling of Negro men."[46]

Often the most crucial problem of interracial marriage centers around the children. They will be treated as members of the minority group by the majority group, and may also be rejected in part by members of the minority group. The member coming from the majority group must face the frustration of seeing his children suffer indignities that he had not

---

[43] Simpson and Yinger, *Minorities,* p. 562.

[44] Vital Statistics of the United States, 1961, vol. 111, secs. 3, 4, and 7, "Divorces," U.S. Department of Health, Education, and Welfare, p. 7.

[45] Thomas P. Monahan, "Interracial Marriage and Divorce in Kansas and the Question of Instability of Mixed Marriages," *Journal of Comparative Family Studies,* Spring 1971, p. 119.

[46] Jessie Bernard, "Note on Educational Homogamy in Negro-White and White-Negro Marriages, 1960," *Journal of Marriage and the Family,* August 1966, p. 776

encountered. The realization that life will be difficult for the children may contribute to the low rate of interracial marriage. Some interracial couples have refrained from having children because of possible difficulties, but they seem to be the exception.[47]

Even though the problems are great in an interracial marriage, it may be that an increasing number of persons who enter such marriages are entering them with the motivations and abilities to make a success of the marriage. One recent study of 95 black-white marriages came to the following conclusion: "It would appear that such intermarriage now occurs between persons who are, by and large, economically, educationally, and culturally equal and have a strong emotional attachment, be it rationalization or real. The external pressures faced by interracial couples are often great but certainly do not appear to be overwhelming."[48]

Interfaith Mate Selection.   Mate selection across religious lines differs from interracial marriage in that it is much more common, no laws prohibit it, and social criticism of it is much less severe. Most Americans identify with their religion and, in varying degrees, view other religious groups with suspicion. Therefore, religious prejudice often enters into the shaping of attitudes towards other religions, particularly when it is related to the intimate relationship of marriage.

As stated earlier, people of the *same* religious faith may often vary greatly in the intensity of their religious beliefs, though such differences between husbands and wives can usually be resolved with little difficulty because religion is felt to be a part of the woman's role. The male can thus shift religious responsibility to the wife and thereby minimize their differences. And some similarity of religious intensity is probably common in mate selection. But the extremely religious person often views life in a way quite different from the person with limited religious interest, and a significant difference in religious intensity between husband and wife can have a negative influence on many areas of interaction.

Various studies show that the frequency of interfaith marriages has been increasing and that such mixed marriages are subject to a relatively high divorce rate.[49] It has sometimes been assumed that religious differences in a marriage would be a source of marital stress leading to mental health problems for one or both of the spouses. However, one study found that persons who marry a partner of a different religion show no greater mental health risk than those who marry a spouse of the same faith.[50]

---

ampson and Yinger, *Minorities,* p. 564.

Pavela, "An Exploratory Study of Negro-White Intermarriage in
Marriage and the Family, May 1964, p. 211.

"The Factor of Religion in the Selection of Marriage Mates,"
ical Review, August 1951, p. 16.

Langner and Stanley T. Michael, *Life Stress and Mental Health*
e Free Press of Glencoe, 1963), p. 327.

A study of 1,167 Manhattan residents by Heiss provides some valuable insights into those who marry across religious lines. He found that Catholics who intermarry are characterized by: (1) nonreligious parents; (2) greater dissatisfaction with parents by the respondent when he was young; (3) greater early family strife; (4) less early family integration (or interdependency of roles); and (5) greater emancipation from the parents at the time of marriage. In the Protestant group, the two strongest characteristics were relatively weak ties to both the family and the religion. For the Jewish group, the only characteristic of any significance was the lower strength of family ties.[51]

Protestants. Because of the many and various subdivisions under the heading of Protestantism, there is no uniform Protestant statement in regard to interfaith marriage. While no Protestant denomination encourages marriage outside the religious group, the different denominations do not agree on the strength of the force they should exert on their members to stay within the religion, or how to treat those who do marry outside the religion. The Protestants' lack of planned program to prevent or control interfaith marriages is due to the lack of organization among the many Protestant denominations.

Most Protestant concern about interfaith marriage is directed at those who marry Catholics, and is a consequence of the long historical struggle of the Protestant movement in breaking away from the Roman Catholic church. The history of this struggle has been one of great bitterness, and, as a result, each group often views the other with suspicion and mistrust. Protestants are also concerned with the loss of offspring to the Catholic church in a mixed marriage, because of the Catholic requirement that such offspring be reared as Catholics.

This negative feeling on the part of Protestants is reflected in attitudes toward interfaith dating and marriage. Generally the attitudes in these areas are more tolerant among Catholics. This is probably because often the Catholic is more limited in number and must turn outside his religion more for dating and possibly marriage partners. The tolerance may be due to necessity rather than liberality.

Estimates place the number of Protestants marrying outside their religion at about 9 of every 100. Of these, the overwhelming majority marry Catholics. It is estimated that only one fifth of 1 percent of all Protestants who marry outside their religion marry Jews.[52] In fact, the only interfaith marriage with which a large number of Protestants are familiar is that of Protestant and Catholic.

Catholics. The Catholic church takes a strong, unambiguous stand on mate selection outside the religion. The Church prefers that the indi-

---

[51] Jerold S. Heiss, "Premarital Characteristics of the Religiously Intermarried in an Urban Area," *American Sociological Review*, February 1960, pp. 53–54.

[52] Paul Landis, *Making the Most of Marriage* (New York: Appleton-Century-Crofts, Inc., 1960), p. 231.

vidual marry within the religion; however, it does allow marriage outside the faith. To be valid in the eyes of the church, a marriage between a Catholic and a non-Catholic must be performed by the Catholic church. Prior to the marriage, the non-Catholic must sign an agreement or contract required by the Church. The non-Catholic, in signing the contract, agrees that:

1. The marriage bond contracted can be broken only by death.
2. The Catholic member shall be permitted the free exercise of religion according to the Catholic faith without hindrance or adverse comment.
3. All children of either sex born of such marriage shall be baptized and educated only in the faith and according to the teachings of the Roman Catholic church, even if the said (Catholic partner) shall die first.
4. No other marriage ceremony than that by the Catholic priest shall take place.
5. He realizes the holiness of the use of marriage according to the teaching of the Catholic church which condemns birth control and similar abuses of marriage.
6. He will have due respect for the religious principles and convictions of the Catholic partner.

These conditions are a part of the Ante-Nuptial Agreement to be signed by applicants for dispensation from impediment of mixed religion or disparity of cult. Whether the non-Catholic signs the agreement is often determined by the strength of the Catholic partner's religion. Failure to sign the agreement means that the Catholic partner is not recognized as married by the Church—and Church recognition of the marriage would be very important to the Catholic partner with strong religious convictions.

One study has indicated that the fact of religious intermarriage by itself is not automatically a determinant of the extent of the religious observance that will be followed by the children. Croog and Teele's research suggests caution in assuming that the Protestant or Catholic sons of an intermarriage "will be less diligent practicers of the faith than those men whose parents share the same religion."[53]

While the Catholic position is very strong in regard to marriage outside the religion, more Catholics than Protestants or Jews enter interfaith marriages. Statistics on the frequency of Catholic mixed marriages are somewhat confusing. One study estimates that about 22 percent of all Catholics marry outside the religion, and indicates that the Catholic, in the vast majority of cases, marries a Protestant. The number of Catholics

---

[53] Sydney H. Croog and James E. Teele, "Religious Identity and Church Attendance of Sons of Religious Intermarriages," *American Sociological Review,* February 1967, pp. 102–3.

marrying Jews is less than one half of 1 percent.[54] The best study of Catholic mixed marriages was done by Thomas, and his estimates are higher. Thomas suggests that between 1930 and 1950 about 30 percent of the marriages performed by priests in the United States were interfaith. "If mixed marriages involving a Catholic but performed outside the church were included, the proportion might be 50 percent."[55]

There appears to be some relationship between social class and the tendency of children of mixed marriages to identify with the Catholicism of their mothers. In particular, to have a Catholic mother tended to lead to a predominantly Catholic identity among the sons at lower social-class levels, "while in the families of college-educated father, presence of a Catholic mother was associated more with non-Catholic identity in the sons."[56]

There are a number of different ways in which the children of interfaith marriages may be affected as to their choice of religion. First, they may choose to identify with the religion of one parent based on a personal choice of that set of religious beliefs. Second, their identity may be brought about through deliberate training by the parents in one religion rather than another. Third, "in situations where offspring are permitted free choice, one parent may serve as a role model, exerting through the power of example and personality a determining influence upon the child."[57]

Jewish. The Jewish faith has maintained an exceptionally high rate of religious endogamy for many years. Because of a long history of religious persecution and the development of a "ghetto" way of life, the pressures are extremely strong for the Jew to marry within his religion. It is estimated that in the United States about 93 of every 100 Jews marry within their religion. Of all the Jewish-gentile mixed marriages, it is estimated that in about 60 percent the non-Jewish spouse is Protestant and in about 40 percent, Roman Catholic.[58]

The Jewish religion recognizes two types of Jewish-gentile marriages. The first is *intermarriage* between a converted gentile and a Jew. This kind of couple can be married by Orthodox, Conservative, or Reformed rabbis. The second type, a *mixed marriage*, occurs when the gentile does not accept Judaism. No Orthodox and very few Conservative or Reformed rabbis can officiate at this type of marriage. However, there is some evidence that a number of Reformed rabbis actually do perform mixed marriages.

In regard to marriage outside the faith, the Orthodox Jewish group

[54] Landis, *Making Most of Marriage*, p. 231.

[55] Thomas, "Religion in Selection of Mates," pp. 488–89.

[56] Croog and Teele, "Religious Identity," p. 103.

[57] Ibid., p. 94.

[58] Bureau of the Census, "Population Characteristics," *Current Population Reports*, series P-20, no. 79, February 2, 1958, p. 3.

takes the strongest position of any religious group. In this group, a Jew who marries outside the religion is considered dead, and the family goes through the bereavement ritual followed when a member actually dies. The Conservative and Reformed groups take a much less severe stand, though both groups emphatically discourage interfaith marriage.

In Jewish-gentile marriages, it is more common for the Jewish male to marry a gentile than it is for the Jewish female to marry outside her religion. In Los Angeles, in 1953, it was found that of all Jewish marriages, 7.4 percent were with non-Jews married to Jews and that almost 80 percent of the non-Jews were females.[59] In Washington, D.C., in 1957, there were 11.3 Jewish households classified as mixed married. Of that group of households, about 70 percent had non-Jewish wives.[60] While both the Jewish male and female are often watched closely in reference to involved social interaction outside the religion, the female is guarded more closely than the male. The role of the male also permits him to get out from under family and community influence more often than does the role of the female. Therefore, it is comparatively less difficult for the male to become involved with gentiles.

There may also be a social-class influence on the tendency for Jews to marry outside their religion. Rosenthal, in his study of interfaith marriage in Washington, D.C., found that "those who engage in traditional Jewish activity, for the most part self-employed work, have a lower incidence of intermarriage. Those who were employed or who were college graduates tended to have a higher incidence of intermarriage."[61]

General Comments. Probably, only a limited number of individuals who enter mixed religious marriages do so deliberately from the start. In most cases, what begins as a relationship of a nonromantic nature moves over into romance and mate selection. Mayer, in his study of Jewish-gentile courtship, makes the following comments, which are applicable to many interfaith marriages. "The emotional vulnerability of the individual to others is not constant and will vary with different situations. At a particular time, a person may be in need of affection and support and, if someone offers him this, he may be strongly drawn to the donor."[62] When the donor has a different religion, the relationship that develops may be stronger than the negative force of the religious difference. In many relationships, as the emotional attachment intensifies, the two individuals spend more and more time with each other. As a

---

[59] Fred Massarik, *The Jewish Population of Los Angeles* (Los Angeles: Los Angeles Jewish Community Council, 1953), p. 44.

[60] Stanley K. Bigman, *The Jewish Population of Greater Washington, in 1956* (Washington, D.C.: The Jewish Community Council of Greater Washington, 1957), p. 125.

[61] Erich Rosenthal, "Studies of Jewish Intermarriage in the U.S.," *American Jewish Yearbook*, vol. LXIV (1963), pp. 21–24.

[62] John E. Mayer, *Jewish-Gentile Courtship* (Glencoe, Ill.: The Free Press, 1961), pp. 83–84.

result, they are increasingly cut off from other influences (or prospective marriage partners), which may lead them to become more and more dependent upon each other.[63] When their religions are different, they may seek out privacy to escape criticism. This leads to an increased interdependency and often results in greater emotional commitment.

It seems that for many persons planning an interfaith marriage there is a strong desire for religious agreement during the premarital stages. Babchuck found that the tendency toward value consensus between spouses had been quite pronounced during the courtship period. "This tendency is further accentuated shortly after the couple have their first child or when their oldest child is ready to attend Sunday school."[64] This would indicate that the couples recognize the stages where their religious differences could be most important and possibly direct extra attention at working them out at those times.

Marriage success studies indicate that interfaith have higher divorce rates than intrafaith marriages, though one caution may be suggested in interpreting the high interfaith divorce rates. A selective factor is operating on many who marry outside their religion that may make them more prone to divorce than those who marry within the religion. The factors that lead a person to marry outside the religion often indicate a tendency of rebellion toward cultural norms; this tendency may also operate in that the person feels less compulsion to continue a marriage if it does not meet his expectations. People who enter interfaith marriages are often less conservative than those who do not. When this characteristic is added to the negative social forces directed at those in interfaith marriages, the higher divorce rate becomes more understandable.

There are some general observations that can be made about interfaith marriages. First, that the highest rates of interfaith marriage are found among religious groups having the smallest community membership. Second, the rates of interfaith marriage are higher among the very young and the older brides and grooms than with the in-between age groups. Third, they are higher in remarriages than in first marriages. Fourth, they are highest in communities where ethnic-group cohesiveness is low. Fifth, the rates are higher among couples considerably emancipated from their parents or whose parents are nonreligious.[65]

HOMOGAMY

The social influences of endogamy may be viewed as a funneling process for the individual. A person starts his life with a theoretically

---

[63] Ibid., p. 95.

[64] Nicholas Babchuck, Harry J. Crockett, Jr., and John A. Ballweg, "Change in Religious Affiliation and Family Stability," *Social Forces*, June 1967, p. 555.

[65] Harold T. Christensen and Kenneth Barber, "Interfaith versus Intrafaith Marriage in Indiana," *Journal of Marriage and the Family*, August 1967, p. 462.

vast market for future mate selection, but as he is socialized and incorporates the value systems of his society, his market is drastically reduced. By the time he reaches marriageable age, he has, in effect, eliminated as potential mates those who, as a result of either social values or the low probability of acquaintance, are not like himself. Even at this point, however, the funnel still has a large spout and the number of potential mates is still fairly extensive. Out of the large number of different individuals still theoretically available to him, he must ultimately focus on one as his marriage choice.

In general, it appears that age of starting to date has little to do with future marital outcome. What may be more important for the success or failure of the future marriage is the length of the dating experience. As individuals move through the process of courtship it is important that they have sufficient experience to make the best choice of mate. So the factors of homogamy are influenced by the intensity of interpersonal experience that the two individuals bring with them through their dating experiences.

The process of homogamy further limits the eventual choice of a marriage partner. By *homogamy* is meant the conscious or unconscious tendency of an individual to select a mate with personal characteristics similar to his own.

Homogamy Factors

Intelligence. People tend to select marriage partners who have a level of intelligence close to their own. Kuhn came to the conclusion, from his analysis of a number of studies of factors related to married partners, that the highest correlations were with respect to intelligence.[66] Intelligence overlaps some of the factors of endogamy that have been discussed. Higher intelligence is related to higher education and more prestigeful occupations, as well as to social class. As with several of the endogamous variables, higher intelligence may be perceived as somewhat more important for the male than for the female. Some evidence indicates that girls tend to play down their basic intelligence while dating and going through courtship, if they believe it is regarded as threatening by the males with whom they are interacting.

Physical Factors. As with intelligence, there is a tendency toward similarity of height in mate selection. One study found a coefficient of correlations of 0.31 for height. "This means that a man above the average height is likely to marry a woman taller than the average but that she will exceed the norm by only about one third as much as her husband

---

[66] Manford H. Kuhn, "How Mates Are Sorted," in Howard Becker and Reuben Hill, *Family, Marriage and Parenthood* (Boston: D. C. Heath & Co., 1955), p. 263.

does.[67] In the United States, the taller man is probably more desirable to most women than the shorter man. A woman usually wants a man to be taller, and often he has to be significantly taller because, wearing high heels, she adds several inches to her own height. It is of interest to note that in the arrangement of "blind dates," the one "matching" variable that is almost always considered is that of height.

Homogamy for health is important because it affects many aspects of the relationship. If there are wide differences in health, the ability to enter into many shared activities will be limited. The physically active usually want a partner who is able to be active with them.

Along with physical health similarities in mate selection there may also be mental health similarities. There is some evidence that individuals of similar mental health are more likely to choose each other as marriage partners than persons of dissimilar mental health. Murstein found that the mental health of the man seemed to be more crucial for the success of the relationship than the mental health of the woman. "In other words, given a disparity in mental health status, the relationship is more likely to flounder if the man is the 'disturbed' one than if it is the woman."[68]

The factor of physical attractiveness is interesting and sometimes confusing. The concept of beauty is relative to cultural and personal values. What constitutes beauty in one society may not be recognized as such in another. In the American culture, the definition of beauty is wide and, except for individuals at the extreme, most people are not viewed as so unattractive they cannot find a mate. Thus, even though the person who most closely meets the ideal requirements of attractiveness generally has a wider market from which to choose, all one has to do is look around to realize that the physically unattractive do find mates—often their counterpart of the opposite sex. Furthermore, in contemporary American society, the sexual appeal of the individual may be as important as the more traditional concern with facial beauty.

Because a young man often considers the attractiveness of girls he dates as reflecting on his prestige in the dating market, he may give this trait greater value than he does the girl herself. In a recent study of college students the only factor that was not rated higher by women than by men was physical attractiveness; "men were much more enthusiastic about having a 'good looking' partner than were women."[69]

Elder has done research relating physical attractiveness to marriage. He suggests there is some evidence of a relationship between a woman's attractiveness and her chances of upward mobility through marriage.

---

[67] Ray E. Baber, *Marriage and the Family* (New York: McGraw-Hill Book Co., 1953), p. 80.

[68] Bernard J. Murstein, "The Relationship of Mental Health to Marital Choice and Courtship Progress," *Journal of Marriage and the Family*, August 1967, p. 450.

[69] Coombs and Kenkel, "Computer-Selected Partners," p. 65.

But it was also found that there were social-class differences in whether or not a girl was defined as attractive. Girls from the working class are likely to be ranked lower in attractiveness than middle-class girls. "As a group, middle-class girls were judged more attractive than girls from the working class on physique, sex appeal, grooming, and overall appearance."[70] However, Elder found that mobile women coming from working-class origins were clearly exceptional in appearance relative to non-mobile women. And in adolescence, mobile women from the working class were also more likely to be seen as well groomed than their less successful counterparts.[71] So physical attractiveness and status aspiration were significantly related to mobility through marriage, "with the former most predictive of marriage to a high-status man among women from the working class. Social ascent from the working class was also associated with a well-groomed appearance and with an avoidance of steady dating and sexual involvement."[72]

Ideal Image.   Many individuals tend to "carry in their head" an image of the person they would like to marry. The individuals they encounter are then measured against this ideal image. The image consists of both physical and personality qualities. Strauss found that "an overwhelming proportion of individuals (59 percent) judged that their mates came very close to, or were identical with, their physical ideal; and, an even larger proportion (73 percent) believed that their fiancés were close to, or identical with, their ideal of personality."[73] What no doubt happens in a number of cases is that after the mate is chosen and the commitment of love is given, the ideal image is altered or elements that once seemed important are discarded as no longer being important.

A common assumption about mate selection is that a person develops an ideal-mate image strongly influenced by his parent of the opposite sex. (This assumption is often presented in the guise of an Oedipus or an Electra complex.) These theories persist although there is little empirical data to support them. Generally, studies indicate that the ideal-mate image of *both* young men and women is one with qualities similar to those of their mother. Furthermore, the data indicates that both males and females show preferential affection for their mothers.[74] Mothers are generally more important in influencing both sons and daughters simply because they are more significant in their parental roles than are fathers.

With the different socialization experience of boys and girls, and with

---

[70] Glen H. Elder, Jr., "Appearance and Education in Marriage Mobility," *American Sociological Review*, August 1969, p. 524.

[71] Ibid., p. 526.

[72] Ibid., p. 531.

[73] Anselm Strauss, "Personality Needs and Marital Choice," *Social Forces*, March 1947, p. 335.

[74] Alfred J. Prince and Andrew R. Baggaley, "Personality Variables and the Ideal Mate," *Family Life Coordinator*, July 1963, pp. 95–96.

their different orientations to future adult roles, we would logically expect differences in their mate-selection values. The research evidence suggests these general sex differences: It is common for young men to place more importance than young women on the physical attractiveness, youthfulness, and popularity of their dates. Men also give high value to the woman's desire for a home and children, and to her housekeeping and cooking skills. In contrast, young women place greater importance on the ambition or industriousness of their dates. Women also see as important general intelligence, financial possibilities, and similarity of backgrounds. And young women are more apt to stress the importance of chastity for themselves and the social skills or degree of the young man's refinement.[75]

There are some aspects of mate selection that may have an influence on biological variables. For example, any divergence from random mating splits the genetic composition of the human population into complex subsystems. These may range from geographically isolated "races" to socially isolated caste, ethnic, or economic groups. Or long-term mate selection for intelligence or educability increases the proportion of like genotypes. So over successive generations this "tends to produce a biotic model of class structure in which a child's educability and, therefore, future social status are genetically determined."[76] The point is that social values that influence patterns of mate selection over a period of time can influence the biological factors seen as valuable. For example, if tall men have a better chance of marriage (and reproducing their own kind) than do short men, then over time the proportion of tall men would increase. The social importance of mate selection vis-à-vis biological factors is an important area almost totally ignored by family sociologists.

COMPLEMENTARY NEEDS

The factors of endogamy help the individual focus on a potential market for mate selection, and the variables of homogamy aid him still further by narrowing the possible marriage partners within this market. Yet, even after individuals are sorted through endogamy and homogamy, a number of possibilities exist. Winch's theory of complementary needs attempts to explain how the range of marriage possibilities is further narrowed.

Winch argues that once the individual has determined the field of eligibles, he then seeks within that field the person who gives the greatest

---

[75] See Burchinal, "The Premarital Dyad," pp. 633–34.

[76] Bruce K. Eckland, "Theories of Mate Selection," in Bert N. Adams and Thomas Weirath, *Readings on the Sociology of the Family* (Chicago: Markham, 1971), p. 227.

promise of providing him the maximum gratification.[77] Winch's major hypothesis is that in mate selection the need pattern of each spouse will be complementary rather than similar to the need pattern of the other spouse.[78]

Winch developed a number of need-gratification areas and showed how they were related to one another through their complementarity. To illustrate, here are several combinations that might be found for two individuals in a marital relationship:

> 1. *Abasement-Dominance.* Abasement means the need to accept blame, criticism, or punishment; to blame or harm the self. Dominance refers to the need to influence and control the behavior of others.
>
> 2. *Recognition-Deference.* The need of recognition is to excite the admiration and approval of others, while the need of deference is to admire and praise another person.
>
> 3. *Nurturance-Succorance.* To give sympathy and aid to a weak, helpless, ill, or dejected person or animal is the need of nurturance. The need of succorance is to be helped by a sympathetic person; to be nursed, loved, protected, indulged.[79]

In testing the hypothesis of complementary needs, Winch found, after using five sets of data, that three supported the hypothesis and the other two, while they did not support the hypothesis, did not show a countertrend.[80]

Winch's theory of complementary needs, while interesting and provocative, is subject to criticism. First, the study sample was made up of only 25 white, middle-class, native-born married couples, and at least one person in each couple was an undergraduate student at Northwestern University.[81] The small size and highly selective nature of the sample raises questions as to the applicability of the theory to couples with different backgrounds. Second, the couples studied were married less than two years and were childless.[82] The study does not show or explain whether the need characteristics of the couple after marriage are similar to what they were when the couple were in the process of mate selection. Once mate selection has taken place, the couple enter into close role relationships prior to their marriage, even closer after their marriage. Quite possibly, some couples at the time of mate selection had like needs, but, through the interactional process of role relationships, one of them altered or modified his needs because the need similarity contributed to role conflict. Certainly we know that the intimacy of marriage role relationships often calls for the individual to redefine his needs. As

---

[77] Robert F. Winch, *Mate Selection* (New York: Harper & Brothers, 1958), p. 406.
[78] Ibid., p. 96.
[79] Ibid., p. 90.
[80] Ibid., p. 119.
[81] Ibid., p. 107.
[82] Ibid., p. 107.

Snyder has pointed out, "If attitude similarity among married pairs exists, as research seems to show, this similarity must be the result of the adjustive interaction shared by the couple and not necessarily an affinity at the onset of the relationship."[83]

Ktsanes, in a study of personality influences on mate selection, writes: "The findings of this study, based upon a sample of recently married, college-age, middle-class couples, indicate that for the population sampled the tendency for an individual to select a spouse unlike himself in a total emotional makeup far exceeds the tendency for him to select a spouse like himself in that respect."[84] Ktsanes, like Winch, used a sample of people already married. A study that would more accurately measure Winch's theory of complementary needs would be a longitudinal one, starting with dating and following the individual through dating-courtship, mate selection, and on into marriage.

Another researcher has suggested that an individual seeks a person with personality traits that he feels he lacks and which he would like to possess. The suggestion is that if one looks at those personality traits which the individual sees himself as possessing and which he sees his ideal-self as not possessing (or vice versa), then the mate will be defined to resemble the individual's ideal-self rather than the individual's actual-self.[85] A testing of this hypothesis found it to be supported by the evidence. That is, there was in general a significant tendency for homogamy between the traits of the subject and the traits of her fiance, as perceived by the subject. "When the traits were not homogeneous, there was a significant tendency for the fiance to resemble the subject's ideal-self rather than her actual-self."[86] This indicates that some personality factors are complementary and some are the same.

Winch's theory of complementary needs is not without value. The selection of a mate is very possibly related to both like and unlike personality needs. Murstein has suggested that role theory is a more logical explanation of marital choice than the theory of complementary needs. This is because various needs may call for complementary behavior and other needs for similarities. So one can argue that individuals select partners to fill key roles they have in mind for such a person.[87]

---

[83] Eloise C. Snyder, "Attitudes: A Study of Homogamy and Marital Selectivity," *Journal of Marriage and the Family,* August 1964, p. 336.

[84] Thomas Ktsanes, "Mate Selection on the Basis of Personality Type: A Study Utilizing an Empirical Typology of Personality," *American Sociological Review,* October 1955, p. 551.

[85] Ellen S. Karp, Julie H. Jackson, and David Lester, "Ideal-Self Fulfillment in Mate Selection: A Corollary to the Complementary Need Theory of Mate Selection," *Journal of Marriage and the Family,* May 1970, p. 269.

[86] Ibid., p. 271.

[87] B. I. Murstein, "Empirical Tests of Role Complementary Needs and Homogamy Theories of Mate Selection." *Journal of Marriage and the Family,* November 1967, p. 696.

The process of mate selection can be summarized, then, as a continuing process of elimination through endogamy, homogamy, and personality needs. The personality influences lead the individual to his final choice through the process of falling in love and having the love returned.

The factors of mate selection discussed in this chapter refer to general patterns of behavior. They do not operate with equal or absolute force, and individuals do not "seek" and are not "selected" according to absolutes. If the factors of homogamy and complementary needs *were* absolutes, no one would ever get married. Relatively strong personal and social requirements for the individual indicate, however, why some never marry. For the vast majority who do marry, the requirements operate with flexibility and the individual is able to choose and be chosen for marriage.

SELECTED BIBLIOGRAPHY

Barnett, Larry D. "Interracial Marriage in California." *Marriage and Family Living,* November 1963, pp. 624–27.

Bayer, Alan E. "Early Dating and Early Marriage." *Journal of Marriage and the Family,* November 1968, pp. 628–32.

Christensen, Harold T., and **Barber, Kenneth** Interfaith versus Intrafaith Marriage in Indiana." *Journal of Marriage and the Family,* August 1967, pp. 461–69.

Elder, Glen H., Jr. "Appearance and Education in Marriage Mobility." *American Sociological Review,* August 1969, pp. 519–33.

Heer, David H. "Negro-White Marriage in the United States." *Journal of Marriage and the Family,* August 1966, pp. 262–72.

Heiss, Jerold S. "Premarital Characteristics of the Religiously Intermarried in an Urban Area." *American Sociological Review,* February 1960, pp. 47–55.

Karp, Ellen S., Jackson, Julie H., and **Lester, David** "Ideal-Self Fulfillment in Mate Selection: A Corollary to the Complementary Need Theory of Mate Selection." *Journal of Marriage and the Family,* May 1970, pp. 269–72.

Murstein, Bernard J. "The Relationship of Mental Health to Marital Choice and Courtship Progress." *Journal of Marriage and the Family,* August 1967, pp. 447–51.

Parke, Robert, Jr. and **Glick, Paul C.** "Prospective Changes in Marriage and the Family." *Journal of Marriage and the Family,* May 1967, pp. 249–56.

Pavela, Todd H. "An Exploratory Study of Negro-White Intermarriage in Indiana." *Journal of Marriage and the Family,* May 1964, pp. 209–11.

Prince, Alfred J., and **Baggaley, Andrew R.** "Personality Variables and the Ideal Mate." *Family Life Coordinator,* July 1963, pp. 93–96.

Rodman, Hyman   "Technical Note on Two Rates of Mixed Marriage." *American Sociological Review,* October 1965, pp. 776–78.

Snyder, Eloise C.   "Attitudes: A Study of Homogamy and Marital Selectivity." *Journal of Marriage and the Family,* August 1964, pp. 332–36.

Strauss, Anselm   "Personality Needs and Marital Choice." *Social Forces,* March 1947, pp. 332–35.

Winch, Robert F.   *Mate Selection.* New York: Harper & Brothers, 1958.

Chapter 7

Those Who Never Marry

It is striking that in the United States, sociology-of-the-family literature almost completely ignores a significant 5 percent of the population—those who never marry. This implies a social bias that people *should* marry and therefore those who don't are not really worthy of study. Yet, whether persons choose not to marry or are not chosen for marriage, they must make adaptations where most of the major adult roles and related values are based on the assumption of marital role experience. Therefore, two basic questions are: "How do people come to choose not to enter or not be chosen for marriage" and "What are the consequences for them?" The family sociologist should not only study those who never marry for their own sake but also for what such studies might tell us about people who do choose marriage.

In the United States the social pressures to marry are overwhelming. They are transmitted from the time of birth not only within the institutional context of the family but also by such other institutions as religion, education, and occupations. The force for marriage is not only in the importance attached to personal needs being met and opportunities for individual achievement but also because all known societies have had some form of marriage and it therefore is assumed to be a necessary condition for society. Even though this is an erroneous assumption the force of the argument contributes to the strong belief by many people about the importance of marriage.

Different pressures influence women and men as to the importance of marriage. The basic and most meaningful adult role for women has been geared to marriage and motherhood. Certainly in the past almost all women were socialized to those values, and the woman who didn't fill them was often seen as both a social and personal failure. By contrast, the work role has been primary for men, with their family roles being secondary. This meant that while the man who didn't marry was still fulfilling his major adult role, the woman who never married was not. However, there is one way in which not being married can hurt a man occupationally and that is when marriage is defined as a measure of his stability and reliability. Some occupations see a married man as more conforming and the type they want as an employee. As a result, in some situations the man is discriminated against in his occupational role for not being married.[1]

The effectiveness of the system to lead people into marriage is often so great that many people probably get married who should not do so. This is also added to by the sanctions against people who would prefer to remain single. David Olsen suggests that "society does this by labeling individuals as deviant and maladjusted if they do not conform to societal expectations in this regard. The continuous push by parents and friends alike is rather persuasive and very effective."[2] There are some research data to support the suggestion that people in general have strong feelings about the desirability of marriage. One study found that only a minority of respondents (9 percent) felt that either the unmarried person or the unmarried state was a legitimate or positive condition. "Furthermore, many of the respondents (40 percent) indicated that they felt such a person would be unhappy."[3]

The negative social attitudes toward those who never marry are reflected in the stereotypes that are held about unmarried women and unmarried men. In the mass media the single woman past age 30 is often portrayed as embittered, frustrated, and displacing her *real* desire for marriage and motherhood with a career. Sometimes she is presented as a home wrecker "who infects the world of the virtuous and happy home-maker and whose only hope for rehabilitation is her own home with her own children."[4] This view indicates that she is going against her "inherent destiny" which largely has been the product of a male-dominated society. In recent years one of the great influences of the women's move-

---

[1] Joseph Veroff and Shiela Feld, *Marriage and Work in America, A Study of Motives and Roles* (New York: Van Nostrand Reinhold, 1970), p. 62.

[2] David H. Olson, "Marriage of the Future: Revolutionary or Evolutionary Change? *The Family Coordinator*, October 1972, p. 384.

[3] Veroff and Feld, *Marriage and Work*, p. 72.

[4] Cynthia Epstein, *Woman's Place* (Berkeley: University of California Press, 1970), p. 30.

ment has been to present role models of women not based on traditional family definitions. As a result many young women are growing up with less overwhelming needs to marry and fill the traditional family roles.

The general image presented about the man who doesn't marry is different from that of the single woman. For many, bachelorhood implies immaturity, selfishness, or some of the other negative consequences. Many see the bachelor as living a carefree life and depriving some woman from marriage.

In 1971, 5 percent of the population age 30 or over were single. The trend well into the 1960s was an exceptionally high marriage rate for the United States. For example, Carter and Glick, in talking about the 1960 Census data, said that only about 3 or 4 percent of the youngest cohort of white persons seemed unlikely to marry when they projected forward to that group as they reached age 49. "This level stands in contrast with the 7 or 8 percent already experienced by those 50 years old at the time of the 1960 Census."[5] However, there is evidence that the very high marriage rate is falling off. Through the 1960s a higher proportion of men and women remained single within that age group. "The percent single among men under 35 years old had increased by about 5 percentage points between 1960 and 1972, while the proportion single among women of the same age had increased by about 7 percentage points."[6] In 1973, of the 48 million single adults in the United States, 12.7 million were between the ages of 20 and 34. That was a 50 percent increase for that age group since 1960.[7] It is also apparent that the population of women who have not married and are in their 20s has increased by one third since 1960.[8]

In talking about those who never marry (single), there are the two major dimensions mentioned earlier that should be examined. First, why do some people choose not to marry or are not chosen for marriage. Second, what are the consequences for those who remain single. Some variables related to persons not entering marriage are discussed under the general headings of Courtship, Marriage and Family, and Nonfamily influences.

Courtship Factors

No Dating Market. An implicit assumption of the dating-courtship market in the United States is that people will have an opportunity to

---

[5] Hugh Carter and Paul Glick, *Marriage and Divorce: A Social and Economic Study* (Cambridge, Mass: Harvard University Press, 1970), p. 302.

[6] U.S. Bureau of the Census, *Current Population Reports*, series P-20, no. 242, "Marital Status and Living Arrangements," March 1972 (Washington D.C.: U.S. Government Printing Office, 1972), p. 3.

[7] *Newsweek*, September 1973, p. 36.

[8] Ibid., p. 36.

meet eligible partners and from that make marital choices. Yet, there are a number of conditions that may limit the market to varying degrees. Some individuals, because of geographical, educational, or occupational isolation may find the chances of meeting eligible mates extremely limited. While they may desire marriage, they simply never have the opportunity to meet a person who meets their basic requirements. This variable can also have an effect on some who do marry in that their opportunities are very limited and their marriage partner is a "forced choice" they might not have made in a market of more eligible partners. Illustrations of men caught in a market with no dating opportunities would be those who take jobs that isolate them from any contact with marriage eligibles. Limits for a woman might be where she enters an occupation made up almost entirely of other women and never has a chance to meet eligible men in the work situation. If she has little or no social contacts outside the job, she finds herself isolated from her potential dating-courtship market, and, as a result, her life is spent with women and ineligible men.

Inability to Perform Courtship. Dating and courtship in the United States can be complex and demanding. There are probably many people who find it very difficult to muster the skills needed for even minimal efficiency. The abilities to perform often include such things as being able to carry on conversation and some minimal level of interpersonal competency. So a person must develop some proficiencies in dealing with the opposite sex to achieve even minimum dating-courtship success. For example, a young man may be socially inadequate when confronted with a young woman and be unable to meet even these minimum requirements of communication. Thus, for him, nothing ever develops beyond the initial contact.

Didn't Get the One. A person may be overinfluenced by the romantic love idea that only one person can really be loved. If the person feels that the "one" love has been found and lost, then no others are possible. For example, a woman falls in love with a man and he rejects her for another. She may feel that no other man will do because the one lost was her only "real and true love." Having loved and lost she must go through life without. Some individuals may desire to treasure the abstract love that ended rather than face the reality of moving into a love relationship that can actually exist. Yet, it seems probable that the romantic influences that effect persons not marrying are decreasing and are of less significance. This is suggested because the overall ethos of romantic love is being reduced in many ways in the United States.

Unattractiveness. While the range of attractiveness adequate for finding a marriage mate is broad in America, individuals at the extremes may find it difficult to marry. Attractiveness can refer to both facial and body characteristics. For example, a young woman may be excessively

overweight and rarely asked for a date; she therefore has little opportunity for taking the initial step necessary for entering the dating-
courtship process leading to mate selection. There are always a certain
number of individuals who are never dated because they go beyond the
minimum limits of attractiveness. Attractiveness is often relative to cultural values and the person defined as unattractive in one culture might
not be defined as such in another society. But it appears that all cultures
have set limits beyond which the person is defined as highly unattractive
and would have great difficulties in finding a mate.

Physical or Mental Health Factors. The person may deviate in
physical characteristics to an extreme, or the health of the individual may
be too poor. For example a dwarf may be "normal" in all respects except
size, but find it nearly impossible to find a mate. Or, a person may be in
such poor physical health that regular dating and courtship is impossible,
and/or these problems frighten away possible marriage partners. Another negative factor for efficient functioning in mate selection is mental
health limitations. There are some individuals who might fit into the
"Inability to Perform Courtship" category because their mental health
problems make courtship impossible for them. This could include individuals who almost totally withdraw from human interaction, who have
great fear of or hostility toward the opposite sex, and so forth. And
mental institutions remove some people from the usual courtship process. About 10 percent of the bachelors and 5 percent of the spinsters in
the United States reside involuntarily in institutions—over one half are in
mental hospitals.[9]

Homosexuality. Homosexual involvement can range from a total commitment to a few contacts over long periods of time. It is certainly true
that some individuals who have defined themselves as totally homosexual
have nevertheless entered into heterosexual marriages. However, many
individuals whose overwhelming focus of love and sexual satisfaction is
directed at members of the same sex often feel that marriage, with love
and sex directed at a member of the opposite sex, is impossible. Homosexuals often reject the social assumption that one's love and sexual involvement must be directed only at the opposite sex. This obviously
implies a rejection of the heterosexual dating-courtship process for those
individuals. However an increasing number of homosexuals have not
totally rejected dating, courtship, and marriage as desirable involvement
—they do enter these relationships with members of the same sex. Also
the concept of being single or married has undergone some change. A
person may be single in the commonly used sense (of not being married
to a member of the opposite sex) but be "married" to a member of the
same sex. The legal systems of the various states have not anticipated and

[9] Paul C. Glick, "Bachelors and Spinsters," in Jeffrey K. Hadden and Marie L.
Borgatta, *Marriage and the Family* (Itasca, Ill.: F. E. Peacock, 1969), p. 71.

do not allow for such marriages, but homosexual marriages have become acceptable in the eyes of some individuals and in some cases even religiously sanctioned marital ceremonies are performed. But society in general continues to overwhelmingly define these people as single or unmarried. It appears quite possible that in the future the right to marry members of the same sex will become more socially acceptable.

Marriage and Family Factors

The categories discussed in the previous section have dealt with influences on remaining single that are related to the dating and courtship stages. In this section we examine some influences that are related to marriage and family variables.

Less Reason to Marry. It has been pointed out that the American woman in the past has been socialized to believe marriage and motherhood were her only real options as an adult. Because social values have always asserted that marriage is a necessary condition for motherhood, remaining single generally represented failure to achieve the desirable adult roles. This view is changing, with options available for many young women—postpone marriage or in some cases not marry at all. The economic and sexual liberation of the young working woman is diminishing her need for marriage. This is reflected in the fact that the proportion of women who remain unmarried into their 20s has increased by one third since 1960.[10]

Among many young people in the United States today there is a problem in defining whether they are single or married because many live together for varying lengths of time without legal ties. Therefore, in the official records they are unrelated people living together. However, in the roles they play relative to each other, many of them in their emotional commitment, and even in how others see them, are the same as persons legally married. Yet, they also often appear to be different from marriages that are legal in that they don't want to make a permanent commitment in their relationship. By contrast, it is generally assumed in legal marriages that the couple have made a commitment to live together for the rest of their lives. Of course, in actuality, many later change their minds and get a divorce. Certainly the new kinds of non-legal marriages are in need of greater study and understanding.

Among older, single women there are often factors mitigating against their marrying. Some women as they get older may feel less motivation for marriage because they see increasingly less to be gained from it. For example, in their analysis of marriage statistics Carter and Glick suggest that the patterns of marriage rates for white women appear to reflect a

---

[10] *Newsweek*, September 1973, p. 36.

reluctance on the part of older, single women to marry available bachelors of similar age (because the men tend to be of lower status) or widowers or divorced men, even if they are of comparable or higher status, on the grounds that they (the single women) could be worse off in marriage.[11] Another study suggests that the greater the economic independence of women, the greater the likelihood that they will stay unmarried. One might project that "the higher the economic achievement of females, the less their desires to accept the confining traditional familial sex-role of wife-mother-homemaker or to be evaluated solely in terms of that sex role."[12]

Hostile Marriage Attitudes.   For a variety of reasons some persons may grow to develop hostile attitudes about marriage. This indicates a failure on the part of society effectively to socialize them into desiring marriage. It may be that often the family itself is the agency for instilling hostile attitudes about marriage. For example, unpleasant childhood experiences in the family of orientation could result in hostile attitudes towards marriage. As an illustration, a child growing up in a home with a great deal of conflict between the parents may come to believe that marriage is undesirable.

Don't Want Responsibilities.   Mate selection implies a willingness on the part of each individual to take on some responsibility for the need satisfactions of the other, as well as for the relationship itself. For example, if in courtship one is unable to give the love the other desires, the relationship has serious problems. Social responsibilities are also inherent in role rights and obligations of husbands and wives. The very nature of significant role interaction implies that each has expectations and responsibilities to the other. Therefore, not to be able or willing to meet the responsibilities toward the other by definition makes the relationship impossible.

Dependence of Others.   Some people remain single because they have others so dependent on them they feel they can't enter into marriage. Or, others may see them as ineligible for marriage because of those dependencies. This is much more common for women than for men. Carter and Glick, in analyzing the 1960 Census data, found that one out of every two persons who entered bachelorhood or spinsterhood was still living with one or both parents. "Spinsters were found to be much more likely than bachelors to live with a brother or sister, whereas bachelors were much more likely to live in the home of a nonrelative."[13]

Single women more often live with, and care for, their parents than do

---

[11] Carter and Glick, *Marriage and Divorce*, p. 323.

[12] Elizabeth M. Havens, "Women, Work and Wedlock: A Note on Female Marital Patterns in the United States," in Joan Huber, *Changing Women in a Changing Society* (Chicago: University of Chicago Press, 1973), p. 218.

[13] Carter and Glick, *Marriage and Divorce*, p. 407.

men because they have been socialized to do so. In the past it has often been assumed that a woman should live with someone if she doesn't marry and, ideally, it should be a relative. This is part of the belief system that sees the family as more important for the woman than for the man. Single women are also more apt to have dependents than are single men. This is because they not only have dependent parents but many single women also have children that have been born out of wedlock.

It is possibly easier in general for single women to live with others than is the case for single men. In general, women have been socialized to be more supportive than men. There are also greater social supports for unmarried women living together than for unmarried men. The men may feel themselves defined as homosexual while women would far less often feel this social definition to be a threat to their living relationships.

Parental Fixation. Parents can have various effects and influences in the socialization of their children. One consequence may be an extremely close relationship where the individual may develop such an emotional identification with one or both parents that he cannot direct to another person the love necessary for marriage. In some cases, the possibility of loving someone else poses a threat to the exclusiveness of the love for the parent. For example, a young man may be so fixated in his love for his mother that he cannot love a girl and, if he attempts to, he has feelings of guilt. Because of this fixation, the guilt feeling over removal of love from the mother becomes psychologically intolerable.

Outside Family Influences

Even given favorable conditions in dating and courtship for entering marriage as well as support from family influences, some individuals still will remain single. The following are some general social conditions that may influence a person not to marry.

Career Desires. For many women in the past, careers were seen as separate from marriage. In the 1920s and 1930s many women who were most successful in their careers remained single. The necessity for keeping careers and marriage separate is much less strong today. Many women who want a career can now think of combining it with marriage. However, there are still some persons who have such high occupational motivations that they perceive marriage as a threat to occupational success. This factor may cause many women to postpone marriage indefinitely. For example, a woman who desires to be successful in pursuing a career may feel that marriage and motherhood will drastically curtail her chances of success or remove her from her career. This factor is probably applicable to women more often than to men because career and marriage are generally not viewed as contradictory for men.

Economic influences. Some individuals are barely able to meet their own economic needs and cannot take on the financial responsibilities of dating, courtship, or marriage. In some cases the person may have financial responsibilities for others, so that the expense of marriage is impossible.

Given the traditional roles of men as breadwinners, their inability to provide for themselves and others operates against their chances for marriage. The proportion of poorly educated men, which represents a large category with limited economic abilities, who have never married is considerably above that of the poorly educated woman. The reverse of this is true among the higher educated. As earlier suggested, top rates of "never married" are found among white women who had completed one or more years of graduate school.[14] To put it another way, the middle-aged bachelors tend to occupy the lowest position on the income scale for men, and the middle-aged spinsters tend to occupy the highest positions for women.[15]

The fact that single men have lower incomes than do married men of the same age is related to several factors. One, it reflects the high marriage rates for men of higher incomes. Carter and Glick found that "virtually none of the middle-aged men in 1960 with high incomes had failed to marry.[16] There are also many younger men who have low incomes because they are students. Even though these biases operate, the fact remains that single men in general have lower incomes than do married men of the same age.

Social Class Influences. Social class influences are related to the economic effects on individuals that remain single. Possibly the most significant group in this category are those women who remain single and achieve upward mobility. Studies show that never-married women tend to be more upwardly mobile than married women. They have often "started life in lower socioeconomic levels and pulled themselves up educationally and professionally."[17] By contrast, bachelors are far more apt to have come from economically advantaged homes. It has been shown that more women than men who do not marry are able to maintain themselves in comfort through work at responsible positions. "Perhaps the greater pressure on upper-class women than on upper-class men to avoid 'marrying down' causes more of the former than the latter to remain unmarried."[18]

It was pointed out in Chapter 6 that the higher the social class of the woman, the less her potential marriage market. Given the fact that she

---

[14] Ibid., p. 407.

[15] Ibid., p. 319.

[16] Ibid., p. 408.

[17] Jessie Bernard, *The Future of Marriage* (New York: World Publishing, 1972), p. 35.

[18] Carter and Glick, *Marriage and Divorce*, p. 299.

generally marries a man of equal or greater social-class level, restricts her choices. By contrast, the man can and often does marry women of lesser achievement in education and income. As Carter and Glick point out there is a general tolerance for men from upper-class families to marry women from lower-class levels particularly when "beauty, charm, wit, and other nondemographic assets serve as substitutes for education and affluence as factors in mate selection."[19] The end result of these two influences is to leave a larger proportion of women than men of favorable social and economic status among those who are single and middle-aged.

Ethnic Background.   While the point has been made that the American value system strongly supports marriage, and at young ages, this system doesn't have the same effect on all people. Some individuals are influenced much more strongly by values they have brought with them from other cultures. Carter and Glick, in their analysis of 1960 Census data, have shown there continue to be ethnic influences on rateş of marriage. They found that the percent single among men 45 to 64 years of age varied a great deal. It ranged from 8 percent single for white, black, and Japanese men in the United States to 34 percent for Filipino men. For women the corresponding figures were from 4 percent single for Chinese women to 22 percent for American Indians. "Undoubtedly because of the continuation of the Irish tradition for late marriage the percent for single middle-aged persons of Irish foreign stock in the United States was nearly twice the level of other persons of European foreign stock."[20]

Nonmarital Occupations.   There are some occupational choices that a person makes that may make marriage impossible or not very probable. This has been most common with religious orders, especially for Roman Catholics. Catholic priests and nuns are still expected to remain single although there has been a movement in recent years to change this. It has been estimated that of all those who never marry in the United States about 5 percent are members of religious orders.[21] Carter and Glick found that rates of nonmarriage of more than 50 percent for women were found among religious workers and private elementary school teachers—occupations with large proportions of Roman Catholic nuns.[22]

It should be reemphasized that any combination of the reasons suggested for failure to marry may operate for the individual. Ultimately, the individual who never marries is one who did not complete the mate selection process. Which factors are most responsible for the individual's not moving through mate selection to marriage is an important question.

---

[19] Ibid., p. 299.
[20] Ibid., p. 407.
[21] Glick, "Bachelors and Spinsters," p. 571.
[22] Carter and Glick, *Marriage and Divorce*, p. 408.

Among those who do not marry, there is a general division between those not selected and those who do not select a mate. To illustrate, it may be that unattractiveness will stop a person from entering marriage more than hostile marriage attitudes. Unattractiveness is a factor in *not being selected,* whereas hostile marriage attitudes refer to *not actively selecting.* Therefore, mate selection must ultimately be viewed as an interaction process wherein the selector and selectee operate mutually on each other. A person may select any number of different individuals as a mate but not be selected in return. On the other hand, a person who is not actively seeking a mate has, in effect, withdrawn from the mate-selection process. In the long run, the person who has withdrawn from the process is more apt to remain unmarried than the person who is in the process but having problems in being selected. Yet, not being selected as against not actively selecting is often ambiguous. For example, a person who is very unattractive may remove himself from the market because he knows or fears he will not be chosen. So when the person says he doesn't *want* to marry he may really feel he would never be selected. Or a woman who enters a Catholic religious order has taken herself out of the market as a result of not being selected. So the general distinction is not always clear.

A number of variables related to people not marrying have been examined. What are some of the consequences for those who never marry? Whether persons choose not to marry or are not chosen to marry they still must make adaptations to a society where almost all major roles and related values are based on the assumption of marital experience. Therefore, a basic sociological question is how do those who never marry adapt to norms and roles generally based on the assumption of marriage?

A great deal in general living patterns and in many aspects of social life of adults is based on the assumption of paired heterosexual couples. Even economically single people must pay for their choice not to marry. They do not receive the income tax deductions that married people do, and they are taxed in a variety of ways to help support the children of those who are married.

Yet, with all the marriage biases that exist in society, it does not appear that those who never marry have a number of special problems. One study came to the conclusion that there was a paucity of significant differences between married and never-married persons.[23] Many who never marry establish a pattern of living alone early in life. One study found that the sense of personal fulfillment was about the same among never-married women as married women. Baker found that the never-married women expressed no feelings of frustration nor any sense of not being a "whole person" because they were unmarried. "Their sense of personal worth comes not from their biological function as a female but from their

---

[23] Elisha M. Rollings, "Family Situations of Married and Never-Married Males," *Journal of Marriage and the Family,* November 1966, p. 490.

social function as a human being, from what they perceive as a creative contribution to their significant society."[24]

In general, what data does exist on the never-married suggests that the background and personality differs very little from the background and personalities of married persons. There have been several attempts to compare rates of mental illness among the single and married. In general, rates of mental illness are lowest for married people as a whole, higher for the widow, still higher for the single, and highest for the divorced. Men and women who remain single into middle age have the greatest risk of being residents in mental hospitals.[25] It appears that single women have lower rates of mental illness than do single men. "Fully 6 percent of bachelors as compared with 3 percent of the spinsters resided in mental hospitals."[26] The lower rate for the single woman may reflect a greater likelihood that she will have a close relationship to another person, either someone who takes care of her or is being cared for by her.

The World of the Never-Married

Because the American society is geared to married people and their patterns of life, the singles have had to make many adaptations. These adaptations can be on the individual or subcultural level. First, a look at some of the assumptions made about the singles; and second, a look at some subcultural elements of single life.

Society assumes that the norms influencing and determining never-married behavior at age 18 will continue to be the same at ages 28, 38, or 48, if the person does not marry. This assumption is beautifully illustrated by our sexual values, which imply the same moral restrictions against nonmarital (people who never marry) sexual behavior as against premarital sexual behavior. The word premarital clearly indicates future marriage and implies actions for young people. While one talks about a 20-year-old, never-married person having premarital sex, the phrase does not seem appropriate for a 50-year-old, single person. Obviously, people who never marry must make some adaptations to a value system that assumes categorical immaturity. This usually means that the person must make discreet adjustments—a social adjustment of values to fit the conditions is not implied, but rather the socially condescending view of "Go ahead and do what you must, but don't get caught." We have no way of knowing to what extent this adjustment to the restrictive nonmarital sexual values, especially for women, leads to feelings of guilt and shame.

[24] Luther G. Baker, Jr., "The Personal and Social Adjustment of the Never-Married Woman," *Journal of Marriage and the Family*, August 1968, p. 478.

[25] Carter and Glick, *Marriage and Divorce*, p. 338.

[26] Alfred C. Kinsey et al., *Sexual Behavior in the Human Female* (Philadelphia: W. B. Saunders, Co., 1953), p. 546.

However, the evidence we do have indicates that the female who does not marry is not the asexual individual that she is often depicted as in various stereotypes. For example, while 96 percent of all married women by age 40 have achieved orgasm from any source, the rate for the never-married women at the same age is 73 percent.[27] When it is taken into account that some women never marry because of no sexual interest, then the differences in orgasm experience between married and never-married women is not very great. The Kinsey data further suggests that active sexual incidence among single women is slightly related to education. For single women in the age group 31 to 35, those with 9 to 12 years of education had an active sexual incidence of 65 percent; those with 13 to 16 years of education, an incidence of 69 percent; and those with 17 or more years of education, an incidence of 75 percent.[28]

As indicated before, more single people are choosing to live alone or with persons not related to them through kinship or marriage. The U.S. population data shows there has been a sharp increase in the number of persons who maintain their own homes while living alone or with persons not related to them. "The greatest percent increase in primary individuals since 1960 occurred in age group 20 to 34 years for both men and women."[29] Many of these living together have decided they don't want marriage, or they are postponing it for some time. But this increased, younger, single population is becoming of more and more importance to American society. For example, the singles have a great deal of money to spend. With the discovery that the unmarried population had an annual spending power in 1973 of about $40 billion, industry's growth exploded in areas trying to satisfy the wants of the unmarried. For example, in 1973 an estimated 100,000 singles-only living units were built throughout the United States. Many of the unmarried are also moving into the suburbs. The number of single-owned homes increased from 2 million to 4.8 million from 1960 to 1970.[30]

The life of the never-married is often presented through the mass media as the "swinging singles" life. This life is seen as a constant stream of parties and good times. While this probably exists for some never-married people, it is doubtful if it is the case for the vast majority of young, never-married persons. One recent study of single, college graduates living in Chicago found that most were uncomfortable about living

[27] Ibid., p. 550.

[28] U.S. Bureau of the Census, *Current Population Reports,* series P-20, no. 233, "Household and Family Characteristics: March 1971" (Washington, D.C.: U.S. Government Printing Office, 1972), p. 2.

[29] *Newsweek* September 1973, p. 40.

[30] Joyce R. Starr and Donald E. Carns, "Singles in the City," in Helena Z. Lopata, *Marriage and Families* (New York: Van Nostrand Co., 1973), p. 159.

arrangements that centered around the single status. Yet, the authors suggest that in a climate that allows year-round, outdoor living the individuals might find the single-living-unit complexes more acceptable. "The party rooms and mixing lounges that abound in cold-climate buildings bent on attracting single populations are anathema to them."[31]

The study of singles living in Chicago found several categories of young women and young men. They suggested that the young women might be placed in three groupings as to how they viewed their occupations: (1) the career women who wanted to develop their work experiences into a full-time career; (2) the women who viewed working as an experience, but who did not view their work roles as ends in themselves; and (3) some young women who begrudged their work roles. (They would have preferred not to work either because they saw themselves as wives and mothers or because they saw themselves at that time, and possibly for the rest of their lives, as not ready to settle down to the responsibility of a job.)[32] The males were also placed into three general categories as related to their work roles: (1) those in conventional career roles and who were striving for success within the corporate world or who believed in the traditional definition of success as prestige and financial gain; (2) the men who consciously rejected traditional work options and values. (They preferred to work at temporary jobs such as driving a cab, construction worker, etc.); and (3) those men who straddled both worlds but belonged to neither. (They typically were craving material success but lacked either talent, skill, or motivation to be successful.)[33] These findings show that both single women and men have a variety of occupational motives.

An important part of the swinging world of the singles, as presented by the mass media, is the development of relationships with the opposite sex. The single people often have an image of almost unlimited opportunity for meeting new people and developing various degrees of relationships. Yet, the Chicago study indicates that developing relationships is not as easy as generally assumed. In that sample the singles often found it very difficult to develop new relationships. "The few relationships that had evolved from casual neighborhood meetings—in shops or laundromats or through a street encounter—were viewed as eventful because they were so atypical. In the city one has only the appearance of youth as a common bond, and even that may be highly suspect."[34] The very fact that the singles are usually transient makes their chances for establishing

[31] Ibid., p. 159.
[32] Ibid., p. 159.
[33] Ibid., p. 159.
[34] Ibid., p. 159.

lasting relationships where they live very difficult. "But most significantly the majority of graduates consider home as a private and inviolate place; they do not welcome intrusion and they avoid making their apartments overly accessible."[35] This would indicate that an open life style is not so common among the singles and therefore opportunities for spontaneous meetings and activities are greatly reduced.

A part of the mass media image of the world of single people centers around their congregating in bars and nightclubs. The Chicago study found that it was a rare woman who, after six months living in that city, continued to seek contacts at singles bars. The males continued to frequent the bars for a longer period of time.[36] Often the bar life appears to be noisy and frantic and seems to offer very little opportunity for single people to meet others.

It was found in Chicago that it was not so much the social life that provided the opportunity for meeting the opposite sex as it was through the work setting. Generally they did not date persons from the work setting because there were very few dating eligibles and because of a resistance to involvement with fellow workers. A more common pattern was to have dates arranged through work friends in a "friend-of-a-friend" pattern.[37] But, in general, the Chicago study came to the conclusion that the popular image of the world of the "swinging singles" developed by the mass media was not accurate. Rather it was found that single people were coping with many of the same problems in life as were the married population. They were trying to find a place to live, looking for satisfaction with their jobs, and seeking friends. This was being done in an "environment for which they have been ill-prepared and which does not easily lend itself to the formation of stable human relationships."[38]

Among older single people there may be less dependency on other singles than among the younger ones. This would be true because there are fewer of them, resulting from the fact that as they get older many of their single friends marry. Also as people get older the world of the unmarried broadens in that it includes more people who have had previous marriages which ended through divorce or death of the spouse. The extent to which the never-married and the previously married interact is hard to determine, but it seems likely that single people tend to stick more with their own because there is often some comfort in being with those who are alike. And in the singles adaptation to a world primarily geared for married people, there may be an extra motivation for them to seek each other out.

---

[35] Ibid., p. 160.

[36] Ibid., p. 160.

[37] Ibid., p. 161.

[38] Ibid., p. 161.

SELECTED BIBLIOGRAPHY

Baker, Luther G., Jr. "The Personal and Social Adjustment of the Never-Married Woman." *Journal of Marriage and the Family*, August 1968, pp. 476–80.

Belcher, John C. "The One-Person Household: A Consequence of the Isolated Nuclear Family." *Journal of Marriage and the Family*, August 1967, pp. 534–40.

Carter, Hugh, and Glick, Paul *Marriage and Divorce: A Social and Economic Study*. Cambridge, Mass.: Harvard University Press, 1970, chap. 10.

Havens, Elizabeth M. "Women, Work and Wedlock: A Note on Female Marital Patterns in the United States," in Joan Huber, *Changing Women In a Changing Society*, Chicago: University of Chicago Press, 1973, pp. 213–19.

Rollings, Elisha M. "Family Situations of Married and Never-Married Males." *Journal of Marriage and the Family*, November 1966, pp. 485–90.

Starr, Joyce R. and Carns, Donald E. "Singles in the City," in Helena Z. Lopata, *Marriage and Families*. New York: Van Nostrand Co., 1973, pp. 154–61.

Chapter 8

Premarital Sexual Attitudes

Americans think and talk a great deal about sex. In the American society of the past, sexual attitudes and behavior were generally felt to be private, at least to the extent that they were not often discussed publicly or between the opposite sexes. Social historians generally regard World War I as the period when American sex attitudes and behavior increasingly came under the influence of forces leading to change. Since World War I, a large number of Americans have been increasingly interested in, if not preoccupied with, sexual matters.

One of man's universal culture characteristics has been his social control of sexual behavior. While societies vary a great deal in how they control sex and what they consider to be the areas of sexual behavior that need to be controlled, some social restrictions are always applied. "Possibly in man's long history there have been peoples who have failed to subject the sexual impulse to regulation. If so, none has survived, for the social control of sex is today a cultural universal."[1]

The relationship of marriage is an important factor in sexual control. Taboos on adultery are widespread; Murdock found they appeared in 120 of the 148 societies for which data were available. However, a substantial majority of societies permit extramarital relations with certain affinal rela-

---

[1] George P. Murdock, *Social Structure* (New York: The Macmillan Co., 1949), p. 260.

tives.[2] In most cultures, the control of sex does not center on the moral condemnation of sexual behavior, but rather on problems that often emerge from uncontrolled sexual behavior, as related to kinship, social stratification, marital status, and so forth.

Societies have tended to be more restrictive about marital than premarital sexual behavior. Murdock found that premarital license prevailed in 70 percent of the cultures for which he had information. "In the rest, the taboo falls primarily upon females and appears to be largely a precaution against childbearing out of wedlock rather than a moral requirement."[3]

When a society does approve certain forms of adolescent sexual activity, it does not usually leave matters of behavior to chance. There are usually special social institutions that provide facilities for the young people to meet and spend time together. However, it is rare in the history of man to find a society like the American—where premarital sexual activity is prohibited but, at the same time, wide opportunity is allowed for private interaction to occur. Ford and Beach point out that in most restrictive societies there is a public conspiracy against the acquisition of any sexual knowledge by children.[4] In restrictive societies, the methods used during adolescence "include segregation of the sexes, strict chaperonage of girls, and threats of severe disgrace or physical punishment."[5] But as Ford and Beach go on to point out, there are probably no societies where any methods of control are completely effective in preventing premarital coitus among young unmarried couples.[6]

Christensen suggests a possible dilemma faced by societies who take *either* a restrictive or a permissive view of premarital sexual relations. "There is a certain amount of evidence that the more permissive the culture regarding premarital sexual intimacy the higher will be the actual occurrence of such intimacy but the lower will be any negative effects deriving therefrom. And, conversely, the more restrictive the culture, the lower will be the actual occurrence but the higher will be the negative effects."[7]

The lesson to be learned from the rich storehouse of anthropological data is that man, through his social institutions, has developed a wide variety of attitudes and controls over sexual behavior. Waller and Hill write, "The sexual impulse can be conditioned to different forms of ex-

---

[2] Ibid., p. 265.

[3] Ibid., p. 265.

[4] Clellan S. Ford and Frank A. Beach, *Patterns of Sexual Behavior* (New York: Harper & Row, 1951), p. 180.

[5] Ibid., p. 182.

[6] Ibid., p. 182.

[7] Harold T. Christensen, "A Cross-Cultural Comparison of Attitudes Toward Marital Infidelity," *International Journal of Comparative Sociology*, September 1962, p. 125.

pression, modified to fit the social order, harnessed to do the work of the world, curbed and encouraged and frustrated and hammered out of shape. But it can never be completely eliminated, never wholly denied, nor can its essential character be destroyed."[8]

In an analysis of premarital sexual attitudes in the United States, two important considerations should be kept in mind: (1) Man, because of his social nature and because he is not biologically restricted in his sexual expression, has created a variety of sexual controls in general, and premarital sexual controls in particular; and (2) the dynamic nature of society often leads to important and significant social changes—as has happened with American premarital sexual attitudes and behavior.

This chapter will focus on American premarital sexual attitudes; the next chapter on American premarital sexual behavior. While behavior is often determined by attitudes, it is also true that verbalized attitudes may be different from actual behavior patterns. In few areas is this better illustrated than with premarital sexual behavior. The commonly stated norms reflected in the attitudes of individuals are that premarital chastity, particularly for the female, is the ideal. However, behavioral studies show that chastity is frequently not the case for a large number of unmarried women. Also, publicly accepting the stated attitudes is often more important than whether or not one actually behaves according to them. A girl who states an acceptance of premarital chastity, but discreetly indulges in premarital sexual intercourse, will receive far less social criticism than the girl who states she does not *believe* in the norms of chastity, even though she does not herself enter into premarital sexual relations.

Many times the inconsistency between attitudes and behavior results from behavior being more subject to rapid social change than attitudes. When there is a general change in behavior patterns, the old attitudes usually continue to prevail, especially if they are a part of a larger value system. Largely as a result of the Kinsey findings, many Americans have been concerned with what they see as the hypocrisy evident in the contrast between attitudes and behavior in premarital sexual relations. Kinsey forced many Americans to recognize that public verbalizations of approved sexual attitudes were not necessarily equivalent to strong individual behavioral controls. This leads to another consideration: The old norms and attitudes do not seem to be working in today's American society. Many Americans react to attitude-behavior differences with the belief that the norms must be strengthened so that behavior will be brought back into line. A minority argue that the norms should be redefined to fit the changes in behavior. The discussion that follows in this chapter will focus on the changing social nature of various premarital sexual attitudes in the United States.

---

[8] Willard Waller and Reuben Hill, *The Family* (New York: The Dryden Press, 1951), p. 58.

Attitude as a Concept. Man's social behavior is learned. The newborn infant does not have attitudes, because he is not social. Through the process of socialization, he acquires the social characteristics made available to him by those already socialized. Therefore, all that is social is initially external to the human infant, but through social interaction with others he internalizes values, norms, and attitudes. Their intensity and significance for different individuals is not constant because of individual variations and differences in experience. In the following discussion of premarital sexual attitudes, the following concepts will be used:

Values—Broad beliefs referring to the appropriateness of thought and action directed at individuals and objects.

Attitudes—The more specific personal internalization of values referring to ideas, perceptions, and dispositions carried over from past experiences and directed at objects, persons, and groups. Attitudes may be general or specific. A woman expressing her attitudes about premarital sexual behavior for girls may state a general attitude for all girls or a more specific attitude if she relates the question to a teen-age daughter.

Norms—Attitudes that are generally accepted as guidelines for conduct by social groups. Generally, the stronger the norms, the more closely behavior will conform to them—indicating that this country's norms against premarital sexual conduct are not very strong.

In this chapter and in the next chapter, then, we will be presenting data from a variety of research studies into premarital sexual attitudes and behavior. However, almost all research in the area of premarital sexual intimacy has taken place within the last 30 years.[9] In Chapter 8 we will discuss in some detail the Kinsey studies because they are our major source on premarital sexual behavior. We will also be referring to a variety of other studies. It should be kept in mind that most of the studies we will be citing apply to white, higher educated groups, and they have generally focused on sexual behavior rather than sexual attitudes.[10]

TRADITIONAL AMERICAN ATTITUDES

That sexual attitudes are in a state of change today can best be seen in light of attitudes of the past. But generalizations about the past run the same dangers as generalizations about present attitudes. Human attitudes are never quite the same for all people or all groups. Therefore, our discussion centers around general traditional American sex attitudes, recognizing that there are many exceptions.

---

[9] See Robert R. Bell, *Premarital Sex in a Changing Society* (Englewood Cliffs, N.J.: Prentice-Hall, Inc., 1966), Ch. 1.

[10] Ira L. Reiss, *Premarital Sexual Standards in America* (Glencoe, Ill.: The Free Press, 1960), p. 74.

The American family of the past approximated the patriarchal model. (See Chapter 2.) The male was dominant in important areas of both marriage and the family, giving him both differential prestige and greater rights and obligations. It was generally assumed that the man had very different sexual needs and drives than the woman. While the male's sexual drive was sometimes seen as "animalistic," people generally believed that the drive had to be satisfied. Sex was expected to be of little or no personal interest to the woman, and was indulged in by her for purposes of reproduction and meeting her husband's sexual needs.

Woman's premarital chastity was very important for several reasons. First, in a patriarchal society the woman was often viewed by men as personal property, at least to the degree that marriages were arranged along economic lines. The worth of the woman was drastically reduced if she could not take chastity into marriage. Second, because the woman was assumed to have little personal interest in sex, any hint of premarital sexual experience might indicate that she was sexually susceptible, thereby threatening the male's image of the sexually pure role expected of the wife.

The sexual attitudes of men were contradictory. On the one hand, the man had strong sexual drives and the need to find a woman for sexual satisfaction. On the other hand, he wanted, for marriage, a woman sexually pure and little interested in personal sex satisfaction. To resolve this contradiction, men often divided women into two categories, the "good" and the "bad." "Good" women were those who were premaritally chaste and maritally restricted in their sexual interest. The "bad" were those women who were available in providing an outlet for the man's sexual needs. The patriarchal male rarely allowed the two female groupings to overlap, because he saw them as absolutes and not different by degree. The distinction had implications for both the man and the woman. The man could satisfy his sexual needs outside of marriage and still maintain belief in the purity of his wife. For the woman, however, any personal sexual satisfaction resulting from marriage could lead to guilt feelings. If she overtly displayed her sexual interests, the husband's suspicion might be aroused that she really was not "good." In many cases, the values effectively removed female sexual satisfaction from the marriage relationship.

Patriarchal beliefs were, in general, supported by religious beliefs in the United States. Early Protestantism, the dominant religion, placed a great emphasis on woman's constant struggle to resist evil and the "temptations of the flesh." While sex outside marriage was sinful for both sexes, it was far more sinful for the woman. In general, it may be said that the Protestant influence, because it included a religiously patriarchal definition of the family, supported the patriarchal family that prevailed.

Many characteristics of the patriarchal concept of sexual behavior still prevail in American society both in traditional, as well as in modified, forms. Thus, the changing patterns of sexual attitudes in the United States have been a matter of degree.

INFLUENCES ON CHANGING ATTITUDES

As previously noted, a shift from the institutional emphasis on the family as a group to the more personal emphasis on the ego-needs of the individual has occurred. This has meant that the impact of family influence on the attitudes of the individual has declined and, therefore, the traditional values of the family no longer have the same significance. Along with a contemporary emphasis on the individual seeking ego-need satisfaction, goes the middle-class concept of personal happiness as a measure of the individual's successful family relationships.

Of great importance to the changes in premarital sexual attitudes has been the increasing social equality of the American woman. Freedom and equality for the woman mean a weakening of the patriarchal traditions. Sex equality and patriarchal values are in contradiction and can rarely exist within the same social group. The emancipation of the American woman implies a number of important social changes. First, she is no longer as rigidly controlled by her family as in the past. Because of increased educational and occupational opportunities, she spends a great deal of time away from the parental home. Therefore, while the values of the parents are important, the young woman has the opportunity to come into contact with other values which may replace or modify the parental ones. This may have a cumulative effect—being out from under the influence of the parents often leads to attitudes that encourage her to move even further away from their control.

Second, increasing sexual equality leads to less female dependence on the male. In the past, the woman was almost totally dependent upon the male for her entire life, first to her father and then to her husband. But today, a woman may leave the influence of the father and not immediately move into a dependency relationship with a husband. While women desire and enter marriage at a high rate today, it is much less a "forced" choice than it was in the past. Many young women also have a period of personal independence between leaving the parental home and entering marriage.

Third, to a great degree the female has broken away from parental influence over the selection of a marriage partner. Because the woman now has an equal role in dating and courtship, she has minimized parental influence and entered into a relationship of near equality with the male in mate selection.

Fourth, one of the most significant developments, particularly in the middle class, is the belief in sexual rights and privileges for the woman. Most young women believe that when they marry they have a right to expect personal sexual satisfaction and fulfillment. Attitudes about sexual rights in marriage have led to a new set of attitudes about sex in general. Females today are less willing to accept the double standard and more likely to expect the same sexual pleasure as the male, or to apply to him the same restrictions.

Yet, while women have just about won the right to sexual equality in marriage, they continue to have far more restrictions placed on them in premarital sexual rights than do men. American values suggest that the American girl can be sexually *attractive* but not sexually *active*. As pointed out earlier, every society imposes some restrictions on sexual behavior, but what is most striking about American codes is a high level of permissiveness in most areas of premarital behavior with the exception of strong restrictions against premarital sex. Lerner writes, "The American girl, with wide leeway in choosing friends, clothes and schools, books and magazines, movies and plays, places to go and people to see, with freedom of movement, education, and opinion, is nevertheless closely watched and admonished on everything affecting sexual relations."[11]

There is evidence of an increase in permissive attitudes towards premarital sex among both males and females. A recent study found that 9 out of 10 men under 25 years of age felt premarital coitus is all right for men, and 8 out of 10 felt it was all right for women, when there is strong affection. Women under age 25 are somewhat less permissive. But 6 out of 10 condone premarital coitus for women where there is only strong affection and 9 out of 10 where there is love.[12] These results clearly show that both men and women hold to a belief in an emotional commitment for women before premarital sex much more than for men.

Secular Society

The American society over the past 50 years has been characterized by a shift away from the sacred values of a traditional society to the more secular ones of a society undergoing rapid social change. The American way of life today emphasizes the right of both sexes to seek personal pleasure and satisfactions out of life. We have a hedonistic approach to living, not an ascetic one. Reiss points out that "we are a nation of people who value rationality quite highly. And the inequality of our traditional sexual customs and the many inconsistencies in them make them a good target for rationalism. The asceticism of these sexual standards is opposed by our hedonism and secularism."[13]

There are various social variables related to more permissive sexual

---

[11] Max Lerner, *America as a Civilization* (New York: Simon & Schuster, 1957), p. 667.

[12] Morton Hunt, "Sexual Behavior in the 1970s," *Playboy*, November 1973, p. 74.

[13] Reiss, *Premarital Sexual Standards*, p. 220.

values. One recent study found that if a woman defines herself as politically liberal this may suggest a more liberal life style that would be reflected in broader sexual experiences.[14] Another study of premarital sexual experiences found that permissive attitudes generally were associated with higher education, political liberalism, white-collar status, and the absence of strong religious feelings.[15]

However, it should be stressed that what is publicly permissive only suggests what is available to a society. It doesn't necessarily mean that many people will follow what is permissable. "Contrary to the would-be censor's predictions, permissiveness did not attract massive portions of the population to the new erotic frontiers. Relatively few people in our society are gourmets of the extremely and/or exclusively erotic."[16]

An increase in religious involvement in the United States has been the subject of some discussion. The evidence usually offered is an increase in church membership. But greater church attendance does not mean that people's attitudes are being greatly affected by religious teachings. While a strong religious restriction in regard to premarital sexual behavior continues, it is questionable that it has a great impact.

Too, there may be some lessening of religious strictures against premarital sexual values as a result of changes internal to religion. For example, one of the most liberal Christian positions on premarital sexual behavior is that of the Quakers. The Quakers condemn as fundamentally immoral every sexual action that is not, as far as is humanly ascertainable, the result of a mutual decision.[17] Grunwald points out that "the implication is strong that, conversely, any act that *is* the result of a mutual, responsible decision may be considered moral. Hence, so continues the implication, only seduction, entrapment, or exploitation make an action immoral."[18] What the long-range impact of this kind of religious view of premarital sexual morality will be is at present impossible to determine.

The traditional influence of religion as *the* determiner of premarital sexual values and behavior is at least in part being replaced by the influence of science and education. For example, the relative influence of the institutional forces of religion and science are reflected in a nationwide study of some attitudes of college students. The students were asked: "How much confidence do you have in these institutions?" With regard to the scientific community, the response, "a great deal," was given by 76

---

[14] Robert Bell and Shelli Balter, "Premarital Sexual Experiences of Married Women," *Medical Aspects of Human Sexuality*, November 1973, p. 112.

[15] Hunt, "Sexual Behavior in 70s," p. 199.

[16] William Simon, "Sex and American Society," in Patricia Sexton, *Readings in Society and Human Behavior* (Calif.: Communications Research Machines, Inc., 1972), p. 53.

[17] Henry A. Grunwald, *Sex in America* (New York: Bantam Books, 1964), pp. 150–51.

[18] Ibid., pp. 150–51.

percent of the interviewees; to higher education, 64 percent; but, to organized religion only 34 percent.[19]

The study also found that those college students who maintained their religious faith while in college seemed to be far less certain of themselves than the nonbelievers.[20] As the number and proportion of young people going on to college increases, it would appear probable that the traditional influence of religion in areas of morality will continue to decline. In general, increased education is related to a decrease in the influence and significance of religion. One study found that "almost 40 percent of the students said their experiences in college had made them question their faith."[21]

It is not just that higher education reduces the influence of religion; institutions of higher education also themselves contribute to new and often different moral values. For example, a *Newsweek* study of college students found that two thirds of all those polled believed that prevailing campus standards encourage promiscuity; "and more than four out of five said their experience in college had made them take a more tolerant attitude toward those who defy traditional sexual morality."[22]

However, the importance of religion on many people's attitudes in regard to premarital sex cannot be ignored. Kinsey vividly showed that the intensity of religious belief is of great significance in influencing sexual behavior. For those with a strong religious orientation, the secular nature of society has limited influence on their sexual attitudes. One study found that "when age, marital status, size of home town, fraternity membership, father's political inclination, and religious affiliation are each held constant, the relationship between sex attitudes and religiosity remains significant. These tests lead one to conclude that there is a relationship between the importance one attaches to religious matters and one's attitude toward premarital sexual relations, a relationship which cannot be accounted for by any of the background factors tested."[23]

Attitudes about premarital sex in the United States have changed greatly. For example, in 1939, 80 percent of a national sample of men said it was either "unfortunate" or "wicked" when young women have sexual relations before they are married. The same study found 83 percent of the women giving the same answers with regard to young men having sexual relations before marriage.[24]

---

[19] *Newsweek*, "Campus '65," March 22, 1965, p. 45.

[20] Ibid., p. 57.

[21] Ibid., p. 57.

[22] Ibid., p. 58.

[23] Jean Dedman, "The Relationship between Religious Attitude and Attitude toward Premarital Sex Relations," *Marriage and Family Living*, May 1959, p. 175.

[24] William Goode, *World Population and Family Patterns* (New York: The Free Press of Glencoe, 1963), p. 36.

Another study looked at values about premarital sex among college-educated women in 1965 and 1970. It was found that while, in 1965, 70 percent of the females felt that premarital intercourse was immoral, only 34 percent of the 1970 females thought so. The authors suggest that traditionally females have been the main supporters of both public and private morality, "but with the present generation of students, it is the male who is assuming the responsibility equally. In response to a liberalization in sexual attitudes on the part of females, it appears as if males are becoming more conservative."[25]

Extended Adolescence

Adolescence is the period between leaving childhood and entering adulthood. Early in adolescence, the individual becomes biologically capable of entering adult sexual relationships, but his—the American—society insists that such relationships should be postponed until adulthood and marriage. An important American social change has been the prolonging of adolescence and, therefore, the prolonging of premarital sexual restrictions. Adolescence has been prolonged by delaying the time when young people can earn their own living, a very important factor in assigning adult status. Social adolescence is also being lengthened by pushing the time of maturing down to an earlier age. As a result of these two influences, the period of social adolescence may be twice as long today as it was 100 years ago. If the trend for younger ages at marriages continues, however, the time period may be somewhat shortened.

While the length of adolescence has increased, few socially approved changes in attitudes toward premarital sexual behavior have occurred. Premarital chastity continues to be the stated ideal. This leads to considerable conflict and strain for the adolescent.

During their extended social adolescence, the two sexes take different views of premarital sexual behavior. A very important part of the adolescent's social involvement is with members of his own sex, and this group influences the individual's attitudes about sexual behavior. The male group often encourages positive attitudes in regard to sexual conquests of females. While there are many variations, the prestige of the boy within the peer group may often be determined by the number of seductions he is able to persuade his peers he has achieved.

Peer group values have a strong influence on the premarital sexual values of its members. One study found that students who were peer oriented and believed their friends were sexually permissive tended to be the most sexually permissive themselves. By contrast, those students

---

[25] Ira B. Robinson, Karl King, and Jack O. Balswick, "The Premarital Sexual Revolution Among College Females," *The Family Coordinator*, April 1972, p. 194.

who were parent oriented and had conservative parents were the least sexually permissive.[26]

During their childhood young boys and girls are socialized to their present and future sexuality in different ways. Basically, girls in our society are not encouraged to be sexual and are often strongly discouraged. And most of us accept the fact that while "bad boys" may mean many things, a "bad girl" almost exclusively implies sexual delinquency. Simon and Gagnon go on to point out that girls appear to be well-trained in the very area that boys are poorly trained. "That is, a belief in and a capacity for intense, emotionally charged relationships and the language of romantic love. When girls during this period describe having been aroused sexually, they more often report it as a response to romantic, rather than erotic, words and actions."[27]

The adolescent girl's group values usually center around popularity, not sexual involvement. She often gains prestige from her female reference group if she has many different dates and if she can draw males into an overt emotional commitment. As the girl enters late adolescence, the emotional commitment of the male becomes even more important to her as a necessary prelude to marriage. Built into adolescent boy-girl relationships are different attitudes that contribute to the struggle between the sexes as to premarital sexual behavior and emotional commitment.

Simon and Gagnon also point out that there are differences by social class as to how boys interact with each other and with girls. They point out that although the sex lives of lower-class males are almost exclusively heterosexual they live in a homosocial world. While they have coitus with girls, the standards and the audience they seek is that of their fellow males. By contrast, middle-class boys shift predominantly to coitus at a significantly later time. "They, too, need and tend to have homosocial elements in their sexual lives. But their fantasies, their ability to symbolize, and their social training in a world in which distinctions between masculinity and femininity are less sharply drawn, allow them to withdraw more easily from an all-male world."[28]

A recent study shows how mothers feel about their children having premarital coitus. A sample of 2,372 married women were asked: "Would you object to a son (daughter) having premarital coitus?" Thirty percent said they would object for a daughter, 22 percent said, "don't know," and 8 percent said, "no." For a son, 19 percent said they would object; 18 percent, "don't know," and 63 percent, "no." The older women objected more for both sons and daughters than did younger women. Sixty-one

---

[26] James J. Teevan, "Reference Groups and Premarital Sexual Behavior," *Journal of Marriage and the Family*, May 1962, p. 290.

[27] William Simon and John Gagnon, "Psychosexual Development," *Trans-Action*, March 1969, pp. 14–15.

[28] Ibid., p. 14.

percent of the women with premarital coital experience answered they would not object for their daughter, as compared to only 23 percent of the women with no premarital coitus taking that liberal a position."[29]

Mass Media Influence

Many observers of contemporary America have commented on the contradiction of a society which holds the traditional sexual attitudes of chastity and asceticism, and simultaneously bombards individuals with sexual stimuli. While the great American interest in sexual behavior has complications for individuals at almost all ages, it has a particular impact on the adolescent and his sexual attitudes and behavior. Because he is in a position of role transition, and because the physical sex drives (particularly in the male) are strong, the adolescent is highly susceptible to the stimuli of an erotic culture. The impact of mass media also has a particular influence on the adolescent because of the insecurity of adolescent roles in reference to desired adult sex status. This insecurity can lead the young person to seek out sex symbols that he believes indicate adult sex status. The images of sexual attraction conveyed to the highly responsive adolescent through movies, television, and various reading materials emphasize the sexually attractive female. Thus, the adolescent girl often wears clothing, adopts hairdos, and plasters on the makeup used by the "sexy" female symbols of mass communication. This then makes her more erotically appealing to the male, who also has been influenced by the symbols of sex huckstered through mass media.

The girl, as a result, must maintain a delicate balance in her relationships with the highly sex-conscious boy. On the one hand, she wants, as a female sex symbol, to stimulate the male, at least to the extent of being popular and desirable. On the other hand, she does not want to be so sexually obvious that she will no longer be defined as a "good" girl. The female's "sexiness" also contributes to the male-female struggles in which the girl tries to pull the boy in her direction of emotional commitment, and the boy struggles to pull the girl in his direction of sexual gratification.

EMERGENT PREMARITAL SEX ATTITUDES

The emerging sexual attitudes in today's society are not clearly defined, and are often confused. A very important contribution to an understanding of different and often conflicting premarital sexual attitudes has been made by Ira Reiss. He suggests that there are two basic types of premarital sexual behavior, with their related attitudes, that may be

---

[29] Bell and Balter, "Premarital Experiences," p. 117.

seen as extremes on a continuum: (1) *body-centered,* with the emphasis on the physical nature of sex and (2) *person-centered,* with the emphasis on the emotional relationship to a given individual with whom the sexual act is being performed.[30] Reiss suggests that individuals' premarital attitudes may usually be classified in one of four categories falling along a continuum.[31]

1. *Abstinence*—premarital intercourse is wrong for both the man and the woman, regardless of circumstances.

2. *Permissiveness with affection*—premarital intercourse is right for both men and women under certain conditions when a stable relationship with engagement, love, or strong affection is present.

3. *Permissiveness without affection*—premarital intercourse is right for both men and women regardless of the amount of affection or stability present, providing there is physical attraction.

4. *Double standard*—premarital intercourse is acceptable for men, but is wrong and unacceptable for women.

The traditional attitude, the double standard, continues to be accepted by many Americans of both sexes. The attitude of abstinence is often found along with the double standard. Historically, the double standard was applied to the male and the abstinence standard applied to the female. The two relatively new categories of permissiveness are the result of many factors of social change in the American culture. Permissiveness without affection places value on the sheer physical satisfaction derived from sex, although it is assumed that individuals will be sophisticated enough to control their pleasure in a careful way. This attitude is probably less accepted than permissiveness with affection, which generally views sex not as an end in itself but as a means of expressing the end of affection.

However, there is some recent evidence that significant changes are occurring about many sexual attitudes among young women. For example, Christensen and Gregg found that while in 1958 more females than males had opposed the censorship of pornography, ten years later the reverse was the case.[32] The same study found in a midwestern sample that while in 1958 only 23 percent of the females stated an acceptance of nonvirginity the rate had gone up in 1968 to 44 percent.[33] They also suggest that "in their new permissiveness Americans are probably less guilt-ridden than formerly, since there seems to be less of a gap between their values and their behavior."[34]

---

[30] Reiss, *Premarital Standards,* p. 80.

[31] Ibid., pp. 83–84.

[32] Harold T. Christensen and Christina F. Gregg, "Changing Sex Norms in America and Scandinavia," *Journal of Marriage and the Family,* November 1970, p. 619.

[33] Ibid., p. 619.

[34] Ibid., p. 623.

The Age Factor

An often-heard stereotype suggests that sexual permissiveness is characteristic of most adolescents today. However, age differences among adolescents are clearly related to different attitudes regarding premarital sexual behavior. Younger adolescents are often under the influence of traditional values communicated to them by their parents. As they grow older and come increasingly under the influence of outside-the-family values, their traditional values are frequently altered. The shift from an age where sexual values are not behaviorally meaningful and only theoretically applied, to an age where the values are behaviorally meaningful and increasingly applied often results in new attitudes related to the new behavior.

Generally the socialization experience of the boy and girl is such that they do not have any sexual experiences before adolescence. And when they do have their initial experiences, for girls more often than for boys, it is generally not immediately related to sexual feelings or gratification but is a use of sex for nonsexual goals and purposes. Simon and Gagnon suggest that the "seductive" Lolita is rare, but she is significant. "She illustrates a more general pattern of psychosexual development—a commitment to the social relationships linked to sex before one can really grasp the social meaning of the physical relationship."[35]

The sexual act is almost always the end stage of a process of increasing sexual intimacy. Premarital intimacy interaction generally moves from kissing to necking to petting to intercourse. Changes in attitudes do not always center on greater liberality in regard to sexual intercourse, but often on a more intimate level of foreplay. Reiss suggests that the real increases in teen-age sexual behavior over the past generation have not been in the area of sexual intercourse, but rather in the area of petting.[36] This may represent a compromise in the sexual attitudes of the girls who continue to accept the ideal of virginity, but at the same time have an opportunity for some sexual involvement. When a girl has indulged in petting, she is still technically a virgin, but at the same time is sexually experienced.

There may be problems for the "technical virgin." On some occasions, the intensity of petting may lead her across the final line to where she is no longer a virgin. Or by engaging in petting, she may find it difficult to stop the male from forcibly moving her across the line.[37] An accepted attitude that intimacy will stop at a certain point is often easier to state theoretically than to practice behaviorally.

It is also possible that for older, unmarried girls the traditional atti-

---

[35] Simon and Gagnon, "Psychosexual Development," p. 11.

[36] Reiss, *Premarital Standards,* p. 59.

[37] See Clifford Kirkpatrick and Eugene Kanin, "Male Sex Aggression on a University Campus," *American Sociological Review,* February 1957, pp. 52–58.

tudes of chastity are less meaningful and forceful. The role of "technical virgin" can be maintained as long as the girl believes that the distinction between petting and sexual intercourse is meaningful. The sharpness of the distinction may be dulled, however, by increasing age and stage of emotional commitment, and the girl may find it difficult to justify the distinction to herself or the boy.

DATING-COURTSHIP STAGES

If attitudes change as the unmarried person gets older, so does the probability of being involved in more intense interpersonal relationships. Even when age is held constant, the different stages in the dating-courtship process often imply different attitudes toward sexual intimacy. The interrelationship of intensity of emotional involvement and attitudes about premarital sexual behavior will, therefore, be examined among the population for which some empirical information is available.

Dating

Dating, it will be recalled, implies no commitment on the part of either individual to the other; ego-fulfillment is the important value in dating. Thus, dating often becomes a battle ground for the ego-satisfaction of the two uncommitted individuals. Because the male has no commitment, he frequently considers the female sexually exploitable. The female wants popularity but often feels that if she allows the male to go too far sexually, she may lose her reputation and desirability as a romantic object and become desirable primarily as a sex object. The situation might be simplified if the girl took a rigid stand and discouraged *any* sexual overtures from the boy. However, the girl may want the boy to indicate that he finds her physically attractive. In fact, the girl often dresses to make herself as sexually attractive as possible. The girl often wants some male aggression, but it must be restricted to her limits. Many girls would probably be disappointed in their dating relationships if the boys never overtly indicated a sexual interest, because the sexual pass indicates sexual desirability, which is generally important to the girl's self-image.

It is clear that for many adolescents and young adults there is a wide difference in sexual attitudes taken into the dating situation by boys and girls. As discussed in Chapter 4, the differences are greatly influenced by the lack of emotional commitment by either individual to the other.

Several studies of college students' attitudes about sexual involvement at the various stages of dating and courtship indicate increasing levels of sexual intimacy associated with dating, going steady, and engagement. A study by Christensen and Carpenter provides some interesting contrasts in the attitudes of three cultures toward premarital sexual behavior.[38] One culture was predominantly Mormon and relatively conservative (Intermountain); the second group was in the midwestern part of the United States and believed to be somewhat typical of the country as a whole (Midwest); and, the third group was in Denmark, which has permissive premarital sex norms.[39] The findings on approval of premarital coitus on random or casual dates assuming mutual desire were, for the males: Intermountain, 6 percent; Midwest, 17 percent; and Denmark, 43 percent; for the females: Intermountain, 1 percent; Midwest, 3 percent; and Denmark, 34 percent.[40] Both of the U.S. populations indicate a low percentage of individuals accepting favorable attitudes toward premarital sexual behavior while dating. In all three groups the acceptance figures are lower for the females than for the males.

In their study of attitudes on premarital sexual behavior, Bell and Blumberg attempted to distinguish levels of sexual intimacy beyond which there were guilt feelings. "The level of guilt for females increases considerably when they go beyond necking during a dating relationship; while the level of guilt for males follows the female trend only beyond petting. Fifty-four percent of the females in contrast to 25 percent of the males said they had gone too far during a date when they had engaged in petting.[41] During dating, the level of approved sexual intimacy is much lower for the female than for the male, illustrating their differential sexual view of dating.

This study not only tried to get at the guilt feelings associated with sexual behavior that had "gone too far," but also at feelings that behavior had not "gone far enough." "About one third of the females indicated that there were dating relationships in which they wished they had been more intimate than they were in fact. About three fourths of the males indicated that they wished they had been more intimate."[42] The finding that a number of girls wished they had gone further suggests for some a definition of sexual fulfillment at a higher level of intimacy in retrospect than that actually engaged in while dating. But the findings most vividly point out that dating implies sexual opportunities for the male, a majority of whom felt that sexual intimacy could have been greater. Thus, the male exhibits greater interest in sex than the female during dating, a time when he feels a limited emotional responsibility for the person dated.

---

[38] See Harold T. Christensen and George R. Carpenter, "Timing Patterns in the Development of Sexual Intimacy: An Attitudinal Report on Three Modern Western Societies," *Marriage and Family Living*, February 1962, pp. 30–35.

[39] Ibid., p. 30.

[40] Ibid., p. 31.

[41] Robert R. Bell and Leonard Blumberg, "Courtship Stages and Intimacy Attitudes," *Family Life Coordinator*, March 1960, p. 62.

[42] Ibid., p. 62.

The findings indicate that in a dating relationship petting and intercourse are the levels of intimacy the male would, if possible, like to reach. The female is interested in some intimacy, at least through necking. The different accepted levels of intimacy while dating clearly indicate the sexual struggle at this level of minimal pair-commitment.

Going Steady

The going-steady relationship is a mutual commitment by two individuals to exclude other members of the opposite sex as possible dates. In some cases, going steady means the individuals are in love and will eventually move into engagement and marriage. For others, particularly the younger, there may be no love involvement. This discussion will be limited to the older group and will assume that some affection or love is usual.

The Christensen-Carpenter and Bell-Blumberg studies examined attitudes on sexual involvement of couples going steady. In the Christensen and Carpenter study, the findings on approval of premarital intercourse for a couple in love and going steady, but not engaged, were for the males: Intermountain, 5 percent; Midwest, 19 percent; and Denmark, 73 percent; and for the females: Intermountain, 2 percent; Midwest, 4 percent; and Denmark, 59 percent.[43] Neither of the two American groups studied show a significant change for either the male or the female in stating approval of premarital coitus when going steady as compared with dating.

The Bell and Blumberg study found that "a little over one third of the females and a little less than one third of the males who had gone steady and who had done any petting, expressed guilt over their behavior. The differences between male and female are greater with respect to intercourse during the going steady period, although the differences are not statistically significant."[44] As with dating, the differences indicate more permissive behavior and attitudes on the part of the male. However, as intensity of relationship increases, the attitudes of the two sexes may converge. Going steady may be an intermediate point that allows fuller sexual expression, sometimes short of intercourse, and provides more emotional protection than dating, but not the strong commitment of engagement.

Attitudes toward sexual behavior while going steady are also influenced by the previous sexual experiences of the individuals involved. We would expect that those with premarital sexual experience would be more liberal in their sexual views. In a study of college students by Prince and

---

[43] Christensen and Carpenter, "Timing Patterns," p. 31.
[44] Bell and Blumberg, "Courtship Stages," p. 62.

Shipman, respondents were asked if they would object to having premarital sexual relations with their "steady." For those with premarital sexual experience, 30 percent of the males and 64 percent of the females answered they *would* object. For those without premarital sexual relations, 63 percent of the males and 91 percent of the females said they would object.[45] Not only were those with experience more liberal, but the males in both categories of experience were more liberal than the females in the same category.

Going steady, when compared with dating, may mean greater liberality in the girls' attitudes on sexual intimacy. For some boys, going steady may mean a decrease in intimacy aspirations because of a commitment to the girl that they did not feel during the dating relationship. Petting, it is suggested, is a commonly accepted level of intimacy for both males and females while going steady.

Engagement

Engagement almost always means a mutual statement of love by two individuals and, usually, an agreement to enter into marriage at some future date. As contrasted with dating and going steady, engagement means a greater commitment to, and a stronger sense of obligation and respect for, the other person.

The Christensen and Carpenter findings on approval of premarital coitus for those couples in love and engaged were for the males: Intermountain, 21 percent; Midwest, 54 percent; and Denmark, 87 percent; and for the females: Intermountain, 7 percent; Midwest, 27 percent; and Denmark, 74 percent.[46] For the conservative American group (Intermountain), the female's attitudes changed little between going steady and engagement, but the male's changed significantly. In the more typical American group (Midwest), both males and females changed significantly from going steady, with the change being greater for the male than for the female.

The Bell and Blumberg study found no significant differences between males and females in feelings of guilt during engagement for either petting or intercourse. When petting was the top limit of intimacy while engaged, 31 percent of the males and 26 percent of the females expressed feelings of guilt. However, 31 percent of the males and 20 percent of the females in the petting group had some regret they had not gone further. Of those who had intercourse during engagement, 41 percent of both males and females had some feelings of guilt.[47] The trend of con-

---

[45] Alfred J. Prince and Gordon Shipman, "Attitudes of College Students toward Premarital Sex Experience," *Family Life Coordinator,* June 1958, p. 58.

[46] Christensen and Carpenter, "Timing Patterns," p. 31.

[47] Bell and Blumberg, "Courtship Stages," p. 62.

vergence of male-female attitudes moves even closer during engagement because of the increased pair-commitment. Petting seems to be a generally accepted level of intimacy during engagement and, for a significant number, sexual intercourse may also be acceptable.

Previous experience with premarital sex appears to influence attitudes about coitus during engagement. Prince and Shipman asked their respondents if they would object to having premarital sexual relations with their engagement partner. For those with premarital sexual experience, 17 percent of the males and 45 percent of the females responded that they *would* object. For those without premarital sexual experience, 47 percent of the males and 76 percent of the females said they would object to having sexual relations with their engaged partner.[48] The females in both experience categories are more conservative in their attitudes than are the males. It is worth noting that girls with premarital sexual experience were as liberal about sex with the engaged partner as were males with no premarital sexual experience.

The stages of interpersonal relationship clearly have a great influence on premarital sexual attitudes. The emergence of different attitudes at different stages of dating and courtship have been primarily the creation of young people, because the general attitudes of the adult population are of a uniform conservative bent. In Chapter 8, differences in sexual behavior at the different dating-courtship stages will be investigated in greater detail.

PREMARITAL CHASTITY OR NOT

The emergence of different attitudes and values regarding premarital sexual intercourse may often lead to conflict and confusion for many of the young unmarried. An attempt to assess the different attitudes and the supporting arguments that are often heard is therefore of value. This will *not* be a statement of what to do, but rather a presentation of some of the factors worth considering in assessing attitudes both for and against premarital chastity.

Background

Before discussing some of the arguments, it is important to look at the background of sexual knowledge and experience the individual has in making a decision as to levels of premarital sexual intimacy. A relevant question is *when, how, and to what extent does the young person learn about sexual behavior?* In a study of urban middle-class boys between the ages of 12 and 16, Ramsey found that 90 percent of their first sex information was acquired from either male companions or from their own

---

[48] Prince and Shipman, "Attitudes," p. 58.

experience. He points out that the most reliable sources are not the ones that contribute.[49] When the boys were asked to rate their parents' contribution to sex education, 60 percent said they had received none from their mothers, and 82 percent had received none from their fathers. Only 13 percent assessed the contribution of either parent as fair or adequate.[50]

No comparable studies for girls could be found, but it seems reasonable to assume that girls, who have a more limited concern with sex during adolescence, know even less than boys. Girls probably also acquire more information from their parents, particularly their mothers. By the time late adolescence is reached, it is assumed that both sexes have a fair amount of sexual knowledge, though it may be somewhat unreliable.

As individuals move into late adolescence and the early adult years, actual premarital sex experience increasingly occurs, though more often for the male than for the female. When individuals move into the relationships of going steady or engagement, previous sexual experiences are differentially viewed by the male and the female. While the male, especially the higher educated, may be less disturbed today than in the past if he discovers his loved one has had previous sexual experiences, he still prefers that she be a virgin. The girl has a somewhat different attitude in viewing her loved one's previous sex experience. Because premarital sexual conquest as a sign of masculinity is a stereotype accepted by a number of girls, as well as by boys, she may actually desire that he not be a virgin. Because she has been taught that sexual satisfaction is important to marriage, she may also feel that his experience will be a positive element in her achieving sexual satisfaction. Kinsey also found that females are less inclined to demand that their husbands be virgins when they marry. "In our sample, something over 40 percent of the males wanted to marry virgins, while only 23 percent of the females expressed the same desire."[51]

Risks

For the male who has no emotional commitment to the female, premarital intercourse has limited risks. When the relationship is transitory, he indulges for the sake of sexual gratification, with little or no emotional involvement. The dangers related to paternity responsibilities in the case of pregnancy, or dangers of venereal disease, are minimal. If his behavior is found out, he is rarely subject to social criticism; in fact, he may gain prestige in the eyes of his male peer group.

[49] Glenn V. Ramsey, "The Sex Information of Younger Boys," in Jerome M. Seidman, *The Adolescent* (New York: Holt, Rinehart, & Winston, Inc., 1960), p. 337.

[50] Ibid., p. 337.

[51] Alfred C. Kinsey et al., *Sexual Behavior in the Human Female* (Philadelphia: W. B. Saunders, 1953), p. 323.

When sexual intercourse results from a close emotional tie with a girl, there are more possible risks for the male. The risks tend to be psychological and often revolve around the double-standard attitudes which many males continue to hold. Since the male often wants the girl to whom he is committed to be "good," he may redefine her as "bad," if his relationship with her becomes sexual. The male may become bothered by the fear that if *he* could seduce her, then so may others. The degree to which this fear prevails in the mind of the young man contributes to his tendency to define the girl as slipping out of the "good" category. As Reiss suggests, "One finds very often an inverse relation, in that boys prefer to have coitus with girls they do not care for, because they regard the girls they do care for as 'too good' for such behavior."[52] An inherent dilemma exists for many young men in their committed relationship with a girl. Because of the close relationship, they push for greater degrees of intimacy; but if they are successful in pushing the relationship to sexual intercourse, their very success may redefine the relationship and lead to its termination. One study has found that both males and females often misread the sexual expectations of the opposite sex, and both always do so in the direction of increased permissiveness. "Both males and females think that the opposite sex's role perceptions are more permissive than they actually are."[53]

The girl has problems similar to those of the male, only more intensified. Social control over sexual behavior is often directed at the girl in terms of strong punishments if she deviates. Strong external social forces, as well as strong internal psychological forces, ensure the girl's conformity. One fear, which is not too important as a middle-class deterrent, is venereal disease. It is doubtful that many middle-class girls consider this a strong reason for refraining from sexual intercourse. A more important deterrent for the female, though probably not as strong as it used to be, is the fear of pregnancy. One study of college students found fear of pregnancy as a reason for not having premarital coitus stated by only 7 percent of the men and 12 percent of the women.[54] Fear of pregnancy will probably be less of a deterrent in the future as contraceptive devices, particularly effective oral contraceptives, become more reliable and available.

One significant change is that the responsibility for control over premarital pregnancy may rest more and more with the girl. If this be true, it suggests a significant change for those girls who engage in premarital coitus with any regularity; they must be willing to anticipate the act and make the necessary preparations. That females are usually responsible for

---

[52] Ibid., p. 57.

[53] Jack O. Balswick and James A. Anderson, "Role Definition in the Unarranged Date," *Journal of Marriage and the Family,* November 1969, p. 778.

[54] Prince and Shipman, "Attitudes," p. 59.

the contraceptive control is shown by the common usage of the diaphragm and increasingly through the various types of oral contraceptives used by the female. Today, it is relatively simple for a girl to go to a physician and say she is getting married and be fitted with a diaphragm or given a prescription for oral contraceptives.

Personal problems within a demanding social setting are a more important restriction on premarital intercourse for the female. If a girl is discovered as having engaged in premarital intercourse, she may be defined as "bad." Her reputation becomes highly suspect and this may curtail relationships with the type of boys and in the kind of emotional setting of commitment she desires. The social penalties for the girl who is found out continue to be severe in American society. She has been reared in a society that stresses the values of virginity, and to a great extent she internalizes the values so that their violation is often also an internal personality violation. Thus, the girl commonly has a high sense of guilt. Internalized values of chastity are probably the strongest female deterrents to premarital sexual intercourse.

An internalized value that premarital sexual intercourse is wrong, and guilt feelings from its violation, continues to be important for a significant number of American girls. If we assume that some of the other restrictive forces are losing strength, then the moral attitudes of the girl take on increasing significance. It is possible that in the future the moral values restricting girls' premarital sexual expression are going to lose some of their force because the girl will have accepted countervalues such as those of secular and hedonistic satisfaction, a belief in marital sexual satisfaction as a right for women, lesser value attached to premarital virginity by the male, a belief in greater equality of the sexes, together with a decrease in adult control and influence.

The adult world generally continues to regard various types of premarital sexual intimacy as deviant behavior. A result of this perspective is that attention is directed to the risks, particularly for the female, who engages in premarital sexual intimacy. But there may also be "risks" for those who do not experience premarital necking, petting, and coitus. Kinsey wrote that a great deal has been said about "the damage that may be done by premarital sexual activities, and particularly by petting; but relatively little has been said about the psychological disturbances and subsequent marital difficulties which may develop when there is such condemnation and constant belaboring of any type of behavior which has become so nearly universal, and which is likely to remain as universal, as petting is among American females and males."[55] It would appear that in a society changing as rapidly as ours, any single standard may have risks for the individual.

---

[55] Kinsey et al., *Female*, p. 261.

ARGUMENTS

Because of the changing state of premarital sexual mores in the American culture, and because of a number of different attitudinal complexes, what the premarital standard *should be* is a matter of controversy. In many instances, the two sides of the argument are clearly divided into male and female arguments.

Popularity

Both male and female, although most often the female, are concerned with popularity. A reputation of being sexually aggressive may decrease the male's opportunities for dates, particularly with those girls who do not want to spend an evening refining their wrestling techniques. The more important popularity problem is for the girl and is often tied up with her emotional feelings about the boy. She has to decide how far she will go, considering her own, as well as his, needs. The girl who is more emotional than the boy in a relationship finds herself in a vulnerable position. She may feel that if she is not permissive enough, she will lose him; yet if she is too permissive, he may define her in a way that will not lead him to a greater emotional commitment.

The most important danger of sexual permissiveness for the girl would seem to be that she may attain popularity through it—but, from her point of view, for the wrong reasons. Few girls probably want the phone to ring constantly with requests for dates because of a "sexual" reputation. The vast majority value a relationship with a boy for present and future emotional involvements, rather than for the physical sex.

On the other hand, there is a relationship between what one does sexually and the reference groups he identifies with. For example, students who have not engaged in coitus tend to be associated with reference groups which discourage premarital intercourse, "while the reference groups of those who have engaged in coitus tend to encourage intercourse."[56] It was found in one study that while 55 percent of the females with premarital sex experience were a part of peer groups which encouraged intercourse, only 3 percent of those without coitus affiliated with such groups. However, among the males, regardless of their sex experience, they tended to associate with peers who encouraged premarital coitus.[57]

Testing

A frequent rhetorical gambit, almost always presented by the boy, is: *Sexual adjustment is extremely important to overall adjustment and hap-*

---

[56] Alfred M. Mirande, "Reference Group Theory and Adolescent Sexual Behavior," *Journal of Marriage and the Family,* November 1968, p. 574.

[57] Ibid., p. 575.

piness in marriage—therefore, we should find out if we are sexually compatible before we are married. The first part of this argument is true enough. The second part makes the highly questionable assumption that sexual intercourse is psychologically and socially the same before marriage as after. The fact that the individuals are not married usually places the behavior in a different context than it will be in after they are married. For many girls, the role of wife gives the sexual relationship a great deal of its significance and satisfaction; not having that role may take something away from the meaning of a sexual relationship. Also, the setting in which the sexual act occurs will often be different. Sexual relations prior to marriage are often carried out in the back seat of a car, for example, or in the parents' home, in a motel, and so forth. The threat of discovery denies the relaxation and removal of apprehension generally important to satisfactory sexual relations, particularly for the girl. As long as social taboos about premarital intercourse exist and are incorporated into the attitudes of the individual, premarital intercourse will not usually be the same as marital intercourse.

The fallacy of the testing argument is its assumption that the sexual act is entirely physical and that therefore physical compatability can be measured. It ignores the important fact that human sexual relations have a highly important psychological and social context.

"Psychological Warfare"

The male and the female have different concerns with the sexual act. In arguing, the male often uses a "scientific" approach to persuade the female of the importance of their having sexual relations. Several variations of the same basic argument center around the assumption that sexual release is important to mental and physical health. The male may argue that the girl "owes it to herself" to have sexual intercourse, that she can't be a really "mature female" until she gives expression to the sexual facet of her personality, or that she is not being mature when she resists, because a sign of adult maturity is the willingness to develop and pursue all aspects of the personality. These arguments are difficult for the female to answer if she accepts the male's premise that sexual expression *per se* is a sign of social maturity.

Many adults believe the ability to give and receive in sexual relations is a sign of maturity, but in the American culture this ability defines maturity after marriage, not before. Psychological maturity in our culture often refers to the ability to fulfill the rights and obligations that go with adult roles. The female's ability to be mature in sexual expression is still defined as a part of marriage maturity. Once again the male's argument ignores the great importance attached to personal and social factors in defining appropriate physical behavior.

On some occasions the male may argue that "you owe it to me." This

argument also centers on a physical approach to sex. The male emphasizes the great force of the sex drive (especially for himself, since individual males like to think of themselves as being well above average in
sex drive) and how, if it is not satisfied, dire consequences will result for
him. He sometimes goes so far as to suggest that if the girl does not provide him with sexual release, his physical health will be dangerously im-
paired. (There seem to be no records of males hospitalized on this account.) The physiological force of the male's sex drive does frequently
build up to the point where semen release is necessary, but to argue that
only the female can bring about this release is ridiculous. Most males
are provided with a biological mechanism of sexual release, the nocturnal
emission or "wet dream." The vast majority of males also use masturbation as a means of satisfying the sex drive, at least occasionally. The argument is again biological, and implies that sexual intercourse is the only
means of satisfying the sex drive. Actually men can and do achieve sexual
release through a variety of sexual outlets—other than the female—as
will be discussed in Chapter 8.

THE PROFESSIONAL CONTROVERSY

Disagreement on premarital intercourse is not limited to the young
unmarried; it is also found among those who professionally study the
American family. Many academic studies, articles, and books have been
presented on questions of premarital sexual behavior. With few exceptions, writers in the past took a conservative and often moralistic point
of view. It is somewhat disconcerting to read marriage and family texts
in which the writers draw logically upon research material related to areas
of the family—until they get to their chapter on premarital sexual behavior. Then the empirical materials are presented, but they are defined
and interpreted within a moralistic context.

For the person writing as a nonscientist, a moralistic approach is justifiable. But when the person approaching the study of marriage and the
family as a social scientist shifts his frame of reference when he deals
with sexual behavior, he violates a basic tenet of scientific inquiry: objectivity. He may point out how premarital sexual behavior is treated and
perceived within the social context, but for him as a social scientist to be
either for or against it is not justifiable. This writer therefore feels it is
important to point out some areas of controversy which are not scientific
disagreements, but rather disagreements between a moral interpretation
and an objective presentation. The two conflicting interpretations will be
referred to as the *conservative* and the *liberal*. Conservative is here used
to refer to various arguments for the maintenance of traditional sex attitudes because they are believed to be right and proper; liberal, to refer
to the arguments that traditional attitudes are subject to scientific investi-

gation and any discovered social inconsistencies, conflicts, and inadequacies should be critically analyzed.[58]

The Conservative Arguments

Probably very few students of the family would adhere to all of the arguments presented in the professional writings, but they are pointed out because all of them have some advocates.

Some conservatives are so committed to the belief that premarital sexual intimacy is bad that they will exaggerate it in amount and consequences. They seem to believe that the United States is today experiencing a great sexual moral decay. For example, the rabbi and psychiatrist Max Levin writes, "Promiscuity we have always had, but where it used to be, in the main, surreptitious, it now has come into the open." He goes on to state that "the coed today will make no bones about the fact that she is no longer a virgin."[59] There is no evidence presented to support these assertions. The available evidence does suggest that virginity may no longer be viewed in the absolute sense it once was, but there is no evidence that premarital sexual promiscuity has increased over the past 40 years, or that girls take loss of virginity lightly. The statements are exaggerated and verge on the irresponsible.

One conservative belief is that premarital sexual intercourse is almost exclusively a promiscuous and lustful physical relationship, with little or no affection and tenderness.[60] While this is true for many sexual relationships, particularly from the male's standpoint, it is clearly not true for all. Studies of sexual relations between those in love and/or engaged show that the relationships are often emotionally strong and the sexual act is far more than simply physical. The logical fallacy is the projecting of characteristics of some premarital relationships to all.

Another conservative belief is that when a couple have premarital sexual relationships, they become sex-oriented rather than emotionally person-oriented. This argument, like the preceding, fails to see that in many premarital relationships the sexual act is only meaningful within broader emotional relationships. Reiss points out that this conservative view is not supported by empirical evidence. He suggests that in reality the opposite may be true. By abstaining from sexual relations one may think more about sex because it has not been attained.[61]

---

[58] See David R. Mace, "Chastity and Virginity: The Case For," and Rene Guyon, "Chastity and Virginity: The Case Against," in Albert Ellis and Albert Abarbanel, *The Encyclopedia of Sexual Behavior* vol. 1 (New York: Hawthorn Books, Inc., 1961), pp. 247–57.

[59] Max Levin, "The American Sexual Tragedy: A Menace to Health," *Journal of Marriage and the Family,* February 1965, p. 108.

[60] Reiss, *Premarital Standards,* p. 73.

[61] Reiss, *Premarital Standards,* p. 183.

The third conservative argument shifts ground to criticize not the sexual relationship, but the possible consequences. Poffenberger argues that the "breakdown of premarital sex mores has damaged group welfare as evidenced by early marriage, premature parenthood, and early termination of education."[62] A vast body of evidence supports this argument as true in many cases; however, the dangers develop around the problem of pregnancy. This problem may be eliminated to a great extent in the future by the wide use of more effective contraceptives.

Poffenberger further argues that "the basic reason that societies control sex behavior at all levels is not fear of pregnancy but experience with the intensity and uncontrollability of sex and the resultant social disorganization when social sanctions are not imposed."[63] There is no reason to assume that premarital sexual behavior must be restricted or social disorganization will occur. As was pointed out at the start of this chapter, many societies have allowed premarital sexual relations; certainly no one would argue that all were socially disorganized.

A fourth conservative argument is that the need for sexual release during adolescence is overestimated and could be conditioned—at least to a degree. If this argument is used in reference to today's American society, it is sociologically naïve. If anything, the American society continues to develop more and more erotic and sexually stimulating influences to titillate the adolescent. In addition, a vast body of psychiatric and psychoanalytic literature points out the possible dangers of sexual inhibition through social conditioning.

Conservatives also believe that the sex drive can be channelized in the direction of nonsexual gratification. A writer of advice to adolescents states, "Be glad if your sexual drives are powerful enough to torment you. This is the fuel you need to drive your way up the economic jungle to security and success. Instead of an illusory escape from poverty, through squandering it, you can win a permanent access to economic well-being by conserving your sexual power and putting it to work for you."[64] This argument—that the sex drive is transferable to a nonsexual drive—is questionable. Even though the individual, through other involvement, may become less concerned with his sex drive, it continues to exist and, given meaningful personal sex stimulus, will probably come forth. So while the sex drive may be temporarily put aside because of other strong interests, the drive itself is not altered. It generally requires a sexual release and it is very doubtful that in an erotic society nonsexual forces can contain the young person's sex drive.

A final conservative argument is that premarital sexual control must

---

[62] Thomas Poffenberger, "Individual Choice in Adolescent Premarital Sex Behavior," *Marriage and Family Living*, November 1960, p. 300.

[63] Ibid., p. 327.

[64] Shailer U. Lawton, *Sexual Behavior Among Teen-Agers* (New York: Wisdom House, 1964), p. 84.

be exerted or the prime motivation for marriage will be removed. This assumes that individuals get married primarily because marriage provides an opportunity for sexual gratification. The studies which show an increase of premarital intercourse over the past 50 years, over the same time that the marriage rate has been going up, indicate the fallacy of this argument.

The Liberal Arguments

Among professionals who study the family, the number who fall into the liberal category make up a minority. Some of the arguments that this group suggest have been presented—in the form of rebuttal—in the discussion of conservative beliefs.

The first rebuttal to the conservative point of view is that liberals maintain that in many relationships of sexual involvement, there are also deep personal and emotional involvements. This argument is best stated by quoting Kirkendall: "The ability to develop a relationship in which communication is free and honest has much to do with the success a couple has in coping with the stresses and strains that are often the consequences of premarital intercourse. The extent to which motives are mutual in nature and each-other centered, as against self-centered, divergent, and opposing, provide important clues to how intercourse will affect a relationship."[65]

The second liberal argument is that an important value commitment made to young people in the American middle class is that they should be taught to think for themselves and that the responsibility of the adult world is to provide them with the necessary knowledge and insight for solving their own problems.[66] This means young people should think for themselves in *all* areas, including sexual behavior, and probably applies best to the unmarried of early adult years who are reaching social maturity. The argument would probably not apply to the adolescent who does not have the social maturity to make a decision on a matter as complex as premarital intercourse. Those who desire to see young people controlled in their sexual activity must work toward giving the young person ability to make decisions, because the constant face-to-face influence of adults will not always be possible. Kirkendall writes, "I think that when we [adults] have talked frankly and honestly, stated our position clearly, and laid our evidence on the line, we have gone about as far as possible."[67]

---

[65] Lester A. Kirkendall, *Premarital Intercourse and Interpersonal Relationships* (New York: The Julian Press, Inc., 1961), p. 181.

[66] Lester A. Kirkendall, "Reply to Mowrer and Poffenberger," *Marriage and Family Living*, November 1960, p. 331.

[67] Ibid., p. 331.

There is evidence to support the belief that the strongest behavioral limits placed on premarital sexual behavior tend to be internal to individuals, not those externally imposed. This belief suggests that controls are more apt to be on the "basis of what the individual *feels* is right rather than on the basis of what he has been *told* is right."[68] Nixon points out that the new mode of internal control "is difficult to achieve, costly, and dangerous: The individual may make mistakes." However, Nixon goes on to say that the old external method "was difficult to maintain, extremely costly, and far more dangerous."[69] The argument for internal controls implies that the young person's ability to make decisions is recognized by the adult world.

A third argument is in rebuttal to the view that because adults assume they are wise and know what is best for young people, they can therefore create wise prescriptions for the control of young people. The liberal criticism of this is that, in reality, adults have come up with few prescriptions to deal with the changing sex role of the young person. If the present confusion over conflicting premarital sexual attitudes is to be eliminated, adults must, because of their maturity and experience, make a significant contribution. What they have done so far is to react with indignation at and disapproval of adolescent sexual behavior. As a result, adolescents have had to try to provide their own prescriptions.

Finally, the last liberal argument points out social inconsistencies. Many times, the punishment directed at the youngster who deviates from adult norms is excessive. Frequently, adult reaction is determined by the degree to which the sexual deviation is known to the community at large. The girl who has premarital sexual relations is much less condemned, particularly in the middle class, if she does not become pregnant. Pregnancy implies that her deviant behavior will be known to many; therefore, her punishment is great.[70] The excessiveness of the punishment, both psychologically and socially, may have long-range personal implications for the girl. The righteously indignant fail to realize that the punishment is often much more problem-creating than was the deviance.

It is important that the reader try to assess the logical and factual base of these professional disagreements. When he does so, he is prepared to arrive at a personal decision on premarital sexual behavior. One reaction that may have already occurred to you is that, factually and logically, no "right" answers are given in the foregoing presentation. Right and wrong answers are given by those who have a moral or ethical frame of reference. The social scientist can only try to provide information and

---

[68] Robert E. Nixon, "Sex or Guilt," in Henry A. Grunwald, ed., *Sex in America* (New York: Bantam Books, 1964), p. 136.

[69] Ibid., p. 136.

[70] See Clark Vincent, *Unmarried Mothers* (Glencoe, Ill.: The Free Press, 1961), chap. i.

some understanding of the social consequences of a given course of action.

SELECTED BIBLIOGRAPHY

Bell, Robert R. *Premarital Sex in a Changing Society.* Englewood Cliffs, N.J.: Prentice-Hall, Inc., 1966.

Bell, Robert, and Balter, Shelli "Premarital Sexual Experiences of Married Women." *Medical Aspects of Human Sexuality,* November 1973, pp. 110–18.

Bell, Robert R., and Blumberg, Leonard "Courtship Stages and Intimacy Attitudes." *Family Life Coordinator,* March 1960, pp. 60–63.

Christensen, Harold T. "A Cross-Cultural Comparison of Attitudes Toward Marital Infidelity." *International Journal of Comparative Sociology,* September 1962, pp. 124–37.

Christensen, Harold T., and Carpenter, George R. "Timing Patterns in the Development of Sexual Intimacy: An Attitudinal Report on Three Modern Western Societies." *Marriage and Family Living,* February 1962, pp. 30–35.

Hunt, Morton "Sexual Behavior in the 1970s." *Playboy,* November 1973, pp. 74–75.

Mirande, Alfred M. "Reference Group Theory and Adolescent Sexual Behavior." *Journal of Marriage and the Family,* November 1968, pp. 572–77.

Robinson, Ira E., King, Karl, and Balswick, Jack O. "The Premarital Sexual Revolution among College Females." *The Family Coordinator,* April 1972, pp. 189–94.

Simon, William, and Gagnon, John "Psychosexual Development." *Trans-Action,* March 1969, pp. 9–17.

Teevan, James J. "Reference Groups and Premarital Sexual Behavior." *Journal of Marriage and the Family,* May 1972, pp. 283–91.

Chapter 9

Premarital Sexual Behavior

Almost all media of mass communications operate under the assumption that where sex is, public interest will be. Tabloid newspapers, confessional magazines and X-rated movies provide "sex" for the lower social classes; the novel, the Broadway play, art movies, and foreign movies provide it for the more "sophisticated" middle and upper social classes; and *Playboy* mazagine and the Playboy clubs provide it for all classes. "Sex" is a success in the commercial marketplace.

Premarital sexual behavior is an area of human behavior that illustrates the "schizoid" nature of American society. Few will accept attitudes of premarital sexual freedom, but many find the actual behavior stimulating and fascinating. Of course, many adults have an honest concern with an attitude toward sexual behavior which they feel is both immoral and socially destructive. Some also feel that something should be done about the hypocrisy evident in the contrast between attitudes and behavior, though few offer any workable suggestions. But the reaction of a large number is either indifference or a kind of fatalism indicating that the younger generation has gone to seed or that youth must, as ever, "sow its wild oats." Some of the reasons for confused attitudes were discussed in Chapter 7. In this chapter, the discussion will center on what is known about premarital sexual behavior.

THE KINSEY STUDIES

No other study of human behavior in the present century seems to have had as great an impact on the American population as the Kinsey reports.[1] Other studies were made on American sexual behavior before the Kinsey studies,[2] and a number of studies have been made since, but the Kinsey studies stand out from the others for two reasons: (1) the size of the population studied (5,300 white males and 5,940 white females) and (2) the vast range of human sexual behavior investigated.

The first Kinsey study—on the male—was published in 1948,[3] the second—on the female—in 1953.[4] In the decade following publication of the first volume, the name *Kinsey* became a household word, and the studies sold in huge numbers. (It is unlikely that very many of the copies were read through, however; they are very long, highly statistical, and written in a pedantic style.) This strong public interest was due in part to appearance of the books at a time when American society was highly receptive to the scientific and to the sexual. The prestige of science soared very high following World War II, and during the war many barriers to sexual behavior were let down; the more open interest developed and continued into the postwar period.

Many Americans reacted to Kinsey's findings with indignation, and many attempts were made to vilify him, his associates, and their work. Since the first appearance of the Kinsey studies, however, a general, if somewhat uneasy, acceptance of studies of human sexual behavior seems to have developed. Those who have engaged in sexual-behavior research since Kinsey owe him a great debt for establishing the right to do this kind of research.

One recent indication of change in the American public's view of sexual research was the reaction in 1966 to the Masters and Johnson study, *Human Sexual Response.*[5] Four weeks after this study's publication, it made the *New York Times* general best-seller list. The Masters and Johnson book is essentially a medical study of coitus and orgasm. It is based upon 11 years of research involving 694 men and women. The subjects were photographed, observed, measured, and interviewed during and

---

[1] Alfred C. Kinsey, Wardell B. Pomeroy, and Clyde E. Martin, *Sexual Behavior in the Human Male* (Philadelphia: W. B. Saunders Co., 1948); and Alfred C. Kinsey et al., *Sexual Behavior in the Human Female* (Philadelphia: W. S. Saunders Co., 1953).

[2] See K. B. Davis, *Factors in the Sex Life of Twenty-Two Hundred Women* (New York: Harper & Brothers, 1929); G. V. Hamilton, *A Research in Marriage* (New York: Albert & Charles Boni, Inc., 1929); and L. M. Terman, *Psychological Factors in Marital Happiness* (New York: McGraw-Hill Book Co., 1938).

[3] Kinsey, *Male.*

[4] Kinsey, *Female.*

[5] William H. Masters and Virginia E. Johnson, *Human Sexual Response* (Boston: Little, Brown & Co., 1966).

after coitus and masturbation. One news magazine observed that even more remarkable than the book's high sales was the minimal public hostility to it. In a short period after the book's publication, its authors had received about 1,000 letters, "10 percent . . . favorable, 20 percent hostile, and 70 percent pleas for help with sexual problems."[6] This public reaction is very different from that which greeted the work of Kinsey and his associates. The response to Masters' and Johnson's second book, *Human Sexual Inadequacy,* in 1970 was also very favorable.[7]

Techniques of Study

Kinsey and his associates used a combined interview-questionnaire approach in which the interviewer could follow formal questions, but could also elaborate or go back to previous questions if he felt it necessary. Interviewing was done only by the authors so, to a great degree, they were able to control variations that might result from using a number of different interviewers. Responses were recorded in a special shorthand that permitted the interview to proceed with a natural conversational flow. Recognizing the importance of social-group differences in vocabulary, the interviewers also attempted to use a level of language understandable to the interviewees. Checks for internal consistency allowed the interviewer to go back to previous questions to check for inconsistencies and to control honesty of response. Individual interviews lasted between one and one half and two hours.

Professional Criticism

An important scientific control is the critical analysis of a study's methods and interpretations by other professionals. Because of the vast breadth of sexual behavior studied and the overall impact of the results, Kinsey's work was subjected to a very complete professional review.[8] Some of the major academic criticisms are considered here.

Sample. No other aspect of the study has been subjected to greater professional criticism than the nature of the sample used. The Kinsey report was not based on probability sampling—in which each individual

---

[6] *Newsweek,* "Response to 'Response,'" May 23, 1966, p. 94.

[7] William H. Masters and Virginia E. Johnson, *Human Sexual Inadequacy* (Boston: Little, Brown and Co., 1970).

[8] See William C. Cochran, Frederick Mosteller, and John W. Tukey, *Statistical Problems of the Kinsey Report* (Washington, D.C.: The American Statistical Association, 1954); Albert Ellis, *Sex Life of the American Woman and the Kinsey Report* (New York: Greenberg, 1954); Seward Heltner, *Sex Ethics and the Kinsey Reports* (New York: Association Press, 1953); and Jerome Himmelhock and Sylvia F. Fava, *Sexual Behavior in American Society* (New York: W. W. Norton & Co., Inc., 1955).

in the universe that is studied has an equal chance of appearing. Because of the impossible problems of acquiring a random sample, Kinsey and his associates attempted to substitute 100 percent participation of persons in various groups.[9] The assumption was that a group's members could persuade fellow members to volunteer for interviews. Through group pressures, this technique did bring in some interviews that would not otherwise have been obtained. However, the groups that participated were not made up of representative members of American society. The overall criticism of Kinsey's sample is that it is not a study of the American male or female, but rather a study of a population sample biased in the direction of individuals from the Northeast, from urban areas, and who were higher educated, and willing to be interviewed.

Physical Emphasis. Another criticism is that the Kinsey studies have too strong an organic or biological emphasis. The basic unit of sexual outlet used in the studies is the achievement of orgasm, and comparisons between various subdivisions are usually made on the basis of cumulation and frequency of orgasm. Orgasm was used as a measure because of the knowledge of almost all people as to this achievement of sexual release; that is, orgasm was believed to be a more objective measure than any emotional evaluation. Some critics argue that Kinsey's emphasis on the biological tends to rule out the significance of emotional elements. They illustrate their point with the question: Can you quantitatively equate an orgasm involving nothing more than purely physical release with one involving both physical and psychological aspects? The logic of the criticism is reasonable. However, the practical question arises of how one objectively gets at the emotional factors related to various types of sexual release. This is an extremely difficult methodological problem for which no one has come up with a research answer. Lerner points out it became fashionable to say that Kinsey's use of the frequency of sexual outlets "no more makes them moral than the frequency of the common cold makes it healthy—an equating of sex with disease which in turn sheds considerable light on the heritage of Puritan repression."[10]

Recall. Any study in which a human being is the source of information is limited by the human being's accuracy of recall. In general, the further you probe back into the past of an individual, the more questionable becomes his recall. A middle-aged man asked to describe the frequency of some sexual outlet during his adolescence must go back over many years to give the answer; how much he will accurately recall is bound to be limited. It may be relatively easier to recall sexual events than many other events in one's life—they are generally significant and meaningful, and the individual often has reason to remember them—but

[9] Kinsey, *Male*, p. 93.

[10] Max Lerner, *America as a Civilization* (New York: Simon & Schuster, 1957), p. 680.

there is a second problem related to recall. A person may honestly believe he is telling the truth, but in actual fact be distorting it. Over a period of time individuals may reach a point where they persuade themselves that something happened to them that is actually a figment of their imagination. This often occurs in the recall of sexual experience. Males are notorious liars in regard to their sexual behavior. If they tell stories long enough, to themselves or others, they may grow to believe the events actually happened. There are no doubt many middle-aged men who sincerely believe they were sexually active during their long past adolescence, when, in reality, they had very limited sexual experiences. An opposite distortion of recall may operate for some women. Women may conveniently "forget" certain sexual experiences of the past. This suggests that recall has a built-in psychological bias that makes the sexual experiences of men and women seem more different than they are in reality.

In the period following the publication of the Kinsey studies, there were some who contended that the data describing the nature and frequency of certain kinds of sexual behavior would serve to encourage many to try those activities. But in the decades that have passed since publication of the studies, there is no evidence to suggest that their readers have been particularly influenced in their sexual behavior. However, there is some evidence that the studies "have played an important part in the reduction of sexual anxiety and the dissemination of tolerance and understanding."[11]

Almost all professional critics do agree that, even with their limitations, the Kinsey studies are far superior to other sexual studies and certainly superior to "armchair speculation." Scientifically, the hope is that the Kinsey studies will be improved upon in future research and better studies will result. Until that happens, the Kinsey studies provide the most objective information on American sexual behavior available.

PREMARITAL SEXUAL BEHAVIOR

Man has developed a variety of methods for satisfying his sexual needs, and all of them are found among both the unmarried and the married. The physical sexual behavior of the unmarried and married is not different, but the social and psychological interpretations are. For the married population, some forms of sexual outlet are approved, but for the unmarried, no outlets receive complete social approval. Yet the sexual needs of the unmarried individual do not lie dormant until his wedding day; they exist, with some change over time and with wide individual variation, during the unmarried years as well as the married. Even though it is assumed that sexual needs can be ignored, conditioned, or trans-

---

[11] John Madge, *The Origins of Scientific Sociology* (New York: The Free Press of Glencoe, 1963), p. 376.

TABLE 8–1

Accumulative Incidence to Orgasm (percent) Related to Various Sexual Outlets up to the Time of Marriage

	Male	*Female*
Masturbation	94	41
Nocturnal dreams	82	12
Petting	26	37
Coitus	80	27
Homosexual	30	5
Animal contacts	8	—
Total outlet	100	64

Adapted from: Alfred C. Kinsey et al., *Sexual Behavior in the Human Female* (Philadelphia: W. B. Saunders, 1953), p. 520.

ferred, in reality they often find expression. Table 8–1, from the Kinsey studies, provides information on various sexual outlets and frequencies up to the time of marriage.

Masturbation

Masturbation is usually a solitary, conscious form of sex outlet. Because it does not involve a partner, it is less subject to moral condemnation than the paired types of premarital sexual outlet. The highly negative interpretation of masturbation that prevailed in the past has been softened a great deal, especially among the higher educated. No authority today accepts the old belief of great physical danger resulting from masturbation. Many authorities hedge, however, by saying masturbation has no biological dangers unless it is excessive; they then fail to say what *excessive* means or to provide evidence of the dangers. The one problem that continues to exist among adolescents is the feeling of guilt associated with masturbation. Guilt will probably continue to be associated with masturbation. Simon and Gagnon suggest that the very guilt and anxiety gives the sexual experience of masturbation an intensity of feeling that is often attributed to sex itself.[12] They go on to suggest that masturbation for many boys is an extremely positive and gratifying experience. "Such an introduction to sexuality can lead to a capacity for detached sex activity—activity whose only sustaining motive is sexual. This may be the hallmark of male sexuality in our society."[13]

However, many fears and taboos continue to be passed on and accepted by the young, and "folk" beliefs are that masturbation leads to "moral" degeneration, feeble-mindedness, and adult sterility. Children

[12] William Simon and John Gagnon, "Psychosexual Development," *Trans-Action*, March 1969, p. 13.

[13] Ibid., p. 13.

are still being told "old wives' tales" about the alleged effects of masturbation. Many students of human behavior feel that this is bad because it would be better for the child to accept his body as pleasurable rather than reject it as a source of anxiety. "Society has progressed to a point where few parents punish their children for masturbating, but it is noteworthy that fewer still encourage it."[14] Masters and Johnson found that all the adult males they interviewed held to a theoretical concern for the imagined effects of excessive masturbation. In every case, "excessive levels," although not defined specifically, were considered to consist of a higher frequency than did the reported personal patterns.[15] For example, one man with a once-a-month masturbatory history felt once or twice a week to be excessive and that that rate might lead to mental illness. Another subject with a masturbatory history of several times a day thought that five or six times a day was excessive and that that rate might lead to a "case of nerves." There is no accepted medical standard for defining excessive masturbation.[16] Masters and Johnson point out in their recent book that contrary to strong cultural beliefs, "masturbatory practices, regardless of frequency or technique employed, have not been identified historically as an etiological factor in the syndrome of premature ejaculation."[17]

Kinsey found in his sample that by the time of marriage, 41 percent of the females and 94 percent of the males had engaged in masturbation to the point of orgasm.[18] The range of variation in sexual activity is generally greater for the female than for the male. Kinsey found there were some women who had masturbated to orgasm as often as 100 times in a single hour.[19] In the unmarried groups, masturbation is the most common sexual outlet for many: In the female, it accounted for 27 to 85 percent of the total outlet; in the male, 31 to 70 percent.[20]

A recent national study found that a little over nine tenths of the men and six tenths of the women had masturbated at some time in their lives. As compared with the past, girls are far more likely today to start masturbating early in adolescence and boys a little bit earlier.[21] All the evidence indicates that masturbation is much more common among younger women today than it was in the past.

---

[14] James Elias and Paul Gebhard, "Sexuality and Sexual Learning in Childhood," in Anne McCreary Juhasz, *Sexual Development and Behavior* (Homewood, Ill.: Dorsey Press, 1973), p. 4.

[15] Masters and Johnson, *Response*, p. 201.

[16] Ibid., p. 202.

[17] Masters and Johnson, *Inadequacy*, p. 96.

[18] Kinsey, *Female*, p. 520.

[19] Ibid., p. 146.

[20] Ibid., p. 173.

[21] Morton Hunt, "Sexual Behavior in the 1970s," *Playboy*, October and November 1973, p. 202.

Among females, a significant change in the use of masturbation is related to higher educational levels, but this is only slightly indicated as true for men. "The accumulative incidence (masturbation at least once) ranged from about 34 percent among the females who had never gone beyond grade school, and 59 percent of the females of the high-school level, to 63 percent among the females who had gone beyond college into graduate work. Among the males, 89 percent of the grade-school group, 95 percent of the high-school, and 96 percent of the college group, had indulged in masturbation to the point of orgasm on at least one occassion.[22]

It is generally overlooked that while masturbation is a solitary sexual act it often has a symbolic interpersonal dimension. The individual frequently fantasizes about another person and in his mind is having sexual relations with that person. So, in that sense, there may be more interpersonal involvement during masturbation than in marital coitus that takes place with a feeling of indifference by one of the partners.

The increasing frequency of sexual experience, by education, is a pattern found in reference to several types of premarital sexual outlet. The higher educated female is more apt to engage in sexual behavior for several reasons. First, she tends more often than the lower educated female to accept the belief that women are equal to men in the area of sexual right. Second, she is less subject to social control through fear, superstition, and a belief in sin. Third, because she marries later, she has more opportunity to indulge in premarital sexual behavior than the lower educated female. Education is one of the most significant social variables used by Kinsey in the analysis of differential female sexual behavior.[23]

Erotica or Pornography

While this category does not refer to a specific form of sexual outlet it may represent an important influence on the individual's sexual interests and expression. In the United States there is a great deal of exposure to explicit sexual materials in the preadolescent and early adolescent years. Probably half of all boys have some exposure to explicit sexual materials by age 15. Exposure on the part of girls lags behind that of boys by a year or two.[24] It is through their friends that the young encounter pornography. One study found that friends were given as most common source of exposure to pictures of sexual intercourse by 70 percent of the male adolescents and 59 percent of the female adolescents. Other mem-

---

[22] Kinsey, *Female*, p. 148.

[23] Ibid., p. 174.

[24] *The Report of the Commission on Obscenity and Pornography* (New York: Bantam Books, 1970), p. 155.

bers of the family were named by 6 percent of the males and none of the females.[25]

The greatest concern with pornography has been its influence on masturbation. The studies indicate that exposure to sex stimuli increases the frequency of masturbation among minorities of various groups. The increase is principally among individuals with either established masturbatory patterns or established but unavailable sexual partners. "In either case, increased frequencies of masturbation apparently disappear within 48 hours after exposure."[26] The studies also indicate that exposure to erotica has no direct relationship to "moral" character. Available research indicates that exposure to pornography does tend to liberalize attitudes with regard to whether such material is itself harmful or whether it should be restricted.[27] So while pornography is frequently used by the young it does not appear to be associated with any problems inherent to its use.

Whether it be erotica, pornography, or other factors, many people fantasize about sexual matters. The ability to become mentally sexually aroused is related to overall sexual satisfaction. A study of young women who were orgastic and nonorgastic in their premarital coitus showed the ones who were having orgasms to be much more apt to be sexually aroused from phantasizing about sex than the young women who were not having orgasms.

Nocturnal Dreams

Nocturnal dreams, erotic dreams that a person has while asleep, are solitary, uncontrolled sexual behavior. Simple eroticism in a dream is not a sexual outlet; for it to be a sexual outlet, orgasm must accompany the dream. Kinsey found that by the time of marriage, 12 percent of the females and 82 percent of the males had achieved orgasm during a nocturnal dream.[28] The reliability of this 12-percent figure for the female is questionable. If the female was asleep, one wonders how she knew she had an orgasm. After awakening, she may or may not recall an erotic dream, but she has no way of knowing whether or not it was accompanied by orgasm. The male has proof of orgasm—the ejaculated semen. No doubt women do achieve orgasm during nocturnal dreams, but the occurrence cannot be reliably measured.

When nocturnal dreams are related to different levels of education, no differences in frequency are found for women, but a higher frequency

---

[25] Ibid., p. 155.

[26] Ibid., p. 222.

[27] Ibid., p. 255.

[28] Kinsey, *Female*, p. 520.

among the college group is found for men.[29] This is probably due to the higher educated male being more prone to fantasy and, therefore, more easily stimulated by his imagination.

Homosexuality

The use of a partner of the same sex for sexual gratification is very strongly condemned in American society for both sexes under all circumstances. Homosexuality may be considered paired, conscious sexual behavior. In the United States, a trend among some sexual experts is to accept homosexuality as a "natural" form of sexual behavior; the vast majority of the population, however, does not. One of the most significant changes over the past 50 years has been a reassessment of the causes of homosexuality. At one time, the causes were assumed to be biological or organic, but today it is believed that most cases of homosexuality have a complex causal explanation primarily of a psychological and social nature. In recent years, it has also been recognized that homosexuality and heterosexuality are not either/or patterns of sexual behavior. For example, of all those who ever engage in homosexuality only 1 to 3 percent of the females and 3 to 16 percent of the males are exclusively homosexual.[30]

Kinsey found that at the time of marriage about 5 percent of the females and 30 percent of the males had engaged in homosexuality to the point of achieving orgasm.[31] Of those who engaged in homosexuality, 71 percent of the females had been involved with one or two partners while 51 percent of the males had one or two partners.[32] At the other extreme, only 4 percent of the women with homosexual experience, compared to 22 percent of the men, had been involved with ten or more partners.[33] The homosexual male tends to be much more promiscuous than the homosexual female, which indicates that the notion of love and exclusiveness of the partner is more important for the female than the male, whether her partner be a man or another woman.

Homosexuality among women increased slightly by level of education. The figures for females who ever had homosexual relationships to the point of orgasm were: grade school, 6 percent; high school, 5 percent; college, 10 percent. For the males, a slightly lower rate was found at the lower level of education: grade school, 27 percent; high school, 39 percent; and college, 34 percent.[34] The figures on homosexuality, by sex, go

---

[29] Ibid., p. 215.
[30] Ibid., p. 488.
[31] Ibid., p. 520.
[32] Ibid., p. 488.
[33] Ibid., p. 488.
[34] Ibid., p. 488.

counter to another popular myth that homosexuality is more frequent among women. The Kinsey figures clearly indicate that the male is much more prone to homosexuality than the female, which, to a great extent, is a result of the greater sexual interests and less restrictive sexual forces that operate on the male in the American society.

Premarital Petting

Petting is paired, conscious behavior that may be defined as physical contact which involves a deliberate attempt to effect erotic arousal.[35] In marital and premarital coitus, some degree of petting as a means to the end of sexual intercourse is usual; however, in petting, the "foreplay" becomes the sexual end. This form of premarital sexual outlet often allows the girl to achieve orgasm in the boy-girl relationship, and still remain a virgin. Kinsey provides information on the sexual experiences of the virgin at the time of marriage. For those females born after 1910, with between 13 and 16 years of education, 100 percent had been kissed, 70 percent had experienced manual stimulation of the breast, and 30 percent oral stimulation. Thirty-three percent had their genitalia manually stimulated, and 22 percent had manually stimulated the male genitalia.[36] Between one quarter and one third of these virgins may be considered highly experienced "technical virgins."

As the adolescent of both sexes became older, petting experience increased sharply: For the female, the percentage rose from 3 by age 15 to 81 by age 18; for the male, from 57 by age 15 to 84 by age 18. By the time the female reached age 20, about 23 percent had achieved orgasm while petting; the figure for the male of the same age was 32 percent. One important difference between the female and the male from the ages of 16 to 25 is that petting accounted for 18 percent of the girls', but only 3 percent of the boys' orgasms.[37]

Whether the boy or girl reached puberty early or late was found to have some relationship to premarital petting experience. Those girls who had reached adolescence at earlier ages (by 11 or 12) were the first to start petting and petting to the point of orgasm.[38] However, Kinsey points out that there was a sharp contrast between the ages at which females and males started their petting experience. "In most instances the male's activity begins quite promptly with or immediately after the onset of adolescence. In the median female, on the other hand, petting did not begin until 15 or 16 years of age, which is three or four years after the average female turns adolescent."[39]

---

[35] Ibid., p. 228.
[36] Ibid., pp. 280–81.
[37] Ibid., p. 267.
[38] Ibid., p. 246.
[39] Ibid., p. 246.

In premarital petting, as in all areas of sexual behavior, the male is sexually more promiscuous than the female. Of the females who had engaged in premarital petting, 42 percent were involved with 5 or fewer partners and 19 percent with 21 or more partners. Of the males, 26 percent had 5 or fewer partners and 37 percent had 21 or more partners.[40] The Kinsey data indicated that about one quarter of the women had ever petted to orgasm by the time they reached age 25. But recent studies show much higher rates. The national study by Morton Hunt found in that sample that more than two thirds of the women had reached orgasm through petting in the year prior to the study.[41] This would indicate that petting is more intense, involved, and sexually fulfilling than was true in the past.

Almost exactly the same percentage of the females at each educational level had engaged in petting to the point of orgasm before marriage,[42] while the percentage of males was highest in the high-school educated group.[43] One reason for the higher educated male having greater experience with petting is that petting is probably more accepted by the higher than the lower educated females. The female usually determines the limits of intimacy, and, for many, petting is accepted in at least some relationships.

In most areas of female sexual behavior, there were significant differences among the Kinsey respondents by intensity of religion, with the more religious being the more restricted in behavior. But religious codes seem to have had little influence on the frequencies of petting to orgasm, even among the most devout females in the sample. "It is particularly significant to find that the devout female, after she has once achieved orgasm in a petting relationship, engages in such activity about as often as the average of the less devout female."[44]

Premarital Coitus

Because it sharply indicated the disparity between norms and behavior, no figure in either of the Kinsey reports was more shocking and upsetting to the American population than that which showed about 50 percent of all the women studied had had premarital coitus. This lack of virginity was viewed by many as categorically the same for all 50 percent, ignoring the variations in number of partners or the frequency of the sexual act. Kinsey pointed out that "a considerable proportion of the female premarital coitus had been in the year or two immediately preceding marriage, with a portion of it confined to the fiancé in a period just before

---

[40] Ibid., p. 683.
[41] Hunt, "Sexual Behavior in 70s," p. 74.
[42] Kinsey, *Female,* p. 239.
[43] Ibid., p. 267.
[44] Ibid., pp. 248–49.

marriage."[45] An important difference in the premarital sexual relations of the female and male continues; a modified double standard still exists. The important distinction between the unmarried male and female, at least for some groups, is no longer the virgin-nonvirgin double standard, but rather a double standard in which nonvirginity is found for both sexes, with the male often sexually promiscuous and the female generally restricted in number of sexual partners.

The variable of education is extremely important to the analysis of premarital coitus. It is important because there is an inverse relationship, by education, between male and female frequency of premarital coitus. By educational level, the percentages for the female are: grade school, 30; high school, 47; and college, 60.[46] The percentages for the male are: grade school, 98; high school, 85; and college, 68.[47] Frequency of premarital coitus for the girl goes up by education because of later age of marriage, more petting, and a less rigid notion as to the importance of virginity. The figures by education go down for the boy because of less coital opportunity and the use of other sexual outlets.

The higher educated girl makes a less rigid distinction between virginity and nonvirginity. One important difference between high- and low-educated females is that while fewer low-educated girls have premarital coitus, those that do have a higher rate of promiscuity. For example, premarital coitus accounted for 38 percent of the grade-school educated females' active sexual experience, but only 18 percent of the college girls'."[48] If we assume that the male to female ratio is roughly equal at the different educational levels, it would mean that, in the grade-school group, there is one girl having premarital coitus for every three boys, while in the college group, the ratio is about one girl for every one boy. While a number of boys, particularly in the lower classes, have their premarital coitus with prostitutes, it must also be remembered that a number of the higher educated boys have their sexual experiences with girls in lower social classes. When girls at all education levels are compared, the college-educated girls are least apt to be virgins at the time of marriage. However, when all girls who have ever had premarital coitus are compared, the "indulging" lower educated girls are the most promiscuous.

Elder has found some relationship between premarital sexual experience and social mobility on the part of young women. He found that coitus during their high school years was much less frequently reported by mobile than by nonmobile women from the working class (10 versus

---

[45] Ibid., p. 286.
[46] Ibid., p. 293.
[47] Ibid., p. 330.
[48] Ibid., p. 331.

70 percent). "The social risks associated with sexual experience, especially a damaged reputation, undoubtedly contributed to this negative relationship between degree of coitus and marriage mobility."[49]

The age factor also becomes important in understanding the higher probability of college-educated females having premarital coitus. Many of them have their sexual experiences at an age when the lower educated girl is already married. Of those girls who had premarital sexual experience, 18 percent of the grade-school group were having premarital coitus by age 15, as compared with 1 percent of the college-educated girls, and, respectively, between the ages of 16 and 20, 38 percent as compared with 18 percent. After age 20, the figures are about the same for all educational levels.[50] That 81 percent of the college-educated females who have premarital coitus have it past the age of 20, suggests premarital coitus is not usually an event of their adolescence, but rather of their young adult years.

Even if a number of girls are not effectively stopped from engaging in premarital coitus by the social attitudes, do they suffer any aftereffects from violating the norms? Moralists direct their indignation at those who violate the norms but do not seem to suffer remorse, and while many Americans are happy to take the errant back into the flock if they will say they are sorry and were wrong, they can become very vituperative toward those who violate the norms and are not penitent.

Kinsey found that "69 percent of the still unmarried females in the sample who had had premarital coitus insisted they did not regret their experience. Another 13 percent recorded some minor regrets."[51] It may be argued that those girls who say they do not regret premarital coitus are rationalizing their behavior. Undoubtedly, many girls say they have no regrets because they feel they must justify their behavior to themselves and, in some cases, to others. However, the degree of rationalization is probably less than many people believe. Kinsey found that an even "larger proportion, some 77 percent of the married females, looking back from the vantage point of their more mature experience, saw no reason to regret their premarital coitus. Another 12 percent of the married females had some minor regret."[52]

One very sharp difference between those unmarried females who did have premarital sexual relations and those who did not is found in their stated intent for the future. Among the unmarried females in the Kinsey study who had never had premarital coitus, 80 percent said that they did *not* intend to before marriage; in contrast, among those who had had

[49] Glen H. Elder, Jr., "Appearance and Education in Marriage Mobility," *American Sociological Review*, August 1969, p. 527.

[50] Ibid., p. 295.

[51] Ibid., p. 316.

[52] Ibid., p. 316.

such experience, only 30 percent said they did not intend to have more.[53]

As previously suggested, one of the strongest arguments made against premarital coitus in the United States centers on the danger of pregnancy. However, in Chapter 7 several studies were cited which indicated that fear of pregnancy was not a common reason given by young women for not engaging in premarital coitus. From the behavioral perspective, an important question is—To what extent does premarital pregnancy occur and what are some of its consequences? Obviously there is no way of knowing exactly how many conceptions occur among unmarried women (we will discuss premarital pregnancies that result in illegitimate births in Chapter 9), but examination of a variety of studies suggests that somewhere between 10 to 25 percent of all brides are pregnant at the time of their marriage.[54] When premarital pregnancy occurs, the engagement period is generally shortened. One study of premarital pregnancy found that for those girls who were not pregnant at marriage, the mean length of engagement was 12 months, but for those premaritally pregnant, the mean length of engagement was 7 months.[55]

Premarital pregnancy is often presented in the mass media as a problem most common among young and immature girls. Given the frequency of premarital pregnancy, what can be said sociologically about it? This: The evidence clearly indicates that even when girls have premarital coitus their chances of pregnancy are not nearly as great when they are in early adolescence as they will be during late adolescence or in the early adult years. This "adolescent sterility" means that coitus is less likely to result in pregnancy in the postpubescent girl than in the mature woman; the average age for full reproductive maturity in women has been estimated at about 23 years.[56] The reason for such relative sterility among girls appears to be that "the number of menstrual periods in which an egg is *not* released from the ovary is much higher among young adolescent females than in older females."[57]

The probability of pregnancy among unmarried girls having coitus is related *both* to "relative sterility" and to age at marriage. For example, if a girl starts having coitus during early adolescence and continues for a number of years without marriage she would have a relatively high probability of premarital pregnancy. The Kinsey data shows that for those girls who had premarital coitus before age 15, only 6 percent be-

---

[53] Ibid., p. 314.

[54] See Paul H. Gebhard et al., *Pregnancy, Birth and Abortion* (New York: Harper & Brothers, 1958), pp. 35–42.

[55] Samuel H. Lowrie, "Early Marriage: Premarital Pregnancy and Associated Factors," *Journal of Marriage and the Family,* February 1965, p. 52.

[56] Clellan S. Ford and Frank A. Beach, *Patterns of Sexual Behavior* (New York: Harper & Row, 1952), p. 72.

[57] Gebhard et al., *Pregnancy, Birth, Abortion,* p. 32.

came pregnant. For those with premarital coitus by age 20, the pregnancy rate was 13 percent, and by age 30 it was up to 21 percent.[58] The point is that with increased age the sexually active unmarried girl's fertility potential increases *and* she has more years in which premarital pregnancy can occur.

A double-standard society directs most sexual restrictions at the female. When social controls on the female begin to lose some of their force, the change in behavior may become cumulative as the deviant behavior further weakens the norms. This would certainly seem to be the pattern for a number of American females for whom the norms no longer have the strength to function as a deterrent or to punish through guilt feelings. Women are becoming more realistic and are much less dependent upon traditional moral reasons for becoming involved in coitus. Many young women feel their coital activity is a natural outgrowth of their sexual relationships with men and should be expected. "There is evidence that women who see sex as a natural part of themselves are more likely to reach orgasm."[59] It is not being suggested that the female has an indiscriminate sex orientation. Rather, many young women no longer consider the line between chastity and nonchastity as absolute, but as a matter of degree. For the majority of young females, love or affection must exist before they enter premarital sex relations.

MALE-FEMALE DIFFERENCES IN PREMARITAL SEXUAL BEHAVIOR

The boy-girl interactional patterns prior to marriage are often characterized by different motivations. The male role, as defined by both sexes, is to be the aggressor in areas of sexual activity; the female role is to determine the extent of sexual intimacy. The assumption made by both sexes is that the male will press for more intimate levels of intimacy unless he is stopped by the female.

There are some general sexual differences between males and females that appear common to most societies. For example, in most societies—as in the United States—men usually start sexual activity at younger ages and participate with greater frequency than women. Men also appear to be somewhat more responsive to psychological and symbolic stimuli associated with sex; however, this difference may be becoming of decreasing significance in the United States. In most societies, men and women do not appear to differ in the initiative taken for starting sexual activity or in speed of achieving orgasm.

---

[58] Ibid., p. 39.

[59] David F. Shope, "Sexual Responsiveness in Single Girls," in James M. Henslin, *Studies in the Sociology of Sex* (New York: Appleton-Century-Crofts, 1971), p. 33.

TABLE 8–2

Percent at Dating Relationship and Erotic Intimacy Level at which Offense Occurred, by Episodes

Date Relationship	Necking and Petting above the Waist	Petting below the Waist	Attempted Intercourse and Attempted Intercourse with Violence	Total
First date	30	16	14	26
Occasional date	31	27	26	30
Regular date, "pinned," and engaged	39	57	60	44
Total	100	100	100	100

Adapted from: Eugene J. Kanin, "Male Aggression in Dating-Courtship Relationships," *American Journal of Sociology*, September 1957, p. 200.

Possibly, females are increasingly the initiators of sexual intimacy. The role of the male as aggressor is probably still dominant today, but is not as rigidly limited to him as it once was. The male is probably the main aggressor in dating relationships, but as the level of interpersonal commitment increases, the female may play a more significant part in sexual initiation.

A study by Kirkpatrick and Kanin among college students shows strong male sexual aggression as quite common. They found that of 291 responding girls, 56 percent reported having been offended at least once during the prior academic year at some level of sexual intimacy. "The experiences of being offended were not altogether associated with trivial situations, as shown by the fact that 21 percent were offended by forceful attempts at intercourse and 6 percent by aggressively forceful attempts at sexual intercourse in the course of which menacing threats or coercive infliction of physical pain were employed."[60]

The girls' feelings that the boy was excessively aggressive were not limited to the dating experience. Table 8–2 shows that offensiveness occurred as follows: first date, 26 percent; occasional date, 30 percent; and regular date, pinned, and engaged, 44 percent.[61] In dating, the girl often defines aggressive behavior by the boy as abrupt and unanticipated. On first-date occasions, 50 percent of the girls said there had been no prior sex play when the male aggression occurred. For the regular date, pinned, and engaged, 63 percent of the girls reported some prior sex play before the aggression occurred.[62] For all the offended girls, ignoring

[60] Clifford Kirkpatrick and Eugene J. Kanin, "Male Sex Aggression on a University Campus," *American Sociological Review*, February 1957, p. 53.

[61] Eugene J. Kanin, "Male Aggression in Dating-Courtship Relationships," *American Journal of Sociology*, September 1957, p. 200.

[62] Ibid., p. 202.

the dating-courtship level, the maximum number of erotic intimacy offenses defined as aggressive on at least one occasion was: necking and petting above the waist, 67 percent; petting below the waist, 14 percent; and attempted intercourse, both with and without violence, 30 percent.[63]

The emotional reactions of the girls to aggression varied: Almost half reacted with anger, about one fifth with guilt, and one fifth with fear.[64] The reactions of the girls on how to deal with the problem varied: Thirty-one percent ended the relationship; 23 percent kept it secret; 30 percent used discussion and warning; and 16 percent made an appeal to parents and other authorities.[65]

These findings indicate the nature of the male-female sex struggle. As long as the boy is the physical aggressor, he is not always going to allow the girl to stop the relationship when she chooses. A common belief among many young men is that a girl often says "no" when she really means "yes," that she must make some pretense of resisting intimacy as a kind of face-saving device. Sometimes a boy feels he can keep being aggressive until the girl really means "no." Different reactions to aggression come because some girls say "no" and mean it, while others says "no" and really mean "go ahead." The girl who says "no" at one level and then allows the boy to go ahead may be in for trouble at the next level when she says "no" and really wants him to stop.

PREMARITAL SEXUAL BEHAVIOR SINCE THE MID-1960s

There are several general points that may be summarized from the various premarital sex studies made during the period up to the mid-1960s. First, while the major studies dealt with quite different samples the findings were in high agreement. In general the studies showed that of those women born after 1900 about half of them were not virgins when they married. And there was no evidence to suggest that when women born after 1900 were compared by decades of birth, there were any significant differences in their rates of premarital coitus. Second, the studies indicated that being nonvirgin at the time of marriage was not an indication of extensive premarital experience with a variety of partners. For the female, premarital coitus usually depended on strong emotional commitments and plans for marriage. Third, if the assumption of a temporary stabilization of premarital sexual coitus was true in the United States, it meant that young people had been engaging in essentially the same types of behavior for three or four decades. It is suggested that these general patterns have been undergoing change in recent years.

---

[63] Ibid., p. 198.

[64] Kirkpatrick and Kanin, "Male Sex Aggression," p. 56.

[65] Kanin, "Dating-Courtship," p. 203.

It is argued that there has been a change in the sexual experiences of unmarried college girls since the mid-1960s.[66] In recent years, even more than ever, the group primarily responsible for rebellion among the young has been the college students. While there has always been rebellion by the younger generation toward their elders, it probably never has been as great in the United States as it has been since the mid-1960s. In recent years youths have not only rebelled, but have also rejected many aspects of the major institutions in American society. The mid-1960s have produced an action generation and their *modus vivendi* has been to experience, to confront, to participate, and sometimes to destroy. Since the mid-1960s a small but highly influencial proportion of college students was deeply involved in the civil rights movement and in the protest over the Vietnam War. What may be most important about that generation of college students was that many were not just alienated as others have been in the past, but they were *actively* alienated.

Many college students believed that many of the norms of adult institutions were not only wrong but were also immoral. That view has been held by many college students toward the treatment of the black, toward the war in Vietnam, toward American political scandals, and so forth. It therefore seems logical that if many of the norms of those institutions are viewed as wrong and immoral by large numbers of the younger generation, they are also going to be suspicious and critical of other norms in various adult controlled institutions. Certainly a social institution that one would expect the younger generation to view with skepticism would be that concerned with marriage and sexual behavior. There are several other social factors that appear to be related to change in premarital sexual experiences.

One important factor of the 1960s was the development, distribution, and general acceptance of the birth control pill. On many large university campuses the pill is available to the coed or it is not difficult for her to find out where to get it in the local community. While studies show that fear of pregnancy has not been a very important deterrent to premarital coitus for a number of years, it now seems to have been largely removed for most college girls. Another influence since the mid-1960s was the legitimization of sexual candor. In part, the new sexual candor has been legitimized by one of the most venerable of American institutions—the Supreme Court. In recent years the young person has had access to a level of sexual expression far greater than just ten years ago. The new sexual candor, whatever its original cause, is often seen by the rebelling younger generation as "theirs" in that it, too, critically subverts the traditional institutions. As a result, the sexual candor of the

---

[66] Robert R. Bell and Jay B. Chaskes, "Premarital Sexual Experience among Coeds, 1958 and 1968," *Journal of Marriage and the Family*, February 1970, pp. 81–84.

late 1960s was often both a manifesto and a guidebook for many in the younger generation.

Finally, it should also be recognized that the rebellion of the younger generation has been given both implicit and explicit approval by many in the older generation. Many adults like to think of themselves as a part of the younger generation and its youth culture. For example, this is seen in the music and fashion of the youth culture which has had a tremendous impact on adults. It would seem that if many adults take on the values of the youth culture, that would raise questions as to the significance of many of their adult values for the youth culture. In other words, the very identification of many adults with youth culture contributes to adult values having less impact on college youths.

There is some evidence that more radical life styles are related to more permissive sexual behavior. A sample of 2,372 married women were asked about premarital sexual behavior. One measurement of more radical life styles is how they defined themselves politically. For those women who defined themselves as politically conservative, 49 percent had premarital coitus; politically moderate, 57 percent; politically liberal, 71 percent; and, politically radical, 91 percent.[67]

Reiss has suggested that in the past the groups that developed a tradition of sexual permissiveness were often groups that had the least to lose. "Men and Negroes would be examples, for men cannot get pregnant and Negroes have less social standing to lose."[68] But he goes on to say that the present movement toward permissiveness among many is based differently than it used to be. This may be occurring within a context of general liberality. "It may be that liberalism emphasizes the types of social forces that maintain high permissiveness, for example, low religious orthodoxy, low value on tradition, high value on autonomy. The stronger the amount of general liberality in a group, the greater the likelihood that social forces will maintain high levels of sexual permissiveness."[69] Reiss's statement very clearly describes the type of college student considered here. It is being argued that the social forces developed since the mid-1960s have led to a rapid increase in rejecting many traditional values and have developed important patterns of behavior common to a general youth culture. And out of this has come an increased rate of premarital coitus among many college girls along with less feelings of guilt about their experiences.

It must be stressed that the change in premarital sexual behavior being suggested is far from total. Rather, the contention is that a degree of

---

[67] Robert R. Bell and Shelli Balter, "Premarital Sexual Experiences of Married Women," *Medical Aspects of Human Sexuality*, November 1973, p. 114.

[68] Ira L. Reiss, *The Social Context of Premarital Sexual Permissiveness* (New York: Holt, Rinehart and Winston, Inc., 1967), p. 54.

[69] Ibid., p. 73.

change has occurred, and that minority has increased in size and significance. But what may be most important is that there is a trend, where one did not exist before. The nature and the degree of change can be examined in several different areas. One possible indication of change is to look at the rates of virginity found in several recent populations that have been studied. During the period from 1945 to 1965 the various studies showed coital rates among coeds of all ages and class standings to be about 25 to 30 percent. This percentage refers to the estimated rate at a given point in time if a sample of college girls could be drawn. Obviously, the rates were much higher among college educated when they married because in many cases several years elapsed from the time they would have been studied until when they married. A study done by Kaats and Davis in the spring of 1967 reported a coital rate of 41 percent for the females studied. However, those females were all 19- and 20-year-old sophomores.[70] Therefore, if the rate was projected to the total coed population in that school it was probably well over 50 percent.

The writer had done a study of premarital sexual behavior among a sample of coeds in a large urban university in 1958.[71] In 1968, the same questionnaire was used with a sample of coeds in the same university. A careful effort was made to match the two samples by age and by class standings. In those studied, the rates of coitus were determined for the different levels of the dating relationship. The coeds were asked about the highest level of intimacy ever engaged in while dating, going steady, and engaged. The number of girls having premarital coitus while in a dating relationship went from 10 percent in 1958 to 23 percent in 1968. The rates of premarital intercourse while going steady went from 15 percent in 1958 to 28 percent in 1968. And the coitus rates during engagement went from 31 percent in 1958 to 39 percent in 1968. "Further examination of the data suggests that in 1958 the relationship of engagement was very often the prerequisite to a girl having premarital sexual intercourse. Engagement often provided her with a high level of emotional and future commitment which she often felt justified having coitus. However, in 1968 it appeared that the need to be engaged and all it implied was much less a condition the coed thought necessary before sexual intercourse. Therefore, the data suggests that the decision to have intercourse in 1968 was much less dependent on the commitment of engagement and more a question of individual decision regardless of the level of the relationship. To put it another way, if, in 1958, the coed had premarital coitus, it most often occurred while she was engaged. But in 1968, girls were more apt to have their first sexual experience while dating or going steady."[72]

---

[70] Gilbert R. Kaats and Keith Davis, "The Dynamics of Sexual Behavior of College Students," mimeographed (University of Colorado, 1968), p. 1.

[71] Bell and Chaskes, "Experience among Coeds," pp. 81–84.

[72] Ibid., pp. 82–83.

Christensen and Gregg have also found evidence of changing rates of premarital coital experience over the same period from 1958 to 1968. In their samples on a midwestern campus and on a Mormon campus (which they refer to as "intermountain") they found no significant change for males over the ten-year period. However, there were changes for the coeds. At the intermountain college the coeds with premarital coital experience in 1958 made up 10 percent of the population studied, but by 1968 the rate was up to 32 percent. The rate was in 1968 almost the same for the males, 37 percent.[73] At the midwestern campus the rates of premarital coitus went from 21 percent in 1958 to 34 percent in 1968. The rates for the males at that school was about 50 percent both in 1958 and in 1968.[74]

There is other evidence of increasing rates of premarital coitus. By comparing respondents by age at the present time it is possible to get rates over time. The older the respondents, the earlier the time period they represent in premarital coitus rates. Hunt did not find much difference for men: For those under age 25, 95 percent had premarital coitus, and the rate for men 55 years of age and older had been 84 percent. But for women, 81 percent under age 25, but only 31 percent 55 years of age and older, had had premarital coitus.[75]

One study of a nationwide sample found that the average age of first coitus of white women was 18.6 years.[76] The same median age of 18.5 years was found by Bell and Balter in their study of 2,372 married women. That study indicates that the average age has been lowered over the years. For those women past age 50 who had premarital coitus, the average age of first experience was 19.2 years, as compared to an average age of 17.3 years for those women 25 years of age and younger.[77]

There is also some evidence that younger women are having premarital coitus with more different partners. Bell and Balter found that 50 percent of the women with premarital coitus experience had one partner, 36 percent had two to five partners, and 13 percent had six or more partners.[78] Generally the younger the woman the more different premarital sex partners she has had. There is also evidence that those having permarital coitus are doing so more often today than was true in the past. For single women age 16 to 20 Kinsey found their rate of coitus was once every three weeks, but for the same age group Hunt

---

[73] Harold T. Christensen and Christina F. Gregg, "Changing Sex Norms in America and Scandinavia," *Journal of Marriage and the Family*, November 1970, p. 621.

[74] Ibid., p. 621.

[75] Hunt, "Sexual Behavior in 70s," p. 74.

[76] Gary Merritt et al., "Association Between Age at First Coitus and Choice of Method of Contraception: An Analysis of Covariance," mimeographed, August 1973.

[77] Bell and Balter, "Premarital Experiences," p. 112.

[78] Ibid., p. 114.

found a rate of more than once a week.[79] The Bell and Balter study also found evidence of greater frequency for younger women. "Of the women 25 years of age and younger 72 percent had premarital coitus nine or more times with each partner, but this was true of only 14 percent of the women respondents past the age of 50."[80]

There is also evidence that younger women are getting greater satisfaction from premarital coitus as measured by their orgasm rates. Kinsey, found that about half of the young women having premarital coitus were having orgasms. The Hunt study found three quarters of the single women were having orgasms. "The median frequency of more than one coital orgasm every two weeks is three times higher than in the Kinsey sample."[81] The Bell and Balter study found that 74 percent of the women 25 and younger had some orgasm in their premarital coitus. This is compared to only 39 percent of the women past 50 years of age.[82]

The achievement of orgasm in premarital sex has been related to several different variables. One study found that when orgastic women were compared with those not achieving orgasm in their coitus they were more apt to like men in general and have a good adjustment with them. "The orgastic girls in this study were significantly more likely to see both their sex drives and their desire for coitus as about equal to their mates'; whereas, the nonorgastic subjects were more likely to feel that their mates' sex drives were much stronger than theirs."[83]

Nowhere in the research literature on premarital sexual behavior has there been any information as to participation in certain types of sexual expression. That is, studies have asked about necking, various types of petting, and coitus but not about oral-genital contact. Yet, the Kinsey study showed that oral-genital sexual experience was common to many married couples and that that area of sexual expression has gained increasing acceptance in recent years, (although it is almost completely ignored in the research literature about the means for sexual fulfillment, even among the married). Hunt found that more than 80 percent of the single men and women between the ages of 25 and 34 "had practiced cunnilingus or fellatio, or both, in the past year."[84] A study in a large Southern university in 1970 found a high frequency of oral-genital sex: Sixty-six percent of the males and 54 percent of the females had engaged in that activity.[85] It is suggested that oral-genital sexual experiences had

[79] Hunt, "Sexual Behavior in 70s," p. 75.

[80] Bell and Balter, "Premarital Experiences," p. 112.

[81] Hunt, "Sexeual Behavior in 70s," p. 75.

[82] Bell and Balter, "Premarital Experiences," p. 116.

[83] Shope, "Single Girls," p. 38.

[84] Hunt, "Sexual Behavior in 70s," p. 88.

[85] Ira E. Robinson, Karl King, and Jack O. Balswick, "The Premarital Sexual Revolution among College Females," *The Family Coordinator*, April 1972, p. 191.

contributed to the wider repertoire of sexual behavior for college students and that not only do they often participate more in coitus but also in these activities. If this is true, it would make them even more sexually experienced than just what the findings on coital experience would indicate.

The recent studies contribute to the general observation that engagement is less important as the stage for justifying premarital coitus than it was in the past. As previously mentioned, the studies in the past have consistently shown that for the coed who had premarital coitus it was usually limited to one partner and then only during engagement. However, in the Bell and Chaskes study, when all girls in the 1968 sample who were ever engaged and who had ever had premarital coitus were analyzed, it was found that only 19 percent had limited their coital experience just to the period of engagement. "Expressing it another way, of all girls who were ever engaged and ever had premarital coital experience, 75 percent had their first experience while dating, 6 percent while going steady, and 19 percent during engagement. For all coeds with premarital coital sexual experience at each stage, 60 percent had coitus while dating, going steady, and engagement."[86]

Closely related to the past condition of engagement before a coed had premarital coitus was the condition of love. It seems clear that this condition has changed and, while coeds do not usually have coitus with males they know only in a casual way, they no longer demand that there be a strong emotional commitment on the part of both. It may also be that the younger generation defined love in a less complex and overwhelming way than it was defined in the past. While many of them say love is important, what they mean by love may be quite different from the past.

When a couple are in love there is some evidence that the love is more likely to remain unchanged or heightened rather than decrease after first premarital coitus. The intensification of love after first coitus most often occurs for those who see themselves as very much in love. Those who state high love are the ones who have the strongest desire for coitus with their love partner. "Clearly, from the subjective point of view, it appears that not only is love compatible with sex but that it tends to be more compatible for those most in love, *both* for males and females."[87]

As earlier indicated, historically in the United States religion has been the force defining appropriate sexual behavior. However, the influence of religious beliefs on premarital sexual activity has steadily been decreasing. In the Bell and Chaskes study it was found that both in 1958 and

---

[86] Bell and Chaskes, "Experience among Coeds," p. 84.

[87] Eugene J. Kanin and Karen R. Davidson, "Some Evidence on the Aim-Inhibition Hypothesis of Love," *The Sociological Quarterly*, Spring 1972, p. 214.

1968 the rates of coitus among coeds was lowest for the Catholics, next for the Jews, and the highest for the Protestants. But what is of particular interest is that the rates went up proportionately about the same for all three religious groups over the ten-year period.[88]

Whatever measurements are used as to religious intensity, regardless of the denomination, they appear to show higher rates of virginity among the more devout. For example, just taking the type of educational institution coeds attended, Packard found that of the coeds in public institutions 49 percent were not virgins and this was true of 42 percent in private institutions but only 12 percent of church-related colleges.[89] There is a strong selection process taking place with the most conservative girls going to the most conservative colleges. Another measurement of religious intensity is that of religious attendance. In the 1970 study by the writer it was found that 67 percent of the nonvirgins had not attended any religious ceremony during the past month, while nonattendance was true of 51 percent of the virgins.

When one examines the various social variables related to present rates of premarital coitus, some of the old and reliable variables are no longer the absolute indicators they once were. For example, it used to be found in whatever group one studied that the rates of premarital coitus for the male would be higher than for the female. Yet when different types of college populations today are compared, the distinction doesn't hold up. Packard writes that at 6 of the 19 schools attended by males, "*fewer* than 50 percent of the males reported that they had ever experienced coitus. And at 6 of 19 schools attended by females, *more than* 50 percent of the females responded that they had at some time experienced coitus.[90] Packard goes on to point out that for the girls the lowest rates of coitus were reported at a Catholic university where less than one fifth reported coital experience. "The highest reported incidence for females was at the eastern women's college with liberal rules, where more than three quarters of them reported coital experience."[91]

As indicated earlier, the Kinsey data showed that many women who had premarital coitus did not suffer from guilt feelings. Given the argument that many coeds are engaged in premarital sex in less emotionally demanding situations today than they were in the past, what are the consequences of that behavior? If the norms of society are incorporated into the personality structure of the individual and are felt by him to be important, any deviation from those norms will usually lead to guilt feelings. Certainly, those who hold to the norms expect that to be true

---

[88] Bell and Chaskes, "Experience among Coeds," p. 83.

[89] Vance Packard, *The Sexual Wilderness* (New York: David McKay, 1968), p. 507.

[90] Ibid., p. 186.

[91] Ibid., p. 187.

and assume that even when young people go "wrong" they will feel bad about it. And what particularly bothers an older generation is not only to have the younger generation go against the norms, but also to not indicate that they are sorry. For the young person to have premarital intercourse and to be little influenced by the norms of the older generation is really the crux of the generational conflict pertaining to premarital sexual manners.

What evidence is there of feelings of guilt in the modern generation? In the Bell and Chaskes study the respondents were asked at each stage of the dating relationship if they had ever felt they had gone "too far" in their level of intimacy. Of those coeds who had coitus, by the level of dating relationship, saying they "went too far" the rates were: "while dating, in 1958, 65 percent and in 1968, 36 percent; while going steady, in 1958, 61 percent and in 1968, 30 percent; and, while engaged, 1958, 41 percent and in 1968, 20 percent. In general, when the data of 1958 is compared with 1968, the coeds were more apt to have had intercourse at all levels of the dating relationship and at the same time felt less guilty than did their counterparts in 1958."[92]

Christensen and Gregg came to the conclusion that there does seem to have been a recent sexual revolution in the sexual activities of the females, although the same is not true for the males. "Even in attitude, the evidence is that females have been changing more rapidly than males which means that the two sexes are now closer together in the way they view sexual matters. But the convergence of the sexes in the area of behavior is also very evident, brought about by female liberalization alone. American females still are more sexually conservative than their counterparts with respect to both attitude and practice, but the differences are less than formerly."[93]

In general, it appears that regardless of the limitations, the available evidence seems to indicate a change in the premarital sexual activity of an important minority of college students since the mid-1960s. From the point of view held by the older members of society there has been no easing up of the traditional restrictive values about premarital coitus. Therefore, the differences by generation contribute to greater potential conflict.

Nature of Engagement

Length of engagement would logically seem—and is—related to a higher probability of premarital coitus. The longer the couple go together, the more they become sexually involved and the greater the tendency becomes to move to more intensive levels of intimacy.

---

[92] Bell and Chaskes, "Experience among Coeds," p. 83.
[93] Christensen and Gregg, "Changing Sex Norms," p. 625.

Kanin studied the impact of the coming marriage on premarital coitus by investigating the sexual behavior of the couple in the last month prior to marriage. He found a slight decrease in activity during the last month for those involved in premarital coitus. Thirty-one percent indicated decrease, 22 percent, increase, and the rest reported their sexual activity unchanged.[94] Kanin's findings did not indicate a slackening off because the marriage was coming near; rather, the slackening off was largely dependent upon the female's failure to achieve orgasm.[95]

The various studies indicate several basic considerations in regard to engagement and coitus, though the nature of the cause-and-effect relationships is very complex. Sexual experience during some successful engagements is probably entered through mutual agreement and mutually defined as contributing to the relationship. The mutuality often means that a relatively high sense of security, particularly for the female, exists in the engagement relationship. The sex experience may then be felt to *add* to the relationship. By contrast, in broken engagements the relationship may not have been strong enough to accept the sexual experience, and it may, therefore, have been a highly disrupting influence.

PREMARITAL EXPERIENCE AS RELATED TO MARRIAGE

A common belief in the United States, based upon traditional attitudes, is that failure to conform to premarital sexual norms will contribute to postmarital problems. This attitude presumes that if sexual intercourse occurs before marriage, negative effects on both the sexual and the overall husband-wife adjustment will result. But behavior studies indicate that this assumption is much less true than many have believed. In the area of sexual adjustment in marriage, the statistical findings on premarital intercourse and sexual success in marriage do not support the theory that coitus before marriage has an adverse effect on the sexual relationships after marriage.

The tendency in the past has been simply to view the act of premarital coitus as bad, without realizing that the act must be related to the social and psychological context of the individuals involved. Contributions of different personality characteristics and of variations in cultural values have been greatly underestimated, and often ignored.

A number of studies have been specifically concerned with the relationship between premarital and postmarital coitus. Kanin and Howard found a relationship between premarital intercourse with spouse and full sex expression during the early weeks of marriage. "Sexual satisfaction was readily attained on the wedding night by wives who had experienced

---

[94] Kanin, "Dating-Courtship," p. 260.
[95] Ibid., p. 261.

premarital intercourse."[96] Of the females who had premarital intercourse with spouse, 71 percent reported wedding-night relations as "very satisfactory" or "satisfactory," in contrast to 47 percent of the females without premarital experience.[97] Of course the nonvirgins may have been less restricted biologically, psychologically, and socially in personal sex expression than the virgins.

It has also been found that the capacity for achieving orgasm in marriage is related to premarital sexual orgasm experience. "The type of premarital experience which correlates most specifically with the responses of the female in marital coitus is premarital coitus—*provided that that coitus leads to orgasm.*"[98] Kinsey found that among the females who had had even limited premarital sexual experience, only 19 percent had failed to reach orgasm in the first year of marriage. By contrast, among the females who had had premarital coitus but who had not reached orgasm in the coitus, 38 to 56 percent failed to reach orgasm in the first year of marriage."[99] Kanin and Howard found that of those women who had reached orgasm in premarital coitus, only 28 percent reported marital sexual difficulties, whereas difficulty was admitted by 47 percent of the women who had failed to achieve orgasm from premarital intercourse.[100] Thus, premarital sexual satisfaction seems to be important to marital sexual satisfaction. However, the higher orgasm frequency for the married women who had achieved orgasm in premarital coitus may also be attributable to the selecting out of those women who are most sexually responsive.

Kinsey, of course, has provided information on the broader area of premarital achievement of orgasm. First, he found "that there was a marked positive correlation between experience in orgasm obtained from premarital coitus, and the capacity to reach orgasm after marriage. Second, among those females who had never reached orgasm from any source prior to marriage, 44 percent had failed to reach orgasm in any of their coitus in the first year of marriage.[101] Kinsey also found that of those females who had reached orgasm at least 25 times in premarital coitus, only 3 percent had failed to achieve at least some orgasm in marital coitus.[102]

Many women may achieve a state of sexual satisfaction in their marriage with limited or even no orgasm. If the love relationship is satis-

---

[96] Eugene J. Kanin and David H. Howard, "Postmarital Consequences of Premarital Sex Adjustments," *American Sociological Review*, October, 1958, p. 560.

[97] Ibid., p. 560.

[98] Kinsey, *Female*, p. 386.

[99] Ibid., pp. 385–86.

[100] Kanin and Howard, "Postmarital Consequences," p. 560.

[101] Kinsey, *Female*, p. 328.

[102] Ibid., p. 329.

factory, then the physical sex satisfaction may not be viewed as too important. However, it seems that the woman's personally felt need to achieve fulfillment in the sexual act, through orgasm, is becoming more important. The young woman of today, particularly the higher educated, is being reared to believe that she has a "right" to expect sexual satisfaction in marriage. Today, many couples go into marriage believing they both can and should achieve sexual fulfillment. A reading of today's sex manuals for marriage shows great emphasis on the theme that both the husband and wife do everything they can to help the wife achieve orgasm as often as possible.

ADULT-YOUTH CONFLICT

In concluding our discussion about premarital sexual values and behavior, we will discuss some generational conflicts and bring together the main arguments both for and against premarital sexual intercourse. In the discussion of generational conflict, we will examine some of the premarital sexual values held by the younger generation and compare those values with those of their parents and other older adults.[103]

Given their different stages in the life cycle, parents and children are almost always going to show variations in how they define appropriate behavior for a given role. Values as to "proper" premarital sexual-role behavior from the perspective of the parents are greatly influenced by the strong emotional involvement of the parent with his child. On the other hand, the child is going through a life-cycle stage in which the actual behavior occurs, and must try to relate his parents' values to what he is doing or may do. There is an important difference between defining appropriate role conduct for others to follow and defining proper role conduct to be followed by one's self. What may be even more important to actual behavior is that often there is more than one significant group of role definers that the young person can turn to as guides for his sex-role behavior. We will examine some recent research that provides data on the attitudes of the younger generation as compared with the values of parents and other older adults.

In many respects there is an almost insurmountable barrier to get over before there can be any significant and meaningful exchange of sexual knowledge between parents and their offspring. There is generally a high degree of discomfort in the communication of sexual material and as a result the young are often condemned by lack of information about what is sexually meaningful from their parents. In other words, because of the cultural taboos, members of the younger generation must continue to make their own mistakes since they rarely have been given the benefits of their parents' past sexual experience—good, bad, or indifferent. Mas-

---

[103] For a more extended discussion, see Robert R. Bell, "Parent-Child Conflict in Sexual Values," *Journal of Social Issues*, April 1966, pp. 34–44.

ters and Johnson go on to point out that the necessary freedom of sexual communication between parents and their children "cannot be achieved until the basic component of sexuality itself is given a socially comfortable role by all active generations simultaneously."[104] Given the wide generation gap on so many matters, this possibility seems a long way off in the future.

In a study of college students and their parents Robert Walsh found that most of the parents felt it was their duty to teach their children about sex and attempted to do so. He found that 93 percent of the mothers had discussed sex with their daughters and 67 percent of the fathers with their sons. But what was most striking was the differential perceptions of the parents in the role of sex informant. "Seventy-three percent of the fathers and 63 percent of the mothers thought that they were indeed the major source of their child's sex information. Only 7 percent of the boys and 29 percent of the girls reported that their parents were the major source of sex information."[105]

A common technique for minimizing conflict is for the daughter not to discuss her sexual attitudes or behavior with her mother. The entire area of sexual attitudes appears to be highly influenced by emotion, especially for the mother as it concerns her daughter. The emotional reactions of some mothers may also be influenced by recollections of their own premarital sexual experiences. The Kinsey study, which provides data on the mothers' generation in their younger years, indicates that the mothers were actually no more conservative in their premarital sexual attitudes and behavior than are their daughters.

However, it is problematic whether the liberal attitudes of the college daughters will continue for very long. It is possible that later in her life the college-educated daughter may be as conservative as her mother, when her attitudinal rationales are not related to herself or her age-peers, but rather to a daughter of her own. It is therefore possible that the "sexual emancipation" of the college girl exists only for a short time in her life span—the time of her own premarital love and/or engagement.

Reiss has done research with several large samples in an attempt to develop scales for the measuring of attitudes with regard to premarital sexual permissiveness, utilizing two major samples: (1) an adult sample of 1,515 individuals aged 21 and older drawn randomly across the United States; and (2) a high-school and college student probability sample of 903 students, ages 16–20, drawn from two high schools and two colleges in Virginia and one college in New York state.[106] This is the first study to draw on a large and randomly selected sample.

---

[104] Masters and Johnson, *Human Sexual Response*, pp. 216–17.

[105] Robert H. Walsh, "The Generation Gap in Sexual Beliefs," *Sexual Behavior*, January 1972, p. 6.

[106] Ira L. Reiss, "Premarital Sexual Permissiveness among Negroes and Whites," *American Sociological Review*, October 1964, pp. 688–89.

Reiss's respondents were asked to express their beliefs about different combinations of intimacy and degree of interpersonal commitment for both unmarried males and females. They were asked if they believed petting to be acceptable when the male or female was engaged. In the adult sample, the belief that petting during engagement was acceptable for the engaged male was the response of 61 percent, and for the engaged female it was the response of 56 percent. Of the student respondents, 85 percent approved for the engaged male and 82 percent for the engaged female.[107] Thus, not only are the adult attitudes about petting during engagement more conservative than those of the student population, but for both the adult and the student groups there is a single standard—that is, the acceptance rates are roughly the same for both males and females.

Reiss also asked his respondents if they believed that premarital petting was acceptable when the individual felt no particular affection toward his partner. To this item, "yes" was the response of 29 percent of the adult group with reference to the male, and of 20 percent for the female. In the student sample, "yes" was the response for 34 percent of the males and 18 percent of the females.[108] (These responses provide some empirical evidence to validate Reiss's concept of permissiveness-without-affection.) Essentially the same rate of unacceptability for petting without affection is given by both the adult and the student samples. The adult responses suggest a single standard of rejecting this kind of behavior, however, while the student sample gives some indication of a double standard—a higher proportion suggesting approval for this behavior pattern for males than for females.

Reiss also asked his respondents if they believed full sexual relations to be acceptable if the male or female is engaged. Approval was the response given by 20 percent of the adult group for males and 17 percent for females. In the student group, acceptance was given by 52 percent for the male and 44 percent for the female.[109] Here, as with petting, there are significant differences between the adult and the student samples, and here both groups suggest a single standard of acceptance for both males and females.

Finally, Reiss's respondents were asked if they believed it acceptable for both males and females to have premarital coitus even if they felt no particular affection toward their partner. In the adult sample, 12 percent stated approval for the male and 7 percent for the female. In the student group, 21 percent approved for the male, 11 percent for the fe-

---

[107] Ira L. Reiss, "The Scaling of Premarital Sexual Permissiveness," *Journal of Marriage and the Family*, May 1964, pp. 190–91.

[108] Ibid., pp. 190–91.

[109] Ibid., pp. 190–91.

male.[110] As with petting with no particular affection, these data suggest that only a small number accept coitus without affection, and in the adult sample the acceptance difference for males and females is not significant. However, there is an indication that for the student population there may be a double standard, with somewhat greater acceptability for the male than for the female.

The data from Reiss's research, along with the data from smaller and more limited studies, clearly suggest important differences in attitudes about premarital sexual intimacy when young unmarried adults are compared with the general adult population.

The values of parents and the adult community in general may in time become more liberal and the conflict between generations reduced. (There seems little possibility that the opposite will occur). But until this happens—if it does—parents and their children will continue to live with somewhat different value systems with regard to premarital sexual values and related behavior. Parents will probably continue to hold to traditional values and assume that *their* child is conforming to those values unless his actions force them to admit otherwise. The youth generation will probably continue to develop their own modified value systems and keep those values to themselves, implicitly allowing their parents to believe they are behaving according to the traditional values. For many parents and their children, the conflict about premarital sex will continue to be characterized by the parent playing ostrich and the youth attempting to keep the sand from blowing away.

In Chapter 7, a number of conservative and liberal views were presented on the subject of premarital sexual freedom. It was not suggested that all of the arguments had equal weight, but that if an individual recognizes them as existing, he might be better equipped to make his own decisions. Although arguments are seldom presented that indicate possible values for premarital intercourse, the social scientist recognizes that they exist, even though those who are morally opposed to premarital sexual freedom may feel they would be better left unrecognized and unstated.[111] Here, to close this chapter, is a summary of arguments presented in Chapter 7.

Arguments for Premarital Sexual Freedom

1. A person may have a strong psychological need for sexual release that can only be satisfied through coitus.

2. A person may derive a high physical and psychological satisfaction from premarital sexual relations.

---

[110] Ibid., pp. 190–91.

[111] See Kinsey et al., *Female*, pp. 308–9. Many of these suggestions were taken from Kinsey and his associates.

3. If little or no guilt exists, the sexual intimacy may intensify the emotional relationships between the two individuals.

4. Premarital coitus is probably more valuable in developing the emotional paired aspect of sexual interaction than the use of solitary forms of sexual release.

5. From premarital coitus, the individual may develop a capacity to make emotional interrelationships that are important to marriage.

6. It may provide an opportunity for learning sexual techniques that can be applied to marital coitus. (Many already assume this is important for the male.)

7. Emotional and physical adjustments are often easier to make at younger ages and therefore may be made with less difficulty before marriage.

8. Heterosexual experiences may prevent the development of homosexual patterns of sexual behavior.

9. Premarital sexual relations may in a positive way lead the couple into marriage.

Arguments against Premarital Sexual Freedom

1. The possibility of pregnancy.

2. Dangers of venereal disease.

3. The problem of a marriage brought about because of premarital pregnancy.

4. The personally disorganizing effects that premarital coitus may have because of the conditions under which it often occurs.

5. The personality dangers of guilt due to breaking the moral standards accepted by the individual. The feelings of guilt are related to the religious values of sin and immorality.

6. The possibility that guilt over the sexual act may end what was otherwise a very satisfactory relationship.

7. Premarital coitus may make some individuals feel obligated to marry the sexual partner.

8. The danger that the male will lose respect for the female and not want to enter marriage.

9. The fear (usually by the male) that his partner may be susceptible to extramarital relations after marriage.

SELECTED BIBLIOGRAPHY

Bell, Robert R. "Parent-Child Conflict in Sexual Values." *Journal of Social Issues*, April 1966, pp. 34–44.

Bell, Robert R., and Balter, Shelli "Premarital Sexual Experiences of Married Women." *Medical Aspects of Human Sexuality*, November 1973, pp. 111–18.

Bell, Robert R., and Chaskes, Jay B. "Premarital Sexual Experience Among Coeds, 1958 and 1968." *Journal of Marriage and the Family,* February 1970, pp. 81–84.

Hunt, Morton "Sexual Behavior in the 1970s." *Playboy,* October and November 1973, pp. 74–75; 85; 88; 194; 197–206.

Kanin, Eugene "Male Sex Aggression and Three Psychiatric Hypotheses." *The Journal of Sex Research,* November 1965, pp. 221–31.

Kinsey, Alfred C., Pomeroy, Wardell B., and Martin, Clyde E. *Sexual Behavior in the Human Male.* Philadelphia: W. B. Saunders Co., 1948.

Kinsey, Alfred C. et al. *Sexual Behavior in the Human Female.* Philadelphia: W. B. Saunders Co., 1953.

Luckey, Eleanore, and Nass, Gilbert D. "A Comparison of Sexual Attitudes and Behavior in an International Sample." *Journal of Marriage and the Family,* May 1969, pp. 364–79.

Reiss, Ira L. *The Social Context of Premarital Sexual Permissiveness.* New York: Holt, Rinehart and Winston, Inc., 1967.

Robinson, Ira E., King, Karl, and Balswick, Jack O. "The Premarital Sexual Revolution among College Females." *The Family Coordinator,* April 1972, pp. 189–94.

Walsh, Robert H. "The Generation Gap in Sexual Beliefs." *Sexual Behavior,* January 1972, pp. 4–10.

Part Three

Marriage, Parenthood, and Other Adult Roles

Chapter 10

Some Legal Aspects of the Family

For most of man's history, the social control of human behavior has rested with the family, the clan, or the tribal unit. No society, past or present, simple or complex, has existed without controls over some areas of human behavior. Without some agreement as to rights and obligations for individuals within a group, there could be no society, only a collection of isolated, nonsocial individuals.

Historically, marriage and the family have been an important area of controlled social behavior. Societies have developed controls over the interactional relationship of marriage, the responsibility for meeting the needs of children, and the transmission of properties, rights, statuses, and knowledge from one generation to the next.

As complex and extended societies developed, social controls became more extensive and far-reaching. Extended social controls came to be vested in the society or its delegates through the emergence of political organization under various systems of government. Out of this development came formalized laws. An important difference between laws and social controls such as norms, or mores, or folkways is that laws are recorded. They therefore provide continuity as well as sanctions for controlling human behavior.

Laws provide formalized sets of controls available (at least in theory) to all members of a society, thus enabling individuals to know their rights and to anticipate the obligations their actions will entail. The human being is socialized to need and desire dependability and predictability in social interaction. The legal system, along with the informal controls of society, provides a social order which allows the individual to proceed through the course of his day making generally accurate assumptions about the behavior of others and, thereby, to function with a sense of personal security in a wide variety of interactional settings.

Although people sometimes tend to perceive laws as being sacred and to attribute to them an intrinsic value of their own, laws are, nevertheless, created by man and are validated through their efficiency as a means of directing the behavior of individuals within the defined social group. Societies often incorporate punishments to ensure the social acceptance and usefulness of laws. But simply because laws exist with stated punishments for nonconformity does not mean that they will always be legally enforced. The vast majority of written laws in the United States are rarely or never applied. For example, in the area of sexual behavior, Kinsey and his associates concluded that "only a minute fraction of 1 percent of the persons who are involved in sexual behavior which is contrary to the law are ever apprehended, prosecuted, or convicted."[1]

Generally, the enactment of new laws or the repeal of old ones is a very slow process. A dynamic legal system to fit the changing nature and needs of society is frequently an ideal, not a reality. Sometimes, too, the laws of a society no longer have their original meaningfulness because of changed social conditions, and they therefore create problems. In the discussion of law and the family that follows, some of the problems of legal and social conflict will be illustrated. The discussion centers on the laws related to entering the marriage role and to the legal role of the child. Some legal aspects relevant to the ending or modifying of the marriage relationship are discussed in Chapter 19. As there is no federal law in regard to marriage and the family, the discussion is general, with reference made to 53 different sets of laws. The 53 legal jurisdictions consist of the 50 states, the District of Columbia, the Virgin Islands, and Puerto Rico.

MARRIAGE LAWS

Legally there have been problems in defining marriage. The problem for courts and legislatures is that marriage can broadly be looked upon as a contract, a status, a relationship, or an institution.[2]

The concept of marriage as a contract has been handed down from

---

[1] Alfred C. Kinsey, et al., *Sexual Behavior in the Human Female* (Philadelphia: W. B. Saunders Co., 1953), p. 18.

[2] Helen I. Clarke, *Social Legislation* (New York: Appleton-Century-Crofts, 1957), p. 73.

English common law as the specific legal definition of marriage. The difficulty in this definition, however, is that while marriage is like the ordinary contract in many ways, it is also different. Clarke points out two ways in which a marriage contract differs from a private contract:[3] (1) Once the relationship of marriage has been legally established, the two members cannot through their own voluntary actions alter or break the contract. "It becomes a legal status that can be severed only by laws and acts of the state itself; whereas in the case of the private contract, the parties can modify or restrict it, enlarge it, or entirely release it by their mutual acts and consent."[4] (2) The requirements of legal capacity to enter into a marriage contract are different from those required for entering into an ordinary contract. For example, a person may contract a valid marriage at an age when he would not be old enough to make a binding contract in the business world.[5]

The laws relating to marriage that have emerged in the United States have basically met one or the other of two social needs, although sometimes the two needs are met within a single law. The two needs are: (1) "the fixing of financial responsibility so as to insure that the state will not have to bear the burden of supporting dependent women and children and (2) the encouragement of marital unions likely to produce acceptable offspring and the confinement of sexual activity within the boundaries of such a marriage."[6] It often appears that the laws with regard to marriage have a minimal social impact; their influence is apparent only when some of the common legal requirements for marriage are changed or introduced for the first time. In the late 1950s and early 1960s, for example, six states (Arizona, New Mexico, South Carolina, Indiana, Mississippi, and Iowa) tightened up or introduced premarital legal requirements. When the combined marriage totals for the last calendar year before the reforms are compared with the marriage totals for the first calendar year after the new legal requirements, the six states show a marriage decline of 47 percent.[7]

Legal Requirements

Age. Historically, the age of marriage was usually related to puberty, the biological age when reproduction is possible. While marriage at a very young age is still possible in some states, the general legal pattern has

---

[3] Ibid., p. 75.

[4] Ibid., p. 75.

[5] Ibid., p. 75.

[6] Harriet Pilpel and Theodora Zavin, "Laws on Marriage and Family," in Albert Ellis and Albert Abarbanel, eds., *The Encyclopedia of Sexual Behavior* (New York: Hawthorn Books, Inc., 1961), p. 614.

[7] Alexander Plateris, "The Impact of the Amendment of Marriage Laws in Mississippi," *Journal of Marriage and the Family*, May 1966, p. 206.

been to move the age for marriage into late adolescence and the early adult years. Furthermore, legal definitions have been made on differences in decision-making rights relative to different ages of marriage. The law has said that while some individuals may marry in late adolescence, legally the final decision is not theirs, but their parents'. Such legal control by the parents is a reflection of thinking handed down from the past, when parents were much more directly involved in controlling the marriages of their children than they are today.

Four legal ages for marriage exist in this country. The four ages are defined by sex and whether the individual may marry with or without the consent of the parents. "The most common age-with-consent is 18 for the male and 16 for the female, while the age-without-consent is most generally 21 for the male and 18 for the female."[8] The law recognizes age differences by sex as to physical and social maturity for entering marriage. Society, through its legal system, maintains marriage control until the minimum ages are reached, then gives the responsibility to the parents for the next few years, and finally gives the individual the right of legal decision-making. In effect, when all factors are taken into account, the legal range of minimum age for marriage in the United States is from 12 to 21.[9] It appears questionable that the consent of parents has much effect on the frequency of young marriages. For example, in 1957 for the first time, a girl in South Carolina had to show with her birth certificate that she was over age 18, or have the written permission of her parents to marry. But there is no evidence from the "data to support the hypothesis that the requirement of parental consent is deterrent to early marriage."[10] It may be that many of the parents feel that when a girl is old enough to want to marry there is little reason to oppose her, or it may be that a young age at marriage is most common among the lower social classes (where there is greater tolerance of such marriages than in the middle class).

Documenting proof of age is not required in all states to get a marriage license. In some states, only one of the partners needs to appear in person before the authority who issues the license. Lying about age is not very difficult and young people who want to get married find it easy to yield to the temptation, even under oath, to make false statements.[11]

It may also be that the minimal age for marriage when relatively higher

---

[8] William M. Kephart, *The Family, Society and the Individual* (Boston: Houghton Mifflin Co., 1961), p. 401.

[9] William M. Kephart, "Legal and Procedural Aspects of Marriage and Divorce," in Harold T. Christensen, ed., *Handbook of Marriage and The Family* (Chicago: Rand McNally & Co., 1964), p. 945.

[10] David A. Gover and Dorothy G. Jones, "Requirement of Parental Consent: A Deterrent to Marriage," *Journal of Marriage and the Family*, May 1964, p. 206.

[11] Max Rheinstein, *Marriage Stability, Divorce, and the Law* (Chicago: University of Chicago Press, 1972), p. 416.

is not too important if there is a nearby state with a younger minimal age. For example, in recent years in Pennsylvania and Virginia, where the specified age for marriage is 21, the largest number of girls who married were of that age. In Maryland, where the specified age was 18, the modal age at marriage was 18. But despite those apparent differences it is quite possible that there actually exists little real difference in average age of marriage in the three states because what may be happening is that the parental consent laws, rather than deterring marriage, contribute to migratory marriage.[12] So many of the 18-year-olds who marry in Maryland have come from the other two states because they could not or would not get legal permission from their parents to marry.

Parents also have certain other legally approved ways of influencing the marriage of their children, even if the children are old enough to marry without the parents' consent. The law supports the idea that parents be given every opportunity short of slander and libel to advise their children on the selection of a mate.[13] Until children leave the parental home, their parents can use a wide variety of influences and pressures—in general, anything that is not specifically prohibited by law.

Family Restrictions. A number of individuals are legally excluded as marriage partners because they are defined as members of the family. Early in history, the church banned marriages of specifically related people, and the legal system gave early support to most of these restrictions. The legal prohibitions involve two categories of family relationships: *consanguinity*, a blood relationship or descent from a common ancestor; and *affinity*, a relationship resulting from marriage. All statutes in the United States prohibit consanguineous marriage with one's son or daughter, mother or father, grandmother or grandfather, sister or brother, aunt or uncle, niece or nephew. With other relationships of consanguinity, less agreement prevails, but over half the states prohibit the marriage of first cousins. Some examples of state affinity restrictions are that the male cannot marry the stepmother in 23 states, the stepdaughter in 22, the daughter-in-law in 17, and the mother-in-law in 13.[14]

Mental Deficiency. The mentally defective are generally unable to control their lives and meet the economic and social responsibilities of marriage. Thus, social concern over their marriage is a practical, economic one; mental inability may result in they and their children becoming the financial wards of the state. A number of states have specific statutes that

---

[12] Ira Rosenwaike, "Parental Consent Ages as a Factor in State Variation in Brides's Age at Marriage," *Journal of Marriage and the Family,* August 1967, p. 455.

[13] John S. Bradway, "What Family Members Should Know About Law," in Howard Becker and Reuben Hill, *Family, Marriage and Parenthood* (Boston: D. C. Heath & Co., 1955), p. 566.

[14] Irving Mandell, *The Law of Marriage and Divorce* (New York: Oceana Publications, 1957), pp. 21–25.

prohibit the marriage of the mentally retarded. However, many states have no satisfactory method of preventing mentally deficient marriages because there is no generally accepted psychological definition of feeble-mindedness.[15] In some cases retarded individuals are placed in institutions to make sure they don't reproduce. If they can be sterilized it is often possible for them to live normal lives in the community. It has been found that even individuals with IQs in the 50s are able to understand the sterilization operation and often ask for it themselves.[16]

Insanity.   Most states have prohibitions against the marriage of the insane. Clarke points out that this restriction is derived from two theories, one legal and the other scientific.[17] The legal is based upon the fact that a marriage contract requires that the two individuals be capable of giving consent; the insane individual is incapable of doing so. The scientific reason is that the mentally incapable can create severe problems for both the family they procreate and society in general. The problem here, as with mental deficiency, is the legal establishment of an acceptable definition of insanity.

Miscegenation.   In the past many of the states restricted marriage across racial lines. Miscegenation laws prohibited a white person from marrying someone of a different race. Originally, the prohibition was based on the belief that significant differences existed between races and that marriage across racial lines would result in a "weakening" of the dominant race. These beliefs have been shown to have no scientific validity; a vast amount of research has failed to demonstrate any crucial differences in intelligence and general biological adaptability among racial groups. In 1967 in the case of *Loving* v. *Virginia,* the United States Supreme Court found a state's prohibition of marriage across racial lines to be unconstitutional.

Marriage Licenses.   Marriage licenses are issued by the state. They serve the dual purposes of withholding legal permission for marriage from those who do not meet the legal requirements and as a means of acquiring marriage statistics. The license laws usually prescribe: (1) that a license shall be obtained for a valid marriage; (2) the form and content of the application, and by whom and where the license will be issued; and (3) the various regulations as to marriage qualifications that must be met by the parties desiring to marry.[18] The agent issuing the license is responsible for obtaining all necessary facts and ascertaining that the parties meet the legal requirements. The legal agent must acquire information in two broad areas. He must get the information that is needed

---

[15] Clarke, *Social Legislation,* p. 98.

[16] Robert W. Laidlaw and Medora S. Bass, "Voluntary Sterilization as it Relates to Mental Health," *American Journal of Psychiatry,* June 1964, p. 1179.

[17] Clarke, *Social Legislation,* p. 98.

[18] Clarke, *Social Legislation,* p. 88.

for complete and accurate records, such as the names of the parties, residence and occupation, time of the proposed marriage, and parental names and addresses, and—of greatest importance—he must acquire the facts needed to establish the legality of the marriage, such as age, race, and the status of any former marriages.[19]

Blood tests are now a legal requirement for marriage in almost all states. The usual purpose of the test is to determine whether either party has syphilis, or that the disease is not in the communicable stage.[20] These requirements operate much more effectively in theory than they do in actual practice. Clarke points out some of the problems connected with serological tests and what might be done to correct them:

1. Examinations are not required of women in some states. There is no sound reason why this should be.

2. Medical examinations are often perfunctory and superficial. Standardized laboratory tests should be required.

3. Statutory fee limitations encourage doctors to make hasty examinations. Public examiners might be designated for all examinations or for some defined classes of persons. Free Wassermanns might also be provided.

4. The laws are often evaded through out-of-state marriages. In those states already having laws forbidding certain kinds of out-of-state marriages, there should be an extension of the prohibition to include those persons seeking to evade the venereal disease provisions.[21]

One other legal requirement directly related to getting a marriage license is the "advance-notice" laws. These laws provide a period of time between when the person applies for or gets the license and when he can legally be married. This period of time is sometimes referred to as the "cooling-off" period. Without the time lag, a couple can marry immediately; with the waiting period, it has been estimated that as high as 20 percent of all applying couples never use the license or return to pick it up. The waiting period thus cuts down on the hasty marriages caused by sudden elopements, intoxication, or "temporary insanity," that have been correlated with high divorce rates.

Three kinds of advance-notice laws are in use in the legal jurisdictions of the United States. The most common is a period of time between the application for and the issuance of the license. The modal period of time between application and issuance is three days, but, in almost as many states, the waiting period is five days and in one state it is one day. This kind of law is generally considered to be more effective than the other two, one of which, found in only three states, requires a waiting period

---

[19] Ibid., p. 89.

[20] Kephart, "Marriage and Divorce," pp. 948–49.

[21] Clarke, *Social Legislation*, p. 103.

between the time the license is issued and when the marriage can take place. The waiting period ranges from one to five days. The method is less efficient than the first because the license is in the hands of the couple, and they may find someone who will marry them ahead of time and postdate the license. The third kind of advance-notice law, found only in New York, is a combination of the first two. The waiting period is three days between license application and issuance and then one more day before the marriage can legally be performed.

The discussion thus far has pointed out a number of legal prerequisites for marriage. If all the requirements are met, the marriage is considered to be *valid*. This does not mean that the legal requirements for marriage of all states must be met, because—with the exceptions already mentioned—a marriage valid where contracted is valid everywhere. For example, suppose a couple are too young to marry in their home state without the consent of their parents and they elope to another state where they are legally old enough to marry without parental consent. They meet the other legal requirements of that state, are married, and return to their home state. This marriage is perfectly valid and will not be annulled or declared void by the home state.

If the legal requirements have not been met, the marriage may be defined as either *void* or *voidable*. In law, any act which is void is null and ineffectual; it has no legal force or binding effect. For example, suppose a woman gets married and later discovers that her husband is still legally married to a first wife. Her marriage is *void* as of the point of discovery of the previous marriage, and its dissolution does not normally call for any court action. A marriage void in its inception does not require the judgment of the court to restore the parties to their original rights.[22] A marriage which is *voidable* is one which may be declared void; it is not void in and of itself.[23] The marriage will be considered valid until it is nullified by the proper court proceedings. The couple cannot together seek to have the marriage voided, and the action must be brought during the lifetime of the two married individuals.[24] The most commonly used and accepted grounds for declaring a marriage void through the actions of the court are nonage and incapacity. For example, if a person marries under the statutory age of consent, the marriage may be annulled by judicial decree.

The distinction between the void and the voidable marriage is blurred in many states because their statutes do not always state clearly whether certain prohibited marriages are void or voidable. Distinctions between the two are necessary because a void marriage may be annulled after the

---

[22] Clarke, *Social Legislation,* p. 110.

[23] Ibid., p. 109.

[24] Ibid., p. 110.

death of the parties, but a voidable marriage may not be. Also, a voidable marriage can usually be ratified or affirmed, but a void marriage cannot be.[25]

Some Implications For Women. The discussion thus far has been about the legal dimension of the marriage as a relationship. Yet, marriage has some different legal consequences for men and women. Once a couple are legally married they do not have legal equality in all ways with each other. The following is a brief discussion of several areas of difference.

In recent years there has been an increasing concern among some women that when they marry they give up their surname. In many ways the loss of a woman's surname at marriage can represent the loss of an important part of her personality as well as implying subservience to her husband. This requirement is not found in all societies. In such countries as Denmark and France both custom and law allow a married woman to retain her maiden name. "By contrast, in the United States, the change in the woman's name upon marriage is not only consistent with social custom, it also appears to be generally required by law."[26] In most states there are statutes that prescribe procedures for changing one's name and thereby have an official record of that change. Yet many of the states specifically exempt married women from their provisions. For example, in Iowa a formal name change can be granted by the court to "any person, under no civil disabilities, who has attained his or her majority *and is unmarried, if a female. . . .*"[27]

A good part of family law as it effects women rests on a patriarchal past. Reeves points out in the past, "those incapable of entering into a contract were infants, children, idiots, the insane, and married women. Family life has changed since then, but family law still lags behind reality."[28] One illustration of this vested right from the past is that the husband has the primary legal responsibilities for family support. This has important implications for property rights. There are 42 states where earnings and property acquired during marriage are owned separately and 8 states (in the West and Southwest) where earnings and most property acquired during marriage are owned in common. In the separate-property states a wife has no legal right to any part of her husband's earnings or property other than basic support. If she has no resources she is in effect dependent upon her husband's "kindness." Today, in the community property states, whatever is achieved during marriage becomes part of a mutual fund, but the husband manages and controls that

[25] Ibid., p. 111.

[26] Leo Kanowitz, *Women and the Law* (Albuquerque: University of New Mexico Press, 1969), p. 42.

[27] Ibid., p. 43.

[28] Nancy Reeves, *Womankind: Beyond the Stereotype* (Chicago: Aldine, 1971). p. 38.

fund."[29] Other instances of different legal rights for men and women are discussed in Chapter 15.

Common-Law Marriages

A common-law marriage is based entirely upon the mutual consent of the two individuals and is not solemnized by any particular form. Common-law marriages were made legally acceptable in the United States as a result of certain historical factors. With only certain groups of people given the legal authority to perform a marriage, sometimes in the past no authority was available for long periods of time. Under the assumption that it would be better for the individuals to be married if they so desired, they were given the legal right to enter into common-law marriage. But a corollary assumption was that they would be legally married when a person with authority to perform marriage was available. The legal right of the common-law marriage has been handed down from a frontier past, when it served a functional social need. Today, a lack of legal authorities to perform the marriage ceremony is rare. However, in the United States today, common-law marriage is recognized in about half the states and another six states recognize it if it occurred prior to a specific date.

While legal definitions of what constitutes a common-law marriage vary, generally three conditions must be met. First, the couple must be legally marriageable. That is, they must be of the proper age, not already married, and so forth. Second, they must live together and hold themselves out to the community as husband and wife. Third, they must, mutually, intend to be legally married at some future date.[30] A popular myth, that has no basis in the law, is that the couple must live together seven years. Generally, no specifically mentioned length of time is needed to establish a common-law marriage.

Common-law marriages are frequently found in the lower socioeconomic classes. Individuals enter this type of relationship for several reasons. They may be fearful of or hostile toward legal authority, or lack knowledge of marriage requirements. Possibly, many see the marriage relationship as tentative, or they plan on getting married, but just never get around to it. In the United States, persons are rarely called upon to give proof that they are married, and presenting themselves as husband and wife is almost always accepted without question by the community.

Problems sometimes develop in common-law marriages when one member attempts to have the marriage defined as valid. It is generally the woman who seeks to have the marriage validated, usually for reasons

---

[29] Ibid., p. 39.
[30] Kephart, *Individual,* pp. 405–18.

of financial help or inheritance questions. In attempting to establish the marriage's legality, the first two legal requirements are not usually difficult to prove, but the third one—or mutual intent to marry at some future date—is often legally difficult to prove, unless the proof of intent to wed is in writing, or very reliable witnesses are available. This is particularly true if one partner does not want the marriage declared valid and contends he never had any intention of legally marrying his partner.

The legal tendency in this country is to do away with common-law marriage, and it will probably be eliminated in many more states in the future. In modern American society, no logical reasons for its maintenance seem to exist, and it creates legal problems, such as legitimacy of children and property rights, that would not exist if the couple were officially married.

Breach of Promise

Breach of promise refers to a suit brought against a person who has agreed to enter into a marriage and then reneged. It is handled in court as a violation of contract. The logic of the action goes against much that is held to be important in engagement today, for example, the belief that engagement is a final testing prior to marriage and should be ended if important flaws in the relationship are discovered. In the past, the right to bring breach of promise actions was often abused—some of the cash awards made ran into hundreds of thousands of dollars. In some states, the breach of promise suit has been abolished and, in other states, its use is much less frequent than was the case in the past.

The policy of the law which allowed breach of promise suits has been condemned by a number of legal authorities. Clarke lists the following objections: (1) It was often used as a method of blackmail. A woman might sue a wealthy man as a source of income and not seek compensation for the loss suffered. (2) The considerable amount of publicity that was given to unhappy love affairs often had unfortunate consequences for the persons involved. (3) In reality, the use of breach of promise was available only to the woman. (4) The amount of damage awarded was often unjust, because the suit was heard by a jury, whose members are sometimes very gullible. (5) Engaged couples should be free to correct their mistakes without the fear of financial suit.[31]

When the woman had little choice of adult role other than marriage, a breach of promise was often viewed as depriving her of the chance to enter the marriage role. It was also based on the assumption of general female inferiority and was provided as special sex-role protection. However, many authorities feel that today the woman, with a wider choice of

---

[31] Clarke, *Social Legislation*, pp. 86–87.

marriage partners, a choice of an adult role other than marriage, and increased social and legal equality, no longer needs such special protection.

Sometimes confused with the breach of promise suit is the right of the parties to keep gifts when a courtship relationship ends. Often the question is whether the girl should return the engagement ring. When these cases have been taken to court, the common decision has been that if the woman was not at fault in bringing about the end of the engagement, she can keep the ring.

Sex in Marriage

There are a number of ways in which legal controls are directed at the sexual aspects of marriage. It is important to recognize that the area of legal control has historically been greatly influenced by religion. While theoretically religion and the legal systems are separate in the United States, we know that in reality religion has greatly influenced American laws. Religious influence has been especially significant with reference to sexual behavior. In the United States, every type of sexual activity *in and of itself* is a crime or a sin. "Marriage removes the stigma of criminality from vaginal heterosexual congress, but many Christians believe that it does not mitigate its sinful quality, unless engaged in for the sole purpose of procreation."[32]

There is also some evidence on a cross-cultural level that during the emergence of the state with its complex and codified legal system, the moral imperatives of traditional values in regard to sexual behavior were influential. Stephens, in a cross-cultural analysis of sexual regulations, analyzed why civilized communities were relatively more strict about the regulation of sex than were primitive societies. He came to the conclusion that ultimately the answer rested in the development of the state.[33]

In an historical study of the emergence of common law in the Western world, Drummond comes to essentially the same conclusion about the significance of the state. She points out that in common law "all the sexual transgressions other than adultery were at first merely torts, or civil wrongs, whatever the punishment inflicted. They were classified as 'sins' and 'wrongs,' the former being offenses against God, the latter against one's neighbor."[34] Drummond further suggests that it was "only when the state became an entity that sins took on the aspect of crimes against the state and became indictable offenses."[35] One consequence has been that

---

[32] Isabel Drummond, *The Sex Paradox* (New York: G. P. Putnam's Sons, 1953), p. 3.

[33] William N. Stephens, *The Family in Cross-Cultural Perspective* (New York: Holt, Rinehart & Winston, Inc., 1963), p. 259.

[34] Drummond, *Sex Paradox,* p. 20.

[35] Ibid., p. 20.

sexual laws have been altered very little over time. "Today, in twentieth-century America, formal sex restrictions are—in their general outline—much the same as they were in the times of Tertullian, St. Augustine, Martin Luther, or John Wesley."[36]

To say that sexual laws continue as a part of the formal legal system is not to say that the laws are generally applied. Pilpel points out that fornication—sexual intercourse between unmarried partners—is a crime but one that is rarely prosecuted in the United States.[37]

One important area of difference between legal definitions and some religious beliefs centers around the function of sex in marriage. All state laws agree that marriage is a sexual partnership and *not* an institution for reproduction. "Reproduction is desirable, but not a condition, whereas sexual cohabitation is a spouse's duty."[38] If a husband or wife refuses or is unable to fulfill sexual partnership in marriage, the partner has the right to contest the marriage or to seek divorce. On the other hand, "childlessness does not give either party the right to have the marriage dissolved."[39] The final legal step of defining sex as only a part of monogamous marriage was reached in 1887, when the Mormons were forbidden to practice polygamy. "Thereafter there existed no State, no sect, no association entitled to depart publicly from the ruling norms of sex-life."[40]

Our legal systems do more than simply restrict sexual expression to marriage. They also attempt legally to define what is permissible sexual behavior *within* marriage. The laws basically assert in most states that all forms of sexual activity "are frowned upon except face-to-face intercourse by husband and wife."[41] Any variation by the couple, "despite the fact that such variation may be described and prescribed by the reputable sex authorities as a form of precoital behavior, is restricted in all states under one law or another."[42] Furthermore, there is the requirement in two states that face-to-face sexual intercourse between the husband and wife must be without contraception. Pilpel points out that while these laws are rarely enforced, "their mere existence challenges a fundamental human right of privacy and their hypocrisy is no less pernicious for being absurd."[43]

In general, married females have often been held to have attained

---

[36] Stephens, *Family in Perspective*, p. 259.

[37] Harriet F. Pilpel, "Sex vs. The Law; A Study in Hypocrisy," *Harpers*, January 1965, p. 36.

[38] Richard Lewinsohn,. *A History of Sexual Customs* (New York: Harper & Brothers, 1958), p. 401.

[39] Ibid., p. 401.

[40] Ibid., p. 389.

[41] Pilpel, "Hypocrisy," p. 36.

[42] Robert V. Sherwin, "Laws on Sex Crimes," in Albert Ellis and Albert Abarbanel, eds., *The Encyclopedia of Sexual Behavior* (New York: Hawthorn Books, Inc., 1961), p. 620.

[43] Pilpel, "Hypocrisy," p. 36.

their majority at 18, but males have had to wait until they were 21 for adult rights. In the area of sexual behavior what was believed to be proper conduct for males and females led to uneven laws in such areas as statutory rape, seduction, and enticement. The young female, but not the male, has been seen as incapable of consenting to sexual relations, though for all other purposes—"contracts, property ownership, capacity to sue and be sued—she might reach the age of majority years before the male."[44]

Once two people are married, the law not only defines their sexual behavior but also restricts all sexual outlets to the marriage relationship. In the United States, adultery is defined by law and is the only legal ground recognized by all states as a basis for divorce. In most states, laws exist that could if applied call for a fine or imprisonment, or both, for those who commit adultery. Also, many state laws with regard to adultery are based on a double standard, with greater punishment directed at the wife. For example, in Texas, "a husband may secure a divorce for a single act of adultery by his wife, but a wife is only entitled to a divorce if her husband actually abandons her and lives with another woman."[45] Or there is the so-called "unwritten law" defense found in a few states. This allows the husband a complete defense of homicide if he kills a man in the act of having sexual intercourse with his wife. However, no state allows a wife to use the "unwritten law" defense if she should become outraged by another woman engaged in an act of sexual intercourse with her husband and should take that woman's life.[46]

THE HAVING OF CHILDREN

Only the very recent historical past has any consideration of the rational decisions as to whether or not to have children had any real meaning. While in a variety of societies, various devices were developed for controlling the number of births, the techniques were for the most part limited in both usage and reliability. The emergence of contraceptive knowledge and its usage by large numbers of Americans are recent social developments. Therefore, most of the legal statutes in the United States in regard to the sale and usage of contraception have been a development of the present century.[47] The various types of contraception are discussed in Chapter 16.

Contraception is often seen as only a negative force—the preventing of conception. While it is true that every time contraception is used effec-

---

44 Kanowitz, *Women and Law*, p. 9.

45 Pilpel and Zavin, "Laws," p. 618.

46 Kanowitz, *Women and Law*, p. 92.

47 John Hejno, "The Contraceptive Industry," *Eros*, Summer 1962, pp. 13–16.

tively a theoretical conception does not take place, it can also be argued that, in the long run, the rational control of conception has a positive side. Medical opinion holds that both the mother's and the child's health are greatly aided by periods of time between births. Thus, the medical emphasis is frequently on the use of contraception as a means of spacing childbirth.

Religious points of view on contraception are not in agreement. Until very recently, the Catholic church has taken the strongest position against it, prohibiting any mechanical, chemical, or physiological interference that will prevent the union of the ovum and the sperm. However, there are indications that the Catholic church is modifying its position. The strength of the Catholic position rests in part on the central authority of the church, while the Protestants and Jews have no central religious authority. But the Committee on Marriage and Home of the Federal Council of Churches, which represents a large sector of United States Protestantism, has stated: "As to the necessity for some form of effective control of the sizes of the family and spacing of children, and consequently of control of conception, there can be no question."[48] In practice, the general position of the Protestant churches centers on the motivation for the use of contraception. If the motives are right, then the use is right. This position defines the sex act of marriage as being both for reproduction and for the exchange and expression of love between marriage partners. The Reformed Jewish position is similar to that of the Protestants, but the Orthodox Jewish position opposes contraception.[49]

Socially, the development of contraceptive knowledge has provided many individuals with a control over their lives rarely before achieved. The ability to determine the number and spacing of children has placed the question of parenthood more and more within the rational decision-making powers of the married couple. It has also removed for many women the dangers and health damages that may result from frequent pregnancies. This greater rational control over pregnancy has had an influence on the emancipation of American women, because the woman is less subject to the problems of "chance" pregnancy.

The Legal Tangle

The fact that contraceptive knowledge is available to the American population in theory does not mean it is always legally available. Although some states have laws that prohibit the distribution of birth control knowledge, most states do not prohibit or restrict the dissemination of birth

---

[48] *Encyclopaedia Britannica*, s. v. "Birth Control." Also see Leon F. Bouvier, "Catholics and Contraception," *Journal of Marriage and the Family*, August 1973, pp. 514–22.

[49] *Encyclopaedia Britannica*, s. v. "Birth Control."

control information. There are still some states that have legal restrictions on the use and sale of contraceptives but it seems likely that these will be eliminated in the near future. This would seem logical from a legal point of view which increasingly argues that the right to control pregnancy and have children should be the right of the individual woman.

The legal tangle historically goes back to the lumping together of birth control information and laws on obscenity; consequently, contraceptive knowledge is identified with obscene writings and cannot be sent through the mails except to "qualified" individuals. The advertising of contraceptives is forbidden in many states,[50] and some states also have statutes that prohibit the teaching of birth control in any school.[51] Because the usual social means for the communication of knowledge is closed to birth control methods, the knowledge is diffused informally and oftentimes haphazardly, cutting down on the basic efficiency of contraceptive knowledge and use. "It is estimated that of the $200 million spent yearly in the United States for contraception, only about one tenth of that sum pays for the kinds recommended as best by physicians and birth control clinics."[52]

The legal tangle may become more complicated in the near future with the further development of oral contraception. For many years birth control authorities have been seeking a method that would be efficient, cheap, and simple to use. Oral contraception may meet all of these requirements in the very near future, but one very important difference exists between the potential use of oral contraception and mechanical and chemical methods. The oral contraceptive *could* be given to people without their knowledge, because it can be mixed with food or liquids. It seems reasonable to assume that with the greater development and use of oral contraception, many legal questions will have to be resolved regarding its usage as a means of applied social control over the fertility of unaware individuals and groups.

Illegitimacy

In the United States, illegitimacy has historically been viewed as morally-wrong, as well as a social threat to the stability of the family institution. Both the unwed mother and her offspring have been subjected to strong moral and legal punishment. Historically, the two primary reasons for the harsh treatment of illegitimate children were the desire to protect property and inheritance rights, and the desire to preserve religious and moral precepts accepted by many as important.[53]

---

[50] Drummond, *Sex Paradox*, p. 261.

[51] Ibid., p. 261.

[52] Ibid., p. 262.

[53] Clarke, *Social Legislation*, p. 365.

In recent years in the United States, the treatment of the illegitimate child has changed both legally and socially. "Legislation has been passed in every state tending to place the illegitimate child on an approximate legal equality with the legitimate child so far as his mother is concerned. Also, in many states he now has certain rights of maintenance, support, and inheritance from his father."[54] While some of the social stigma has been removed from the child, it still continues to exist for the unwed mother.[55] The new social attitude is that there are no illegitimate children, only illegitimate mothers.

Even though moral condemnation of the unwed mother continues, it seems to have limited influence on the behavior leading to unmarried pregnancy. In 1965 there were approximately 291,000 illegitimate births in the United States. From 1938 to 1958, the estimated number of illicit births per 1,000 live births in the United States increased slightly from 38.4 to 49.5,[56] though for the most part this rise in illegitimacy parallels the rise in all births. Herzog writes that it is "not that, suddenly and erratically, illegitimate births have shot up, and that this is an isolated aberration," but rather that this is a part of an evolution, not a revolution.[57]

During the period from 1960 to 1964, 28 percent of the nonwhite and 4 percent of the white women who were marrying for the first time had a child before that marriage. There had been a rise between the 1940s and the 1950s in the proportion of nonwhite women who had a child prior to marriage but no further increases in the 1960s. "Among whites there apparently has been an increase in the proportion of women who bear a child before marriage."[58]

There are several factors related to the increase in illegitimacy. One factor related to the increase is the decline in the incidence of induced abortion. With more girls having premarital intercourse and it still being difficult to get an abortion, the number of women having illegitimate children will increase. Another factor that may help to account for the rise in illegitimacy is the reduction of sterility associated with venereal disease.[59]

---

[54] Ibid., p. 365.

[55] Clark Vincent, *Unmarried Mothers* (Glencoe, Ill.: The Free Press, 1961), chap. 1.

[56] Ibid., p. 1.

[57] Elizabeth Herzog, "The Chronic Revolution: Births Out of Wedlock," *Clinical Pediatrics*, February 1966, p. 130.

[58] Reynolds Farley and Albert I. Hermalin, "Family Stability: A Comparison of Trends between Blacks and Whites," *American Sociological Review*, February 1971, p. 11.

[59] Alice J. Clague and Stephanie J. Ventura, "Trends in Illegitimacy," in Jeffrey K. Hadden and Marie T. Borgatta, *Marriage and the Family* (Itasca, Ill.: P. E. Peacock, 1969), p. 558.

It is commonly supposed that a large number of children are born to unmarried adolescent girls, and it is true that the proportion of all illicit births occurring to females under 15 years of age has remained about the same—2.3 percent in 1938 and 2.1 percent in 1963.[60] (In 1963, for those mothers between the ages of 15 and 19, about 39 percent of their births were out of wedlock.[61]) So the mothers of illegitimate children are often quite young. In the mid-1960s, 44 percent of the unmarried mothers giving birth were under 20 years of age.[62] But while teen-agers do represent a large proportion of unwed mothers, they constitute an even larger proportion of *all* unmarried females. Thus, when teen-agers are considered as a proportion of *all* unmarried females, they actually represent a smaller proportion of unmarried mothers today than they did in the past.[63] To put it another way, very few teen-agers are married in comparison with older women. Therefore, a smaller proportion of teen-age girls are in a position to have a legitimate child. "The result is that even though only a very small percent of the women aged 15–19 years have an illegitimate child (1.7 percent in 1965), a much larger percent of all births to teen-age mothers are classified as illegitimate."[64] Therefore, while illegitimacy is a characteristic of fairly young women, it is not particularly common among young adolescent girls. Thus, illegitimate babies are most often born during the years when their mothers are physically best able to bear a healthy child. This is important when it is realized that half or more of these children are placed out for adoption.

When the mother has an illegitimate child, she has several possible courses of action. She may give up the child by having it placed for adoption. Or, if she decides to keep the child, she may either take on complete responsibility for the child's rearing or seek financial help from the father by bringing a paternity suit against him. In most paternity cases, the burden of proof rests with the accused to prove he is *not* the father. Generally, the courts will award a paternity responsibility to the male if he has great difficulty proving he is not the father. Blood tests are usually not legally accepted as evidence of nonpaternity. The old, accused-male tactic of having a number of friends claim they had sexual relations with the girl no longer acquits the accused. Instead, what often happens is that the court makes *all* of the males financially responsible for the support of the child. In a paternity suit, the court is anxious to find someone who will be financially responsible, knowing that if it doesn't, the responsibility will rest with the state.

Since the burden of proof rests with the male in a paternity suit, males

---

[60] Vincent, *Unmarried Mothers*, p. 54; and Herzog, "Out of Wedlock," p. 132.

[61] Herzog, "Out of Wedlock," p. 132.

[62] Clague and Ventura, "Illegitimacy," p. 555.

[63] Herzog, "Out of Wedlock," p. 131.

[64] Clague and Ventura, "Illegitimacy," pp. 551–52.

who are actually not the fathers may be exploited. There is nothing to stop a pregnant girl from selecting a male, claiming he is the father, and having the suit taken to court. In most cases, the accused can do very little about it and may be given financial responsibility for the child. (Some legal opinion holds that, while this could happen in theory, it does not occur very often in reality.)

CHILDLESSNESS[65]

If a married couple are unable to have a natural child of their own, they may, through legal procedures, go about attaining one. The number of couples who are unable to have biological offspring of their own is higher than many realize. One very extensive fertility study found that "approximately 10 percent of the couples with the wife 35–39 years old are childless *and* have a fecundity problem."[66] This suggests that 10 percent of these couples where the wife has almost completed the childbearing years, are not biologically able to beget children. A discussion of two different ways in which the childlessness problem can be solved, and the legal aspects of the two procedures, follows.

Solutions to Childlessness

Adoption. In adoption, a child is taken bodily and completely from one family and legally made a part of another. This differs from custody, which shifts only the care and control of the child from one family to another.[67] The ultimate consequence of adoption is that it creates reciprocal rights and duties between adoptive parents and child, and a number of states provide that the legal relationship shall be the same as between natural parents and child.[68]

The procedural features of adoption legislation usually include the following steps. First, the petition of the adopting parents or their substitutes. Second, notice to the child's parents or their substitutes and receipt of their consent. Third, the presence of the necessary parties in court, where the final judicial decree is handed down.[69]

While the procedure varies from one state to another, here is how these steps operate, for example, in Pennsylvania. Generally, the first

---

[65] The social-psychological implications of childlessness are discussed in Chapter 16.

[66] Ronald Freeman, Pascal K. Whelpton, and Arthur A. Campbell, *Family Planning, Sterility and Population Growth* (New York: McGraw-Hill Book Co., 1959), p. 47.

[67] Bradway, "Members Should Know," p. 587.

[68] Clarke, *Social Legislation*, p. 329.

[69] Ibid., p. 317.

step is the agreement of the natural parent or parents to place the child for adoption. Permission may be given by the parent or a legally delegated authority. After the adopting parents file a petition, there is a waiting period of six months before the final decree can be handed down. During that time, the adopting parents are usually investigated by a county social worker as to their fitness to be parents. Even though the adopting parents have the child during the waiting period, it is often a time of great anxiety for them because the child is not legally theirs. If the natural parent or parents should change their minds and want the child back, the adopting parents would in most cases have to give up the child. When the time for the final decree is reached, the natural parent or parents must be notified of the time and place of the legal hearing. They normally do not appear and the only ones present are the adopting parents with their lawyer and the child. Often the hearing is brief and held in the privacy of the judge's chambers. Once the decree is handed down, the child is then legally a member of the adopting family. The original birth certificate is impounded in the state capitol, and a new one is issued with the adopting parents' names. The new birth certificate is exactly like one issued to the parents of a natural born child.

In many states, the various social agencies have waged a legal battle for their complete control of all adoption and against the maintenance of legal rights of other specified individuals to place children for adoption. The trend has been to give the social agencies control over adoption under the assumption that they are best able to make an assessment of what will constitute a good home for the child. In 1963 there were 127,000 adoptions in the United States and almost half of the adoptions were made by other relatives, most often by step-parents. But of the remaining 67,000, the majority (44,000, or 66 percent) were arranged by adoption agencies.[70] Social workers seem to be in limited agreement on objective procedures for determining a good home, and many times their criteria are highly questionable. For example, some adoption agencies ask the prospective adopting parents to write essays on "Why I Think I Can Be a Good Parent" or "Why I Want a Child." Even family authorities would disagree on what would be the "best" answers to these highly subjective questions. Very often the prospective parents write what they think the adoption agency wants to hear—not what they themselves really feel. Further techniques for screening out potential parents are often used, not because of meaningful differences between the various couples, but because the demand for white infants for adoption far exceeds the supply. It has been estimated that there are approximately ten times as many applicants as there are children available for adoption.[71] (Two groupings

[70] Statistical Abstract of the U.S., *U.S. Bureau of the Census* (Washington, D.C.: U.S. Government Printing Office, 1964), p. 312.

[71] Hugo G. Beigel, "Illegitimacy," in Albert Ellis and Albert Abarbanel, eds., *The Encyclopedia of Sexual Behavior* (New York: Hawthorn Books, Inc., 1961), p. 513.

of children sometimes lead to the impression that a large number of infants and children are available for adoption. One is the number of black infants and children up for adoption; but rarely are black children placed in white homes. The second is a common tendency to think of foster children as being available for adoption. There are about 175,000 children living in foster homes and 95,000 children in public institutions, but only about 5 percent of these are available for adoption.[72])

In making its final decision for placement, a social agency may not be so much objective as simply arbitrary. Too, the adopting parents often do not get the child before four to six months of age because the agencies want to keep the infants long enough to make a rather careful check on them. As a result, the adopting parents are not given the chance of rearing the very young infant. In acquiring a child for adoption through a legally qualified individual (often a physician or lawyer), the infant may be brought home six or seven days after birth.

There has been some concern about the consequences for the young infant who is held in an institution against being placed in the adopting home. One British study found no significant differences in the emotional and social development of children who were adopted early (before six months of age) and children reared by their natural parents. "However, children adopted later than six months of age were inclined to exhibit behavioral problems such as lying, stealing, being destructive toward property, being cruel to animals, and having temper tantrums."[73]

It is estimated that about 100,000 petitions for adoption are made each year in the United States. It is further estimated that about 70 percent of all white illegitimate children are given up for adoption and that they constitute about 40 percent of the total adoption market.[74] The relationship between the two social problems of illegitimacy and childlessness is an interesting one. Illegitimacy is viewed as a social problem that should be eliminated; however, a significant decrease in illegitimacy would result in an increase in the number of marriages that would have to remain childless because of the lack of adoption opportunities. A marriage which is without children when they are desired is also viewed as a significant social problem. So one social problem (illegitimacy) helps to resolve another (childlessness). But there is a social-class difference in the two solutions. The higher the social-class level, as measured by education, the less the belief that the unwed mother should raise her child and the greater the belief that the child will be better off reared by adoptive parents. Kirk found that for those respondents with some high-school education or less, 73 percent thought the unwed mother should

---

[72] Ibid., p. 513.

[73] Michael Humphrey and Christopher Ounsted, "Adoptive Families Referred for Psychiatric Advice—I: The Children," *British Journal of Psychiatry*, vol. 109 (1963), p. 601.

[74] Vincent, *Unmarried Mothers*, pp. 13, 195.

rear her own child and 27 percent that the child should be reared by adoptive parents; however, for college-educated respondents, only 27 percent said the unwed mother, while 73 percent said adoptive parents should rear the child—or exactly the reverse.[75]

The values reflected by legal and social agencies mean that children placed out for adoption most often go to upper middle-class couples. Furthermore, among childless couples there is a highly selective process operating. First, those couples are selected out of the total childless population by their decision to try to solve their problem through adoption. Second, once the decision to adopt is made, there is a further selection process determined by the ability of the couple to find and obtain a child for adoption, either independently or through agencies.

Usually the greatest pressure to adopt comes from the wife in a marriage. This seems logical, given the generally greater commitment to the parental role by the woman than by the man. Kirk found that 94 percent of his female respondents and 85 percent of his male respondents said they would adopt if they could have no children of their own.[76] Because many couples may spend several years trying to have natural children without success, and because they often have to wait some length of time before getting a baby for adoption, adopting parents become parents at older ages. Kirk found that adopting parents were about seven years older than their biological counterparts when they received their first child.[77]

There is some evidence of a preference for sons by parents prior to the birth of their first natural child. However, Kirk suggests that there may be a tendency among adoptive parents to prefer girls,[78] arguing that with the wife feeling the most deprived in not being able to fill her parental role, and the husband often the hesitant spouse with regard to adoption, a girl may represent a compromise solution.[79] There may also be a belief that as a girl grows older, and begins to see the importance of her future mother role, she will have fewer concerns and anxieties about her own adoption than would a boy. It may also be that many times the adopted child had unwed natural parents, and being of illegitimate birth status may have less stigma for the girl than for the boy.

Often when a couple have made the important decision to adopt and have gone through all the demands necessary for adoption, they are not overly concerned with what may appear to be unimportant questions. For example, Kirk found that adoptive parents were fairly detached about

---

[75] H. David Kirk, *Shared Fate* (New York: The Free Press of Glencoe, 1964), p. 28.

[76] Ibid., p. 134.

[77] Ibid., p. 9.

[78] Ibid., pp. 126–28.

[79] Ibid., p. 143.

matching their physical appearance to that of the child, with only 48 percent of the husbands and 50 percent of the wives saying they thought this factor important. There was even greater detachment with regard to the child's nationality background. Only on the question of racial background was the large majority of adopting parents in favor of a homogeneous family. Three quarters of all the respondents said that matching by race was very important.[80]

Artificial Insemination. For a number of childless couples, artificial insemination is the only way their problem may be biologically resolved. Artificial insemination was first attempted with a human in 1799 by the English physician Dr. John Hunter; the first recorded attempts in the United States were not made until 1866, by Dr. Marion Simms of North Carolina. She performed 55 inseminations with varying degrees of success.[81]

There are two types of artificial insemination. The first type, AIH or artificial insemination with sperm from the husband, is a medical procedure often used because of conception problems related to the sperm meeting the ovum through the natural method of sexual intercourse. This type of artificial insemination generates little social concern or legal interest. The second type is AID, artificial insemination with sperm from a donor. The donor is almost always anonymous. Much social and legal confusion has developed around AID.

Theoretically, AID could solve the childless problem of a large number of married couples. Conception inability among married couples is estimated to rest with the husband in about 40 percent of the cases. In many of these cases, the husband produces no sperm, or the sperm count is so low or the sperm are so sluggish that biologically fathering a child is impossible or extremely difficult for him. AID substitutes sperm from an anonymous donor so that the wife may become pregnant. When the sperm is contributed, some of the inheritable physical characteristics of the male donor are often recorded. The physician may then try to match the physical characteristics of the donor with those of the husband. The physician usually gets the sperm from a "sperm bank," so that neither he nor the couple know the identity of the contributor. Success of conception through AID has reportedly been achieved in 50 to 80 percent of the cases where it has been used. Estimates suggest that there are about 20,000 persons in the United States who were conceived through AID.

Clearly, AID is used in only a very small number of cases in which it theoretically could be applied. Of the several reasons for this, one is that probably only a limited number of Americans are aware of its possibili-

[80] Ibid., p. 60.

[81] Alan F. Guttmacher, *Planning Your Family* (New York: Macmillan, 1961), p. 254.

ties. Second, it has had some religious opposition, particularly from the Catholic church.[82] Third, two studies both indicate resistance to AID even when it is explained or known to the respondents, although the two studies show sharp disagreement in the stated approval of AID. In one study, 52 percent said they approved of AID, while in the other, only 17 percent approved. (In the second study, 27.5 percent were "undecided," while in the first, the respondents were forced to answer "yes" or "no.")[83] Vernon and Boadway found some difference in acceptance by sex. For the males, 22 percent indicated acceptance of AID, compared with 14 percent of the females.[84] The reasons given by the respondents for rejecting AID were: would prefer adoption, 40.6 percent; morally wrong, adultery, etc., 16.6 percent; church disapproval, 16.6 percent; source of marital friction, 9.7 percent; others, 15.5 percent.[85]

The writer has many times presented the following question to his students: "If you were married and you both wanted children, and it was discovered that the husband was absolutely sterile, which method of resolving your childlessness would you prefer to use, adoption or AID?" About 90 percent of the students chose adoption. The main reason given is that if both husband and wife can't contribute to the genetic make-up of the child, then neither spouse should. When it is pointed out that if the inheritable traits of the wife are valued, it might make sense to transmit at least those, students may see the logic of AID argument, but they will still emotionally reject it; for them, half a genetic loaf is *not* better than no genetic loaf at all.

A legal judgment was not passed on AID in the United States until 1948, although at an earlier date the Canadian case of Oxford vs. Oxford in 1921 held that artificial insemination was adultery.[86] "In 1948 the New York courts established the legitimacy of a child born to a woman artificially impregnated with a donor's semen and with the husband's consent."[87] Drummond suggests that on the basis of legal principles, if AID were performed "without the husband's prior consent, it seems likely that he would have [a legal] action for damages against the doctor performing it."[88]

There are no federal or state laws in the United States that govern

---

[82] Glenn A. Vernon and Jack A. Boadway, "Attitudes Toward Artificial Insemination and Some Variables Associated Therewith," *Marriage and Family Living*, February 1959, p. 45.

[83] Ibid., p. 44; and Joseph H. Greenberg, "Social Variables in Acceptance or Rejection of Artificial Insemination," *American Sociological Review*, February 1951, p. 88.

[84] Vernon and Boadway, "Artificial Insemination," p. 46.

[85] Ibid., p. 43.

[86] Clarke, *Social Legislation*, p. 181.

[87] Ibid., p. 181.

[88] Drummond, *Sex Paradox*, p. 252.

the use of artificial insemination. The only local ordinance is in New York City where "a section of the sanitary code imposes regulations for checking the health of a semen donor."[89] In six different states, bills have been introduced that deal specifically with artificial insemination; however, none of the bills has been enacted into law. In two states, "the bills were unfavorable and aimed at stigmatizing donor insemination as unlawful, the child illegitimate and the parties of the act subject to fine and imprisonment." In the other four states, "the bills were favorable with the objectives of legalizing the procedure, legitimizing the offspring, and assuring their full rights of inheritance."[90] One student of society and the law suggests that "as in all other scientific achievements, the law's response to artificial insemination has been, and will be, perfect horror; skepticism; curiosity; and then acceptance."[91]

As one would expect, there have been wide differences by organized religion with regard to both AIH and AID. Most Jewish and Protestant groups in the United States approve of AIH and AID. However, the Orthodox Jewish faith stipulates that AIH is permissible only after 10 years of a childless marriage and after all medical means of having children have failed. The Orthodox Jew believes that children born as a result of AID are legitimate, but the practice is forbidden. A woman who gives birth to a child as a result of AID, regardless of permission by the husband, may be sued by him for divorce.[92] The Catholic church rejects both AIH and AID. On this subject, Pope Pius XII in 1956 said, "Artificial insemination is not within the rights acquired by a couple by virtue of the marriage contract, nor is the right to its use derived from the right of offspring as a primary objective of matrimony."[93]

LEGAL RIGHTS OF THE CHILD

From the earliest days of American colonization, the courts have set up certain legal rights for the child. The general principle is to allow the parents flexibility in handling their children unless certain treatments are felt to be detrimental to the child or to society. Today, the welfare of the child is of paramount legal consideration, and the mother has been given rights equal to the father in the custody of their children. The legal changes have corresponded roughly with the shift from patriarchal rights to the more democratic view of equal parental rights.

---

[89] Guttmacher, *Planning*, p. 269.

[90] Albert P. Massey, "Artificial Insemination: The Law's Illegitimate Child?" *Villanova Law Review*, vol. 9 (1964), pp. 79–82.

[91] S. B. Schatkin, "The Legal Aspects of Artificial Insemination," *Fertility and Sterility*, vol. 5 (1954), p. 40.

[92] See Guttmacher, *Planning*, p. 267.

[93] Quoted in Ibid., p. 266.

Usually only in "extreme" cases will the courts move in on the parents and take the custody of their children out of their hands. "Almost all cases where parents have been deprived of custody are those in which they were shown to be unfit or in which they had relinquished their right for a time and then sought the aid of the court to regain custody."[94]

Not only must parents legally meet basic requirements in the care of their children, but they must also provide for the children's education up to some legally specified age or grade or both. A system of legal equity for the education of children beyond the basic requirements may also lead to extended educational responsibility for the parents. The courts "will exercise their discretion in civil suits to determine whether 'higher education' is necessary."[95]

In custody cases, most courts tend to follow the same legal reasoning in contests between the mother and father for the child. Courts generally award the mother custody of infants and young children, especially girls, "even where the mother's conduct has been such that if the children were older or of the other sex, their custody would be placed elsewhere."[96] The legal attitude reflects a general social belief that if there has to be a choice of one parent for the child, the mother is the more important one.

In the support of the child, the responsibility both in common law and by statute rests upon the father. During the father's lifetime, the mother has no obligation to support the children in the absence of statutory provisions.[97] The father's responsibility to his children remains even if the marriage is ended. "Today, the courts ordinarily hold that the father remains liable for the support of his minor children when he and his wife are divorced, legally separated, or living apart on an agreement, although there are circumstances when this is not true."[98] The courts' position is based upon the fact that if the father does not meet the economic needs of his children and the wife is unable to, then the costs would be the responsibility of the state.

Inheritance

The rights of inheritance in the United States have changed with the legal shift from patriarchal to a more democratically oriented concept of the family. The change is reflected in the legal rights of inheritance for the wife and children. In a patriarchal society, the wife had few legal rights of inheritance. Inheritance followed the principle of *primogeniture,* in which inheritance or succession of authority was passed on to the first

---

[94] Clarke, *Social Legislation*, p. 224.

[95] Ibid., p. 251.

[96] Ibid., p. 224.

[97] Ibid., p. 242.

[98] Ibid., p. 243.

born, specifically the eldest son. The law of primogeniture as understood in England has been abolished throughout the United States, and male and female relatives inherit equally.[99]

As with all legal interpretations in the United States, no two states have identical roles of descent, although the passing on of real and personal property tend to be essentially the same. The usual form of statute gives the wife one half when there is but one child. When there is more than one child, the wife takes the same size share as each of the children.[100] These rights are legal rights provided by the state for cases in which the deceased has not made a formal designation for inheritance. There are two mutually exclusive legal procedures in reference to inheritance, absolute rights of *bequest* and *inheritance*. "In general, by an absolute right of bequest is meant the freedom to leave one's possessions exactly as one pleases, whereas an absolute right of inheritance is an unalienable right to possess what someone has left."[101]

In practice, when the individual has a fairly large amount of wealth, he makes his bequests through a will. Under a will, the person can "cut off" any member of his family he chooses, and if the will is legally valid it is very difficult to have it changed. But when no will exists, the inheritance statutes of the state determine the distribution of property and wealth.

The discussion of some legal and social aspects of marriage and the family suggest several generalizations: (1) Society, through the development of a legal system, sets up minimum requirements felt to be basic to the family. Because the legal framework is broad, the range of legally acceptable individual behavior is fairly wide. (2) The legal system tends to be resistant to social change and, as a result, a dysfunctional relationship often exists between the law and social attitudes and behavior. (3) Finally, a legal understanding of marriage and family laws is very difficult because there is no federal law, only the laws of 53 distinct legal jurisdictions.

SELECTED BIBLIOGRAPHY

Clarke, Helen I. *Social Legislation.* New York: Appleton-Century-Crofts, 1957.

Drummond, Isabel *The Sex Paradox.* New York: G. P. Putnam's Sons, 1953.

Kanowitz, Leo *Women and the Law.* Albuquerque: University of New Mexico Press, 1969.

Kephart, William M. "Legal and Procedural Aspects of Marriage and Di-

---

[99] *Encyclopaedia Britannica,* 1962 ed., s. v. "Inheritance."

[100] Ibid., p. 357.

[101] Ibid., p. 358.

vorce," in Harold T. Christensen, ed., *Handbook of Marriage and The Family.* Chicago: Rand McNally & Co., 1964, pp. 944–68.

Kirk, H. David   *Shared Fate.* New York: The Free Press of Glencoe, 1964.

Pilpel, Harriet F.   "Sex vs. the Law: A Study in Hypocrisy." *Harpers,* January 1965, pp. 35–40.

Reeves, Nancy   *Womankind: Beyond the Stereotype.* Chicago: Aldine, 1971.

Rheinstein, Max   *Marriage Stability, Divorce, and the Law.* Chicago: University of Chicago Press, 1972.

Vernon, Glenn A., and Boadway, Jack A.   "Attitudes Toward Artificial Insemination and Some Variables Associated Therewith." *Marriage and Family Living,* February 1959, pp. 43–47.

Vincent, Clark   *Unmarried Mothers.* Glencoe, Ill.: The Free Press, 1961.

Chapter *11*

The Nature of Marriage

Probably no other society in the world, past or present, has shown as great a social and personal concern with marriage as the United States today. All areas of mass communications devote time and energy to the question of marriage, and a great amount of their interest is directed at the "problem" areas of marriage: marital frustrations and unhappiness, sexual maladjustment, role confusion, and divorce. These areas, and many others, have also been of great interest to the social scientist studying the family institution.

Anthropological literature shows a wide range of social adaptations to the relationships of marriage and the family. It is important to keep in mind that the patterns of marriage common to other societies may be quite different from those found in the American middle class. While all societies, past and present, have had some form of marriage, they have not always been monogamous nor have they always even been assumed to be permanent. Nor in all societies has it been necessary for husband and wife to live together, "nor do necessarily they 'cleve together and forsake all others,' nor need they be the main source of either their own livelihood or the care, protection, discipline, and legal identification of their children."[1]

There is in the middle-class American family a strong belief in mar-

[1] Conrad M. Arensberg, "The American Family in the Perspective of Other Cultures," in Eli Ginzberg, ed., *The Nation's Children* (New York: Columbia University Press, 1960), p. 60.

riage being a relationship of togetherness. That is, in the United States, marriage generally involves a high degree of intimacy and sharing between husband and wife: "going together to parties, on visits, and to various recreations; jointly owning house, car, and other possessions; and so forth. This degree of togetherness is usually *not* found in other societies."[2] In some societies, the husband and wife do not "live" together in the sense that we use the word. In those societies, "the most common living arrangement is for each wife to have her own house (or hut); the husband either has another house of his own, or divides his time between the houses of his various wives."[3] And in many societies, characterized by the extended family, the young couple at the time of marriage usually move in with the husband's family of orientation. In the United States, on the other hand, the pattern has increasingly been that married couples will, as soon as they possibly can, have their own households. That this value is very strong is reflected in the statistic that in 1960, 98 percent of all married couples maintained their own households.[4]

One other important and almost special value placed on marriage in the American middle class is that the success of the marriage relationship generally determines the broader stability and success of that family of procreation. Our American ideals almost represent a cultural extreme, both in the reduction of the family in size and because of the major value placed on the success of the marriage relationship.[5] And even with the many changes in American marriage, and the increased availability of divorce, the institution of marriage appears to be stronger than ever in the United States.

Our interests in this chapter will be with the nature of marriage as it is found in the middle class today, and will focus on changes in patterns of marriage, the wedding and the honeymoon, reasons for entering marriage, and different marriage orientations. The next chapter, Chapter 12, will deal with marriage roles and marital adjustment.

PATTERNS OF MARRIAGE

American marriage rates are among the highest in the world. Close to 95 percent of all Americans will be married at least once before they die. In 1900, two out of every three women in the total population of the United States had been married at some time in their lives, while at the present time this is true for four out of five women.[6] In 1970, for

---

[2] William N. Stephens, *The Family in Cross-Cultural Perspective* (New York: Holt, Rinehart & Winston, Inc., 1963), p. 270.

[3] Ibid., pp. 270–71.

[4] U.S. Bureau of the Census, "Characteristics of the Population: Part I," *U.S. Census of Population,* vol. 1, table 79, 1960.

[5] Arensberg, "American Family," p. 60.

[6] Margaret Mead and Frances B. Kaplan, eds., *American Women: The Report of The President's Commission* (New York: Charles Scribner's Sons, 1965), p. 80.

the third consecutive year, there were over 2 million marriages in the United States. The rate of marriage had continued to increase so that the 1970 rate of 10.7 marriages per 1,000 individuals was the highest annual rate since 1950.[7] However, as pointed out in Chapter 7, there is some evidence that the marriage rate has fallen off slightly in the early 1970s.

Americans are now marrying at the youngest ages recorded over the past 80 years, and, with a few exceptions, over the years the pattern of movement has been steadily toward younger ages at marriage for *both* men and women. Between 1890 and 1972 the median age of marriage dropped from 22.0 to 20.9 years for women and from 26.1 to 23.3 years for men.[8] These figures also show that the age difference between husband and wife has been decreasing—from 4.1 years in 1890 to 2.4 years in 1972. Another way of illustrating the increasing pattern of marrying at young ages is that during the 1950s and early 1960s about one half of all women entered their first marriage by the time they were 20 years of age; by contrast, in 1940, about half of all women had not entered their first marriage until they were about 21.5 years.[9] The evidence available at the present time suggests that the high marriage rate and the young marriage ages will continue into at least the near future. There is also a common tendency to combine marriage and higher education by many young people. In 1970, 27 percent of the men and 19 percent of the women enrolled in U.S. colleges and universities were married.[10]

However, there are variations in age at marriage related to certain social variables. For example, early marriage has a strong attraction for some young people. Some see early marriage as the best means to achieve adult status and related privileges. It is also seen as providing a daily and nightly partner who serves to reduce the psychological cost extracted from the lone individual by the mobility-achievement system which pervades much of our society. In other words, early marriage is seen by many as providing them with a "significant other at a time when they have a strong need for that type of relationship."[11]

As suggested earlier, there are also possible negative consequences to early marriage. The earlier the marriage the more apt it is to be dis-

---

[7] David H. Olson, "Marriage in the Future: Revolutionary or Evolutionary Change?" *The Family Coordinator,* October 1972, p. 383.

[8] U.S. Bureau of the Census, *Current Population Reports,* Series P-20, No. 242, "Marital Status and Living Arrangements, March 1972" (Washington, D.C.: U.S. Government Printing Office, 1972), p. 2.

[9] Paul C. Glick, "Demographic Analysis of Family Data," in Harold T. Christensen, ed., *Handbook of Marriage and The Family* (Chicago: Rand McNally & Co., 1964), p. 301.

[10] U.S. Bureau of the Census, *Current Population Reports,* Series P-20, No. 222, "School Enrollment, October 1970" (U.S. Government Printing Office, 1970), p. 1.

[11] Clark E. Vincent, "Sex and the Young Married," *Medical Aspects of Human Sexuality,* March 1969, p. 15.

solved by the couple. Also, the earlier the marriage, the more likely it is to be characterized by negative effects.[12] Very often the question of success or failure in a marriage may be less determined by chronological age than by personal and social maturity.

While a great deal of criticism has been directed at elements of the dating-courtship process in the United States, the process must be recognized as being successful at least in respect to the large number of individuals who move from it into marriage. In several respects, the high marriage rate in the United States is surprising because of social and personal influences that might, on the surface, appear to reduce the desire for marriage. For example, it might be argued that any one of the following factors would reduce the interest in marriage:

High divorce rate. Because so many marriages end in divorce, some might choose not to marry because they are not willing to chance the psychological and social costs of having a marriage fail.

Marital adjustment. The image sometimes projected to young people is that in many cases marriage is a relationship of conflict and dissatisfaction. Individuals might feel they do not want a relationship that has a chance of going contrary to the values of personal happiness felt to be so important in the American society.

Freedom of women. In the past, women had little choice other than marriage for their adult role but, today, many occupational roles are open to them. Some might choose not to marry because the other alternatives provide more attractive adult role opportunities than does marriage.

Greater sexual freedom. The pleasures of sex were traditionally seen as something to be achieved from marriage. The evidence today clearly indicates that many achieve at least some sexual satisfaction without marriage, so the sex inducement to marry has been reduced.

Familiarity with opposite sex. In the past, marriage often meant the first close contact with a "mysterious" member of the opposite sex. With today's long and intimate dating-courtship relationship, each sex learns a great deal about the other and is, therefore, less mysterious to the other.

Less need to marry. In very recent years the social pressure to marry, especially for the young woman, has been somewhat reduced. There are more occupational options, as well as living arrangements, different from the past that are now available. The overwhelming need to marry in the United States is being altered.

While all of these factors might logically seem to be forces in reducing the desire to marry, they are not, in fact, marital deterrents of any great strength. The positive reasons for marriage seem to be overriding in their significance for the individual.

---

[12] Karen W. Bartz and F. Ivan Nye, "Early Marriages: A Propositional Formulation," *Journal of Marriage and the Family*, May 1970, p. 265.

THE WEDDING

In all societies, the transition from single to married roles involves some ceremony—that is, some applied sanctions that are part of the social system. The individual also incurs new rights and obligations with his newly achieved status. The nature of the ceremony and rituals of marriage vary a great deal. Most societies celebrate marriage with extensive marriage ceremonies and in many societies marriage involves a series of wedding ceremonies. The marriage customs of the United States, when looked at in a cross-cultural perspective, are characterized by simplicity, informality, and cultural poverty.[13] In the United States the couple have a range of choices—from being married in a few minutes by a justice of the peace to a wedding ceremony and receptions that may last for several days.

At present, entering marriage means entering a role that will exist for a long period of time. The great attention and publicity that centers around the high divorce rates in the United States causes many to overlook the fact that most marriages last for long periods of time, and will be ended only through the death of one of the partners. Also, the years of marriage have been extended by the early age of marriage and the greater life expectancy of both sexes.

In the United States, the act of marriage has two important institutional focuses, the legal and the religious. All individuals must meet the legal requirements for marriage—those discussed in Chapter 10. Marriage, in the legal sense, is an act that places a man and woman under legal and social obligations to each other.[14] With the exception of a few states, however, a religious ceremony is not a legal requirement. The couple have a choice as to type of ceremony because 47 out of the 50 states permit either a clergyman or a civil official to preside over the marriage ceremony.[15] (Most couples choose to be married in a religious ceremony. In 1961, 83 percent of all brides and grooms entering a first marriage were wed in a religious rather than civil ceremony.[16])

While all individuals have to meet certain legal requirements for marriage, many also choose to meet the religious requirements, because religious approval is of great importance to them. This is particularly true for the Catholic, because his church defines marriage as a sacrament. However, all clergymen perform the ceremony not in their capacity as

---

[13] Stephens, *Family in Perspective*, p. 239.

[14] Helen I. Clarke, *Social Legislation* (New York: Appleton-Century-Crofts, 1957), p. 27.

[15] William M. Kephart, "Legal and Procedural Aspects of Marriage and Divorce," in Harold T. Christensen, ed., *Handbook of Marriage and The Family* (Chicago: Rand McNally & Co., 1964), p. 949.

[16] Vital Statistics of the United States, "Marriages," vol. III., sections 1, 2, and 7 (United States Department of Health, Education, and Welfare, 1961), p. 4.

ministers, but as civil officers constituted for that purpose by the state. The words and rituals of the religious ceremony do not make the couple legally married; the formal start of marriage begins with the signing of the marriage license by the delegated legal authority.

The religious as opposed to the nonreligious wedding ceremony has been of interest to a number of family researchers as it relates to success in marriage. Statistically, marriages with religious ceremonies have a higher rate of success than marriages without religious ceremonies—possibly for several reasons. First, the more conforming members of society, who would be less prone to ending their marriages through divorce, are more likely to have a religious ceremony. Second, starting marriage with a religious ceremony may provide an added incentive for the couple to achieve success. Third, religious group supports and sanctions add to the importance of maintaining the marriage.

Since the wedding ceremony differs in importance to different couples, their marriages take place in several different ways. They may elope or marry secretly, which means a minimum of social ritual. When persons choose to invite a number of guests, they may be married in a church, at home, or in a hired hall. Since both number of guests and site of wedding and reception can vary a great deal, the total cost of getting married ranges widely. For many middle-class families, the cost of launching a daughter on her marriage may be several thousand dollars.

The reception following the wedding publicly presents the couple as husband and wife for the first time. Their first acts as a married couple are frequently symbolic; their joined hands making the first cut in the wedding cake, for example. In the American culture, no single pattern socially defines the marriage ceremony. For some groups, marriage is a solemn and almost sad occasion, which may reflect an attitude that the young couple are leaving their carefree single years behind them and entering their responsible adult years. The traditional American wedding ceremony and reception often has this overtone. However, other groups view marriage as a time of great happiness, the start of a period of pleasure that now lies ahead for those who have acquired the privileges of marriage. This joyousness is often seen in the ceremonies and receptions of groups more recently transplanted to the American culture and it reflects "old country" values.

In Chapter 4, it was pointed out that engagement represents a period of high personal prestige and glamour for the girl, with her prestige reaching its peak on the wedding day. The folk cliché is that "all brides are beautiful." In American middle-class culture, the wedding, like the engagement, is female centered, and usually the responsibility of the girl's family, with the planning generally done by the bride and her mother. The bride's central role in the wedding is symbolized by the time and expense devoted to her bridal gown, a gown that will be worn only once. By contrast, the groom may buy something new to wear, but it is put to use after marriage.

The groom is not necessarily the second most important figure at the wedding. Both domination and prestige tend to center on the female, and the glory spreads from the bride to her mother, the groom's mother, the matron or maid of honor, and the bridesmaids. The female's importance at weddings is related to several historical factors. First, the bride was traditionally given in marriage in the sense that she left the parental home for that of the husband. This is still true in many ways and is symbolized by the bride giving up her family name for that of the husband's. Second, marriage has been and continues to be entrance for the female into her most important adult status, wife-mother. Therefore, the marriage symbolizes the significance of role change for the woman getting married as well as for those women who have been or will be married. Marriage is often seen as a "rite of passage" for the female into adult status.

The marriage ceremony also has a more extended social function related to prestige. For example, the dress and the overall material display associated with the wedding and the reception are often matters of social prestige. The family may desire to have an impressive wedding so as to launch the young couple into marriage with deserved fanfare. In other cases, the girl's family may have a costly wedding either in hopes of gaining prestige or out of fear of losing social face if they do not. The latter concern is illustrated by the success of business firms that completely take over the planning of a wedding and reception with the guarantee that it will be done "right" and family prestige will be retained or enhanced.

THE HONEYMOON

The honeymoon is increasingly accepted as a part of getting married. This is particularly true for middle-class couples, most of whom take a honeymoon that usually lasts for a period of a few days to a few weeks.

Honeymoon Functions

Recuperation. The period leading up to the wedding and ending after the ceremony and reception makes great demands on the physical and psychological stamina of the couple, particularly the bride. Once the day is over, the couple, who are often near exhaustion, need to go somewhere where they can relax. However, the tendency for some to take a long trip for a honeymoon, particularly if they are driving an automobile, often creates a situation in which rest and recuperation are extremely difficult. And being rested and relaxed is probably a contributing factor to the initial success of marital interaction.

Initial Adjustment.   The honeymoon can provide favorable conditions in which to start filling the new roles of husband and wife. The couple can devote most of their attention to their new marriage roles and temporarily put aside other, possibly distracting, role demands. The honeymoon removes the person from the environment in which his established habits function and encourages him to concentrate on the formation of new patterns. The newness of the honeymoon setting goes with the newness of the marriage roles.

While each partner has already made certain definitions of both his own and his spouse's marital roles, actual participation in the roles is, of course, new. Thus, one important element of adjustment in marriage is the individual's adjustment to the new role. While aspects of adjustment are discussed in Chapter 12, several factors may be pointed out here. First, the individuals rarely come back from their honeymoon fully adjusted either to their own new role or to the relationship between the husband and wife roles. The more common achievement may be some initial sense of ease with being a husband or a wife. Because adjustment in marriage is a dynamic process, a start in developing the facilities of adjustment would seem a reasonable expectation for the honeymoon. The negative influences of an unsatisfactory honeymoon may have unfortunate long-range consequences. Because the honeymoon relationship is highly idealistic, an unsatisfactory initial adjustment may destroy the early idealism in marriage and lead to a feeling of great loss for the couple.

Second, when the couple return to their everyday lives, other role demands will again be made and must be shared with the new marriage role demands. If very limited success results when full effort is directed at the marriage roles on the honeymoon, greater marriage role success may be even more difficult to achieve when some attention must be directed to other roles. Regardless of the honeymoon's success, when the couple leave it, they must move from an exclusive marriage-role orientation to one shared with other role demands.

Sexual Expression.   Sexual adjustment in marriage is one subdivision of the total adjustment process, but it probably has an even more dynamic quality of change over time than most other areas. The sex needs and feelings of individuals are not constant and often change drastically with length of marriage. Therefore, the achievement of sexual adjustment on the honeymoon only means the couple have reached a point in their sexual relationship satisfactory at that time. This initial sexual adjustment makes no guarantee for the future. However, sex and the honeymoon are given great attention in American society because the folklore of the honeymoon equates it almost entirely with sexual behavior.

In the literature that gives sex advice to the newly married, great emphasis is placed on early sexual satisfaction for the bride. While the male usually enters marriage with great sexual anticipations, the female is probably more apt to enter marriage with some sexual anxiety and apprehension. Most of the professional advice given to the newly married couple for the honeymoon period stresses the need for the female to be encouraged and helped by an "understanding and skillful" husband.

Because the female is conditioned to believe that she must reserve her sexual expression for marriage, she may enter the honeymoon with some problems. To the extent that she accepts the belief that sexual relations go with being married, her entering into marital coitus with increasing degrees of freedom will be associated with her being accustomed to being married. As she comes to accept her new overall role as natural, she will also be increasingly apt to enter into marital sexual behavior with a minimum of inhibitions and anxieties.

The "romantic" nature of American sex training may also create problems for some girls on their honeymoon. A part of the rationale for abstaining from coitus before marriage is that sex after marriage will be worth waiting for. The girl may have developed an idealistic image or romanticized version of the marital sexual relationship that is behaviorally unobtainable. Some girls may have a feeling of letdown after their initial sexual experience in marriage—not because the experience was unpleasant, but because it did not reach the idealistic peaks they had imagined it would.

REASONS FOR MARRIAGE

As already indicated, some of the reasons for marriage have changed, and various combinations of old and new influences operate for different individuals. The following discussion will refer to some common influences that operate in today's American society.

Social Values

Since there are few clear-cut role definitions providing adult status for the young adult, the acquiring of what are believed to be particular adult roles takes on the added importance of providing meaning to the unclearly defined general role. The role distinction between the single and the married person is clear and unambiguous; the role distinction between adolescent and adult is not. Being single and adolescent are related roles filled by the same individual; being an adult and married are also generally seen as related. Therefore, a part of the desire to seek and achieve adult status is felt to be accomplished by getting married, and many young people are anxious for marriage for this reason.

The consideration of adulthood and marriage as related roles can also be seen in a common attitude toward the older single person. The bachelor is sometimes perceived as someone who will not "grow up" and take on responsibilities; that is, he won't get married. The spinster may be perceived as an unfortunate person unable to fill important adult roles. For example, people may consider her able to take care of someone's children but simultaneously believe that she does not *really* understand children because she has not personally experienced the roles of wife and mother.

Related to the above points is that marriage may be considered a means of sex-role fulfillment. This is probably much more important for the woman than the man, even today when the woman has a number of adult-role alternatives to marriage. The male has been socialized toward his important role of occupation, but, implied in his role indoctrination is that success in the occupational role will be given added significance when he uses it as the means of being a good provider as husband and father. Being a good provider contributes to his overall role as an adult male.

For the female, marriage is even more important. Generally speaking, no alternative adult roles are available to her that are of equal social value. A woman who pursues a career and never marries will normally be given less social recognition than the man who pursues a career and never marries. The reason, of course, is that marriage is still the female adult career most socially valued. Given the social pressure for the woman to marry, her personal motives become very strong and, for many women, a failure to marry indicates a failure to achieve the most important and significant female adult role. In American society, marriage provides a sex-role fulfillment for the woman greater than remaining single; however, the more complete fulfillment comes with the added role of mother. The woman who has become a wife and mother has, in most cases, achieved the highest adult status and sex-role fulfillment available.

Another social pressure to marry is through the force of conformity. Because marriage is achieved by the vast majority, the unmarried individual stands out as being different and, as he grows older, he may find himself excluded from the world of paired-relationships. Americans believe strongly that social life across sex lines must be carried out by pairs. For example, the hostess who wants to invite a single man to a party finds herself trying to find a single woman with whom to match him off for the evening (and if possible forever after). The single person quickly learns that the pressure is on him. If he finds himself functioning extensively in the paired world, he may find the pressure to join those ranks increasingly difficult to resist.

Some married people view the single person as something of a threat to their paired commitment. If the married believe that their state is the natural one, they must develop a rationale to account for the unmarried. Some single persons may be defined as single for negative reasons such as immaturity, poor personality characteristics, other responsibilities, and so forth. If no rationalizations can be applied to account for the single person, his married friends may often feel he should join them as soon as possible. If he is a "normal" person (like the married), then he should get married, and if he does not marry, then he must be peculiar (unlike the married).

The married couple's self-definition of their own marriage also influences their desire to see the single get married. They may feel that their marriage is so good and so satisfactory that they would like to see the single friend marry and achieve the same bliss. At the opposite extreme may be those who envy the single person's life and want him to join the ranks of marital misery. Those who have very unsuccessful marriages often make some of the strongest attempts to get single friends married.

Paired Relationship

When the couple are engaged, their private world takes on new significance and is projected to the time after marriage when it will become even more exclusive. The engaged couple who derive a great deal of pleasure and satisfaction from their exclusive relationship are often anxious to marry and extend the closed world even further.

It is generally during engagement that the middle-class couple move away from their involvement with unmarried friends and move more into their intense paired relationship. It has been suggested that the young woman begins to orient herself away from close friends during the period of engagement and to turn more and more to her partner for his determination of the kinds of activities they will pursue, and the people with whom they will associate.[17] Out of this increasingly dependent paired interaction grows the feeling of belongingness.

Marriage is generally viewed as the *most* intimate relationship that can be achieved by two adults. The belongingness of marriage is very different from the belongingness of engagement because it is a continuous, rather than periodic, relationship. The male no longer takes the girl to her home and then goes to his; they go to their home together. The external world can be excluded for long periods of time and the couple can have extended privacy. Ego-satisfactions become of great significance in their private paired world; each individual realizes that the other wants only him most of the time. Hence, one's sense of self-importance is affirmed by being important to the other. In a society often characterized

---

[17] Nicholas Babchuk, "Primary Friends and Kin: A Study of the Associations of Middle Class Couples," *Social Forces*, May 1965, p. 486.

by impersonal relationships, one in which a given individual is important to only a few, the most "significant other" takes on great importance in giving the individual a sense of personal value. Society helps contribute to the belief that the "significant other" of the spouse is special through the belief that the marriage relationship has something special in it that *cannot* be found in any other relationship. Martinson found in his study that "persons who marry demonstrate greater feelings of ego deficiency than do persons who remain single. It may be that it is the immature or not-so-well adjusted person for whom marriage has its strongest appeal."[18]

Social Relationships

As suggested above, one of the important role shifts from being single to being married is the increased involvement in social relationships as a pair rather than as an individual. While the male may see himself as an individual in pursuing his occupation and the female may see herself as an individual in taking care of the home, when two marriage partners enter a wide range of social activities in the extended community, they often do so as a pair. Babchuk, in his study of middle-class couples, found that couples constitute the basic unit with respect to primary friendship relations. "Not only is there a tendency for spouses to see themselves as a unit in the friendship network but for their friends to see them as a unit."[19]

The development of friendship groups between married couples appears initially to be dependent more on the husband than on the wife. It was found that "husbands are likely to initiate friendships for the pair early in marriage and continue to exercise greater influence throughout the period of marriage."[20] Implied here may be that the men must first determine if they have anything in common; for example, occupation, sports, politics. If the men have something in common, it is assumed that the wives will find something in common because of their being wives, mothers, and housekeepers.

Clearly implied in middle-class marriage friendships is that the husbands will be friends and the wives of the husbands will be friends. Babchuk writes that "many respondents stated explicitly that it would not be morally appropriate to be equally close to both married persons who were mutual friends, and a majority of subjects supported this position indirectly."[21] What seems to be clear in the social relationships of

---

[18] Floyd M. Martinson, "Ego Deficiency as a Factor in Marriage," *American Sociological Review*, April 1955, pp. 163–64.

[19] Babchuk, "Primary Friends and Kin," p. 491.

[20] Ibid., p. 492.

[21] Ibid., p. 487.

two married couples is that they may share things as two married couples, or as two individuals of the same sex, but not as two individuals of the opposite sex.

In Chapter 3, it was stated that in the lower class the social life of the husband and wife was generally pursued separate from one another and in sex-peer groups. But in the middle class, the spouse often fills the role of being the mate's best friend. Babchuk found that middle-class couples do not maintain extensive friendship networks independently of each other. "Indeed, approximately half of the husbands and wives in our study claimed not to have a single primary friend independent of their spouses."[22]

Personality Relationships

An important part of marital-pair interaction centers around the relationships of the two as individual personalities. Prior to marriage, many young people probably feel that they understand both their own and their loved one's personality. However, the intensity and complexity of the marriage paired relationship brings forth for the couple new dimensions of each personality in the interactional relationship.

Before marriage, people in love have the tendency to emphasize the similarities in their ways of thinking rather than the differences. The engaged couple discuss many areas, tending to put aside those that do not strike a responsive cord with the other, and to become thrilled over the things they have in common. After marriage, some of the areas passed over in the excitement of sharing begin to come forth. Because they are living together without social restrictions and because the "best foot forward" element of courtship is now past, new aspects of the personality emerge that may be received with feelings ranging from great pleasure to severe shock.

The marital partner's personality is important because in marriage, with its close paired relationship, personal abilities must be developed for predicting the personality of the other in many situations. Personality is never quite the same in each social situation and the partner has never been observed before in the situation of marriage. Therefore, personality learning and adaptation is an ongoing process in marriage.

Sexual Satisfaction

Though probably very few individuals marry only to achieve a sexual outlet, the sexual nature of marriage is nevertheless a contributing factor to an interest in marriage. The importance attached to marital sex is

---

[22] Ibid., p. 491.

generally different for the male and the female. Studies on premarital sexual intercourse show that marriage is often not the first time for sexual experience for either sex, but rather it is the relationship in which social approval and personal ease of mind can be achieved in sexual experience.

The type of orientation to marriage is related to expectations about sexual satisfaction. For example, the greater the joint organization of marital roles, the more significance the couple attach to being able to arrive at a mutually satisfactory sexual relationship. By contrast, in societies where the "roles of husband and wife are segregated the couple will not usually develop an ardent sexuality, and the wife will not consider sex relations with her husband as an attractive source of gratification."[23] The kind of joint relationship that leads to sexual compatibility is often the same kind of relationship that leads to overall marriage compatibility.

Many males see marriage as an opportunity to satisfy sexual appetites that, in most cases, were at least partially starved during their single days. The single male often envies what he imagines to be the married man's always available sexual gratification. Many young men probably go into marriage perceiving the sexual relationship almost exclusively as a means of personal satisfaction, rather than as that and also a means of expression and love for the spouse. Sometimes it is assumed that males go into marriage with a highly idealistic version of marital sex. The single male has often experienced sex as a periodic event and thus may visualize sex in marriage as an unlimited series of events with a desirable sex partner. The young woman may look forward to the sexual relations of marriage with some degree of anticipation or apprehension. Sex is probably not initially viewed by most young women as a series of unlimited events to be entered into after marriage; rather, she may view the sexual experiences as a means of expressing love.

Economic Security

In the past, marriage was important to the female as a means of achieving economic independence from her father. Today, this is probably less of a motive for marriage because she has economic alternatives to marriage, though economic independence continues to be very important to the young woman in her desire to achieve adult status. Because of the alternatives, however, the economic force of marriage has decreased.

When a woman does agree to marry, she makes a great investment in her husband's ability to provide future economic security. This aspect of her decision may be more important today than in the past, because she

---

[23] Leonard Benson, *Fatherhood: A Sociological Perspective* (New York: Random House, 1968), p. 87.

often has the ability and opportunity to pursue a career of her own. When she chooses marriage, she is, therefore, by choice, placing her economic future in her husband's hands, placing an extra burden on the male for success because he not only must fulfill the traditional expectations that go with the bread-winner role, but must also show his wife that her "sacrifice of career" was a wise decision.

Expectation of Success

Most people entering marriage are firmly convinced that it is what they want and that they will make a success of it. The stated beliefs indicate not just a relative lack of fear of marriage, but often the opposite —many individuals "know" they will be good at the relationship and cannot wait to marry.

While most couples go into marriage with the belief that they will be successful, they also believe that the marriage can be ended if it is not successful. The vast majority enter marriage with the notion that their individual marriage will be successful; and yet, by their belief that if it is not successful it can be ended by divorce, they imply the possibility of failure. Most individuals probably see themselves as being successful in marriage with divorce being available for "unsuccessful others."

As a summary of reasons for moving into marriage, probably no other human activity has a more perfect blending of Thomas' "four wishes": *The new experience* achieved through the new and different role relationships of marriage; *security* reached through the sense of belongingness inherent in the paired relationship of marriage; *response* brought about by the exclusive nature of the husband-wife relationship, and *the recognition* each gives to the other in being defined as important and meaningful.

MARRIAGE ORIENTATIONS

The ensuing discussion of the different social orientations to the husband-wife relationship that exist in the United States today takes the changing nature of marriage roles into consideration. Different orientations place different emphases on the rights and obligations that go with the husband and wife roles. The orientations that are presented are not, however, completely distinct from each other and may, in fact, often overlap.

Patriarchal

Historically, the dominant marriage relationship was based on male authority and power. The traditional cultural values that determine the power relationships within the family appear to have been constructed by men. For example, deference customs are almost always wife-to-husband and rarely husband-to-wife.[24] Or, as Jessie Bernard puts it, the Christian mode of marriage is one in which, as Paul commanded, wives submit to their husbands, and as a result it is most likely to be the wife that does the adjusting to marriage.[25] Historically, the common pattern of the patriarchal family has been that the husband is dominant in most areas; his wife's authority is in areas of childrearing, and caring for the home and is delegated to her by him. This pattern of marriage relationship is based upon a sharp distinction between the sexes and places a premium on masculinity and femininity that derive their meaning and significant difference by contrast to each other. Patriarchal marriages in a somewhat modified form are still found in some segments of American society, including some rural areas, immigrant families, and (as discussed in Chapter 3) the lower and upper social classes. The middle-class urban family represents the segment of American society from which the patriarchal family has, for the most part, disappeared.

Matriarchal

The matriarchal relationship vests authority and power in the wife-mother. Some observers have suggested that this pattern exists in the United States in the lower class, particularly for the black family. The wife-mother is the adult responsibility in many lower-class families, because the husband-father is totally absent or may disappear for periods of time. But the woman gains her authority by default and not by agreement or consent. When a husband-father is in the home, the marriage is often patriarchal, and becomes matriarchal once again only if the male leaves. The lower-class male's role is often different from that of the traditional patriarch in that he frequently wants the authority but not the responsibility.

It has also been suggested by some writers that the suburban family of today tends to be matriarchal because the husband is away from home for long periods of time and the wife takes over many of the family responsibilities. But this, too, may be authority and responsibility by default; when the husband is home, the marriage authority may be shared by the husband and wife. A matriarchal marriage relationship does not seem to be common in contemporary America, for, in a true matriarchy, the wife-mother is the power figure with or without the husband's presence.

---

[24] Stephens, *Family in Perspective*, p. 305.

[25] Jessie Bernard, "The Adjustments of Married Mates," in Harold T. Christensen, ed., *Handbook of Marriage and The Family* (Chicago: Rand McNally & Co., 1964), p. 681.

Companionship

Burgess and Locke have argued that, because of the impact of social changes on the family, a new form of relationship has emerged in the modern urban family. They suggest that the unity of the new marriage and family relationships are much less determined by community pressures and values, and more and more in "such interpersonal relations as the mutual affection, the sympathetic understanding, and the comradeship of its members."[26] From the concept of the companionship family, some have drawn the suggestion that the husband and wife always make decisions as a democratic pair and, as a result, their individual marriage roles are often essentially the same.

One study found that companionship and being able to express their true feelings to each other were most often chosen as the most rewarding aspects of the marriage relationship. By contrast, having different values and philosophies of life and a lack of mutual interests were most often the aspects of the marriage defined as most troublesome.[27]

Certainly many of the rights and obligations of marriage roles have been drastically modified in the modern middle-class family. These modifications have often had the effect of making the husband and wife increasingly alike in their attitudes and behavior. Yet the husband and wife are not filling roles that are completely interchangeable. Patterns of responsibility and decision making that separate one role from the other in many otherwise democratically oriented marriages, continue to operate.

There is sometimes the belief that companionship is enough to ensure marital satisfaction. While in the middle class it is usually very important, other elements are also important. For example, one study found that instrumental factors such as the husband's achievement of desired standards of living as well as coordinated divisions of labor were important to marital satisfaction.[28] This further illustrates the point that in many middle-class marriages there is a need for a combination of shared as well as individual roles to be filled.

Colleague

The colleague family provides a framework for taking the concept of the companionship family with its emphasis on mutual, shared behavior and adding the recognition of role differences. The colleague family is

---

[26] Ernest Burgess and Harvey J. Locke, *The Family* (New York: American Book Co., 1953), p. 97.

[27] Nick Stinnett, Linda M. Carter, and James E. Montgomery, "Older Persons' Perceptions of Their Marriages," *Journal of Marriage and the Family*, November 1972, p. 669.

[28] James L. Hawkins, "Associations Between Companionship, Hostility, and Marital Satisfaction," *Journal of Marriage and the Family*, November 1968, p. 650.

not drastically different from the companionship family; the distinction is probably more important theoretically than practically. In both types of families, decisions are partially determined through the acceptance of other family members. Colleague-family orientation indicates that the modern middle-class family is *not* in reality an association of complete equals.

Miller and Swanson point out that, while women and men in marriage are increasingly equal, they are also separate and different. The development of specializations within marriage has led to new relations between the married couple.[29] In different areas, both recognize that authority is vested in the role or in the interests and abilities of only one of them. This recognition allows each one to defer to the other in different areas of competence, without loss of prestige. Furthermore, in most middle-class families, there is no absolute equality between parents and children. The younger children are not given equal voice in decision making with either older siblings or parents, and the adolescent and young single adult often continue to be partly under the authority and influence of the parents. The colleague family recognizes equality of rights in many areas, but differential rights and obligations in others.

Blood and Wolfe in their study found that "two decisions are primarily the husband's province (his job and the car), two the wife's (her work and food), while all the others are joint decisions."[30] In the more minor day-by-day decisions, a clear division of labor and authority exists in most middle-class marriages. However, the division of labor in the colleague marriage is not based on a belief of complete differences between the husband and wife roles and often, if conditions demand, one partner can temporarily take over the role of the other. For example, not too many years ago many men would have been unwilling to do the family wash, and this chore is still generally assumed to be the role responsibility of the woman. However, today, if the wife is indisposed, the male may do the wash and fear no personal loss of role prestige. But as soon as the wife is able to do the chore again, it is usually assumed that she will return to her role responsibility. Or, if the wife is working, the usual role responsibilities of the woman may be shared, but they generally revert back to her when she stops working.

The concept of power in decision making can be misleading in many marriages. Equalitarianism often doesn't exist where power takes different forms. An influential spouse may not be recognized as such by the other spouse because he (she) may be able to make his (her) ideas and wishes prevail without any "public" recognition of this fact. One

---

[29] Daniel R. Miller and Guy E. Swanson, *The Changing American Parent* (New York: John Wiley & Sons, Inc., 1958), p. 200.

[30] Robert O. Blood and Donald M. Wolfe, *Husbands and Wives* (Glencoe, Ill.: The Free Press, 1960), p. 20.

spouse may relegate one or more decisions to the other spouse because he or she finds those decisions unimportant or time consuming. "This relegation of decision-making power does not mean lesser power for the relegating spouse."[31]

Power is also related to the differential degree of commitment by each of the spouses. Usually the husband or wife who has a lesser stake in the marriage will care less as to whether or not his or her spouse is displeased and, as a result, will have a greater chance of imposing his or her will. "The wife whose husband loves her more than she loves him is more likely to have her whims obeyed. Husbands who enjoy fighting will win more often, at least as long as the marriage lasts."[32]

The colleague or companionship marriage characterized by the notion of "togetherness" is most often among upper-middle-class professional and managerial couples. "Frequent churchgoing, family recreation and entertaining, and various mutual commercial recreations are extremely prevalent among these persons. Such togetherness is less as one moves either direction in the occupational status continuum."[33]

Implied in some of the approaches to marriage is the belief in equality and sharing of power. But these assumptions have recently come under serious questioning. The belief that the American family is equalitarian is a reflection of American values and has been perpetuated even though there is little supporting research evidence. "Neither decision making nor the division of labor in the family (even among middle-class spouses) has been found to be equalitarian, nor has the conception of marital roles by married people been reported as companionate or equal in any sense."[34] A true equalitarian marriage is one where both spouses are primarily friends and companions to each other, "joined in a mutually supportive and complementary relationship rather than a dominant-subservient one, and sharing all the familiar tasks, responsibilities, and privileges."[35] It is doubtful that very many marriages meet this definition and can therefore be defined as equalitarian.

The person socialized to any of the marriage orientations suggested may carry them into his own marriage. If the husband and wife come into marriage with different orientations because of differential socialization, they may have an adjustment problem. For adjustment to be

---

[31] Constantina Safilios-Rothschild, "The Study of Family Power Structure: A Review 1960–1969," in Carlfred Broderick, *A Decade of Family Research and Action* (Minneapolis: National Council on Family Relations, 1971), p. 80.

[32] William J. Goode, *The Contemporary American Family* (Chicago: Quadrangle Books, 1971), p. 26.

[33] Bert N. Adams and James E. Butler, "Occupational Status and Husband-Wife Social Participation," *Social Forces*, June 1967, p. 507.

[34] Safilios-Rothschild, "Power Structure," p. 64.

[35] Ibid., p. 65.

achieved, they must arrive at some common orientation that is mutually acceptable and workable.

This discussion of marriage orientation has described some social patterns that operate in various ways and degrees on general social perspectives to marriage. The next chapter looks more specifically at marriage roles and adjustment in marriage. The discussion therefore moves from the general concern with the nature of marriage to the more specific interest in various aspects of marital adjustment.

SELECTED BIBLIOGRAPHY

Adams, Bert N., and **Butler, James E.** "Occupational Status and Husband-Wife Social Participation." *Social Forces,* June 1967, pp. 501–7.

Babchuk, Nicholas "Primary Friends and Kin: A Study of The Associations of Middle Class Couples." *Social Forces,* May 1965, pp. 483–93.

Bernard, Jessie *The Future of Marriage.* New York: World Publishing, 1972.

Foote, Nelson N. "New Roles for Men and Women." *Marriage and Family Living,* November 1961, pp. 325–27.

Hawkins, James L. "Associations Between Companionship, Hostility, and Marital Satisfaction." *Journal of Marriage and the Family,* November 1968, pp. 647–50.

Olson, David H. Marriage of the Future: Revolutionary or Evolutionary Change? *The Family Coordinator,* October 1972, pp. 383–93.

Safilios-Rothschild, Constantina "The Study of Family Power Structure: A Review 1960–1969," in Carlfred Broderick, *A Decade of Family Research and Action.* Minneapolis: National Council on Family Relations, 1971, pp. 79–90.

Stinnett, Nick, Carter, Linda M., and **Montgomery, James E.** "Older Persons' Perceptions of Their Marriages." *Journal of Marriage and the Family,* November 1972, pp. 665–70.

Chapter 12

Adjustment in Marriage

Some aspects of marriage roles as related to adjustment, and various factors both within and outside of marriage related to possible problem areas for marriage interaction and adjustment, will be discussed.

MARRIAGE ROLES

A person does not move into the role of husband or wife without at least some knowledge of marriage roles. For example, the young woman entering marriage generally has expectations on how she will perform as a wife. She must in her marriage achieve some basic agreement between her marital role expectations and her own personality needs. However, the wife's role expectations for herself may need to be altered if they are not congruent with what the husband believes is the appropriate wife role. Therefore, a second area of adjustment is between the role perceptions of the person filling the role and the spouse's beliefs about the role. A third aspect is the interactional nature of the two roles; that is, whether the husband and wife roles, as filled by the two individuals, are mutually satisfactory and compatible.

Marital-role adjustment also has a dynamic quality because the needs of the individuals and their role relationships frequently change. For example, the bride may at first enjoy the role demands placed on her for taking care of the house, but later view them as unpleasant, Or, the wife may at first view her husband's solicitous actions as an expression of his love, but later as a lack of his recognition of her ability to do things for herself.

How the marital-role beliefs have been acquired is important. For most young people, the parents have served as important marriage role models. In the socialization of the individual, the relationship of the parents as husband and wife generally is the only marriage with which the person has had a lasting, intimate association. Because the learning has been going on all of one's life, this socialization to marriage roles is often deeply rooted in the marriage role expectations of the offspring.

Studies have shown that a person coming from a home in which the marriage of the parents was ended through divorce or bereavement has less statistical chance of success in his own marriage than does the individual coming from a home in which the parental marriage remained intact. While the reasons for this are complex, one important factor is the influence on the youngster of the remaining parent's distorted role performance. If one parent is left with the main responsibility of rearing the child, the child no longer sees that parent in a marriage role. In effect, the parent no longer functions as a marriage model because one role is meaningless without a partner in the counter role. In addition, the parent is playing the role of both parents and therefore functioning differently than when a spouse is also available as a parent. For example, when a youngster sees his mother not only in the mother role, but also doing many things that are normally a part of the father role, he may get a distorted image of the combined parental role played by the mother.

The child socialized in the one-parent setting may take into his own marriage an exaggerated definition of the rights and obligations of that parent's role. If he marries a person who has been reared by two parents who were both active in their marriage and parent roles, strong differences in role definitions may be taken into marriage by each person. As a result, each may have a conflict in defining his own role and the role of his partner.

Another possible way that parents as marriage models influence the child is through their relationships to him. The most favorable relationship seems to occur when the child does not overidentify with one parent. There is evidence that poorly adjusted wives tend to have experienced greater intimacy and affection with one parent. Overinvolvement with one parent may lead to a role distortion, resulting in an exaggerated definition of the marriage role played by that parent. The distorted role image may be carried by the offspring into his own marriage, leading to possible problems with both his own role definition and that of his marriage mate.

The parents may also have influence after marriage, especially for the wife. While the young wife can compare herself with other women in the wife role, she often sees herself in contrast to her own mother and her mother-in-law. The mother-in-law becomes important as a wife-role model because of the young wife's emotional commitment to her husband. In a study by the writer, college-graduate wives were asked to compare themselves in their roles as wives with both their mothers and their mothers-in-law. In comparing themselves to their mothers as wives, 72 percent said they were about "the same or better"; 10 percent, "not as good"; and 18 percent, "can't answer." In comparing themselves with their mothers-in-law as wives, 58 percent said they were "the same or better"; 9 percent, "not as good"; and 33 percent, "can't answer."[1] Although the daughters made little distinction between the mother and mother-in-law when comparing themselves as wives, only a few of the young wives defined themselves as not being at least equal to the two older important role models.

For many young women during the early years of marriage, their family of orientation has high significance. The young woman starting out in her roles of wife, mother, and housekeeper can, with social approval and without loss of face, turn to her family (usually her mother) for some help and reassurance as to how she is filling her new roles. By contrast, the male's activities and interests are much more apt to be occupationally oriented and he has less reason to turn to his family of orientation.

The individual enters marriage socialized by parents and other influences to the role he will play. One may wonder how accurate the premarriage role beliefs turn out to be. In the writer's study, wives were asked: "Would you say that your image of what is meant to be a wife before you were married has proved to be realistic?" Eighty percent of the respondents answered "yes," 20 percent "no."[2] There is bound to be some distortion between the actual premarriage beliefs and how they are recalled after moving through the experiences of marriage, but the findings indicate that many wives think their premarital beliefs proved realistic.

Since the two roles are interacting, it is obvious that one partner does not always play his role in the same way and cannot always choose that part of his role he wants most to play at a given time. An important quality of role playing is the ability to take the role of the other, so as to understand and predict the other's behavior and to relate it to one's own behavior—in short, having one's behavior influenced in part by the desires of the "significant other."

The ability and willingness to take the role of the other varies with

---

[1] Robert R. Bell, unpublished data.
[2] Ibid.

different settings within the marriage relationship. The important point is that even in very well-adjusted marriages, the altruism of the individual is not so great that he will always resolve a problem by looking at it from the perspective of the "significant other." He may weigh the other's desire against his own and choose his own. Too, the influence of the other's desires varies with different situations.

There is some evidence to suggest that women have a better understanding and grasp of their husband's views about his marriage roles than does the husband about his wife's perceptions of her roles.[3] Given our general assumption of greater involvement in marriage and family roles by the woman than by the man, we would expect this. There is also some evidence of changes in the importance of role expectations and behavior with length of marriage. The findings of one study suggest that "the husband's role definitions and expectations may be more important to the early success of a marriage than the wife's. Since our culture tends to define her role as centering around her family, there may be greater pressure on her to develop an accommodative pattern in relation to other members of the family."[4] This is reflected in the findings from various studies that married women are more often docile than aggressive, cautious rather than daring, and not very self-sufficient. They tend to be women who have reached an "adjustment" standard of mental health. They fit the situation they have been trained from infancy to fit and enjoy conformity to it.[5]

For many young women marriage is the most important new role they will take on during their adult years. This is often true when pregnancy follows closely after marriage. If the young woman does not have a child right away, there is a greater spreading out of the new marriage and mother roles. And for most middle-class women it is accepted and increasingly expected that they will work after marriage. When this happens she spreads out the new wife, occupational, and mother roles over time. But when she marries and has a child fast, there is often no occupational role and she compresses together the wife and mother roles.

If an individual does not always sacrifice his own needs for the marriage partner, neither does he always ignore the needs of the other. In well-adjusted marriages, the two partners can probably meaningfully take the role of the other and pursue it as an end, even if it means some loss of personal role gratification. There is a balance between the complete "other-" and complete "self-" orientation in successful marriages.

Ultimately, success in marriage roles depends upon the satisfaction

---

[3] See Robert R. Stuckert, "Role Perception and Marital Satifaction—A Configurational Approach," *Marriage and Family Living*, November 1963, pp. 415–19.

[4] Ibid., p. 419.

[5] Jessie Bernard, "The Paradox of the Happy Marriage," in Vivian Gormick and Barbara K. Moran, *Woman in Sexist Society* (New York: Signet Books, 1971), p. 150.

achieved by the two individuals. The well-adjusted marriage is often one in which the roles for the two persons are not in significant conflict, when the desires of the individuals are given minimal satisfaction by both themselves and the other. The writer's study found some information on the interaction relationship through the wife's image of herself in the wife's role and her assessment of her husband in his role. When the wife was asked, "How would you evaluate yourself as a wife?," 72 percent answered "good" or "very good"; 26 percent, "average"; and 2 percent, "poor" or "very poor." When they were asked, "How would you evaluate your husband as a husband?," 82 percent answered "good" or "very good"; 15 percent, "average"; and 3 percent, "poor" or "very poor."[6] In regard to filling their respective roles, the wives gave their husbands somewhat higher evaluations than they gave themselves.

The complexity of marriage and family roles places a high significance on the difference in personalities brought into marriage. The abilities to meet and reach compatibility between one's own needs and the roles filled both by one's self and by one's spouse are important. Jessie Bernard suggests that when the major importance is placed on the relational pattern between husband and wife, "the spouses adjust to one another primarily and to the role secondarily."[7] She goes on to stress that marital satisfaction is a team as well as an individual or personality matter.[8] But it should also be recognized that there is no one marriage relationship that leads to better results for all husbands and wives. For example, Hurvitz found no evidence that couples who hold companionship values were any happier in their marriage than husbands and wives who held to traditional values.[9]

Very often society makes certain assumptions about the types of roles husbands and wives will fill. Frequently, the wife who is dominant is seen as a misfit in the relationship while a husband who is dominant is not. In part this is because among men, power and prestige are seen as going together, but very often "women have to pretend they do not have power and convince the world they do not."[10]

On the basis of this discussion of marriage roles, some general theoretical criteria of successful marriages will be suggested. These should not be thought of as universal to all adjusted marriages, but rather as patterns that are frequently found in marriages defined by the couples as success-

---

[6] Bell, unpublished data.

[7] Jessie Bernard, "The Adjustments of Married Mates," in Harold T. Christensen, ed., *Handbook of Marriage and The Family* (Chicago: Rand McNally & Co., 1964), p. 688.

[8] Ibid., p. 729.

[9] Nathan Hurvitz, "Control Roles, Marital Strain, Role Deviation and Marital Adjustment," *Journal of Marriage and the Family*, February 1965, p. 31.

[10] Jessie Bernard, *The Future of Marriage* (New York: World Publishing, 1972), p. 132.

ful. In various successful marriages, not all the criteria will have the same significance or be related in the same way.

1. *Satisfaction is achieved in one's own marriage role and that of the mate.*   The individual entering marriage moves into a role that offers him a range of alternative courses of behavior within socially defined limits. He usually has no great problem in playing his role so long as his desired behavior falls within the defined limits. However, problems may emerge if his personal desires go outside of·what he or his spouse define as appropriate role behavior.

In some cases, the individual who conforms to role expectations feels a sense of personal frustration. Few, if any, individuals will fill their marriage role for any length of time without some dissatisfaction; but for most, role dissatisfactions are not crucial enough to define the total marriage as unsatisfactory. For example, many women feel a sense of specific role frustration over the demands of housework, but do not usually find this basically disturbing to the total marriage satisfaction. By contrast, when a wife finds her role as a sexual partner very disturbing, her overall feelings about her marriage role may thereby be strongly influenced and may result in her negatively defining the marriage relationship.

As with one's own role, a person is also not always satisfied with how the spouse fills his role. Generally, the effects of this do not drastically disturb the total marriage relationship. A wife may feel that a part of her husband's role is to perform certain chores around the house. The fact that he does not always fill this role when she wants him to will not usually be seen as endangering the marriage relationship. However, if the husband in his role of provider gambles away his paycheck, the wife may consider this a role failure on his part that has serious implications for the total marriage relationship.

It is important to recognize that the paired unit of marriage is the primary setting for the emotional balance to be achieved by the husband and the wife. This is where their psychic wounds can be taken care of. "Thus, the emotions within marriage are likely to be intense, and the relationship between husband and wife may well be intrinsically unstable, depending as it does on affection."[11] This emotional depth contributes greatly to the demands each places on the other.

The congruence of role perception may be another problem. The partners may or may not essentially agree in their definition of whether one role is being filled satisfactorily. One of them may be quite satisfied that he is fulfilling his role, but the other person may not be. For example, the wife may feel that she is fulfilling the sexual role demands of the marriage very well, but the husband may perceive her as inadequate in her role of sex partner.

---

[11] William J. Goode, *World Revolution and Family Patterns* (New York: The Free Press of Glencoe, 1963), p.9.

2. *Each partner in the marriage has some opportunity to express his own personality.* In some marriages, the role demands made by one's own role as well as that of the other may lead to a sense of personal frustration. The individual may feel that he never has the opportunity to develop personality interests of his own because the demands of the marriage interaction overlooks the need for individuality by placing all the emphasis on the paired role relationships. While similarity and agreement are important in marriage, so too are individual differences. In many marriages, the relationship may actually be one of some accommodation—the couple agree to disagree and be different in some ways.

The opportunity for individual expression in marriage varies by sex and with time. The wife usually has less opportunity for individual expression than the husband because her life is more routinized and restricted. The demands made on the woman which restrict her individual expression often vary over time. For example, the young mother with preschool children may find that she must temporarily put aside most of her own personal desires; she may be able to accept this, because she knows that when the children get older her role demands will lessen and she will have more opportunity to pursue her individual interests.

In most marriages it is important to each of the spouses, and possibly to the marriage relationship itself, that each have or do some things *not* shared by the spouse. Because the spouse is often one's most important "significant other" it may help the adjustment of each mate if his spouse has some illusions about him that are not put to the test of reality. For example, the area of sports is increasingly presented as an area of activity for the middle-class husband and wife to share. Because we assume that men are (and should be) athletically superior to women, shared activity may place a strain on the husband to perform better than he can, and on the wife to urge him to. If there are activities that the couple can pursue independently, they are not faced with the need to compete. In sports this would allow one (usually the husband) to convey to his spouse the impression (real or exaggerated) of his masculine competency achieved in an all-masculine world.

There may also be some activities that the individual enjoys doing with others—but does not want that other to be his spouse. Once again sports may be used as an illustration. For example, one of the pleasures of playing golf for many husbands is to play the game with a group of male friends. It appears that pleasure for the individual through involvement with groups of his own sex is more common for men than for women. It seems quite possible that in the American middle class, women are psychologically and socially much more dependent on men than men are on women. And this appears to be true both in and out of marriage.

3. *Each marriage partner is an important focus of affection for the*

other. Because love is an important reason for getting married and because it is important in giving the ongoing marriage a basic reason for existence, the partners usually must be reassured that love continues to exist. It is generally through the continuation of love and affection in marriage that the person maintains the feeling of being wanted and being important to the other. The reciprocal nature of the love relationship provides an important aspect of ego-need satisfaction for each partner. If one no longer sees the partner as the "significant other" of affection, a feeling of great loss in the marriage relationship may result.

In almost all marriages, the nature of the husband-wife affectional relationship changes and shifts with time. When children come, the parents direct affection at them, but this is not usually viewed as a threat to the affection given by the spouse to his partner. On occasion, a young father will perceive his child with some jealousy because his wife is directing a great deal of affection to the child and he may feel that, in a sense, this affection has been taken away from him. However, since people generally have no fixed limits of affection, they do not take from one relationship to give to another.

In a number of marriages, a partner may not substitute another person as an affectional recipient, but rather lose interest in his because of various demands in life or change in personality needs. The partner's withdrawal of affection may represent a severe loss for the spouse who continues to desire the affection. This may be illustrated by the husband who, as he grows older, simply loses affectional interest in his wife and lives with her more out of habit than emotional feeling. For the wife who wants and needs his affection, this loss can be a severe shock. It also means that the relationship is continuing without the reciprocal affection so highly valued in middle-class marriage.

4. *Each partner derives some pleasures and satisfactions from the marriage role relationships.* Mutual satisfaction may be considered the opposite to the individuality stressed in the second point above. If some individual expression in marriage is needed, the couple also usually need to interact in their roles as husband and wife. If the individuals do not, their marriage roles will have little meaning because these roles derive their meaning and importance through the interrelationships.

The importance of the role relationship of marriage is related to different definitions of happy and unhappy marriages. One study found that those individuals who report very happy marriages tended to stress the relationship to the spouse as the major source of their happiness, "while those reporting less happiness in marriage tend to concentrate on the situational aspects of marriage (home, children, social life) as sources of their marital happiness."[12]

---

[12] Gerald Gurin, Joseph Veroff, and Shiela Feld, *Americans View Their Mental Health* (New York: Basic Books, 1960), p. 98.

When two married people fill certain roles as a result of living together, but are not personally significant to each other, then an arrangement between two individuals, and not a marriage in terms of role interrelationship, exists. The husband and wife who live together but do not participate together, are married in name only.

MARRIAGE ADJUSTMENT

Given the various ways in which modern middle-class marriage roles may be filled, the ultimate measurement of successful marriage is the degree of adjustment achieved by the individuals in their marriage roles and in interaction with one another. In the following discussion, adjustment and success are both used in essentially the same way to refer to the degree of satisfaction with marriage.

All living things are modified by their environment, and their ability to adjust is crucial to survival. However, when we attempt to make distinctions between good and bad adjustments in the social and psychological areas it is often very difficult. For example, it is clear that historically some of the most creative and useful people have failed to make a "good adjustment" in terms of what this usually means in a clinical sense. Far too often—if not always—a "good adjustment has come to mean social conformity."[13] It is important to keep this danger in mind as we look at the concept of marital adjustment.

The concept of adjustment is applied to many aspects of social behavior. It may be used in reference to the individual being adjusted to external social expectations or to the internal relationship between personal desires and socially expected behavior. Because all human behavior is social, the patterns for adjustment either within or between individuals, which were originally external to the individual, had to be internalized through the process of socialization. Adjustment is of importance in both the social and psychological sense. *Social* refers to the interactional role relationships between individuals, and *psychological* to the relationship of internalized social roles and the personality desires operating for the individual.

Adjustment is a basic requirement of social participation and social organization. A society develops minimal requirements of adjustment in areas of social relevance and, if a given individual cannot meet them, he may be viewed as dangerous to himself and/or others and may be institutionalized or even eliminated. However, if he meets the minimum requirements, individual variations within the acceptable behavior range are generally permitted. All functioning members of a society are adjusted to at least a set of basic social requirements and maladjusted to the de-

---

[13] Wainwright Churchhill, *Homosexual Behavior among Males* (New York: Hawthorne Books, 1967), pp. 255–56.

gree that no individual can accept and conform to all of the requirements. Social adjustment is not an either/or proposition, but a matter
of degree.

Given the complexity of the roles and role relationships, as well as the
personalities of different individuals, no marriage is absolutely adjusted or
maladjusted. Even in marriages assessed as highly adjusted, some areas
of conflict for or between the partners will exist. A marriage in which
absolute personal and social acceptance and satisfaction always prevails
is hard to imagine. Even in marriages that end in rapid divorce, some
areas of adjustment for or between the couple existed.

Whether or not a marriage is successful is determined by the interaction between the two partners over the time span of their marriage. That
is, a marriage is not simply the sum of the two individuals that make it
up, but rather it is a unity of two interacting personalities, "neither one
of which alone determines the success of the relationship. An outcome
which has an extremely low value for the wife married to one may have
a high value for her if married to another, and vice versa."[14] In other
words, there is no type of personality that is a failure in marriage, but
rather two individual personalities that have through interaction with one
another failed in marriage. And while marital failure might not have
occurred with a different mate, it is also true "that even happily married
people might have been happier if married to someone else."[15]

Marital adjustment implies "that the individual or the pair has a good
working arrangement with reality, adulthood, and expectations of others."[16] The definition points out the individual and paired nature of marital adjustment. One may be adjusted in one area, but not the other; for
example, a person may fill his role demands in his relationship to the role
of the other, but feel personal frustration while filling the role. This dual
stress on marital adjustment is more common in the United States today
than it was in the past. When roles were clearly defined, marriage was
more apt to be assessed on the basis of the ability of the two individuals
to meet the rights and obligations of the role relationship. But with the
development of the emphasis on the individual achieving ego-need satisfaction in marriage, and the confusion in marriage role definitions, an
individual may increasingly find a conflict between the role demands
made on him and his own desires and wishes.

There are important differences related to adjustment in marriage by
social class. In part this is true because the worlds in which marriage takes
place are often very different. For example, lower-class men and women
have a greater tendency to live in separate social and psychological

---

[14] Bernard, "Adjustments," p. 730.

[15] Ibid., p. 729.

[16] Willard Waller and Reuben Hill, *The Family* (New York: The Dryden Press, 1951), p. 362.

worlds with limited communication in marriage. But in the middle class there is generally a great stress placed on communication and shared activities and these are seen as closely related to adjustment in marriage. These differences are also reflected in what is felt to be important in marriage by social class. One study concluded that "the evidence indicates that spouses in the middle-class marriages were more concerned with psychological and emotional interaction, while the lower-class partners saw as most salient in their lives financial problems and the unsubtle physical actions of their partner."[17]

Over the years, social scientists have attempted to develop techniques for determining success or adjustment in marriage.[18] The earliest attempts used a *single* criterion, such as happiness with marriage.[19] Ratings were achieved through self-evaluations of marriage or through evaluations by others who were familiar with the marriage. The limitations of single-criterion evaluation were that the criterion one person might use to make an assessment of a marriage might not be used by another and, even if the same criterion were used, the insight and ability of assessment would vary a great deal among different observers.

Later, a score system with several criteria was set up, under which a marriage's success rating was determined by responses of the married person to a number of items.[20] This led to the use of a *composite* index that recognized different facets of marital success. However, this technique was criticized because the total ncore concealed the various contributions made by each of the criteria.[21] An overall success score tells little about the various parts that make up the whole.

Burgess and Wallin argue that the *multiple* criteria of marital success measurement meet the objections of the composite index, because each contributing criterion is composed of a number of items.[22] In their method, a total score for overall adjustment can be seen and used, as well

---

[17] George Levinger, "Sources of Marital Dissatisfaction among Applicants for Divorce," in Jeffrey K. Hadden and Marie L. Borgatta, *Marriage and Family* (Itasca, Ill.: F. E. Peacock, 1969), pp. 519–20.

[18] See Ernest W. Burgess and Leonard S. Cottrell, *Predicting Success or Failure in Marriage* (New York: Prentice-Hall, Inc., 1939); Ernest W. Burgess and Paul Wallin, *Engagement and Marriage* (Chicago: J. B. Lippincott, 1953); Gilbert V. Hamilton, *A Research in Marriage* (New York: Albert & Charles Boni, Inc., 1929); Harvey J. Locke, *Predicting Adjustment in Marriage: A Comparison of a Divorced and a Happily Married Group* (New York: Henry Holt & Co., 1951); and Lewis M. Terman, *Psychological Factors in Marital Happiness* (New York: McGraw-Hill Book Co., 1938).

[19] See Harvey J. Locke, *Predicting Adjustment in Marriage* (New York: Henry Holt & Co., 1951).

[20] See Ernest W. Burgess and Leonard S. Cottrell, *Predicting Success or Failure in Marriage* (New York: Prentice-Hall, Inc., 1939).

[21] Burgess and Wallin, *Engagement and Marriage,* pp. 504–5.

[22] Ibid., p. 505.

as scores for the various categories that make up the total. Burgess and Wallin suggest that the "multiple criteria" method has been successful as an instrument in differentiating between successful and unsuccessful marriages by the practical test of validation, divorce.[23]

After a careful survey of the many research attempts to investigate marital relationships, Jessie Bernard distinguishes a variety of criteria that have been used. The criteria include: "(a) how well a marriage meets the needs and expectations of society; (b) its permanence or endurance; (c) the degree of unity and/or agreement or consensus developed between the members; (d) the degree to which it facilitates personality development; and, (e) the degree of marital satisfaction or happiness it achieves."[24]

One very important aim of all scientific disciplines is to expand the knowledge of an area so that a means of prediction may be developed. In the marriage and family field, prediction research and the development of reliable instruments have two major objectives. The first is the practical aim of gaining reliable prediction material which would be useful to the many individuals in positions of counseling the premarried as well as the married. The second is the general contribution which could be made to knowledge of human behavior in marriage.[25]

While many variables have been shown to have a statistical relationship with adjustment and success in marriage, none of them has been found to be absolute. The researcher must make a constant and concerted effort to distinguish the variables that make a successful or well-adjusted marriage. Few researchers would assume that all successful marriages will be made up of the same variables in the same relationships. While distinguishing variables in successful marriages is very important, it may also be suggested that adjustment in marriage is a "naming stage" for most married couples. The couple who feel that their marriage is good, and honestly see themselves as adjusted, are adjusted within their frame of reference. To say they are not is to imply a knowledge of what marital adjustment really *is* and of its application to all marriages. If the couple feel that their marriage is good and successful, their attitudes and behavior will generally reflect the belief. We would suggest that most couples who "name" their marriage as at least mimimally satisfactory would meet two general criteria: first, a marriage is successful if the satisfaction is positive, "that is, if the rewards to both partners are greater than the costs"; and second, if the marriage relationship is preferable to any alternative.[26]

---

[23] Ibid., p. 505.

[24] Bernard, "Adjustments," p. 730.

[25] Ibid., p. 555.

[26] Bernard, "Adjustments," p. 732.

There also appears to be a common tendency for many married couples to exaggerate the success of their marriages. This is reflected in the fact that a definite majority of couples rate their marriages as better than most others. In part this is a tendency to distort the appraisal of their marriages in the direction of social desirability. "There seems little question but that the tendency to deceive one's self and others that one's marriage is better than it really is is intensive and widespread."[27]

INTERACTION CHANGES WITH LENGTH OF MARRIAGE

One very important adjustment that has to be made by many couples early in marriage is the redefining of their inexperienced, premarital marriage role expectations on the basis of newly experienced reality. Waller and Hill write, "now gently, now with startling brutality, the real person and the reality of marriage pound at the portals of thought, and at length enter. One may struggle against disillusionment. As a hitherto unperceived facet of a personality reveals itself and destroys an illusion, one may build a mental bulwark around the old illusion or rationalize the new behavior into some sort of agreement with the old configuration."[28] Redefinition of the marriage roles is usually called for if the couple are to maintain a relationship that is satisfactory to them in light of their new experience. But very often marital adjustment over time is not a conscious or deliberate activity by either spouse. "People are sometimes surprised, in fact, when they become aware of the changes which have occurred in their relationship over a period of time; they have been adjusting to one another without even recognizing the fact."[29]

Studies indicate that an increase in length of marriage is accompanied by an increase in unfavorable perception of the spouse. The longer a couple are married, the less favorable personality qualities each tends to see in the mate. It appears that persons in happy marriages see their spouses as less admirable than formerly, while those in unhappy marriages see their spouses as being more undesirable than formerly.[30]

Disenchantment with the romantic relationship in marriage also will vary over time. Pineo's study suggests that "men have apparently suffered more disenchantment in the early years than have the women. This is in sharp contrast to where the losses in adjustment from early marriage to the middle years were almost invariably larger for wives than for hus-

---

[27] Vernon H. Edmonds, Glenne Withers, and Beverly Dibatista, "Adjustment, Conservatism, and Marital Conventionalization," *Journal of Marriage and the Family*, February 1972, p. 103.

[28] Waller and Hill, *Family*, pp. 258–59.

[29] Bernard, "Adjustments," p. 680.

[30] Eleanore Luckey, "Number of Years Married as Related to Personality Perception and Marital Happiness, *Journal of Marriage and the Family*, February 1966, p. 46.

bands."[31] This may be the result of the males' illusions being less realistic or the females' being slower to react to the reality of the marital relationship.

There are other differences between husbands and wives and what affects their marital adjustment. For example, one study found that women tend to adjust more in marriage than do men. As a consequence, this tendency may influence the wife to be more attentive to the fulfillment of her husband's needs. There is also some evidence that adjustment in marriage is easier for the man because he expects less. Stinnett points out that research from various cultures show that husbands "generally tend to report higher marital satisfaction scores partly because they possess more conservative expectations of marriage than do wives."[32]

There are also differences between husbands and wives in handling disagreements in their marriages. Husbands, more than wives, seem to use a "wait and see" strategy when their wives go against their expectations. By contrast, it has been found that wives more often meet a violation of expectations with an open sharing or talking about the situation or by reacting negatively.[33] It was also found that when difficulties occurred in marriages they were handled differently by married couples. "Husbands say they talk openly about violations of expectations in the area of finance but not in the area of sexual intimacy."[34]

The above study also found that about half of the nonadjustive responses for both husbands and wives came about as a result of an open sharing of the feelings about the violation of expectations. So, contrary to what might have been expected, even though a couple openly talk about the violation of expectations on the part of the other it does not always lead to adjustment. Furthermore, the data shows, especially for the wives, that in a "large percentage of times, a negative reaction on the part of one partner does not lead to an adjustive response by the other. Negative reactions are apparently not always followed by reciprocal negative reactions."[35] In many marriages the individual response of the person in a disagreement can be either negative or positive, which may or may not lead to a resolution.

A positive development usually occurs as the disillusionment with the romantic idealism of premarriage unfolds—the increasing number of common experiences as husband and wife. New values are developed in the

---

[31] Peter C. Pineo, "Disenchantment in the Later Years of Marriage," *Marriage and Family Living*, February 1961, p. 10.

[32] Nick Stinnett, Janet Collins, and James E. Montgomery, "Marital Need Satisfaction of Older Husbands and Wives," *Journal of Marriage and Family*, August 1970, p. 432.

[33] Beverly R. Cutler and William G. Dyer, "Initial Adjustment Processes in Young Married Couples," in Hadden and Borgotta, *Marriage and Family*, p. 291.

[34] Ibid., p. 290.

[35] Ibid., p. 291.

marriage relationship to replace the disappearing romantic illusions. The very fact of sharing experiences as a husband and wife provides a strong bond for many couples; they can derive satisfaction from the situations they have encountered and resolved. They may have developed a universe of discourse in which they can give and take in ways and areas they consider to be important. The increasing experience with the other also leads to the ability of many to predict the behavior of the spouse and, as a result, an intimacy of behavior develops not found in many other pair-relationships.

One of the realities of marriage is that the couple must face many problem areas, whereas in courtship the emphasis was generally on the pleasurable areas. The sharing of problems may lead to a closer tie between the pair because they can give aid and support to the other and gain satisfaction in successfully dealing with their problems. In many marriages, the husband and wife relationship will, with time, minimize personal pretense on the part of both partners. Each partner can therefore turn to the other for support and help with a minimum threat to his ego because of less need to "cover up."

It has been argued that even after marriage many of the romantic qualities of courtship and early marriage should continue. This argument overlooks the fact that romantic forms of expression frequently have their meaning only when the couple have no other shared areas for interaction with each other. If the marriage relationship brings a sense of security and satisfaction, the behavior patterns of the romantic stage are often no longer appropriate. They operated during a period of minimum interpersonal security and satisfaction. The wife who is upset because her husband does not bring home flowers every week may be reacting because she wants to hang on to the symbolism associated with the romantic courtship period. Or, if she wants the flowers as a sign of her husband's love, it might indicate that she doesn't feel other signs exist.

As time goes on, the husband-wife roles undergo change. Most family research has been directed at the early changes in the marriage relationship. The transfer from single to married roles offers the most dramatic change and, as a result, alterations later in marriage have usually been ignored.

Earlier, we suggested some changes that occur in marriage over time. We know that with time, and as the married couple move through the various family-life stages, the importance of their marriage and family roles undergoes a variety of changes. One characteristic of most marriages is that with time the knowledge and predictability with regard to the spouse's feelings and behavior increases. The observation has been made that often the longer a couple are married, the less they verbally interact with each other. While this is no doubt true, it is also the case that the longer the couple are married, the less may be their dependency on conversation as their chief means of communication. The husband and wife often get to know each other so well over time that they can anticipate what the other will say, or a few words or gestures may be all the cue that is needed. Communication and attempts to influence each other in marriage show somewhat different patterns for men and women. Men tend more than women to use such verbal techniques as discussion and persuasion, while women more often use such nonverbal techniques as "sweet talk and affection," "pouting," or "silent treatments." However, the more a spouse (male or female) feels he(she) has a considerable say in family decision making, the more he(she) relies on verbal rather than nonverbal techniques to influence the other.[36]

The indications have been that husbands have somewhat less involvement in marriage than do their wives. This difference appears to be true at most stages in the life cycle of marriage. It also appears that different stages in the life cycle have less effect on husbands than on wives. The subjective evaluations of marital satisfaction vary little from marriage through the childbearing and childrearing phases for the male. "However, the wives have a substantial decrease in general marital satisfaction and a high level of negative feelings from marital interaction during the childbearing and childrearing phases until the children are ready to leave home. After the childrearing phase both husbands and wives have a substantial increase in marital satisfaction through the 'retirement' stage with an apparent temporary setback just before the husband retires."[37]

The evidence also suggests that over time the spouses' knowledge and assessment of each other is such that they may gradually turn less to each other. This may be an adaptation to an *over*dependency that existed early in marriage. Blood and Wolfe found that young wives turned very often to their husbands both for sympathy as well as when they were angry. But they found that over time and with the involvement of children, "the husband assumes a less significant role as audience, being replaced by such alternatives as God, other people, and housework."[38]

It becomes clear that as time passes, new attitudes toward marriage develop. For many couples, the happiness ratings of their marriages go down with increasing age and with length of marriage. The happiest years of marriage may be the early years, even though it is generally during those years that most problems of marital adjustment occur. Gurin found that "feelings of inadequacy and problems progressively decrease with age. One might suspect that over time there tends to be an increas-

---

[36] Constantina Safilios-Rothschild, *Toward a Sociology of Women* (Lexington, Mass: Xerox College Publishing, 1972), p. 9.

[37] Boyd C. Rollins and Harold Feldman, "Marital Satisfaction over the Family Life Cycle," *Journal of Marriage and the Family,* February 1970, pp. 26–27.

[38] Robert O. Blood and Donald M. Wolfe, *Husbands and Wives* (Glencoe, Ill.: The Free Press, 1960), p. 189.

ing adaptation to the marital partner and to the distresses in the marriage."[39] Or, as Jessie Bernard suggests, the "marital relationship that comes with age may, therefore, reflect resignation rather than happiness."[40]

There is a very strong tendency to define marital happiness as it characterizes the early years of marriage and to hold to that definition for persons as they grow older and are married for longer periods of time. This bias is reflected in the common assumption that when a marriage relationship is described as "resigned" or "low in happiness," these descriptions refer to undesirable characteristics of a poor marital relationship. But with many years of marital interaction and the spouses' great familiarity with one another, it may be that most of the relationships in marriage must become routine and predictable. In fact, one might speculate that certain kinds of interaction that would end a marriage during the early years might become a reason for maintaining it in later years. For example, some older couples appear to detest each other. But this hostility may actually have a positive value because it indicates that the other is still "significant." While most of us would desire positive expressions directed at us by a "significant other," we might, in their absence, prefer negative expressions rather than none.

Because of the generally greater commitment of the woman to marriage, we will direct some attention to how she is affected and influenced with increasing length of marriage. When women enter their late 40s, their lives usually undergo drastic changes. First, since their children are growing up and leaving home, many women, especially those who have largely devoted themselves to their children, must make a difficult adjustment. The greater the degree to which the woman has involved and immersed herself in the rearing of her children, the greater the loss of function she suffers when they grow up. Some women may be able to adjust to this role loss by taking on other interests, but for the rest the role commitment to being mother has been so great that it is very difficult for them to move successfully into new roles.

Second, as the middle-class woman enters her middle years, her husband is often at his occupational peak and very often deeply involved in his career. Earlier in marriage, the wife might have been very helpful to the husband's career, but at this point her assistance is often limited. Thus, the husband's important occupational role may call for little involvement by the wife. A third important change is that the woman enters the menopause at about 47 years of age. This change is associated with an ovarian-hormone decrease which leads to a variety of physical and functional changes. The psychological impact of the menopause is often

---

[39] Gurin, Veroff, and Feld, *Mental Health,* p. 102.
[40] Bernard, "Adjustments," p. 732.

very strong because it dramatically ends what many women believe to be their most important function—the having of children. It also forces the woman to realize her youth is now over and she is moving toward old age.

When these elements of change are combined, the impact on the middle-aged woman may be very great. As a result, she may seek roles outside the family to give new meaning to her life. The two prescriptions often offered as substitutes for the loss of the childrearing role are volunteer activities and part-time employment. The real function of many social activities which suggest high social goals is often the attempt to provide the middle-aged, middle-class woman with a meaningful role. One may wonder how long and to what degree the many "busywork" middle-class organizations can really delude the intelligent woman into believing she is filling a new and significant role. While some may believe that what they are doing is important, many others probably go along with the myth because they have nowhere else to turn. This may be the price many women pay for not maintaining and developing an individuality during their childrearing years.

Pauline Bart has examined in some detail the consequences of the traditional family roles for the middle-aged woman. She found that few clear norms govern the relationship between a woman and her adult children. As a result, when her children leave, the woman's situation is often normless."[41] She found that role loss was associated with depression and that middle-aged women suffering from depression were more apt to have suffered maternal role loss than had nondepressed women. The depression is due to their lack of important roles and subsequent loss of self-esteem, rather than the hormonal changes of the menopause.[42] Bart also found that Jewish women had the highest rates of depression because in the traditional Jewish family the most important tie is between the mother and her children and the mother has a very high identification with them. As a result Jewish women are about twice as apt to be diagnosed as depressed than are non-Jewish women.[43] She summarized her study by stating that her data showed that it was the women who assumed the traditional female role "—who are housewives, who stayed married to their husbands, who are not overly aggressive, in short who 'buy' the traditional norms—who respond with depression when their children leave."[44]

The role changes are less severe for the middle-aged male, but exist to some degree. He has his occupational involvement, which may give

---

[41] Pauline Bart, "Depression in Middle-aged Women," in Gornick and Moran, *Sexist Society*, p. 168.

[42] Ibid., p. 176.

[43] Ibid., p. 178.

[44] Ibid., p. 184.

him his most important role satisfaction. When a man has reached his late 40s, his occupational success has been pretty well determined. Some men are satisfied with their position and their expectations for the future, but many men may not be satisfied and a sense of occupational failure may force its way into their thinking.

Also at this time, a man's sexual interests and capabilities are often decreasing. If the male has associated his sense of masculinity with sexual behavior, he may undergo a drastic role shock. As a further complication, if the wife's sexual interests are still at a relatively high level, the husband may find himself in the highly disturbing position of being sexually inadequate. The sexual drive of the middle-class male may also be influenced by the occupational role. Foote raises the question of "what happens to sexual potency when the masculine ego is damaged by being occupationally conquered by a junior."[45]

MARRIAGE IN THE POSTPARENTAL YEARS

In Chapter 19 and Chapter 20 we will discuss various aspects of parent-child relationships. At this point we want to look at some aspects of marriage during the years after the children have grown up and left home. What is new and significant in the family life cycle after the children have left home has been the expansion of the period where the couple live together as husband and wife. The recent emergence and significance of the postparental years is reflected in the statistics that in 1890 the average woman was a widow before her last child left home.[46] By contrast, today the average woman can expect about 15 years of marriage after her youngest child has grown up and left home.[47] In the discussion that follows, the age range of the postparental marriages will be defined as 45 to 64. Old-age marriages (as 65 years of age and older) are discussed in Chapter 13.

For many young people older marriages seem to have little of the ingredients that they feel to be important to marriage. The young often see the older married couples living together as the result of habit and not deriving any of the romantic satisfactions. This is a reflection of the belief by many young people that older persons are by the very fact of their age unromantic and unexciting in their relationships with one another. But there are variations among young people in how they view older marriages. One study found that female college students have a more favorable view toward older marriages than do college males. It was also

[45] Foote, p. 326.

[46] Irwin Deutscher, "The Quality of Post-parental Life: Definitions of the Situation," *Journal of Marriage and the Family*, February 1964, p. 52.

[47] Margaret Mead and Frances B. Kaplan, eds., *American Women: The Report of the President's Commission* (New York: Charles Scribner's Sons, 1965), p. 89.

found that persons from a rural background also had a more favorable image of older marriages. This may be because "rural life is more favorable to the status of aged persons than is urban life, because the larger and more flexible rural household offers many opportunities for the aged to make a contribution."[48]

One might reasonably assume that when a couple have for many years participated minimally in their marital roles and maximally in their parental roles, problems might emerge when suddenly they find that most of their family-role involvement centers around their roles of husband and wife. Yet there is some evidence that the adjustment to postparental marriage is not as great as has often been assumed, and that there are some available social means for adjusting to the new role demands. Deutscher suggests that "when urban middle-class post-parental couples describe their life, the hurdle does not appear to have been insurmountable and the adaptations are seldom pathological."[49]

In his study of older marriages Stinnett has suggested several generalizations. First, that many older couples state that their marriages are as satisfactory as, if not more than, they had been in previous years. Second, by contrast he found in other studies that there was evidence that marital satisfaction decreased during the later years. However, it is suggested that that appears to be characteristic of lower-class husbands and wives where only a small amount of companionship and satisfaction existed in the earlier years of marriage.[50] Third, that marriages that are defined as satisfactory in later life have usually been satisfactory from the beginning, whereas those seen as unsatisfactory have usually been defined as such from the start. Fourth, older persons who were living with their spouses were usually found to be better adjusted and to have higher morale than those older persons who were widowed, divorced, or single. Fifth, Stinnett found that persons over 65 and living with their spouse experienced less loneliness and engaged in less daydreaming than did their unmarried counterparts.[51]

Because of her generally greater involvement in the parental role, one would expect that the wife would be more concerned with postparental adjustments than would the husband. Deutscher found that a larger percentage of wives assessed the postparental period *both* more favorably and more unfavorably than did their husbands.[52] This would suggest that

---

[48] Nick Stinnett and James T. Montgomery, "Youths' Perceptions of Marriages of older Persons," *Journal of Marriage and the Family*, August 1968, p. 396.

[49] Irwin Deutscher, "Socialization for Postparental Life," in Arnold Rose, ed., *Human Behavior and Social Processes* (New York: Houghton Mifflin Co., 1961), p. 509.

[50] Stinnett, Collins, and Montgomery, "Marital Need Satisfaction," p. 428.

[51] Ibid., p. 429.

[52] Deutscher, "Post-parental Life," p. 58.

men were less influenced either negatively or positively than women because there were fewer adjustments and adaptations for them to make. With the relationship between higher social class and greater commitment and satisfaction derived from marriage, it is not surprising that Deutscher found that upper middle-class spouses had a more favorable outlook with regard to their postparental life than did their lower middle-class counterparts.[53]

There may be certain transitional learning experiences that directly contribute to the parents' adjustment to their children leaving home, and indirectly to their adjustment to the new demands placed on the marriage relationship. Deutscher suggests that adaptations to children leaving home are helped by the initial parental interpretation of it as a temporary phenomena, often with the parental expectation that the children will at some time again return to live at home. This means that the "temporary" can often change to a permanent separation without any traumatic transition.[54]

SOME PROBLEM AREAS

Many individuals enter marriage roles and move through marital interaction encountering few significant problems. To some people, the concept of adjustment implies that individuals are making the best of a rather unpleasant situation. However, adjustment as it has been used in this discussion applies to the relationship of the individual to his marriage role and his role as related to the role of his spouse. For many, the search for adjustment is the search for the most workable and satisfying marital relationships. The characteristic of marital difficulties is common to all societies—at least to the extent that no society has found the means of achieving perfect marital harmony. In some societies, marital conflict is so great that the anthropologist devotes a great deal of space to explaining its nature. But, as Stephens points out, "I know of no case where marriage is so blissful, so free from strife, as to receive special comment from the ethnographer."[55] In the ongoing nature of marriage, some areas inevitably lead to problems.

There may also be a broad social context in which marital problems occur that is related to how individuals get along with other individuals. One study has found that people who have few intimate associations are more likely than others to be dissatisfied with their marriages. That is, marital satisfaction was found to be closely related to the number of intimate relatives and friends that one claimed. "Social isolates—those

---

[53] Ibid., p. 58.

[54] Ibid., p. 88.

[55] William N. Stephens, *The Family in Cross-Cultural Perspective* (New York: Holt, Rinehart and Winston, Inc., 1963), p. 231.

who claimed no more than two close friends and no more than two close relatives—were much more likely than others of the same race, sex, and age to be unhappily married."[56] This indicates that one's ability or inability in general interpersonal relationships are related to the more intimate interpersonal relationship of marriage.

Consistent with the greater commitment to marriage of the woman is a greater tendency for women to report problems in their marriages. This appears to be true at most educational and age levels. Furthermore, when "men do report marriage problems, they are less likely to attribute the cause of these problems to their wives than women are to attribute these problems to their husbands."[57]

It has been argued that women have traditionally had a greater commitment and vested interest in marriage. This has meant that marriage has some different meanings and consequences for women. In every marriage there may actually be two marriages—his and hers—which do not always coincide. Often the happiness of the woman is more dependent on marriage than is the man's happiness. As a result, women have to pay more, and all studies show women make more concessions in marriage than do men. Wives are "reflecting objective circumstances when they report more problems and dissatisfactions in their marriages than their husbands do. *Their* marriages are more problem-laden and dissatisfaction-prone than their husbands' are."[58]

Further evidence of each marriage in a sense being two marriages is the different perceptions the two people have. While they agree on such verifiable items as how many children they have, they often disagree on length of premarital acquaintance and of engagement, on age at marriage, and interval between marriage and birth of first child. "Indeed, with respect to even such basic components of marriage as frequency of sexual relations, social interaction, household tasks, and decision making, they seem to be reporting on different marriages."[59]

Wives, in general, report a lower degree of marital satisfaction than men. But men have been socialized to expect their fulfillment and self-actualization primarily from work and secondarily from marriage and fatherhood. There is also evidence that marriage is much more important to women who stay at home than it is for those who work.[60] Those who stay home simply have fewer options to turn to for personal satisfaction.

The problems for married women are seen in their comparison with

---

[56] Karen S. Renne, "Correlates of Dissatisfaction in Marriage," *Journal of Marriage and the Family*, February 1970, p. 65.

[57] Gurin, Veroff, and Feld, *Mental Health*, p. 110.

[58] Bernard "Paradox," p. 149.

[59] Bernard, *Future of Marriage*, p. 7.

[60] Safilios-Rothschild, *Sociology of Women*, p. 67.

single women. Studies show how married women have more feelings of depression and unhappiness. They are also reported to be more passive, phobic, and depressed. When married women are compared with husbands, more wives report marital frustration and dissatisfaction; "more report negative feelings; more wives than husbands report marital problems; more wives than husbands consider their marriages unhappy, have considered separation or divorce, have regretted their marriages; and fewer report positive companionship."[61]

There are social-class differences in the kinds of problems found in marriage. For example, lower-class wives are far more apt to complain about financial problems, physical abuse, and drinking than are middle-class wives. By contrast, the middle-class wives are significantly more likely to complain about lack of love, infidelity, and excessive demands. "Middle-class husbands paralleled the wives in their significantly greater concern with lack of love; on the other hand, they were significantly *less* likely than lower-class husbands to complain of the wife's infidelity."[62]

For some couples, a more basic problem in marriage may be a disillusionment with the partner. In this writer's study of the problem, the wives were asked a question which they answered as follows: "If you had your life to live over, would you—"marry the same person," 85 percent; "marry a different person," 12 percent; "not marry at all," 3 percent.[63] In a Canadian study, twice as many wives (about a fourth) as husbands (about 12 percent) said they would not remarry the same person or they had doubts about it.[64]

Many of the satisfactions as well as problems in marriage involve the ability of the couple to interact effectively. The nature of role interaction is not quantitative, but qualitative, and as such, definable by the couple. In marriage, the individual's ability to fulfill the marriage role for his own sake, as well as for the related personality and role filled by the spouse, is of central importance. This means the individual must not only be adaptable to his own personality and role needs, but to those of his spouse as well.

Some of the problems found in marriages are related to feelings of happiness or unhappiness. Hicks and Platt, after an extensive review of studies related to happiness in marriage, found a positive relationship between marital happiness and higher occupational statuses, incomes, and educational levels for husbands. "The strongest, most compelling data emerging from research in the 60s have, however, added a new dimension to these accepted findings: The significance of the positive relationship

---

[61] Bernard, p. 27.
[62] Levinger, p. 519.
[63] Bell, unpublished data.
[64] Bernard, p. 152.

between the instrumental aspects of the male's role and marital happiness has been strongly demonstrated by research in this decade."[65]

One of the most common assumptions about happiness in marriage has been that children and happiness go together. Yet, an examination of research does not provide support for that assumption. For example, one study found the "higher the ratio of children per years of marriage, the less satisfactory the marital experience will be."[66]

Studies indicate that even though the higher educated tend to be happier in marriage, they also tend to have more feelings of inadequacy and more problems than the less educated. "With more education, marriage apparently becomes more central in one's life, a factor which also gives it a greater potential of being satisfying or stressful."[67]

However, the measurement of happiness in marriage has a restricted value—at least to the extent that marital stability is often not contingent upon happiness. Yet, very little interest has been paid to low happiness–high stability marriages. The strength of the marriage bond can only be partially assessed by the variable of marital happiness. Unhappiness may be the bond that holds some marriages together.[68] For some an unhappy marriage may be seen as better than no marriage.

Blood and Wolfe found that the main satisfactions for wives in marriage were: (1) companionship in doing things together with the husband; (2) the chance to have children; (3) the husband's understanding of her problems and feelings; (4) the husband's expression of love and affection.[69] The writer's study asked the respondents what the most satisfying part of being a wife was: companionship was for 35 percent; being needed and loved, for 28 percent; helping and making the husband happy, for 15 percent; and, all other satisfactions, 22 percent.

It may be estimated that roughly half of all married couples will encounter some important problems in their marriages. If the problems become very severe, many couples will end the marriage, but others will work out, ignore, or live with the problems. The impact of problems on a marriage is evidenced by the number of couples that are or have been so dissatisfied with their marriages that they have thought about ending them. In the writer's study of college-educated wives, 14 percent said they had seriously considered divorce.

---

[65] Mary W. Hicks and Marilyn Platt, "Marital Happiness and Stability: A Review of the Research in the Sixties," in Carlfred Broderick, *A Decade of Family Research and Action* (Minneapolis: National Council on Family Relations, 1971), p. 68.

[66] John R. Hurley and Donna D. Palonen, "Marital Satisfaction and Child Density Among University Student Parents," *Journal of Marriage and the Family,* August 1967, p. 483.

[67] Hicks and Platt, "Marital Happiness," p. 66.

[68] Ibid., p. 69.

[69] Robert O. Blood and Donald M. Wolfe, *Husbands and Wives* (Glencoe, Ill.: The Free Press, 1960), p. 81.

It needs to be stressed that the wife bears the greater burden or responsibility in marital adjustment. Some initial adjustment to marriage is probably greater for the wife than for the husband. Marriage, for many women, means a whole new daily routine of taking care of a home, while the occupational role for the man continues pretty much as it did before marriage. However, given the woman's greater commitment to marriage, she often has a greater personal and social investment in its being successful.

The woman's greater involvement in the family often means that she may be playing any one of several different role possibilities reflecting different views held toward her husband and toward her relationships to him. The following types of female role definitions of husband and family have been suggested in the work of Helena Lopata.[70] First, there is the wife who is *primarily husband oriented.* For this woman, even though she may be very involved in her role as mother, or in other roles, her major personal identification and life is built around her husband. A second role definition is the wife who is *sometimes husband oriented.* She may shift away from the husband as she devotes more time and energy to her children or when the husband becomes involved in his career. Third, is the woman who has a basic role identification and *orientation to her children.* The husband is seen as outside this basic unit of mother and children, as someone who provides and performs tasks for the unit, or toward whom specific duties must be directed. Fourth, may be a *home orientation.* Here the woman's basic role commitment is not to husband or children, but to the home and her possessions in it.

It also appears that when many people complain about marriage they also have a number of other problems. Renne found that marital dissatisfaction is seldom an individual's only complaint. But often it is one of a number of physical and psychic symptoms, ailments, and disabilities. Because the state of the individual's marriage both influences and is influenced by his general feeling of well-being, marital satisfaction is strongly related to various indices of health and morale. Renne found that "the people with the most serious health problems were most likely to be dissatisfied with their marriages."[71]

The strain of marriage on many women is reflected in the finding from one study that about twice as many married women (25 percent) as married men (12 percent) have felt a nervous breakdown was impending. More women than men experience both physical and psychological anxiety and immobilization. "More wives than husbands, especially among college women, have feelings of inadequacy in marriage."[72]

[70] See Helena Z. Lopata, "The Secondary Features of A Primary Relationship," *Human Organization,* Summer 1965, pp. 116–23.

[71] Renne, "Correlates," p. 63.

[72] Bernard, "Paradox," p. 152.

Men very often tend to gain in mental health when they are married, if they are compared with single men. Although the physical health of married men is no better than that of single men until middle age, their mental health is far better, fewer show serious symptoms of psychological distress, and fewer of them suffer mental health impairments.[73]

Husband-Wife Disagreement

Couples can disagree about many things, but certain areas are most common. Blood and Wolfe found that the four most common were money, children, recreation, and personality.[74] As to disagreements and arguments in marriage, this writer asked his respondents two questions. To the first question, "How would you estimate the amount of arguing in your marriage" they answered: "never," 1 percent; "rarely," 34 percent; "sometimes," 55 percent; "often," 10 percent. The second question and their answers were: "When disagreements arise, do they usually result in: your (the wife) giving in," 20 percent; "husband giving in," 5 percent; "agreement by mutual give and take," 75 percent.[75]

Instead of arguing, some individuals may resort to pouting, icy or frozen treatment, or withholding privileges. But in general, these techniques are considered immature and unworthy of the married couple. The more common recourse is to vent disagreements in arguments; because the couple are also close and know each other well, they are usually uninhibited and tend to be frank in what they say.

Family specialists sometimes find themselves in a dilemma over marriage arguments because they are not sure whether they are for them or against them. They sometimes play with words and talk about *quarreling,* which is bad, and *constructive argument,* which is good. This writer suggests that in most marriages disagreements and arguments are going to occur. In fact, it seems probable that the couples who go through married life with a normal amount of daily interaction without ever becoming irritated to the point of disagreement are very deviant social beings. When a couple never argues, it may mean that the persons have no individuality, that one does not recognize the other as being significant enough to disagree with, or that one may not disagree because of fear of the other. In these situations, the reasons for not arguing may be more detrimental to the marital relationship than arguments.

Many marriages develop a closeness of paired relationship never achieved with any other individual outside of marriage. When the relationship is open and unpretentious, the couple may be so frank with each other they are bound to disagree. Some married couples find that

---

[73] Ibid., p. 17.

[74] Blood and Wolfe, *Husbands and Wives,* p. 241.

[75] Bell, unpublished data.

arguments can be stimulating and enjoyable. For the married couple who enjoy a give-and-take relationship, arguments can add an important positive dimension to marital interaction.

Along with the positive elements of arguing in marriage go, of course, some dangers. These arise when one of the individuals lets his emotions take over, gets mad and strikes out in every direction he can. The type of person who does this can endanger the marriage relationship. Some writers make a great deal out of this possibility, but whether or not it occurs in any significant number of marriages is not known. Furthermore, to project from the destructively arguing type to the generalization that all argument in marriage is bad is highly questionable. Individuals who randomly strike out at their mate may have severe marital limitations in other directions; their argumentativeness may be a manifestation of more important problems.

Implied in the above discussion are relative degrees of power in marriage. There was some discussion of power in Chapter 11, but a few more observations at this point seem appropriate. There have been many studies that stated an intent to look at power relations in marriage. But, generally, in measurements of power all decisions are given equal weight even though they don't have the same importance to the family members. For example, which job the husband should take and which doctor to call have been decisions considered to be equal. Of course, some decisions are made less frequently than others—some decisions are "important" and "frequent" and others frequent but not important.[76]

It appears clear that the authority of the male is used as a justification of power where it is useful, as in the case of the working class. But new justifications will arise as they are useful, as in the case of professional men, "who demand deference because of their work, thus enabling them to accept the doctrine of equality while at the same time undermining it for their own benefit as males."[77] But if the wife is to gain much power in the marriage relationship she must usually attain it from external sources. "She must participate in the work force, her education must be superior to that of the husband, and her participation in organizations must excel his."[78]

There appear to be some general patterns of reacting to marital problems and some general patterns of attempts to solve them that are common to middle-class couples. Though of course not all problems are of equal significance in various marriages, or in the same marriage over time, very often the problems defined as important are those close to

---

[76] Dair L. Gillespie, "Who Has Power? The Marital Struggle," *Journal of Marriage and the Family,* August 1971, p. 446.

[77] Ibid., p. 451.

[78] Ibid., p. 457.

the basic needs of the spouse doing the defining. One study found that the "two most important areas of disturbance in unhappy marriages concern the fulfillment of each other's needs and the kind of interaction which prevails between the spouses if basic needs are not satisfied."[79]

The belief that "talking out" is an important means of achieving·some resolution to marriage problems is common, but it is most often found among higher educated and higher social class couples.[80] Some topics lend themselves to discussion more readily than others. For example, one study reports that "husbands say they talk openly about violations of expectations in the area of finances but not in the area of frequency of sexual intimacy."[81]

Also basic to problem-solving in marriage is the relative degree of commitment to the marriage by each of the partners. Here we have the principle of least interest, "namely that the one who cares more in any relationship is at a disadvantage vis-à-vis the one who cares less. The person who cannot tolerate quarreling and bickering will give more concessions than the spouse to whom it means less."[82]

One of the ironies of life is that solving one problem may result in a new problem. One partner may effectively bring about changes in the behavior of the spouse only to find that the changed behavior creates new problems. For example, in studies of wives of alcoholics who had learned to control their problem, the wives were greatly disappointed by the results. Some women found "that they preferred the man who, however difficult he might have been intoxicated, was more lovable when sober than the man who is sober always."[83]

Parent and In-law Problems

Before looking at in-law relationships a few comments on kinship and friendship ties. There is some evidence that men participate in more voluntary groups than women, but they do not join sexually exclusive groups more often. Men exceed women only in number of affiliations and not in time spent in them. The same study found that females maintain more kinship ties than do males. "Their ties limit their participation in other social relationships, particularly those calling for strong effective investments such as friendship. Women with modest kin commitments

[79] Vincent D. Mathews and Clement S. Mihanovich, "New Orientations on Marital Maladjustment," *Marriage and Family Living,* August 1963, p. 304.

[80] See Mirra Komarovsky, *Blue-Collar Marriage* (New York: Random House, 1962), p. 195.

[81] Beverly R. Cutler and William G. Dyer, "Initial Adjustment Processes in Young Married Couples," *Social Forces,* December 1965, p. 201.

[82] Bernard, "Adjustments," p. 730.

[83] Ibid., p. 695.

are comparable to men in other affiliations." This study also found that women's ties of kinship are stronger than the mens'. Women are more spontaneous with friends and kin, and devote more time to voluntary organizations to which they belong.[84]

There is some social-class difference in the extent of kinship involvement. The working class are more involved with kin than are the middle class. But Adams writes that to say the working classes are more "kin oriented" should not be interpreted in either-or terms. "Middle-class individuals keep in contact with nonproximate relatives and express quite generally the feeling that kin are an important part of their lives, and tend to be particularly close to their parents. Yet in terms of daily living, kin seem more salient to working-class people."[85]

The relationship of parents and in-laws to their young, married children provides a logical point for concluding the discussion on marriage. The initial relationship is commonly a problem and involves both the couple who are starting marriage and their parents who are well along in the marriage relationship.

After marriage, the young couple have generally moved into adult status; however, for many, the movement is not sharp and distinct, but rather slow and evolving. Because the new roles of marriage are not always clearly distinguished from certain of the role aspects of being single, problems may emerge. One problem area develops from the fact that after marriage the couple do not always move completely away from the control and influence of their parents. A popular image in the United States is that in-law conflict is an expected consequence of marriage. Many young people think of marriage and in-law conflict as being inevitable and, for them, it may turn out to be a "self-fulfilling prophecy." Of course, many times conflict with parents is due to more than simple anticipation. The nature of different family roles and their relationship to one another in the American middle class contribute to potential difficulties. The parents are faced with certain problems when their children marry. They see their young adult child not only in his present role, but also in all the roles he has filled from infancy on. The parents have taken the responsibility for rearing their child and making many of his decisions for him, and they often continue this to some degree right up until he marries. But once he marries, the parents often find that their child no longer listens, or that he no longer considers they have the right to instruct him. Some parents find this sudden shift in their role difficult

---

[84] Alan Booth, "Sex and Social Participation," *American Sociological Review*, April 1972, pp. 191–92.

[85] Bert N. Adams, "Isolation, Function and Beyond: American Kinship in the 1960s," in Broderick, *Decade*, p. 174. Also see Geoffrey Gibson, "Kin Family Networks: Overheralded Structure in Past Conceptualizations of Family Functioning," *Journal of Marriage and the Family*, February 1972, pp. 13–23.

to accept. In some cases, the role loss may lead to hostility directed at the offspring's spouse. Because of their emotional commitment to their own child, it may be difficult for the parents to recognize that the relationship has changed; the spouse may provide a convenient scapegoat.

The parents must also face the fact of "losing" their offspring to someone for marriage. The parents may have an exaggerated notion of their child's worth and they may view the person he marries as unworthy of him. "The father and mother of the newly married person necessarily overvalue their own child and cannot believe that anyone is quite good enough for him; they are thereafter highly critical of the newcomer in the group."[86] The parents' relationships to the offspring and his mate are complicated because each parent, in reference to the young married couple, is cast both in the role of parent and parent-in-law, and each member of the new marriage is cast as an offspring and an offspring-in-law.

The young married couple must also recognize that they have been through many roles in relationship to their parents, and that this may lead to difficulty when they marry and move into new role relationships with their parents and with their spouse. A long pattern of turning to parents for help has been established for many; it is not always easily ended with marriage. It may be viewed as threatening by the spouse in the new marriage. The young wife who feels her husband is turning to his mother when she feels he should be turning to her, will often see her wife role as being threatened.

Each of the newly married pair may also have a tendency to compare his spouse with his own parent of the same sex. This may have unfortunate consequences; the two compared are not role equals: One has been in the role for a long time and the other is just beginning it. The husband who compares his wife to his mother as a cook is comparing a novice to a woman with years of experience. He is also comparing what his mother, who has, in many cases, conditioned his tastes, thinks is "good cooking," to what his young wife, who may have very different tastes, thinks is "good cooking." The very fact that the young wife is in a new role often means role insecurity for her; comparing her to her mother-in-law may play upon this insecurity.

Another important element of the parent-married child relationship is that each has been a member of his family of orientation since birth. The cliché that at marriage "one doesn't lose a son (or daughter), but gains a daughter (or son)" is not wholly accurate. The son or daughter gained is an adult son or daughter, shaped and influenced by another family of orientation. When he enters into interaction with his in-laws, they enter with a limited knowledge of experience with his family's back-

---

[86] Waller and Hill, *Family*, p. 290.

ground. Over the years, each family acquires a family culture both like and unlike other families. In the area of the unlike, the new in-law is a stranger. The wife and her family may talk about people and events of the past that mean nothing to the husband. While they may try to bring him into things by telling him about the past, he can never directly be a part of it.

A distinction must be made between conflict with in-laws and conflict with one's spouse about kin. These are often two separate problems. In the first there may be agreement between the married couple toward a relative, while in the second they are in disagreement with each other about the relative.[87] In-law problems are fairly common in the American middle class of today. Yet there are very often contradictions with regard to the in-laws as problems. For example, one study found that the commonest complaint by young couples about their in-laws was that they were meddlesome and dominating. But the second most common complaint was that the in-laws were "distant, indifferent, thoughtless, and unappreciative."[88]

Mother-in-law and Daughter-in-law. The most common in-law trouble is between the wife and the husband's mother. In part this is because in both spouse and kin conflicts the husband's side of the family is most involved. The content of the conflict can center around feelings of rejection or neglect by kin, or interference of kin in family affairs.[89] In the writer's study, college educated wives estimated their relationships with the mother-in-law, when they could be assessed, as: "very good and good," 75 percent; and "fair or poor," 25 percent.[90] There was some evidence that in the frequency of conflict with specific in-laws, the mother-in-law led the list and coming second, slightly ahead of the father-in-law, was the sister-in-law. This indicates the female nature of in-law conflict. This is further supported in a study by Komarovsky, who found that one third of the wives revealed serious dissatisfactions with their in-laws, whereas the husbands enjoyed fairly satisfactory in-law relationships.[91] Because the wife is involved in kinship and is, as a result, more sensitive to subtleties of the relationships, and because involvement with her own kin is considered more legitimate by males, relations between husband, wife, and his kin are more likely to result in such conflicts."[92]

The adult roles of the mother-in-law and the daughter-in-law contribute to the frequency of conflict in their relationship. The important fact is that though their adult roles are essentially the same, they are

---

[87] Adams, "Isolation," p. 173.

[88] Quoted in Bernard, "Adjustments," p. 727.

[89] Ibid., p. 173.

[90] Bell, unpublished data.

[91] Komarovsky, *Blue-Collar Marriage*, p. 259.

[92] Adams, "Isolation," p. 173.

two individuals with many differences in role experience. The young wife usually brings into marriage the training she received from her mother, and as a result may have ways of doing things different from her mother-in-law's ways. If the daughter-in-law rejects suggestions by the mother-in-law, she is questioning the way the mother-in-law has been doing things for many years; she is indirectly criticizing the mother-in-law's fulfillment of her role. On the other hand, for the daughter to accept the mother-in-law's way of doing things may indicate to her own mother a rejection of the way *she* has played her role. Thus, the young wife may be caught between two experienced women trying to show her how she should fill her new role. It is also important to note that many aspects of the woman's role and her efficiency and success are publicly available for assessment. How a woman manages her home or prepares a meal can be evaluated and compared, particularly by her relatives.

Competition between the mother-in-law and daughter-in-law for the son and husband may also occur. With the effective development of her marriage role, the daughter-in-law inevitably replaces her mother-in-law in many areas in which the mother-in-law in the past received her son's love and admiration.

Mother-in-law and Son-in-law.   In more than half of the cultures of the world, a man and his mother-in-law are expected to avoid each other. Shlein points out that Americans have developed patterns of hostility and rejection that are never directed at the son or daughter-in-law, but only at the mother-in-law. This strong hostility is reflected in our humor. For example—Definition of conflicting emotions: You see your mother-in-law driving over a cliff in your new Cadillac.[93] The mother-in-law and son-in-law are of the opposite sexes in their role performances and cannot be personally compared. The mother-in-law may become critical of the son-in-law in his role of husband if he does not treat her daughter in the way she thinks he should. But because his world is so different from hers, possible areas for criticism are limited.

Probably the more important source of conflict comes from the feelings of the son-in-law. Because controls over behavior are usually longer and greater for the girl than the boy, the mother may have greater difficulty giving up the controls over her daughter when she marries. The son-in-law may feel that his mother-in-law is overstepping her rights and treading on his as husband if she continues to influence his wife.

Because of the mother's close emotional involvement with her daughter, and because she herself has been a wife for many years, she may feel that her daughter should listen to her advice on the role of the husband. Some mothers may want to shape their daughters' husbands into an

---

[93] John M. Shlein, "Mother-in-Law: A Problem of Kinship Terminology," in Hyman Rodman, ed., *Marriage, Family and Society* (New York: Random House, 1965), p. 199.

image they have had for but not realized in their own husbands. Others may tell their daughters how to behave in the role of wife in a way that worked for them in their marriages, forgetting that the daughter's husband may be very different from their own. Komarovsky, in her study of the lower middle class, found that the following conditions tended to be associated with an unsatisfactory relationship between the husband and his mother-in-law: "marriage to a better-educated wife; wife's hostility towards her mother; wife's emotional dependence upon her mother; and economic and social interdependence, including a joint household with in-laws."[94]

Father-in-law and Daughter-in-law. Few young wives have a problem in this relationship, making it the one of least frequent conflict. The father generally has much less influence on the day-to-day rearing of his children and is therefore less involved after they marry. Also, because the daughter-in-law is filling an opposite adult sex role, he has little reason to compare her role with his.

The husband's father may see the daughter-in-law in a somewhat romantic light. Their relationship may be characterized by a kind of flirting, very ego-satisfying to the father because of his older age and the youthfulness of his daughter-in-law. The daughter-in-law herself may be attracted, because many times the father-in-law has many of the same characteristics that her husband has. Hence, the role relationships between a father-in-law and daughter-in-law may provide a socially approved role relationship between a male and a female in which some degree of intimacy is acceptable.

Father-in-law and Son-in-law. The jealousy of the father toward his son-in-law does not seem to exist, at least to the degree that is troublesome. The important role difference, when compared with the mother-in-law and daughter-in-law relationship, is that, while the two males have the same primary role responsibilities, they are not usually subject to detailed and public comparison.

Both have the primary responsibility of earning a living, and if the father-in-law accepts the son-in-law's ability to do so, conflict is not apt to emerge. *How* the one fills his occupational role is not usually subject to observation by the other; the variety of occupations that a male can fill are almost endless, and most of them are known only in a very general way to persons not in them. It is probably important that the father-in-law respect the occupational role of the son-in-law, but he usually does, because of the social class similarity of individuals who marry.

Unlike the mother, the father is much less apt, even though experienced as a husband, to try to influence his son-in-law in that role. However, the father's concern may emerge if he feels the son-in-law is over-

[94] Komarovsky, *Blue-Collar Marriage*, p. 261.

stepping the rather broad limits of the husband's role. He may then feel called upon to perform as his daughter's protector. But generally, if the son-in-law is at least adequate in his important occupational role, his behavior in the husband's role is not of major importance to the father-in-law.

In-laws as Grandparents.   One of the contradictions in stereotyped role images in the American society centers around the same person filling two different roles, the mother as mother-in-law and the mother as grandmother. Often the stereotype of the mother-in-law is of a hard, interfering battle-ax, while the stereotype of grandmother is a kindly lady handing out sugar cookies to her adoring grandchildren. The fact is that neither stereotype is very accurate.

In some situations of in-law conflict, the influence of grandchildren may be positive. They may provide a common focus of emotional and social involvement for both parents and grandparents. Many times the grandparents get a great deal of pleasure out of their grandchildren; they can deal with them pleasurably and without the responsibility of rearing them.

In other situations, grandchildren may provide an area of conflict. The dispute often involves the question of how the children should be reared, and it usually occurs between the mother-in-law and the daughter-in-law. Disputes arise because one has reared children in the past while the other is doing it in the present, and because of differences in training and attitudes. The mother-in-law has a rather devastating argument to use in support of her notions on childrearing if she chooses to use it. She can argue that her methods were obviously successful—the daughter-in-law chose to marry her son. To this argument, the wife has little recourse; she can hardly say that her husband grew up the way he did despite his mother.

While this discussion has pointed out possible in-law conflicts, it should not be assumed that they are inevitable. In most marriages, adjustments with the parents of both the husband and the wife will have to be made. Perhaps, certain social changes are emerging in the American middle class that are decreasing or will decrease the extent of in-law conflict.

One factor of change, a decrease in the generational difference between the parents and their married children, has several causes. Two of these are the younger ages of marriage and the changes in "aging" resulting from increased knowledge in the medical and health areas. The young married couple and their parents are, therefore, much more apt to be closer age peers in a social and psychological sense than they were in the past. As a result, their pattern of life may be closer than has previously been the case.

A second factor is that in the middle class, with a high degree of geographical mobility for the younger generation, the parents and children often have limited contact after marriage. Increasingly, they are not living near each other and they may have to travel long distances to visit. Because they see less of each other, chances of strain that develop over long and continuous contact are reduced. When they do get together, it may be within a vacation setting rather than one of duty or obligation relationship. In some cases, however, this less frequent but more intense visiting may cause problems because the interactional demands are continuous.

SELECTED BIBLIOGRAPHY

Adams, Bert N. "Isolation, Function and Beyond: American Kinship in the 1960s," in Carlfred Broderick, *A Decade of Family Research and Action.* Minneapolis: National Council on Family Relations, 1971, pp. 163–85.

Bahr, Stephen, and **Rollins, Boyd C.** "Crisis and Conjugal Power." *Journal of Marriage and the Family,* May 1971, pp. 364–68.

Ballweg, John A. "Resolution of Conjugal Role Adjustment after Retirement." *Journal of Marriage and the Family,* May 1967, pp. 277–81.

Bart, Pauline B. "Depression in Middle-Aged Women," in Vivian Gornick and Barbara K. Moran, *Women in Sexist Society.* New York: New American Library, 1971, pp. 163–86.

Bernard, Jessie "The Adjustments of Married Mates," in Harold T. Christensen, ed., *Handbook of Marriage and The Family.* Chicago: Rand McNally & Co., 1964, pp. 675–739.

Bernard, Jessie *The Future of Marriage.* New York: World Publishing Co., 1972.

Blood, Robert O., and **Wolfe, Donald M.** *Husbands and Wives.* Glencoe, Ill.: The Free Press, 1960.

Booth, Alan "Sex and Social Participation." *American Sociological Review,* April 1972, pp. 183–93.

Cutler, Beverly R., and **Dyer, William G.** "Initial Adjustment Processes in Young Married Couples." *Social Forces,* December 1965, pp. 195–201.

Edmonds, Vernon H., Withers, Glenne, and **Dibatista, Beverly** "Adjustment, Conservatism, and Marital Conventionalization." *Journal of Marriage and the Family,* February 1972, pp. 99–103.

Gillespie, Dair L. "Who Has The Power? The Marital Struggle." *Journal of Marriage and the Family,* August, 1971, pp. 445–58.

Hicks, Mary W., and **Platt, Marilyn** "Marital Happiness and Stability: A Review of the Research in the Sixties," in Carlfred Broderick, *A Decade of Family Research and Action.* Minneapolis: National Council on Family Relations, 1971, pp. 59–78.

Pratt, Lois "Conjugal Organization and Health." *Journal of Marriage and the Family,* February 1972, pp. 85–95.

Renne, Karen S. "Correlates of Dissatisfaction in Marriage." *Journal of Marriage and the Family*, February 1970, pp. 54–67.

Rollins, Boyd C., and **Feldmann, Harold** "Marital Satisfaction over the Family Life Cycle." *Journal of Marriage and the Family*, February 1970, pp. 20–28.

Safilios-Rothschild, Constantina *Toward a Sociology of Women.* Lexington, Mass.: Xerox College Publishing, 1972.

Chapter *13*

Family Patterns of the Elderly

In recent years an increasing interest has developed in many societies in the study of older people, as the traditional family patterns of caring for the aged have been replaced by other agencies and institutions of society. However, family sociologists have not shown a great deal of interest in studying the elderly, and there is not very much known about the family structures of the aged or what alternatives society has created to replace the past family forms that cared for them. This chapter in general concerns the overall setting of the elderly person in the United States and, more specifically, the significance of marriage and family roles for them.

In many ways the elderly are becoming more distinct and set apart from the rest of society. As the rates of social change have increased, more older people have become aware of how different they are from the youth-oriented society in which they live. Toffler has pointed out that the elderly often become drop-outs from society and withdraw into a private environment, "cutting off as many contacts as possible with the fast-moving outside world and, finally, vegetating until death."[1]

There are many problems in defining who are elderly or when old age starts. Old age has started at various times during different historical

---

[1] Alvin Toffler, *Future Shock* (London: Pan Books Ltd., 1970), p. 45.

periods as well as in different societies. Unlike the transitions into young adult status that have been recognized in many societies of the past, there has not appeared to be any society with a ritual ceremony for the entrance into old age. It may also be noted that in most societies, including the United States, there are few legal distinctions made in the rights of people during their adult years. Throughout life the adult retains the same political rights, and civil law makes no distinctions between the rights of a person aged 40 or one of 70. From the perspective of legal definitions the aged are not looked upon as a class apart from other adults.

The concept of "old" has a number of dimensions. It can refer to psychological and sociological factors as well as the physical changes in the body and related health problems. Therefore, a person may be old in some ways but not in others. These kinds of discrepancies can present problems for the aging individual who does not define himself as old but is required to interact within a social structure which often sees him as a dependent, nonproductive member of society.[2] Often there is a struggle, with society defining the individual as elderly and the individual not willing to accept the definition.

The defining of aging is further confused because it often has different meanings and implications for men and women. Very often aging has an earlier impact on women. Inge Bell argues that women must endure the specter of aging much sooner than men because the cultural definition of aging gives men a decided psychological, sexual, and economic advantage over women. "The multimillion dollar cosmetics advertising industry is dedicated to creating a fear of aging in women."[3] She goes on to point out that a man's wrinkles do not define him as sexually undesirable until possibly his late 50s. "For him sexual value is defined much more in terms of personality, intelligence, and earning power than physical appearance."[4]

The fear of aging among many women has a real basis in the fact that society deprives them of many rights when they are defined as old. As a result many women often distort their age, hoping to delay society's categorical stigma. Even professional women, who presumably have roles which should not be threatened through middle age, are much more likely than men to feel their advancing age is a serious impairment to them. Bell points out that in the listings of the Directory of the American Psychological Association, "women are ten times as likely to omit their age as men."[5]

---

[2] James E. Birren and Kathy Gribbin, "The Elderly," in Don Spiegel and Patricia Keith-Spiegel, *Outsiders USA* (San Francisco: Rinehart Press, 1973), p. 76.

[3] Inge Powell Bell, "The Double Standard," in Helena Z. Lopata, *Marriage and Families* (New York: Van Nostrand Co., 1973), p. 216.

[4] Ibid., p. 216.

[5] Ibid., p. 219.

Women generally see little reason to look forward to old age. While some may look forward to the new roles of grandmother they generally don't see that as a role of an old person. Simone de Beauvoir, in her outstanding study of aging, observes she has never come across one single woman, either in real life or in books, who had looked forward to her own old age cheerfully. "In the same way no one ever speaks of a 'beautiful old woman'; the most one might say would be a 'charming old lady.' "[6]

The view of general society is often that the elderly are somehow vaguely defined and should not force themselves on society as a clearly defined group seeking special recognition and dispensations. This social reaction was illustrated in many of the reactions that Simone de Beauvoir received when she was writing her book on old age. She said that by acknowledging that she was on the threshold of old age was like saying old age was lying there in wait for every woman and it had already reached many of them. "Great numbers of people, particularly old people, told me, kindly or angrily but always at great length and again and again, that old age simply did not exist. There were some who were less young than others, and that was all it amounted to. Society looks upon old age as a kind of shameful secret that it is unseemly to mention."[7] The very fact of using such words as "elderly," "old," and "the aged" is often seen as being insensitive and unfair. In their place many would have our society use such euphemisms as "senior citizen" and "golden years." All this really shows is that the truth of old age is to be camouflaged by the use of synonyms that fool very few.

This social attempt sometimes to try and pretend that old age doesn't really exist has other consequences. It means that we don't know a great deal about the social and psychological factors of being old. One popular newsmagazine has observed that while the subculture of youth has been studied, "psychoanalyzed, photographed, deplored, and envied, few have wanted even to admit the existence of a subculture of the aged, with its implications of segregation and alienation."[8] The same article goes on to point out that the aged have much in common with youth. Both groups have high unemployment, their bodies and personalities are undergoing change, and they are both heavy users of drugs. Both groups are very much concerned with time. "Youth, though, figures its passage from birth, the aged calculate backward from their death day."[9]

---

[6] Simone de Beauvoir, *Old Age* (Great Britain: Cox and Wyman Ltd., 1972), p. 277.

[7] Ibid., p. 1.

[8] *Time Magazine,* "The Old in the Country of the Young," in Arlene S. Skolnick and Jerome H. Skolnick, *Family in Transition* (Boston: Little, Brown & Co., 1971), p. 433.

[9] Ibid., p. 433.

Still, far more is known about the social world of youth than of the elderly.

Given the social values against recognizing the elderly it is understandable that defining old age is difficult. Certainly one can't talk about old age as something that arrives on a given birthday. Rather the entrance into old age is through a transition stage and this is usually during the 60s. Before age 60 very few people would be defined as elderly, and once they enter their 70s very few would not be defined as elderly. It is during the 60s that the significant changes in life patterns and styles usually associated with old age take place.

Old-Age Rates.   The usual age for computing old age in the official records is that of 65. In 1850 there were 2.5 million people in the United States who were 65 years of age and over. Today, there are more than 20 million Americans in this group, and they now constitute more than 10 percent of the total population.

There is a common misconception that people are now living much longer than they did in the past. This confusion appears to come about because an infant born in 1900 could at that time expect only to live to be about 50 years of age, but an infant born in 1970 could expect to live to about 70 years of age. However, this difference is almost entirely due to a sharp reduction in infant mortality. In 1900 many infants and young children died, pulling the average life expectancy age for all their cohorts down. But a more meaningful comparison is the life expectancy that persons at age 65 still have ahead of them. Today, the average life expectancy for a man 65 years of age is 14 more years. In 1900 the 65 year old man had 13 years of life expectancy ahead of him. "We have prolonged life in general; thereby creating a large group of the aged; but we have not prolonged the life of the aged."[10]

Life expectancy has had different implications for men and women. Over the years women have continued to outlive men at increasing rates. Around 1940 the life expectancy for women was 4.3 years more than for men, but by 1967 this had increased to 7.2 years. This difference for men is stronger in the United States than in most other countries possibly because higher mortality of men reflects the differential burdens of the roles men and women are expected to perform in American society."[11] For example, American men have high rates of heart attacks that are clearly related to the demands and tensions of the economic system.

The various statistics on the distribution of variables related to the

---

[10] Beauvoir, *Old Age*, p. 547

[11] Jeanne Clare Ridley, "The Effects of Population Change on the Roles and Status of Women: Perspective and Speculation," in Constantina Safilios-Rothschild, *Toward a Sociology of Women* (Lexington, Mass: Xerox College Publishing, 1972), p. 375.

elderly person in the United States allows for a general descriptive picture. The "typical" older person in the United States is a widowed white woman, and she probably has about nine years of formal education. She is not employed in any fashion, lives in central city, and receives most of her income from social security. She has at least one chronic health condition that does not limit her mobility, and she will live into her 80s.[12]

Living Patterns of the Elderly

What are some of the options available to the elderly in how they live their lives? We first examine the importance of kinship for the elderly person. In the past, in many societies including our own, the extended family had as a major function the care of the aged. Very often the elderly maintained control of the family until their death so they were never really dependent on their children. An examination of some of the early families to settle in New England shows that the father maintained control over his adult children until they were well into middle age and he was well into old age. That was part of a patriarchal system that not only gave authority to the male but even more to the older man. However, this has changed as the male authority and the extended family have been greatly altered, while at the same time the high value and authority accorded the elderly has been greatly reduced.

At the present time the importance of kinship is greatly confused. Our society has set up other institutions to care for the aged. These usually have been under the institution of government: for example, social security and medicare. Often the elderly turn to their kin to look after them in a social and psychological sense, if not in an actual physical way. Kinship carries with it special demands. When the ties of kinship are the strongest they are based on positive concern, which is a function of its permanence, plus obligation and affection.[13] Implied here is a sense of duty and very often there is no guarantee of positive rewards or satisfactions for the kin. This reflects an important difference between kinship and friendship. In friendship there is consensus. That is, one can choose as a friend a person whose ideas agree with his own and who enjoys the same sorts of activities which he does.[14] One can feel

---

[12] Richard A. Kalish, "Of Social Values and the Dying: A Defense of Disengagement," *The Family Coordinator,* January 1972, p. 83.

[13] Bert N. Adams, "Isolation, Function and Beyond: American Kinship in the 1960s," in Carlfred Broderick, *A Decade of Family Research and Action* (Minneapolis: National Council on Family Relations, 1971), p. 178.

[14] Ibid., p. 178.

friendship toward their kin but there is no guarantee that such must or will occur.

There is also evidence that generational kinship ties tend to be stronger than are lateral ties. In other words, obligation and mutual concern seem to outweigh the age similarity of siblings in determining comparative involvement with parents and siblings.[15] There is also some indication that older persons would prefer to turn to their children than their siblings. It would appear, then, that the parent-child tie is stronger, even though it cuts across generations, than is the sibling tie, even though of the same generation.

Not only is there a greater closeness between parents and their adult children but this closeness tends most often to be with the daughter. Almost all studies show that women are more involved in kin affairs of all types than are men. Yet, in spite of the stronger linkage in the kinship interaction of women, more older men than women actually live in families. This is because women tend to live longer than men. "There are more nonmarried women (including widows) and women living alone than single men or men living alone."[16] Also, mobile older women probably are more self-sufficient than older men.

As parents get older and turn to their adult children, this often implies for all parties an important role reversal. During their previous adult years the parents had been responsible for their children and now their children have become responsible for them. Older persons, because of different levels of ability, find themselves in different types of relationships with their children. But ultimately the older persons who give much less than they receive find themselves in a dependent status with regard to their children.

The number of older people who live with their children in the United States is quite high. One third of all people who have living children do live with them. Such joint households are usually two generational, though, not three generational. "Only 8 percent of American families are true three-generational households, with grandchildren in them."[17] Usually the middle-age parents have one of their parents move in with them after the grandchildren have left home. This kind of family is different from the common model because it is made up of elderly and middle-age adults. There has been practically no research into this kind of family— its structure and its needs.

Even when the elderly do not move in with their children they will often move so as to live close to them. Adams found that the aged,

---

[15] Bert N. Adams, "Occupational Position, Mobility and the Kin of Orientation," *American Sociological Review*, June 1967, p. 377.

[16] Lillian E. Troll, "The Family of Later Life: A Decade Review," in Broderick, *Decade*, p. 193.

[17] Ibid., p. 190.

regardless of social class, frequently migrated to live with or, more often, near their offspring.[18] There are a number of studies that show that the great majority of older Americans who have children live within one-half hour's driving distance of at least one child. Moreover, they see one another quite frequently. One nationwide sample found that 65 percent of the elderly had seen at least one child in the 24-hour period prior to the interview.[19]

When the elderly have frequent contact with their children there can be problems. Studies indicate that often the relations between young adults and their parents are characterized by frequent contact, affection, and an obligation to help out in time of need. It is when obligation to help becomes the dominant element in the relationship that trouble frequently enters. If actual aid enters the relationship it can weaken the affectional and enjoyable aspects of it.[20] It is quite possible that the shifting of the help patterns from the older to the younger creates the basis for problems because it is something neither is used to.

Problems between the elderly and their children can be related to other factors. Because they are of different ages their interests may vary. The things one age group holds to be important may not be important to the other. For example, you can often have sharp differences in religious values, political beliefs, and so forth. This means that these topics can be a source of conflict if they see much of each other. Or to minimize conflict they may leave out discussion of those topics. When this happens the two generations are often thrown back on their family ties, and the demand placed on those ties strain them or are not satisfying to all concerned. The important point is that for many possible reasons the relationships between the elderly and their adult children may not be satisfactory and often lead to problems that the emotional bond cannot overcome.

While the discussion has been about the elderly turning to their children, this is not an option for many older persons. For example, 8 percent of all persons over age 65 have never married. Furthermore, not all married persons ever had children or have surviving children. Of the noninstitutionalized population over 65 about 25 percent do not have any living children.[21] While some of these persons may have siblings to turn to, many older persons may in effect have no kinship structure. Certainly as the extended family of cousins and aunts and uncles continues to shrink, it means fewer kinship relationships available to persons at all ages.

---

[18] Adams, "Isolation," p. 177.

[19] Gordon F. Strieb, "Older Families and Their Troubles: Familial and Social Responses," *The Family Coordinator*, January 1972, p. 13.

[20] Adams, "Isolation," p. 170.

[21] Strieb, "Older Families," p. 13.

The stress has been on the need of many older people to have involvements with their children. But, at the same time there is, for most elderly people, a strong need to maintain independence. There is a fear among many people as they get older that they will have to be dependent on others. As a result there is a great concern with retirement plans that provide independence. Today many people as they get older are inclined to use their money rather than simply to accumulate it. One aspect of this is the smaller interest today in the idea of "building up an inheritance" for children. More and more the older generation are coming to believe they have the right to spend their own money on their own needs.[22]

Studies indicate that it is often of great importance to the elderly to be able to keep their own home. This provides the opportunity for independence. Adams, in his study of kinship, found that both the aged and their children are most satisfied with relationships when they include separate residences and friendly interaction.[23] It is not only that the house symbolizes independence for the elderly but also because it provides a setting for them to lead their lives as they choose. Their day-to-day patterns might often lead to conflict if they were living with their children because their routines are different.

The research also shows that as people get older they change their residence much less. Montgomery has suggested that the anchoring variables "include limited income, declining health, a strong sense of place, and an unwillingness to face adjustment problems occasioned by moving."[24] This often implies they will have less contact with their adult children who are subject to far more movement. The younger generation increasingly enter occupations that insist on moving them a great deal. Also a difference exists in the symbolic importance of the home. For many in the older generation the home has been "the old homestead" in the sense that they have lived there for many years, reared their children there, and have a strong emotional identification with it. Therefore to leave is to tear out important roots of the past. But the younger generation, often moving every few years, rarely develop these emotional bonds to any house.

Homes are also important to the elderly because often as they get older they are more and more dependent on them. Older people leave their houses less. It has been estimated that persons over 65 spend 80 to 90 percent of their lives in their homes. "Of all people, only small children, the chronically ill, and those institutionalized for law violations are

[22] William J. Goode, *World Revolution and Family Patterns* (New York: The Free Press of Glencoe, 1963), p. 79.

[23] Adams, "Isolation," p. 170.

[24] James E. Montgomery, "The Housing Patterns of Older Families," *The Family Coordinator*, January 1972, p. 39.

so house and neighborhood bound."[25] Other studies indicate that with increasing age the life space used continues to diminish. If people become old and enfeebled or ill, their life space becomes reduced to a house or apartment, "to a room, and ultimately to a bed with four restraining walls."[26]

There has been a trend in recent years for many older people to give up their homes after their children have grown up and move to new locations. Many of them move to retirement areas in such states as Arizona, California, and Florida. This raises problems for many because they may move many miles from their adult children and other relatives. Yet, one study found that postretirement migration did not lead to greater family isolation for the aged than if they had remained in their home communities. "Many of the migrants who presently see their children only infrequently were unlikely to have had much greater contact with them had they retired instead in their homes."[27] What frequently happens is that personal interaction between the aged and their children is increasingly tied to holiday and vacation periods. The above study found that "older persons who retire to Florida and Arizona typically find this as convenient a locale for receiving or initiating family visits as was their previous residence in the Midwest.[28]

Studies indicate that most older persons do not wish to live in retirement communities, many cannot afford to do so, and the health of many will not permit it. "But the leisure-oriented who possess the health, the money, and the desire seem to find these communities highly satisfactory."[29] The community setting provides expanded opportunities for friendships. The proportion of friendships among the elderly appears to be related to the number of aged peers who live nearby. As previously suggested, the values of the elderly are often more rigid than for younger persons, and, therefore, they can, in the community of peers, find persons who share their values. The retirement communities provide some protection against social change and the threat of conflicting values and beliefs.

Retirement

Chapters 14 and 15 discuss the relationships of occupations to marriage and family roles. It need only be pointed out at this time that the occupational role is usually the most important adult role filled by the

---

[25] Ibid., p. 37.

[26] Ibid., p. 37.

[27] Gordon L. Bultena and Douglas G. Marshall, "Family Patterns of Migrant and Nonmigrant Retirees," *Journal of Marriage and the Family*, February 1970, p. 92.

[28] Ibid., p. 92.

[29] Montgomery, "Housing Patterns," p. 43.

male. Therefore, when he leaves that role it will usually indicate a sense of loss and the need for adaptive behavior. In part this can be understood in that there are strong similarities between retirement and unemployment. The implications of retirement for the wife will be discussed shortly. Among men, the one who has the greatest trouble adjusting to retirement is the one who identifies himself most closely with the breadwinning role. For some men, avocations help them adjust, but a "flexible view of what it is that constitutes masculinity, a fundamentally equalitarian approach to the marital interaction, will also help enormously."[30]

For many men, retirement produces a feeling that they have lost their main adult identity. For example, a former mechanic is no longer a mechanic—he is occupationally nothing. "It therefore means losing one's place in society, one's dignity, and almost one's reality. In addition to this, the retired do not know what to do with their leisure, and they grow bored."[31]

Various studies indicate that when persons are asked whether they would rather go on working or retire, the reasons given for either choice are usually negative. When they say they want to continue working, often it is because they fear poverty if they stop; and if they say they would prefer to stop work, it is often because of poor health. But in neither type of situation do they look forward to retirement as a way of life that is pleasurable. They tend not to see either work or leisure as a form of self-fulfillment because neither one nor the other is freely chosen.[32]

Retirement is an arbitrary decision to have people leave the work force. It is arbitrary because it picks a specific age, and generally that age cannot be altered to fit different cases. This means that some persons are forced out of their occupations when they still have the ability to give a great deal, while others hang on long after they have nothing to give simply because they are not old enough to retire. There is also discrimination based on age that occurs well before retirement. In the United States about half the states have laws that forbid all discrimination on the basis of age. Yet, various employers give semiofficial instructions to agencies that result in age discrimination. For example, one study of eight large cities found that employment agencies fixed the upper age limit as 35 and one third at 45. It was also found that 97 percent of the advertisements in newspapers set 40 as the limit.[33] So job discrimination against the aged and increasingly against the middle-aged is already a fact. Yet, while nearly 40 percent of the long-term unem-

---

[30] Myron Brenton, "New Ways to Manliness," in Nancy Reeves, *Womankind: Beyond the Stereotype* (Chicago: Aldine Publishing Co., 1971, p. 199.

[31] Beauvoir, *Old Age*, p. 266.

[32] Ibid., p. 274.

[33] Ibid., p. 227.

ployed are over 45, only 10 percent of the federal retraining programs are devoted to men of that age. To add to the problems it is also often difficult for older people to get bank loans, home mortgages, or automobile insurance.[34]

There is some argument that restrictions on job opportunities and other activities for the aged are justified because of inabilities on their part. While certainly some older people are handicapped in what they can do, this is not true for most. For example, studies show that the elderly are able to memorize and recall new information, but they need more time than younger people. "Their responses are apparently slowed down by anxiety; an older person's goal is less to achieve success than to avoid failure."[35]

As suggested, society takes a confused and sometimes contradictory view about retirement. This is because often occupations seem to imply that age limits eliminate those who can successfully fulfill them. For example, in American society the athlete is in an occupation that calls for early retirement. In some areas, like swimming, you can be too old to be a champion by the time you reach your early 20s. Occupations at the other extremes can be best illustrated by politics where often there is no mandatory retirement age. This is most vividly illustrated in the United States Senate and House of Representatives where seniority means power. It is often assumed that congressmen well into their 70s are able to effectively function, and rarely has there ever been any serious charge of malfunction due to senility. Given the wide range of retirement ages it is important to note that often a given individual feels frustration because he sees persons older than himself effectively functioning in occupations.

Simone de Beauvoir has suggested that society takes an ambiguous view of aging with such as doctors, lawyers, and professional men in general. She suggests this is especially true for doctors because, for a certain period of time, age adds to their value. It is thought to bring experience, and a person with a long career behind him is preferred to a novice. But later the picture changes. "The old doctor is looked upon as worn out, in biological decline, and as one who had therefore lost much of his ability. And above all he is thought to be out of date."[36]

As mentioned earlier, with the movement of the elderly from under the care of the extended family, society has had to take over. Among the capitalist countries there are three that look upon it as an important duty to care for all citizens of all ages. Those three are Denmark, Norway, and Sweden. For example, in Sweden there is a system of supple-

---

[34] *Time Magazine*, "Country of Young," in Skolnick and Skolnick, *Transition*, p. 434.

[35] Ibid., p. 436.

[36] Beauvoir, *Old Age*, p. 385.

mentary pensions, and the retired person draws two thirds of his average annual wage based on the 15 best-paid years of his life.[37] Compared to this it can be seen that the United States has a long way to go.

What has happened in many countries, including the United States, is that the elderly are very overrepresented among the poor. In the United States elderly people, who make up about 10 percent of the population, comprise 20 percent of the poor. According to the 1970 Census there were 4.8 million older persons living in poverty. As a result, one out of every four older persons is poor. And of that group of aged poor, two thirds of them are women.[38]

Marriage and the Elderly

As the number of elderly has increased in the United States the number of them married has also increased. The number of older persons who are married and living with their spouses has increased from a little under 7 million in 1955 to well over 9 million in 1970. The marriages of those elderly couples are different in many respects from what they were during their younger years.

The marriages have often had to make important adjustments in middle age when the children have all left home. What may be most important to the postparental marriage is how the couple define it and what they expect from their relationship. If, for a number of years, the marriage stayed together because of the children, then the couple must decide if they want to stay together now that they no longer fill active parental roles. Some couples who appear to have had a smooth marriage surprise their friends by suddenly getting a divorce. Yet as Hunt points out, "there is no mystery about it; they had simply been too busy to notice that they were no longer friends, until their aloneness made it obvious."[39] But it appears that most couples either make a satisfactory adjustment to the postparental years or decide that staying married is the lesser of alternative evils.

By the time the couple reach old age, they constitute a family unit generally made up of only the husband and wife, and that may have been true for a number of years. In 1961 in the United States "only 4 percent of the 4.9 million husband-wife families with the head 65 years old and over had any children of their own under 18 still at home."[40]

We have discussed many of the implications of retirement for the

---

[37] Ibid., p. 225.

[38] Birren and Gribbin, "Elderly," p. 8.

[39] Morton Hunt, *Her Infinite Variety* (New York: Harper and Row, 1962), p. 219.

[40] Paul C. Glick, "Demographic Analysis of Family Data," in Harold T. Christensen, *Handbook of Marriage and the Family* (Chicago: Rand McNally and Co., 1964), p. 302.

husband, but it is just as important to look at the consequences of retirement for the elderly wife. The occupational retirement of the husband has many implications for the marriage relationship. What is especially important in contemporary American society is that retirement is a new form of social life, in that it is different from previous patterns of old age and has not achieved any specific institutional integration. "Past societies have had numbers of aged people, but these were not *retired persons*. They remained integrated in traditional institutional orders through work and kinship roles and relationships."[41] Our interest here is with the impact of retirement on the marriage roles—the man retires from his occupation and spends most of his time at home with his wife.

Donahue suggests that in the normal life cycle a woman has often experienced two or three "retirements" by the time her husband is facing his first retirement. What Donahue means by "retirement" experiences of the woman are that many left jobs for childrearing and thus had experienced that retirement experience during early adulthood. Women also experience retirement in other activities: For example, "when their children grow up and leave the parental home, women experience another retirement from an essential function and have to make adjustments to the cessation of the maternal role."[42] Yet in some cases the woman may find it more difficult to accept her husband's retirement than it was to accept her own retirements. Several studies show that a significant proportion of women do not want their husbands to retire because they believe that they will have more housework to do, "that their daily routine will be disrupted, that they do not want their husbands home all day, and that they will have to live on a lower income."[43]

To suddenly have the husband around for long periods of time puts a strain on many marriages because the husband and wife must interact far more extensively than in the past. As Donahue and her associates describe it, the "daily absence from the home except over the weekends may have enabled many husbands to adjust to marital relationships which under conditions of closer contact they might have found explosive or intolerable."[44]

There are several factors that may lessen the problems for the couple after the husband's retirement. When the household activities are contrasted before and after retirement, often the home in which the husband has retired is more likely to show increased activity on the part of the husband and decreased involvement by the wife than it did before re-

---

[41] Wilma Donahue, Harold L. Orbach, and Otto Pollak, "Retirement: The Emerging Social Pattern," in Clark Tibbitts, *Handbook of Social Gerontology* (Chicago: The University of Chicago Press, 1960), p. 334.

[42] Ibid., p. 372.

[43] Ibid., p. 371.

[44] Ibid., p. 371.

tirement.[45] Ballweg found there were two factors which tended to lessen the possibility of upsetting family balance even though there was a change in task distribution. First, the retired husband did not share tasks with his wife any more than he did when he was working. Second, those jobs which the retired husband did "appeared to be masculine or marginal in orientation rather than those which would have a significant influence on the self-conception of the wife. The supposed invasion by the retired husband thus became more of an emancipation from tasks which the wife could have relinquished at any time the husband was willing to accept them."[46]

Often the social view of marriages among older people is one of life in set and routinized relationships, based upon shared experiences of many years. As Beauvoir has pointed out, if old people show the same desires and some of the requirements of the young, they are looked at with some ridicule or disgust. Among the old the idea of love and jealousy often seem to the young to be absurd. What many want is for the old to represent the virtues of society. "Above all they are called upon to display serenity: The world asserts they possess it, and this assertion allows the world to ignore their unhappiness."[47]

Sexual Behavior.   Where the above limitations on the elderly are the strongest is with regard to sexual behavior. For many younger people the idea of sexual relations between elderly people is shocking and even disgusting. Sometimes the elderly accept the definitions against their sexuality. They may become ashamed of their desires or deny having them. "He refuses to be a lecherous old man in his own eyes, or a shameless old woman. He fights against his sexual drives to the point of thrusting them back into his unconscious mind."[48] These kinds of values not only hurt the elderly but also others. The widespread denial of sexuality in older people can make it difficult to diagnose correctly many of their medical and psychological problems. It may also distort interpersonal relations in marriage, disrupt relationships between children and parents thinking of remarriage, "perverts the administration of justice to older persons accused of sex offenses, and weakens the whole self-image of the older man or woman."[49]

With few exceptions, the approach to marital sex has traditionally been presented by family textbook writers as something peculiar to the

[45] John A. Ballweg, "Resolution of Conjugal Role Adjustment after Retirement," *Journal of Marriage and the Family*, May 1967, p. 278.

[46] Ibid., p. 281.

[47] Beauvoir, *Old Age*, pp. 3–4.

[48] Ibid., p. 320.

[49] Isadore Rubin, "The 'Sexless Older Years'—A Socially Harmful Stereotype," in Ann McCreary Johasz, *Sexual Development and Behavior* (Homewood, Ill.: Dorsey Press, 1973), pp. 82–83.

young and newly married, with discussion centering around the early stages of sexual expression and adjustment in marriage. The implication seems to be that with time the married couple will either achieve some sexual adjustment or that sex will become of lesser importance to them. That marital sex for middle-aged and elderly married couples has generally been ignored by text writers has been in part due to little research knowledge to draw upon. One of the major contributions of the research of Masters and Johnson has been their findings with regard to sex and the aging.

Another study by Pfeiffer and his associates was with 254 subjects between the ages of 60 and 94. They found that the percentage of women indicating no sexual interest was higher than that among men in all the age categories. They also found that the percentage indicating a strong sexual desire or interest was lower than that found among men in all age categories.[50] This suggests that the somewhat greater sexual involvement of men is common to all ages—young, middle-aged, and elderly.

For the woman, the first strong feeling of aging usually occurs at the time of the menopause. But while this represents the end of her child-bearing years, it does not mean the end of her sexual interests or abilities. The menopause does not occur all at once but may represent a transition over many months. The menopause may start as early as age 35, but it more commonly begins at 45 to 47, and it may not occur until the early or even middle 50s. The majority of women, about four fifths in fact, pass through this period without any ill effects whatever and, so far as regular health is concerned, without even being aware of it. Masters and Johnson found no reason why the menopause should be expected to slow down the female's sexual capacity, performance, or drive. "The healthy aging woman normally has sex drives that demand resolution—there is no time limit drawn by the advancing years to female sexuality."[51]

As the woman moves into older age, her sexual activity shows some decrease, usually due to two main causes: (1) her own decrease in sexual interest and (2) the fact that a large number of older women have no spouse or have a spouse with little or no sexual interest and/or ability. Christenson and Gagnon found that for married women at age 55, 89 percent were coitally active; by age 60 the rate was 70 percent, and by age 65 the rate was 50 percent.[52] Also at age 65, of the married women, 25 percent were actively involved in masturbation; and of women of the

[50] Eric Pfeiffer, Adriaan Verwoerdt, and Glen C. Davis, "Sexual Behavior in Middle Life," in Juhasz, *Sexual Development,* p. 73.

[51] William H. Masters and Virginia E. Johnson, *Human Sexual Response* (Boston: Little, Brown & Co., 1966), pp. 246–47.

[52] Cornelia Christenson and John H. Gagnon, "Sexual Behavior in a Group of Older Women," *Journal of Gerontology,* July 1965, p. 352.

same age no longer married, 33 percent were engaging in masturbation.[53]

The use of masturbation by older people often comes as a surprise. It is generally seen as an activity that ends with maturity and rarely would be associated with the elderly. But the Pfeiffer study also found that for many older people masturbation continues to serve as a satisfactory form of sexual release from sexual tensions when a partner is, for one reason or another, not available.[54] It should also be kept in mind that coitus is a far more complex and difficult undertaking than masturbation because it constitutes an involvement with another person. Harsh as it may sound, many elderly people may prefer their fantasies to their mate's age-worn body.

The major limiting factor on the older woman is not lack of sexual interest but rather the lack of a sexually active partner. Christenson and Gagnon found that "in terms of both incidence and frequency of coitus the relative age of the husband was a strongly determining factor: The wives with husbands younger than they showed higher figures and those with older husbands considerably lower ones, at successive ages for the females." Masters and Johnson came to essentially the same conclusion—that the sexual activity of women at 70 years of age and over was greatly influenced by male attrition.[55] In the Christenson and Gagnon sample, there was not a single case of a woman at 65 or over involved in postmarital coitus.[56] Pfeiffer found that only 7 of the 101 single, divorced, or widowed subjects reported any sexual activity with partners. "Apparently, the strength of the sexual drive of most elderly persons is usually not great enough to cause them to seek sexual partners outside of marriage in the face of social disapproval and the difficulties of such an endeavor."[57]

For the male, the central problem of aging is the fear of impotency. A male at any age may have temporary impotency. It may occur only on occasion or for varying periods of time. In almost all cases, impotency is believed to be caused by psychological factors such as overwork, anxiety, fear, and fatigue. For the male in a temporary state of impotency, the inability may contribute to his problems and intensify his impotency. He worries about his inability to have an erection, and, as a result, the worry contributes to even greater difficulty. Generally, the cure for impotency is rest and mental relaxation—which for many men may be easier said than done.

Generally speaking, as the male grows older his fear of impotency becomes increasingly important. Masters and Johnson state that there

---

[53] Ibid., p. 352.

[54] Pfeiffer, Verwoerdt, and Davis, "Middle Life," p. 87.

[55] Masters and Johnson, *Response*, p. 245.

[56] Christenson and Gagnon, "Older Women," p. 352.

[57] Pfeiffer, Verwoerdt, and Davis, "Middle Life," p. 91.

is no way to overemphasize the importance that "fear of failure" plays in the aging male's withdrawal from sexual performance. "Once impotent under any circumstances, many males withdraw voluntarily from any coital activity rather than face the ego-shattering experience of repeated episodes of sexual inadequacy."[58]

As suggested, the fear of impotency is not something that waits for old age, but it is often a characteristic of middle age. Fears of impotence "were expressed under interrogation, by every male study subject beyond 40 years of age, irrespective of reported levels of formal education."[59] As the male reaches middle age, there are often many concerns on his part that repress his sexual interests for long periods of time. "This sensitivity of male sexuality to mental fatigue is one of the greatest differences between the responsiveness of the middle-aged and the younger male."[60]

Increasing age sometimes offers an excuse for the man who is suffering from sexual insecurities or problems. A man who is having impotency problems, or is indifferent to sex, or is worried about it may be relieved that old age allows him refuge in abstinence that will seem normal afterwards. It provides him with a socially acceptable way of getting out of doing something he wants to get out of.[61]

As the male moves into old age, there are other factors that restrict his sexual interest and/or sexual ability. Masters and Johnson state that "loss of coital interest engendered by monotony in a sexual relationship is probably the most constant factor in the loss of an aging male's interest in sexual performance with his partner."[62] At the same time, many of these men may be married to women who have little or no sexual interest, and many of the women "by their own admission . . . no longer showed either sexual interest or sexual concern for their husbands."[63]

What appears to be most significantly related to active marital sexual expression in old age is whether there has been an overall pattern of active sexual interaction during the marriage. "When the male is stimulated to high sexual output during his formative years and a similar tenor of activity is established for the 31–40-year age range, his middle-aged and involutional years usually are marked by constantly recurring physiologic evidence of maintained sexuality."[64] But what is of great importance in the research of Masters and Johnson is that the "male over 50 years old can be trained out of his secondarily acquired impotence in a high

---

[58] Masters and Johnson, *Response,* pp. 269–70.

[59] Ibid., p. 202.

[60] Ibid., p. 267.

[61] Beauvoir, *Old Age,* p. 320.

[62] Masters and Johnson, *Response,* p. 264.

[63] Ibid., p. 265.

[64] Ibid., p. 262.

percentage of cases. If he is in adequate health, little is needed to support adequacy of sexual performance in a 70- or even 80-year-old male other than some physiologic outlet or psychologic reason for a reactivated sexual interest."[65]

Masters and Johnson do find some changes in the sexual response in the older man—for example, reduction in seminal-fluid volume and decreased ejaculatory pressure—"but *he does not lose his facility for erection at any time.*"[66] They go on to point out that fears of performance are brought about by a lack of knowledge about the natural changes in male sexual responsivity that go with the aging process. *"Really, the only factor that the aging male must understand is that loss of erective prowess is not a natural component of aging."*[67]

Nearly everyone has a varying number of years without a partner after the death of the spouse. The elderly person without a spouse is assumed to have little or no sexual interests. Society tends to see them, as they do an elderly person with a sick, feeble, or impotent spouse, as persons to be shunted off with the suggestion that continence and self-control should be exercised as seemly virtues for the aging members of the community. One of the contributions of the Masters and Johnson research has been that the elderly can and do have sexual lives. The topic of sex and the elderly is still very restricted, but it is a little more open than it was in the past.

Grandparent roles.   One other family role which many older people find themselves in is that of grandparent. Grandparents can often look at their grandchildren in a way they couldn't view their own children. They often can be generous because they have few rights or obligations. The grandparents don't have the task of bringing them up, of saying no, and of sacrificing the present to the future. "So the children often show a great deal of affection for them, looking upon them as a refuge against their parents' severity."[68]

Frequently, contact with the grandchildren is very important to the lives of the elderly. It is important to them, quite apart from any family ties, because it gives them contact with changing times and they can to some extent relate to the present through the children. Simone de Beauvoir suggests that it helps carry them along the infinity of the future and is the best defense against the gloom that threatens old age. But she says that, unhappily, relationships of this kind are not too common because the young and the old very often belong to two separate worlds between which there may be little communication.[69]

---

[65] Ibid., p. 263.

[66] Ibid., p. 326.

[67] Ibid., p. 329.

[68] Beauvoir, *Old Age,* p. 475

[69] Ibid., p. 475.

A number of factors have altered the role of the grandparent in recent years. First, given the great increase in the number of older people there are more persons to be grandparents. Second, given the fact of younger ages at marriage and having children, people become grandparents at younger ages. Third, the roles of many older people make them different from the grandparent of the past. For example, the grandmother today is very apt to be a working woman. What those changes mean is that becoming a grandparent for the first time often occurs during middle age rather than old age. As a result, there has been an increase of four-generation families and the great-grandparent is now a fairly common role. The fact that many grandparents are middle-aged means that the "rocking chair" image must be changed, and this has far reaching consequences for adult socialization and role modeling as well as family interaction.[70] The change also suggests that we need to know more about the great grandparent role and its implications for the elderly. This is another area of neglected research in the sociology of the family.

Problem Areas. In concluding this chapter it is useful to look briefly at some of the problems related to the elderly. These are problems not only for the older person but also for society because it must provide means for dealing with them. This is especially true since the extended family takes less responsibility for the elderly.

Anywhere from one third to one half of the aged are poorer, are employed less, work in lower-status occupations, have less education and poorer health than similar proportions of the nonaged population. And too, the "aged, like certain minority groups, tend to be concentrated in rural areas and in the central city and are underrepresented in the suburbs."[71] But his should not be taken to mean that large numbers of elderly are totally dependent on society. Actually, the overwhelming majority of the elderly can take care of themselves reasonably well. "Only 5 percent of aged Americans live in institutions; perhaps another 5 percent remain bedridden at home."[72]

While most of the elderly make no special demands on society, some of them do. Obviously as people get older their medical problems increase. This is because the aging body suffers from some deterioration and they become more prone to various illnesses. While the aged account for about a twelfth of the population they occupy about one fifth of all hospital beds. Also the number of medical consultations increases with old age. Because there are far more women among the aged, they

---

[70] Troll, "Later Life," p. 202.

[71] Erdman Palmore and Frank Whittingham, "Trends in the Relative Status of the Aged," *Social Forces*, September 1971, p. 89.

[72] *Time Magazine*, "Country of Young," in Skolnick and Skolnick, *Family in Transition*, p. 436.

account for a majority of older persons in hospitals as well as seeking all kinds of medical help.

A large number of elderly Americans (close to a million) are living in nursing homes or convalescent facilities provided by medicare. In fact, as a new growth industry, nursing homes now provide more beds than do hospitals.[73] "These kinds of facilities are in part a social means for handling the aged outside of their children's homes. There is no agreement that this is a satisfactory solution. On one hand it does take the elderly away from a private home where they may not be able to look after themselves or their demands are seen as too much for others. But on the other hand it puts them in a highly segregated setting of aged and often ill persons. This means that their lives are distorted and frequently very repressive and sad. Often the big event in many of these homes is when one of the patients dies. Their world becomes not only institutional but also very fixed in that they are all basically alike. Unfortunately there may be no really good social solution to caring for the dependent aged.

As people get older not only do they suffer increasingly from physical problems but also mental ones. In fact, sometimes the two are closely related. Aging brings about in some people both physical and mental changes that are reflected in mental health problems. The most obvious illustration is senility. The rate of mental illness among the aged is about 236 per 100,000 population. By contrast, the rate is about 76 per 100,000 in the 25 to 34 age group.[74]

The most vivid measurement of problems among the elderly is reflected in their suicide rates. In the United States about 22 out of every 100,000 people in their 40s kill themselves. This figure continues to rise with age, and at 80 it reaches 697 in every 100,000. "Some old people kill themselves after neurotic depressions that have not yielded to treatment, but most of these suicides are the normal reaction to a hopeless, irreversible situation that is found to be unbearable."[75]

In general, the status of the elderly in society is not very good. It is clear that the gaps between the aged and the rest of the population in such crucial areas as income, employment, and education are steadily and substantially increasing. It is probably only in the area of health that there is any relative gain for the aged. "This means that despite all the public and private programs to help the aged, and despite many adequate gains, they are actually falling further behind the nonaged in most ways. Thus the evidence from the past 30 years in the United States

---

[73] Ibid., p. 435.

[74] Beauvoir, *Old Age,* p. 493.

[75] Ibid., p. 276.

supports the theory that the relative status of the aged tends to decline in industrial society."[76]

From the perspective of marriage and the family the greatest demand placed on the elderly couple is in their marriage relationships. Their roles as husband and wife become more important because their family roles have been reduced by their children growing up and their work roles no longer filled because of retirement. Add to this the anxieties for many of aging and the possible fears of death for the spouse and the self and it means that the potential strains on marriage are probably greater for the elderly than at any other time in life.

SELECTED BIBLIOGRAPHY

Adams, Bert N. "Isolation, Function and Beyond: American Kinship in the 1960s," in Carlfred Broderick, *A Decade of Family Research and Action.* Minneapolis: National Council on Family Relations, 1971, pp. 163–85.

Ballweg, John A. "Resolution of Conjugal Role Adjustment After Retirement." *Journal of Marriage and the Family,* May 1967, pp. 275–80.

Birren, James E., and **Gribbin, Kathy** "The Elderly," in Don Spiegel and Patricia Keith-Spiegel, *Outsiders USA.* San Francisco: Rinehart Press, 1973, pp. 75–95.

Bultena, Gordon L., and **Marshall, Douglas G.** "Family Patterns of Migrant and Nonmigrant Retirees." *Journal of Marriage and the Family,* February 1970, pp. 90–96.

de Beauvoir, Simone *Old Age.* Great Britain: Cox and Wyman Ltd., 1973.

Kalish, Richard A. "Of Social Values and the Dying: A Defense of Disengagement." *The Family Coordinator,* January 1972, pp. 78–83.

Montgomery, James E. "The Housing Patterns of Older Families." *The Family Coordinator,* January 1972, pp. 37–46.

Palmore, Erdman, and **Whittengham, Frank** "Trends in the Relative Status of the Aged." *Social Forces,* September 1971, pp. 84–101.

Pfeiffer, Eric, Verwoerdt, Adriaan, and **Davis, Glen C.** "Sexual Behavior in Middle Life," in Ann McCreary Juhasz, *Sexual Development and Behavior.* Homewood, Ill.: The Dorsey Press, 1973, pp. 69–79.

Strieb, Gordon F. "Older Families and Their Troubles: Familial and Social Responses." *The Family Coordinator,* January 1972, pp. 5–19.

Troll, Lillian E. "The Family of Later Life: A Decade of Review," in Carlfred Broderick, *A Decade of Family Research and Action.* Minneapolis: The National Council on Family Relations, 1971, pp. 187–214.

---

[76] Palmore and Whittingham, "Trends," p. 90.

Chapter *14*

The Male and Marriage, Family, and Occupational Roles

In the American middle class, the most important adult role filled by the male is usually that of his occupation, and the most important adult role for the female is usually that of wife-mother. Nonetheless, the middleclass male's involvements in his family roles are often strong, and there are many women adding to their traditional adult roles of wife and mother by participation in occupational roles. However, the *relationships* between occupational roles and family roles have not been the subject of much study.[1] One pair of researchers has observed that the relationships between work and family life have seldom been studied explicitly by family sociologists and that other approaches—such as those of industrial sociology or occupational psychology—have usually treated each institution as a relatively closed system.[2]

In American society today, the work settings of men and women generally function separately; the man goes off to his place of work and the woman does her work at home. But this pattern of sex separation is of fairly recent origin. Before the industrial revolution, most men and

[1] Jesse R. Pitts, "The Structural-Functional Approach," in Harold T. Christensen, ed., *Handbook of Marriage and Family* (Chicago: Rand McNally & Co., 1964), p. 102.

[2] Robert Rapoport and Rhona Rapoport, "Work and Family in Contemporary Society," *American Sociological Review*, June 1965, p. 382.

women were co-workers on the land and in the home. "Women worked in the fields when the chores of the home and childrearing permitted, so that there was not only close association between work and home for both sexes, but even a certain amount of overlap in the sexual division of labor."[3] As Benson points out, in traditional societies the structures of work and domestic activities were closely bound together and each was unambiguously an extension of the other. But, by contrast, in both our business and our psychological accounting we assign work and the running of the home to separate spheres.[4] One of the most important historical changes in the family was the removal of the woman (and children) as contributors to economic production; and with increasing specialization of occupational roles, the man was increasingly removed physically and psychologically from the home.[5]

At the same time that the man was being pulled out of the home to fill his occupational role, the family was becoming increasingly specialized in the functions of socialization and emotional support for its members. It was then that in those areas the woman took on her major role responsibilities.[6] The generally strong emotional commitment acquired by middle-class wife-mothers continues to exist to the present day. Therefore, when they take on occupational roles, it is often to supplement their traditional roles rather than to replace them.

One important consequence of the man's great involvement in his occupational role and the woman's in her family roles is that a good part of their individual daily life occurs in quite different social settings. Hunt describes the different worlds for the upper middle-class man and woman as follows: "Between his twenties and his forties he spends about five thousand working days dealing with other human beings, acquiring knowledge in his field, experiencing something of the larger world he lives in, and attaining a measure of personal and professional stature."[7] By contrast, his wife during the same years spends them with "her children, her housekeeping, and her fellow homemakers; she is very likely to emerge from motherhood in her 40s with little more than the talents and stature she had in girlhood, somewhat faded from disuse."[8]

In the discussion that follows, we will examine the occupational roles of the middle-class male to see how those are related to his marriage

---

[3] Carl N. Degler, "The Changing Place of Women in America," *Daedalus*, Spring 1964, p. 654.

[4] Leonard Benson, *Fatherhood: A Sociological Perspective* (New York: Random House, 1968), pp. 272–73.

[5] Degler, "Women in America," p. 654.

[6] Hyman Rodman, "Talcott Parsons' View of the Changing American Family," *Merrill-Palmer Quarterly*, vol. 11, no. 3 (1965), pp. 217–18.

[7] Morton M. Hunt, *Her Infinite Variety* (New York: Harper & Row, 1962), p. 220.

[8] Ibid., p. 221.

and family roles. This will provide a contrast with the changing nature of adult female roles to be discussed in the following chapter. Because the various roles of men have changed little in contrast with those of the woman there is far more to examine in the following chapter on the woman than in this one on the man. The conflicts and problems related to the male and female roles and to middle-class marriage are best understood within the context of social change.

OCCUPATIONAL AND FAMILY ROLES OF MEN

In the American middle-class family the primary role of the man is performed *outside* the family setting. For example, Lopata found that of her female respondents 87 percent gave the breadwinner role as the most important role for the man.[9] The role of the breadwinner is at the core of the significance of the father in the American society. This is not only seen as true among men but also among women. For example, in a study of women about two thirds of them considered the breadwinner role to be the father's most important function; "husbanding and child-rearing ranked a poor second and third."[10]

Another study found that what the male finds most meaningful to his sense of manliness are the fruits of his work. This includes the pay he gets, the prestige the job has, and the status it provides him in the community. It often includes the material things he can buy and the better life it enables him to give his family. "His wife views his bread-winning role the same way: Many wives have little comprehension of what their mates actually do for a living."[11]

One variation in how the husband is seen as breadwinner is at different social-class levels. The higher social classes give him recognition according to how well he provides materially *and* also for the prestige of his occupation. However, in the lower classes, the important requirement is that he be a good provider; the nature of the occupation is often of little importance. Komarovsky found that lower middle-class women sometimes do not even know the specific occupations of their close relatives, and while they see a good job as the means to a good living, they do not see achievement in a specialized vocation as the measure of a person's worth.[12]

How much income there is in a family is often related to the degree

---

[9] Helena Z. Lopata, "The Secondary Features of a Primary Relationship," *Human Organization,* Summer 1965, pp. 118–19.

[10] Benson, *Fatherhood,* p. 271.

[11] Myron Brenton, "New Ways to Manliness," in Nancy Reeves, *Womankind: Beyond the Stereotype* (Chicago: Aldine, 1971), pp. 191–92.

[12] Mirra Komarovsky, *Blue-Collar Marriage* (New York: Random House, 1962), p. 57.

of marital satisfaction or dissatisfaction. Renne found that income was more closely related to marital dissatisfaction than was either education or occupation, "probably because it has an independent and very concrete impact on the couple's daily life. Other aspects of social status count for relatively little if the family's income is not adequate to its needs."[13]

In the lower classes there is often a different relationship between occupational and family roles than is the case in the middle class. Aldous found that heightened domesticity was not always associated with work alienation. She found that when men are alienated from their work that their kin or cronies can provide alternative sources of emotional support.[14] Aldous goes on to point out that on his job the lower-class man often has little opportunity to associate with men in other occupations or specialties that hold different values from his as well as possessing different skills. The lack of a variety of role contacts means that many lower-class men don't have the chance to develop their role-taking abilities. "Many lower-class men interact with others on the basis of routinized reactions and projections of their own views. Because women play a different role lower-class men find their projecting strategy in interpersonal relations ineffective. As a consequence marital communication is limited."[15]

Aldous has further found in her research that the companionship family is most frequently found in the lower middle class. She suggests that this is the case because men, "far from seeking to carry over job-related behaviors to the family often look to their homes as havens from job monotonies and as sources of the satisfactions lacking in the occupational sphere."[16]

In the discussion that follows we will refer primarily to the upper-middle-class male's involvement in his profession. The term *profession* is used simply to designate occupations that require a high level of formal education and generally imply high prestige and income. While we will be discussing some prestige aspects of professions for men, it should also be kept in mind that a part of his occupational prestige results from the material things that he gives his family. In this sense, his family directly translates his occupational prestige to the community through the material symbols his economic success provides.

It should also be stressed that while in the past kinship was closely related to the economic system, this is no longer of very great impor-

---

[13] Karen S. Renne, "Correlates of Dissatisfaction in Marriage," *Journal of Marriage and the Family*, February 1970, p. 61.

[14] Joan Aldous, "Occupational Characteristics and Males' Role Performance in the Family," *Journal of Marriage and the Family*, November 1969, p. 712.

[15] Ibid., p. 712.

[16] Ibid., p. 712.

tance. The life stream of individual societies, even though we often deny it, "is money not blood, and production, not reproduction, has transcendent value. Kinship institutions, therefore, in the present period have but marginal utility and peripheral importance."[17]

It should also be mentioned that the man's overall prestige in the middle class is related to age for him in a way quite different than for his wife. It seems quite possible that women lose ground in their personal development and self-esteem during the early and middle years of adulthood. But by contrast men gain ground in these respects during the same years. Rossi has suggested that the retention of a high level of self-esteem may depend on the adequacy of the socialization for major adult roles. "Men's training adequately prepares them for their primary adult roles in the occupational system, as it does for those women who opt to participate significantly in the work world. Training in the qualities and skills needed for family roles in contemporary society may be inadequate for both sexes, but the lowering of self-esteem occurs only among women because their primarily adult roles are within the family system."[18]

The difference for men and women basically means that the man is out of the home and is constantly challenged in his work—even if it is only to keep a firm hold on his job. So he is required to measure himself against criteria external to the family. "The woman, since she is using *his* motion to propel *her* onward, is immune both to challenge and to criteria. Wives and mothers are good wives and mothers by definition, not by performance."[19]

Occupational Roles. The vast majority of American men leave their homes and their family members to pursue their occupations. This means that the adult male's life is often carried out in two separate worlds—the world of his family (and residential community), and his world of work. While occasionally his world of work may intrude on his family world —that is, working at home, moving his family, etc.—rarely does he physically bring his family into his work world—that is, take his wife or children to his place of work to interact with his occupational peers or work procedures.

One important dimension of family and occupational roles is how they synchronize. This may vary widely because of many variations in occupational demands. Aldous points out that his dimension encompasses such aspects of the job as hours, the amount of geographical mobility, and at what stage of the family life cycle the occupation makes its

---

[17] Reeves, *Womankind*, p. 77.

[18] Alice S. Rossi, "Transition to Parenthood," *Journal of Marriage and the Family*, February 1968, p. 35.

[19] Reeves, *Womankind*, p. 33. See also David R. Goldman, "Managerial Mobility, Motivations, and Central Life Interests," *American Sociological Review*, February 1973, pp. 119–26.

greatest demands. "Occupations having irregular hours or requiring night work, as well as taking the man away from home for days at a time, all limit his opportunities to assist with family decisions and tasks as well as to become acquainted with his children."[20] It is not surprising that friction between husband and wife is greater for night than for day workers. "Night workers develop crony cliques to supply the sociability and emotional support their families, geared to a daytime existence, are literally too asleep to provide."[21]

Aldous also found a relationship between kinds of occupations and the kind of marriage that some men participate in. For example, science-oriented technologists tended to make more decisions with their wives on an equalitarian basis than did technologists concerned with equipment. The difference may be interpreted in terms of the carry-over from occupation to home of the universalistic norms that underlie science. "Professionals, organization men, and others heavily concerned with the interpersonal relations of the job hold high expectations of the companionship aspects of marriage. They appear to be demanding professionalization of the marital roles, perhaps in order partially to redress the balance between occupation and family."[22]

There is also some evidence of differences between how men perform as fathers and the kinds of occupations they fill. Men who work mainly with things appear to place a high value on obedience in children but are not disposed to value self-control very highly. It also appears that "men who work mainly with ideas tend to stress self-control and to devalue obedience; men whose work consists essentially of dealing with people fall somewhere in between."[23]

The fact that a man spends many hours away from home in his occupational role has a number of implications for his family. It seems probable that many upper middle-class males strongly identify with and for the most part enjoy their professions. This kind of job involvement and satisfaction is generally not a characteristic of lower-class males. One study of factory workers found that only 24 percent of those studied could be labeled job-oriented in their life interests.[24]

But what is most important is that the kinds of jobs that a man fills has implications for his family. The characteristics of the job the man holds in the occupational structure can have profound effects on his marital and parental functions. Basically, there is the question of how com-

---

[20] Aldous, "Occupational Characteristics," p. 709.

[21] Ibid., p. 709.

[22] Ibid., p. 710.

[23] Benson, *Fatherhood*, p. 276.

[24] Robert Dubin, "Industrial Workers' Worlds: A Study of the 'Central Life Interests' of Industrial Workers," in Erwin O. Smigel, ed., *Work and Leisure* (New Haven. Conn.: College & University Press, 1963), p. 60.

patible occupational characteristics are with family participation. "The *relative salience* of the job in comparison with family roles is important in this connection. If the occupation is of intrinsic interest to the man, it often competes with or even supplants the family as his major concern."[25] And just in terms of time involvement the man often spends more time in the work situation than he does in the family setting.

It appears that given a choice between filling his occupational role or his family role, a professional man will choose his occupation. Yet the man is generally expected to put his family roles above all other roles *if* there is a choice. But if it appears necessary for him to pursue his occupational role over his family roles for the good of his family, then that is not only socially acceptable but often socially applauded. He may be defined as performing above and beyond the call of duty as a breadwinner and making special sacrifices for his family. We would suggest that often the professional man who says he doesn't want to work late or he doesn't want to make a trip is rationalizing his actions to his family (and possibly himself) by blaming his job.

What is of particular interest is that because the man does usually work away from his family, he is not subject to comparisons in those two role settings. And with those two roles filled in separate settings, the man may sometimes play off one role against another. For example, at home he may play off his occupational role either because he *wants* to go to his place of work or to escape the family setting and its demands. And usually in leaving for his occupational setting he conveys the notion to his family (and even an extended community) that what he is doing is for the family's good.

On other occasions a man may play off his family role to escape from occupational role demands. For example, if he doesn't really want to work, he might say that his family is expecting him or that he promised them he would be home. This implies that he would like to stay on the job but has a responsibility to meet the demands of his family role. This explanation allows him to meet the expectations of his occupational peers as to the primary importance of his professional role. It appears that it is rare for a man either in a professional setting or in any exclusively male setting to openly state that he would prefer to leave it and be with his family. That is, it is rare for a man to explain leaving his occupational world because he *wants* to join his family; he uses the explanation of being *expected* by his family.

It is clear that the wife is usually faced with the responsibility for the basic care of the family. It may be that the husband is too busy or too disinterested to apply much assistance in running the home. So very often the husband uses the family's consumption patterns and the wife's

---

[25] Aldous, "Occupational Characteristics," p. 708.

interpersonal skills in the service of his mobility strivings. And he may even use his family as an excuse to change positions. Aldous gives an illustration of the academician who finds his colleagues unexciting and his position at a dead end; he may suddenly discover his family's "unhappiness with the climate and begin looking openly for a more satisfactory appointment. A strategic retreat into family roles disarms critics while permitting continued occupational striving."[26]

Often within the context of the occupational world, the rewards for the man are not there. Frequently he finds that his work, which he has been socialized to believe is his most meaningful adult role, is by and large meaningless. The great ego investment a man makes in his job, the great emphasis he places on it in terms of his masculinity, and the work he does will not, generally speaking, reward him commensurately; and he often shows it. The increasing problems of stealing, "restriction of output, malingering, 'putting something over' on the company, expense account cheating, and heavy drinking at lunch or after work—all are, in part at least, manifestations of job alienation."[27]

The Family Setting. There is a great investment on the part of the wife and her children to their husband-father's success in his occupational role. This investment seems increasingly to imply a willingness by his family to do whatever they can to help him in his occupational role because they feel that the whole family stands to gain or lose by his performance in it.

There is some evidence that the very fact of marriage may contribute to the success of the husband in his occupation. One study of a group of professionals in the mental health area found that of those who were married, regardless of whether the marriage was their first or a subsequent one, were far more likely to be highly successful than colleagues who were not married. It was also found that those who were not currently married, but who were formerly married, tended to be more successful than those who had never been married. "Marriage *per se*, but not marital stability, is strongly related to occupational success and marital disruption is not a liability, particularly when followed by remarriage."[28] In general, it may be that some of the negative forces that operate against occupational success are the same factors that operate against success in the courtship process.

For a woman, her commitment to marry a man implies at that time that she is betting on his future occupational role success. So in the long run the crucial economic decision made by most women occurs at the

---

[26] Ibid., p. 709.

[27] Brenton, "Manliness," p. 191.

[28] John H. Marx and S. Lee Spray, "Marital Status and Occupational Success among Mental Health Professionals," *Journal of Marriage and the Family*, February 1970, p. 117.

time they agree to marry. The wife may help or hinder her husband's occupational future, but ultimately what the wife can do is determined by the husband's particular abilities, motivations, and opportunities.

Frequently in the American middle class the young wife not only wants her husband to be occupationally successful for all the usual reasons, but also to justify for her the occupational future *she* gave up by marrying him. If the wife has a better background than her husband, she may feel a strong need to push him. One study found that when the wife had the superior education she was more apt to put achievement pressure on her husband and depreciate his ability to reach the goals she had set for him.[29] There is also some difference by social class as to wives defining their husbands as successful or unsuccessful. For example, lower-educated wives refer to "bad luck" when explaining the economic failure of their husbands, while higher-educated wives married to men they see as poor providers tend to accuse their husbands of a lack of drive.[30]

However, there are several different ways in which the middle-class wife can be important to her husband in his occupational role. Blood and Wolfe suggest several categories in which wives may contribute to their husband's success in his occupation: (1) The *Collaborative* wife may be found where the couple own their own business (farm, store, or office) and the wife works directly with the husband in running the business operation. (2) The *Working* wife is one who has as her primary function the supplementing of her husband's income so as to improve his occupational position. (3) The *Supportive* wife is generally young and in the upper middle class. She sees herself as providing emotional support as well as home entertaining as a means of helping her husband to get ahead. (4) The *Peripheral* wife is one who sees herself as minimally involved with her husband's occupation. This type of wife is most common to the lower social classes and among old couples, where the wife sees her main function as taking care of the house.[31]

There is sometimes a danger for the wife who helps her husband get ahead: he may "outgrow" her. If the husband greatly outdistances his wife intellectually, she is less able to function as his confidante and partner. Hunt points out that the "average top-level executive talks less to his wife about business than he did as a junior executive, not only because they spend less time together, but because she has fallen too far behind him to be an adequate listener."[32] So, ironically, the wife who is successful in driving her husband *ahead* occupationally may also drive him *away* as a partner.

---

[29] Robert O. Blood and Donald M. Wolfe, *Husbands and Wives* (Glencoe, Ill.: The Free Press, 1960), p. 96.

[30] Komarovsky, *Blue-Collar Marriage,* p. 77.

[31] Blood and Wolfe, *Husbands and Wives,* p. 94.

[32] Hunt, *Variety,* p. 221.

Still another possible area of involvement by the wife with her husband's occupation may be in their social life. While this marital activity is common to the upper middle class, it is not nearly so common in the lower middle class. Komarovsky found that the great majority of wives in her study had no social contact with their husband's workmates. "The friendships husbands form on the job do not include their wives."[33] But in the upper middle class, the wife is very often intimately involved in a social world that pivots around her husband's occupational associates.

As we have mentioned, the wife of the professional man is often very strongly committed to his occupational success. This commitment is not only assumed by herself and by her husband, but may also be assumed at the place of the husband's work. A part of the expectation by both the couple and many business establishments is that the wife believe the company's demands to be of primary importance. Furthermore, it is generally assumed that, over time and if the husband is successful in his occupation, the wife will become even more actively involved. Rostow points out that the "job descriptions of many leading positions presuppose the active participation of a wife. No couple—ambassadorial or company president—is paid a double salary, although the wife may give as much in her part as her husband in his."[34]

The wife is generally expected to put up with social demands that her husband's occupation makes on them. If occupationally they see it as important to attend a dinner or party, even though it may not be what they really want to do, they are expected to attend. To absent themselves would be to run the risk of jeopardizing the husband's occupational future—and of course also the future of his wife and their children. This frequently means that social gatherings are not activities for relaxation and enjoyment, but rather social gatherings that function with a formal and clear-cut set of role relationships that the husband and his wife are expected to know and abide by.

With the husband's occupational future often significantly influenced by the success or failure of the wife in entertaining his occupational associates, she may often be conservative in what she does. For example, the wife may be very concerned with the image her home furnishings or her means of entertainment project to those who will be significant to her husband's occupational future. As a result of her apprehension, she may be conservative in how she decorates her home, the food and drink she serves, and even in the clothes she wears.

There are several other important consequences of a high occupational commitment by the husband. For example, often his great involvement with his occupation not only means that he may not be around the home

---

[33] Komarovsky, *Blue-Collar Marriage*, p. 153.

[34] Edna G. Rostow, "Conflict and Accommodation," *Daedalus*, Spring 1964, p. 752.

very much, but that when he is he is less involved in the care and upkeep of the home than are other men. For example, higher-status men do less work around the house than lower-status men, and for everything that the successful man does less of, his wife does correspondingly more.[35]

Many men spend a good part of the time they are home working on matters related to their occupations. This is not only true about work directly related to their occupation—for example, bringing home paper work from the office—but, it may also be seen in how some men use what they consider to be leisure time at home. Gerstl found these differences among three professional groups (admen, dentists, and professors) on how they would use a hypothetical free two hours at home: Thirty-three percent of the admen said they would use the time for a hobby or recreation and 24 percent said they would spend the time with their family; 32 percent of the dentists said a hobby or recreation and 29 percent said relaxation; among the professors, 50 percent said they would use the time for work or work-connected reading and 28 percent said for recreational reading.[36] We see in these three occupations a wide variation in spending leisure time, but for all three groups there is implied a belief that the home is in part a place for pursuing at least some individual interests that may have little to do with the rest of the family or the home.

In many middle-class families there are differences in the expectations of husbands and wives as to what the husband will do in the home. In general, the husband does less than the wife would like him to do. And certainly many men view things to do around the house as having low priority unless they are things the man likes to do for their own sake rather than because they are chores to be done. It is also true that generally women expect the husband to spend more time around the house than he chooses to spend. In part, this is because the man places less value on the home than does the wife and often his lack of interest in the home raises questions as to how important the home is in the mind of the woman. His not taking it too seriously may lead her to wonder if her definition of importance is really justified. One study found that in the area of spending time at home wives checked a violation of expectations in that area six times more frequently than did husbands. The wives also had more non-met expectations in the area of care of the home.[37]

There is also evidence that what the husband does in the home can

---

[35] Blood and Wolfe, *Husbands and Wives*, p. 60.

[36] Joel E. Gerstl, "Leisure, Taste and Occupational Milieu," in Smigel, ed., *Work and Leisure*, p. 149.

[37] Beverly R. Cutler and William G. Dyer, "Initial Adjustment Processes in Young Married Couples," in Jeffrey K. Hadden and Maria L. Borgatta, *Marriage and Family* (Itasca, Ill.: F. E. Peacock, 1969), pp. 290–91.

contribute to greater family success when the wife is working. For example, when the father participates in more household tasks, the adolescent children are more accepting of their mother's employment. This is true for both sexes but is somewhat greater for daughters than for sons. It was also found that "the sons are influenced more than daughters by their mothers' activities; and the daughters are influenced more than the sons by their fathers' activities."[38] The question of the wife working is closely related to how the husband responds in terms of her feelings of satisfaction. In other words, the occupational and family roles of the man to a great extent determine the success or failure of the woman when she fills an occupational role.

It should be recognized that for many middle-class men there is a close relationship between the effective involvement of the home and their work situations. This is related to the suggestion that it may be argued that assumed contrast between family and occupational roles is overdrawn. That is, the entire human relations approach found in industrial management came from the recognition that there existed an informal structure of communication and friendship networks that often circumvented the formal rules of the work situation. "As a result, the 'highly charged effective relations' found in the family are also present in the occupational world and influence what goes on there from job selection to job performance."[39] So for many men in the middle-class professions the kinds of interpersonal relationships they have on the job are not too different from what they participate in at home.

Probably one of the most important consequences of the male's occupation for his family is its implications for his wife's and children's mobility—both social and geographical. If the husband-father is economically successful, his family may move to a higher-priced home and community. Or the man may be asked to move to another part of the country. While this latter move is often presented to the man as something he may choose to do or not, a refusal may be defined as a lack of commitment to his occupation and be held against him in the future.

While there are still many complementary relationships between the male's occupational roles and those of his family roles, there are many situations where the two sets of role demands are in conflict. Increasingly it seems that for many middle-class males to become successful in their occupational roles, they must become less involved and committed to their family. Or, to put it another way, for the successful man, increasingly his occupational role setting functions more and more as his major

[38] Karl King, Jennie McIntyre, and Leland J. Axelson, "Adolescents Views of Maternal Employment as a Threat to the Marriage Relationship," *Journal of Marriage and the Family*, November 1968, pp. 636–37.

[39] Aldous, "Occupational Characteristics," p. 707.

reference group. His occupational role limits his direct family involvement, but represents greater indirect rewards economically and socially for his wife and children.

As discussed in an earlier chapter, the occupation of the male may take on great importance when he loses it through retirement because for many men that represents the loss of their major adult role. It has generally been through his occupational position that the worker has defined his general social role. But once he has retired he no longer has access to the occupation for performing that social role and reinforcing his self-image. "In addition, the retired worker is excluded from participation with co-workers and finds himself evaluated differently from the evaluation he received as a member of the active work force. The retired worker is beset with the problem of replacing the sources of satisfaction and respect which his former job and co-workers had accorded him."[40] The individual who retires may find that he has lost far more than just the work role. When the individual retires, most of his friends continue to be employed and he becomes a deviant in his social group. All of a sudden he becomes an outsider. "The conversation about business in which he had been able to join freely when he had still been working becomes after retirement a sign of his no longer being in the in-group and a barrier to continued association with his employed friends."[41] This means that for many men who retire the occupational role is gone and the family role is greatly altered by their coming into the home.

There is one aspect of family and occupations that still continues to have some importance in the United States. That is the family-owned and operated business. One study of family businesses found that participants often see them as fraught with problems and are usually not outstandingly successful. "Conflicts among kin were frequent in businesses that were not doing well financially, but were reported in a few cases even in those that were successful."[42]

A very common problem is the extent to which positions can be given in the business on an objective basis. Kinship can cloud the objectivity of who is hired, promotions, and salary. The obligations of kinship sometimes limit the flexibility of the business. The hierarchy of kinship positions may influence the business hierarchy, and this makes it more difficult to maintain the latter, especially if the two hierarchies do not correspond. "Relationships between generations, that is, father-son re-

---

[40] John A. Ballweg, "Resolution of Conjugal Role Adjustment after Retirement," *Journal of Marriage and the Family,* May 1967, p. 277.

[41] Zena Smith Blau, "Structural Constraints on Friendships in Old Age," in Rose Coser, *Life Cycle and Achievement in America* (New York: Harper's, 1969), p. 218.

[42] Hope Jensen Leichter and William E. Mitchell, "Family-Kin Business," in Bert N. Adams and Thomas Weirath, *Readings on the Sociology of the Family* (Chicago: Markham, 1971), p. 347.

lationships, appear to have a particularly strong carry-over into business dealings."[43]

THE LEARNING OF OCCUPATIONAL ROLES

Given the great importance of the occupational role for the male in the American society it is of interest that there has been very little research or even speculation into how one learns his future occupational roles. In past societies the young boy was taught his future occupational role by his father or by men with various skills who transmitted them through an apprenticeship method. This has meant that the father was in the role of transmitting stability through his son. In general, the position of the father in the sociological analysis of society centers around him as an agent of social stability. Benson suggests that the father is almost never seen as an instrument of social change in any society. "When the father is used as an explanation for reform or social invention, it is the impact he has upon his son that is considered to be the dynamic force, not the innovations that he makes in the father role per se."[44] So one consequence of the father losing control of the socialization of his sons has been that they can be socialized to change in a more complex society. Today, in the United States, the father has little direct influence on his son's occupational choice.

The child enters the school system at a young age and is there prepared in a general way for his occupational future. The very fact of continued education becomes a crucial factor in the categories of occupations that the person will eventually fill. The decision to end education with high school or to go on to college has far more to do with the future of the person than any specific choice of an occupation. The schools, especially elementary and high school, provide the background for future occupational choice. Which one the person will choose is a result of a number of social and personal factors.

As the young person is going through the school system, his future choices may be affected by his relationship to his parents. The young man's development of ability and motivation to achieve are heavily contingent on which one of his parents is dominant. Elder found that for boys "paternal dominance and maternal overprotection have the most negative effects. Furthermore, in an authoritarian, father-dominated family boys seem to receive little achievement training from the father."[45] It would appear that the father's very dominance means that he has little

---

[43] Ibid., p. 351.

[44] Benson, *Fatherhood*, p. 13.

[45] Glen H. Elder, Jr., "Family Structure and Educational Attainment: A Cross-National Analysis," in Coser, *Life Cycle*, p. 55.

interest or ability to direct the training of his son. That is, the very dominance that may make him effective in his occupation may inhibit his
abilities to help his son's achievement development.

As children grow up they develop vague notions of what future adult
roles are really available to them. In part, this is because they have little
interpersonal involvement with adults who are filling occupational roles.
The only one they really experience is that of the teacher and this does
become the role choice for many girls as they grow up. But basically the
children in our society face the crucial task of finding their future place
in the vast division of labor while poorly informed and ill-prepared.
"They formulate their occupational preferences and make their choices
on the basis of information supplied for the most part by unsystematic
sources of unknown validity about which we know relatively little."[46]

The child in his personal development learns about the labor force as
a ranked system of occupational roles in the same way as his development
of concept formation is acquired. That is, learning proceeds from the sim-
plest to the most complex as well as from the most concrete to the most
abstract. But in general children begin to acquire definite ideas about
occupational roles and how certain occupations compare with others at
an early age. For example, they learn early that a doctor has more prestige than a trash collector. But while role information begins to be acquired early, "status-ranking abilities are acquired more slowly. Generally, as age increases, so does the acquisition of knowledge about the
occupational system."[47] But before he is too old he has a pretty good idea
of the differential prestige accorded the various occupations.

There are also important differences by social class in what and how
children growing up learn about occupations. In general, lower-class children have much less contact with occupations than do the children of the
middle class. Also, many lower-class children quickly learn that many
occupations are not for them. Their family, peer groups, and teachers
may indicate to them directly and indirectly that to grow up to fill middle-
class occupations is not really a part of their futures. The DeFleurs found
that social class played a clear part in influencing the acquisition of occupational knowledge among children. "Upper and middle class children
had significantly more role knowledge concerning the occupations studied
than did the lower class children."[48]

One important source of learning about occupational roles for children
today is through television. But unfortunately TV often provides children
with a great deal of misleading and superficial information. From this
experience children often develop occupational stereotypes. "Given the

---

[46] Melvin L. DeFleur and Lois B. DeFleur, "The Relative Contribution of Television as a Learning Source for Children's Occupational Knowledge," *American Sociological Review,* October 1967, p. 777.

[47] Ibid., p. 788.

[48] Ibid., p. 788.

deep significance of occupational roles for both the individual and society, any learning source which distorts reality concerning this aspect of the social structure and the child's 'generalized other' may be laying the foundation for difficult personal and social problems."[49] So many children either grow up with no knowledge of an occupation or highly distorted information. The American society really has no systematic way for socializing individuals to make intelligent, knowledgeable choices about occupations for their futures. Once they make a decision society has very complex means for training them—but how they get there in the first place is often due to no more than chance.

In general, it appears that the young middle-class boy growing up has little first hand information even about his father's occupation. It also seems clear that many boys reject the idea that they fill the occupations of their fathers. This may be one important measurement of their developing independence and autonomy. It doesn't appear that fathers are too concerned that their sons do the same kinds of jobs that they do. Rather, the middle-class father wants the son to fill an occupation at the same general level or higher. But middle-class fathers do generally transmit to their sons the belief that whatever occupation they fill it is very important because it will be their most important adult role.

SELECTED BIBLIOGRAPHY

Aldous, Joan "Occupational Characteristics and Males' Role Performance in the Family." *Journal of Marriage and the Family,* November 1969, pp. 707–12.

Axelson, Leland J. "The Marital Adjustment and Marital Role Definitions of Husbands of Working and Nonworking Wives." *Marriage and Family Living,* May 1963, pp. 189–95.

Ballweg, John A. "Resolution of Conjugal Role Adjustment after Retirement." *Journal of Marriage and the Family,* May 1967, pp. 277–81.

Benson, Leonard *Fatherhood: A Sociological Perspective.* New York: Random House, 1968.

DeFleur, Melvin L., and **DeFleur, Lois B.** "The Relative Contribution of Television as a Learning Source for Children's Occupational Knowledge." *American Sociological Review,* October 1967, pp. 777–89.

Goldman, David R. "Managerial Mobility, Motivations, and Central Life Interests," *American Sociological Review,* February 1973, pp. 119–26.

Komarovsky, Mirra *Blue-Collar Marriage.* New York: Random House, 1962.

Marx, John H., and **Spray, S. Lee** "Marital Status and Occupational Success among Mental Health Professionals." *Journal of Marriage and the Family,* February 1970, pp. 110–18.

Rapoport, Robert, and **Rapoport, Rhona** "Work and Family in Contemporary Society." *American Sociological Review,* June 1965, pp. 381–94.

Rossi, Alice S. "Equality Between the Sexes." *Daedalus,* Spring 1964, pp. 607–52.

---

[49] Ibid., p. 789.

Chapter 15

The Female and Marriage, Family, and Occupational Roles*

The most basic factor related to the changing nature of the American family has been the changes in the roles filled by women. This has been true of their roles as wives, mothers, and in occupations. There has also developed a new interest in the roles that women might fill both within and outside the family. Therefore, this chapter will explore the changing nature of women's roles in America today. To better understand the present changes taking place it is necessary to present a brief historical discussion of the roles of women in the United States over time. This chapter will also discuss the meaning and influence of the Women's Liberation Movement.

In the late 1960s in the United States a new militancy seeking female equality or liberation emerged. The United States has had a long history of feminism that has brought about many significant social changes. But the new militancy has been much more aggressive and demanding than anything that had gone before. To a great extent this is because the female liberation movement has developed out of such militant movements of the 1960s as civil rights, student protests, and the politically radical left. There are many who see the militant women's movement

---

* This chapter is based primarily on materials from my book, *Social Deviance: A Substantive Analysis* (Homewood, Ill.: The Dorsey Press, 1971).

as a temporary fad that will quickly fade away because women really are not discriminated against and have no basis for protest. However, it is suggested that the movement will not fade away and quite possibly may become one of the most important social movements of the 1970s. This suggestion is based on the contention that there are many ways in which American women are still treated as second class citizens and oftentimes as being inferior to men. To better understand the roles of women today it is necessary to first look at how women have been defined and treated in the past.

HISTORICAL BACKGROUND

It has been pointed out that almost all societies of the past have been patriarchal, meaning in effect that women have had second-class status. If we go back to early Greek civilization, it can be seen that the powers the Greek husband had over his wife were no less than what he had over his children. If they had no children, he could divorce her. The dowry of the wife became the husband's property during his lifetime and he had the rights to any separate earnings she might acquire. She was under his jurisdiction almost entirely and could not even leave the house without his permission. By contrast, the Early Roman wife stood in a place of complete social equality to her husband and was seen as having dignity and honor both within the family and the state. She was both honored and subordinated: "she was highly respected, and yet she was given no tangible legal rights."[1]

Whatever status the woman had gained during the Roman period she began to lose with the rise of Christianity. In that period a tendency developed to increasingly restrict the woman's legal and social rights. Women were given no special position or recognition in early Christian teaching. Jesus expressed no new ideas with respect to the position of women. The Apostle Paul advocated that women take a subordinate position to man and over time this became the dominant attitude among early Christian leaders. Therefore, the status accorded to women was a step back compared to what they had had in Rome. Eventually women were excluded by Christians from any offices. Still less were they men's equals in private life. "In marriage wives were bidden to be subject to their husbands."[2]

Christianity developed an obsession with sexual matters which also placed a great strain on women. Treated by the Saxons as property,

---

[1] Helen I. Clarke, *Social Legislation* (New York: Appleton-Century-Crofts, Inc., 1957), p. 35.

[2] Richard Lewinsohn, *A History of Sexual Customs* (New York: Harper and Brothers, 1958), p. 92.

woman by the Middle Ages often was seen as the source of all sexual evil. "It was argued that sexual guilt really pertained to women, since they tempted men, who would otherwise have remained pure."[3] The combined views of her as inferior to man and as repository of sin has placed her at a level of inferiority from which she has never completely recovered in the eyes of traditional Christian thought. With time, and due to Christian influence, she also came to be legally defined as inferior. In the English common law the husband's rights over the wife's personal property were almost unlimited. After the end of the 13th century the common law put the absolute property in the wife's chattels with the husband. She was not even permitted to make a will without the husband's consent. In many respects, up until the 20th century the woman had a status not too different from a slave. This was the general state of affairs that existed at the time the American colonies were founded and developed.

In many ways early American women were treated almost like slaves. Both were expected to behave with deference and obedience toward owner or husband. Both had no existence officially under the law and had but few rights with regard to education. "Both found it difficult to run away; both worked for their masters without pay; both had to breed on command, and to nurse the results."[4] It is of interest that from the very start the woman and the black have been compared in terms of their second-class status and this comparison is basically as appropriate today as it was during the colonial period.

The inferior status of American women in part comes from the feeling that they, like their prototype, Eve, are provocateurs of sin. As suggested, they were constantly condemned during the early history of the church and during the Puritan eras in England and America. Even the horrible practice of witch burning was in part due to the belief that women "are servants of satan."[5]

The 18th Century. Women continued to be treated in many respects as second-class persons. They received very little formal education because it was commonly believed that girls were unfit in brain and character to study seriously. It was argued that girls should be taught how to run a household, "and, if suitable, how to display the graces of a lady." However, near the end of the 18th century there were voices being heard that no longer accepted the traditional definition of the woman. And if helplessness was one common female adaptation to the world around

---

[3] G. Rattray Taylor, *Sex in History* (New York: Ballentine Books, Inc., 1954), p. 64.

[4] Andrew Sinclair, *The Emancipation of The American Woman* (New York: Harper and Brothers, 1965), p. 4.

[5] Wainwright Churchill, *Homosexual Behavior among Males* (New York: Hawthorne Books, 1967), p. 24.

her, for other women a new militancy was coming to be an alternative. For a few women there was the choice of either barricading herself in the home with the myth of frailty or to struggle to get outside the home and find some new definitions of femininity.

In 1792, the first comprehensive attack on marriage as it then existed and the way in which it subjugated women was made by Mary Wollstonecraft in a book called *A Vindication of the Rights of Women*. She did not want to do away with marriage but rather to correct some of the inequalities that existed. She argued that women should have increased social and economic rights as well as greater education so that in marriage they would not have to be submissive, but rather equal to their husbands. Women were also being heard in other areas of protest. In general, in the 18th and 19th centuries when voices of protest were heard they were from women. It was primarily women who fought against slavery, against child labor, and against the development of slums. They also fought for schools, libraries, playgrounds, and legislation to protect children. Women have historically been the social conscience of American society.

The 19th Century. During this century great changes occurred in the United States. Industrialization meant a change in life patterns, as the productive unit shifted from the family to the individual going away from the home to work. For some women, where the home had been the setting for all their work, the chance to work in a factory appeared like freedom. Hard work for 12 hours a day, or more, had been normal for most American women and their tasks had been heavy, endless, and unpaid. For many of them the early factory system represented a semiskilled and repetitive job which demanded little physical exertion.

As the 19th century unfolded female rebels became more and more common. The first females in rebellion were basically rebels who happened to be women. That is, they were not champions of their sex, but rather were champions of themselves. They fought for the right to be treated as individuals, without distinction being made by sex. However, they did not consider themselves to be other than exceptions. "They never questioned that the general rule was the rule of women by men. Thus, they were not feminists so much as female rebels, made so by the accidents of birth and place and inspiration."[6] The early feminists also saw how the role of lady had enslaved American women because the very definition of a lady was based on inferior status and ability. Yet, many of the early feminists only felt free when they were playing the role of ladies. They never came to terms with this anomaly, and, as a result, feminism in the 19th century remained primarily a middle-class and ladylike business. "In fact, most American ladies—by their very social

---

[6] Ibid., p. 32.

position—opposed anything other than safe and mild reforms of a religious or educational nature."[7]

In the decades prior to the Civil War in the United States a changing definition of women had developed on the part of men. The "animal" nature of women came to be stressed less by men, and women came to be seen as more spiritual. So the new explanation for their exclusion from politics came to be not because they were inferior, but rather because of their superiority. They were seen as not so much sinful but as too good for the world. As a result, their moral value placed them above the nasty business of politics and making money. The men turned over to them the matters of "culture" and the rearing of children. Women were encouraged to believe that their sex gave them a distinct function that was different from and better than the mere getting of money. It is doubtful that very many men really believed that what women did was important. The really important world was their world—the man's world of money making and politics. So they could keep women out of their world and feel morally superior about it at the same time.

Despite all the forms of resistance, the women's rights movement did develop and grow. The factor of industrialization continued to remove many women from the home and freed many of them from the functions they had performed in the past. There were a number of landmarks in the movement. For example, in 1833 Oberlin was the first men's college in the United States to admit women, and four years later Mount Holyoke, the first women's college, was opened. The first Woman's Rights Convention was held at Seneca Falls, New York in 1848. The first to speak out in public for women's rights were Fanny Wright, the daughter of a Scotch nobleman, and Ernestine Rose, the daughter of a rabbi. There was great hostility toward those women and the first was referred to as "the red harlot of infidelity" and the second as "a woman a thousand times below a prostitute."[8] The declaration that came out of Seneca Falls brought forth an outcry of revolution and insurrection directed at the women and the hostility was so great that some of the women withdrew their signatures from the declarations.

By the 1850s such respected intellectuals as the New England Transcendentalists were aligning themselves with the women's rights movement. During that period in England the Unitarians and other liberal elements were also becoming involved. In 1869 John Stuart Mill wrote his work, *The Subjection of Women*, which gave the mark of respectability to English feminism. By the 1860s women began to discard their crinolines and slowly slimmed down their skirts until only the bustle was left. "Once again they could and did begin to take exercise and play

---

[7] Ibid., p. 109.

[8] Betty Friedan, *The Feminine Mystique* (New York: W. W. Norton and Co., Inc., 1963), p. 86.

simple games of sport such as croquet and lawn tennis; and unchaperoned they could once again walk arm in arm with men."[9]

However, the major force in the growth of the feminist movement in the 1800s was the slavery issue. So the concern that turned many women into pioneer reformers was less an attack on sexual bondage than an assault on the slavery of the blacks. In their seeking to free the slaves many radical women became more conscious of their own lack of freedom. "Through helping others, they learned to help themselves. The destiny of American women and American Negroes had been interacting, and still is."[10]

As suggested, most men were strongly against the women's rights movement. The man was, of course, a double standard male who saw his way of life being threatened and the possibility of some of his conveniences being taken away from him. The man had no desire to change his world but only to increase his rights as a male. On economic grounds he found his world ideal. A subjugated wife, even if cranky, was simpler and cheaper to deal with than an equal before the law who could leave with her property if she wanted or who could sue for redress if mistreated. From the business point of view the woman's low position made good sense to him. So any plea for female education or reform in marriage was often linked with atheism, socialism, abolition, teetotaling, sexual immorality, and other despicable forces by the male.

The male often took on a pious posture in arguing against the women's rights movement. By supporting the image of the female as submissive, dependent, and inferior, he could argue that her basic being was under attack. So he could intone as did one senator in 1866 that to give women equal rights would destroy that "milder gentler nature, which not only makes them shrink from but disqualifies them for the turmoil and battle of public life."[11] Against this image he could then picture the feminists as violating their very nature as women, and the picture they often presented was in sharp contrast to the traditional docile women. Some of the early feminists cut their hair short, wore bloomers, and tried to be like men. So the hostile image held of the feminists came to be one of inhuman, fiery man-eaters who had none of the traditional feminine qualities.

Near the end of the 19th century new forces for women's rights were developing. Over the long run one of the most important developments was higher education for women. In the late 19th century there was the founding and establishing of a number of women's colleges. The rise of those new colleges created a demand for the services of academic women, and the demand, under the circumstances of the time, created the supply.

---

[9] Morton M. Hunt, *The Natural History of Love* (New York: Alfred A. Knopf, 1959), p. 332.

[10] Sinclair, *Emancipation*, p. 37.

[11] Friedan, *Mystique*, p. 86.

These schools came about as a result of the great reform ferment that had started in the 1840s and, while slowed down by the Civil War, reached a peak at the turn of the century. "Abolition, women's rights, temperance, prison reform, labor organization—these were only a few of the many causes which had been fostered in the great reform movement. The higher education of women had been one of the many."[12] In the first two decades after the turn of the century many of the elitist women's colleges were in conflict with themselves. "The academic women who staffed them were still for the most part women with causes, still reformers at heart, but action was becoming less attractive than contemplation within the ivy-covered walls. The feeling began to grow that the academic role was not an activist one."[13] But the colleges had provided the rallying point and the training grounds for many of the women involved in women's rights that occurred around the turn of the century.

By the end of the 19th century some women began to believe in an option to the traditional role of marriage and motherhood. This came about as customs changed and more women were able to work and support themselves without losing their self-respect. Also, during this period some women entered business and moved into the professions. Toward the end of the century essays appeared that argued that for a woman to remain single and support herself was better than to become the wife of a dissipated man. The rights of lowly and genteel women to work provided the means of escape from unhappy or loveless marriages. So while the work pattern was not common for most women, it was there and provided the roots for rapid development in the 20th century. But at the same time the battle to keep the woman in the home continued. While anthropology and biology had destroyed the old belief that women were inferior, new arguments developed. Some men contended that immigration and eugenics provided reasons for keeping women in the home. Their argument was that old stock women were needed at home to bear children that would be necessary to preserve and protect the destiny of the nation. Those middle-class women were told how important they were and how they should stay home and bear more superior beings like themselves to compensate for the "inferior" offspring of the immigrants. It is clear that historically whenever one argument against women lost its effectiveness new ones were invented.

The 20th Century. As suggested, during the 19th century the battle for women's equity was closely related to the fights for various social reforms. The feminist movement was tied in with Jane Addams and Hull House, the rise of the union movement, and the great strikes against intolerable working conditions in the factories. And the final battle for

---

[12] Jessie Bernard, *Academic Women* (University Park: Pennsylvania State University Press, 1964), p. 31.

[13] Ibid., p. 36.

the right of the female to vote was fought primarily by the college-trained women. Social reform continued to be seen as something for which women could be concerned. These concerns were linked with man's stereotype of women being compassionate and impractical creatures. The American man has always underestimated the influence of the woman as society's conscience. A reading of history indicates that man's inhumanity would have been much greater if women had not functioned to force about a more compassionate view of the world and human beings.

The most dramatic change in the image of women came after the First World War. This resulted from the upsurge in women's employment outside the home. The 1920s saw the emergence of the white-collar class in the United States, and the women were a large part of it. For example, over twice as many women entered the labor force during that decade as during the previous one.[14] But the major event, and one that had been fought for many years, was the passing of the 19th Amendment to the Federal Constitution in 1920. It read that the "rights of citizens of the United States to vote shall not be denied or abridged by the United States or by any state on account of sex." This was an important landmark in the fight for women's rights. However, it did not bring about any great changes in the political life patterns of women.

The 1920s were the period of greatest change in the roles and rights of American women. That decade saw a revolution in morals that were most vividly reflected in the behavior of women. During the 1920s many taboos of the past against women were thrown aside. For the first time women began to smoke and drink in public. As recently as 1918 it was considered daring for a New York hotel to permit women to sit at the bar. But during the twenties, despite prohibition, both sexes drank in public. As Degler points out, in the years since the 20s there have been few alterations in the position of women that were not first evident during that decade. "The changes have penetrated more deeply and spread more widely through the social structure, but their central tendency was then already spelled out."[15]

The 1920s were also the period of great change in the sexual behavior of women. It was the period when women began to believe that they had the same rights to sexual satisfaction as did the man. And it was during that decade that the increased frequency of premarital coitus among females occurred. The sexual superiority of the male was no longer an accepted belief for many woman as well as men.

Once women had the legal right to vote in 1920, they found that this did not lead to legal equality. This was because there could be no real

---

[14] Carl N. Degler, "Revolution Without Ideology: The Changing Place of Women in America," *Daedalus*, Fall 1964, p. 657.

[15] Ibid., p. 659.

sex equality until women actually participated on an equal basis with men in politics, occupations, and the family. "Law and administrative regulations must permit such participation, but women must want to participate and be able to participate."[16] Actually, in the 1920s the grip of the traditional political machines became even stronger with women voting. This was because the female relatives of every man connected with the political machines were registered to vote. For many of those city bosses the vote of the women was merely a multiplication factor. In fact, women refused to vote against antifeminists in Congress, and sent them back with increased majorities as their representatives. While the women had the vote, they generally continued to use it as their men told them to.

Since 1920 the number of women who have attained positions of power in the federal and state governments have been unbelievably few. There have been only three women elected state governors. Two women have held cabinet rank in the federal government and only six have served as ambassadors or ministers. At the present time the United States has one female senator out of one hundred. And while women hold about one fourth of all jobs in the federal civil service, they hold only 2 percent of the top positions. But this also appears to be true in many other countries, although somewhat less severe than in the United States. For example, even with the Soviet Union's wide base of professional personnel the number of women decreases disproportionately as one goes toward the top in the Soviet hierarchy.[17]

Western World Today. The treatment of women has changed in most countries of the West. How women are treated in most countries appears to be related to the educational and social class level of men and women. Goode found in his cross-cultural studies that in the lower classes, women had somewhat more authority. This was because the low standard of living gave the women a key position in the family. In the higher classes, where the men are better educated than in the middle classes, they are often more willing to concede rights and women are eager to demand them. "Men in the lower strata, by contrast, are much more traditional minded than their counterparts in the upper strata, and are less willing to concede the new rights being demanded; but they have to do so because of the increased bargaining power of their women."[18]

But when the countries of the Western world are examined, it can be seen that they are changing rapidly and in some cases women have received greater rights than in the United States. The right of the vote is

---

[16] Alice S. Rossi, "Equality Between the Sexes: An Immodest Proposal," *Daedalus*, Spring 1964, p. 610.

[17] Women's Bureau, *1969 Handbook of Women Workers*, bulletin 294 (Washington, D.C.: United States Department of Labor), 1969, p. 3.

[18] William J. Goode, "Industrialization and Family Structure," in Norman W. Bell and Ezra F. Vogel, *The Family*, rev. ed. (New York: The Free Press, 1968), p. 118.

now common to the woman in most countries. In 1968 women could vote and run for office in 117 countries. There were only seven countries that prohibited voting for women and four others that imposed some limitations. Women have also gained in the number who go on to college. In the 1960s women in the United States and Great Britain made up a little over 30 percent of the college population, while in *USSR* women made up well over 40 percent of the student population. While the proportion remains small in most countries, women in the professions in Sweden, Great Britain, the Soviet Union, and Israel have doubled or more over the past 20 years.

In Russia, a woman would be expected to explain why she is *not* working while in the United States the woman is often expected to explain why she *is* working.[19] The Russian women do not have the domestic help or the household appliances commonly taken for granted in the United States. Furthermore, the Russian men, like other European men and unlike American, typically do not, and are not expected to, help in the household.[20]

Sweden is probably the country most affected by feminist reform. In 1970, 14 percent of its parliamentary seats and two of its cabinet ministeries were filled by women. Swedish women do such jobs as running cranes and driving cabs and buses. The fathers must support their children, although divorced women are expected to pay their own way. The schools have compulsory coeducational classes in metalwork, sewing, and childcare. The new tax structure of Sweden is forcing many wives to go to work and a start has been made on the development of day-care centers. There has been a recent government ordered revision of textbooks that is expected to start eliminating the stereotype images of both sexes that has traditionally been presented.

The trend clearly has been one where societies have legislated reforms and the legal framework to provide economic opportunity for women. However, there is probably no modern society, with the possible exception of those of the Communist countries, "in which expectations of female-role behavior include a constellation keyed to women's participation in the productive and prestigious work of the economy."[21] In the United States the contribution of women to the economy is seen as secondary to men and not equal to their contribution in social worth.

One expert on the family suggests that there will be no family system emerging in the next generation that will grant full equality to women, although the general position of women throughout the world will greatly improve. "The revolutionary philosophies which have accompanied the

---

[19] Cynthia F. Epstein, *Woman's Place* (Berkeley: University of California Press, 1970), p. 43.

[20] Ibid., p. 103.

[21] Ibid., p. 46.

shifts in power in Communist countries or in the Israelic *kibbutzim* have asserted equality, and a significant stream of philosophic thought in the West has asserted the right to equality, but no society has yet granted it."[22] Goode goes on to argue that it is possible to create a society where full equality could occur but to do so would call for radical reorganization of the social structure. A new socialization process would need to be developed because families continue to rear their daughters to take only a modest interest in careers in which they would have responsibility equal to men.[23] Young girls continue to be reared in most societies to fill the secondary roles they have always filled.

AMERICAN WOMEN TODAY

An examination can now be made of the traditional roles of women as they are filled in the United States today. The interest is in looking at the roles of wife, mother, and housekeeper. In the next section an examination will be made of the work role of women and how that role is related to their traditional roles.

Wife Role. As discussed in Chapter 10, the most modern and democratic view of the wife role is within a colleague family setting. This type of marriage is not in reality an association of complete equals but is based on the notion of the development of specializations within marriage. In different areas, both partners recognize that authority is vested in the role or in the interests and abilities of only one of them. This recognition allows each one to defer to the other in different areas of competence, without loss of prestige. The division of labor in the colleague marriage is not based on a belief of complete differences between the husband and wife roles and often, if conditions demand, one partner can temporarily take over the role of the other. But even in this setting various duties are sex assigned. While a husband might take over the washing of laundry if his wife is ill, as soon as she is well she takes it over in most cases. Even the most democratic marriage is generally one where the husband has more privileges and does more of the things important and interesting to society.

As pointed out in Chapters 12 and 13 an examination of power in marriage indicates differences for wives and husbands. It has been observed that women are often caught up in a vicious circle because of their economic dependence upon their husbands and their lack of contact with the work world, and their being tied down to the house restricts, to a great extent, the kind of decisions over which they can claim expertise

---

[22] Goode, "Industrialization," p. 119.
[23] Ibid., p. 119.

and, ultimately, control. "Women, therefore, as a 'class' have not had the chance to obtain the 'resources,' skills, and expertise that would allow them a share in most important types of family power."[24]

Mother Role. Rossi has pointed out that for the first time in the history of any known society motherhood became a full-time occupation for adult women in the United States.[25] In the past that was an impossibility because the woman had far more things to do and more children to look after. Full-time motherhood came about as the result of technological development and economic affluency. Once full-time motherhood came about, women were told how important it was, and the fact that mankind had previously functioned without it was generally forgotten. It seems clear that continuous mothering, even in the first few years of life, is not necessary for the healthy emotional development of the child. What is more important is the nature of the care rather than who provides it.

In fact, there is strong evidence that not only is the fulltime mother not necessary to the growth of the child but she may also contribute to problems for her children. In a number of cases the etiology of mental illness is linked to inadequacies in the mother-child relationship. It is often the failure of the mother which perpetuates problems from one generation to the next that affect sons and daughters alike. Alice Rossi writes that full-time motherhood is neither sufficiently absorbing to the woman nor beneficial to the child to justify the modern woman devoting 15 or more years to it as her only occupation. "Sooner or later—and I think it should be sooner—women have to face the question of who they are besides their children's mother."[26] (For a further discussion see Chapters 17 and 18.)

Housekeeper Role. As industrialization developed and the means of taking care of the house increased, many women have not been released from household efforts, but rather have continued to spend as much time on them as before. The American woman often has become subject to Parkinson's Law that "work expands to fill the time allotted for it." As cleaning aids have been improved, standards of cleanliness have been upgraded far beyond the thresholds of sanitation necessary for health.[27]

Regardless of the propaganda, housework is basically low-status work. This is reflected in a number of ways. Our society rewards occupational efforts with money and yet housework is not within the money economy.

---

[24] Constantina Safilios-Rothschild, *Toward a Sociology of Women* (Lexington, Mass.: Xerox College Publishing, 1972), p. 2.

[25] Rossi, "Equality," p. 615.

[26] Ibid., p. 624.

[27] Epstein, *Woman's Place*, pp. 104–5.

In fact, it is not always defined as real work. Many women who do not hold income-producing jobs will say they don't work—only take care of a house. Nancy Reeves has pointed out that a recent study of the mentally retarded reports that feeble-minded girls make exceptionally good housekeepers and nursemaids. "It should be added that they are also adequate sex partners and have the organic potential to reproduce themselves."[28] Among women who work for money, domestic work is at the bottom of the occupational hierarchy. Lower-class young women prefer to work in offices and factories rather than to hire out and care for children and a house. Because they can't get domestic help, many middle-class women must do their housework themselves. So the low-prestige occupation of housework has become a major specialty of the educated woman.

Another reflection of how many women feel who take care of the house themselves is reflected in what they are willing to pay domestic workers. When it comes time to hire a woman, they want to pay her the lowest salary possible. In fact, many women who are quite liberal about increasing the pay of grape pickers are all for substandard wages for the domestics they try to hire. As a result, they often show their own low assessment of housework by saying that the women should be satisfied with the low pay because it is only housework.

There are also persons of some respectability and influence telling women how important housekeeping is. They change the name to homemaking because that sounds more creative. For example, one female author writes "homemaking during the early family years is a full-time job, and that the skills required are probably quite as exacting as those necessary in many of the professions."[29] What the professional skills of homemaking are she doesn't say. It appears that in spite of all the attempts to sell women on housekeeping as a means of life fulfillment it is failing in the middle class. Many women can understand housework as something that has to be done—but not something that will give them any real personal satisfaction. Yet the American system continues to socialize girls to want to grow up to fill the traditional roles. It is difficult to persuade girls during their high-school years to look beyond their goals of marriage and a family.

The value of "housewife" may vary with the different levels of the social-class system within which the position occurs. The position of the upper-class housewife may be much more highly valued in the overall social structure than the position of lower-class housewife. Joan Acker goes on to suggest that it may be that the value of this position rises as its

---

[28] Nancy Reeves, *Womankind: Beyond the Stereotype* (Chicago: Aldine, 1971), p. 36.

[29] Gladys E. Harbeson, *Choice and Challenge for The American Woman* (Cambridge, Mass.: Shenkman Publishing Co., 1967), p. 59.

functions become more symbolic and less utilitarian. "Or, to put it another way, the value may rise as functions become centered more around consumption and less around productive activities."[30]

Traditional female roles in the family have been discussed for the middle class. However, there are some sharp differences among women in the lower-middle and lower social classes. Most of those women continue to live in a world that is patriarchal—at least when the male is present. For many there is little in marriage that is shared between the husband and wife. For example, Komarovsky found in her study of a working-class group that the husband and wife shared little other than the immediate daily tasks. "The impoverishment of life and of personality curtails the development of shared interests."[31] In the sexual realm the great majority of the wives felt that men were more highly sexed than women. And less than a third of the women in her sample expressed high satisfaction with their sexual relations.[32]

In the lowest social-class levels frequently the husband participates very little and the wife carries the responsibility for the home and the children largely by herself and seldom participates with her husband in outside activities. About the working-class wife, there is nothing "collective" because she is basically unorganized. She is neither a joiner nor a participant. She may be quite religious but is much less likely to attend church regularly than her middle-class counterpart. She is virtually isolated from life outside the confines of her family and neighborhood.

Yet with all the restrictions on the life of lower-class women there does not appear to be a high degree of status frustration among them. They expect to be housewives—that is their reason for being and there is no real alternative. Komarovsky found in her study hardly a trace of the low prestige that educated housewives attach to that role. Rarely did she find a woman saying, "I am just a housewife." The women did have discontent, but it was not caused by a low evaluation placed on domesticity; rather, it was from the frustrations of being a housewife.[33] When some of the women did show a dislike for housework, they often felt guilty about their dislike of what they saw as the normal female responsibility. "Unlike some college-educated housewives who detest housework, our respondents never say that they are too good for it, that housework is unchallenging manual labor."[34]

---

[30] Joan Acker, "Women and Social Stratification: A Case of Intellectual Sexism," in Joan Huber, *Changing Women in a Changing Society* (Chicago: University of Chicago Press, 1973), p. 180.

[31] Mirra Komarovsky, *Blue-Collar Marriage* (New York: Random House, 1962), p. 155.

[32] Ibid., p. 85.

[33] Komarovsky, *Blue-Collar Marriage*, p. 49.

[34] Ibid., p. 55.

MALE-FEMALE DIFFERENCES

Before looking at women in the work force and in occupational careers it is necessary to examine the basic differences between males and females. This is important because so much of the discrimination against the female has been and continues to be rationalized on the grounds of unchangeable, physical differences. It is argued here that almost all significant differences between the sexes can be explained on the basis of differential socialization and that the biological differences have been greatly exaggerated insofar as the differential behavior patterns attributed to them.

It is obvious that men and women are somewhat different as sexual beings and often perform in complementary ways. However, there is no inherent reason for believing that either sex is dependent on the other for sexual satisfaction. Heterosexuality, as well as homosexuality or solitary sexuality, are adaptations to sexual needs that are made by individuals. The fact that the vast majority of adults prefer heterosexuality as a means of expression is because they have been socialized to do so.

Probably the most important biological difference between the man and woman is the differential reproductive burden. The man is needed only to provide the sperm and he doesn't even have to be present to do that, while the woman in a normal pregnancy and birth must carry the fetus for nine months. In the past, the pregnancy period of the woman led to many restrictions being placed on what she could do. However, it seems clear that most women, who have no pregnancy complications, can work on most jobs with no more than a loss of a week or two for the birth of the child. So there is no reason why many women, if they choose, cannot pursue a career at the same time that they have children. It is common to argue that time off for pregnancy interferes with a career for women. Yet many men must also take time off from a career for illnesses and other reasons and this doesn't usually affect their careers. Or some flexibility could be set up to allow women to use vacation time to have children. The point is that there is little that is inherent in the birth experience for women that *necessarily* must restrict them in the ways that have been done in the past.

Another common argument for differential treatment of women centers around the fact that the *average* woman is not as strong as the *average* man. That is, she has been excluded from certain jobs because it has been argued that she doesn't have the strength to perform. The range of physical strength among women is as wide as it is among men. This means there are some women who are stronger than some men. Strength, by sex, is not an absolute difference, but a relative one. Many times men are rejected from jobs because they are not strong enough. "Men only" becomes irrelevant; the job requirement should be simply the strength to qualify. In that way work would be available to individuals on the basis of abilities, skills, strengths, and motivation regardless of sex. A woman might be turned away from a job because she wasn't strong enough but some men would also be turned away for the same reason.

It has also been argued that because women do have some physical differences, this results in personality differences based upon their being female. A psychoanalytic view is that there are personality types that represent femininity.[35] Yet there are no personality qualities found in women that are not also found in men. Once again it is a question of relative differences rather than absolute ones. And whatever it means to be a woman is dependent on the socialization experience and what the individual personality brings to bear. Any combination of so-called female personality traits if applied to male and female samples would find them in some men and absent in many women.

In the United States male and female infants are immediately subjected to different socialization experiences. They are dressed differently and are provided with toys seen as appropriate to their sex. As they grow up, social values are often exerted on girls to be more gentle and emotionally demonstrative than boys, but the differential socialization is never total and boys are sometimes reared like girls and vice versa. When that happens, the impact of the socialization experience is clear. As they grow up, boys and girls learn about their future roles and they quickly learn that the male adult is the adult of greatest prestige and influence. For example, seldom do even educated girls develop a mental picture of a family basking in the glow of the mother's achievement as a scientist or judge unless she is also seen as a good homemaker. No one asks if a male Nobel Prize winner is also a good father. But the headline in a recent article about a female Nobel Prize laureate scientist read, "Grandmother Wins Award," as if having grandchildren had some relevance to high professional achievement.[36]

It should also be pointed out that one of the most common sexist arguments against the equality of women is to ask where are all the great women in arts, science, and business. But, as Linda Nochlin points out, "there have been no great women artists, as far as we know—or any Lithuanian jazz pianists, or Eskimo tennis players, no matter how much we might wish there had been."[37] To condemn women on sex grounds for not achieving what was culturally impossible is erroneous and sexist in the worse sense.

---

[35] Clara Thompson, "Femininity," in Albert Ellis and Albert Abarbanel, *The Encyclopedia of Sexual Behavior* (New York: Hawthorne Books, 1961), p. 423.

[36] Epstein, *Woman's Place*, p. 66.

[37] Linda Nochlin, "Why Are There No Great Women Artists," in Vivian Gornick and Barbara K. Moran, *Women in Sexist Society* (New York: New American Library, 1971), p. 483.

An important part of the assumed difference between males and females has been a part of the American historical heritage. Basically, the difference has been intellectualized to not only be inevitable but also desirable. The most powerful intellectual influence has been that of Freud. The propaganda that women should marry early and breed often has prevailed. The psychologists and psychiatrists have replaced clergymen as the authorities. In this century the belief came to be that it was best for a woman to become a mother, not because God said so, but because Freud said so.[38] Freud's view of women was to define them as inferior human beings. The castration complex and penis envy, two ideas basic to his thinking, were based on the belief that women were inferior to men. Freud's view of women reflected the times in which he lived. In his middle-class world there were highly conservative beliefs about the proper roles for men and women in marriage and society. Those views have little validity for the kind of world that exists today. But the Freudian view has continued to be perpetuated. For many years American women have been told through Freudian followers that there can be no greater destiny for women than through their traditional femininity. Women have been told to pity the neurotic, unfeminine, unhappy women who have wanted to be poets or physicians.[39]

Freud's followers generally have seen women in the same image as he did—as inferior and passive. They have argued that women will only find *real* self-fulfillment by affirming their natural inferiority. One of his followers writes that for women there must be a willingness to accept dependence on the male without fear or resentment and that she must not admit of wishes to control or master, to rival or dominate. "The woman who is to find true gratification must love and accept her own womanhood as she loves and accepts her husband's manhood. The woman's unconscious wish to possess the organ upon which she must thus depend militates greatly against her ability to accept its vast power to satisfy her when proffered to her in love."[40]

In recent years both Freudian and some other psychiatric interpretations have lumped the increased employment of women with many social and personal problems. Their working has been linked with increased divorce, more crime and delinquency, and increased alcoholism and schizophrenia among women.[41] American society has also been inundated with the psychoanalytic viewpoint that believes that any conflict in per-

---

[38] Sinclair, *Emancipation,* p. 359.

[39] Friedan, *Mystique,* pp. 15–16.

[40] Ferdinand Lundberg and Marynia Farnham, "Woman: The Lost Sex," in Edwin Schur, *The Family and The Sexual Revolution* (Bloomington: Indiana University Press, 1964), p. 230.

[41] F. Ivan Nye and Lois W. Hoffman, *The Employed Mother in America* (Chicago: Rand McNally and Co., 1963), p. 7.

sonal or family life must be treated on the individual level. "This goes with the general American value stress on individualism, and American women have increasingly resorted to psycho-therapy, the most highly individualized solution of all, for the answers to the problems they have as women."[42] The psychiatric influence has been such that any problem is seen as individually based rather than socially determined. As a result, many women who have felt miserable and unhappy as housewives have defined themselves at fault or inadequate rather than recognizing that in many cases they are victims of social situations that cause their problems.

While the Freudian influence in the thinking about keeping the woman in the home has declined in recent years, other "intellectual" spokesmen have come along. Both Dr. Spock and Dr. Bettelheim in books and in their advice columns in popular women's magazines argue that women should not be employed during their children's early years. "Thus the mothers not only have difficulty finding good care for their children but they also feel guilty about it."[43] It has only been with the literature of the Women's Liberation Movement that women are being presented with information that counteracts the traditional views of the woman's place being in the home.

There is another area of difference across sex lines and that is the evidence of greater problems related to mental health for women than for men. But this can be understood within the context of social values. There are several reasons to assume that women, because of the roles they usually fill, are more likely than men to have emotional problems. Most important is that many women are restricted to the single social roles of housewife. But a man has more role options if one of his roles is unsatisfactory. In contrast, if the woman finds her family role unsatisfactory, she usually has no alternative source of gratification.[44]

The women's greater role restrictions has several important consequences. For example, there is considerable evidence that women have more negative images of themselves than men have of themselves. There is also evidence that women are more likely to become depressed than men. The overall evidence on first admissions to mental hospitals, psychiatric treatment in general hospitals, psychiatric outpatient clinics, private outpatient care, the practices of general physicians, and community surveys all indicate that more women than men are mentally ill.[45] These findings reflect the consequences for women of living in a society of inequality in the roles available to them in contrast to men.

---

[42] Rossi, "Equality," p. 613.

[43] Epstein, *Woman's Place*, pp. 109–10.

[44] Walter R. Gove and Jeanette F. Tudor, "Adult Sex Roles and Mental Illness," in Huber, *Changing*, p. 52.

[45] Ibid., p. 69.

THE WOMAN AND WORK

In one respect the general disregard of the significance of the female in the work force is seen in the fact that women are rarely, if ever, mentioned in the academic literature that deals with work and occupations. When they are considered, it is almost always within the context of the family structure. That is, they are characterized as *still* single, the secondary jobholder in an *organized* family, or the major jobholder in a *disorganized* family.

It should also be recognized that female labor today is, as it has been for decades, a marginal section of the labor force. In this respect the current increase of women in the work force cannot be interpreted as progress because the provisional status of female labor has not been altered.[46] A sharp economic depression would probably see women lose most of what they have gained in the work force.

About nine out of ten women work outside the home at some time during their lives. In general, marriage and the presence of children tend to limit their employment, while widowhood, divorce, and the decrease of family responsibility tend to bring them back into the work force.[47] The percentage of the work force being female has steadily increased over the years. In 1900 only 18 percent of all workers were women, in 1940 it was 25 percent, and in 1968 it had increased to 37 percent.[48] Furthermore, in 1968, 42 percent of all women of working age were in the labor force, and of that group three out of five were married. Put another way, in 1972, 40 percent of all married women were in the work force. Among the married women the highest rates of participation in the labor force were where the husband's income did not represent poverty levels, but rather the lower range of middle-income levels. The rate than declined as the husband's income reached higher levels. About two fifths of all married women and many single women as well were both homemakers and workers. "During an average workweek in 1968, 50 percent of all women were keeping house full time, and about 42 percent were either full- or part-time workers. Most of the remainder were girls 16 to 20 years of age who were in school."[49]

There have been changes in the work patterns during the life cycle of the woman. In 1900, if the woman worked at all during her lifetime it was usually only before marriage and children, and the proportion employed declined steadily with age. By contrast, in 1970 between 49 and 54 percent of women in the 35–59 age groups were in the labor force. Also the number of years in the work force has increased greatly. The

---

[46] Reeves, *Womankind,* p. 57.
[47] Women's Bureau, *1969 Handbook,* p. 7.
[48] Ibid., p. 9.
[49] Ibid., p. 12.

work expectancy for women born in 1900 was 6.3 years. For those born in 1940, 12.1 years; in 1950, 15.2 years; and in 1960, 20.1 years.[50]

Working mothers with children under 18 years of age represented 38 percent of all mothers in the population and 38 percent of all women workers. Of those mothers who worked (with at least one child under 14 years of age), 46 percent of the children were cared for in their own homes, with 15 percent looked after by their fathers, 21 percent by other relatives, and 9 percent by maids, housekeepers, or babysitters. Another 16 percent of the children were cared for outside their own homes, about half by relatives. Thirteen percent of the children were looked after by their mothers while they worked, and 15 percent had mothers who worked only during school hours. Eight percent of the children were expected to care for themselves, while only 2 percent of the children were in group care, such as day-care centers, nursery schools, and after-school centers.[51]

Of great importance with reference to women who work is what they earn relative to the income of men. For example, in 1966, for women who were year-round full-time workers, they had a median income or salary of $3,973 while men had $6,848. Not only is the income of women considerably less than for men but the gap has been widening in recent years. In 1956, among full-time year-round workers, women earned 63 percent of what men earned. In 1966 they earned only 58 percent.[52]

Another area of discrimination is that not only does the working woman earn less than the man for doing the same job but she is also subjected to greater taxes and other working costs. The woman's income is emasculated by the government's refusing to recognize household and child-care expenses as essential business deductions. In addition to paying between 20 and 50 percent of her income for domestic help, she must also pay income tax on the higher bracket into which her second salary places the family. It is estimated that if a husband earns $10,000 and a wife $5,000 her contribution to the net family income would be only $2,175 and she couldn't afford full-time domestic help with that amount. Or if the husband earns $15,000 and wife earns $10,000, the wife after paying for nondeductible domestic help will add only $650 to the yearly family income.[53]

More specific facts about the American work force and some variables related to women's participation are of interest here. Before the Industrial

---

[50] Women's Bureau, "Facts about Women's Absenteeism and Labor Turnover," in Nona Glazer-Malbin and Helen Youngelson Waehrer, *Woman in a Man-made World* (Chicago: Rand McNally and Co., 1972), p. 267.

[51] Women's Bureau, *1969 Handbook*, p. 49.

[52] Ibid., pp. 133–34.

[53] Julie Ellis, *The Revolt of the Second Sex* (New York: Lancer Books, 1970), p. 161.

Revolution most men and women were co-workers on the land and in the home. But the Industrial Revolution removed work for most men from the home and they became both psychologically and physically separated in their work from the home. This same industrial process that separated work from the home for men also provided the opportunities for women to follow men outside the home to work. In one sense the entrance of married women into the work force is a resumption of the part they had played in the past as co-worker with the husband. It should be recognized that the Victorian heritage that a man's work alone should support his family continues to be accepted. When this notion emerged it was a new one in human history—that one sex should support the other entirely.

Education is also related to women working. The more education women have the more likely they are to be in the work force. In March 1970, the rate for all wives who had 11 years or less of education was 34 percent. This compared with 44 percent of those who had completed high school and 47 percent of the wives with one year or more of college. The more education they bring to their jobs the higher the earnings.[54] But when compared to men with the same education and type of job, they earn less.

As mentioned previously, when women began to enter the work force in large numbers, the belief developed that their husbands and children were suffering as a result. Nye and Hoffman, in their extensive study of working women, found that there were some problems in the husband-wife relationship associated with the woman working. This may have been due to the husband holding to the Victorian view of his being the only family wage earner, and, as a result, his sense of masculinity was threatened. And it may also have been that some women entered employment because they were dissatisfied with their marriage relationship.

Research indicates that the reasons for the wife working can have an impact on her marriage. One large study of four different communities found that marital happiness was lower for both partners when the wife was working, only because she needed the money as against when she worked by choice. When the wife works out of necessity the husband has greater negative feelings in marriage and the wife sees a significant reduction in the positive side, especially in sociability with her husband.[55]

Nye and Hoffman found none of the studies they examined showed any meaningful differences between the children of working mothers in general and the children of nonworking mothers.[56] Alice Rossi also came

---

[54] Elizabeth Waldman and Anne M. Young, "Marital and Family Characteristics of Workers, 1970," *Monthly Labor Review*, March 1971, p. 46.

[55] Norman M. Bradburn and David Caplovitz, *Reports on Happiness* (Chicago: Aldine, 1965), p. 399.

[56] Nye and Hoffman, *Employed Mother*, p. 191.

to the same conclusion and reports that children of working mothers are no more likely than children of nonworking mothers to become delinquent, to show neurotic symptoms, to feel deprived of maternal affection, to perform poorly in school, to lead narrower social lives, etc.[57]

Another study found that adolescents' perception of parental interest, parents' help with school and personal problems, and closeness to parents were largely unrelated to mothers' employment status. This serves as evidence against the belief that parents are more likely to reject their children or deny them emotional support because the mother is working. As Margaret Poloma points out, while there is no evidence from existing research that working mothers as a group are better mothers than those who do not work, the data suggest that professionally employed women perceive their employment as making them better mothers than they otherwise would have been.[58]

Career Women. We now look more directly at women who pursue occupations in the same way as most men. That is, as a potential life work that will be long range for them and to which they will have a commitment. In the past most American women have been interested in jobs and not in careers. This is the primary reason why the United States, with one of the highest proportions of working women in the world, ends up with a very small proportion of its women in such professions as medicine, law, and the sciences. To argue, as many feminists have, that men have opposed and resisted the opening of career opportunities to women is only partially true. The complete truth is that American society in general, including women, has shunned like a disease any feminist ideology directed at high occupational commitment.[59]

An absolute requirement for entering most careers is that the individual have the formal education necessary for qualification. Therefore, it is important to look at women in higher education and how they fare as compared to men. In general, in most families there continues to be a somewhat greater stress on the boy going to college than the girl. However, once girls enter college, their chances of staying in are the same as that of the boy. The college dropout ratio is the same, about four out of ten who enter. However, the reasons for dropping out are different. Boys are more apt to leave school because of academic problems or difficulties in their personal adjustment, while the most common reason for girls' dropping out is to get married.

At the present time just about half of all high-school graduates are girls, while in 1900 they represented 60 percent of all high-school graduates. The percentage of all bachelor's degrees going to women has been

---

[57] Rossi, "Equality," p. 615.

[58] Margaret M. Poloma, "Role Conflict and the Married Professional Women," in Safilios-Rothschild, *Sociology of Women*, p. 191.

[59] Degler, "Revolution," p. 665.

steadily increasing. In 1900 females received only 19 percent, but in 1970 it was up to 41 percent.[60] As to higher degrees, there has been little change in the percentage of women receiving masters or doctorates since 1930.[61]

Women have been attracted to specific subject areas for earning their degrees. Jessie Bernard points out that a field like political science, which emphasizes power, attracts or fosters relatively few women, whereas anthropology, "at least where it emphasizes kinship more than kingship, finds much more place for women."[62] Or on the doctorate level, although only 12 percent are earned by women, their share in certain fields has been considerably higher. "Women received 20 percent of the doctorates conferred in 1967 in education, in the humanities, and the arts, and 19 percent in psychology. On the other hand, when half of all doctoral degrees conferred in 1967 in the United States were in the basic and applied sciences, the women's share was only 6 percent."[63]

One of the consequences of achieving higher education is a greater interest in entering the work force. Not very many women are going to be satisfied with receiving a higher education and never using it in any occupational way. So the more education that a woman receives, the more likely it is that she will seek employment, irrespective of her financial status. "The educated woman desires to contribute her skills and talents to the economy not only for the financial rewards, but even more to reap the psychic rewards that come from achievement and recognition and service to society."[64] In 1968, 71 percent of all women 18 years of age and over who had completed five years of college or more, and 54 percent of those who had earned only a bachelor's degree were in the work force. The percentage dropped to 48 percent among those who were high-school graduates and to 31 percent among those who did not go beyond the eighth grade.[65] A study of 10,000 Vassar alumnae showed that most graduates in the mid-1950s wanted marriage, with or without a career, while in the mid-1960s graduates were strongly insisting on careers—with or without marriage.[66]

What kind of occupations do women enter? Of all the women in the work force a large number of them fall into low-skilled clerical jobs. But the women who enter professional careers tend to go into teaching, nursing, social work, and related occupations. These are commonly seen by both men and women as occupations appropriate to the "special"

---

[60] Epstein, *Woman's Place*, p. 57.
[61] Women's Bureau, *1969 Handbook*, p. 191.
[62] Bernard, *Academic Women*, p. XX.
[63] Women's Bureau, *1969 Handbook*, p. 198.
[64] Ibid., p. 9.
[65] Ibid., p. 205.
[66] Ellis, *Revolt*, p. 8.

qualities of women. However, the definition of what is appropriate work for men or women changes over time. For example, during the colonial period elementary school teaching was seen as a male occupation, supposedly because women did not have the necessary stamina of mind to educate the young. Or one rarely hears of an American woman dentist, but 75 percent of the dentists of Denmark are women and dentistry is considered to be a female occupation in some South American countries.[67]

Whatever the specific occupation it is clear that if women are given the chance to pursue satisfying careers they pursue them just as consistently as men. For example, the percentage of law degree holders who are in practice is similar among women and men, and figures for female and male doctors are also alike.[68]

The cultural definitions of the professions as linked to one sex or the other are often based on what are believed to be special characteristics of one sex. In illustration, many times women are thought to be good elementary school teachers because as females they are believed to have compassion, sympathy, and feeling for children that men do not have. Or as Epstein points out, in the same way that it has been argued that blacks "have rhythm" and are therefore good jazz musicians, so women are said to have "intuition" and a gift for handling interpersonal relations and are therefore encouraged to become social workers. The image of women also includes some noncharacteristics: "lack of aggression, lack of personal involvement and egotism, lack of persistence (unless it be for the benefit of a family member), and lack of ambitious drive."[69] The career woman who is seen as having many of the above characteristics often has been viewed as the antithesis of the feminine woman.

It also appears to be important in how women perceive themselves and their careers. One woman observer from the business world says that the difference between the women who have "made it" and those who have not makes it clear that the women who *have* behave as if they expected to be treated equal. "They know the myths about women, but they do not believe them."[70]

Randall Collins has argued that women constitute the subordinate class in a system of sexual stratification. What is meant is that the principle of the system is that women take orders from men but do not give orders to them. Hence only men can give orders to other men, and women can give orders only to other women. This is seen in the fact that

---

[67] Epstein, *Woman's Place*, pp. 157–58.

[68] Elizabeth Waldman, "Changes in the Labor Force Activity of Women," in Glazer-Malbin and Waehrer, *Man-made World*, p. 33.

[69] Ibid., p. 22.

[70] Roslyn S. Willett, "Working in a Man's World: The Woman Executive," in Gornick and Moran, *Sexist Society*, p. 514.

professional women are concentrated in specialties where they deal mainly with children or other women, rarely with men of high status. The highest ranking women's job is likely to be president of a women's college or mother superior of an order of nuns. "Similarly, women can be given high status as actresses or singers, but not as movie directors or symphony conductors, because they do not give orders to anyone."[71]

In some occupations consisting of a large proportion of women, men have replaced them in the positions of power and influence. For example, the decline in the percentage of female elementary school principals has been very great. In 1928, 55 percent of the principals were women; in 1948, 41 percent; in 1958, 38 percent; and in 1968 the figure was reported to have dropped to 22 percent.[72] The assumption seems to be that while the woman can be a teacher she is not qualified to administrate the school. In many occupations there appears to be a distinction made where women can be the professional field workers, whether it be teachers, social workers, or nurses, but when it comes to administration those positions should be filled by men. As Epstein points out, "no matter what sphere of work women are hired for or select, like sediment in a wine bottle they seem to settle to the bottom."[73]

One common myth about employment is that women—far more than men—leave their jobs or take more time off. But the evidence indicates that women workers have favorable records of attendance and labor turnover when compared to men employed at the same job levels and under similar circumstances. A Public Health Service survey of time lost from work by persons 17 years of age and over because of illness or injury shows an average of 5.6 days lost by women and 5.3 days lost by men during the calender year.[74]

Because the career woman, whether married or single, is filling a social role with a great amount of social confusion, she is often defined by others in a variety of ways. For example, many housewives see the career woman as a threat to themselves. "The career woman is often seen as a competitor for their husbands (the working woman, though deprecated, also seems more glamorous—and often is, because she usually takes care of her appearance and is more interesting). The career also provides an alternative model to the domestic life and may cause the housewife to question her own choice of life style."[75] If the career woman is married and is a mother and gives the appearance of being happy and satisfied

[71] Randall Collins, "A Conflict Theory of Sexual Stratification," *Social Problems,* Summer 1971, p. 5.

[72] Epstein, *Woman's Place,* p. 10.

[73] Ibid., p. 2.

[74] Women's Bureau, "Absenteeism," p. 266.

[75] Epstein, *Woman's Place,* p. 120.

with her life, she often becomes a severe threat to the woman who has rejected a career and is not very happy with her life.

Many men react to career women with confusion. If the woman is attractive, they can't quite cope with her as a nonsexual being. Because so many men are geared to women primarily as sexual objects, they find it very difficult to see them as something more. It is probably also true that many American men are uneasy in the presence of highly intelligent women in a way which they would not be with very intelligent men. But most men probably react to career women as potential threats to themselves and in this sense their opposition is not ideologically based but rather based on vested interest. "Because men typically have more power, they suspect and fear encroachment on that power. The situation is, of course, analogous to the fears of whites about retaining job priorities in the face of advancing opportunities for Negroes."[76]

Very often women who choose both marriage and career find their situation one where the norms are confused and unclear. There are no clear guidelines for her to apportion time and resources between the two major role responsibilities. The ability to handle the roles of wife, mother, and career is still for the most part a matter of individual adaptation. So while fewer career women today are spinsters, among those who marry there is a high rate of divorce. "The proportion of divorced professional women is substantially higher than that of professional men."[77]

There have been some recent studies of the dual professional family where both partners are involved in careers. There is some evidence of husbands' support for their wives' careers. Generally the women choose a career for personal rewards and expect their husbands to adjust. The husbands frequently support their wives' independence. Also the independence of the wives was met by the husbands' pride in their wives' accomplishments and individuality. "Often the husbands were more interested in getting their wives involved in careers than were the women themselves."[78]

Another study found that some restrictions were seen by the woman in the dual-career marriage. Garland found that in no instance did any of the wives want to be more successful than their husbands. When the women had children, guilt feelings did occur, but they were occasional and situational rather than overriding. "Very few mothers revealed any signs of being guilt-ridden and all such cases were employed on a full-time basis and because of the family's economic need."[79] But, among the

---

[76] Ibid., pp. 117–18.

[77] Ibid., p. 98.

[78] Catherine C. Arnott, "Husbands' Attitudes and Wives' Commitment to Employment," *Journal of Marriage and the Family,* November 1972, p. 683.

[79] T. Neal Garland, "The Better Half? The Male in the Dual Professional Family," in Safilios-Rothschild, *Sociology of Women,* p. 714.

husbands, the most commonly cited benefit of the dual-career marriage was that the wife's professional involvement made her happier and a more interesting marriage partner."[80]

Alice Rossi has argued that these problems of different roles can be worked out by what she calls socially androgynous roles for men and women. These would be roles where the two are equal and similar in such spheres as intellectual, artistic, political, and occupational interests and participation. But they would be complementary in only those spheres required by physiological differences between the sexes. "An androgynous conception of sex role means that each sex will cultivate some of the characteristics usually associated with the other in traditional sex role definitions."[81] Rossi goes on to point out that this is one of the points of contrast with the early feminist goals. That is, rather than a one-sided plea for women to adapt a masculine stance in the world, "this definition of sex equality stresses the enlargement of the common ground on which men and women have their lives together by changing the social definition of approved characteristics and behavior of both sexes."[82] This suggestion is based on the assumption that men and women can work out a solution together and that there is no inherent incompatibility between the male and the female that cannot be worked out. However, this is not an assumption that is shared by some of the present day feminists in the Women's Liberation Movement.

THE WOMEN'S LIBERATION MOVEMENT

There is a risk in talking about a movement that is emerging because what is happening at a given time can become obsolete within a short time. However, the Women's Liberation Movement is so important that it should be looked at even though it is in the state of emergence. This movement has a long history, and one of the purposes of this chapter has been to provide a background for looking at the contemporary Women's Liberation Movement. Basically, what the movement wants is complete equality for women and they want it fast. This makes its basic aims the same as the Black Militant Movement. The new militant feminism has taken hold in territory that at first glance looks like an unlikely breeding ground for revolutionary ideas; "among urban, white, college-educated, middle-class women generally considered to be a rather 'privileged lot.' "[83] As the movement developed in the late 1960s, it came out of two primary influences. One was the influence of Betty Friedan's book, *The Feminine*

---

[80] Ibid., p. 713–14.

[81] Rossi, "Equality," p. 608.

[82] Ibid., p. 608.

[83] Susan Brownmiller, "Sisterhood Is Powerful," *New York Times*, March 15, 1970, p. 27.

Mystique, published in 1963. The second was the influence on young women of the civil rights and radical left movements.

Friedan's Influence. Through the 1950s and into the 1960s there was little in the way of a feminist movement in the United States. During those years no one argued whether or not women were inferior or superior; they were simply seen as different. Women during that period were assumed to be happy with being a wife and mother. Given the great influence of psychoanalytic thought, it was assumed that if a woman felt frustrated she had a personal problem and if she could work her problem out she could once again be happy doing what women should do. During that period words like "emancipation" and "career" sounded strange and embarrassing; no one had used them for years.[84] It should be remembered that the 1950s were conservative thinking years in American history. It was a period characterized by political conservatism of McCarthyism, student complacency, and the benevolent paternalism of the Eisenhower years. When Betty Friedan's book appeared, it sold in large numbers and brought forth great indignation from the traditional and conservative forces of society.

The major thesis of Friedan's book was that the core of the problem for women was not sexual but rather a problem of personal identity. She wrote, "it is my thesis that as the Victorian culture did not permit women to accept or gratify their basic sexual needs, our culture does not permit women to accept or gratify their basic needs to grow and fulfill their potentialities as human beings, a need which is not solely defined by their sexual roles." She went on to say there was growing evidence that woman's failure to develop to complete identity had hampered rather than enriched her sexual fulfillment and this "virtually doomed her to be castrative to her husband and sons, and caused neuroses, or problems as yet unnamed as neuroses, equal to those caused by sexual repression."[85]

Friedan saw the answer to the woman's achievement of a personal identity to be reached through work. She felt that work was the key to the problem because the identity crisis of American women had started a century before, as "more and more of the work that used their human abilities and through which they were able to find self-realization, was taken from them."[86] She goes on to say that one of the first things that women must do is reject the housewife image. "The first step in that plan is to see housework for what it is—not a career, but something that must be done as quickly and efficiently as possible."[87]

In the years following the publication of her book, Betty Friedan was

---

[84] Friedan, *Mystique,* p. 19.

[85] Ibid., p. 77.

[86] Ibid., p. 334.

[87] Ibid., p. 342.

the most influential spokeswoman for the little female rebellion that did exist. The passage of the Civil Rights Act of 1964 made it clear to a number of women that there was a need for a civil rights organization that would speak out for women. In June 1966, Betty Friedan met with a number of other women and they agreed that an organization would be founded. At that time NOW (National Organization for Women) was founded and its initial purpose was to take action to bring women into full participation in the mainstream of American society and to have all the privileges and responsibilities that would make them completely equal to men. In August 1967, NOW organized its first picket line. The members dressed in old-fashioned costumes to protest the old-fashioned policies of the *New York Times* in its male and female help wanted ads. They handed out thousands of leaflets and were for the first time featured on television news and given wide mass media coverage.

The big issues for NOW came to be: (1) the Equal Rights Amendment which has been kicking around Congress since 1923 (This amendment states: "Equality of rights under the law shall not be denied or abridged by the United States or by any state on account of sex."); (2) abortion law repeal; (3) day-care centers for everyone; and (4) equal employment opportunities and equal pay for equal work.[88] The NOW group includes men in their membership so long as they are men concerned about the civil rights of women. However, the more radical groups in the liberation movement do not accept men, regardless of whether they are sympathetic to the cause or not.

Civil Rights and the Radical Left. The Betty Friedan influence on the Women's Liberation Movement has had its greatest appeal to older and less radical women. By contrast, many of the younger and more radical women have come out of the civil rights and radical left movements. And some of their terms are a reflection of their past influence. For example, *sexist* is a women's liberation term for a male supremist and its similarity to racist is clear. This was inevitable in a movement that drew much of its rhetoric and spirit from the civil-rights revolution and that, like America's first feminist movement, evolved out of the effort to liberate blacks.

Jo Freeman says that 1967 was the crucial year. That was when the blacks threw out the whites from the civil rights movement, student power had been made suspect by SDS and the organized New Left was fading out. Only the draft resistance movement was on the increase. "And this movement more than any other exemplified the social inequalities of the sexes. Men could resist the draft; women could only counsel resistance."[89]

Yet many of the young women left the other movements because they

---

[88] Ellis, *Revolt,* pp. 47–48.

[89] Jo Freeman, "The Origins of the Women's Liberation Movement," in Huber, *Changing,* p. 40.

found that often the men in those groups were as chauvinistic as men in more conservative groups. As "movement women" they were tired of doing the typing and fixing the food while "movement men" did the writing and leading. For example, during the student takeover at Columbia University a call went out for women volunteers to cook for the hungry strikers. One young female revolutionary protested that "women are not fighting the revolution to stay in the kitchen," and the call was amended to ask for *people* to man the kitchen.[90] Many of the movement women were living with or married to movement men who, they believed, were treating them as convenient sex objects or as somewhat lesser beings. This is illustrated in an often quoted statement of Stokeley Carmichael to S.N.C.C. that "the position of women in our movement should be prone." So many of the young radical women felt the men were taking a condescending approach to women's problems, while they felt their problems were important and it was up to them to do something about them.

So the radical liberation groups are made up of only women, although many of their tactics have been borrowed from the radical left and civil rights groups. It is common in the liberation literature to see similarities made to the civil rights movement and analogies drawn between the problems of blacks and of women. This, as suggested throughout this chapter, has been a characteristic of the feminist movement in the United States. Morton Hunt, in a *Playboy* article, has argued that this analogy is misleading. He says that whites and blacks do not have innate differences that commit them to different roles in education, politics, employment, and so forth. However, men and women can eliminate all role differences "only by ignoring and suppressing a vital part of their inherent natures and by accepting the frustration that results from unmet needs and unfulfilled desires."[91] However, there is no clear evidence of different "inherent natures" and Hunt's arguments in the *Playboy* piece are really those of a male chauvinist, sophisticated, but nevertheless chauvinistic. No one would deny that there is a biological basis for people's being black, but no one argues that it should be treated with a biological solution. In the same sense sex is also a biological fact but the problem is a social one in the same way as is the problem of race.

There is another way that the radical liberation groups are like the militant black groups. Many of the liberation women feel that like the blacks with their Uncle Toms, they are also hampered with an enormous fifth column of women referred to as "Aunt Tabbies" or "Doris Days." Also like the blacks, the militant women are asking that their "hidden history," the study of the feminist movement, be taught in schools and

[90] Epstein, *Woman's Place*, p. 34.
[91] Morton Hunt, "Up Against The Wall, Male Chauvinistic Pig," *Playboy*, May 1970, p. 207.

colleges. The intellectuals in the movement are challenging many of the psychiatrists, psychologists, sociologists, and anthropologists that have held to the theory that for women their "anatomy is their destiny."[92]

In 1969 and 1970 a wide range of women's liberation groups developed. The most conservative is NOW and the spectrum moves leftward to the highly radical and revolutionary groups. Groups presently in existence besides NOW are FLF (Female Liberation Front), W.I.T.C.H. (Women's International Terrorist Conspiracy from Hell), Redstockings, and so forth. The revolt is growing with rapid speed and "instead of Lucy Stone in bloomers, we have Abby Rockefeller in bare feet, dungarees, and work shirt."[93]

Barbara Polk describes these groups as independent, and they typically are composed of no more than 10 to 15 women who come together in "consciousness-raising" or "rap" groups for the purpose of developing their own understanding of the condition of women on the basis of their own experiences. These groups inherited from their radical roots the belief that structures are always conservative and confining.[94]

The loosely defined rap groups have been very successful at changing individual attitudes; but they have not been very successful in dealing with social institutions. Individual rap groups often flounder when their members have used up the possibilities of consciousness raising and decide they want to do something more concrete. "The problem is that most groups are unwilling to change their structure when they change their tasks. They have accepted the ideology of 'structurelessness' without realizing its limitations."[95]

The ultimate goal of the radical groups is revolution. As one radical journal writes, revolution must occur because the condition of female oppression does not "depend on," is not "integrated to," the structure of society; it is the structure. "The oppression of women though similar to that of blacks, differs from it in that it depends not on class division but rather on a division of labor premised on private property and resulting in the family as the primary unit for the function of the economy."[96]

Another radical liberation group, the FLM, through their journal, *No More Fun and Games,* urges women to leave their husbands and children and to avoid pregnancy. They also want women to dress plainly and simply, to cut their hair very short, and to "reclaim themselves" by discarding their husbands' or fathers' names. The journal also urges the women to live alone and to abstain from sexual relations. The FLM

---

[92] Ellis, *Revolt,* pp. 9–10.

[93] Ibid., p. 19.

[94] Barbara Bovee Polk, "Women's Liberation: Movement for Equality," in Safilios-Rothschild, *Sociology of Women,* p. 322.

[95] Freeman, "Liberation Movement," in Huber, *Changing,* p. 47.

[96] "I am Furious (Female)," *Radical Education Project* (Detroit: No date).

women refrain from wearing makeup—though Chap Stick and hand lotion (for karate callouses) are allowed.[97]

All of the liberation groups see the present conjugal family structure with its traditional division of labor as destructive to full female identity. Much of the focus has been on trying to alleviate the burdens of housework and get help through free collective childcare. The more radical groups, such as the FLM, have contempt for the family. Roxanne Dunbar, a leader of that group, writes: "The family is what destroys people. Women take on a slave role in the family when they have children. People have awful relationships. It's a trap, because you can't support it without a lot of money."[98] Another spokesman writes that marriage which is made to seem attractive and inevitable is a trap for female children as well as mothers. "Most women do not grow up to see themselves as producers, as creators—instead they see their mothers, their sisters, their women teachers, and they pattern themselves after them. They do not see women making history."[99] Still another spokeswoman, Ti-Grace Atkinson, said at a conference of the Women's Liberation in New York City that the prostitute is the only honest woman left in America. According to Atkinson, prostitutes are the only honest women because they charge for their services rather than submit to a marriage contract which forces them to work for life without pay.[100]

It seems clear that for most groups in the Women's Liberation Movement marriage is a clear definition of relationship, making the woman subservient and secondary. The possible solutions for this can range from ending marriage to modifying it. But what is most important is the belief that marriage implies a secondary status for women. It is clear that many men as well as women believe that a woman in marriage is a second-class citizen. For example, in the recent article on the Women's Liberation Movement in *Playboy*, Morton Hunt wrote that for the American woman today and in the foreseeable future the most workable answer—"the scheme of life that most nearly fits her own needs and those of the American man—is a combination of marriage and career in which she accepts a secondary part in the world of work and achievement in order to have a primary part in the world of love and home."[101] This statement is a good example of the kind of male thinking that women's liberation groups of all types are fighting against.

Another role activity which many of the liberation women object to is that of motherhood. They rebel against the belief that childbearing and

---

[97] Ellis, *Revolt*, p. 54.

[98] Ibid., pp. 54–55.

[99] Laurel Limpus, *Sexual Repression and The Family* (Boston: New England Free Press, 1970), p. 65.

[100] *Philadelphia Bulletin*, May 29, 1970, p. 2.

[101] Hunt, *Variety*, p. 209.

the rearing of children is the fulfillment of a woman's destiny. Limpus writes that this belief is by far the most damaging and destructive myth that imprisons women. Having children is no substitute for creating one's own life, for producing. And since so many women in this culture devote themselves to nothing else, they end up becoming intolerable burdens upon their children, because in fact these children are their whole lives.[102] The women are objecting to the fact that not only is there a mystique about parenthood but that the mystique *really* equates motherhood with parenthood. People frequently say how important a father is to his children, but the empirical evidence shows that when there is no father the children suffer no more psychological problems than when the father is present. However, no one has ever studied those families where there is no mother present and the children are reared by the father. It may be that those children are not significantly different from those reared with a mother.

It is not that most liberation groups are opposed to women having children if they so desire. What they object to is the woman's being required to fill the mother role and care for the children. The liberation women insist that society should take care of the children. They argue that childcare centers are needed not just for women at the poverty level, but to be put at the disposal of all working women and be used the same as any other public facility, such as a museum, library, or park. At the present time the United States is the only industrialized country which does not provide childcare services. There are close to 4 million children in the United States who need supervision while their mothers work and the present facilities can handle less than one half a million.

Because most liberation groups see themselves as women who have been sexually exploited by men, there is a great deal of concern with sexual participation with men and what it means. Yet, in the areas of male-female interaction women have in recent years felt freer to speak of their rights in the sexual sphere than in the social sphere. And as suggested earlier, sexual rights for the woman have been gained and women increasingly have the means of sexual equality. In fact, the right of women to sexual equality is now established and even treated as acceptable in the mass media. For example, such conservative national women's publications as *Ladies' Home Journal* and *McCall's* carry articles almost every month dealing with some aspects of sex in detailed clarity.[103]

However, the objection that many liberation women have to sex is how it is used as a means of manipulating both men and women by various agencies in society. Much of the resentment results from women

---

[102] Limpus, *Repression*, p. 66.
[103] Epstein, *Woman's Place*, p. 37.

feeling they are being treated by men as sexual objects. "Fashion, advertising, movies, *Playboy Magazine,* all betray the fact that women are culturally conceived of as objects and still worse, often accept this definition and try to make themselves into a more desirable commodity on the sexual market."[104] The objection is not that females or males make themselves sexually attractive but rather that mass media focuses on the sexual attractiveness of the woman and does not present her as a human being.

One writer for the liberation movement, a female sociologist, sees the problem of sexuality as a dual one. When she speaks of female liberation, she refers to liberation from the myths that have enslaved women in their own minds as well as in the minds of others. "Men and women are mutually oppressed by a culture and a heritage that mutilates the relationships possible between them."[105] She further suggests that the problem of sexuality illustrates that men and women are oppressed together. She argues that women shouldn't become obsessed with freeing themselves from sick male sexuality, but rather, that it is more important for both males and females to free themselves from structures that make them sexually sick. "The male definition of virility which makes women an object of prey is just as much a mutilation of the human potential of the male for the true love relationship as it is the female's." Limpus goes on to say that even though it is the female who experiences the predatory attitude, they as women also contribute to it. "We must both be liberated together, and we must understand the extent to which our fear and frigidity, which had been incalcated in most of us from infancy onwards and against which most of us have had to struggle for our sexual liberation, has hurt and mutilated them."[106]

Limpus further points out that the socialization to female sexual repression is so strong that even most highly liberated women cannot completely shake their earlier restrictive sexual training. She observes that even in supposedly radical circles girls can still be labelled "promiscuous." "There are tremendous residual moral condemnations of female sexuality in all of us, in spite of our radical rhetoric. A woman, even a relatively sexually liberated one, often finds it hard to approach a man sexually the way a man can approach her."[107]

Probably the most publicized and most important statement about sexual expression made in the Women's Liberation Movement was by Anne Koedt called "The Myth of the Vaginal Orgasm." She points out that frigidity has usually been defined by men to mean that women have failed to have a vaginal orgasm. The myth of the vaginal orgasm has pri-

---

[104] Limpus, *Repression,* p. 70.
[105] Ibid., p. 61.
[106] Ibid., p. 67–8.
[107] Ibid., p. 69.

marily been perpetuated by psychoanalysts. In actual fact, the vagina is not a highly sensitive area and is not physiologically constructed to achieve orgasm. All physiologically based orgasms in the female come from the clitoris. Koedt points out that men have orgasms primarily through friction of the penis in the vagina, not with the clitoris. "Women have thus been defined sexually in terms of what pleases men; our own biology has not been properly analyzed. Instead we have been fed a myth of the liberated woman and her vaginal orgasm, an orgasm which in fact does not exist."[108] She goes on to say that women must redefine their sexuality and discard the "normal" concepts of sex and establish new guidelines. "We must begin to demand that if a certain sexual position or technique now defined as 'standard' is not mutually conducive to orgasm, then it should no longer be defined as standard."[109] It is also important that from Freud on, it has been men who have defined the standards of sexual satisfaction and adjustment for women. Actually, the "vaginal orgasm" has been a part of the overall view of many followers of Freud related to the belief in the inferiority of women. The myth of the physical vaginal orgasm is recognized by most sexual authorities today.

Constantina Safilios-Rothschild argues that women's sexual liberation includes the right to refuse to make love with any man and for a variety of reasons other than just fear of pregnancy or belief in a double standard. "But it seems that few men are liberated enough to grant this right to a woman they desire. True sexual liberation means the woman can determine with whom, when, how often, and in which way to have sexual relations in order to derive maximum gratification and, therefore, be able truely to satisfy her partner."[110]

The Women's Liberation Movement, like that of the militant black, the militant college student, and the Hippie has been greatly influenced by television. If a group of women interested in the liberation movement meet and carry on their session without theatrics, they are not covered by the mass media. As a result, many people believe that the Women's Liberation Movement is made up of nothing more than far-out, deviant types of women. In one sense there develops a reaction against a kind of caricature of the movement. So a common reaction is to not take the movement seriously and to respond with ridicule—which has been the reaction to feminists for decades. However, some men have begun to react to the liberation movement with anger, and many members are expecting an increased backlash from men and women.

Women often have reacted to the liberation movement with confusion

---

108 Brownmiller, "Sisterhood," p. 130.
109 Ibid., p. 130.
110 Safilios-Rothschild, *Sociology of Women,* p. 102.

and hostility. What they hear goes contrary to their socialization experiences as females. Women are often their own worst enemies and are willing to attack one another in ways that men will not do to each other. Women everywhere refer to female "cattiness" and disloyalty. "They claim to dislike other women, assert they prefer to work for men, and profess to find female gatherings repugnant. This set of attitudes constitutes a barrier to women's aiming high in the occupational world."[111] There are also many women who have established careers in male dominated fields who are resentful of the liberation movement because their individual success gives them a sense of superiority over other women. Some of these women say they encounter no discrimination. It may be that the men who work with them, like with blacks, show respect to indicate that they are not prejudiced. Many organizations not only have token blacks but also have token women in their employment.

But probably the most hostile reaction to the Women's Liberation Movement comes from the many women who have spent a good part of their adult years doing the things the liberation women are saying are demeaning and valueless. To a great extent the hostility is a generational one. The middle-aged woman who has spent her adult years as a wife, mother, and housekeeper is very threatened by the young woman who tells her that her life has been empty and she is a victim of male viciousness. For her to admit that the liberation women may be right is to admit that her life has been a charade. So one can predict increasing resistance and hostility from the majority of American women who are wives, mothers, and housewives.

There is a great deal of disagreement among the various factions of the Women's Liberation Movement on what they want, but most of them want gender difference to become secondary to human equality; that is, that all persons are human beings first and male or female second, but what is often overlooked is that full equality may mean equality in areas that are not always desirable. As women have achieved greater equality to men in the United States, their rates of alcoholism, drug addiction, and so on have increased. But many women are quite willing to accept these negative possibilities along with the more desirable ones.

It may also be that many women have an idealized image of the freedom of some men, because the only really independent people are those with no interpersonal relationships at all. Yet this is not something that very many persons want. And many of the women in the liberation movement who reject husbands and family turn to each other to meet their interpersonal needs. One writer suggests that few of the women she met in the liberation movement accepted the notion that life itself was unfair.

---

[111] Epstein, *Woman's Place*, p. 125.

"Most of them cherish an apocalyptic conviction that a society that assumed the drudgery of child-rearing would free women."[112] The question is to free women for what? To fill the jobs that men now fill and often hate? Very few men could be described as creating their own histories by transcending themselves.[113] Many women believe that the fight for total sexual equality is the issue and if it is achieved and women find themselves along with men in undesirable life patterns, then the fight can be made for overall human betterment. It seems clear that this movement is going to have far reaching effects on marriage and family roles in the United States.

SELECTED BIBLIOGRAPHY

Acker, Joan   "Women and Sexual Stratification: A Case of Intellectual Sexism," in Joan Huber, *Changing Women in a Changing Society.* Chicago: University of Chicago Press, 1973, pp. 174–83.

Bernard, Jessie   *Academic Women.* University Park: The Pennsylvania State University Press, 1964.

Brownmiller, Susan   "Sisterhood Is Powerful," *New York Times,* March 15, 1970, pp. 27–28, 30, 132, 134, 136, 140.

Degler, Carl N.   "Revolution Without Ideology: The Changing Place of Women In America." *Daedalus,* Fall 1964, pp. 653–70.

Ellis, Julie   *Revolt of The Second Sex.* New York: Lancer Books, 1970.

Epstein, Cynthia F.   *Women's Place.* Berkeley: University of California Press, 1970.

Friedan, Betty   *The Feminine Mystique.* New York: W. W. Norton and Co., Inc., 1963.

Glazer-Malbin, Nona, and Waehrer, Helen Youngelson   *Woman in a Manmade World.* Chicago: Rand McNally and Co., 1972.

Gornick, Vivian, and Moran, Barbara K.   *Women in Sexist Society.* New York: New American Library, 1971.

Huber, Joan   *Changing Women in a Changing Society.* Chicago: University of Chicago Press, 1973.

Reeves, Nancy   *Womankind: Beyond the Stereotype.* Chicago: Aldine, 1971.

Safilios-Rothschild, Constantina   *Toward a Sociology of Women.* Lexington, Mass.: Xerox College Publishing, 1972.

Sinclair, Andrew   *The Emancipation of The American Woman.* New York: Harper and Brothers, 1965.

Women's Bureau, *1969 Handbook of Women Workers,* bulletin 294. Washington, D.C.: U.S. Department of Labor, 1969.

---

[112] *Newsweek,* March 15, 1970.

[113] Limpus, *Repression,* pp. 62–63.

Chapter 16

Birth Control and Human Sexuality

Historically in the majority of cultures, marital sex has been defined as important two ways: first, as the means of reproduction, and second, as a means of satisfying the sexual needs of the husband. With few effective methods of controlling conception, pregnancy frequently occurred as a consequence of marital coitus. This resulted in a large number of children, high rates of maternal mortality, and a short life span for the reproductive wife. In the past, while women could and did receive personal satisfaction from the sexual aspect of marriage, it was not usually an expected right. In the patriarchal system, sexual need was generally assumed to be a need of the man. The woman who also received sexual satisfaction was sometimes viewed by her husband (and herself) as somewhat "unnatural." "Good women," at least in terms of accepted social values, did not usually derive pleasure from the sexual act. Their role as sexual partner was one of duty to the husband.

In contemporary middle-class America, the traditional patriarchal beliefs about marital coitus have been altered and expanded. No longer is the relationship of the sexual act and conception viewed as beyond control of the individual. Through the development and use of birth-control methods, conception is increasingly controlled. A second change in the traditional beliefs about marital sex is today's assumption that the wife has as much right to expect sexual fulfillment in marriage as her husband. Thus, the two general social changes in regard to marital coitus have had their greatest impact on women. Because these two social changes are of importance, each is presented in some detail before discussing the broader area of sexual adjustment in marriage.

First, the various methods of birth control, their uses and reliability. Second, human sexuality, the similarities and differences in male and female sexual expression. Chapter 17 is directed at a more specific discussion of sexual expression in marriage and out of marriage by married couples.

BIRTH CONTROL

Birth control, in a broad sense, refers to the various methods used to stop either pregnancy or live birth. Sometimes birth control is used in reference to "positive" aspects of controlling family size through the spacing of children over time, but ultimately this means not having children except when desired. Birth control may be applied in a number of ways. First, *destruction* after conception; this may range from destroying the fetus by induced abortion or by giving birth to the child and then destroying it. Second, through *sterilization,* a process in which a person is made biologically incapable of producing or transmitting the ovum or the sperm. Third, the *processual* ways of controlling pregnancy. This may be through the withdrawal of the penis prior to ejaculation of sperm, or through a system where the sperm is present but no ovum is available for fertilization. Last, are the various *contraceptive* methods. The term contraception is generally applied to mechanical or chemical barriers that prevent the access of spermatozoa to the uterus and fallopian tubes when fertilizable ova are present.

While most societies, preliterate and literate, past and present, have accepted large birth rates as natural and inevitable, it is also probably true that in many of those societies at various times there have been some people who have attempted to control conception. To the problems of birth control there have always been two general approaches. The first has been a mystical formulae, and practices stimulating emotional responses. The second approach has been one based on rationality. This approach has centered around whatever had been believed in a given society to be the processes whereby procreation occurred on the one hand and the powers of the substances used to stimulate or defeat them on the other. These approaches were not only used among primitive tribes but also among the civilized nations of antiquity. The Egyptians, the Jews, the Greeks, and the Romans all possessed beliefs about the reproductive process and some knowledge of contraceptive devices.

In most societies of the past there was no knowledge of how conception occurred and therefore no awareness of a process that could be halted by some contraceptive measure. The rational development of birth control methods assumes the knowledge that conception occurs as a result of sexual intercourse. When this knowledge did not exist, societies had to wait to try to do something about birth control until pregnancy could be seen or the infant was born. Therefore, in primitive societies the chief method of birth control was abortion and in many societies infanticide was also used. A study of anthropological monographs shows that there were other practices also used by some preliterate groups. For example, "delayed marriage and celibacy, both almost negligible among primitive peoples; sex taboos limiting the time and frequency of connection, prepuberty coition, sex perversions (more or less neglected by most writers), prolonged lactation, and conception control, both magical and rational."[1]

Historically, the techniques of abortion and infanticide were used much more widely than contraception to control family size.[2] This was true because knowledge of the reproductive nature of sexual relations and the means of controlling conception through the uses of contraceptive devices was limited. Only in recent years and particularly in the Western world, has the emergence of effective contraceptive devices used by large numbers of the population occurred. For example, Margaret Sanger opened the first birth-control clinic in New York City in 1917—an act for which she served a prison sentence.[3]

Because the modern techniques are efficient they control conception. However, even the less effective techniques of the past could have been more effective if used consistently and with care. Had such attempts been made the population of Europe would not have risen so greatly during the 18th and 19th centuries. "We must instead say that the modern *demand* for better control has led to the *development* of more adequate techniques—that is, has created a large market for the new, improved devices."[4]

During the past decade, as there has emerged an increasing concern with the rapid expansion of the world's population, birth control has become of increasing interest on an international level. It was not until 1830 that the world's population reached its first billion, but only 100 years later, in 1930, the world's population was 2 billion, and 30 years later, in 1960, it had reached 3 billion. It is estimated that the 4-billion

[1] Norman E. Himes, *Medical History of Contraception* (New York: Gamut Press, 1963), p. 4.

[2] Ronald Freedman, Pascal K. Whelpton, and Arthur A. Campbell, *Family Planning, Sterility and Population Growth* (New York: McGraw-Hill Book Co., 1959), p. 57.

[3] See Chapter 10 for a discussion of the legal and religious aspects of contraception.

[4] William J. Goode, *World Revolution and Family Patterns* (New York: The Free Press of Glencoe, 1963), p. 53.

mark will be reached by 1975 and 5 billion by 1985. The United Nations estimates that world population is growing by 8,000 every hour or approximately 70 million a year.[5] Given this population explosion, the development of new, effective, and inexpensive means of birth control is increasingly seen as important to all of mankind.

The use and effectiveness of controlling contraception in the United States has been documented through several extensive studies of large populations.[6] One of the studies, made with a probability sample of wives on a national level, found that 70 percent of the respondents had at some time used contraception and only 6 percent said "they did not intend to use preventive methods at some time."[7] Another study of couples in eight of the nation's nine largest metropolitan areas found that 53 percent of the couples first used contraception before the first birth, and 30 percent more before the second birth.[8] These two studies indicate both the frequency of use and the early starting point of pregnancy control in marriage.

Generally speaking, by the 1930s in the United States there was an acceptance of birth control by many. For example, a poll in 1936 asked, "Do you believe in the teaching and practice of birth control?" and 63 percent of the respondents answered "yes." In 1943 another poll asked a group of women ages 21 to 35: "Do you believe that knowledge about birth control should be available to all married women?" and 85 percent of them answered "yes." By 1965 when a national sample of women were asked "Do you think birth-control knowledge should be available to anyone who wants it?" about 80 percent of *both* Protestant and Catholic women answered "yes."[9]

Contraceptive Methods

Abstinence. This is obviously the most reliable method of birth control but it is also the most extreme. It represents the total linking of coitus with reproduction because coitus would never be engaged in unless the intention was pregnancy. This method has been used by many individuals or groups of individuals in various cultures. Of course, if it were used completely by a social group, that group would never replace itself unless it did so by bringing in new members from the outside.

---

[5] Elizabeth Ogg, *A New Chapter in Family Planning* (New York: Public Affairs Committee, Inc., 1964), p. 4.

[6] See ibid.; and Charles F. Westoff et al., *Family Growth in Metropolitan America* (Princeton, N.J.: Princeton University Press, 1961).

[7] Freedman, Whelpton, and Campbell, *Family Planning*, pp. 61–62. This study will be referred to as the "national" study.

[8] Westoff, et al., *Family Growth*, p. 72. This study will be referred to as the "metropolitan" study.

[9] *Trans-Action*, April 1967, p. 3.

Sterilization. Sterilization prevents parenthood without destroying the sexual abilities of the individual. The usual methods are the cutting of the *vas deferens* (vasectomy) of the male or the fallopian tubes (salpingectomy) of the female.[10] Sterilization should not be confused with castration, which does destroy the sexual ability of the male. Other operations may also result in sterility, even though that is not their stated intent; for example, a female hysterectomy.

The vasectomy operation is safe and only takes about 20 minutes. There is no resulting interference with the testicles' ability to manufacture sperm nor with the normal secretion of hormones. The sperm are reabsorbed by the body. This operation is totally reliable and is the most effective means for making sure that pregnancy does not occur. However, it does have one major disadvantage for some who use it and that is that the effects of the operation are often permanent. If at a later date a man wants to undergo an operation that reverses the effects of the vasectomy, there is only about a 50 percent chance of success.

There have been some fears associated with the male vasectomy. First, it does not in any way influence the sexual ability or drive of the male. Second, there has been anxiety by some women that it will lead to unfaithfulness by their husbands. The available evidence indicates this is not common. Follow-up studies find that rarely do men have regrets about the operation. For example, one study found that 98 percent of the men would have the operation again. Of those men, 73 percent said they had increased sexual pleasure while 2 percent said it had decreased. "The health and sexual enjoyment of the wives improved even more than that of the husbands."[11]

The female operation costs far more and requires about ten days in the hospital. It is estimated that in the United States about 2 million couples have had surgical birth control. For most of them there is probably no great concern about changing the operation at some later date because they do not want children or already have all the children they want.

The "national" study found that 9 percent of all couples questioned controlled pregnancy by this method. Variations occur by education—with the college-educated representing only 6 percent and the grade-school educated 13 percent—and by religion, with the Protestants representing 11 and the Catholics 5 percent.[12]

Rhythm System (Safe Period). The rhythm method of contraception is the refraining from sexual intercourse during that period when the fe-

---

[10] Helen I. Clarke, *Social Legislation* (New York: Appleton-Century-Crofts, Inc., 1957), p. 193.

[11] Helen Edey, "Psychological Aspects of Vasectomy," *Medical Counterpoint*, January 1972, p. 23.

[12] Freedman, Whelpton, and Campbell, *Family Planning*, p. 30.

male ovum is at the stage in the menstrual cycle when conception is possible. The fertility period during each menstrual period is determined by taking the midpoint of the cycle and subtracting two days and adding three to five days to give the period of greatest possible conception. This, then, is the unsafe period, during which couples abstain from coitus if they do not desire pregnancy. Temperature charts are often used to determine the midpoint of a cycle; most commonly it is the 12th day. About 90 percent of the time, ovulation takes place between the 10th and 16th day. The reason each woman determines her own midpoint (or ovulation) before adding and subtracting days for the period of sexual abstinence is that the midpoint varies among different women.

For the period 1938–39 until 1955, the "national" study found an increase in the usage of the rhythm system from 11 to 24 percent of the couples studied.[13] The "metropolitan" study found the rhythm system in current usage among 19 percent of the couples studied.[14]

Several problems are associated with the use of the rhythm system. First, extreme care must be exercised in the calculation of dates. This generally means that the more irregular a menstrual cycle, the less dependable the rhythm system. And absolute regularity of the menstrual cycle is a myth. "Eighty percent of women have cycles averaging 28.6 days, with a span between 26 and 34 days. The remaining 20 percent have either shorter or longer cycles, or exhibit considerable variation in cycle length. Variations of between 21 and 90 days occur in women who appear to be physiologically normal."[15]

The second problem is the enforced restriction placed upon sexual relations. The spontaneity of sexual satisfaction must be put aside for at least part of every month because of the dangers of conception, and sometimes human inability to restrict sexual desire leads to pregnancy. For those who accept these factors, however, the rhythm system can often be used with high efficiency. The "national" study points out that "rhythm is most likely to be used as an exclusive method by couples who have both the sophistication to understand and the special religious motivations that will compensate for the self-denial and risk in depending on it."[16] The effective use of the rhythm system by higher-educated Catholic women is an illustration.[17] However, the rhythm system is not to be used indiscriminately by Catholics. To be used without guilt by them, three conditions must be present: "(1) there must be a justifiable reason . . .

[13] Ibid., p. 174.

[14] Westoff, et al., *Family Growth*, p. 78.

[15] George W. Corner, Jr., "Menstrual Cycle," in Albert Ellis and Albert Abarbanel, eds., *The Encyclopedia of Sexual Behavior* (New York: Hawthorn Books, Inc., 1961), p. 729.

[16] Freedman, Whelpton, and Campbell, *Family Planning*, p. 192.

[17] Westoff et al., *Family Growth*, p. 215.

(2) it must be agreed upon, and (3) the mutually agreed-upon abstinence must not be a proximate occasion of infidelity on the part of one or both spouses."[18].

Withdrawal (Coitus Interruptus). Like the rhythm system, withdrawal is a "processual" means of controlling conception in that it does not involve artificial impediments. Sexual intercourse is interrupted immediately before the male orgasm by withdrawal of the penis and ejaculation outside the vagina. Withdrawal is one of the least used methods in the United States today. In the "national" study, it was reported by 11 percent of the couples, and in the "metropolitan" study by even fewer, 5 percent.[19]

A number of problems are associated with this method. First, it demands very great willpower on the part of the male. He must be willing to give up the final and often most satisfying stage of sexual intercourse. While the method does permit a physical release through orgasm, it may lead to a feeling of psychological incompletion for both the male and female. A second problem involves the ability of the male to anticipate accurately when he is ready to ejaculate. Sometimes ejaculation happens with little or no warning; or he may know it is coming but feel he can wait a little longer, and wait too long. Third, even if the male withdraws ahead of ejaculation, some possibility of pregnancy still exists. The danger rests with the sperm cells in the few drops of seminal fluid which often escape from the penis before the orgasm is reached.

Douche. Douching is the cleaning of the vagina with a mild acid, sperm-killing solution after sexual intercourse. In the 1930s douching was the most common method of birth control used in the United States. But from 1938–39 to 1955, a strong shift away from its use occurred. In the "national" study, it was reported as used by 44 percent of the couples in 1938–39, but only by 11 percent in 1955.[20] In the "metropolitan" study, douching was used by only 4 percent of the couples as an exclusive means of controlling conceptions.[21]

In many cases, a douche may be used to supplement other methods; for example, it may be used with the diaphragm. There are several difficulties in using the douche as the only means of controlling conception. It must be used immediately after intercourse, which may be psychologically upsetting to the woman, and there is no guarantee that all of the sperm will be reached and destroyed by it.

Condom. The condom is a sheath of rubber or animal membrane

---

[18] Alphonse H. Clemens, "Catholicism and Sex," in Ellis and Abarbanel, eds., *Encyclopedia of Sexual Behavior* (New York: Hawthorn Books, Inc., 1961), p. 230.

[19] Freedman, Whelpton, and Campbell, *Family Planning*, p. 174; and Westoff et al., *Family Growth*, p. 78.

[20] Freedman, Whelpton, and Campbell, *Family Planning*, p. 176.

[21] Westoff et al., *Family Growth*, p. 78.

placed on the penis to catch the ejaculated sperm. The popularity of the condom has increased a great deal over the past 25 years. One reason for this is the wide publicity given the condom during World War II as a protection against venereal disease.[22] The "national" and "metropolitan" studies found the condom used, respectively, by 30 and 31 percent of the couples.[23]

One of the great advantages of the condom over most other methods of controlling conception is its simplicity. It can be placed on the penis quickly and it has little effect in influencing the natural development of the sexual act. However, it may dull the sensations of the nerve endings in the penis for some men (although this may have the positive effect of slowing down their orgasm) and it may be defective or broken so that sperm do escape.

Diaphragm. A diaphragm is a flexible rubber disc that is coated with a spermicidal jelly and covers the cervix, thereby preventing the sperm from reaching the ovum. It is left in place from 8 to 12 hours after coitus. The "national" study found 25 percent of the couples used this method; in the "metropolitan" sample, it was used by 18 percent.[24] Use of the diaphragm has increased, particularly among the higher educated. In recent years, a great deal of medical stress has been placed on the use of the diaphragm, and it is often recommended by planned-parenthood clinics.

The diaphragm is generally considered to be one of the most reliable and efficient of all contraceptive methods in use today. Its advantage, besides efficiency if correctly fitted and inserted, is that the women may insert it long before intercourse occurs, precluding any need to destroy the continuity of the sexual act. However, if the diaphragm is not inserted ahead of time, a breakoff in sexual foreplay is required for its insertion. When it is not inserted prior to foreplay, some women find the squatting position usually needed for its insertion unromantic and destructive to their sexual interest.

Intrauterine Contraceptive Devices (IUCD). These are small plastic or metal devices of various sizes and shapes. They are designed to fit into the womb and act as an irritant to prevent implantation of the fertilized ovum in the uterine wall. The process is simple and usually painless. The placement can be made without danger by any physician or other trained medical technician.

At first IUCDs seemed ideal—they were almost as effective as the pill, they did not affect the body's natural hormone balance, and once in place they could be forgotten. But now there is some controversy as to

---

[22] Freedman, Whelpton, and Campbell, *Family Planning*, p. 177.

[23] Ibid., p. 174; and Westoff et al., *Family Growth*, p. 78.

[24] Ibid., pp. 174 and 178.

their having possible hazards. This is important because in 1973 about 3 million American women were using them. One problem is that the IUCD is not as reliable as originally thought. The average pregnancy rate is 3 percent as compared with 00.1 percent for those using the pill. There is some evidence of their causing perforation of the uterus, pelvic infection, spontaneous expulsion, and excessive menstrual bleeding. But there is also evidence that the negative claims are exaggerated. One clear fact is that the risk of death from pregnancy far exceeds the risk associated with the IUCD.[25]

Oral Contraception. Of increasing significance as a means of birth control, are the oral contraceptives. They work through: (1) the suppression of ovulation or spermatogenesis; (2) prevention of fertilization; or (3) preventing the implanting of the fertilized ovum in the uterus. The so-called "steroids," pills that contain synthetic hormones, have been the most effective of the oral contraceptives. When they are taken daily from the 5th to the 25th day of the menstrual cycle, they halt conception by halting ovulation.

In November 1959, the Federal Food and Drug Administration (FDA) approved for public sale the first pill to be used for purposes of birth control. Since that date, other oral contraceptives have been approved by FDA. The various pills are manufactured by a number of firms and are promoted through extensive advertising campaigns. Their sale is rapidly expanding.

One of the major problems resulting from the use of oral contraceptives is the control of undesired side effects. The most common of these are the same as those usually associated with pregnancy; that is, nausea, weight gain, breast discomfort, swelling of hands and feet, changes in skin and hair, vaginal spotting, and improvement of acne. In one study of a sample of more than 11,000 women who had used oral contraception for more than two years, about 7 percent had experienced nausea and some swelling. The number dropped to about 5 percent for women who remained on the pills for 37 to 42 months. (Most of the women who stopped using the pills did so because of weight increase.) A five-year study based on a sample of 18,000 women found that pill users had higher blood pressure, faster heart rates, higher blood-sugar levels, and a greater tendency to form blood clots than nonusers. On the plus side, the pill users seemed to have better hearing. And those over age 40 had lower blood-cholesterol levels than women of the same age not taking the pill.[26]

By 1969 the use of the pill had reached an estimated 7 million women in the United States. This meant that approximately one seventh of all

---

[25] *Newsweek,* "The Risks of the IUD," June 25, 1973, p. 54.
[26] *New York Times,* September 23, 1973, p. 8.

women in the childbearing years were using the pill. It was estimated that the wholesale value of domestic sales was about $100 million per year and export sales about equal to that. All indications were that the pill would increasingly be used by a greater proportion of women, but in 1969 came the "pill scare."

The pill scare came about as a result of congressional hearings on oral contraception. At that time testimony was heard that the pill was dangerous and had not been adequately tested as to side effects and possible dangers for the user. The hearings received a great deal of publicity and panic set in among many users. By the winter of 1970 it was clear that many users of the pill had stopped. A Harris poll found that 50 percent of a national sample of women said they had stopped the pill because they thought it to be injurious to their health. The same poll asked: "From what you have heard or read, do you feel the birth control pill is dangerous to use or not?" To this question 80 percent of the respondents felt the pill was dangerous. However, most of the respondents did not feel that the pill should be outlawed.

There were other indications of the panic related to the pill. A number of New York City obstetricians say they have been approached to perform abortions on women who stopped using the pill. Also, birth-control clinics in New York funded by the Office of Economic Opportunity reported that before Senator Nelson's congressional hearings on the pill about eight out of ten women asked for the pill, but after the hearings only about 60 percent chose oral contraception.[27]

Some counter support for the pill has developed, but it has received much less publicity. Most of the congressional testimony emphasized the hazards of the pill and did not pay much attention to it as the most effective means of family birth control. Guttmacher has argued that blood-clotting problems, some of which can be fatal, are the only proven risks associated with oral contraceptives. Death from clot complications occurs in about three out of every 100,000 women on the pill, but for women who become pregnant the risk is 15 times greater.[28] Guttmacher further points out that if all the women who quit the pill turn to the next most effective method, the intrauterine device, almost 50,000 will become pregnant because of the higher failure rate of that method.[29] There is a need for careful and objective study of the pill with a clear statement on the dangers and the advantages from that method.

There is no evidence that using the pills has a negative effect on those who desire a future pregnancy. "In every study so far, a high percentage of women who stopped taking the pills after one to 48 months of use

[27] *Newsweek*, March 9, 1970, p. 46.

[28] Ibid., p. 46.

[29] Ibid., p. 46.

promptly conceived—many in the very first cycle after stopping—and bore normal babies. The longer oral contraceptives had been used, the higher the pregnancy rate after women stopped taking the pills.

The cost of oral contraception continues to be high enough so that it is not economically feasible for use on any mass, public health basis. At present, the most commonly used pills cost between $1.25 and $3.50 for a month's supply. If we average that to $2.50 and estimate that a couple have coitus on ten different occasions in a month, then the contraceptive cost per coital protection would be about $0.25. This would compare to the cost per coital protection of other methods as follows: foam, liquid, and sponge, $0.04; jelly and diaphragm, $0.06; aerosol foam or foam tablets, $0.08; and jelly or cream alone, $0.11.[30] Of course, while the cost is greater for the oral contraceptive, its reliability is also greater.

Oral contraception seems to be the contraceptive method of the future, though it will probably take some little time before it will be accepted and used with confidence by the majority of American women. Its advantages over older methods are that it offers a high degree of reliability —not only biologically but also psychologically, in that the human errors often found with the use of the condom and diaphragm are minimized. Oral contraception can also contribute to greater spontaneity in the sexual act because the pill can be taken prior to sexual intercourse. Because of its great simplicity of use, it can also be taken by many not willing or able to correctly use the condom or diaphragm.

At the present time, there appears to be agreement among the officials of FDA, the pharmaceutical companies, and physicians about the general assets and liabilities of oral contraceptives. The agreement is that: (1) the pills are at present the most effective means of birth control; (2) for most young women they are safe to take within the time limits set up by FDA; (3) there is no evidence that the pills are the cause of any disease; and (4) the pills do produce certain side effects, or unpleasant reactions, in some women. There will undoubtedly emerge in the near future great changes in oral contraceptives. At the present time, several drug companies are working on an injection that will prevent ovulation for from one to three months.

There are a number of other possible birth-control methods being worked on for the future: (1) lower dosage minipills whose lower hormonal concentration will, hopefully, cause fewer side effects; (2) an implanted capsule of slowly released birth-control hormones which could be changed yearly, lowering the chances of failure through forgetfulness; (3) a pill that a woman would take before intercourse which would change the chemical makeup of the mucous in the cervix so that sperm could not fertilize an egg; (4) vaginal pessaries containing prosta-

---

[30] Ogg, *Family Planning*, p. 13.

glandins that are inserted once a month so that menstruation occurs whether the woman is pregnant or not (If she is pregnant, then she has an early abortion without being aware of it.); and (5) a male pill which would combine progesterone with the male sex hormone, androgen, rendering the man infertile.[31]

These methods of birth control provide the means for controlling pregnancy. While they vary in their degrees of reliability, so do the individuals using them. The "national" study found that one pregnancy in eight was accidental, occurring in spite of preventive efforts.[32] The percentage of accidental pregnancies by type of birth-control methods used was also found to vary. For those using rhythm, 30 percent reported accidents; appliance methods, 20 percent; and withdrawal, 13 percent.[33]

In general, the most effective methods for controlling conception are the oral contraceptives, IUCD, diaphragm and jelly, condom, and withdrawal; the least effective are the rhythm system and douche.[34] Many times the failure of contraception is attributed to the method, rather than the persons using it. The fact is that the most reliable methods used by careful individuals can and do effectively control pregnancy. This is illustrated by the fact that one five-year study found that one third of all couples using contraception to avoid or delay pregnancy have children anyway. The study found that whatever the method chosen, it is only as effective as the commitment to its use.[35] From the point of view of significant social change, this fact has been revolutionary in affecting the married role of the woman. Today's middle-class wife now has the means of determining the number and spacing of her children.

Social Correlates of Birth Control. In the discussion of the various methods of birth control some references have been made to how their use varies according to certain social variables. There are wide variations in how and why certain groups of individuals use or do not use the various contraceptive knowledge. For example, among young adolescent girls the failure to practice birth control may stem more from limited knowledge and access rather than from any pattern of sexual promiscuity outside marriage. In a study of adolescent unwed mothers it was found that if birth control had been available to them many would not have become unwed mothers.[36]

The most important social factor related to the use of birth control is

---

[31] *New York Times,* September 23, 1973, p. 8.

[32] Freedman, Whelpton, and Campbell, *Family Planning,* p. 70.

[33] Ibid., p. 208.

[34] Westoff et al., *Family Growth,* p. 77.

[35] *New York Times,* September 23, 1973, p. 8.

[36] Frank Furstenberg, Jr., Leon Gordis, and Milton Markowitz, "Birth Control Knowledge and Attitudes Among Unmarried Pregnant Adolescents: A Preliminary Report," *Journal of Marriage and the Family,* February 1969, p. 42.

that of religion—particularly among Catholics. As suggested earlier, with the exception of the rhythm method, the Catholic church opposes all forms of birth control. Yet, between 1955 and 1965 the proportion of Catholic wives using methods of birth control other than rhythm increased steadily. But this did not bring about any change in the Catholic church's stand. In 1964 and again in 1966 Pope Paul VI affirmed: "The thought and the norm of the Church are not changed; they are those in force in the traditional teaching of the Church."[37] In general, it seems that from 1955 to 1965 the proportion of Catholic women conforming to their Church Magisterium's position on birth control has been decreasing and that deviation has been occurring at consistently younger ages over that period.[38] A national fertility study in 1965 showed that a majority of all Catholic wives between the ages of 18 and 39 were not conforming.[39]

There are variations among Catholic women and whether or not they use birth control methods. For example, Catholic women who have married Catholic men report a higher proportion conforming than do Catholic women who have married Protestant men. Conformity is also associated with amount of education received in Catholic schools and, as would be expected, with the frequency of attending mass and especially with the frequency of receiving communion. It is also important that refraining from the use of birth-control methods is more common among Catholic white-collar groups and among the better educated.

The relationship between frequency of sexual activity in marriage and the use of birth-control methods is an area of study generally overlooked. Couples who have a higher frequency of intercourse have a greater potential for conception when contraceptive practices are held constant. So whatever definitions of sexual frequency are decided upon in a marriage can be seen as a contribution to birth control potential. Also involved are the relative interests of the husband and wife as to sexual frequency and birth control. For example, a couple may agree that sexual relations should continue but pregnancy should be avoided. Often there is the feeling that birth-control methods are annoying, especially for the person who has the primary responsibility. One study has suggested that in this kind of situation bargaining often takes place between the husband and wife. If other factors are equal, the person who tends most often to assume ambiguous role responsibilities in the marriage will probably assume responsibility for contraception as well. However, this may be modified. "If the husband wishes sexual relations much more frequently

[37] Raymond H. Patvin, Charles F. Westoff, and Norman B. Ryder, "Factors Affecting Catholic Wives' Conformity to Their Church Magisteriums' Position on Birth Control," *Journal of Marriage and the Family*, May 1968, p. 263.

[38] Ibid., p. 262.

[39] Ibid., p. 263.

than the wife, then the wife may systematically use fear of pregnancy as an excuse for avoiding relationships and may therefore refuse to take responsibility for contraception."[40]

Whatever the feeling about birth control among various groups in general, there is a high level of acceptance that birth-control methods should be used by the American people. There may be disagreements on what methods should be used but not that having children should be out of the control of the individual. And the evidence indicates a continuing acceptance of birth-control methods in the United States.

THE SEXUAL "RIGHTS" OF THE WIFE

The second important change in the American middle class in regard to marital coitus has involved the "rights and expectations" of the wife. Today she is often taught that when she enters marriage she has a right to sexual fulfillment; in fact, some modern marriage manuals give this attainment the highest emphasis. Such a change in expectations is closely related to the development of effective methods of birth control; these methods allow the wife to enter the sex act as an end in itself, rather than with the traditional belief that it can, on any given occasion, lead to pregnancy.

A brief look at some past professional attitudes provides a vivid contrast to marital coital attitudes for the female in today's society. Up to and well through the 19th century, both moral and "scientific" criticism was directed at female sexual satisfaction. Dr. William Acton, in a standard text on the reproductive system, wrote "that the belief that women had a sexual appetite was a vile aspersion." William Hammond, surgeon-general of the United States, wrote "that nine tenths of the time decent women felt not the slightest pleasure in intercourse"; and at the University of Basel, an eminent gynecologist named Fehling labeled "sexual desire in the young woman as pathological."[41]

Female sexual interest was even negatively tied in with the woman's reproductive function. "In 1839 a highly successful English marriage manual written by a physician named Michael Ryan warned that female sterility was due, among other causes, to an excessive ardor of desire or 'passion strongly excited.' . . . It is well known that compliance, tranquility, silence, and secrecy are necessary for a prolific coition."[42] Sexual satisfaction for the woman was to be achieved only by the prostitute—

---

[40] David A. Rodgers and Frederick J. Ziegler, "Social Role Theory, The Marital Relationship, and Use of Ovulation Suppressors," *Journal of Marriage and the Family*, November 1968, p. 591.

[41] Morton M. Hunt, *The Natural History of Love* (New York: Alfred A. Knopf, Inc., 1959), p. 319.

[42] Ibid., p. 319.

this attitude of the past was often voiced not only by the clergy, but also by poets and physicians.

Many sources could be drawn on to illustrate how historical attitudes about the sexual role of the woman have completely changed. In fact, it would be next to impossible to find any reputable writers in the United States today voicing the old beliefs. A common view today is that "it is necessary that she [the wife] share the grandeur of the topmost heights with him—orgasm, the sexual climax—or else the enterprise becomes meaningless for both."[43] To emphasize the great importance of sexual satisfaction for the woman, the same writer says, "to serve as the cornerstone of happy marriage, sexual intercourse must be welcome and delighting not to the husband alone but to the wife as well."[44] Sexual satisfaction as often viewed today not only is of prime importance for the personal satisfactions of the woman, but also for the overall marriage relationship.

In the past it was assumed that female sexuality was based on receptiveness and this meant the whole structure of personality was viewed as dependent, passive, unaggressive, and submissive. Female sexuality has been seen in the past to involve long arousal and slow satisfaction, inferior sex drive and romantic idealism, rather than lustful reality. Those are stereotypes commonly presented through the mass media, and many men and women have conformed to them in reality. But more important is that the ability to respond sexually is to a great extent a function of experience for both sexes. Women have started all forms of sexual activity later than men and as a result are slower to reach a masculine level of sexual response. "If the figures are adjusted to take account of the difference in experience of the two groups, their responses to sexual stimulation are very alike."[45]

Many of today's marriage manuals emphasize the sexual problems centering around the wife's achievement of orgasm. Attention is directed at the need for extended foreplay so that actual coitus does not start until the wife is near her sexual peak; the couple together may then reach "the ultimate summit of mutual orgasm." The assumption usually made is that the male should control his sexual selfishness to make sure his wife reaches her sexual peak. Seldom is any attempt made to understand that prolongation by the male is not always susceptible to rational control. In addition, Himes and Taylor point out that "rarely do contemporary books have anything to say about the need of the woman's helping the man to prepare himself, especially when there is difficulty or

---

[43] Maxine Davis, *The Sexual Responsibility of Women* (New York: Permabooks, 1959), p. 24.

[44] Ibid., p. 95.

[45] Ann Oakley, *Sex, Gender, and Society* (Melbourne: Sun Books, 1972), p. 104.

slowness in erection."[46] The overall assumption is that the husband is usually sexually ready and all he must do is help his wife reach the same state.

The sexual world of both men and women is being expanded. This is seen in an examination of sex manuals. For example, oral-genital and anal intercourse were previously ignored or were seen only as foreplay. But they are now seen, at least on some occasions, as ends in themselves and represent a freer orientation toward sexual expression. The boundries of human sexuality are slowly being expanded. Hedonism, within the context of marriage for many, is the new norm.

The importance that is placed on the wife achieving sexual satisfaction is for the most part characteristic of the middle class. For example, Rainwater found in his lower-lower-class sample that 67 percent of the respondents said the husband enjoyed coitus more, 7 percent said the wife, and 26 percent about equal, as contrasted with the middle class where 33 percent said the husband enjoyed coitus more, 8 percent said the wife more, and 59 percent about equal.[47] Masters and Johnson found that husbands with fear of sexual performance were confined primarily to the higher educated. They found that only 14 percent of those men with no college education expressed the slightest concern with responsibility for their partner's sexual satisfaction. "These men felt that it was the female's privilege to achieve satisfaction during active coition if she could, but certainly it was not the responsibility and really not the concern of the male partner to concentrate on satisfying the woman's sexual demands."[48] By contrast, of those males with college matriculation, 82 percent of them expressed concern with coital-partner satisfaction.[49]

One assumption that is rarely verbalized is that mutual orgasm is important and, as a corollary, that the interests, drives, and abilities of the two sexes are equal. This may well be a reaction to the second-class sexual rights allotted the woman in the past. Given the vast variations in sexual interests and abilities within *either* sex, however, the assumption that each partner can reach an optimum level of satisfaction is often unrealistic. Some writers confronted with this possible dilemma resolve it by stating that the couple's sexual differences are handled by working out a compromise. This may be far more difficult for many couples than is often recognized.

The human female has a unique distinction among female animals. "As far as can be discovered, only the human female is capable of orgasm, or

---

[46] Norman E. Himes and Donald L. Taylor, *Your Marriage* (New York: Rinehart & Co., Inc., 1955), p. 163.

[47] Lee Rainwater, *Family Design* (Chicago: Aldine Publishing Co., 1965), p. 68.

[48] William H. Masters and Virginia E. Johnson, *Human Sexual Response* (Boston: Little, Brown & Co., 1966), p. 202.

[49] Ibid., p. 202.

reaching a sexual climax."[50] Furthermore, "the anatomic structures which are most essential to sexual response and orgasm are nearly identical in the human female and male."[51] This means that, at least in theory, males and females, equally, have the capacity for achieving sexual satisfaction.

The potentiality for sexual expression in the human female is very great. There is good reason to suspect that many women, if they could be fully freed from their sexual inhibitions, would be more sexually able than the average male. It is known that sexually uninhibited women have more orgasms and they are more intense and longer lasting than those experienced by equally released men. If a woman was freed of the cultural taboos she could behave like other primate females—"copulating all day long, day after day, with one male after another, until physical exhaustion puts an end to it."[52]

Masters and Johnson found that the female orgasm usually results in clearly recognizable physical changes and "the grimace and contortion of a woman's face graphically express the increment of myotonic tension throughout her entire body. The muscles of the neck and the long muscles of the arms and legs usually contract into involuntary spasm."[53] The potential range of difference in the female's experience of orgasm is great, and there are significant differences between different women, as well as marked variations in the individual female's orgasmic experience. Masters and Johnson write that "day to day, and week to week, she presents an entirely different picture of sexual activation for the observer."[54] They go on to point out that "there is great variation in both the intensity and the duration of the female orgasmic experience, while the male tends to follow standard patterns of ejaculatory variation."[55]

Masters and Johnson have through their research, for the first time, distinguished the female cycle of sexual response. During the cycle, many physiological, psychological, and social influences are interrelated as the woman moves through the four phases, or stages, in the cycle. The first stage is the *excitement phase* which may be brought about by any physical or psychological sexual stimulation. If the source of sexual stimulation is maintained, the female enters the second or *plateau phase*. At this stage the degree of sexual feeling is intense and a state of complete tumescence of the breasts, perineum, and vagina are reached.

---

[50] Ira L. Reiss, *Premarital Sexual Standards in America* (Glencoe, Ill.: The Free Press, 1960), p. 22.

[51] Alfred C. Kinsey et al., *Sexual Behavior in the Human Female* (Philadelphia: W. B. Saunders Co., 1953), p. 593.

[52] Mary Jane Sherfey cited in Edward M. Brecker, *The Sex Researchers* (Boston: Little, Brown & Co., 1970), p. 190.

[53] Masters and Johnson, *Response*, p. 128.

[54] Ibid., pp. 57–58.

[55] Ibid., p. 6.

Third is the *orgasmic phase* which is brief and explosive and may erase for some women all other conscious stimuli. And finally is the *resolution phase,* in which the physiological residuals of sexual tension are slowly dissipated.[56]

Important differences exist in the development of sexual intensity for the male and the female. "The responsiveness of the human male develops earlier than that of the female. By 15 years of age, 92 percent of the human males have experienced orgasm, but the female population is 29 years of age before a similar percentage has experienced first orgasm."[57] The slower development of the woman is not attributed to biological reasons so much as to cultural and psychological influences. For example, males become aware of orgasm at a much younger age than females and they do not have to be taught how to bring it about. "Women more rarely experience orgasm spontaneously during waking hours; most of them have to learn how to bring themselves to climax. Many do not even know what they are supposed to be experiencing until they learn from observing their husband or male partners."[58]

The cultural values of American society have led to different sexual concerns and fears by men and women. Increasingly for middle-class women, fears of performance concern their ability to achieve orgasm. For the male, the fears are related to attaining and keeping a penile erection; his orgasmic capacity is assumed.[59] Beyond these fears there are two major areas of physiological difference between the orgasm experience of men and women. "First, the female is capable of rapid return to orgasm immediately following an orgasmic experience, if restimulated before tensions have dropped below plateau-phase response levels. Second, the female is capable of maintaining an orgasmic experience for a relatively long period of time."[60]

Another difference between the male and female involves sexual arousal and speed of achieving orgasm. Kinsey writes "there is a widespread belief that the female is slower than the male in her sexual responses, but the masturbatory data do not support that opinion. It is true that the average female responds more slowly than the average male in coitus but this seems to be due to the ineffectiveness of the usual coital techniques."[61] After intensive study, Kinsey and his associates concluded

---

[56] Ibid., pp. 56–57.

[57] Alfred C. Kinsey, "Sex Behavior in the Human Male: Physiological and Psychological Factors in Sex Behavior," *Annals of the New York Academy of Sciences,* May 1947, p. 636.

[58] Jessie Bernard, "The Adjustments of Married Males," in Harold T. Christensen, ed., *Handbook of Marriage and the Family* (Chicago: Rand McNally & Co., 1964), p. 713.

[59] Masters and Johnson, *Response,* p. 218.

[60] Ibid., p. 131.

[61] Kinsey, *Female,* p. 164.

that "in spite of the widespread and oft-repeated emphasis on the supposed differences between female and male sexuality, we fail to find any
anatomic or physiological basis for such differences."[62] Therefore, any
difference in sexual behavior between the male and female "appears to
be the product of learning and conditioning."[63]

For women there may be some personality factors related to success
in sexual performance. There is some evidence that "submissive" women
are sometimes unable to assert themselves sexually and can only enjoy
one kind of satisfaction, that which is totally dependent on the skills of
the male. "They cannot tell their lovers even what they want done to
their own bodies, and the awareness of this acts as a barrier to the
physical sensation of the experience itself. 'Dominant' women are not
repulsed by the physical needs and sensations of their own bodies."[64]

There are a number of social and psychological variables that are related to experience with sexual materials. For example, men are more
likely to be exposed to erotic materials than are women. Younger adults
are more likely to be exposed than are older adults. People with more
education are more likely to have experiences with erotic materials.
Also people who read general books, magazines, and newspapers more,
and see general movies more also see more erotic materials. Finally,
people who are more socially and politically active are more exposed to
erotic materials, while people who attend religious services more often
are less likely to be exposed to erotica.[65]

Some comparison of the psychological differences between males and
females illustrates their differences in susceptibility to erotic influence.
The chart which follows gives the percentages of females and males
that reported definite and/or frequent erotic response to observing
various stimuli.[66]

	Percent Females	Percent Males
Portrayals of nude figures	3	8
Genitalia of opposite sex	21	many
Own genitalia	1	25
Moving pictures	9	6
Burlesque and floor shows	4	28
Portrayals of sexual action	14	42
Animals in coitus	5	11
Fantasies of opposite sex	22	37
Fantasies during masturbation	50	72
Stimulation by erotic stories	2	16

---

[62] Ibid., p. 164.

[63] Ibid., p. 644.

[64] Oakley, *Sex, Gender*, p. 126.

[65] *The Report of the Commission on Obscenity and Pornography* (New York: Bantam Books, 1970), p. 23.

[66] Kinsey, *Female*, pp. 652–71.

These findings indicate a higher erotic response by males to almost all sexual stimuli. The male and female are closest together on those items involving some "love" and furthest apart on those items related to "pure sex." It is possible that the difference in male and female responses to erotic stimulation either is becoming less or may have always been less than was generally believed. For example, Masters and Johnson found that 75 percent of the women they studied showed a reaction of the clitoral glands when they were exposed to pornographic literature.[67] The Commission on Pornography also casts doubt on the assumption that women are vastly less aroused by erotic stimuli than are men. It appears that among the younger generation males and females are coming to be more alike. A commission survey found that men and women in their early twenties reported a higher frequency of erotic dreams and sexual fantasy after exposure than did older people. "Thirty-five percent of men in their 20s and 30 percent of women in their 20s report having erotic dreams frequently or occasionally, as against smaller proportions for later ages."[68]

"Our sexual behavior is essentially the result of our attitudes toward sex; and these attitudes, in turn, are a product of how we have been brought up."[69] Given the emergent middle-class assumption of sexual rights in marriage for the wife, a new kind of social conditioning is taking place. The woman enters marriage expecting sexual satisfaction; if she does not achieve it, she may feel that something very important to marriage is missing. The implications of this assumption for the husband-wife relationship will be discussed in the next chapter.

Whatever changes that do occur, any new sexual morality is going to argue for equal rights of sexual expression for both men and women. This means that women will increasingly demand the same sexual rights for themselves as do men, whether in or out of marriage. "No matter what the outcome of the academic and ethical debates, women are going to continue to demand equal time and equal rights to erotic pleasure, to self-realization, to self-respect—and, if they can't find these qualities within marriage, they will quietly go on seeking them elsewhere."[70]

Differential Reproductive Burden

The significant reproductive difference between the male and female is the absolute biological requirements of sex. The woman must carry the

---

[67] Masters and Johnson, *Response*, p. 102.

[68] *The Report of the Commission on Obscenity and Pornography*, p. 228.

[69] Allan Fromme, *Sex and Marriage* (New York: Barnes and Noble, Inc., 1955), p. 95.

[70] Nancy Love, "The 70's Woman and the New Marriage," *Philadelphia Magazine*, February 1970, p. 56.

fetus from time of conception until she gives birth; the male need only provide the sperm. Even in "emancipated" contemporary American society, the woman may find that her greater reproductive burden leads to various kinds of sexual discrimination. If married, she may not get the kind of a job she wants or a promotion in a job she has because it is assumed that if she becomes pregnant, she must leave the job for at least several months.

Historically, the reproductive load on the woman has been viewed as inevitable. Yet there is a possibility that, in the future, this could be reduced a great deal. Suppose that a woman could have her own natural child, but not have to go through pregnancy and the giving of birth. Could a woman have a child through a "proxy mother"? Winchester feels there is reason to believe that it is possible.[71] An egg from the wife, fertilized by a sperm from the husband, could safely develop in the body of another woman with young, healthy reproductive organs and the couple could have a child which was entirely their own—just as much so from the standpoint of heredity as if the wife had borne it."[72] While the proposal is probably of little appeal for the vast majority of women, it does offer a startling means of reducing the traditional reproductive burden of women. As Winchester points out, "For thousands of years, women have often depended on the so-called 'wet nurse' to feed their babies after birth. Why not then carry the process a step further and have prenatal 'wet nurses'?"[73]

Another biologist has made even more radical suggestions for the future. Possibly within 10 or 15 years a woman will be able to buy a tiny frozen embryo, take it to her doctor, have it implanted in her uterus, carry it for nine months and give birth. The embryo would be sold with a guarantee that the baby would be free of genetic defects. Given even more time it may be possible to do away with the female uterus altogether.[74]

SELECTED BIBLIOGRAPHY

Draper, Elizabeth   *Birth Control in the Modern World.* Baltimore, Md.: Penguin Books, 1965.

Edey, Helen   "Psychological Aspects of Vasectomy." *Medical Counterpoint,* January 1972, pp. 19–24.

Freedman, Ronald   *Population: The Vital Revolution.* New York: Anchor Books, 1964.

---

[71] A. M. Winchester, *Heredity and Your Life* (New York: Dover Publications, Inc., 1960), p. 52.

[72] Ibid., p. 52.

[73] Ibid., p. 53.

[74] Cited in Alvin Toffler, *Future Shock* (London: Pan Books, 1970), p. 185

Guttmacher, Alan F., et al.   *The Complete Book of Birth Control.* New York: Ballantine Books, 1961.

Havemann, Ernest   *Birth Control.* New York: Time Inc., 1967.

Himes, Norman E.   *Medical History of Contraception.* New York: Gamut Press, Inc., 1963.

Oakley, Ann   *Sex, Gender and Society.* Melbourne: Sun Books, 1972.

Sherfey, Mary Jane   "The Evolution and Nature of Female Sexuality in Relation to Psychoanalytic Theory." *Journal of the American Psychoanalytic Association,* 1966, pp. 28–128.

Winchester, A. M.   *Heredity and Your Life.* New York: Dover Publications, Inc., 1960.

Chapter 17

Marital and Extramarital Sexual Expression

The focus of the first part of this chapter is on sexual attitudes and behavior in marriage. This deals with overall sexual adjustment in marriage and some problem areas of sexuality. The second part of the chapter examines extramarital sexual behavior.

Because of the great interest and attention directed at sexual adjustment in marriage, sexual and overall adjustment in marriage are sometimes thought of as being synonymous. But while the sexual aspect is of great importance, it is not the same as overall marital adjustment. To assume that good sexual adjustment will make a marriage, or that poor sexual adjustment will destroy it, does not seem to be the usual case. Burgess and Wallin came to the conclusion in their study that "although good sexual adjustment increases the chances of high marital success, poor sexual adjustment by no means precludes it."[1] Terman found that of those he studied, intercourse was almost as frequent in the most unhappily married group as in the happily married group.[2]

It is commonly overlooked that probably very few marriages are always completely satisfying to both partners in every area including that

[1] Ernest Burgess and Paul Wallin, *Engagement and Marriage* (Chicago: J. B. Lippincott Co., 1953), p. 692.

[2] L. M. Terman, *Psychological Factors in Marital Happiness* (New York: McGraw-Hill, 1938), p. 277.

of sex. It may be that the only marriage where the sexual adjustment is always perfect is where the couple have no interest in sex and therefore no sexual activity. But in practically all marriages there are times when one member wants sex and the other doesn't or one partner is bored by the proceedings. As Comfort points out, probably most couples, if they are quite honest, sometimes desire a sexual holiday from one another.[3]

As discussed in Chapter 11, the honeymoon and early stages of marriage are of great importance for developing the paired abilities related to the changing nature of sexual adjustment in marriage. Marriage provides the setting for sexual expression but, as Kirkpatrick points out, marriage has a dual influence on sexual behavior. "On the one hand, a more favorable environment for love is usually provided, with privacy, social approval, freedom from guilt feelings, and a more exclusive direction of erotic responses to the marriage partner. On the other hand, there is some extinction of sex responses with loss of novelty and with intimate association."[4] The initially exciting novelty of sex in marriage may quickly move into the realm of marital routine. If it does, the ability to redefine the sexual situation becomes important for many couples.

The importance of human sexual expression is very great. However, it is inaccurate to equate it with certain other basic human needs. While sexual functioning is a natural physiological process, it does have the unique facility that no other natural physiological process, such as respiratory, bladder, or bowel functions can imitate. "*Sexual responsivity can be delayed indefinitely or functionally denied for a lifetime.* No other basic physiological process can claim such malleability of physical expression."[5]

The Changing Nature of Sexual Adjustment

Sexual adjustment in marriage calls for at least minimum satisfaction for the self and the other in sexual interaction. The sexual-role relationship is less often guided by open verbal communication than are other areas of interaction in marriage. Frequently, each partner may have to try and "read" the sexual desires of the partner. Because of the failure to communicate, one partner may mistakenly believe that the techniques and frequency of marital coitus are satisfactory to the other. Role-relationship efficiency is based on the assumption of symbolic interaction and if it does not exist, the persons may feel a sense of role frustration. Because the sex act and the marriage role are new to the young married

---

[3] Alex Comfort, *Sex in Society* (Great Britain: Penguin Books, 1963), p. 119.

[4] Clifford Kirkpatrick, *The Family* (New York: The Ronald Press Co., 1955), p. 439.

[5] William H. Masters and Virginia E. Johnson, *Human Sexual Inadequacy* (Boston: Little, Brown & Co., 1970), p. 10.

woman, and because taboos against open sex verbalization—even after marriage—still exist, the woman may not be able psychologically to free herself for open communication. The young wife may desire greater frequency of intercourse, different methods of foreplay, or different techniques of sexual expression, but be too inhibited to let her husband know it, either by action or word. As time goes along and the wife's role as a sexual partner becomes more internally a part of her self-concept, many of her inhibitions may be dropped. Over the years, most females become less inhibited and develop an interest in sexual relations which they may then maintain until they are in their 50s or even 60s.[6]

The older woman with a strong interest in sex may be becoming a more common role in American society. Jessie Bernard talks about her as a new subsex—a new kind of woman. "She is the result of cultural forces, technological as well as normative, and of advances in medicine, nutrition, and health care, especially obstetrical."[7] These women are attractive and have strong sexual interests whether they be married or not.

The importance of sexual communication in marriage is stressed by Masters and Johnson. They suggest that "rather than following any preconceived plan for stimulating his sex partner, the male will be infinitely more effective if he encourages vocalization on her part. The individual woman knows best the areas of her strongest sensual focus and the rapidity and intensity of manipulative technique that provides her with the greatest degree of sexual stimulation."[8] The above suggestion helps to get away from the idea that the male, in some intuitive way, is an expert on the female's sexual feelings and desires. Masters and Johnson further point out that the most unfortunate misconception in our society has been to assign to sexual functioning the assumption, held by both men and women, "that men by divine guidance and infallible instinct are able to discern exactly what a woman wants sexually and when she wants it. Probably this fallacy has interfered with natural sexual interaction as much as any other single factor."[9] On the same point, Vincent states that few young men are aware of the complex nature of sexuality because there is no place where they would have learned. This means that to learn more about human sexuality the man must admit there are some things he does not know. However, for many men to admit lack of knowledge and skill in the sexual area is seen by them as questioning

[6] Alfred C. Kinsey et al., *Sexual Behavior in the Human Female* (Philadelphia: W. B. Saunders Co., 1953), p. 353.

[7] Jessie Bernard, *The Future of Marriage* (New York: World Publishing, 1972), p. 262.

[8] William H. Masters and Virginia E. Johnson, *Human Sexual Response* (Boston: Little, Brown & Co., 1966), p. 66.

[9] Masters and Johnson, *Inadequacy*, p. 87.

their masculinity. "The majority of young husbands are 'boxed in' by their childhood indoctrination that masculinity is synonymous with knowing all about sex."[10]

Because of the different sexual needs of males and females, as well as variations for either sex at different times, the achievement of sexual expertise will be the result of the effective interaction between the two individuals, rather than resting only on the skills of the male partner. What often happens is that the man thinks himself an expert and the female is reluctant to point out otherwise. The woman is always faced with the problem of the male wondering how she acquired her knowledge "and arousing his anxiety about her ability to make invidious comparisons. Consequently, the sexual relation is learned by and large through the exchange of cues and gestures rather than through discussion or direct experimentation."[11]

In the discussion that follows reference will be made to a *Marital Sex* study done by the writer and several co-workers. The data to be reported come from a sample of 2,372 married American women. The respondents do not represent a random sample. When compared to married women in general, they are biased in the direction of higher educated, working women who were willing to answer detailed, anonymous questionaires about their sexual values and behavior. The answers should be interpreted as somewhat more liberal than what would be expected for American women in general.

The women in the *Marital Sex* study were asked if they discussed their intimate sexual feelings with their husbands. Overall, 72 percent said they did. However, it was more common for the younger women, with 83 percent of those 30 years of age and younger saying they discussed their sexual feelings with their husbands but only 52 percent of the women past age 50 giving the same answer.[12]

When there is a failure of communication between the husband and wife over sexual matters, that failure may be further reflected in broader areas of marital maladjustment. Masters and Johnson have found that the failure to communicate in the sexual area often extends rapidly to every other phase of the marriage. "When there is no security or mutual representation in sexual exchange, there rarely is freedom of other forms of marital communication."[13]

A majority of young women are probably able to achieve at least some

---

[10] Clark E. Vincent, "Sex and The Young Married," *Medical Aspects of Human Sexuality,* March 1969, p. 17.

[11] John H. Gagnon, "Sexuality and Sexual Learning in the Child," *Psychiatry,* August 1965, p. 214.

[12] Robert R. Bell and Phyllis L. Bell, "Sexual Satisfaction among Married Women," *Medical Aspects of Human Sexuality,* December 1972, p. 136.

[13] Kinsey et al., *Female,* p. 348.

degree of sexual satisfaction early in marriage. Kinsey found that 49 percent of the females in his sample had experienced orgasm in their coitus within the first month of marriage. By the end of the first year, 75 percent had experienced orgasm in at least some of their coitus.[14] Later in marriage, sexual satisfaction decreases for both the male and female. By the time the wife reaches her late 50s, about 65 percent were reaching orgasm.

The frequency of sexual relations in marriage is closely related to age. The average frequency of marital coitus in the Kinsey sample had started at 2.8 per week for the females who were married in their late teens.[15] This coital frequency dropped to 2.2 per week by 30 years of age, to 1.5 per week by 40, to 1.0 per week by 50, and 0.6 per week by age 60.[16]

In the *Marital Sex* study the average number of àcts of coitus per month for women 30 years of age and under was 9.4; ages 31 to 40, 7.4; 41 to 50, 6.1; and past age 50, 4.1.[17] In that study two thirds of the women felt the frequency of intercourse was about right. Frequency also showed a relationship to personal happiness. Of those women who were happy most of the time, 74 percent said the sexual frequency was about right. By contrast, of those women who were unhappy most of the time, 37 percent said the sexual frequency was about right.[18]

The degree of satisfaction with sexual intercourse is also important. One common measurement used is the achievement of orgasm, though this is a measurement of satisfaction with given sexual acts and not a measurement of whether or not the person feels his sexual needs are being satisfied over the long run. In reference to the sexual act itself, the male almost always achieves orgasm but the married female reaches orgasm in only a portion of her coitus; and some percentage of all the females in the Kinsey sample had never reached orgasm at any time, in any of their marital coitus.[19] Of all those women who achieved orgasm in marital coitus, Kinsey estimates the average female in the sample had reached orgasm in something between 70 and 77 percent of her marital coitus.[20]

In the *Marital Sex* study, data was also gathered about orgasm in marriage. Of the total sample 59 percent said they reached orgasm all or most of the time; 32 percent said sometimes or once in a while; and, 9 percent never reached orgasm during coitus. Orgasm success was also related to how the women rated their marriages. Sixty-three percent of the women who rated their marriages as "good" or "very good" achieved

---

[14] Ibid., p. 349.

[15] Ibid., p. 348.

[16] Ibid., p. 349.

[17] Bell and Bell, "Sexual Satisfaction," p. 141.

[18] Ibid., p. 141.

[19] Kinsey et al., *Female*, p. 352.

[20] Ibid., p. 375.

orgasm all or most of the time. But this was true of only 41 percent of those who rated their marriages as "fair," "poor," or "very poor."[21]

It is of interest to note that Kinsey found the higher educated female had a distinctly higher frequency of achieving orgasm in marriage than the lower educated female. Rainwater, in his study, found that 50 percent of the middle-class wives stated a very positive gratification about their sexual relations as compared to 20 percent of the lower-lower-class wives.[22] He also found that 78 percent of the middle-class husbands were "very interested" in marital coitus as compared to only 35 percent of the lower-class husbands.[23] Contributing to the higher educated woman's greater sexual satisfaction is the fact that she is less restricted by fear and ignorance, and that there is also probably more extended foreplay and general sexual sophistication on both her part and the part of her husband.

MALE-FEMALE COMPARISONS

One major theme of this book has been that the rights of women are coming more and more to the forefront, and this is certainly true in the sexual area. This is a sharp break from the past. Mary Jane Sherfey has argued that the rise of modern civilization, while coming from many sources, was dependent on the suppression of the cyclical sex drive of women. She says that if women had remained hypersexual it would have drastically interfered with maternal responsibility. With the rise of agricultural economics man became very involved in property rights and kinship laws. "Large families of known parentage were mandatory and could not evolve until the inordinate sexual demands of women were curbed."[24] Whatever the historical reasons, the sexuality of women is becoming increasingly important in American society.

However, women are influenced in their sexual needs and expression by a variety of factors. One is their view of the sexual nature of men being greater than that of women. One study found that 90 percent of all married women who never had reached orgasm in marital coitus believed that men had stronger sexual drives than women. "The more that women were able to find satisfaction and pleasure in the sexual relationships, the more nearly they regarded their sexual needs and desires as equal to the males."[25] There is also evidence of personality traits being related to

---

[21] Bell and Bell, "Sexual Satisfaction," p. 142.

[22] Lee Rainwater, *Family Design* (Chicago: Aldine Publishing Co., 1965), p. 64.

[23] Ibid., p. 67.

[24] Mary Jane Sherfey, "The Evolution and Nature of Female Sexuality in Relation to Psychoanalytic Theory," *Journal of the American Psychoanalytic Association*, vol. 14 (1966), p. 128.

[25] Eustace Chesser, *Women* (London: Jarrolds, 1958), p. 101.

sexual satisfaction for women. For example, studies show that women with a low capacity for orgasm were less confident and less sure of themselves, "more emotionally unstable and sensitive, and more conformist in their attitudes towards authority and convention."[26]

While there are no comparative data from the past it seems clear that women are becoming more sexually aggressive in marriage. In the *Marital Sex* study the women were asked if they ever initiated sex in marriage. There were significant differences by age. For those married women 30 years of age and younger, only 22 percent said they did so less than 15 percent of the time. But 34 percent of the women ages 31 to 40; 41 percent ages 41 to 50; and, 43 percent past age 50 said they initiated sex in their marriages less than 15 percent of the time.[27] This reflects a reduction in the traditional notion that in marital sex the husband plays the active role and the wife the passive role. These roles are becoming much less linked just to the female or the male.

Because of the differential socialization process, young men and women enter marriage with different attitudes in regard to marital coitus. Burgess and Wallin found that 10 percent of the husbands and 26 percent of the wives entered marriage with sex attitudes of disgust, aversion, or indifference.[28] But what is of greatest importance is that while some sex differences continue, the differences are not great. That 90 percent of the husbands and 74 percent of the wives entered marriage with sex attitudes of interest, anticipation, or eager longing shows the overall high interest for both males and females.

This writer in a study of college-educated wives asked: "Looking back to before you were married, in light of your married experience, how would you assess your estimate at that time as to the importance of sex in marriage?" The responses were 29 percent, "overestimated"; 58 percent, "about what was estimated"; and 13 percent, "underestimated."[29] The fact that three out of ten wives made a downward reassessment of the importance of sex in marriage is of interest. Further, a relationship existed between the assessment of the importance of sex in marriage and the overall evaluation of happiness with marriage. The importance of sex in marriage was about what they had estimated for 67 percent of those who rated their marriage "very happy," as contrasted to only 36 percent of those who rated their marriage happiness as "average" or less.[30]

In the same study, the wives were asked to estimate their own and their husband's feelings about the sexual adjustment of their marriage.

---

[26] Ann Oakley, *Sex, Gender and Society* (Melbourne: Sun Books, 1972), p. 121.

[27] Bell and Bell, "Sexual Satisfaction," p. 140.

[28] Burgess and Wallin, *Engagement and Marriage*, p. 660.

[29] Robert R. Bell, "Some Factors Related to the Sexual Satisfaction of the College Educated Wife," *Family Life Coordinator*, April 1964, p. 44.

[30] Ibid., p. 44.

Seventy-nine percent of the wives rated their sexual adjustment as "very good" or "good" and 78 percent rated their husband's feelings at the same level. Of those women who rated their marriages as "very happy," 95 percent rated their own sexual adjustment and 94 percent their husband's sexual adjustment as "very good" or "good." This is in contrast to 51 and 46 percent ratings of self and husband's sexual adjustment as "very good" or "good" by those women who assessed their marriage as "average" or less.[31] The general sexual satisfaction of the husband and wife, at least as seen by the wife, seems to be the same at different levels of marital happiness.

Experts today generally believe that, no matter how high or low the incidence of intercourse may be, the frequency of sexual relationships is not the question; rather, the question is how the couple define the relationship, and that is a matter of agreement between them. As one writer puts it, "happiness in sexual relationships comes most readily to the couple who have been able to adjust their desires so that approximately the same amount and type of sexual intimacy satisfies both."[32]

Some writers believe that sexual satisfaction can be reached through the will and desire to do so. They base this belief on the assumption that the couple can and will articulate their sexual needs to one another, and act on them. However, if needs are different, an agreement on a sexual relationship may be reached that does not meet the needs of one of the individuals. Too often, the implication of some writers is that simply by reaching agreement the basic sexual needs are changed. This assumption is illustrated by the statement of one writer that "the two share intercourse just as they share dancing, picnics, or music."[33] If the sexual needs of the couple are quite different, they may reach a point of compromise which is workable for their relationship, but which may not meet their individual sexual needs. To say that you will have intercourse less, because your partner wants it less, does not mean that you will no longer continue to wish it were more frequent. Frequency of marital coitus is a more complex and interpersonally meaningful decision than whether to take hard-boiled or deviled eggs on a picnic.

Given the importance of need satisfaction in the sexual nature of marriage, contemporary emphasis on the interests of the woman adds an increasingly important dimension to the problem of sexual adjustment in marriage. One implication of this change is that not only are women increasingly achieving sexual satisfaction, but they are also increasingly conscious of *lack of achievement*. An implied assumption has been that once restrictions on marital sex are removed, the wife will catch up to the

---

[31] Ibid., p. 44.

[32] Ruth S. Cavan, *The American Family* (New York: Appleton-Century-Crofts, Inc., 1957), p. 261.

[33] Ibid., p. 261.

husband in sexual desire and will then be his sexual equal. What generally has not been recognized is that some women may pass their husbands in sexual interest. In the writer's study, when the wives were asked to assess the frequency of sexual relations in their marriages, 25 percent said that it was "too infrequent."[34] One out of four wives was saying that for a variety of reasons, there was not enough coitus in her marriage to satisfy her. This is a recent and generally unanticipated sexual response for wives.

As more and more restrictions are removed from the woman and she is encouraged to achieve sexual satisfaction, it seems logical that the change in her sexual desires will include the desire for greater frequency of sexual intercourse. Theoretically, the woman's ability to indulge in sexual intercourse is not biologically restricted. In other words, she continues to be sexually limited by social and psychological influences, but as these are altered or removed, the biological restrictions remain few. It is suggested that through the loss or modification of inhibiting values, women are moving in a less inhibited direction. If this be true, then the biological differences between the male and female in regard to sexual frequency become of increasing significance. In illustration of male-female differences, "actively masturbating women controlling their own sexual response levels will experience five to twenty recurrent orgasmic experiences with sexual tension never allowed to drop below a plateau phase maintenance level until physical exhaustion terminates the session."[35]

Thus, a number of married couples may find themselves in a situation where the sexual interests of the wife have increased past those of the husband. But because of the biological limitations on the man, he, unlike the woman, cannot normally, without some interest, function as a sex partner. While this difference is probably not an important problem early in marriage, it may become one as the couple grow older, with the sexual interest of the woman often increasing and many of her early inhibitions removed. As the male grows older, his sexual drive—as well as, in some cases, his sexual interests—are often decreasing. Thus, the older wife may desire more frequent coitus, while her husband is neither physically nor psychologically capable of satisfying her need. This can be extremely important to the male who makes a close association between his sexual potency and his sense of masculinity.

A somewhat extreme case will illustrate the implications of this situation for the male. Suppose that the wife for some reason hates her husband and wants to hurt him. She could do this sexually by insisting on intercourse until he is no longer able to have an erection, and then accusing him of not being a man. It is the male who must always quit; no

---

[34] Bell, "College Educated Wife," p. 45.
[35] Masters and Johnson, *Response,* p. 109.

equivalent of erection is required for the woman to indulge in sexual intercourse.

In the future, the number of marital sexual problems involving a lack of satisfaction for the woman may possibly increase. While this would be an ironic switch from the past, the results may be far more serious for the inadequate or uninterested male than they were for the restricted female.

Noncoital Sex. The discussion thus far has been on coitus in marriage. This is because sex in marriage is almost always equated with coitus between wife and husband. Yet, there are other sexual activities or methods that may be used. Often those other activities are seen as foreplay which will end in coitus, but they sometimes become sexual ends in themselves. However, marital coitus in the traditional view is the only really acceptable sexual outlet for "mature, adult" couples. The other types of sexual behavior have often been labeled as immature and generally not worthy of major interest and participation.

Sexual intercourse for the woman has a basic dependency on the sexual satisfaction of the male. That is, he must be able to sexually perform for the woman to achieve sexual satisfaction through coitus. In the past the man was almost always assumed to be ready and able, and rarely was the question raised as to the sexual needs of the woman. As long as the female's sexual satisfaction is determined by the ability of the male to maintain an erection she is limited. This was true so long as it was assumed that the only way women could achieve sexual satisfaction was through vaginal penetration by the penis. As Anne Koedt has pointed out, the establishment of the clitoral orgasm threatened the heterosexual institution. It meant that female sexual pleasure was obtainable from men, women, or by one's self. Within this context heterosexual coitus is not an absolute but rather an option.[36] As long as the female's sexual satisfaction is determined by the ability of the male to maintain active coitus beyond a few moments many women turn to means other than coitus to meet their sexual needs.

Oral-Genital Sex. Traditionally the attitudes toward this type of sexual outlet have been negative. For many the idea of oral-genital sex has been repulsive. This appears to have been based on two beliefs. One, that the sex organs in some manner are physically dirty and therefore those acts are hygienically repulsive. Second, the belief that there is something perverted in the activity because it is associated with homosexuality. In fact, some will even define oral-genital sex as homosexual even when it takes place between a man and a woman. However, it is clear that many couples engage in what they see as sexually pleasurable and do not worry much about the legal or moral taboos.

---

[36] Ann Koedt, "The Myth of the Vaginal Orgasm, *Women's Liberation,* 1970, p. 166.

Kinsey, in his study of the female, treated oral-genital sex as a pre-coital technique and did not discuss it as a sexual end in itself. However, in recent years more and more people have found oral-genital sex to be a highly satisfying sexual end in itself. The *Marital Sex* study shows that oral-genital sex is important as a means to an end and as an end in itself.

The women in the *Marital Sex* study were asked: "Has your husband ever performed oral-genital sex on you?" The responses were: never, 20 percent; once-in-awhile, 49 percent; and often, 31 percent.[37] (The rates were almost exactly the same for the wife performing oral-genital sex on her husband.) Kinsey, in his sample, found that a little more than half (54 percent) of the women had had oral-genital stimulation of their genitalia by the male.[38] Though Kinsey doesn't give any indication of how often that happened, it seems clear that women in the *Marital Sex* study represent a definite increase in this area of sexual activity compared to those women he studied.

In the *Marital Sex* study it was striking that only 13 percent of the women 30 years of age and under said they *never* had oral sex performed on them. It is reasonable to assume that some of those 13 percent will experience it in the future, thus lowering the rate even further. By con-trast, 43 percent of the women over age 50 said they never had oral sex. Given their age, it is doubtful that many of them are yet to have the experience for the first time.[39]

Masturbation. This is generally ignored as a sexual outlet for the married. There is a tendency to think of masturbation as childhood and adolescent behavior and something that adults, and certainly those who are married, do not do. The general view exists that masturbation is somehow inappropriate for the adult. Masturbation is also often seen as something men do, but generally not women.

The women in the *Marital Sex* study were asked: "Have you ever masturbated since your marriage?" Nine percent of the women answered, "often"; 50 percent, "once in awhile"; and 41 percent, "never." The woman under age 25 has the highest rate of never masturbating, but past that age there were no significant age differences.[40]

Kinsey discovered a relationship between education and masturbation. He found that the accumulative incidences at age 40 ranged from 34 per-cent among those who had never gone beyond grade school to 63 percent among females who had gone beyond college into graduate work.[41] The *Marital Sex* study found that of those women with a high-school educa-

---

[37] Robert R. Bell and Janet Connolly, "Non-coital Sex in Marriage," (Toronto: National Council on Family Relations, October 1973), p. 4.

[38] Kinsey et al., *Female,* p. 361.

[39] Bell and Connolly, "Non-coital Sex," pp. 4–5.

[40] Ibid., p. 12.

[41] Kinsey et al., *Female,* p. 148.

tion or less, 49 percent had never masturbated in marriage but this was true of 31 percent of the women who had some graduate education. Masturbation was also most common among those women with no religious attendance. One third of the women with no church attendance had never masturbated since marriage, but this was true for over half of the women with five or more church visits a month.[42]

The respondents in the *Marital Sex* study were also asked: "If you did masturbate did you find the experience sexually satisfying?" Three fourths of the women answered "yes." The main reason for the high level of satisfaction was that masturbation was a very efficient way of achieving orgasm.[43]

There are two other techniques of noncoital sex that might be used by married women. One is homosexual contacts which only 4 percent of the women in the *Marital Sex* study had experienced since they were 18 years of age;[44] and two, anal intercourse with their husbands was another possibility. To that activity only one percent said they did it often; 23 percent, once-in-awhile; and 76 percent, never.[45] It did not appear to be a sexual activity at all popular among the married women in that study.

SEXUAL PROBLEMS IN MARRIAGE

The nature of the problems related to both personal and paired sexual satisfaction in marriage are complex, because in varying degrees they are causally related to biological, psychological, and social influences. The discussion that follows focuses on several important sexual problem areas in marriage.

Masters and Johnson, in their new book on sexual inadequacy, take as a major point of approach that sexual dysfunction is a marital problem and never *only* a wife's or only a husband's concern.[46] Another major theme in their dealing with sexual problems is the overwhelming importance of fear. That is, fear of inadequacy is "the greatest known deterrent to effective sexual functioning, simply because it so completely distracts the fearful individual from his or her natural responsibility by blocking reception of sexual stimuli either created by or reflected from the sexual partner."[47]

Frigidity

Generally, frigidity is defined as the failure of the woman to be sexually aroused or to reach orgasm in sexual relations. The definition implies

---

[42] Bell and Connolly, "Non-coital Sex," p. 12.

[43] Ibid., p. 12.

[44] Ibid., p. 9.

[45] Ibid., p. 7.

[46] Masters and Johnson, *Inadequacy*, p. 3.

[47] Ibid., pp. 12–13.

several possible dimensions. One indicates an incapacity to function sexually, which is sometimes attributed to biological causes. But most of the evidence today indicates that the causes of frigidity are primarily psychological, rather than physical. Masters and Johnson found that for most women who have failed to reach orgasm it was due to the repressed expression of their sexual identity because of ignorance, fear, or authoritarian direction. These kinds of influences led to the initial inhibiting failure of their sexual functioning.[48] The authoritarian influence was reflected in the fact that of 193 women who had never achieved orgasm 41 were products of rigidly religious backgrounds. Eighteen were from Catholic, 16 from Jewish, and 7 from fundamentalist Protestant backgrounds.[49]

So the causes of frigidity may be due to negative socialization to sex, or may be a result of the female's feelings for her sex partner. For example, some women become frigid if they develop a dislike for their husbands; for them the necessary condition of love has been destroyed. For many women one of the most frequent causes of orgasm failure is a lack of complete identification with their marital partner. "The husband may not meet her expectations as a provider. He may have physical or behavior patterns that antagonize. Most important, he may stand in place of the man who had been much preferred as a marital partner but was not available or did not choose to marry the distressed woman."[50]

Many women may have problems of sexual satisfaction although they are not frigid. Very often their feelings about sex are closely linked to their feelings towards their husbands. In general women who have mutual love and respect in their relationships with their husbands tend to be fairly high on sexual response and become more so with increased coital experience. "Women whose marriages are persistently negative in quality tend to remain relatively low on responsiveness."[51]

In most instances frigidity seems to have been caused by guilt and shame which have been inculcated in the frigid woman early in her life and which she has been unconsciously reiterating to herself for many years. The frequency of frigidity is difficult to estimate. In the Kinsey study of the female, it was found that ultimately 10 percent of the wives never achieved orgasm in marital coitus.[52] However, the failure to achieve orgasm does not necessarily mean that the woman is frigid; some women may achieve sexual satisfaction in marriage without orgasm. They may find the act pleasurable to themselves and their husbands because of

---

[48] Ibid., p. 223.

[49] Ibid., p. 230.

[50] Ibid., p. 235.

[51] Alexander L. Clark and Paul Wallin, "Women's Sexual Responsiveness and the Duration and Quality of Their Marriages," *American Journal of Sociology*, September 1965, p. 189.

[52] Kinsey et al., *Female*, p. 392.

psychological satisfactions. The woman who honestly defines her sexual activity as satisfactory, with or without orgasm, has from her point of view achieved sexual satisfaction. In some cases, she may feel some sense of sexual frustration but still perform the sexual act so that her husband believes she is achieving complete satisfaction. The husband will rarely do this.

Impotency

As a sexual problem, impotency for the man is quite different from frigidity in the woman. The most common type of impotency is *erectal* impotence, which means the inability to have an erection sufficient for sexual intercourse. A second type, called *ejaculatory* impotence, is the incapacity to ejaculate even when aroused and in erection. This second type is very rare; Kinsey and his associates found it in only 6 out of 4,108 males they studied.[53]

The Kinsey study found that impotency in the male was less common than many experts have believed. "There is a rare male never able to have intercourse for anatomical or physiological reasons." Kinsey found erectal impotence in less than 1 percent of the males under 35 years of age, and of this group only a small number had lifelong impotency.[54] Impotency increases as the male ages, but not at a rapid rate; of males 70 years of age, only 27 percent have become totally impotent.[55]

There are some social variables that are related to the occurrence of impotency in men. One frequent factor in the onset of impotence is related to the incidence of acute ingestion of alcohol or to a pattern of excessive alcohol use.[56] Another variable, as with the woman and frigidity, is the influence of religious orthodoxy. After clinical treatment, Masters and Johnson report there was a 67 percent immediate failure to reverse symptoms of primarily impotent men, "and a 50 percent failure to reverse symptoms of secondary impotent men influenced by religious orthodoxy."[57]

Impotency for the male has generally far more important implications than frigidity for the female. The impotent male cannot usually indulge in sexual relations, while the frigid female can, and sexual potency is usually more closely linked to masculinity than sexual desire in the woman is to femininity. As suggested earlier, a decrease in the husband's sexual interest and ability may have implications for the wife with strong sexual interests and unrestricted ability.

---

[53] Ibid., p. 237.
[54] Ibid., p. 237.
[55] Ibid., p. 237.
[56] Masters and Johnson, *Inadequacy*, p. 160.
[57] Ibid., p. 213.

Adultery

In the United States, the stated attitudes and values are that sexual outlet after marriage will be restricted to the marriage partner. In the past, the male might discreetly indulge in sexual relations outside of his marriage. Sometimes he was expected to, because of sexual needs that could not be met by the good, nonsexual woman he married. But only under rare circumstances was the wife expected to have a sexual outlet outside of marriage. The traditional double-standard attitudes have changed to the extent that both partners are expected to restrict their sex needs to marriage and any extramarital "rights" of the husband are not much greater than those of the wife.

Anthropologists find that in some societies, a need is recognized for some extramarital coitus for the male. Generally, this permission is given to relieve for him the pressures of society's insistence on stable marital partnerships. These same societies, however, less often permit it for the female.[58] Some primitive societies reflect the same patriarchal distinctions of sexual outlet for the husband and wife as did the American society of the past. But there have been some societies where adultery for the female was an accepted pattern of sexual behavior and did not result in any undue conflict.

As suggested, when one actually examines the many cultures, past and present, it is seen that the taboos against extramarital involvement are widespread—although sometimes more honored in the breach than in actual practice. Murdock found in his sample of 148 societies that taboos against adultery appeared in 120 (81 percent). "In 4 of the remaining 28, adultery is socially disapproved though it is not strictly forbidden; it is conditionally permitted in 19 and freely allowed in 5. It should be pointed out, however, that these figures apply only to sexual relations with unrelated or distantly related persons. A substantial majority of all societies permit extramarital relations with certain affinal relatives."[59]

Many societies reflect a double standard with regard to extramarital rights. Ford and Beach in their study of various societies found that 60 percent of them forbid a married woman to engage in extramarital relationships. They point out that in some societies the married man is also restricted, although most societies are much more concerned with the behavior of the wife. Yet, in those societies, very often any man who seduces a married woman will be punished.[60] They go on to point out that "although in theory many societies accept a double standard of restric-

---

[58] Kinsey, *Female*, p. 413.

[59] George P. Murdock, *Social Structure* (New York: Macmillan Company, 1949), p. 265.

[60] Clellan S. Ford and Frank A. Beach, *Patterns of Sexual Behavior* (New York: Harper and Bros., 1952), p. 115.

tions on extramarital liaisons, it is only in a few cases that the mated man can take advantage of his theoretical liberties."[61]

When it is seen that in most societies women have fewer opportunities for extramarital sex and even where the opportunity exists they have lower incidences and frequencies, it must be recognized that this is due to cultural differences rather than biological ones. That is, the evidence clearly indicates that if women are given the opportunity without strong social and psychological restrictions, many find extramarital sexual involvement attractive and enjoyable. As Harper points out, in those countries where strong progress has been made toward social equality of the sexes, "such evidence as exists indicates increased incidences among married women of extramarital sex behavior that approximates the male pattern."[62] This appears to be a pattern of an increasing number of American women—especially among the higher educated.

Compared to many other societies, the United States takes a strong position against adultery. Hunt points out that various American studies suggest that roughly 80 percent of American women do not expect or intend to seek extramarital relations, "while 36 percent of a sample of French and Belgian women—though not asked exactly the same question —said that a wife's fidelity is unimportant to the marriage, and another 37 percent termed it desirable but not necessary."[63] Christensen, in comparing the responses of a midwestern American sample with one from Denmark, found several important differences. He found that 41 percent of the Danish males and 36 percent of the females indicated approval of sexual infidelity if the need arose during a long absence from the spouse. Approval was stated by only 12 percent of the American males and 5 percent of the females.[64] Christensen also asked for reactions to infidelity if one was in love with another married person. Approval for sexual relations under this condition was stated by 27 percent of the males and 29 percent of the females in the Danish sample, but only 7 percent of the males and 2 percent of the females in the midwest American sample.[65]

Adultery is used here to refer to sexual intercourse with a partner outside the marriage. Adultery is legally punishable in the United States, but actual prosecution is rare. Adultery has its greatest legal importance as

---

[61] Ibid., p. 115.

[62] Robert A. Harper, "Extramarital Sex Relations in Albert Ellis and Albert Abarbanel, *Encyclopedia of Sexual Behavior* (New York: Hawthorne Books, Inc., 1961), p. 386.

[63] Morton M. Hunt, *Her Infinite Variety* (New York: Harper and Row, 1962), p. 127.

[64] Harold T. Christensen, "A Cross-Cultural Comparison of Attitudes Toward Marital Infidelity," *International Journal of Comparative Sociology*, September 1962, p. 130.

[65] Ibid., p. 130.

grounds for divorce. The traditional taboos against adultery are reflected in the fact that adultery is the only legal ground for divorce recognized by all legal jurisdictions in the United States.

The attitude in this country is that, after marriage, one will want to concentrate his sexual drive exclusively on the marriage partner. Implied in discussions of marital sexual adjustment is that the adjustment is between the two married individuals. Rarely is it argued that a married couple might turn to other partners to achieve sexual adjustment, or that, if the needs are different, one might use masturbation, or manual or oral means of achieving a greater sexual outlet without the partner's outlet also increasing. The fact that these possibilities are rarely seriously presented indicates the great influence the legal, religious, and moral values of monogamous coitus have in the United States.

Monogamous sexual values are further implemented by the personalized attitudes that individuals have in regard to sex. The female is generally conditioned to believe that love is a precondition for sexual behavior. If a woman is in love, she gets married if at all possible, and then the relationships of marriage, love, and sexual outlet are usually seen by her as inseparable. The male often views his wife as his exclusive sexual property; any tampering with her is viewed as a severe threat to that which he feels very possessive about. And for both partners, the exclusive, ego-centered nature of the love relationship implies the spouse is not interested in any other age-peer of the opposite sex in any romantic or sexual way. If one shows a romantic or sexual interest in someone else, this may be viewed as catastrophic to the ego-relationship of marriage. But even in this area, male and female differences continue. Many men feel that adultery on the part of the woman is an irreparable blow to their marriage. Women are less inclined to see male adultery in the same extreme way. The husband who has what is seen by the wife as a single sexual encounter may be forgiven; however, if he has an affair of some length, the wife is much more threatened because, to her, a lengthy affair implies that her husband must care about the other woman—thus, the "other" woman becomes an emotional threat.

Yet one often gets the impression through the mass media that adultery is very common to the American middle class. Hunt suggests that, if one accepts the view of mass media, "the major reason for the prevalence of adultery is that it no longer poses moral problems to women, but only tactical ones—the choice of how and when, and the avoidance of detection."[66] But adultery is certainly not common to the vast majority of American middle-class women. "She does not view sexual straying as one of her rights, nor adulterous love as a pleasure she deserves to enjoy in

---

[66] Hunt, *Variety*, p. 118.

addition to those of her married life. In our society adultery does not coexist with marriage, but combats it; the affair rarely achieves balance and equilibrium, but nearly always is a cause of change and upheaval which ends in its own termination or in marriage."[67]

The stated attitudes against extramarital coitus are extremely strong; yet the behavior patterns indicate that a number of individuals deviate from the norms. The extent to which behavior deviates from the stated values indicates the weakness of the values in effectively influencing behavior. The deviancy also raises questions about the total acceptance of monogamy, with exclusive and total sexual satisfaction being achieved through the marital partner.

As suggested, one element of marital sex is the extent to which the partner serves as the exclusive sexual outlet. While it is almost always believed that the total sexual outlet of the married person will be achieved through the marriage partner, many realize that some seek out other sex partners. However, some who do not use the marriage partner as the total sexual outlet do not find other partners. Kinsey estimated that, in the married population studied, the woman achieved about 10 percent of her total sexual outlet through masturbation, and the man 4 to 6 percent.[68] He further estimated that about 89 percent of the married woman's total sexual outlet was with her husband and 81 percent of the husband's with his wife.[69]

When the Kinsey study on the female was first published, several statistics startled the American public, including those on extramarital coitus. Kinsey found in his sample that by age 40, 26 percent of the married women and 50 percent of the married men had had an extramarital coital experience.[70] In the *Marital Sex* study it was also found that 26 percent of the women had extramarital coitus. However, the average age of the women in that sample was 34.5 years, somewhat younger than the women in the Kinsey study. So a projection of a few years to equalize the age variable makes it likely that this extramarital rate will be higher than Kinsey's. In the *Marital Sex* study, the differences by ages of the women clearly point to this suggestion. Seventeen percent of the women 25 years of age and younger had had an extramarital coital experience. This was true of 34 percent of the women between the ages of 26 and 30, 29 percent between the ages of 31 and 50, and 16 percent of those past age 50. The key age group may be that of 26 to 30; and as they move to age 40 their rate will continue to increase, as will the 25-year-old-and-younger group coming behind them. Ultimately the rate of extramarital

---

[67] Ibid., p. 119.
[68] Kinsey et al., *Female*, p. 173.
[69] Ibid., p. 393.
[70] Ibid., p. 416.

coitus for women 30 years of age and under may be somewhere between 40 and 50 percent.[71]

Kinsey found that 41 percent of the women he studied had limited their extramarital coitus to one partner. Another 40 percent had contacts with two to five partners, and 19 percent had had more than five partners. The rates for the 2,372 married women in[72] the *Marital Sex* study were almost the same. Coitus with one extramarital partner, 42 percent; 2 to 4 partners, 41 percent; and five or more partners, 17 percent. There were a few women in the study who had extramarital experiences with a large number of men. For example, 10 women had more than 30 partners, and three of those had more than 100 different partners.[73]

One striking finding in the *Marital Sex* study was that extramarital sex *as a single event was not the common pattern.* The average number of times a woman had sexual relations with each extramarital partner was almost six times. Only 16 percent of the women had limited themselves to one sexual experience. By contrast, one third had extramarital coitus more than ten times with each partner. Therefore, extramarital coitus was not usually an isolated event but clearly implied a willingness to maintain a series of experiences with the sexual partner.[74] Extramarital coitus frequently implied a conscious planning, and this fits the pattern of greater sexual aggressiveness for women.

One should not underestimate the great importance of love to sexual involvement for most women. This was discussed in some detail with regard to premarital sexual attitudes and behavior, and the variable of emotional feeling is important to all female sexual relationships, including the homosexual. For example, one study found that "the majority of female jail house turnouts have genuine love affairs with their sexual partners, and have repeated contact with the same person."[75] A second study found that the woman who "terminates affairs too quickly is held in scorn by the inmates, as her behavior is held to be promiscuous. This behavior draws forth words of scorn from the inmates because the ideal cultural pattern in the prison is to establish a permanent relationship."[76]

For the female, the Kinsey studies found no overall relationship between frequency of extramarital coitus and educational level, but for the male, the rates were higher in the less educated.[77] By religion for women,

---

[71] Robert R. Bell and Dorthyann Peltz, "Extramarital Sex," *Medical Aspects of Human Sexuality,* March, 1974, pp. 32–36.

[72] Kinsey et al., *Female,* p. 425.

[73] Bell and Peltz, "Extramarital Sex,"

[74] Ibid., p.

[75] David A. Ward and Gene G. Kassebaum, *Women's Prison* (Chicago: Aldine Publishing Co., 1965), p. 193.

[76] Rose Giallombardo, "Social Roles in a Prison for Women," *Social Problems,* Winter 1966, p. 284.

[77] Kinsey et al., *Female,* p. 437.

the active incidence of extramarital experience was highest among the less devout and was true of all the Protestants, Jews, and Catholics in the sample. The same general relationship to devoutness of religion was also found for the male.[78]

As pointed out earlier, Kinsey also found a relationship between premarital and extramarital coitus for the female. For example, by age 40, 20 percent of the females without premarital coitus and 39 percent with premarital coitus had experienced extramarital coitus.[79] Of those women in the *Marital Sex* study with premarital coitus, 31 percent had had extramarital coitus; but this was true of only 15 percent of those without premarital coitus. These findings suggest a pattern of greater sexual liberality, and chronologically it would indicate that if a woman has premarital coitus, her future has a greater probability of being sexually liberal than is true for the woman with no premarital sexual experience.[80]

Kinsey found that in the available sample, about 85 percent of all those females engaging in extramarital activity were responding at least on occasion to orgasm. However, as Kinsey points out, selective factors may have been involved, and the more responsive females may have been the ones who had most often engaged in extramarital coitus.[81] Of greater importance than the women's physical response to extramarital coitus— given the strong social taboos against it—are their psychological reactions. If the norm and values of society were fully accepted and incorporated into the personality structure of the individual, then one might expect strong feelings of remorse and guilt by the adulterous females. Kinsey found that "among the married females in the sample who had not had extramarital experience, some 83 percent indicated that they did not intend to have it, but in a sample of those who had extramarital experiences, only 44 percent indicated that they did not intend to renew their experiences."[82] These findings indicate that a number of women did not have strong enough feelings about their past experiences to be deterred from future experiences.

Given the traditional importance attached to the husband's exclusive sexual rights to his wife, it might be assumed that a husband who found his wife guilty of adultery would either end or drastically alter the nature of the marriage. But Kinsey found that of the females who had extramarital coitus, about 49 percent believed that the husband knew or suspected. And in those marriages where the husband suspected or learned of the wife's extramarital activities, 42 percent of the women

---

[78] Ibid., pp. 424, 437.

[79] Ibid., p. 427.

[80] Bell and Peltz, "Extramarital Sex," p. 35.

[81] Ibid., p. 418.

[82] Ibid., p. 431.

stated they had no difficulty.[83] While some of the women may have been reading their husbands' reactions in a distorted way, it is also possible that many were not. If they were not, it indicates a very drastic change for at least some husbands from the traditional notion of the wife's sexual exclusiveness. Certainly the feeling of jealousy would be common to the spouse who finds that his partner has been engaging in adultery. But as Stephens points out, in some societies that allow adultery, "the jealousy problem still exists; some people are still hurt when their spouses engage in perfectly proper and virtuous adultery."[84]

Realizing the limitations of the Kinsey studies, they nevertheless offer important suggestions about the changing nature of adultery and the influence of traditional attitudes in the United States today. It seems clear that a significant number of both husbands and wives seek and find sexual partners outside of marriage. It also seems clear that this cannot be attributed in all cases to a series of chance circumstances, especially in the case of the woman who has more than one partner and plans on continuing her extramarital coitus experience in the future. While no stated changes in the attitudes toward extramarital coitus have been made, it is obvious that the old norms no longer exert effective control over a number of husbands and wives. Most significant is the indicated behavioral change in the sexual experience of wives; the philandering of husbands has generally had latent acceptance, but the philandering of wives has not, past or present.

The increase in extramarital coitus is no doubt due to many factors. A brief discussion of a number of variables that may enter into extramarital coitus follows. It should be recognized that, for any given individual, the suggested variables may operate in various combinations with various degrees of intensity.[85]

1. *Variation of sexual experience.* As suggested earlier, the monogamous sexual relationship of man and woman is culturally conditioned, and the conditioning may not be as strong for some individuals as for others. In some cases, the sexual relationship of marriage becomes routinized and boring and the idea of a new partner suggests the different, new, and exciting. In others, the person may feel his marriage partner is inadequate in meeting his sexual needs and, consequently, may seek out a person believed to be a superior sexual partner. The basic motivation may be the desire for new experience.

2. *Retaliation.* If one person in the marriage discovers that his partner has had an extramarital affair, his reaction may be, "If he can, so can

---

[83] Ibid., p. 434.

[84] William N. Stephens, *The Family in Cross-Cultural Perspective* (New York: Holt, Rinehart & Winston, Inc., 1963), p. 252.

[85] Ibid., pp. 432–35. The following list of variables is in part drawn from those compiled by Kinsey and his associates.

I." The motivation is not one of sexual desire for another partner, but of revenge. An affair by the husband of a woman who believes in sexual equality may be interpreted by her as something she too must have to show her sexual equality. In these situations, getting even is a greater factor than sexual interest.

3. *Rebellion.* Some may feel the monogamous nature of marriage is placing an undesired restriction on them and, through extramarital coitus, show their independence. The rebellion may be directed at the spouse, whom they feel restricts them, or against social codes. Some who may feel that the social norms are unreasonable show their objection and contempt by entering a sexual liaison. Here, too, the motivating factor is not the extramarital sex partner, but "showing" the spouse or society in general.

4. *New emotional satisfaction.* Many individuals obviously do not feel their personal ego-needs are being met in the marriage relationship. This may lead some to seek satisfaction from a partner outside the marriage. If the wife feels that the extramarital partner is satisfying her emotional needs, sex often enters the picture. It may also enter as a result of the man meeting other needs she has. The primary motivation here is the search for emotional and/or sexual needs outside of the marriage relationship.

5. *Development from friendship.* It has been suggested that one reason why cross-sexual friendships among adults are very difficult is the possibility of their moving into romantic or sexual intimacy. In some cases, the man and woman may be friends, and if they spend time together, they may find themselves developing an emotional and sexual interest in each other. Here the motivations may not all be conscious and are possibly related to increased interest and feeling for the person, which ultimately includes sex.

6. *Spouse encouragement.* In some cases in the Kinsey sample, the husbands had encouraged their wives to engage in extramarital activities. The motive of a number of husbands originated with their desire to find an excuse for their own extramarital activity.[86] What is sometimes referred to as "wife swapping" usually involves this kind of situation. Kinsey found that "most of the husbands who accepted or encouraged their wives' extramarital activity had done so in an honest attempt to give them the opportunity for additional sexual satisfaction."[87]

7. *The aging factor.* As mentioned earlier, the highest rate of extramarital coitus for women occurs in the age group 36 to 40. Several factors may operate for women in this age group. First, their sexual desires and interests are high as a result of a strong sex drive and the loss of many

---

[86] Ibid., p. 435.
[87] Ibid., p. 435.

sexual inhibitions that operated when they were younger. At the same time, many of their husbands have had a decrease in sexual drive and interest. Second, the woman is entering middle age and leaving her youth behind. She may want to prove to herself (and sometimes others) that she is still a desirable female; extramarital affairs may be seen as one way of doing so.

8. *Hedonism.* One final category centers around the fact that while sex is usually highly enjoyable, most people will often forego the pleasure because of various types of social conditioning. If the moral restrictions are not meaningful for the individual, then the individual may take an amoral, hedonistic view toward sex. So some people may have extramarital sexual intimacy simply because new sexual relationships are pleasurable and they do so with no negative consequences. Of course, in this day and age of belief in deep-seated and hidden motives (many of which are never empirically proven), a simple hedonistic approach to extramarital sex is denied. Yet we would suggest that some people enter "illicit" sexual activity not to prove a thing—but simply because sex is pleasurable and they are not subject to many of the usual social restrictions.

When adultery does occur, whatever the reasons, it tends to be of short duration, because the sexual act is not usually treated separately from the general values of love and interpersonal commitment by the woman. Hunt writes that "the adulteress in America generally makes a rather poor mistress, even when she is sexually responsive and suitably flattering to a man's ego, because she wants too much of her lover—she wants him to be her mainstay in life, her be-all and end-all, and, inevitably, her legal mate. It is enough to frighten any sensible philanderer away."[88]

Implied in the discussion thus far is that extramarital sex may follow many different patterns. One writer has suggested that today the two extremes are the new open and accepted affair and the old secret and guilt-ridden one.[89] The variation as well as the changing pattern of extramarital sex is reflected in what they are called. Not too many years ago it was *cheating*, but now it's an *affair*. In fact, it is increasingly getting to be that only the lower-middle and lower class call it *cheating*. "In fact, adultery is getting to sound old fashioned and almost quaint."[90]

One type of extramarital sexual involvement that has always existed but has changed a great deal in recent years is the mistress relationship to the married man. This is an intimate relationship that involves far more than sex. It usually lasts for some period of time and there are generally no real expectations that marriage will ever occur. By contrast, an "affair"

---

[88] Hunt, *Variety*, p. 139.

[89] Nancy Love, "The '70's Woman and the Now Marriage," *Philadelphia Magazine*, February 1970, p. 56.

[90] Ibid., p. 56.

is much more sexually oriented and has much less interpersonal commitment between the two individuals. Cuber has described the mistress relationship in some detail. He found that the mistress was just as apt to be married as unmarried. When two married people move into a mistress relationship, it is usually because they feel their respective marriages are lacking in interpersonal or sexual fulfillment. "However, for one reason or another they do not wish to terminate their marriages legally and so find their fulfillment in what is really a *de facto* marriage, without any legal or moral sanction by the community."[91]

Cuber found no simple configuration of attitudes and life style which distinguished the wife from the mistress. Just as with a wife, a mistress may fit a wide variety of attitudes, life styles, fulfillments, and frustrations. Also, the importance of sex to the mistress relationship can be overdone. "Some mistresses are primarily intellectual companions, women who share some intellectual pursuit with their men, some important hobby, some political or ethical commitment in a way which neither has had or is not able to have with anyone else."[92] He goes on to point out that the stereotype of the young mistress and the aging man does not fit the fact. In fact, he found that a number of men even in their later middle ages had mistresses who were about the same age. Cuber suggests that perhaps the most startling finding of his study was that a considerable number of the mistress relationships endured for long periods of time.[93]

As suggested, in Cuber's discussion of the "mistress" affair sex may not always be important and in some cases may not occur. There may be some nonsexual affairs that are based upon fairly strong emotional attachments. In fact, an emotional attachment that is nonsexual may be a far greater threat to a marriage than a brief sexual nonemotional affair.

Many other variables are related to extramarital coitus, but the ones suggested point out some of the ways in which this kind of behavior may be influenced. When we relate our discussion of extramarital sexual behavior to premarital sexual behavior, it becomes clear that the stated attitudes and actual behavior are often in conflict in today's American society. More important, it indicates to the social scientist that the attitudes are not effective deterrents of nonmarital coitus and are not incorporated by a number of individuals to the extent that their violation leads to any great guilt or remorse. The question of whether individuals "really" feel guilt is a problem for the psychiatrist to study. The lack of agreement between the moral sexual norms and the sexual behavior of many individuals points up the "schizoid" nature of sex in America.

---

[91] John F. Cuber, "The Mistress in American Society," *Medical Aspects of Human Sexuality,* September 1969, p. 86.

[92] Ibid., pp. 85–86.

[93] Ibid., p. 87.

SELECTED BIBLIOGRAPHY

Bell, Robert R., and **Bell, Phyllis L.** "Sexual Satisfaction among Married Women." *Medical Aspects of Human Sexuality,* December 1972, pp. 136–45.

Bell, Robert R., and **Connolly, Janet** "Non-coital Sex in Marriage." Toronto: *National Council on Family Relations,* October 1973.

Bell, Robert R., and **Peltz, Dorthyann** "Extramarital Sex." *Medical Aspects of Human Sexuality,* March, 1974, pp. 32–36.

Christensen, Harold T. "A Cross-Cultural Comparison of Attitudes Toward Marital Infidelity." *International Journal of Comparative Sociology,* September 1962, pp. 124–37.

Christenson, Cornelia, and **Gagnon, John H.** "Sexual Behavior in a Group of Older Women." *Journal of Gerontology,* July 1965, p. 352.

Cuber, John F. "The Mistress in American Society." *Medical Aspects of Human Sexuality,* September 1969, pp. 81–91.

Dentler, Robert A., and **Pineo, Peter** "Sexual Adjustment, Marital Adjustment and Personal Growth of Husbands: A Panel Analysis." *Marriage and Family Living,* February 1960, pp. 45–48.

Masters, William H., and **Johnson, Virginia E.** *Human Sexual Response.* Boston: Little, Brown & Co., 1966.

Masters, William H., and **Johnson, Virginia E.** *Human Sexual Inadequacy.* Boston: Little, Brown & Co., 1970.

Oakley, Ann *Sex, Gender, and Society.* Melbourne: Son Books, 1972.

Sherfey, Mary Jane "The Evolution and Nature of Female Sexuality in Relation to Psychoanalytic Theory." *Journal of the American Psychoanalytic Association,* vol. 14 (1966), pp. 1–128.

Vincent, Clark E. "Sex and the Young Married." *Medical Aspects of Human Sexuality,* March 1969, pp. 13–21.

Chapter *18*

Entrance into Parenthood

In all societies, marriage is generally expected to be followed by parenthood. Positive values about children are basic to societies because the birth of infants is an obvious necessity for their continuation. Murdock points out, "even if the burdens of reproduction and child care outweigh the selfish gains to the parents, the society as a whole has so heavy a stake in the maintenance of its members, as a source of strength and security, that it will insist that parents fulfill these obligations."[1]

The view of children as we see them today is quite different from what it has been in the past. Aries, in his historical study of family life, points out that medieval art until about the 12th century did not know childhood or at least did not portray it. He goes on to say that the discovery of childhood began in the 13th century, and its development can be traced in the history of art to the 15th and 16th centuries. "But the evidence of its development became more plentiful and significant from the end of the 16th century and throughout the 17th."[2] Aries goes on to point out that the first concept of childhood was characterized by "coddling" and made its appearance in the family circle, in the company of little children. But the later second concept of childhood came from outside the family. It came from churchmen who were eager to ensure disciplined rational

---

[1] George P. Murdock, *Social Structure* (New York: The Macmillan Co., 1949), p. 9.

[2] Philippe Aries, *Centuries of Childhood: A Social History of Family Life* (New York: Vantage Press, 1962), p. 47.

manners. "They were unwilling to regard children as charming toys, for they saw them as fragile creatures of God who needed to be both safeguarded and reformed. This concept in its turn passed into family life."[3]

Historically, parents have had a variety of personal and social obligations in childbearing and childrearing. The first function of parents is simply that of reproduction. Societies have generally accepted the belief that reproduction should be a function of marriage, and taboos of varying strengths against birth outside of marriage have been developed to keep the reproductive function within marriage. Second, societies have almost always delegated the responsibility for meeting the needs of the totally dependent infant to the parents, especially the mother. The parents continue to meet the child's needs until he reaches the social age of independence. Third, the parents are expected to make the child a functioning member of society.

It is through society that the agencies and the agents of socialization are brought to bear on each newborn infant. Socialization is not only basic to the social development of each individual, but it is also necessary to the future of any society. For a society to continue, there must be institutionalized means through which the young are trained to take on a positive orientation to significant cultural values. "This socialization is not only basic to personality development, but also has manifest implications for and is requisite to social organizations."[4]

The three basic functions of parent-child relationship could and have been met by other agencies of society, but usually they have been fulfilled by the parents. Because the parent-child relationship has been in existence so long and in all societies, many view it as "natural," rather than socially determined. Historically, it has been assumed that if adults were capable of having children they were capable of rearing them. The fact that many adults in all societies are poor parents, by any criteria, is generally ignored. In most cultures of the world, including the United States, society is so "loath to interfere with the ultimate primary relationships of the family that only in extreme cases will it take the child from its parents."[5]

There are a variety of social pressures that can influence the birth rate. Certainly the long-held value that having children was the "natural" role of women has been very powerful. This value was almost always reinforced by a woman's family and her friends. Even today many women want to have children because their friends have them. One study found that many young married women wanted to have a baby just so they would: (1) have something to do (For them motherhood was seen as

---

[3] Ibid., pp. 132–33.

[4] Edward Z. Dager, "Socialization and Personality Development in the Child," in Harold T. Christensen, ed., *Handbook of Marriage and the Family* (Chicago: Rand McNally & Co., 1964), p. 747.

[5] Ibid., pp. 252–53.

better than working in an office with very little future and where they were *expected* to leave and become mothers.); (2) have something to hug and possess, to be needed by and have power over; and (3) have something to be—a baby's mother.[6]

Becoming a parent is different from most other roles because this is a combination of biological change and social definitions. That is, one can decide to marry and then change his mind. But once a woman is pregnant and on the way to becoming a parent it is much more difficult to change her mind. As Rossi points out, once pregnancy occurs there is little possibility of undoing that commitment to parenthood that is implicit in conception. "We can have ex-spouses and ex-jobs, but not ex-children."[7]

THE HAVING OF CHILDREN

The having of children sometimes seems to many Americans to be inevitable. Yet a number of American couples will have problems or be completely unable to become biological parents. In the "national" fertility study, it was found that, according to the criteria the investigators used, about one couple in three had a fecundity impairment.[8] Fecundity refers to the capacity of a couple to have children in the future. Ultimately 10 percent of all couples in the "national" study will have no children.[9] In their study of couples in Detroit, Blood and Wolfe found that 11 percent were childless.[10] The "national" study found that less than 1 percent of the couples studied intended to have no children,[11] and the "Detroit" study found that of all the couples, with or without children, only 3 percent "wouldn't want any children if they had their life to live over again."[12] In general, about 5 to 8 percent of all married couples with the wife in the 18-to-39 age range are unable to have children.[13] In the 1960s it was commonly estimated that only about 1 percent of all married couples wanted to remain childless. However, there has been some evidence that more couples prefer not to have children. In 1973 it was reported that among married women under age 24, one in 25 expected to

---

[6] Betty Rollins, "Motherhood: Who Needs It?" in Arlene S. Skolnick and Jerome H. Skolnick, *Family in Transition* (Boston: Little, Brown & Co., 1971), p. 354.

[7] Alice S. Rossi, "Transition to Parenthood," *Journal of Marriage and the Family,* February 1968, p. 32.

[8] Ronald Freedman, Pascal K. Whelpton, and Arthur A. Campbell, *Family Planning, Sterility and Population Growth* (New York: McGraw-Hill Book Co., 1959), p. 26.

[9] Ibid., p. 26.

[10] Robert O. Blood and Donald M. Wolfe, *Husbands and Wives* (Glencoe, Ill.: The Free Press, 1960), p. 137.

[11] Freedman, Whelpton, and Campbell, *Family Planning,* p. 48.

[12] Blood and Wolfe, *Husbands and Wives,* p. 137.

[13] Leslie Aldridge Westoff and Charles F. Westoff, *From Now to Zero* (Boston: Little, Brown & Co., 1968), p. 34.

have no children, against one in 75 only six years before.[14] However, in general, the high positive values about having children are accepted by the vast majority of Americans, and the majority of couples without children are not that way by choice.

Fertility problems and the possibility of childlessness, are generally seen as more personally serious by women than by men. For example, Kirk found that involuntary childlessness represented a serious problem for women: "The terms used by wives have an emergency quality about them. Men, although they may be disappointed by childlessness, appear to feel less deprived. However real their loss, it is probably more readily compensated for by occupational activity."[15]

The "national" study found some relationships between childlessness and social variables. For example, there was "relatively more subfecundity found among the twice-married wives than the others when the comparisons are restricted to wives of the same age or duration of marriage."[16] Perhaps those women who did not have children may have been more prone to divorce than those who did have children. It is also found that working wives had higher incidence of fecundity impairments than those who did not work.[17] (This, however, reflects the fact that a woman without children is more apt to enter the work force than a woman with children.)

There is a common belief that not only do blacks have more children than whites but that childlessness is also less common among blacks. Data from the 1960 census were analyzed to check that assumption. The study found that "a greater proportion of the nonwhite couples are childless than are white couples. This difference was not diminished when age cohort, age married, and husband's age were controlled separately or simultaneously."[18]

In marriage, two crude dimensions of sterility or infertility are made. *Relative* sterility refers to a couple who are having problems of conception, but whose problems may be treated and corrected medically or in some cases are resolved with time. *Absolute* sterility refers to those couples who, on the basis of present knowledge, are incapable of having biological children of their own. One reason for a decrease in the number of childless couples in recent years has been some shift of diagnosis and treatment from absolute to relative sterility. Some infertility problems

---

[14] "Kidding You Not," *Newsweek*, November 5, 1973, p. 82.

[15] H. David Kirk, *Shared Fate* (New York: The Free Press of Glencoe, 1964), pp. 2–3.

[16] Ibid., p. 43.

[17] Ibid., p. 53.

[18] Philip R. Kunz and Merlin B. Brinkerhoff, "Differential Childlessness by Color: The Destruction of a Cultural Belief," *Journal of Marriage and the Family*, November 1969, p. 719.

defined as hopeless a few years ago are susceptible to corrective medical treatment today, because of increased scientific knowledge.

To say that a marriage is sterile says, of course, that the two people cannot be natural parents, even though in most cases the responsibility rests with just one of them. Until recent years, it was generally assumed in most cultures that a childless marriage was the "fault" of the wife. In recent years, the role of the sterile husband has come to be increasingly recognized. Today it is estimated that in about one third to one half of all infertile marriages, the inability to conceive rests with the husband.

Sterility

Male. Sterility is more easily diagnosed in the male than in the female, although the male is not always more easily treated. Farris found that in 80 percent of the male sterility cases with which he worked, the problem was physiological in origin, not psychological.[19] Sterility in the male is related to number, vigor, and structure of the spermatozoa. The medical assessment of male fertility focuses primarily on an analysis of the cellular components of the ejaculate to determine: (1) if a large number of spermatozoa are present and (2) if a large enough number of those spermatozoa have a degree of motile activity sufficient for them to move through the uterus and fallopian tubes to the ovum.[20]

Farris, on the basis of his research findings, set up three levels of fertility in the male: (1) *high fertility*, indicated by a count of above 185 million active spermatozoa on the first day and above 80 million on the next day; (2) *relative fertility*, with a range of 80 to 185 million on the first day, but less than 80 million on the next day; and (3) *subfertility*, with a count of less than 80 million in the majority of semen examinations. On the basis of his studies, Farris suggests that "about 40 percent of the males were highly fertile, about 35 to 40 percent relatively fertile, about 15 percent subfertile, and the rest sterile."[21]

Female. Because the reproductive system of the woman is so much more complex than that of the man, her sterility is often more difficult to diagnose and treat. Some of the most common problems of infertility in the woman are: (1) failure to ovulate; (2) the egg cannot or does not pass through the tubes into the uterus; (3) sperm cannot get through the cervix; (4) vaginal or cervical secretions are hostile to sperm; and (5) in ovum cannot be developed and maintained after fertilization. Many times the diagnosis and treatment of the woman extends over long periods of time, because the use of various corrective measures is ultimately tested

---

[19] Edmond J. Farris, "Male Fertility," in Marvin Sussman, *Sourcebook in Marriage and the Family* (Boston: Houghton-Mifflin Co., 1955), p. 135.

[20] John MacLeod, "Fertility in Men," in Albert Ellis and Albert Abarbanel, eds., *Encyclopedia of Sexual Behavior* (New York: Hawthorn Books, Inc., 1961), p. 428.

[21] Ibid., p. 139.

by the result of pregnancy. Each new medical approach must normally be tried in a new menstrual cycle; therefore, medically, it may not be possible to work with the patient more than once a month. In many cases, the woman may undergo medical treatment for years.

There is also the fact that the fertility potential of the woman is not the same at all periods during her theoretical childbearing years. As discussed earlier, the fertility of a girl at age 15 is not as great as it will be when she reaches age 20. The greatest fertility age period for women is in the age range of 21 to 25.[22] From then on the woman's fertility potential decreases and by age 35 to 39 the average conception rate is estimated to be about 50 to 75 percent of what it was at the ages of 21 to 25.[23] Only about 1 out of every 1,000 births is to a woman 45 years of age and over.[24]

While pregnancy impairments may emerge after the birth of one or several children, probably the greatest degree of dissatisfaction exists among those couples who are unable to have any children. The existence of fertility problems often takes time to become known and be recognized by married couples. Most people when they marry never think about the possibility of infertility—they simply assume their own fertility potential. Kirk found that with only 9 out of 70 couples adopting a child, neither spouse could recall ever considering the possibility that they might not be able to have a child until they were actually faced with the problem.[25] Another study found that women did not become seriously upset about their slowness to conceive until they had been trying for about a year.[26]

For couples who want children, the difference between none and one is usually much greater and important than between one and two. The different degrees of desire for children have not been studied. At one level, couples go through a number of years of marriage without children, but do nothing medically. At another level are those who find they cannot have natural children of their own and stop at that point. Finally, some couples who find out they cannot have biological children of their own seek out a child through adoption. Yet, couples on all of these levels may say and honestly believe they want children.

In childless marriages, the wives are probably more ready to take the necessary steps to try to resolve the problem than are husbands. Because of sex differentials in socialization, the wife sees the child as a greater necessity to her adult role than the husband does to his. Husbands often put up a strong resistance to medical checkups because of a fear that they will be found infertile, a possibility viewed by some men as threatening to

[22] Paul H. Gebhard et al., *Pregnancy, Birth and Abortion* (New York: Harper & Brothers, 1958), p. 81.

[23] Charles F. Westoff, Robert G. Potter, Jr., and Philip C. Sagi, *The Third Child* (Princeton, N.J.: Princeton University Press, 1963), p. 23.

[24] Gebhard et al., *Pregnancy, Birth, Abortion*, p. 82.

[25] Kirk, *Shared Fate*, p. 6.

[26] Westoff, p. 31.

their personal sense of masculinity. Husbands may also be more resistant to the possibilities of adoption because they feel less compulsion to be a father and are more threatened than the wife by the idea that the child "would not really be their own."

As suggested in Chapter 8, there are differences among couples as to their willingness to turn to adoption to solve their problem of childlessness. Also suggested, women are generally more willing to turn to adoption than are men. One study relates the degree of dogmatism in the minds of persons and their willingness to turn to adoption. They found that dogmatism and adoption scores did not correlate for females. They suggest that this is because the role of mother is so emphasized that it transcends any negative attitudes. They also suggest that perhaps adoption may be considered a well compartmentalized area for females "which does not share the open-closed minded dimension which might be applied to areas such as religion and politics."[27] They also found that willingness to adopt children was influenced by possible problems that children might have. They found that prospective urban adoptive parents would accept for adoption children who had remedial physical handicaps. However, children with indications of less than average intelligence were not acceptable.[28] So the potential parent is not willing to solve his childlessness under all conditions.

Before leaving the topic of childlessness it is important to say something of that factor as related to marital satisfaction. As pointed out, a majority of married couples who have no children did not do so by choice. But one study has found that, contrary to popular belief, childless marriages are more satisfactory than others. "Parents, especially those currently raising children, were definitely less apt to be satisfied with their marriages."[29] Of course, people without dependent children can divorce or separate easier than those raising children. "Presumably the unhappiest marriages among childless couples and those whose children have grown up have already been dissolved, while the unhappily married with children remain married longer."[30] Jessie Bernard suggests that the positive effects of childlessness are even more marked for the husband's view of marriage than for the wife's view. More childless men than fathers are happy. "Conversely, more fathers felt marriage to be restrictive, and more reported problems."[31]

---

[27] Betty Giles Dembroski and Dale L. Johnson, "Dogmatism and Attitudes Toward Adoption," *Journal of Marriage and the Family*, November 1969, p. 792.

[28] Ibid., p. 792.

[29] Karen S. Renne, "Correlates of Dissatisfaction in Marriage," *Journal of Marriage and the Family*, February 1970, p. 61.

[30] Ibid., p. 61.

[31] Jessie Bernard, *The Future of Marriage* (New York: World Publishing, 1972), p. 57.

Mortality

Maternal Mortality. Maternal mortality refers to the death of the mother at the time of childbirth. Over the years, maternal mortality rates have been steadily decreasing and they have continued to decrease through recent years. For example, in 1952 the maternal mortality rate was 6.8 deaths per 10,000 live births while in 1961 it had dropped to 3.2 per 10,000 live births. Or, described in another way, the maternal mortality rates dropped an amazing nine tenths in the two decades between 1940 and 1960.[32] But one population group that still has a relatively high maternal death rate are nonwhite women. In 1960, the maternal mortality rate was 2.8 per 10,000 live births for white women as compared to 10 per 10,000 for nonwhite women.[33]

One important reason for the decrease has been the greater tendency for women to have their babies in hospitals—over 90 percent of all births today take place in hospitals. This has taken many births out of the hands of midwives and placed them where medical facilities are available should complications arise. Maternal mortality rates could be still lowered, particularly in the lower social classes and in rural areas.

A relationship exists between maternal mortality and the age of the mother at the time of birth. In 1959, for white women ages 20 to 24, the maternal mortality rate was 1.4 per 10,000 live births; for women age 30 to 34, it increased to 3.3; and for women 45 and over to 14.0.[34]

Infant Mortality. Before discussing infant mortality, some mention must be made of *fetal deaths,* which refer to deaths during pregnancy. Many fetal deaths occur too early in pregnancy to be recognized. "It has been estimated that the complete reporting of fetal deaths in the United States might bring the fetal death rate to 150 or even 200 per 1,000 fetuses."[35] The "national" study found that "one in four of the wives in their sample who were ever pregnant had at least one fetal death."[36]

For many women who experience fetal death, it occurs once or twice and is interspersed with other pregnancies that are healthy and successful. But some childless women also fall into this category; they have no trouble conceiving, but cannot carry a fetus full term and give live birth. Some in this category can be helped by proper medical attention and are eventually able to give live birth.

---

[32] Paul C. Glick, "Demographic Analysis of Family Data," in Harold T. Christensen, ed., *Handbook of Marriage and the Family* (Chicago: Rand McNally & Co., 1964), p. 301.

[33] Mortality Analysis and Summary," *Vital Statistics of the United States, 1961,* vol. 2, sec. 1 (U.S. Department of Health, Education, and Welfare), p. 11.

[34] Metropolitan Life Insurance Company, *Statistical Bulletin,* vol. 42 (August 1961), p. 6.

[35] Freedman, Whelpton, and Campbell, *Family Planning,* p. 35.

[36] Ibid., p. 31.

In the past, the chances of an infant surviving the first year of birth were often limited. As recently as 1940, there were 47.4 deaths per 10,000 live births in the United States, but this dropped to 26 per 10,000 by 1960.[37] Generally, the older the infant the greater his chances for survival. Twice as many babies die in the first month as in all the other months of the first year. Premature babies account for almost half of all infant deaths within the first month after birth. There are several other social factors related to different fetal and infant mortality rates. There is a higher probability of fetal deaths when there are plural births, when the fetus is male, and when the pregnancy is among nonwhites.[38] Infant mortality is higher for males as well as nonwhites.[39]

Child spacing is also related to infant mortality. When births are one year apart, the loss of babies is nearly 50 percent higher than when the births are two years apart. As with maternal mortality, the rate of infant mortality has decreased with greater use of medical facilities. Here, too, improvements can be made in the lower social classes and in rural areas. Both maternal and infant mortality rates could be lowered by earlier medical attention during pregnancy. For example, in many lower-class areas, the mother receives her first medical attention at the time of birth. Problems discovered at that time might not have developed, or could have been medically planned for, if the mother had been under medical supervision earlier in pregnancy.

Pregnancy Fears

There has long been a belief that childbirth should be a traumatic event for the woman. Often pain was associated with the significance of the event of giving birth to a child. Pain was seen as the price the woman paid for becoming a mother. For example, after Sir James Simpson invented chloroform he was attacked for using it at the time of birth because it was "unnatural" to take away the pangs of childbirth. "Chloroform was a 'decoy of Satan'; did not the Bible enjoin, 'In sorrow thou shalt bring forth children?' "[40]

One final problem, though probably not as severe as the others discussed, is the apprehension among some women about pregnancy and birth. While the girl in the American culture is socially conditioned for the day when she will become a mother, her first pregnancy is usually an

---

[37] "Infant Mortality," *Vital Statistics of the United States, 1961*, vol. 2, sec. 3 (U.S. Department of Health, Education, and Welfare), p. 7.

[38] "Fetal Mortality," *Vital Statistics of the United States, 1960*, vol. 2, sec. 4 (U.S. Department of Health, Education, and Welfare), p. 8.

[39] "Infant Mortality," *Vital Statistics of the United States, 1961*, vol. 2, sec. 3 (U.S. Department of Health, Education, and Welfare), p. 4.

[40] E. S. Turner, *Roads to Ruin* (Great Britain: Penguin Books, 1966), p. 11.

impressive personal experience and she is forced to think about its culmination while it is still months away. Because she is *the* pregnant woman and because she has heard many stories about pregnancy and childbirth, she may face the future birth with some concern.

A part of the mythology of the American culture is that when a young married woman discovers she is pregnant for the first time she becomes flushed, coy, and radiant; in actual fact, she is very likely to be frightened and depressed, masking these feelings in order not to be considered contemptible. The belief that pregnant women live in a euphoric state is as misleading as the idea that pregnant women are characteristically anxiety ridden. Brodsky found that while some expectant mothers fall in the categories of euphoria and anxiety there was no tendency in either direction among pregnant women significantly different from control groups of nonpregnant women with children and married women never pregnant.[41] While pregnant women do not show a deep antagonism to motherhood, it does sometimes happen that the arrival of pregnancy interrupts a pleasant dream of motherhood and awakens them to the realization that they have too little money, or not enough space, or unresolved marital problems, or have not yet acquired the skills of housekeeping, and so on.

Some women pregnant for the first time probably also tend to make the most out of their pregnancy. When this is added to the common human fear of the unknown and unexperienced, the pregnant woman may build up a state of anxiety. If the first birth turns out to be not too difficult, the second one is usually viewed with much less apprehension.

There is in American society a certain romanticism centered around the birth experience and its significance for the mother. A part of the romantic belief is that giving birth to the first child symbolizes achieving "complete" female role fulfillment. Yet today the birth experience has increasingly become a technical event where the administrative and technical needs of the hospital have top priority and the emotional needs and personalities of the mothers often get in the way of efficiency. "Birth itself may be subordinated to the schedule: Some doctors schedule their deliveries, and induce labor to keep them on time. Even 'natural' labor may be slowed down or speeded up by drugs for convenience."[42]

Sexual Relations and Pregnancy. There is often confusion as to what is sexually appropriate when the woman is pregnant, especially for the first time. One common belief has been that the pregnant woman loses interest in sex and her husband finds her sexually less attractive as she moves through pregnancy. If there is any question of possible danger, either physical or psychological, to the pregnant mother or her unborn

---

[41] Stanley L. Brodsky, "Self-Acceptance in Pregnant Women," *Marriage and Family Living*, November 1963, p. 484.

[42] Marian G. Morris, "Psychological Miscarriage: An End to Mother Love," *Transaction*, January–February 1966, p. 9.

child through sexual relations, then the sexual aspect of the marriage is almost always put aside. This, when it occurs, symbolizes a role decision for the married couple that will prevail for many years—that is, the role demands of being parents will generally take precedence over the role desires of being husband or wife.

Through the research of Masters and Johnson, we now have some data on changes in sexual tensions and effectiveness of sexual performance through the stages of pregnancy.[43] The nine months of pregnancy are divided into three three-month periods referred to as the first, second, and third trimesters. The women studied were divided into two groups, those going through a first full-term pregnancy (Nulliparous) and those attempting a second or more, full-term pregnancy (Parous).

During the first trimester (first three months) of pregnancy, 77 percent of the nulliparous women reported a reduction in sexual tensions or effectiveness in their sexual performance, while 14 percent reported no change and 9 percent an increase. Many of these women were suffering from nausea, and all of them were affected by sleepiness and symptoms of chronic fatigue. Probably because of being pregnant for the first time and unsure of themselves, 60 percent of the nulliparous women reported "fear of injury to the conceptus (frequently not vocalized to their partner) as affecting the freedom of their physical response in coital activity during the first trimester."[44] Possibly due to their previous experiences with pregnancy, very few of the parous women noted any sexual changes during the first trimester; 84 percent reported no change, 10 percent reduction, and 6 percent increase in their levels of sexual interest or effectiveness in sexual performance.[45]

During the second trimester (middle three months), "sexual patterns generally reflected a marked increase in eroticism and effectiveness of performance regardless of parity or ages of the women interrogated." Only 26 percent of the nulliparous and 12 percent of the parous stated no improvement in sexual interest or performance.[46]

In the third trimester (last three months) of pregnancy, there was a significant reduction in coital frequency. About three quarters of the women studied had been advised by their doctors to sexually abstain for periods of time varying from four weeks to three months prior to delivery. Although strongly influenced by medical restrictions, 82 percent of the "nulliparous women reported that they personally gradually lost interest in sexual activity during the third trimester."[47] Among the parous women, 75 percent were medically restricted from coitus for various periods of

---

[43] William H. Masters and Virginia E. Johnson, *Human Sexual Response* (Boston: Little, Brown & Co., 1966), pp. 156–60.

[44] Ibid., pp. 156–57.

[45] Ibid., p. 158.

[46] Ibid., p. 158.

[47] Ibid., p. 159.

time during the third trimester, and 67 percent of this group reported "a significant reduction in eroticism and frequency of sexual performance as the estimated date of confinement approached."[48]

Masters and Johnson also found that 88 percent of those women "for whom coition was interdicted medically expressed concern with the prescribed period of sexual continence and its possible effect upon their husbands' sexual requirements." Fifty-five percent of the medically restricted nulliparous and 70 percent of the parous women "reported that they made deliberate attempts to relieve their husbands during the period of prescribed continence."[49]

Once the mother has given birth to her child, there is often confusion as to how long the couple should wait before reactivating their sexual life. In many societies there are *post partum* sex taboos and in many societies the sex taboos last for several years.[50] In the Masters and Johnson study, 47 percent of the women described themselves as having low or essentially negligible levels of sexuality during the interviews conducted early in the third post partum month. However, the highest level of postpartum sexual interest in the first three months after delivery was reported by the group of nursing mothers. Not only did they report sexual stimulation induced by suckling their infants, but as a group they also described interest in as rapid return as possible to active coition with their husbands.[51]

It may also be added that overwhelmingly the sex act of marriage is entered with no anticipation of pregnancy. One estimate based on a 6.7 average frequency of intercourse per month came to the conclusion that about 2 billion sex acts occurred in the United States in one year. Given the fact that 3.5 million births occur each year to married women living with their husbands indicates a ratio of about one live birth for about every 600 acts of sexual intercourse.[52]

In Chapter 16 the means available today for the planning of families in regard to number and spacing of children was discussed. It was suggested that along with the rise of contraceptive knowledge has emerged the belief by the married couple that childbearing is a matter of choice rather than fate. However, a number of couples exert little or no control over pregnancy for a variety of personal and social reasons.[53] It is estimated that the probability of conception occurring when there is coitus with no protection against conception occurs in about 2 to 4 percent of all coital acts. The "national" study found that of the couples they studied, 85 per-

---

[48] Ibid., p. 160.

[49] Ibid., pp. 159–60.

[50] William N. Stephens, *The Family in Cross-Culture Perspective* (New York: Holt, Rinehart & Winston, Inc., 1963), pp. 348–49.

[51] Masters and Johnson, *Response*, pp. 161–62.

[52] Westoff and Westoff, *Zero*, p. 24.

[53] Freedman, Whelpton, and Campbell, *Family Planning*, pp. 79–81.

cent either completely or partially planned their pregnancies. It is also pointed out that completely planned families are small families. "Not one of the 86 families with six or more births was completely planned."[54] Personal motivation and interest on the part of the wife is also related to child planning. "Among fecund couples, working wives are much more likely than nonworking wives to have completely planned fertility."[55]

Most American couples attempt to control fertility. But it has been estimated that about one fifth of all births are unwanted. The percent of unwanted births increases sharply by birth order: 5 percent of first births, 30 percent of fourth births, and 50 percent of sixth or higher-order births. There is also a social-class relationship to unwanted births. "Fifteen percent of births to nonpoor families were declared unwanted, compared to 23 percent among the near poor and 37 percent among the poor."[56] It also appears that the timing for births is often not what the parents would have preferred. It has been estimated that two thirds of wanted births would have occurred at another time if the woman had been successful in controlling the timing of births.[57]

The ideal number of children in the United States ranges from two to four. Very few women state they want one or no children, and few say they want more than four. In a survey done in 1970 wives from 14 to 24 years of age reported expecting an average of 2.9 children.[58] This is still well above the number of children necessary for population replacement. However, as they get older there may be some reduction in the actual number of children they have.

So the evidence clearly indicates that possibly as high as 90 percent of the American population approves of the concept of family planning. There is also some evidence that families with more than four children, even when controls are established for differences in socioeconomic level, are less likely to be viewed by their children as having happy families. There is also evidence that the large families are less likely to produce self-reliant children who achieve well in school. There is also some evidence that children from large families have lower tested intelligence on the average and achieve less well occupationally.[59]

---

[54] Freedman, Whelpton, and Campbell, *Family Planning*, p. 81.

[55] Ibid., p. 137.

[56] Larry Bumpers and Charles Westoff, "Unwanted Births and U.S. Population Growth," in Daniel Callahan, *The American Population Debate* (New York: Doubleday and Co., 1971), p. 269.

[57] Jeanne C. Ridley, "The Effects of Population Change on the Roles and Status of Women: Perspective and Speculation," in Constantina Safilios-Rothschild, *Toward a Sociology of Women* (Lexington, Mass.: Xerox Publishing, 1972), p. 380.

[58] Ibid., p. 381.

[59] Catherine S. Chilman, "Fertility and Poverty in the United States: Some Implications for Family-Planning Programs, Evaluations, and Research," *Journal of Marriage and the Family*, May 1968, p. 213.

Rossi has suggested that when a couple have a small family it is for one of two primary reasons. First, that the family wanted to be small and were successful in achieving that end. Second, that they wanted a large family but were unsuccessful in achieving that end. In either case, there is a low probability of unwanted children. Therefore, "small families are most likely to contain parents with a strong and positive orientation to each of the children they do have."[60]

The question might be raised as to why the vast majority of adults want children. Many of the reasons that existed in the past for having children no longer seem important. The economic motive has not only disappeared for the middle class, but in some respects reversed itself. In the past, children made an economic contribution to the family from a rather early age, and also gave economic security and aid to the parents in their old age. When children work today, they do it primarily as a "valuable learning experience," or for "spending money" and not usually to contribute to the total family income. Few middle-class parents expect their children to take care of them in their old age. In fact, in middle-class families, many parents continue to help their children financially long after the children are married.

The old motive of having children to carry on the family name also has much less middle-class relevance today than in the past, as a result of the shift in importance from the family unit to the individual. In a society that stresses and rewards individual achievement, family ties and background have lost most of their past significance, except for a few ancestor worshippers. No doubt many couples today see their children as extensions of themselves who will be living after they are gone, but, for most, this does not have the significance it did in the old patriarchal society.

Parents may also have an influence on the number of children their offspring will have when they grow up. One theory argues that children acquire values in their family of orientation which will later influence their own family planning decisions in such a way as to "cause them to recapitulate, in so far as possible, the demographic structure of their families of orientation.[61] In a test of the above theory it was found that family sizes were related to the size of the family of orientation. It was further found that the relationship of family size preferences was stronger among those who felt closest to their families as well as among first-born women.[62]

Because of the highly emotional and personal emphasis placed on the individual within the family setting today, the most important reason for having children probably centers around the ego-needs of the parent. This

---

[60] Rossi, "Transition," p. 33.

[61] Gerry E. Hendershot, "Familial Satisfaction, Birth Order, and Fertility Values," *Journal of Marriage and the Family*, February 1969, p. 28.

[62] Ibid., p. 33.

does not imply a selfish motive, but rather that the parents want to give and receive love in relationship to their children. Because the infant is totally dependent, the parents are of great importance to the child. An adventurous and challenging aspect to childrearing may operate for many future parents. Many adults without children look at those with children and are sure they can do a better job of childrearing; many married couples anticipate the kind of child they can help create and develop.

Problems may accompany the positive factors of having children. Some parents are surprised to find that the reality of childrearing may be quite different from the idealized beliefs they had prior to becoming parents. Parents must constantly reconcile their idealized images of their child with the reality of the child's personality. Parents may encounter problems with their children in many different areas, from birth on through the years.

There are several variables that appear to be related to the probability of parents defining themselves as having problems with their children. One study found 72 percent of the parents reporting that they had some problems with their children and this rate was about the same for all social class levels.[63] However, in the same study, only 4 percent of the high-status parents said their children gave them more trouble than pleasure, as compared to 21 percent of the lower-status parents.[64] Another study found that the greater the number of children, the higher the rate of parents saying they had problems in raising their children, but at the same time there was "no relationship between number of children and feelings of inadequacy."[65]

Given the historical changes in the importance of children, and the emergence of many new considerations that parents must take into account in rearing children, the motives for having children are somewhat confusing. Dager raises the question of what functions children serve and points out that: "They are strictly economic liabilities; they keep parents awake; they prevent parents from going anywhere of any significance for several years; they create continuous anxiety in parents lest they not grow up in accordance with 'established' psychological principles, break a leg, fail a grade, get pregnant; *ad infinitum*."[66] Dager then goes on to suggest that it is no wonder that many parents are ambivalent about having and rearing children.

Premarital pregnancy can also be a factor in marriage and parenthood. In the period 1964 to 1966, 22 percent of first births occurred to women

[63] Thomas S. Langner and Stanley T. Michael, *Life Stress and Mental Health* (New York: The Free Press of Glencoe, 1963), p. 335.

[64] Ibid., p. 338.

[65] Gerald Gurin, Joseph Veroff, and Sheila Feld, *Americans View Their Mental Health* (New York: Basic Books, 1960), p. 134.

[66] Dager, p. 775.

married less than eight months. Assuming that most of those births were due to premarital conception means they were undoubtedly a factor in determining the timing of marriage. This suggests that one consequence of better contraception might be an increase in the age of marriage.[67]

The average-size family in the United States in 1960 was 3.68 individuals, which was somewhat greater than in 1950 when it was 3.54.[68] To put it another way, in 1960, 67.7 percent of all families had from three to six persons and 32.3 percent had only two persons.[69] The two-person families were predominantly the young married couple prior to their childbearing years and the older married couple after the children had grown up and left the parental home. That many American families have very young children is illustrated by the fact that, in 1960, almost one third (30.5 percent) of all families in the United States had one or more children under six years of age.[70]

The actual number of years in her life that the wife is bearing children is quite limited. In 1950, the median age of marriage for the wife was 20.1 years and she gave birth to her last child at the median age of 26.1 years.[71] That means that the median childbearing years cover a period of six years. Glick estimates that, on the average, women today are through their childbearing years about six years younger than were their grandmothers.[72] When the average woman today reaches 45, about the period when her biological capacity for childbearing ends, she often finds her youngest "baby" is about 18.

In recent years the average spacing interval between children has increased. The combination of younger age at marriage now than before and the smaller size of family, with a longer interval between children, has had the effect of lowering the average age of women at the birth of their last child and also at the time when the last child marries. As a result, the proportion of couples who survive jointly until the last child has married and left home has risen sharply: "Formerly it was barely one half, but currently is about four out of five."[73]

Many couples have a preference as to wanting sons or daughters. There are more males conceived and born than females. There are different variables related to the greater probability of the birth of males. For

---

[67] Ridley, "Roles and Status of Women," p. 380.

[68] U.S. Department of Commerce, Bureau of the Census, *Population Characteristics,* Current Population Reports, Series P-20, November 2, 1960, p. 4.

[69] United States Department of Commerce, Bureau of the Census, *Statistical Abstract of the United States,* 1961, 82nd annual edition, p. 39.

[70] Ibid., p. 39.

[71] Paul C. Glick, *American Families* (New York: John Wiley and Sons, Inc., 1957), p. 54.

[72] Ibid., p. 195.

[73] Hugh Carter and Paul Glick, *Marriage and Divorce: A Social and Economic Study* (Cambridge, Mass.: Harvard University Press, 1970), p. 394.

example, there is a greater chance of the first born being a male if born to a woman under age 25 as against women past age 35.[74] There is also some evidence that a conception occurring early in the menstrual cycle has a greater chance of being a male than if the conception occurs later. This would suggest that couples with a high coital rate would be more likely to produce males because the greater frequency would mean they would be more apt to be having coitus early in the menstrual cycle.[75]

In the past there was often a strong preference for having sons. However, the preference for one sex over the other has decreased a great deal. This has been true since the economic importance of sons is no longer an important consideration in industrial societies. "Currently, however, the desire for at least one son appears to be a universal one."[76] This means that the birth of a son can effect the birth rate. For example, significantly more families stop having children after they have a boy than after they have a girl. One consequence of this is that more youngest children are boys. One other interesting aspect of gender choice among parents in what would happen to the sex ratio if parents had a free choice. One estimate is that if parents had a free choice there would be about 121 boys born for every 100 girls. If this did happen it would lead to many problems. "The shortage of females would produce an increase in the proportion of males remaining single, an increase in the age of marriage for males, as well as an increase in prostitution and homosexuality."[77]

Christensen has suggested a general, descriptive picture of the process of child spacing in the American middle-class family. The first child is born about one and one half years after the marriage takes place. The subsequent births occur after intervals that grow progressively longer with each birth. And there exists "a negative correlation between average interval separating births and total number of births. This last mentioned fact demonstrates how number and spacing are interrelated, which can make possible the prediction of eventual family size once the early spacing intervals are known."[78]

As discussed in previous chapters, adjustment to marriage roles develops and changes over time. Because the role relationships of marriage are dynamic, it was suggested that in many successful marriages each one is able to reach general satisfaction with the demands of his own role and the role of his partner. Therefore, couples who enter the parent roles shortly after marriage have had very little time to develop exclusively the

---

[74] William H. James, "Cycle Day of Insemination, Coital Rate, and Sex Ratio," *The Lancet,* January 6, 1971, p. 112.

[75] Ibid., p. 113.

[76] Ridley, "Roles and Status of Women," p. 381.

[77] Ibid., p. 381.

[78] Harold T. Christensen, "Children in the Family: Relationship of Number and Spacing to Marital Success," *Journal of Marriage and the Family,* May 1968, p. 283.

new roles of marriage. Glick found that half of the women 30 to 35 had their first child less than 1.7 years after marriage.[79] This means that half the couples had less than a year in the husband-wife roles before moving into "expectant parents" roles.

Other studies also point out some negative association between children and marriage. One study reported a substantial decline from the beginning of marriage to the preschool stage in the frequency of positive companionship experience in marriage.[80] Other research identifies the happiest time in marriage as before the arrival of the first child and after the departure of the last.

Limited time spent in nonparental husband-wife roles may have both long- and short-range implications for marriage. In the long run, it may mean that the demands of being parents influence the marriage relationship before the couple have had time to develop their husband and wife roles. After children enter, the couple have much less time or opportunity to function exclusively as husband and wife. Later in their marriage, after the children grow up and the couple revert back to the exclusive husband and wife roles, they may have little to return to in the way of a husband-wife relationship.

The short-run problems center around the couple's ability to relate their new parental roles to their marriage roles. The success of the husband and wife role relationships is often related to the maintaining of some autonomy in the face of the new parental roles. However, it is doubtful if any marriage role development is going to be unaffected by parental roles. While individuals are husbands and wives both before and after parenthood, being a husband-father or wife-mother is bound to be different because the roles are not mutually exclusive.

There is some research that indicates that the experiences of childbearing and childrearing may have a profound and negative effect on the marital satisfaction of wives even in their basic feeling of self-worth in relation to their marriage. This may be a result of the reduction in the companionship experiences with their husbands because of the pressures of childrearing. Yet, the same study found that the loss of companionship seemed to occur for the husband without a decrease in marital satisfaction.

The interrelationship of marriage and parent roles may be illustrated in a number of ways. Since the relationship of marriage is between two individuals assumed to be mature adults, and the relationship of the parents to the infant and child is between the mature adult and the immature child, the element of adult responsibility enters. The young child in real

---

[79] Glick, *American Families*, p. 64.

[80] Boyd C. Rollins and Harold Feldman, "Marital Satisfaction over the Family Life Cycle," *Journal of Marriage and the Family*, January 1970, p. 27.

need of his mother must normally be given preference over the need of the husband for his wife.

Together, the couple are also bound to meet many cases of role conflict between their marriage and parent roles. For example, the couple who plan on going out as husband and wife, but discover they have a child who is ill, must usually put aside their husband-wife roles and stay home as parents. As the child grows older, they may, in a role-conflict situation, choose to pursue the marriage roles, because the demands of the child become less pressing.

SELECTED BIBLIOGRAPHY

Aries, Philippe   *Centuries of Childhood: A Social History of Family Life.* New York: Vantage Press, 1962.

Benson, Leonard   *Fatherhood: A Sociological Perspective.* New York: Random House, 1968.

Brodsky, Stanley L.   "Self-Acceptance in Pregnant Women." *Marriage and Family Living,* November 1963, pp. 483–84.

Brody, Grace F.   "Socioeconomic Differences in Stated Maternal Child-Rearing Practices and in Observed Maternal Behavior." *Journal of Marriage and the Family,* November 1968, pp. 656–60.

Christensen, Harold T.   "Children in the Family: Relationship of Number and Spacing to Marital Success." *Journal of Marriage and the Family,* May 1968, pp. 283–89.

Figley, Charles R.   "Child Density and the Marital Relationship." *Journal of Marriage and the Family,* May 1973, pp. 272–82.

Hendershot, Gerry E.   "Familial Satisfaction, Birth Order, and Fertility Values." *Journal of Marriage and the Family,* February 1969, pp. 27–33.

Masters, William H., and Johnson, Virginia E.   *Human Sexual Response.* Boston: Little, Brown & Co., 1966.

Rollins, Betty   "Motherhood: Who Needs It?" in Arlene S. Skolnick and Jerome H. Skolnick, *Family in Transition.* Boston: Little, Brown & Co., 1971), pp. 346–56.

Rossi, Alice S.   "Transition to Parenthood." *Journal of Marriage and the Family,* February 1968, pp. 26–39.

Winchester, A. M.   *Heredity and Your Life.* New York: Dover Publications, 1960.

Chapter **19**

Parent-Child Interaction: Infancy and Childhood

The specific nature of later acquired parental roles will be examined with the realization that the parents are first husband and wife. As indicated in the last chapter, becoming parents for the first time is probably the most significant and demanding new role that most individuals encounter during their lifetime, and the new experience demands an extended emotional involvement. New parenthood is somewhat different for the mother role and the father role, though it should be emphasized that these roles derive an important part of their meaning in relationship to one another. The interactional importance of the parent roles has two interrelated dimensions: parent-child and mother-father. The mother-father relationship is important as a division of labor and responsibility, as well as a buttressing paired role relationship in interacting with the children. For example, a mother and father not supporting each other in their role relationships as parents may create confusion for the children or set up a situation in which the children play one parent off against the other.

Mother Role

The mother role as filled in the American middle class is very different from that of most other cultures. Cross-cultural studies show that many societies do not have the kind of mother-child role relationships that are seen as "natural" in the United States.[1] In traditional societies, the mother and father roles were most sharply defined because the father had an authoritarian and exulted position with regard to his children. But in present middle-class American society, the contrast between father and mother roles insofar as control and influence over the children is concerned has for the most part disappeared.[2]

The role of mother has become highly exaggerated in American society. Research indicates that the mother's absence need not always be negative nor is her presence always positive for the children. However, the "prevailing ideology of the family seems to ascribe an almost mystical effect on children in the mother's mere presence."[3]

On the social significance attached to the mother role, Alice Rossi writes that "for the first time in the history of any known society motherhood has become a full-time occupation for adult women."[4] She goes on to suggest from her studies that full-time motherhood is not sufficiently absorbing (nor beneficial to the children) to justify today's woman devoting 15 or more years to it as an exclusive occupation. "Sooner or later —and I think it should be sooner—women have to face the question of who they are besides their children's mother."[5]

But it seems clear that the role of wife-mother continues to be the basic role aspiration and achievement for most middle-class women. One study found that for the wife, marriage was not as great a role transition as becoming a mother.[6] This is true because greater demands are placed on the woman as mother than as wife. The young mother finds herself moving into the new role when, because of the total dependency of the newborn infant, the demands of that role are the greatest. Moving from the non-mother role to the mother role is not transitional, but abrupt, and demands an extensive revision of her daily life.

Becoming a mother calls for important changes in a wife's behavior and often over time calls for highly important adaptations. One study asked a sample of mothers "How is a woman's life changed by having children?" By far the most common response was that children meant less freedom,

---

[1] Edward Z. Dager, "Socialization and Personality Development in the Child," in Harold T. Christensen, ed., *Handbook of Marriage and the Family* (Chicago: Rand McNally and Co., 1964), p. 770.

[2] William N. Stephens, *The Family in Cross-Cultural Perspective* (New York: Holt, Rinehart & Winston, Inc., 1963), p. 320.

[3] Arlene S. Skolnick and Jerome H. Skolnick, *Family in Transition* (Boston: Little, Brown & Co., 1971), p. 306.

[4] Alice S. Rossi, "Equality Between the Sexes, *Daedalus,* Spring 1964, p. 615.

[5] Ibid., p. 624.

[6] Robert O. Blood and Donald M. Wolfe, *Husbands and Wives* (Glencoe, Ill.: The Free Press, 1960), p. 43.

particularly that they restricted the mother's freedom of movement.[7] Also, the greater adaptability to crisis by the mother than by the father has been shown in a study of families with a severely retarded child. It was found that fathers were less adaptable than mothers and were more vulnerable to social stigma and extrafamilial influences such as children's physical appearance and sex.[8]

Because the role is so demanding and entails such extreme responsibility, the new mother often feels anxious and apprehensive. In the day-to-day care of the infant and child, she must make constant decisions and, because of her inexperience, the decisions can be dangerous to the infant. Some women may also have conflicting feelings about the mother role. The female is socialized to want to be a mother, but she is given little direct preparation for the role; on the other hand, she wants and loves the child, but is faced with some role insecurity. Therefore, the idealized image of wanting children may be altered by the reality of having and caring for them. In a study by Miller and Swanson, mothers were asked about their reactions and feelings to the period of their children's infancy. In that sample, 66 percent reported "very pleasant experiences," 19 percent "mildly pleasant experiences," and 14 percent "unpleasant experiences."[9]

Children often place a great demand on the mother. She often finds her role of mother takes precedence over all other roles and sometimes even over her personal feelings and needs. The mother may be called upon in ways other family members are not. One study observed that unless the mother can expect assistance in caring for her family she often cannot afford to adopt even the sick role. She often must put aside sickness that other family members can allow to alter their roles.[10] Generally, whatever the problems of being a parent, the mother is limited in her options because, unlike a disappointing marriage, disappointing motherhood cannot be terminated by divorce.

Child Abuse. Before moving on, it is important to look at child abuse. Physical mistreatment and even killing of the child go against all the images of parenthood and beliefs in human decency. That some mothers severely reject their children either psychologically or physically is often overlooked, but the truth is that many American women do not love or want their babies. And though few mothers actually kill their infants,

---

[7] Gerald Gurin, Joseph Veroff, and Sheila Feld, *Americans View Their Mental Health* (New York: Basic Books, 1960), p. 30.

[8] Irving Tallman, "Spousal Role Differentiation and The Socialization of Severely Retarded Children," *Journal of Marriage and the Family*, February 1965, p. 42.

[9] Daniel R. Miller and Guy E. Swanson, *The Changing American Parent* (New York: John Wiley & Sons, Inc., 1958), p. 216.

[10] H. Reed Geertsen and Robert M. Gray, "Familistic Orientation and Inclination toward Adopting the Sick Role," *Journal of Marriage and the Family*, November 1970, p. 644.

"the crippling effects of early maternal rejection on children can hardly be exaggerated—or glossed over."[11] The following statistics give an indication of the extent of this problem: There are about 50,000 to 70,000 children neglected, battered, or exploited annually and there are about 150,000 children placed in foster homes for these reasons. There are over 300,000 children in foster care altogether. Eight to 10 percent of all school children in one 20-county study were found to be in need of psychiatric examination and some type of treatment for their problem.[12]

One study of parents who had engaged in child abuse points out some contributing factors. It is usually only one of the parents who abuses the child, and in the reported study it was the mother in 50 instances and the father in 7 cases.[13] However, other studies show it more apt to be about evenly divided between mothers and fathers. If the rate is higher for mothers one obvious reason would be that they are around the children more than is the father.

The study by Steele and Pollock suggests that with few exceptions the patients they saw who had abused their children had emotional problems severe enough to be accepted for treatment. The abusing parents placed demands on their children that were great and were also premature. The demands were clearly beyond the ability of the infant to comprehend, to know what was wanted and what he should do. "Parents dealt with their children as if they were much older than they really were. Furthermore, their expectations for their children had always been high. From early in infancy the children of abusing parents were expected to show exemplary behavior and to be respectful and submissive toward adult authority and society."[14]

In addition to the many thousands of children who are believed to be physically abused each year there are many thousands of others who are neglected and abandoned. Parental roles are usually assumed to be positive, and rarely is it recognized that many parents don't want their children and physically and/or mentally abuse them. Far more attention should be directed at the negative costs, both physically and mentally, of some parenthood instead of assuming that it inherently is the most desirable means of raising all children.

Role satisfaction for the mother is learned experience. While most mothers probably derive a sense of role fulfillment from parenthood, a number clearly do not. As with many roles in the American society, the problem may be the conflict between the idealized image of the role and

---

[11] Marian G. Morris, "Psychological Miscarriage: An End to Mother Love," *Trans-Action*, January 1966, p. 8.

[12] Ibid., p. 8.

[13] Brandt F. Steele and Carl Pollock, "The Battered Child," in Skolnick and Skolnick, *Transition*, p. 358.

[14] Ibid., p. 362.

its realities. The image of the cuddly, happy infant may be quite different from the reality of a messy, screaming infant demanding immediate attention.

Father Role

The transition to the father role is probably not as great as the transition to the mother role. This would seem to be true if for no other reason than that the father role is usually not nearly so demanding and time consuming. Benson points out that fatherhood is a role that does not call for training, discipline, or high-priority effort. And any attempts to get fathers to take careful stock of themselves is sporadic and unorganized. "One review of the literature revealed about 15 times as many publications dealing with the mother-child relationship as with that between father and child."[15]

And because the male's occupational role is performed in a setting different from his family roles, the child often has only an indirect influence on this role. Even when many new fathers are at home, the new child may have less influence on their new father role than on the longer established husband-wife roles. The husband may find he has to make a more drastic readjustment to his wife as mother than to his new role as father.

The male in his occupational role is affected by the obligations of his new role as father. Because the male through his occupation must provide his wife and children with their material needs, children place a greater financial responsibility on him. In middle-class occupations, the male's income gradually increases over the years. Yet, at the time when the children are young and the financial demands may be the greatest, he is at a relatively low point in his lifetime income level. The husband may feel frustrated if increases in income seem inadequate to meet the increasing costs of the children. Children may also mean a loss of occupational mobility because the male, aware of his financial responsibilities, may be very hesitant to leave his job with its security for a more risky new job with more potential.

Walters and Stinnett examined a number of studies dealing with aspects of the father role. They concluded that the research suggests that children perceive fathers as being "more fear arousing, more punitive, more restrictive, colder, and less understanding than mothers."[16]

Marriage and Parent Roles. The acceptance of parental roles and their impact on marriage roles will vary a great deal for different couples.

[15] Leonard Benson, *Fatherhood: A Sociological Perspective* (New York: Random House, 1968), p. 6.

[16] James Walters and Nick Stinnett, "Parent-Child Relationships: A Decade Review of Research," *Journal of Marriage and the Family*, February 1971, p. 85.

Satisfaction is theoretically related to the ability of the individuals to perceive their roles as parents in relationship to themselves, each other, and the children. The parent who feels a basic role conflict involving his parental role is bound to feel some dissatisfaction with both that role and the one it is frustrating. Therefore, the ability to fill parental roles calls for adaptability to the new role needs and a redefinition, where necessary, of other role requirements.

With the entrance of children a variety of changes usually occur in marriages. First, often the pregnancy and postnatal periods are times of stress for both parents. Second, there are all kinds of role changes related to the additional responsibilities of becoming parents. Third, very frequently the morale level of the marriage decreases with the addition of children. The couple are less able to meet each others' needs plus the problems introduced by the children.[17]

During the early years of childbearing many problems may emerge. In the period after the first child is born, but before he is old enough for school, is when many women leave the work force. During this period the wife becomes isolated and almost totally socially, economically, and emotionally dependent upon her husband. "The boundaries of her world contract, the possibilities of growth diminish."[18]

Other research has shown that school-age children from 6 to 14 appear to have an especially distressing effect on marriage. This period appears to be especially difficult for wives. It has also been found that being the father of teen-agers is especially difficult because the variable of "satisfaction with children" at that stage of life is at its lowest ebb. Studies have further shown that young, unmarried sons and daughters over 18 can be devastating to a marriage. "For both husbands and wives, this is the time when fewest say that the present stage of the marriage is very satisfying."[19] The research findings seem to suggest that almost all stages of child development can contribute to problems in some marriages.

As was pointed out in Chapter 12 children may, in the long run, be a negative factor in satisfaction in marriage. One study concluded that "people raising children were more likely to be dissatisfied with their marriages than people who never had children or whose children had left home, regardless of age, race, or income level."[20] Or, as pointed out in the statement by Hicks and Platt after a review of the literature, the

---

[17] Charles R. Figley, "Child Density and the Marital Relationship," *Journal of Marriage and the Family*, May 1973, p. 273.

[18] Dair L. Gillespie, "Who Has the Power? The Marital Struggle," *Journal of Marriage and the Family*, August 1971, p. 456.

[19] Jessie Bernard, *The Future of Marriage* (New York: World Publishing Co., 1972), pp. 67–68.

[20] Karen S. Renee, "Correlates of Dissatisfaction in Marriage," *Journal of Marriage and the Family*, January 1970, p. 60.

most striking finding to emerge from research was "that children tend to detract from, rather than contribute to, marital happiness."[21]

CHILDREARING

Historically, childrearing had a strong parental orientation. That is, parents tended to rear their children according to their own needs and values. But over time in the United States, a transition from the parental to the child orientation has been made. The following quotation briefly describes the major historical emphases in childrearing in the United States:

> It is convenient to divide this history of American child training into four broad periods. The first extends from the middle of the 1700s to about the time of the Civil War. Those years saw the decline of techniques for "breaking the child's will" and the beginning of attacks on corporal punishment. In the second period, roughly from 1869 to the First World War, corporal punishment and the arbitrary use of parental authority drew less and less support. The 1920s and 1930s represent a third phase in rearing children. The great theme of those decades is the training of children who would be highly independent. Finally, in the fourth period, a span of years from about 1945 to the present, there occurred many drastic changes in ideas about child care. For the first time in American history, it became proper to let the child set the age at which he was ready to be disciplined, weaned, and trained to use the toilet. Thumbsucking and genital play were tolerated.[22]

The period of the 1940s and 1950s was one in which motherhood and the having of children reached a peak in the United States. That period had very high birth rates and turned motherhood into something of a cult. Betty Rollins says about that period that they wallowed in the aesthetics of it all "—natural childbirth and nursing became maternal musts. Like heavy-bellied ostriches, they ground their heads in the sands of motherhood, only coming up for air to say how utterly, happily fulfilled they were."[23] That was also an era greatly influenced by psychoanalytic theory. Parents came to believe they were responsible for whatever went wrong with their children's lives. Many came to believe that almost any parental act could have permanent traumatic results for a child. And if they, as parents, insisted that their children perform

---

[21] Mary Hicks and Marilyn Platt, "Marital Happiness and Stability: A Review of the Research in the Sixties," in Carlfred Broderick, *A Decade of Family Research and Action* (Minneapolis: National Council on Family Relations, 1971), p. 75.

[22] Miller and Swanson, *Changing Parent*, pp. 5–6.

[23] Betty Rollins, "Motherhood: Who Needs It?" in Skolnick and Skolnick, *Transition*, pp. 348–49. See also E. E. Lemasters, *Parents in Modern America*, rev. ed. (Homewood, Ill.: The Dorsey Press, 1974).

according to what had been minimal standards, they were afraid they would turn their children into repressed neurotics.

The changes in childrearing and child care have been so great in the American middle class that often there are very significant differences in beliefs from one generation to another. In a study by Kell and Aldous, it was found that in "comparisons of the mothers' childrearing values with their mothers . . . only in the area of discipline were the two generations significantly more likely to have values alike than unlike."[24]

Childrearing practices have undergone such rapid change in recent years that mothers sometimes feel frustration not over whether what they are doing *is* basically right, but whether it is still *believed* to be right. One can almost choose at random his beliefs in childrearing and then, by looking around, find various experts to support them. The concern here is not with the pros and cons of various schools of childrearing, but with the social context in which the child is currently perceived and how social values shape rearing practices.

As has been pointed out, the modern, urban, middle-class family is no longer strongly bound together by traditional family ties. Without the strong kinship supports and the related dependency of women on men, new family ties had to be developed. The new ties center around the emotional setting of the family in meeting the ego-needs of its members; but the nature of the need relationships within the family setting are influenced by social values outside the family.

A commonly accepted belief in the United States is that the small family can provide security for children. Many other countries have developed patterns based on the belief that parents can't attend to all things for their children. Many countries believe that the community has a responsibility to help every child to a healthy physical and social development. For example, this is the case in eastern European countries as well as Israel and Sweden.[25] There is increasing evidence that the American system leads to severe problems. Some recent theories of schizophrenia argue that the isolated nuclear family provides a setting for driving children mad. "In the isolation of the nuclear family, the parent can easily deny some aspect of reality, usually the parents' behavior or motives, thus causing the child to doubt his own perceptions. For example, the parent may act very angry or sexy, yet deny he or she is doing so."[26]

It has long been recognized that there are general social-class differences in childrearing patterns. For example, one study found that

---

[24] Leone Kell and Joan Aldous, "Trends in Child Care Over Three Generations," *Marriage and Family Living*, May 1960, p. 176.

[25] Alice S. Rossi, "Sex Equality: The Beginnings of Ideology," in Constantina Safilios-Rothschild, *Toward a Sociology of Women* (Lexington, Mass.: Xerox College Publishing, 1972), p. 350.

[26] Skolnick and Skolnick, *Transition*, p. 306.

middle-class mothers tended to use a stimulating and emotionally warm means of childrearing. Emphasis was placed on the child's achieving autonomy through satisfactions from his own efforts rather than on the basis of maternal rewards and punishments. By contrast, working-class mothers were inclined to play a more passive and less stimulating role with the child, "with more emphasis upon control through rewards and punishments. These differences have apparently persisted in spite of the homogenizing influence of the child-rearing education offered by the mass media."[27]

Another study contrasts childrearing in Italy and the United States by social class. It was found that American parents were more likely than Italian parents to value happiness, popularity, and consideration, regardless of social class. Italian parents were more apt to value manners, obedience, and seriousness. American values appeared to be more child-centered, "emphasizing the child's own development and gratification, while Italian parental values seem more adult-centered, emphasizing the child's conformity to adult standards."[28] When they compared the two countries by social class, they found them to be very much alike. Furthermore, the conservatism apparent in American working-class parental values, "far from being a peculiarly American phenomenon, is even more apparent in Italian working-class values. It seems the lot of the worker that he must accord respect to authority and teach his children to do so."[29]

Miller and Swanson suggest that the middle-class family of today is increasingly bureaucratic because there is a complex relationship between a society that stresses bureaucratic values and the family that prepares its children to move into this kind of social setting. "The adult, as the child, must be warm, friendly, and supportive of others. The powerful ambitions and desires for independence cherished by our middle classes for two centuries would unfit a youngster for participation in a society that requires him to be relaxed and cooperative."[30] The middle-class family, in rearing its children, is faced with the basic problem of teaching the children to be competitive enough to stand out to some degree, but not to be so different they will be viewed as threatening to generally accepted social values. In the "bureaucratic" middle-class family, the child "increasingly meets his peers as colleagues whose favor he must court and whose respect he must win."[31] In a society where being liked is important, the child is often taught not to select one or two close friends

[27] Grace F. Brody, "Socioeconomic Differences in Stated Maternal Child-Rearing Practices and in Observed Maternal Behavior," *Journal of Marriage and the Family*, November 1968, p. 660.

[28] Leonard I. Pearlin and Melvin L. Kohn, "Social Class, Occupation, and Parental Values: A Cross-National Study," *American Sociological Review*, August 1966, p. 469.

[29] Ibid., p. 471.

[30] Miller and Swanson, *Changing Parent*, pp. 55–56.

[31] Ibid., p. 202.

and ignore the others, but to learn to fit in smoothly with all of his age peers. "He must learn to be a 'nice guy'—affable, unthreatening, responsible, competent, and adaptive."[32]

This picture of the basic values implied in middle-class childrearing today seems to be sociologically accurate; a society where many of the new and prestigeful adult occupations stress the facility of relating to others, getting along, and not being an "odd ball" will stress the same values in the rearing of children. In many ways, today's parents want their children to fall within a more restricted behavioral spread than did parents of the past. The parent may want the child to learn the rudiments of playing the piano but not to be a pianist, to be bright but not brilliant, to be attractive but not handsome or beautiful, and to be a good student but not an excellent one. It may be that, given an American society increasingly dominated by middle-class values, parents are preparing their children in the most socially efficient manner. But the long-range social implications of a society oriented to the mediocre, conforming middle range is frightening to many social observers.

THE NATURE OF THE CHILD

The discussion thus far has concerned the parents' roles and childrearing. A further understanding of the relationship of parents to their children necessitates some discussion of the nature of the child. The question of how the child emerges from the stage of total infant dependency to a social being able to function independently has interested observers for many centuries, and many theories of human development have been put forth. One theory or way of looking at the social development of the infant and child is presented here. Most experts today assume that the infant's development as a social being is a result of internal factors such as inheritance and physiological make-up and the initially external social factors. At one time there was great controversy as to which of these two areas was the most important, but today it is recognized that a biological and social interrelationship is needed to explain human development. Generally speaking, the infant *inherits* his original nature and *acquires* his human nature.

Biological

Each child enters life having received half of his genetic makeup at the time of conception from his father and half from his mother. The factors of inheritance are passed on through 23 chromosomes from each of the parents, and each chromosome is made up of many genes related

---

[32] *Ibid.*, p. 203.

to specific inherited characteristics. Because of the vast number of genes and possible combinations, "the chance that any two human beings, now living or having lived, having identical sets of genes is practically zero, identical twins always excepted. The hereditary endowment which each of us has is strictly our own."[33]

At the time of conception, the genetic structure determines one fact about the individual which is of greatest importance in determining his social development—that is, the sex of the individual. Genetically, the structure of inheritance differs between the male and female. The male like the female has 46 chromosomes, but the male has only 22 matched pairs; the 23rd pair consists of one large and one small chromosome. The father determines the sex of the child. If a sperm carrying the X chromosome (the large one) fertilizes the egg, there will be 23 matched pairs and a girl will result. If a sperm carrying a Y chromosome (the small one) fertilizes the egg, there will be only 22 matched pairs, plus the unequal pair, and the result is a boy.[34]

The original inheritance places limits on many aspects of future personal and social development. For example, one inherits from his parents a range of possible height and, given the most favorable environmental conditions in the world, the individual will not grow beyond the upper limits set genetically. How many human qualities of development are limited in this way is unknown, but, in general, the inherited factors set a variety of limits within which social factors enable the ultimate achievement.

An important biological factor in the development of the child is *maturation*. This term is generally defined in biological terms, though it has a direct relationship to human functions of a social nature. Maturation is coming to be defined as the personal and social behavior that becomes possible through changes in the physical characteristics of any part of the human organism. Some understanding of maturation is important in knowing what the child can achieve socially. For example, before a child can walk he must have matured enough so that he has the motor skills needed for walking. Many parents attempt to train their child to an activity before the child is biologically capable of performing the activity. This often happens with toilet training and, in some instances, explains why the child who has developed some skills in toilet training "regresses." He may not have developed adequately to anticipate his needs, or not have been completely socialized as to the function of the toilet. In some cases, the child may be old enough biologically to be toilet trained but not socialized enough to accept its use.

---

[33] L. C. Dunn and Th. Dobzhansky, *Heredity, Race and Society* (New York: The New American Library, 1952), p. 56.

[34] A. M. Winchester, *Heredity and Your Life* (New York: Dover Publications, Inc., 1960), p. 108.

The relationship between biological and social variables is a complex one. Often children are left at a low level of development because they are seen as biologically limited. However, in some cases environmental changes may alter what was assumed to be a biologically limiting condition. This has been shown with children defined as mentally retarded. In a study of children under two years of age who were moved from emotionally unresponsive orphanages to one where they received emotional stimulation and support, significant changes occurred. After a period of two years the children showed a gain of close to 30 I.Q. points. In follow-up studies over the years, those children completed an average of a 12th-grade education.[35] This would suggest that many children seen as biologically unable to cope with life could cope if better social conditions were provided for them.

There are also ways in which social conditions may have negative effects on the physical development of children. The concept, "failure to thrive," refers to deficient physical development in the absence of any organic impairment. Failure to thrive in the infant may be associated with such symptoms as chronic vomiting, feeding problems, and irritability. Failure to thrive appears to be caused by disturbed relations between the baby and his parents. "Usually the parents show serious inadequacies in their functioning as persons and parents."[36]

Social Learning

In addition to biological factors, the process of acquiring social characteristics is also significant. It should be remembered that no one is born social, but that he must acquire social characteristics from others and incorporate them into his own personality. Social learning or socialization is the process by which someone learns the ways of a given society or social group so that he can function within it. Because he starts life with no social experience, socialization is most crucial to the infant and child although, because it is never completed, the process continues during the total life span of the individual.

For a child to become socialized, three conditions must operate. First, there must be an ongoing society. Society provides the necessary background of social factors to be transmitted to the child. Second, the child must have the basic genetic and biological background for the acquisition of social factors. For example, the mentally defective infant can only be partially socialized, because he falls below the minimum level of the basic

[35] Harold M. Skeels, "Adult Status of Children with Contrasting Early Life Experiences," *Monographs of the Society for Research in Child Development*, no. 105 (1966), p. 56.

[36] M. F. Leonard, J. D. Rhymes, and A. J. Solnit, "Failures to Thrive in Children, *American Journal of Diseases in Children*, vol. 11 (1966), p. 610.

requirements for learning. Third, "a child requires 'human nature,' defined as the ability to establish emotional relationships with others and to experience such sentiments as love, sympathy, shame, envy, pity, and awe."[37] It is through these sentiments that many social relationships are learned and developed.

Given the necessary conditions and background for socialization, the process of social development in the infant occurs. The child is taught the realities of his society not in the abstract, but by encountering his culture through already socialized individuals. In most cases, the important agency for transmitting the culture is the immediate family of the child. The family is important because it "gets him first, keeps him longest, is his major source of cultural imperatives, and proscribes them with emotional finality. It is important because it not only satisfies the wishes of the individual but it is instrumental in shaping those wishes into a form which only the family can satisfy."[38] The family initially sets up goals and many times offers the means of achieving them. Furthermore, the role models the family provides for the child provide directions for his developing attitudes and behavior.

As the young child starts to explore avenues of action, his behavior has to some degree been predetermined by the family, and, with future action, the family helps him to refine his roles. In this process, the child defines the meaning of his own acts by the behavior which these acts evoke in adults. For example, the child who throws his food on the floor elicits forms of disapproval from the mother, showing him that his behavior is wrong. While the mother's disapproval may have little influence on a single occasion, over the long run her reactions will usually channelize the child's behavior in the approved direction.

From a broader point of view, the parents in setting up controls and direction over the child's social development are communicating the values of society. This provides the high agreement in the socialization of most children in the same society. The meanings communicated by the parents are, for the most part, not arbitrary, but a part of the culture in which the process takes place. Because the parents have been through essentially the same socialization process, a basic continuity is provided for individuals to relate with each other in meaningful ways.

Initially, the child's learning moves from the broad to the more narrow, the general to the specific. This is particularly true in the acquisition of language. To be social, the individual must be able to communicate, and all human communication ultimately rests on the ability to use language. While the newborn infant has the capacity for learning a

---

[37] Frederick Elkin, *The Child and Society* (New York: Random House, Inc., 1960), p. 7.

[38] Willard Waller and Reuben Hill, *The Family* (New York: The Dryden Press, 1951), p. 33.

language, the specific language must be provided for him through experiences with members of society already capable of using the accepted language forms. The socially meaningful vocabulary of the child is acquired gradually, and then over time develops more rapidly. The child initially gives only a general meaning to the words he uses. For example, at first "doll" may be applied to all toys and, only later, to a specific type of toy.

Along with learning a more specific application of language, a more specific definition and understanding of role behavior generally develops. The role is a primary means of social growth for the child. The child adds to his understanding of the roles he plays by learning from others in the roles they play. One important function of role learning is through "playing the role of another." The child who plays the role of the mother may project himself into the mother role in reference to himself, thus seeing himself, in part, as his mother does. For example, the child playing the role of the mother in relationship to a doll may say to the doll "don't do that." The importance of this kind of behavior is that the child is developing an awareness of how his actions are perceived by others. It is through these various experiences that the child develops a generalized concept of himself. The generalized concept of how others view him becomes a meaningful determinant of action. In other words, the child is becoming social by being influenced by others and internalizing those values.

"As the child develops, the 'generalized other' becomes an internalized model consisting of the standards from which he views and judges his own behavior, the perspective which determines whether he is pleased or displeased with himself."[39] This may be illustrated by the child who starts some behavior and then, realizing that the behavior has been defined as wrong and having accepted, as a part of his own internal structure, that it is wrong, refrains from the action. "Since we grow into favorable roles, we tend to become what we imagine that we are, or rather, what we imagine that others imagine that we are. We grow away from unfavorable roles and elaborately avoid imagined unfavorable judgments."[40]

The initial stages of socialization, then, are provided the child through the primary influence of family models and controls in his role development. Socialization is not smooth and many times it involves conflict, refusal to accept presented roles, and regression into earlier socialized behavior. But ultimately socialization wins because the child reaches a point where his behavior and self-image fall within the limits defined as acceptable by society. Because the individual accepts the values the family transmitted as socially important, he may think they were a matter

---

[39] Elkin, *Child and Society*, p. 35.
[40] Waller and Hill, *Family*, p. 48.

of choice or are peculiar to him as an individual. However, society determines not only the "things the child thinks about but also what he thinks about the things he thinks about."[41]

In the middle class, the parents are not only concerned that the child learn from others to develop his self-awareness but also that he learn how to relate and get along with others. To be able to interact effectively with others is a highly valued middle-class skill. One study found that the highest social-class level respondents showed the greatest concern for the interpersonal relations of their children and they point out that the "higher status child gets pushed in the direction of caring what the other fellow thinks."[42]

After initial socialization, as the child's experiences and capacities increase and as he becomes more familiar and proficient with his roles, the rights and obligations that go with his roles change. The complexity of the child's roles increases for a variety of reasons. First, he comes into contact with new role models that have significance for him. The child entering the playgroup is encountering a new kind of model, a model close to himself in age and without the emotional commitment to him that his parents have. When he was in his own home with his parents, the toys he played with were often his own; but now he has to learn the attitudes and behavior related to possessiveness. A three-year-old joining the playgroup for the first time may grab the toy of another child. The other child may grab the toy back and hit him over the head with it: The three-year-old is being socialized in reference to peer-group behavior.

Second, the child finds that he no more than reaches a level of proficiency in filling a role than the role may no longer be appropriate for him. What may have been viewed as acceptable role performance at four years of age may not be at six years of age. Adults constantly force the child to recognize different role behavior for different ages. The six-year-old is told to quit acting like a baby. He is also presented with contrasts between his present age role and future roles he will fill. He may be told that he cannot do something because he is not old enough. This often has the important influence of moving the child along in new age roles because the future roles are frequently presented as including rights that seem desirable. Thus, future roles sometimes function as a dangling carrot to lead the child into new age roles. As a result, many children live in anticipation of the future because of the greater rights that go with older age roles. Often adults do not show the child that along with the rights of older age roles also go greater obligations.

Another important factor associated with the social development of the

---

[41] Ibid., pp. 42–43.

[42] Thomas S. Langner and Stanley T. Michael, *Life Stress and Mental Health* (New York: Basic Books, 1960), p. 336.

child is his love relationship to his parents. Kirkpatrick writes "it seems justifiable to conclude that the infant in our culture has a love need in the sense that denied love response from parents or parent-substitutes, he will be handicapped in his emotional development. It should not be forgotten, however, that a hypothetical love need is probably a matter of aspiration and expectation based on past experience."[43]

How parents treat their children makes a difference in their development. One study of four-year-old boys found that the parents of the most competent children had treated them more as children and less as adults. "It was also found that the parents of the competent children were significantly more permissive, less restrictive, warmer, and less hostile. There was also some indication that parents, especially mothers, of competent children spent less, though better, time with their sons."[44]

It should also be pointed out that the world of the child is quite different from the world of the adult. Although the child achieves socialization from adults, he translates this into a world determined by his own immaturity and influenced by other children. In one important way, the world of the child is different from both the infant and adult worlds: The child often develops a fantasy world and dreams his way out of conflicts and defeats. His fantasy world sometimes provides him with an opportunity to experiment emotionally with role possibilities. The young boy may dream he is another Willie Mays; while this is an unrealistic role expectation, it gives him an experience with the process of role identification that becomes valuable in identifying with roles he will ultimately seek to achieve. The fantasy world of the child often makes an important contribution to his breadth of social knowledge and understanding and, therefore, contributes to socialization.

Sex Roles.   A combining of biological and social factors lead to the development of sex-role identification. The child's learning of his own gender label as male or female takes place early, usually near the end of the second year. It does not mean he has a clear understanding of classification but rather a general physical category. The label "boy" may be seen as a name just like that of "Billy."

The individual comes to develop a sex-role identity which includes his belief about how his physical and personal characteristics match his ideal of being a male or female. Of course the ideal sex role is based on the values of the culture, and those can vary greatly in different societies. The ideal sex-role images have traditionally been that the American male wants to prove he is strong and powerful; the female to prove that she

---

[43] Clifford Kirkpatrick, *The Family* (New York: The Ronald Press Co., 1955), p. 201.

[44] William F. Clapp, "Dependence and Competence in Children: Parental Treatment of Four-Year-Old Boys," *Dissertation Abstracts*, vol. 28 (1967), p. 1703.

was capable of forming a deeply emotional relationship that brought satisfaction and growth to the partner. "Boys and girls have grown up with variations on their ideal sex-role images."[45]

The mother role has been of great significance in shaping the sex-role attitudes of young people. It has been found that there appear to be two important and fairly distinct dimensions of the mother role that effectively influence children. First, the degree to which the mother dominates the attitudes to which the children are socialized; and second, the degree to which the mother exhibits attitudes of social achievement in her own right. These mothers present very distinct images to their children of what women can be and can do.[46]

The mother obviously has great influence on her daughters as a role model. One thing seems clear and that is if the woman has focused her life on the mother role she will usually try to teach her daughters to grow up and want the same role.[47] The mother often believes her role is the only real one for an adult woman, and this is the cause of a great deal of mother-daughter conflict because the daughter doesn't buy the traditional mother role for herself.

It cannot be overlooked that all very young children are dependent on adults for their physical well-being and for the knowledge that they have personal worth and value. In the past, the girl's self-esteem has remained dependent on other people's acceptance and love, and girls continue to use the skills of others instead of developing their own; "the boy's impulsivity and sexuality are sources of enormous pleasure independent of anyone else's response; these pleasures are central to the early core-self."[48] Very often when boys are pressed to give up what are seen as childish ways, it is because their behavior is seen as feminine by parents. "Boys have to earn their masculinity early. Until puberty, femininity is a verbal label, a given attribute—something that does not have to be earned."[49]

The sex-role learning of children is also affected by school experiences. In elementary schools 85 percent of all the teachers are women. Although schools are run at the top by men, they are essentially feminine institutions. "Women set the standards for adult behavior, and many favor

---

[45] Suzanne Keller, "Does the Family Have a Future?" *A Warner Modular Publication,* reprint 64 (1973), p. 10.

[46] Harold C. Meier, "Mother-Centeredness and College Youths' Attitudes toward Social Equality for Women: Some Empirical Findings," *Journal of Marriage and the Family,* February 1972, p. 120.

[47] Rollins, "Motherhood," p. 354.

[48] Judith M. Bardwick and Elizabeth Douvan, "Ambivalence: The Socialization of Women," in Vivian Gornick and Barbara K. Moran, *Women in Sexist Society* (New York: New American Library, 1971), p. 227.

[49] Ibid., p. 228.

students who most conform to their own behavior norms—polite, clean, obedient, neat, and nice."[50] In her study of 1,000 boys and girls in the ninth grade Patricia Sexton found that when a boy scored high on masculinity measurements, his report-card average was low. In fact, the less masculine boys had better marks in most school subjects. "Only in physical education and science did boys with middle masculinity scores tend to get the best marks. Low-achieving boys got their highest marks in shop and physical education."[51]

REWARDS AND PUNISHMENTS

The child may be coerced, encouraged, and indoctrinated in many different ways, but with few exceptions the methods are based on a reward and punishment system. For example, even the child who emotionally and intellectually responds to social demands is often doing so because he sees some personal gain or reward. Or, put the opposite way, a child will not usually change voluntarily if he anticipates little or no gain for himself.

Discipline for the child must always originate externally, because it is related to social expectations he must learn. At first, discipline seems to come entirely from the parent's side, and obedience to be wholly the function of the child. But as development takes place, discipline shifts from its position of outward authority to an inner position of self-control, there blending with obedience until the two are indistinguishable. Obedience becomes then not a yielding to superior force but the spontaneous expression of self-discipline.

So in the middle class the value of self-discipline becomes important in the socialization of the child. The parents place a high value on self-direction when the children are quite young. It is of high importance to those parents that the child be able to decide for himself how to act and that he have the personal resources to implement his decisions. "Working-class parents, on the other hand, stress conformity to external standards and are themselves quite willing to give obedience, obedience to 'authority,' in return for security and respectability."[52] Another study found that it is primarily in the lower middle-class levels that boys get more punishment than girls, and the latter receive greater warmth and attention. "With an increase in the family's social position, direct discipline drops off, especially for boys, and indulgence and protectiveness

---

[50] Patricia Sexton, "How the American Boy is Feminized, "*Readings in Society and Human Behavior* (California: Communications Research Machines, Inc., 1972), p. 41.

[51] Ibid., pp. 43–44.

[52] Benson, *Fatherhood,* pp. 280–81.

decrease for girls. As a result, patterns of parental treatment for the two sexes begin to converge."[53]

Discipline or obedience is a requirement made by all societies. The individual must conform and accept at least a minimum set of social requirements; if he did not, social relationships would have no order or predictability. The question is not discipline or no discipline, but rather what degree and type of discipline. Even in the most "permissive" up-bringing of a child, some adult social discipline must be exerted on the young child or he would not survive.

As to type of discipline, experts disagree. Some argue for spanking and others against it. One type of discipline will probably work with some children and not others. It seems important, whatever the form of punishment, to relate the punishment to the act and not to give the child the feeling of rejection or loss of love. Because the love of the parents is socially important, punishing through withdrawal of love may create for the child a situation more harmful than the behavior that led to the punishment.

There are some research data to suggest that when parents are restrictive, rather than permissive, there is more apt to be aggression on the part of the child. This appears to be especially true for boys. This may mean that restrictiveness leads to aggression as a consequence which the child sees as natural.[54]

Many psychologists now believe that in the socialization of the child to positive techniques of social control the techniques of rewards or praise are better than their negative counterparts of punishment or aversion stimulation. "This belief is based upon accumulated research findings which indicate a variety of undesirable concomitants which stem from the use of these negative techniques."[55]

Parents sometimes use excessive love as a means of controlling their children. In some middle-class families, the parents saturate their children with love and, as a result, the love of the parent means little. The child may feel he can do anything because the love of his parents is not altered by his behavior. Or the child may be convinced that his parents love him so much that not meeting their expectations means letting them

---

[53] Urie Bronfenbrenner, "The Changing American Child: A Speculative Analysis," in Rose Coser, *Life Cycle and Achievement in America* (New York: Harpers, 1969), p. 11.

[54] Eva J. Delaney, "Parental Antecedents of Social Aggression in Young Children," *Dissertation Abstracts*, vol. 26 (1965), p. 1,763.

[55] Gerald Marwell and David R. Schmitt, "Attitudes Toward Parental Use of Promised Rewards to Control Adolescent Behavior," *Journal of Marriage and the Family*, August 1967, p. 500. See also Howard S. Erlanger, "Social Class and Corporal Punishment in Childrearing: A Reassessment," *American Sociological Review*, February 1974, pp. 68–85.

down, which may result in strong feelings of guilt when he does not meet their expectations.

The types of reward and punishment used in the American society vary greatly; no single system is used by all parents. The Miller and Swanson study indicates some of the types of punishments used by mothers for a child ten years of age "who had done something with which the mother was extremely upset or angered." The most common punishments were "restrict behavior and withdraw privileges," 44 percent; "scolds and threatens," 25 percent; and "physical punishment," 22 percent. A much higher agreement was found in rewards for a ten-year-old: "psychic reward or other verbal praise," 68 percent; and "material reward, money, gifts, etc.," 19 percent.[56]

These are some of the patterns of socialization frequently found in the American middle class. While actual procedure varies widely, the variations normally fall within an acceptable social range. In all aspects of socializing the child, parents are given alternative courses of action, and it is only if they go beyond the accepted limits that society steps in and takes responsibility for childrearing out of their hands.

When compared to the rest of American society, the middle class has certain values that it stresses with regard to child care and rearing. For example, one study reports that "middle-class parents train their children earlier, are more affectionate, and employ 'conditional love' techniques of discipline to a greater extent than lower class parents."[57] Middle-class parents are more concerned with "developing internalization of self-control by the child, and in this sense are future oriented, while lower-class parents are more concerned about immediate consequences of child behavior and maintaining order and obedience."[58] Lenski found that among upper middle-class Protestants 90 percent valued intellectual autonomy above simple obedience, as compared to 48 percent of the lower-working class.[59]

The evidence from various studies generally suggests that middle-class parents tend to be more supportive and controlling of their children than are lower-class parents. The middle class are more likely to discipline their children by utilizing reason and appeals to guilt and are less likely to use physical punishment. "Differential treatment of male and female children seems to occur primarily among lower-class families."[60]

Ultimately the test of socialization is the end product. The fact that some children turn out to be inadequate in a social and/or personal way

---

[56] Miller and Swanson, *Changing Parent,* p. 221.

[57] Bernard C. Rosen, "Family Structure and Value Transmission," *Merrill-Palmer Quarterly,* January 1964, p. 74.

[58] Dager, "Socialization," p. 750.

[59] Gerhard Lenski, *The Religious Factor* (New York: Anchor Books, 1963), p. 223.

[60] Walters and Stinnett, "Parent-Child Relationships," p. 124.

is a reflection on society, as well as the adults who were responsible for the socializing. With so many children and adolescents (as well as adults) experiencing severe psychological problems, the American system of childrearing often seems to be inadequate. In most of these cases, the responsibility probably rests with those who did the childrearing, rather than society in general. This is suggested because so many individuals *are* reared to emerge as well-socialized individuals in reference to both social and personal criteria. It is difficult to define a good or effective personality in psychological terms; however, it is possible to make some suggestions within a social context. To say a person has a "good" personality in the American middle class usually means that the person is able to make the social adjustments required of him and, at the same time, maintain enough individual flexibility to deal effectively with new situations. Another way of saying essentially the same thing is in terms of social and psychological maturity: That is, the individual is able to function as an adult in society. Probably the best single index of maturity is the extent to which a person has progressed from the utter self-centeredness of childhood toward full acceptance of the responsibilities of social living.

Implied in the above discussion is that some balance should exist between the demands of society and individual desires. Some degree of conformity is needed for the individual to function in society; however, an opportunity for expression of individual desires must also be given. The social and personal demands will not always balance and, in many instances, the individual may go counter to social demands and expectations. Deviancy from social norms leads to degrees of individual personality variations as well as possible social change.

THE FAMILY SETTING AND INTERACTION

The parents provide the children with direction not only in the roles they are playing at a given point in time, but also in reference to their future roles. As indicated earlier, the childrens' experiences in learning from their parents the roles of husband and wife have long-range implications for their own future marriage. This is also true in regard to the future roles of the children as parents.

One very important role the parents play during the growth of the child is as sex-role models. The children learn to a great extent, at least in their early years, role conceptions of adult masculinity and femininity from their parents. This is important not only in learning the sex role that the child will play, but also in learning something of the opposite sex role. The middle-class child has limited experiences with adult males, and therefore the influence of the father as a male-role model is important to both sons and daughters. Because the role of the father is generally less developed in relation to the child than is the role of the mother, the children may be influenced more by male-role models provided through the mass media than by their own father.

A stated ideal that may not always be easy to carry out is that parents have equal feelings for all of their children, or at least show no overt preference. Even if their emotional commitment to their children is essentially the same, their treatment of each child will be different because of personality and age-sex differences. When this happens, the child may "see" the brother or sister receiving different treatment and define it as preferential treatment. The older child may feel that the parents let the younger one get away with more, not realizing the younger is given greater leeway because he is less mature. On the other hand, the younger child may feel that the older sibling has more privileges, not realizing that that is a result of the parents recognizing greater maturity.

In any family the personalities of the children differ, and because their age and sex differ too, the parents must treat them differently. Some children are very cooperative and are not subjected to parental control to the same degree as a sibling who is not cooperative. To the child, the reason and the logic for variations in parental treatment are usually difficult to understand.

Finally, many parents do, in fact, have a preference for one of their children. A great deal of research has been done on birth order and sex of children in relationship with their parents, but it has not established any definite tendency for a specific type of child to be selected as a favorite. As examples, one might argue that a mother would feel closer to her oldest child because he was her firstborn, or one might equally argue that she will feel closer to her youngest because he continues to be her "baby." It might be argued that a father would feel closest to a son because the son is an extension of himself or, in contrast, that he would feel closest to the daughter because of the attractiveness of the child of the opposite sex. What evidence there is would seem to indicate that the choice of a favorite child will be determined by the peculiar personality factors of both the parents and the children.

The Relation of Mother and Child

The mother will generally be perceived by the children in a different light than the father because the "mother role tends to be anchored between family and mother-child systems, the father role between family and extrafamilial systems."[61] The fact that the mother spends time in a

---

[61] Talcott Parsons and Robert F. Bales, *Family, Socialization and Interaction Process* (Glencoe, Ill.: The Free Press, 1955), p. 81.

variety of role activities means that her children see her role as more extended than that of the father.

A study of children between the ages of 6 and 12 found that a majority of both boys and girls perceived their mothers as friendlier, less punitive, less dominant, and less threatening than fathers.[62] Winch suggests that in the "middle-class American society there is a tendency for: (*a*) the mother to be the preferred parent, (*b*) the son to be the preferred child, and (*c*) for the mother-son relationship to be the strongest of the four parent-child relationships."[63] While a good deal of evidence supports the first two suggestions, the third seems questionable. The mother-son relationship is the Freudian Oedipus tie that seems to perpetuate itself in family writing, but has very little empirical support. The evidence appears to clearly illustrate that the mother is the major parental influence for both sons *and* daughters. For example, Langner found that a "worrying mother" was somewhat more harmful with respect to the offspring's mental health than a worrying father. "A third of the [disturbed subjects'] mothers were worriers, but only a tenth of the fathers."[64]

There are various reactions among males and females in identifying with their parents. Often the male identifies with the culturally defined masculine role while the female tends to identify with her mother. It appears that both males and females tend to identify more closely with their mothers than with their fathers. The closer identification of the son with the mother tends to be most revealed in personality variables which are not clearly sex typed.[65] Males are more anxious regarding sex-role identification than females and tend to hold stronger feelings of hostility toward females than females toward males.[66]

The Relation of Father and Child

In middle-class American society, children see much less of their father than their mother. The period of time between when the husband returns home in the evening and when the children go to bed may be short and not particularly centered around father and children interaction, and on the weekend, many middle-class fathers are involved in personal activities and have limited time to spend with their children. The children also have interests of their own and often want to pursue them

---

[62] Jerome Kagan, "The Child's Perception of the Parent," in Jerome M. Seidman, *The Child* (New York: Holt-Dryden, 1958), p. 139.

[63] Robert F. Winch, Robert McGinnis, and Herbert R. Barringer, *Selected Studies in Marriage and the Family* (New York: Holt, Rinehart & Winston, 1962), p. 299.

[64] Langner and Michael, *Life Stress*, p. 221.

[65] David R. Lynn, "The Process of Learning Parental and Sex-Role Identification," *Journal of Marriage and the Family*, November 1966, p. 468.

[66] Ibid., p. 469.

on the weekend. The father who "gives" Saturday morning to his son may really be "taking" the son from something he would rather be doing.

Some fathers see in their sons an opportunity to project their own ambitions. (This may also be true for mothers.) The father's projection to his son may be in the area of physical success through athletics. The father may play games with his son not so much for the pleasure of playing the games, but rather to help the boy become more athletically proficient. This is illustrated by the middle-class "little-league syndrome." Anyone who believes that little-league baseball is always performed for the pleasure that the boy will derive from the game should attend a few little-league practices or games.

Often the father responds to his son's behavior as if that behavior was taking place within his occupational world. That is, fathers in the middle class often evaluate their children's behavior in terms of aggressiveness and competitiveness which is expected in their own occupational world, "despite their explicit contention that the two spheres should be kept quite distinct. Thus, the fathers regard the characteristics essential to their work as virtues, not simply means to occupational goals."[67] This is also further evidence that for many men the occupational role is more important than the father role—at least in terms of major values adhered to.

For many a father, relationships with his son are to help him be a "real boy" according to the definitions accepted by the father. The father's control over the daughter tends to be much less direct and concentrates more on the pleasurable aspect of the relationship than on a responsibility of her rearing. While many fathers are concerned that the son is not meeting their expectations, they are inclined to leave the setting of daughter expectations and behavior to the mother. Many parents assume that because the father was a boy and the mother a girl they are qualified to understand, diagnose, and prescribe behavior for the child of the same sex. There is evidence that parents tend to exert more power toward their same-sex children than toward their opposite-sex children.[68] Though the father assumes that the mother can take care of the son in the everyday requirements of childrearing, he also believes that he should move in and give the son the masculine direction he needs. While it is important that the parent of the same sex perform as a sex-role model, it does not necessarily mean that simply because they are the same sex they are best qualified to know what is appropriate for the child.

---

[67] Benson, *Fatherhood*, pp. 279–80.

[68] Walter Emmerich, "Variations in the Parents' Parent Role as a Function of Sex and the Child's Sex and Age," *Merrill-Palmer Quarterly*, vol. 8 (1967), p. 10.

In most texts about the family, the assumption is made that two parents, with positive role relations, are needed for successful socialization of their children. It seems highly probable that the most favorable family socialization occurs for children when they do have a positive and ongoing relationship with both their parents, but simply having both parents present and actively interacting with their children does not necessarily lead to positive patterns of parent-child relationships. More relevant is the corollary assumption that *not* having a parent (almost always the father) present is highly negative to the process of socialization. If the assumption is true, one would expect a strong body of evidence showing negative consequences for children reared in fatherless families.

The number of one-parent families in the United States is very large. In 1969 more than 25 percent of all nonwhite families were headed by females. The proportion of all white families headed by women was about 10 percent. However, it is relatively rare for a child to live with someone other than his mother. In 1960, 99.1 percent of all white children under five years of age lived with their mothers. Of the 10 percent of all white children in 1968 not living with both their parents, 7 percent were living with the mother only, 1 percent with the father only, and 2 percent with neither parent.[69]

In a study by Nye, broken (one-parent) and remarried homes were compared with intact, but unhappy, homes. Nye found broken homes were somewhat superior to the intact, unhappy homes but, in general, no evidence of more adjustment problems for children in any one of the three types.[70] Burchinal, in a study of homes similar to Nye's types, found no significant differences in most aspects of adolescent adjustment.[71] Perry and Pfuhl, in comparing one-parent homes to remarried homes, found among the children studied no differences in delinquency, psychosomatic complaints, or school grades.[72] Crain and Stamm used two groups of second-grade children to test the hypothesis that regular prolonged absence of the father affected the child's perceptions of both the mother and the father. "The results did not support the hypothesis. Generally, nonsignificant differences are found between father-present and father-

[69] Reynolds Farley and Albert I. Hermal, in "Family Stability: A Comparison of Trends between Blacks and Whites," *American Sociological Review*, February 1971, p. 14.

[70] F. Ivan Nye, "Child Adjustment in Broken and in Unhappy Unbroken Homes," *Marriage and Family Living*, November 1957, pp. 356–61.

[71] Lee G. Burchinal, "Characteristics of Adolescents from Unbroken, Broken, and Reconstituted Families," *Journal of Marriage and the Family*, February 1964, pp. 44–51.

[72] Joseph B. Parry and Erdwin H. Pfuhl, "Adjustment of Children in 'Sole' and 'Remarriage' Homes," *Marriage and Family Living*, May 1963, pp. 221–23.

absent children in the child's perception of father and mother as sources of authority and love."[73]

The studies raise serious questions about the general assumption as to the absolute need of the father. The point is not that a father makes no significant contribution, but rather that absence of the father (the one-parent family without a father) may not, in fact, be *the* cause of almost all personal and social problems. (The one-parent family *has* been used to "explain" delinquency, mental illness, crime, sex-role and sexual inadequacies, school problems, and poverty.)

The assumption has been that the presence of the father is needed to serve as a sex-role model in the socialization of his children. But as we have decreased the amount of time and degree of involvement of the father—even in an "ideal" family—the influence of the father as a sex-role model may have become greatly diminished. Children often find sex-role models outside the family to supplement or replace the father, that is, males tending to identify with a cultural stereotype of the male role. The stress placed on the great importance of sex-role models also implies a society where there are important sex role differences, but there is a good deal of evidence to suggest that masculinity-femininity differences are decreasing in America.

In brief, in today's American middle-class family, parents are less involved in the socialization of their children than they were in the past. The father role is primarily supportive and the functions he performs are often minor and replaceable either by the wife or by outside-the-family agencies—without evidence of significant negative costs to the child. The mother role is comparatively more important than formerly—when compared to the father role—because increasingly the mother includes in her role combined parental functions.

Sibling Relationships

How siblings react to each other is to some degree influenced by how their parents treat them as children. The evidence indicates that parents often respond to their first child somewhat differently than they respond to later children. One study found that parents tended to be more supportive of, and to exert more pressure for, achievement upon first-born children. "Because the first-born children are more accustomed to receiving supportive behavior, they also tend to be more dependent upon others for support when placed in stressful situations."[74] It appears that

---

[73] Alan J. Crain and Caroline S. Stamm, "Intermittent Absence of Fathers and Children's Perceptions of Parents," *Journal of Marriage and the Family*, August 1965, pp. 344–47.

[74] Walters and Stinnett, "Parent-Child Relationships," pp. 123–24.

as parents have more children they become more authoritarian and decrease their communication with children. These variables would appear sometimes to affect how siblings treat each other.

When the sex differences of children are analyzed, it is clear that the socialization process has many areas of difference. Parents in most cases rear daughters differently than they do sons. Sex differences in the socialization of children are not peculiar to the American society. A survey of 110 cultures showed that "in childhood there is, as in our society, a widespread pattern of greater pressure toward nurturance, obedience, and responsibility in girls and toward self-reliance and achievement striving in boys."[75]

Many parents start to stress sex distinctions long before the infant is aware of his own sex. The dressing of boys in blue and girls in pink, or the sex-differentiated toys given to infants are examples. As boys and girls grow up, the whole family is consciously aware of their sex differences and, as a result, sibling conflict and competition may be minimized. Because the boy and girl are often reared within somewhat different frames of reference, they are less compelled to make comparisons with each other than are siblings of the same sex.

When the siblings are of the same sex, they are developing with essentially the same socialization emphases and are apt to view each other and be viewed in a competitive light. But the younger sibling may also have the advantage of using the older brother (or sister) as a role model. The older sibling, who is further along in the socialization process but still relatively close in age actions to the younger sibling, may be a more effective agent of model expectations than the much older, adult parents.

Many younger children view their older siblings with mixed feelings. On one hand, the older siblings may do things that the younger would like to do but cannot because he is not old enough; on the other hand, they are perceived as helpful by the younger because of their greater experience and prestige.

If siblings are similar in age, there is companionship at the price of possible rivalry. If they are widely separated in birth order, there is lack of competition but sacrifice of companionship. This indicates that there is no ideal relationship in age for siblings. Research has shown by its inconclusiveness that little of a reliable nature can be said about any particular birth position, age, or sex sibling relationship making a greater positive contribution than any other.

Brim found that through interaction and taking the role of the other, cross-sex sibling relationships lead to some differences in the acquiring

---

[75] Herbert Barry III, Margaret K. Baron, and Irvin L. Child, "A Cross-Cultural Survey of Some Sex Differences in Socialization," in Winch, McGinnis, and Barringer, *Selected Studies*, p. 274.

of masculine and feminine traits. For example, a girl with an older brother is more masculine than her counterpart with an older sister, and the boy with an older sister is more feminine than is his counterpart with an older brother.[76] Research on the two-sibling family indicates some important differences in the learning of sex roles. "While the younger, as contrasted with the older, girl with a brother manifests only a slightly greater degree of masculinity, this difference for boys is quite striking: The younger, as contrasted with the older, boy with a sister is substantially more feminine."[77]

One study shows that there is no evidence for the notion that a girl with a brother will tend to have a more traditional orientation toward the female role or more traditional beliefs about female personality traits than girls without brothers. It has been found that the girl who has an older brother is more apt to have a conception of female personality traits which denies there is a great difference between males and females.[78]

There are some advantages of having siblings. First, the child is usually provided with age peers, which means that he has others of about the same age with whom to interact, and who generally contribute to his overall socialization. Second, the siblings help bring him into contact with other children. His siblings will have their friends who will be around him, and this will extend his experiences. In some cases, this may have unpleasant implications if the older sibling's friends are the younger child's primary reference group and they reject him. Third, the sibling functions as a role model in teaching the younger sibling his future role behavior. Fourth, because children other than himself are in the family, the child must learn to share with them the rights and privileges of the family. This is important in the social sense that a child must learn that his wishes cannot always be satisfied or must sometimes remain unsatisfied because of the needs of others.

There has long been an interest in the question of whether or not the birth order of children has any significance. This interest has been based on the assumption that ordinal positions of children subject them to different patterns of interaction leading to different learning experiences. Rossi has suggested that last-born children are more likely to be unwanted than are first- or middle-born children, particularly in large families. "This is consistent with what is known of abortion patterns among married women, who typically resort to abortion only when they have

---

[76] Orville G. Brim, Jr., "Family Structure and Sex Role Learning by Children: Further Analysis of Helen Koch's Data," in Winch, McGinnis, and Barringer, *Selected Studies*, p. 286.

[77] Ibid., p. 287.

[78] Kenneth Kammeyer, "Sibling Position and the Feminine Role," *Journal of Marriage and the Family*, August 1967, p. 498.

achieved the number of children they want or feel they can afford to have."[79]

Rossi also suggests that last born children may experience less verbal stimulation as well as less prompt and enthusiastic response to their demands—"from feeding and diaper change as infants to requests for stories read at 3 or a college education at 18—simply because the parents experience less intense gratification from the parent role with the third child than they did with the first."[80] Kammeyer found that first born girls were more in agreement with their parents' attitudes about proper feminine role behavior than were later born girls. This is explained on the grounds that parents have more time and energy to devote to the socialization of the first child. "As a result of this characteristic it is likely that first-born children will tend to hold views that are similar to their parents."[81]

Some general problems related to family siblings also exist. First, the personalities of the different children may conflict. The very fact that they are different in age and personality structure will lead to some differences. In many families, sibling relationships seem to be one long series of conflicts. Second, there will be some sibling rivalry. The fact that what the child wants is not always available to him just when and to the degree he wants it may be due to the competition of a sibling. Therefore, the child often perceives the sibling as a threat and a rival. Many experts have suggested that sibling rivalry is inevitable in the family, and there seems good reason to believe this is true. A third problem may be the development of family cliques. While this sometimes happens with a parent and child, it is probably more common among the children themselves. For example, two children of the same sex may organize against a child of the opposite sex, or two older siblings against a younger. Some kinds of alignments among siblings seem inevitable, though in many families these may be shifting and temporary.

The family relationships among children and with the parents are a pattern of complex interaction in the middle class. This is true because of the numbers as well as the demands made in learning to fill appropriate age-sex roles. With the entrance of an added child, the family takes on greater numerical complexity. When only the two parents and one child are in the family, only three interactional relationships exist. The addition of the second child increases the interactional relationships to six, the addition of a third child to ten, and so forth. It has been argued that large families in the past had fewer problems than today; however, if this was true, it may have been because the social and psychological

---

[79] Rossi, "Equality," p. 33.

[80] Ibid., p. 34.

[81] Kammeyer, "Sibling Position," pp. 77–78.

demands made on both parents and children in the past were probably fewer and simpler than in today's American middle class.

SELECTED BIBLIOGRAPHY

Benson, Leonard   *Fatherhood: A Sociological Perspective.* New York: Random House, 1968.

Dager, Edward Z.   "Socialization and Personality Development in the Child," in Harold T. Christensen, ed., *Handbook of Marriage and the Family.* Chicago: Rand McNally & Co., 1964, pp. 740–81.

Dunn, L. C., and **Dobzhansky, Th.**   *Heredity, Race and Society.* New York: The New American Library, 1952.

Elkin, Frederick   *The Child and Society.* New York: Random House, Inc., 1960.

Erlanger, Howard S.   "Social Class and Corporal Punishment in Childrearing: A Reassessment." *American Sociological Review,* February 1974, pp. 68–85.

Kammeyer, Kenneth   "Sibling Position and the Feminine Role." *Journal of Marriage and the Family,* August 1967, pp. 494–99.

Lynn, David R.   "The Process of Learning Parental and Sex-Role Identification." *Journal of Marriage and the Family,* November 1966, pp. 466–70.

Marwell, Gerald, and **Schmitt, David R.**   "Attitudes Toward Parental Use of Promised Rewards to Control Adolescent Behavior." *Journal of Marriage and the Family,* August 1967, pp. 500–504.

Miller, Daniel R., and **Swanson, Guy E.**   *The Changing American Parent.* New York: John Wiley & Sons, Inc., 1958.

Pearlin, Leonard I., and **Kohn, Melvin L.**   "Social Class, Occupation, and Parental Values: A Cross-National Study." *American Sociological Review,* August 1966, pp. 466–79.

Walters, James, and **Stinnett, Nick**   "Parent-Child Relationships: A Decade Review of Research." *Journal of Marriage and the Family,* February 1971, pp. 70–111.

Chapter 20

Parent-Child Interaction: Adolescence and Launching Years

As pointed out in the previous chapter, the first few years of the young child's life are centered almost completely within his family of orientation. As the child grows older, other agencies and influences in society take on relevance for him. The influence of the playgroup and the school start early in the life of the child and take on greater and greater significance as the child grows older. This generally means that the influence of the family decreases. It is important to recognize that the family is "helped" to give up some of its influences over the child by the other agencies becoming increasingly important to the child. This "help" normally occurs whether the parents want it or not.

In the American middle class, adolescence is a transition stage in which the youngster is no longer socially defined as a child but is not yet an adult. The period of adolescence roughly corresponds to the teen-age years; the young person is neither "fish nor fowl" in filling child or adult roles. Many primitive societies had no similar period of role confusion in moving from child to adult status because the individual was treated as a child until he qualified for adult status and underwent the "puberty rites" of his society. From that point on, he was recognized as an adult.

That the American society has no clear-cut age when adult status is

reached is illustrated by the different legal ages giving rights and obligations to the young person in the United States. Over time and in different states a variety of ages may be set for marriage, voting, going into
the armed forces, and so forth. For purposes of discussion, it is suggested
that in the middle class, adolescence corresponds with the teen ages and
the "launching" years run from about 18 into the early 20s. Of course,
individual exceptions will occur; some persons may be socially recognized
as adults at 18 or 19. Before discussing the social nature of adolescence,
however, it is necessary to say something of the biological influences
during this period.

Social change occurs so rapidly that not only may there be wide differences between parents and children but even among young people a
few years apart. Toffler has suggested that the pace of change is already
so blinding that "some brothers and sisters, separated in age by a mere
three or four years, subjectively feel themselves to be members of quite
different generations."[1]

EARLY ADOLESCENCE

Pubescence taken in its literal sense refers to the period of time during
which the pubic hair is developing. This means that the youngsters are
moving physically through changes that make them sexually mature
males and females. Pubescence is a stage or period of development for
the youngster, and while the duration varies to some degree, it is rarely
less than two years and may be considerably longer. By the time pubescence is ended, the boy has completed the development of pubic hairs,
facial hair, voice change, and enlargement of the genitals. For the girl,
the physical changes are growth of pubic hair, rounding of the hips,
enlargement of the breasts, some vaginal changes, and the first menstrual
period.

The concept of adolescence is recent in the historical development of
mankind. The concept as it is generally understood and applied today
did not exist before the last two decades of the 19th century. In the early
books that were written about youth the primary concern was related to
the problem of authority. "In one form or another, they all imparted the
same message; the authority of parents must be established early in the
child's life and firmly maintained throughout the years of growth."[2] It was
believed that even the smallest infant showed a "willfulness that came of
a depraved nature and that was intensely selfish." The written belief in
the early days was that that depraved nature had to be suppressed by

---

[1] Alvin Toffler, *Future Shock* (London: Pan Books Ltd., 1970), p. 267.

[2] John Demos and Virginia Demos, "Adolescence in Historical Perspective," *Journal
of Marriage and the Family,* November 1969, p. 633.

strict training in obedience "or it will rapidly develop beyond the possibility of control with dire implications for the later (adult) personality."[3] The tendency of youth toward mental instability—"melancholy for males and hysteria for females—was set down by medical writers from the 1830s onward under the rubric 'pubertal insanity.' "[4] The growth of the concept of adolescence came about in response to an observable fact—the fact of a youth culture. Americans needed some means of understanding the problems of, and the problems created by, these young people."[5]

During the 20th century, many physical characteristics of the American population have undergone change. With the development of new knowledge in medicine, nutrition, sanitation, and disease control, the younger generations are somewhat more physically advanced at earlier ages than previous generations. For example, in 1888 the average Yale freshman was 5 feet 7½ inches tall and weighed 136 pounds, as compared to the freshman of 1957 who was 3 inches taller and 20 pounds heavier. And coeds at Vassar and Smith in 1957 were almost 2 inches taller and 10 pounds heavier in the 1950s than were their counterparts at the start of this century.

Puberty occurs in girls at an average age of 12, in boys at an average age of 14. Girls start out ahead of boys in physically maturing and maintain the lead through adolescence; they reach physical maturity at about the age of 18, 2 or 3 years ahead of their male contemporaries. The important phenomena of menstruation occurs about a year after the girl enters the period of pubescence. The average age of first menstrual period for girls in the United States is about 13. The range of usual occurrence is between 11 and 15, with about 3 percent falling below and 3 percent above the limits. It appears that this average has become somewhat earlier in recent years and that girls reach the menarche on the average a few months earlier than did their mothers.

The reaching of puberty, and particularly the menarche, does not mean that girls are completely adult females in reproductive ability. The evidence suggests that conception is extremely unlikely to occur during the first year following the menarche, and that for a period of four to six years it is less likely than after full maturity. Conception can occur very early, but it seldom does so before the age of 16, regardless of the age at the menarche.

There are important differences in the physical growth of boys and girls around the time of puberty. Girls gain in height at an accelerating

---

[3] Ibid., p. 633.

[4] Joseph F. Kett, "Adolescence and Youth in Nineteenth-Century America," in Theodore K. Rabb and Robert I. Rotberg, *The Family in History: Interdisciplinary Essays* (New York: Harper and Row, 1973), p. 103.

[5] Demos and Demos, "Adolescence," p. 638.

rate from 9 to 12 years, whereas boys do so from 11 to 14 years. Thus, in the age group 11 to 13, the girls are frequently taller than the boys. Relationships are often difficult for youngsters in this age group because of the reversed physical differences in height and the general awkwardness of the social relationships.

The age range for reaching pubescence has different implications for girls than it does for boys. While early or late pubescence is a biological fact, its occurrence is treated within a variety of social definitions. Harold Jones did a study of the physically most precocious 20 percent and the physically most retarded 20 percent in a random sample of girls from a public school. The two groups were matched according to intelligence, social class, race, and childhood health records.[6] His general findings were that "the early-maturing (girls) were below the average in prestige, sociability, and leadership; below the average in popularity; below the average in cheerfulness, poise, and expressiveness."[7]

The Jones study indicates that the girl who goes through pubescence at a later age has definite advantages over the early bloomer, and suggests several reasons for this advantage. The first is a physical advantage. Those girls who are later in sexual maturing have less sudden physical growth, which involves fewer hazards of physiological imbalance and physical distortion for them than for the early maturing girls. Jones writes that the longer period of growth "affects particularly the legs, and the late maturing girl is therefore long-legged, and tends to conform closely to our American standards of beauty of figure, which in the present code of commercial advertising must always be long-legged and usually a bit hypo-feminine."[8]

A second important factor is that the early-maturing girl moves abruptly into being physically a young woman, but her age and social abilities do not keep pace with the sudden change. With a later maturation, the parents and the girl herself have a longer time in which to get used to the new interests, new impulses, and new requirements as to behavior. A third factor is that the late-maturing girl is more nearly in step with the boys in her age group than is the early-maturing girl. The two-year lag in the average maturity patterns of boys as compared with girls is reduced or eliminated among those girls who mature late and, as a result, various social activities are more immediately satisfied.

It has been argued that since adolescence begins earlier for females they are inclined by a "need for social comparison" and by parental push to become more peer oriented in early adolescence than do boys. With the onset of puberty girls are faced with their first crisis: "they must

[6] Harold E. Jones, "Adolescence in Our Society," in Jerome M. Seidman, *The Adolescent* (New York: Holt-Dryden, 1960), pp. 50–51.

[7] Ibid., p. 56.

[8] Ibid., p. 58.

come to terms with and find pleasure in their physical femininity and develop the proper psychological 'femininity'."[9] Probably most adolescent girls remain dependent on others for their feelings of affirmation. Because there are few independent and objective achievements girls know their worth only from others' responses, "know their identity only from their relationships as daughters, girl friends, wives, or mothers and, in a literal sense, personalize the world."[10]

For the boy, the consequences of early maturing are just the opposite. "The early-maturing boy enters adolescence at a time when girls in his age group are appreciative of male acquaintances who no longer insist upon being children. He also acquires traits of strength and athletic ability which give him prestige with his own sex." By contrast, the boy who matures late is out of step with all the others in his age group and is often treated by them as a little boy. It was found that those boys who were physically accelerated had little need to strive for status and from their ranks come the outstanding leaders in senior high school.[11]

The variations in achieving physical maturity, by sex, provide a contrast in the social definition of early adolescent roles. For the boy, early physical maturity, if accompanied by appropriate coordination, provides him with an advantage in the valued activities of boys. Being nearer to male adult physical development provides him with an advantage over other boys. But socially just the opposite is often true for the girl. The early-adolescent girl who stands out from most of her age peers in physical development is, like the early-developing boy, closer to female adult physical growth. She is often viewed by adults as a little girl with a woman's body and it is often feared that her social and psychological immaturity will get her into trouble. (However, her physical development may provide her with advantages in acquiring dates.)

In many groups of girls, there is a tendency to conform in physical appearance. The girl with greater physical development may try to hide it, or the underdeveloped girl may try to give the impression of being more developed. The second is probably a more common trait in today's American society. For example, in the past the girl with early breast development might wear loose clothing or become stoop shouldered to hide her "deformity." In contrast, the slower-developing girl today may buy "falsies" to catch up with the "honest" girl who reflects the norms of the group.

Because early adolescence signals the period of rapidly developing interest in the opposite sex, general physical attractiveness becomes of great

---

[9] Judith M. Bardwick and Elizabeth Douvan, "Ambivalence: The Socialization of Women," in Vivian Gornick and Barbara K. Morgan, *Women in Sexist Society* (New York: New American Library, 1971), p. 230.

[10] Ibid., p. 231.

[11] Jones, "Adolescence," p. 59.

importance. One study found that 57 percent of both sexes were concerned about blackheads and pimples—a concern that led all other concerns about attractiveness.[12] Also at this age, girls tend to be greatly concerned with weight. "Almost one third of the girls see themselves as heavy, with more than half of them expressing some concern. Only 3 percent of the boys describe themselves in this manner, and little concern is expressed by them."[13]

Clearly, physical characteristics become important for the early adolescent within the context of social definitions. Physical maturity continues to emerge fairly rapidly for the adolescent; however, he is not necessarily attaining social maturity at the same rate. "In terms of growth, strength, fecundity, and mental capacity, full maturity tends to be attained only a short time after puberty; but socially the adolescent still has a long way to go, in most cases, before full status is reached."[14] This is particularly significant for the middle-class girl who may achieve physical maturity at about 17, but is still 4 or 5 years away from achieving adult role recognition.

The description of the teenager as being neither child nor adult during adolescence is generally accurate in terms of both appearance and behavior. Kirkpatrick writes, "A significant and baffling aspect of adolescence is the fact that there is often an erratic, inconsistent, and shifting pattern of maturity. The girl is half child and half woman and the male adolescent is half boy and half man, each capable of unpredictable behavior which violates expectations. The baffled parent does not quite know whether to spank or trust, and either course may have its dangers."[15] Consequently, both the parents and the adolescent are often erratic in their interactions, so that sometimes when the youngster wants to be an adult the parent treats him as a child and, on other occasions, just the opposite occurs.

In reality adolescence is a lengthy and cumbersome stage of its own rather than a time of transition from childhood to adulthood. The stage is confused by values of parents. Increasingly, children, from an economic point of view, are distinct liabilities. While only a few years ago the motive to have children was easy to explain, parenthood is becoming increasingly difficult for many to justify.

---

[12] Alexander Frazier and Lorenzo K. Kisonbee, "Adolescent Concerns with Physique," in Jerome M. Seidman, *The Adolescent* (New York: Holt-Dryden, 1960), p. 145.

[13] Ibid., p. 142.

[14] Kingsley Davis, "Adolescence and the Social Structure," in Jerome M. Seidman, *The Adolescent* (New York: Holt-Dryden, 1960), p. 42.

[15] Clifford Kirkpatrick, *The Family* (New York: The Ronald Press Co., 1955), p. 241.

THE ADOLESCENT AND HIS PARENTS

The relationships of parents to their adolescent children are in part affected by the stage of the parents' adulthood. One important fact is that when their children are in adolescence, many parents have left their young adult years behind and are moving into the middle-age years. The adolescent period is thus made more difficult for both parents and children, because the parents' adjustment problems to middle age are often occurring at the same time.

At this point in time both the parents and their children may be caught in feelings of role confusion and frustration. Sebald points out that the parents are constantly exposed to the American youth "cult" and they cannot fail but to have some feelings of inferiority in the face of their declining strength, prowess, and youthful appearance. "On the other side, youth cannot help but feel inferior in the face of many formal and informal restrictions that limit their activities and privileges."[16] This also indicates that probably at no time does one ever fill a role that doesn't lack some things the person would like that exist in another role.

In the youth-oriented culture that characterizes the American middle class, the problems of the adolescent are often stressed to the point of ignoring the personal problems of the parents. Leaving the young adult years behind is not easy for many parents and when they are faced with the youthful images of themselves presented by their children, the problem may be further intensified. Some parents react by doing everything possible to keep from moving into the middle-age category. The mother who is mistaken for the older sister of her adolescent daughter often feels that she has achieved the ultimate in compliments. One common middle-class belief is that the parents who successfully stay close to their children in "psychological age" are to be admired. This belief reflects a lack of social value and prestige associated with being older psychologically—and is questionable in terms of an ongoing socialization process. The parents may "regress" to the psychological and social level of the adolescent rather than perform at their own age level and serve as adult role models for their children as they grow older.

The middle-class belief that a parent should be a "pal" to his children reflects a social value which gives importance to a common world for parents and children. The belief in a common world has developed around notions of democracy between parents and children and implies they are equals socially, psychologically, and intellectually. If this is true, it is a devastating picture of the parents because it implies they are still essentially teen-agers. The fact is that a mature adult is usually su-

---

[16] Hans Sebald, *Adolescence: A Sociological Analysis* (New York: Appleton-Century-Crofts, 1968), pp. 505–6.

perior to his children in almost every way and, as a role model, this superiority is very important.

Given the fact that parents went through adolescence at an earlier period when things were very different means their children have had very different experiences from them. Goode illustrates this point by the fact that many modern parents have tried some of the illegal drugs that are a part of the youth world. However, as Goode points out, no parents have actually grown up in the so-called drug culture. "Nor did the current generation of parents grow up in a culture in which the contraceptive pill was taken for granted."[17] So the very fact of age differences means the shared experiences of parents and children are limited.

It may be that the adult's belief in being a "pal" to the teen-ager has little relationship to what the adolescent wants. The adults, whether parents, teachers, or youth activity leaders, are almost always in a position of power and the adolescent may find it to his advantage to pretend an enthusiasm for adults in the "pal" role. There are many adults who serve as youth leaders and believe they are "reaching" the adolescent, when in reality the adolescent contemptuously sees them as "jerks, creeps, and squares" to be conned in the "pal" relationship so long as it is advantageous to do so. There is a certain arrogance and lack of perception in the adult belief that an adolescent wants him for a pal. We tend to feel most comfortable with peers who share our interests and have no strong power over us and these are two characteristics generally missing from adult-adolescent "pal" role relationships. At any rate, there is evidence that adolescents don't really think of an adult as a pal.

While some of the problems of parent-adolescent relations rest with the parents' personal problems and their effect on the adolescent, others result from a lack of social clarity in the treatment of the adolescent. One basic problem for parent and adolescent alike is the degree of freedom and independence the youngster should expect or be encouraged to take All societies must develop procedures for moving their youth into adult roles. Stephens has examined a number of cultures with regard to the emancipation process; that is, the transition from the childhood dependence on parents to the freedom and autonomy of adulthood.[18] "In this area our society also appears to be unusual, but in this case it is not because we are 'late.' Rather, it is because emancipation is so sudden, radical, and early in our society."[19] Because the parents have the child from the early age of total dependency, it is sometimes very difficult for them to assess the adolescent's ability to handle independency. The Miller and

---

[17] William J. Goode, *The Contemporary American Family* (Chicago: Quadrangle Books, 1971), p. 34.

[18] William N. Stephens, *The Family in Cross-Cultural Perspective* (New York: Holt, Rinehart & Winston, Inc., 1963), p. 393.

[19] Ibid., p. 393.

Swanson study found that the start of adolescence was a period of important change in the central relationship of mothers to their children. In the 13th or 14th year, the median mother no longer keeps track of what he (the youngster) is doing most of the time.[20] However, almost a third (28 percent) of the mothers felt that close supervision should go on for 17 years or more.[21]

The self-image of early adolescence often undergoes significant change or disturbance. Often, there is an increase in disturbance when the child is about 12. During early adolescence, when compared to the years 8 to 11, children often show increased self-consciousness, instability of self-image, lower self-opinions, and a reduced belief that their parents, teachers, and peers hold favorable opinions about them. One of the main reasons 12-year-olds are more apt than 11-year-olds to show an increase in disturbance about their self-image appears to be because they have entered junior high school. "Movement into junior high school at puberty is a significant event for the child."[22]

Entering high school is also of importance at this age. It not only implies a social definition of greater independency for the adolescent but may also alter his daily life patterns to the extent that the mother is less able to keep track of him even if she wants to. The fact that about one third of the mothers believe that close supervision should go on until 17 years of age means that for a number of adolescents conflicts will arise between the demands of the mother and the individual freedom of adolescent behavior associated with the high-school ages.

The father has some influence in the direction of interest his sons take in school. Kahn found there was a significantly greater tendency for the vocational interests of sons who strongly identified with their fathers to resemble their fathers' occupations. "The degree to which sons see their fathers as satisfied in their work tends to affect their experienced vocational interests."[23]

The Miller and Swanson findings also point out another area of possible conflict between young adolescents and their parents. Since different mothers give freedom at different ages, adolescents sometimes run into difficulty with their age peers. The fact that his mother is still watching him closely can be very disturbing to a youngster. This is especially true for the boy, because his untactful peers point out to him that he is tied

---

[20] Daniel R. Miller and Guy E. Swanson, *The Changing American Parent* (New York: John Wiley and Sons, Inc., 1958), p. 224.

[21] Ibid., p. 224.

[22] Roberta G. Simmons, Florence Rosenberg, and Morris Rosenberg, "Disturbance in the Self-Image at Adolescence," *American Sociological Review*, October 1973, pp. 564–65.

[23] Edwin M. Kahn, "Sociometric Variables, Parental Identification and Son's Interest," *Dissertation Abstracts*, vol. 29 (1968), pp. 757–58.

to "mother's apron strings." The problem is not so much which of the mothers is right as it is their lack of agreement in the treatment of children; and the lack of agreement reflects the lack of clearly defined social norms. Because adolescents are often strong conformists, they may use any differential treatment as a weapon in trying to "con" their mothers. The mother (and sometimes the father) is constantly asked, "Why can't I do (have) something all the others kids do (have)?" The mother who believes what her child tells her may change if she feels that she is wrong or if she does not want her child to be too different. Through this process, youngsters probably manipulate their parents far more than many parents realize.

Because the interaction of parent and adolescent in many middle-class families is based upon some different values and ends, conflict seems inevitable. From the conflict, certain changes in the relationship develop. "When the child's will collides with that of the parent, the relation begins to be pervaded by ambivalence."[24] Through conflict and ambivalence, independency may emerge. If nothing else, the changed feelings indicate that the child no longer accepts the parent as the final arbiter and begins to question what he once accepted as absolute authority. And until parental authority is questioned, the youngster is not achieving independence. Ideally, this conflict can have a great deal of psychological and social value because it allows the youngster to reach for independence at a time when the parents can partially control the reaching. However, a balance between the reaching of the youngster and the controls of the parents is often difficult to achieve.

One major difference between generations is how each views the future and the necessity for preparation. Many young people do not show the same degree of concern as did their parents about preparing themselves for a career and "getting ahead in the world." Many adults get concerned by what they see as attitudes of youth which stress pleasure, fun, and enjoyment without a counterbalancing concern for disciplined and sustained work effort. However, there is no evidence that a majority of young people are unwilling or incapable of productive and disciplined work performance. "In fact, the great majority of young people are performing their tasks in industry, the professions, and education quite effectively."[25]

Probably every generation views the adolescent as a problem, but this view seems to be even more intense among the present adult generation, if for no other reason than the greater attention directed at the adolescent. As mass media often "makes" a crime wave, they may also "make"

[24] Willard Waller and Reuben Hill, *The Family* (New York: The Dryden Press, 1951), p. 390.

[25] *Marihuana: A Signal of Misunderstanding*, The Official Report of the National Commission on Marihuana and Drug Abuse (New York: New American Library, 1972), pp. 125–26.

an upsurge in adolescent "problems." It is interesting that while most of the mass media presents the adolescent as the cause of problems, there are a number of professional "adolescent experts" who see the adolescent as suffering from problems created by the adult world. This position—one taken by some educators and psychologists—is that the adolescent instead of riding roughshod over helpless adults, is actually being segregated, shunned, manipulated, discriminated against, and forced to live in a deluxe ghetto where tastes and mores of a distinct subculture flourish only for lack of meaningful integration into a stable adult society. It is quite probable that the adolescent as the cause of many social problems *or* as the object of destructive manipulation by adults are both exaggerations.

While to some degree conflict between parents and children is inevitable, in most cases it is not severe enough to lead to breakdown in either the interactional relationships or the personality of the individual. However, the vast body of psychiatric literature indicates that the relationships of the child to his family are an important causal factor in mental illness. Many individuals may accept the mobility aspirations projected by parents and satisfactorily meet them or, through personal experience, redefine their own expectations. Nevertheless, the emphasis is that the relationships of the offspring to his parents from infancy on may have important implications for many of the mental health problems found in the United States today.

THE ADOLESCENT SUBCULTURE

In sociology, the concept of subculture refers to a fairly cohesive cultural system within the larger system of the total culture. The adolescent subculture in the American middle class is, basically, a system created over time by adolescents themselves. The adolescent, being neither child nor adult and having no clearly defined role made available to him by the overall culture, has created a loose cultural system to provide some role meaning for his adolescence. Adolescents accept *most* values of the adult world (often, unquestioningly), but the emphasis here is on those areas in which adolescent values differ from those of the adult world.

The adolescent subculture develops for several important social reasons. It is caused by basic characteristics in the social structure and cultural ethos of the country rather than by imitating what exists in another country. "The development of adolescence is basically due (1) to a finely divided division of labor, which produces a very technical and complex social structure; and (2) to the failure of a culture to provide its members with a convincing and compelling ideation, which would result in a strong identity and a feeling of purpose."[26]

---

[26] Sebald, *Adolescence,* p. 8.

Because the adolescent subculture is to some degree self-developing, it has certain conflict points with the dominant adult cultural system. However, the inconsistency of adult definitions of adolescent behavior has also contributed to the emergence of subcultural values. The very fact that the adult views the adolescent with indecision as to appropriate behavior means that the adolescent is treated one way on one occasion and in a different way on another. Since the adolescent often desires decisiveness and some precision in role definitions, he consequently tries to create his own. When he does, he often demands a high degree of conformity by other adolescents as "proof" of the rightness of his definitions. It is ironical that the adolescent often thinks of himself as a social deviant. What he fails to realize is that his adolescent group deviates from the adult world, but that the requirements for conformity within his subculture are extremely strong.

Prior to puberty, sex distinctions among age peers are not as strong as later. As a result it appears that until puberty academically successful girls evolve a "bisexual" or dual self-concept. Both sexes are rewarded for achievement, especially academic achievement. "Girls, as well as boys, are permitted to compete in school in athletics without significant negative repercussions. "But once they pass puberty the peer group pressures become stronger with regard to differential behavior for boys and girls. It has been shown that for both boys and girls, peer orientation increased until about the tenth grade where there is a leveling off for males and some reduction for females."[27]

It appears that the group nature of adolescent subcultures has different meanings and significance for boys and girls. Henry argues that different sex patterns develop before adolescence and subcultural involvement. He suggests that in boys' groups most of the games they play require teams and it would be very difficult for a boy to avoid group life and teamwork with his age and sex peers.[28] By contrast, "little girls play with their dolls, their sewing, their cut-outs, or their jacks. Boys flock; girls seldom get together in groups above four, whereas for boys a group of four is almost useless. In boys' groups the emphasis is on masculine unity; in girls' cliques the purpose is to shut out other girls."[29] The sex differences described by Henry carry over into adolescence, with boys generally interested in sports with their own sex and in dating, the latter often for the prestige it will give them with their male peers. On the other hand, the adolescent girl is generally not interested in large female group activities. She would rather be with one or two girl friends to talk to about boys.

---

[27] H. Hugh Floyd, Jr., and Donald R. South, "Dilemma of Youth: The Choice of Parents or Peers as a Frame of Reference for Behavior," *Journal of Marriage and the Family,* November 1972, p. 632.

[28] Jules Henry, *Culture Against Man* (New York: Random House, 1965), p. 150.

[29] Ibid., p. 150.

And increasingly the girl's orientation is to herself and *a* boy, with decreasing interest in age peers.

One study found a closer correspondence between behavior and peer group expectations for females than for males. This goes along with other studies that indicate that in the area of sexual behavior the female is more subject to influence by social factors. It was also found that conformity existed along the lines of sexual experience. None of the male or female respondents with sexual experience fell into the category where both of their best friends had not engaged in intercourse. "Among students without sexual experience, on the other hand, 67 percent of the females and 29 percent of the males have both friends who have not experienced coitus. Apparently student premarital sexual behavior is influenced not only by the expectations of associates but also by their behavior."[30]

In addition to parents, other adults have been partially responsible for the development of the adolescent subculture. The school is of particular importance because, during weekday hours, the teacher and other school adults are responsible for placing adult limitations on the adolescent's behavior. The primary historical function of the school was to educate the child. However, the adolescent finds that many times the adults at school want to be democratic in defining adolescent roles, and, like his parents, they treat him in a contradictory fashion. As a result, the adolescent often perceives the school adults as having the same lack of clarity in providing him with role definitions as do his own parents, and again turns to his own subcultural values.

In part, the adult world of parents, teachers, and others contributes negatively to the development of the adolescent subculture. In the middle class, they make few role demands on the adolescent and as a result he has a great amount of free time. Our teenage culture—in contradistinction to the teen-age culture of the past or of other societies—is a product of affluence. This means that the middle-class adolescent has both the time and the money to develop patterns of behavior and values peculiar to himself. The adolescent subculture partly results because we can afford a large leisure class of youngsters not in the labor force but yet consumers on a vast scale. Because they have money to spend and do spend it on specific goods, they become recognized by at least one segment of the adult world—the businessman who produces the goods that adolescents buy. And because the businessman caters to him, the adolescent gains a sense of adult recognition in some areas he has defined as important.

When looking at general characteristics and interests of adolescents, one must keep in mind that among adolescents are many individuals who are exceptions and whose values may be in complete opposition to the

---

[30] Alfred M. Mirande, "Reference Group Theory and Adolescent Sexual Behavior," *Journal of Marriage and the Family,* November 1968, p. 575.

more common teenage values. While some individuals deviate as individuals from the common adolescent pattern, there are also some deviant subgroups within the overall adolescent subculture. For example, because of the selectiveness of its student population, a high school may have group values that place high prestige on outstanding academic achievement. When this subgroup pattern exists, the factor of conformity to group norms is often just as strong as in those schools where the values are just the opposite. The following discussion, however, concentrates on the more general subcultural values of middle-class adolescents in today's society.

One way in which adolescents make themselves different from the adult world is through a special language. This language serves to maintain barriers between themselves and the world of adults. A youngster may speak over the phone with his age peer in a jargon that leaves the parents wondering what he is talking about.

The adolescent often goes along with peer values, not because he likes them, but because he fears negative consequences if he rejects his peer group's values. The negative consequences may not only be directed at him by his peers, but may also result from his own fear of threatening what have become personal, internalized values.

It should be emphasized that values of the personality cult and anti-intellectualism are not at variance with those of the adult culture. What is of particular social relevance is that, historically, youth have usually been those with the least commitment to tradition and the *status quos* and therefore rebellious. However, today adolescents and young adults have created a subcultural value system different from that of the adult world only in areas of what are essentially social irrelevancy. Being different from adults in dress, music, and aspects of language is not of great social significance. Especially relevant is when both youth and adults tend to be alike in the acceptance of such social values as personal conformity and intellectual mediocrity. An important result of these likenesses is a limitation on social change and a restriction of individual expression.

In one other respect, the adolescent value system reflects the shift in middle-class values from a commitment to others to a commitment of self. The fact of high social conformity does not necessarily mean a high identification with others, but rather that the "significant others" provide security for the individual's behavior because the others do not question it. Thus, the person who is really different is defined as an "oddball," implying that something is wrong with him. Defining *his* behavior as wrong implies that *your* behavior is right; therefore his behavior is much less threatening. For the adolescent, with his age and social insecurities, the need to account for the nonconformist often takes on great significance.

As suggested, the adolescent in most areas of behavior is not very different from his parents. Teenagers and young adults for the most part want what the adult world wants them to want, and they are essentially content with their way of life. Furthermore, they have little doubt that their tomorrows will be even better than their todays. This suggests that the compatibility between most adolescent peer group values and those of the adult community is very high and that for the most part the peer group of adolescents has assumed a position that is complementary to both the school and the family.

While the world of the adolescent seems removed in many respects from the adult world, there comes a time before reaching adult status when the young person must make certain decisions that will have a very important influence on his future. In today's American middle class, probably the most important decision that the boy must make is whether to continue his education after high school. If he does not go on educationally, his occupational future will be increasingly limited; if he does pursue·education, he must often simultaneously make his occupational choice by deciding what he is going to study in college. Yet, in the American middle-class society it is questionable that the 18-year-old has the background for making an occupational choice on any extended rational basis. Whether or not to go on to college is probably becoming less of a choice for the middle-class boy because he is being socialized with parental values that simply assume that he will go on to college. He unconsciously assimilates this assumption into his own value system.

With the increase in population of college age, plus the percentage increase in that age group going on to college, new anxieties are created for both the high-school graduate and his parents. Will he get into the college of his choice or even get into any reputable college? In recent years, new attitudes about higher education may have developed for both adolescents and their parents. One possible change may be a reduction in antiintellectualism and greater social recognition given to those with intellectual ability. If the colleges and universities force students to come up to higher academic standards, there may be even more drastic changes in the intellectual values and attitudes of the middle class over the next 25 years. And when today's adolescents become the parents of tomorrow's generation, the parent-adolescent relationship may be quite different from what it is today.

The schools are important for the adolescent and the young adult in that they take up a great part of the young person's time and activity. Home life has been preempted by the high school because adolescents spend most of their week days there. When after-school activities are added to classroom time (plus, often, the time involved in bus rides to and from school), the adolescent's day may run from 8 A.M. to 6 P.M. In the schools, adolescents make most of their friends, learn most of their lessons, and are advised, encouraged, analyzed, console, and profoundly influenced by specialists in surrogated parenthood, the guidance coun-selors. Our economic system increasingly is demanding specialized train-ing of youth for their adult futures. The kind of training needed for their futures indicates that "children are increasingly dependent on agencies other than the family for the functional means of fitting themselves for their future roles."[31]

THE LAUNCHING STAGE

At various points, the preceding discussion of adolescence has over-lapped with what may be called the "launching stage"—the period when children are ending adolescence and starting to leave the parental home for college, occupations, and marriage. "During the 'launching stage' the family is variable in size, expanding on holidays and vacation periods and contracting quickly thereafter. It is an unpredictable family, spas-modically familistic and individualistic."[32] In effect, the launching stage in the family is the transitional stage between the family of orientation and the establishment of the offspring's family of procreation.

As with adolescence, the young adult years are often seen as years of great rebellion against parents and other adults. The mass media give the impression that many college students are "protesting" something or other most of the time. But it appears that the majority of college students are not rebels and are little concerned with social problems—except as those problems affect them personally. Nor are they for the most part con-cerned with continued graduate education because of strong intellectual motives, but rather because extended formal education leads to greater economic rewards. Most college students have no strong feelings about wanting to change the social system; they seem quite satisfied with the *status quo*.

The launching stage is also important because in many situations, it symbolizes the period of role transition from adolescent to adult. It is at this time that independence for the young person becomes very impor-tant, because increasing independence is a major criterion in his being socially recognized as an adult. Yet independence must mean a break-down of the long existing dependency ties with the parents. While both parents and children may have been leading up to this role change, it is not always easily accepted by all involved. Often the "launching stage" provides a setting in which the expectations of parents and their young adult children are incompatible.

One basic problem during the launching stage centers around the par-

---

[31] Edward Z. Dager, "Socialization and Personality Development in the Child," in Harold T. Christensen, ed., *Handbook of Marriage and the Family* (Chicago: Rand McNally & Co., 1964), p. 774.

[32] Waller and Hill, *Family*, p. 431.

ents being able to let go of their offspring. A part of the problem is that there is no cultural preparation for those parents who want to give up control and guidance. In the past, the task of socialization was to prepare the child to remain with the family rather than depart from the family for an independent existence. When the time for independence is reached, the parents are expected to let go, but since this must occur after many years of interacting with a dependent child, letting go may be very difficult to carry out in actuality. The situation is sometimes further complicated because some young adults do not want or are not ready for independence when their parents want them to have it. For "letting go" to be successful, the parents and the offspring must both be willing and able.

This period in time often represents a low point in the marriage of the parents. One study found that both husband and wife rated highly the childbearing and early childrearing phases of their marriage and the low point when they were launching their children from the home. It may be that this is an indication of satisfaction with parenthood more than with marriage.[33] But whatever the reason, the low feeling by some parents at this time makes it more difficult to deal with their children leaving home without personal strain and frustration.

Because the offspring has reached the young adult years does not mean that the parents no longer have a strong emotional and vested interest in his future. Davis points out how this situation may lead to a conflict of interests for many parents. "Because his [the child's] acquisition of independence will free the parents of many obligations, they [the parents] are willing to relinquish their authority; yet, precisely because their own status is socially identified with that of their offspring, they wish to insure satisfactory conduct on the child's part and are tempted to prolong their authority by making the decisions themselves."[34]

One other problem for parents during the launching stage is that the move of the young person is often not to complete independence. The young person is not leaving his parents behind; in fact, he often continues to live at home, although it may be for specific periods of time rather than consistently as at younger ages. And with the extension of formal education, a common pattern in middle-class society is the continued economic dependence of the son or daughter on the family. Nevertheless, the offspring are at the same time biologically mature, psychologically capable of making individual and independent decisions, and socially competent to fit into an adult society.

A closer look at some of the role relationships at the time of the launch-

---

[33] Boyd C. Rollins and Harold Feldman, "Marital Satisfaction over the Family Life Cycle," *Journal of Marriage and the Family*, February 1970, p. 26.

[34] Davis, "Adolescence," p. 381.

ing stage will be useful in distinguishing some of the differences during this period for the mother and father, as well as the son and daughter.

The Mother. The findings of some studies presented earlier indicate that the mother role is the one laden with the greatest emotional significance of all family roles. In American society, pathos and sentimentality are often attached to the image of the mother. When her children grow old enough to leave her, she is often seen as coming to the end of her most important adult role. If the mother then has nothing to turn to with some roles significance, she often experiences severe personal frustrations. Even when she has other interests, she may have a period of difficult adjustment to the loss of the mother role; maternal roles do not taper off gradually, as they did when families had more children more widely spread in age. Furthermore, today's mothers are physically and psychologically not nearly so ready as their grandmothers were to retire to their knitting in the easy chair by the fireplace as their children leave home.

As we have previously discussed, some of the consequences of the mother role in American society have led to unfortunate results both for the mother and for her children. Because the mother is more involved in the parent role than the father, it is not surprising that she has the greater number of parental problems. One study found that while only 19 percent of the sample of adolescents said they had disagreements with their fathers, 33 percent said they had disagreements with their mothers.[35] When mothers and fathers are each linked to daughters and sons, the most common relationship for disagreement between an adolescent child and one of his parents is that of mother and daughter. One study found disagreement problems for 36 percent of the mothers and daughters and 29 percent of the mothers and sons, and for 24 percent of the fathers and sons and 16 percent of the fathers and daughters.[36]

There also appears to be a strong body of evidence that links many problems manifested in the adult years to inadequacies in the earlier mother-child relationship. When the son is the one with the problems (the "failure"), he is often visible to the broader community. Female failures are not as socially visible. But as Rossi suggests, "It is a short-sighted view indeed to consider the immature wife, dominating mother or interfering mother-in-law as a less serious problem to the larger society than the male homosexual, psychoneurotic soldier or ineffectual worker, for it is the failure of the mother which perpetuates the cycle from one generation to the next, affecting sons and daughters alike."[37]

Recognizing the problems that face the mother, it is not surprising that

---

[35] Thomas S. Langner and Stanley T. Michael, *Life Stress and Mental Health* (New York: The Free Press of Glencoe, 1963), p. 258.

[36] Ibid., p. 259.

[37] Alice S. Rossi, "Equality Between the Sexes," *Daedalus*, Spring 1964, p. 621.

many of them consciously or unconsciously resist the growing independence of their children during the launching stage. Many parents, and
especially mothers, maintain a new and modified parental role with their
children even after the children have left home and are married. In the
middle class has emerged the "help pattern": The parents continue to be
involved with their children even after the children are married, which
often allows the mother to play at least a modified mother role.

Adams found that all types of aid to the married couple were the
greatest during the first ten years of marriage and that financial aid was
little influenced by differences in residential distance between the couple
and the parents. Adams also found that in both middle-class and working-
class marriages the parents of the wife gave more frequent total help than
did the parents of the husband.[38] These patterns represent some modification from the traditional role of parents and their married children.
The continuation of help after the children's marriages makes the behavior similar to some aspects of the interactional relationship that existed
when the children were younger and, from the married children's side, is
a change from the traditional pattern of the independency of the male
after marriage. Often, the children may accept financial help as well as
some influence in decision making from the parents. In the majority of
cases, this help pattern is probably between the parents and the married
daughter, since the daughter tends to maintain closer relationships to her
parents after marriage than does the son. If this is the case, the young
husband is not only accepting help *for* his family of procreation, but that
help is coming *from* his in-laws. It appears that the young middle-class
husband and father is increasingly willing to accept help after he is
married and does not feel his role threatened, even when the help comes
from his in-laws.

The Father.   Some of the comments above on the middle-class "help
pattern" also have application to the father in and after the launching
stage. Because the father's commitment to his role is usually not as great
as the mother's to hers, when the children grow up and leave home, he is
usually not so greatly affected as his wife. "Usually the adjustment that
the father makes is relatively less painful, since he often continues secure
in his earner role and in his more detached position as representative of
the family in the business community. His paternal roles in father-child
activities are frequently more peripheral than central to his life organization, and the departure of the children to college and later to jobs and
marriage does not threaten his way of living drastically."[39] However, because the loss of children may mean a great deal to his wife, he may be

---

[38] Bert N. Adams, "Structural Factors Affecting Parental Aid to Married Children,"
Journal of Marriage and the Family, August 1964, p. 330.

[39] Waller and Hill, *Family*, p. 429.

greatly needed to help her adjust to her loss of the mother role; thus, in some situations he becomes involved—not directly in his father role, but indirectly in his husband role.

Some of the father's problems at the launching stage may involve the age period he is going through, rather than the actual loss of his children from home. About the time his children are growing up, the man must face certain facts that may be personally disturbing. He may find that he is not going to reach his earlier occupational expectations and must try to adjust to occupational reality, and as mentioned in an earlier chapter, the middle-aged man is often faced with decreased sexual interest and ability. The combination may result in a feeling of threatened masculinity. Finally, the father is often forced to contrast himself with the youthful vigor of his sons and daughters, and their friends.

The Daughter.   Generally, daughters have a closer attachment to their parents, both before and after marriage, than do sons. The female tends to be more attached to the parental family in that the wives reported being homesick more frequently and seeing their parents more often than did the males. Because girls are generally given less personal freedom and are thus reared in a close association with their parents, ties to their parents often continue to be strong after they marry.

There is some evidence to support the impression that the girls who are not emancipated have a greater than average probability of becoming engaged in marriage. Perhaps the girl who is more emancipated from her parents has less interest in marriage. But even if this is true, it is important that the girl can remain to some degree dependent on her family without jeopardizing her possibilities of achieving the wife role. For this kind of daughter-parent relationship, the transition from family of orientation to family of procreation is often relatively smooth.

There is evidence that educational level of the parents is related to the image and degree of closeness by daughters to their parents. In a study which compared a variety of attitudes and images by college daughters of their parents, analysis was made by the educational level of the mothers. In this study, the daughters were divided into three groups by mother's education: "college graduate," "some college," and "no college." Where differences existed between the daughters, those with "college graduate" mothers had a higher and more positive relationship to their mothers. The "college graduate" group also had the highest positive image of the father and the closest relationship to him.[40] One important factor was that because the daughter was in college and both parents had college educations, parents and daughters tended to have fewer areas of disagreement; they accepted the same general values.

A study by this writer attempted to analyze the daughter's role during

---

[40] Robert R. Bell, unpublished research.

the launching stage.[41] In this study, 229 daughters and their mothers responded to questions in reference to the daughter's role. The findings indicate a number of areas of conflict between mothers and daughters in defining the daughter's role. A summary of the overall mother and daughter findings were:

> In the area of mate selection, mothers were less influenced by the "romantic" attitudes when thinking of husbands for their daughters, and the mother's values lead her to believe that her daughter should place greater stress on "rationality" in selecting a mate. Added to this was the belief by the mothers that they should have a greater veto power, if they feel it necessary, over their daughter's mate selection than the daughters feel they should have. These different attitudes suggest that during the "launching stage" mate selection is a potential source of conflict between mothers and daughters. The fact that daughters placed a greater importance on establishing some close ties with a girl friend, as well as attributing greater importance to the father, indicates a second possible area of conflict. Financial aid from the parents may constitute a third area of conflict. Daughters feel less willing to accept financial help and have a greater suspicion of it when given, than do the mothers.[42]

The findings indicate that the launching stage as perceived by mothers and their in-college daughters has a number of potential areas of disagreement and conflict. The daughter is in the process of making the break away from her parental home. "She lives in a society that both encourages and demands that she increasingly be her own decision maker. Yet, the daughter is often torn between her love for and obligations to her mother and her increasing desire for independence. Many of the mothers still adhere to the traditional belief that the parents are the important, right, and ultimate decision makers."[43]

A part of the conflict between the mother and daughter centers around defining of appropriate role behavior for the daughter. In her younger years, the daughter's role is defined to a great degree by her mother. As she grows older, she is influenced by other definitions, which she internalizes and applies to herself in her movement toward self-determination. However, the mother often continues to visualize the daughter's role as it was defined in the past and assigns the same importance to her function as mother in defining her daughter's role. "But given the rapid social change associated with the family roles the definer, as well as the definitions, may no longer be institutionally appropriate. Therefore, the daughter's concept of her role during the 'launching stage' will differ at least

---

[41] Robert R. Bell and Jack V. Buerkle, "Mother-Daughter Conflicts During the 'Launching Stage,'" *Marriage and Family Living*, November 1962, p. 384–88.

[42] Ibid., p. 386.

[43] Ibid., p. 388.

in some degree from that of the mother, because the function of role definition is changing."[44]

The middle-class daughter in a "launching" relationship to her parents will be influenced by several factors. First, the need for a high degree of emancipation is probably less for those girls who still accept many of the values and role functions that their parents accept. Second, those girls who find the greatest conflict are often those who are operating within a role concept of self which is different from that of the parents, particularly the mother. This often happens when the daughter is strongly influenced by a value system different from that of the parents. Third, for many daughters conflict occurs during the launching stage, but once she is fairly well established with her own family of procreation, the conflict will probably decrease.

The Son.   The son entering the launching stage probably has a greater need for emancipation from the family of orientation than the daughter. The pressures from society in general are very strong for him to express his independency, which is often taken as the sign of his having achieved adulthood. Independence is probably more readily attained by the son than the daughter, because male emancipation from the family will usually be more clear-cut. One indication of the need for the male to attain emancipation, particularly from the mother, is that a close relationship with the mother is correlated with low courtship progress. However, it is possible for the son not to make a strong break with his father and still achieve his adult occupational role. This situation often arises when the son goes into the father's business or into the same, or a related, occupation. The need for the son's independence from the father may occur when the son's occupation is the father's choice, not that of the son.

It also seems likely that the family helps and encourages the son's independence more than it does the daughter's. His earlier and more distinct emancipation may be brought about as the result of several factors: (1) The parents provide the sons with earlier and more frequent opportunities for independent action; (2) the parents give boys more privacy in their personal affairs; and (3) the son is held to a less exacting code of filial and kinship obligations than is the daughter.

Once the children have been launched into their adult roles, the relationships with the parents undergo change as the parents move into the roles of grandparents and, as the parents grow older, in relationship to their adult children. Eventually, roles may be reversed, with the aged parents dependent upon their adult children. A more extended set of family relationships may be emerging in the middle class. When the middle-age parents are launching their children into independency, they may simultaneously be developing a relationship with *their* parents of an

---

[44] Ibid., p. 388.

increasingly dependent nature. This series of separate, but interrelated families, probably will become more and more common with increasingly greater life expectancy and earlier ages at marriage; in the future, a whole new series of family relationships may develop. For example, a married couple in their early 20s with young children could have both of their parental families in their 40s and up to four pairs of grandparents in their 60s. Such a situation would alter many aspects of family living. For instance, the young couple's children would grow up not only with grandparents, but also with various great-grandparents during childhood and adolescence. What the implications of these sets of related families would be remains to be determined.

One other possibility may also be mentioned. A point that has been made on several occasions is that when the children grow up and leave the parental home, the demands on the husband-wife role relationship become very important. Because many couples end the launching years of their children while still in their 40s, they have 20 or 30 years of life expectancy left to them. In the near future, perhaps more couples who reach this age period will realize little is left in the husband-wife relationship, and decide that the years ahead with the partner seem intolerable. As a result, it is possible that the divorce rate for couples in their 40s will increase in the future.

SELECTED BIBLIOGRAPHY

Bardwick, Judith M., and Douvan, Elizabeth "Ambivalence: The Socialization of Women," in Vivian Gornick and Barbara K. Moran, *Women in Sexist Society*. New York: New American Library, 1971, pp. 225–44.

Bell, Robert R., and Buerkle, Jack V. "Mother-Daughter Conflicts During the 'Launching Stage.'" *Marriage and Family Living*, November 1962, pp. 384–88.

Demos, John, and Demos, Virginia "Adolescence in Historical Perspective." *Journal of Marriage and the Family*, November 1969, pp. 632–38.

Elder, Glen H., Jr. "Parental Power, Legitimation and Its Effects on the Adolescent." *Sociometry*, vol. 26 (1963), pp. 50–65.

Floyd, H. Hugh, Jr., and South, Donald R. "Dilemma of Youth: The Choice of Parents or Peers as a Frame of Reference for Behavior." *Journal of Marriage and the Family*, November 1972, pp. 627–34.

Kett, Joseph F. "Adolescence and Youth in Nineteenth Century America," in Theodore K. Rabb and Robert I. Rotberg, *The Family in History: Interdisciplinary Essays*. New York: Harper and Row, 1973, pp. 95–110.

Sebald, Hans *Adolescence: A Sociological Analysis*. New York: Appleton-Century-Crofts, 1968.

Simmons, Roberta G., Rosenberg, Florence and Rosenberg, Morris "Disturbance in the Self-Image at Adolescence." *American Sociological Review*, October 1973, pp. 553–68.

Part Four

Marriage Breakdown and Alteration

Chapter 21

The Ending of Marriage

The divorce rate in the United States has climbed over past decades, and as a result there has developed an increasing concern with the ending of marriage—through divorce. In addition to the greater number of marriages ended by divorce, the number in which death ends the marriage has also increased. (Because of the increasingly greater life expectancy of the woman, an increasing proportion of the latter are terminated by the death of the husband.) However, the ending of marriage through death does not elicit the same social concern as the ending through divorce. Divorce implies the failure of a marriage, and while all marriages, successful or unsuccessful, must ultimately end, the greatest social concern is directed at those marriages ended through the deliberate choice of the individuals involved. Implied in this reaction is the continued acceptance by our society's members of the belief that marriage should continue until ended by death.

Sometimes the mass media give the impression that today's American marriages are of short duration. But a couple marrying today can statistically expect about 35 years of marriage before the relationship ends either through divorce or with the death of one spouse. That is, because of greater life expectancy and younger age of marriage, the young couple of today enters marriage and remains in the marital relationship longer than did their grandparents. And even with today's high divorce rate, the average person spends about half his life with one marital partner.

Divorce is an important influence on many Americans and more are becoming involved all the time. In 1970, there were 715,000 divorces and annulments in the United States, which was almost double the number in 1950. And since 1967, the divorce rate has increased by 30 percent. When all the minor children are considered as well as the spouses of marriage terminated by divorce, the total number of persons involved in a given year runs over 1.5 million.[1]

This chapter focuses on social and legal factors related to the different ways in which marriages may be altered or ended. Chapter 22 concentrates on social-psychological factors related to divorce and remarriage.

BEREAVEMENT

All marriages not dissolved in some other manner eventually end with the death of one marriage partner; and bereavement accounts for the ending of well over half of all first marriages. The legal start, and eventual finish, of marriage coincides with the social view of start and finish. The marriage has its legal and social start at the time of marriage and is terminated at the death of one of the partners. When the partner dies, the surviving spouse takes on the new legal and social role of widow or widower.

When bereavement is compared with divorce in the ending of marriages, the death of the spouse accounts for about twice as many terminations as does divorce. Divorces are most common as a means of ending marriages of short duration, but as the couple are married longer, divorce becomes less common and the chances of bereavement increase.

In one important sense, the comparison of marital termination through divorce with bereavement is misleading. Divorce must occur through the deliberate actions of the married couple, while death occurs without choice. Therefore, many individuals have experience with marriages ending through more than one means. Even the divorced person who remarries, and stays married, ultimately has the second marriage end through death.

In all types of marital termination, one area of great interest is the impact and consequences of the ending of a marriage on its children. The significance for the child is of importance because of the psychological, social, and economic factors related to the rearing of the child by the single responsible parent. The differential effects of bereavement and divorce on the child are discussed in Chapter 22.

The greater life expectancy of the woman, plus the fact that the father is statistically about three years older than the mother, means that it is the death of the father that most often ends the marriage. Of all orphans un-

---

[1] Max Rheinstein, *Marriage Stability, Divorce and the Law* (Chicago: University of Chicago Press, 1972), p. 4.

der 18 in the United States, about two thirds were orphaned as the result of the death of their fathers. But when compared with divorce, bereavement less often affects children under 18 years of age because it occurs later in the parental marriage than does divorce. Also, the chances of the child being orphaned before he is 18 are less today than they were in the past because of the earlier age of marriage and greater life expectancy of the parents.

DESERTION

While desertion is frequently used as a legal ground for divorce, it is considered here as an informal means of altering or ending marriage. Marriage starts at the same point in time socially and legally; however, when one of the marital partners deserts, the marriage ends only socially, not legally. The fact that a marriage altered by desertion is not legally recorded means that the estimates of desertion in the United States are very crude. Only those that reach the courts are recorded.

A conservative estimate of the number of desertions per year at about 100,000 and this would be roughly one desertion for every four divorces. A study by Kephart of desertion and divorce in Philadelphia indicates that for that city, the ratio of desertion to divorce has been about one to one.[2]

Desertion is typically a male phenomenon, though it is possible for the woman to desert. When the woman deserts, it is often used as a ground for divorce. For example, in many states the wife must move with the husband if he must change residence for occupational reasons, and if she refuses she may be legally defined as guilty of desertion. When the man walks out on his family, he often returns after a period of time although he will then often desert again at a later date.

Kephart has provided valuable information on some social characteristics related to desertion in his Philadelphia studies. In family literature, desertion has often been characterized as "the poor man's divorce," the implication being that in the lower social classes, individuals desert rather than get divorces. Kephart, after careful study, writes: "When Philadelphia desertion cases were analyzed by occupational level, the idea of the 'poor man's divorce' failed to materialize, at least to the degree that had been expected."[3] Kephart found that 43.6 percent of the white desertions are derived from the upper half of the occupational ladder.[4]

Children are involved more often in desertion than divorce cases. Monahan and Kephart found that "for the native white primary marriages in the *divorce* sample all religious groups showed between 57 and 61 percent

---

[2] William M. Kephart, "Occupational Level and Marital Disruption," *American Sociological Review*, August 1955, p. 460.

[3] Kephart, "Marital Disruption," p. 464.

[4] Ibid., p. 461.

to be childless couples. In the same type of desertion cases only 19 percent were childless, and the average number of children was 1.32 per family."[5] The higher number of children involved in desertion cases is due to several factors. (1) There is a selective factor, because women with dependent children are often placed on the records as having a deserting husband. The fact that she has children means she is more apt to seek financial help than is the childless woman whose husband has deserted. (2) Because the deserting husband often returns to his wife, the probability of their continuing to have children increases. (3) There is some evidence that the overall social length of marriage is shorter in divorce than in desertion, thereby increasing the probability of the deserted family having more children. (4) It is possible that the children are responsible for some husband-fathers deserting because the fathers feel unable to cope with the demands of the family, feel personally inadequate, or desire to escape responsibility.

Of great concern to the courts is the financial responsibility for the children in desertion cases. As discussed in Chapter 10, the court knows that if the father does not assume the financial responsibility, then costs must often be met with tax dollars. Monahan points out that a "basic revolution has taken place in the field of family law and social control over deserting spouses. Family fugitives can no longer flee to the frontier or the anonymity of the metropolis, as they have done before."[6] Many states now have working agreements with other states in returning the deserting spouse to his home state and financial responsibility for his family. The legal concern is not so much with the stability of the family as it is that the husband-father meet his economic responsibilities. So long as he meets them, the court has little interest in whether or not he lives with his family.

Even with the tightening of laws in regard to the deserting husband-father, many husbands are still able to escape their financial responsibilities. Monahan further points out that authorities "remain reluctant to confront a man with his marital responsibilities and to energetically insist that he be responsible for the wife or children he has abandoned, or suffer imprisonment."[7]

An important contrast between desertion and divorce is that in the majority of desertion cases it is the husband who "rejects" his wife by leaving her, while, in a majority of divorce cases, it is the wife who "rejects" the husband by bringing suit against him for divorce. With the

---

[5] Thomas P. Monahan and William M. Kephart, "Divorce and Desertion by Religious and Mixed Religious Groups," *American Journal of Sociology*, March 1954, p. 463.

[6] Thomas P. Monahan, "Family Fugitives," *Marriage and Family Living*, May 1958, p. 150.

[7] Ibid., p. 150.

great importance that most women attach to the wife-mother role, their husbands' rejecting them by walking out may be psychologically very upsetting. Although this is probably most true in the middle class, the middle-class woman may reverse the "stigma" by bringing a divorce suit against the husband for desertion, thereby "rejecting" *him*. In the lower class, desertion is often viewed with some indifference while, in the middle class, the social reactions are usually those of pity or even scorn.

LEGAL SEPARATION

Legal separation (*divorce a mensa et thoro*) is a partial or qualified divorce for cause by the judgment of a court, which forbids the parties to cohabit. It does not affect the basic obligations of the marriage, and under it there is no right to remarry.[8] Limited divorces (or legal separations) are granted in about half of the legal jurisdictions of the United States. Of the total number of marital dissolutions in the United States, limited divorce or legal separation probably account for no more than 2 to 3 percent of the total.[9]

Because the husband and wife cannot live together, the marriage socially ends with legal separation. Legally, however, the marriage is altered, not ended. From the male's point of view, a legal separation means that he continues to have the responsibilities of marriage, but not the rights. If the couple should decide to live together again, they would have to go back through the courts; if they should decide to get an absolute divorce, they would have to go through the usual divorce proceedings.

Legal separation is not a popular means of resolving marital problems. It is used if there are strong reasons for not getting a divorce, or as a means of economic protection for the wife. Suits are generally brought by the wife for permanent maintenance and support. Since most decrees are concerned with questions of property settlement and custody of the children, a majority are contested. This is in contrast with divorce, where very few are contested.

ANNULMENT

A decree of annulment means that no marriage ever legally occurred. Hence, neither party ever acquired any marital rights and upon the issuance of the decree, the parties returned to the *status in quo* at the time of marriage. No property rights accrue, and in the absence of a statute to

[8] Helen I. Clarke, *Social Legislation* (New York: Appleton-Century-Crofts, Inc., 1957), p. 119.

[9] William M. Kephart, *The Family, Society and the Individual* (Boston: Houghton Mifflin Co., 1961), p. 584.

the contrary, children are illegitimate.[10] It is estimated that annulments account for about 3.5 percent of the total marital dissolutions in the United States.[11]

A marriage ended through annulment has a very different meaning when viewed legally and socially. Legally the marriage never had a starting point and therefore cannot be legally ended. However, socially the marriage started at the time the couple were married and ended when the couple stopped living together as husband and wife. While an annuled marriage may never have existed legally, it usually had a social meaning in marital role relationships for the couple.

Annulment of a marriage is based upon fraud committed prior to the marriage. It is based upon the legal definition that the couple were not eligible for marriage for such reasons as duress, bigamy, nonage, and insanity. The term fraud is a broad term and is the most popular cause for annulment; it covers a number of specific causes generally related to some premarital disrepresentation.

What constitutes fraud in an annulment case is vague, and the courts have used it without clearly defining what facts are essential. The common pattern has been to limit it essentially to those facts related to the sexual aspects of marriage, such as venereal disease, false representation by the woman that she was pregnant, concealed intent not to consummate the marriage, or not to have intercourse to produce offspring. "Annulments have been rarely granted for fraudulent misrepresentations of character, past life, or social standing and hardly ever for misrepresentation on matters of property or income."[12]

In 1961, California reported 5,643 annulments and New York reported 2,310. The 7,953 annulments granted by these two states constituted over two thirds of all reported annulments in the United States during 1961.[13] It is common knowledge that annulments in these two states generally serve to circumvent certain aspects of their divorce laws. (In New York, up until 1968, divorce was granted only for adultery, so that annulment was frequently used as an alternative to divorce.)

DIVORCE

Most writers, both academic and nonacademic, view divorce as a social problem. Frequently, the assumption is that divorce is evil or destructive to both the personal and social make-up of the American population. In

---

[10] Clarke, *Social Legislation*, p. 120.

[11] Kephart, *Individual*, p. 587.

[12] Rheinstein, *Marriage Stability*, p. 95.

[13] U.S. Department of Health, Education, and Welfare, Public Health Service, National Office of Vital Statistics, "Divorce," *Vital Statistics of the United States, 1961*, vol. III, sections 3, 4, and 7, p. 6.

Chapter 22, the use of divorce will be discussed as a part of contemporary American society.

In ecclesiastical dogma divorce has been seen as rupturing the marriage union of its functional oneness. It was seen as a sin to permit such rupture unless on the basis of guilt, and the most significant guilt was that of adultery. Over the years there has been a great religious clash about divorce. This started with Martin Luther who opposed the Catholic doctrine of indissolubility of marriage.[14] Over the years the major clash has been between the religious positions of Catholicism and Protestantism.

In New England, divorce was recognized from the beginning (see Chapter 2). In the lists of legal grounds adultery and desertion were thrown together with impotence, "fraudulent contract," premarital fornication with a relative of the spouse, and bigamy. The number of early divorces that can be determined was fairly high. In the small community of Plymouth Colony at least six divorces were granted between 1661 and 1692. "At the end of the colonial period, divorce was an established institution in New England, unknown to the laws of the Southern colonies and of New York, and of occasional occurrence in Pennsylvania and New Jersey."[15] However, the idea that a marriage might be ended simply because it had broken down and without putting the blame on either party did not find expression in any American statute until after the first half of the 19th century.[16]

It should be emphasized that divorce is not new or peculiar to the American society. Some kind of divorce arrangements are universal in all the cultures of the world, both past and present. Historically, the right of divorce in most cultures was given to the husband. Two common historical grounds used by the male in divorcing his wife were "barrenness" and adultery. Generally, if the wife did not bear children the fault was assumed to be hers. In many societies where great value was attached to the continuity of the family line through offspring, the failure to reproduce was viewed with great concern; therefore, the husband often had the right to divorce his wife and acquire a new one. In patriarchal societies, the dual sex standards operated around adultery. The husband was not usually punished for adultery but the wife was often subject to severe criticism, and this many times took the form of divorce. Divorce in the past provides a sharp contrast with divorce in the United States today, for the legal grounds today are more favorable for the wife than for the husband, and the wife more often than the husband gets the divorce.

---

[14] Rheinstein, *Marriage Stability,* p. 22.

[15] Ibid., p. 33.

[16] Ibid., p. 35.

In general the Western world adhered to the belief that the best way to deal with marital breakdown was to prevent it and the method of prevention was deterrence. But the force of deterrence has been greatly reduced in the 20th century, and as a result divorce has become far more common in many countries. In the past several countries have had higher divorce rates than has the United States, but at present the United States has the highest divorce rate among all Western nations. The opportunity for divorce ranges greatly between various countries. For example, in Japan a marriage is terminated by both parties notifying the registrar of their agreement to disagree. By contrast no divorce at all is permitted in Andorra, Argentina, Brazil, Chile, Columbia, Eire, Paraguay, the Philippines, or Spain.[17]

In the United States "absolute divorce, or *divorce a vinculo matrimonii*, is the legal separation of man and wife effected for cause by the judgment of a court totally dissolving the marriage relation."[18] Socially and legally the marriage started at the same point in time, but in many cases the social relationship of the marriage ends before the marriage is legally terminated. This is true because the couple often cease living together as husband and wife before the final decree of divorce is granted.

It has sometimes been argued that the increase in divorce rates in the United States represents an increase in unhappiness or maladjustment in marriage. But there is no way of knowing whether or not married couples are more or less happy in marriage today than they were in the past. Divorce is more socially and personally acceptable today than it was in the past; therefore, the increase in divorce may be influenced by a growing unwillingness to *endure* unhappiness in marriage. Also, divorce is legally more available today than it was in the past. All legal jurisdictions of the United States grant absolute divorce, South Carolina in 1949 being the last to do so.

Unquestionably, divorce rates have been increasing in the United States. At about the time of the Civil War the divorce rate per 1,000 population was 0.3, but by 1920 the rate had reached 1.6 and by 1945 the rate was 3.5.[19] "The divorce rate hit an all-time peak in 1946, as an aftermath of World War II, when many marriages deteriorated. It then declined steadily until the late 1950s, at which time the number of divorces per 1,000 married persons under 55 years of age reached approximately the same level as that for 1940. Since the mid 1950s the proportion of first marriages ending in divorce has increased sharply. This is shown by the fact that in 1955, 10.5 percent of the women who had been born from 1920 to 1924 had their first marriages end through divorce. By compari-

---

[17] Ibid., p. 8.

[18] Clarke, *Social Legislation*, p. 119.

[19] Hyman Rodman, *Marriage, Family and Society* (New York: Random House, 1965), p. 290.

son, in 1970, 15.8 percent of the women who had been born from 1935 to 1939 had their first marriages end in divorce.[20] The increase in the divorce rate in recent years is illustrated by the statistic that in 1960 there were 28 divorced men for every 1,000 men with wife present; by 1972 this ratio was 38 per 1,000. There were 42 currently divorced women for every 1,000 women with husband present in 1960, as compared with 66 per 1,000 in 1972.[21] Thus, within roughly a century, "with almost one out of every four marriages ending in divorce, it was evident that one of two things would happen: (*a*) The divorce laws would be made more liberal or (*b*) the enforcement of the laws—the divorce procedure itself—would become more lenient. As it turned out, it was the latter practice which came to the fore, hence the development of the American divorce paradox: relatively stiff laws on the one hand versus lax law enforcement on the other."[22]

Rates of divorce often vary when related to different social conditions or variables. For example, the divorce rates varies somewhat by geographical region. During 1960, 1 married couple out of every 104 was divorced. However, the rate was lowest in the Northeast with 0.8 divorces for every 100 marriages, 2.2 in the North Central states, 2.8 in the South, and 3.5 in the West. "Thus the divorce rate in the West was more than four times as high as that in the Northeast."[23] The high divorce rate of the West reflects a large number of people from the Northeast, particularly from New York, going to Nevada for their divorces.

One explanation for the fact that divorce rates by states generally increase from East to West and from North to South has been a greater "frontier atmosphere" of independence, self-reliance, and adventurousness. It also appears that divorce rates are highest in those states with high migration rates. One reason suggested is that communities having a large number of new members will not show the same amount of integration that is found in older, more stable communities. "The social costs of divorce, therefore, will be lower in areas of high migration because enforcement of norms in these areas will be comparatively relaxed."[24]

There is also some relationship between divorce rates and economic

[20] U.S. Bureau of the Census, *Current Population Reports,* Series P-20, No. 239, "Marriage, Divorce and Remarriage by Year of Birth, June 1971," (Washington, D.C.: U.S. Government Printing Office, 1972) p. 5.

[21] U.S. Bureau of the Census, *Current Population Reports,* Series P-20, No. 242, "Marital Status and Living Arrangements: March 1972," (Washington, D.C.: U.S. Government Printing Office, 1972), p. 3.

[22] William M. Kephart, "Legal and Procedural Aspects of Marriage and Divorce," in Harold T. Christensen, ed., *Handbook of Marriage and The Family* (Chicago: Rand McNally & Co., 1964), p. 952.

[23] U.S. Department of Health, Education, and Welfare, "Divorce," p. 3.

[24] Bill Fenelon, "State Variations in United States Divorce Rates," *Journal of Marriages and the Family,* May 1971, p. 326.

conditions. Divorce, like marriage, closely follows the business cycle. It is low in periods of depression and correspondingly high during periods of prosperity. One primary reason for the decrease in divorce during periods of economic depression may be the cost; when money is limited, divorce may be temporarily postponed. This would also explain in part why divorce goes up with increased prosperity. With greater affluency, there are not only those who have reached the point of wanting a divorce, but also those who have postponed it because of the cost in the past, but are now able to afford it.

In the United States today, divorce is a common means of ending marriage. Glick estimates that "under current conditions, close to one out of every five marriages is likely to end in divorce."[25] However, one point that is often overlooked is the high rate of remarriage among those who get divorces. Glick points out "that about two thirds of the divorced women and three fourths of the divorced men will eventually remarry."[26] For the majority, divorce does not indicate disillusionment with marriage in general, but rather with a specific marriage. (An extended discussion of remarriage is presented in Chapter 23.)

THE LEGAL NATURE OF DIVORCE

Anyone who studies the legal nature of divorce in the United States is forced to the conclusion that little relationship exists between the legal approach to and the social reality of divorce. As stated before, the United States has no federal divorce law, but rather the various laws of 53 different legal jurisdictions. Therefore, the laws vary from state to state and, even when agreement seems to exist on certain legal points, in reality disagreement prevails between states and even on interpretation of a specific point within a given state. Several of the most important legal considerations related to divorce are presented in the following discussion.

Legal Considerations

Collusion. Suppose that a couple have been married for a few years and reach a point of mutual agreement that their marriage is miserable and they would both like to end it with a divorce. They might go to court and ask for a divorce on the grounds that they have conscientiously tried marriage but theirs has failed, they are unhappy, and after careful consideration have mutually agreed they would be better off not married to each other. The court's response would be to tell the couple they cannot have a divorce for the legal reason that they are guilty of collusion. "Col-

---

[25] Glick, *American Families,* p. 198.
[26] Ibid., p. 199.

lusion is any agreement between the parties by which they endeavor to obtain a divorce by an imposition on the court."[27] A number of courts have held that "any agreement between the husband and wife whereby they attempt to obtain a divorce by imposing upon the court is collusion."[28]

Legally speaking, any couple who mutually decide they want a divorce cannot have it. Yet, in a vast number of cases, divorce is sought because the marriage partners find they are incompatible. Except in a few states, however, incompatibility is not a legal ground for divorce; therefore, one party must find some legal ground he can use to divorce his partner. While legally there can be no collusion, in reality the spouse's agreeing to divorce does occur. The law insists on the myth of noncollusion although in reality collusion exists in the majority of divorce cases.

Contest.　The legal restriction against collusion is based upon the assumption that divorce is a contest between the innocent and guilty (referred to legally as the plaintiff and defendant). However, suppose that our couple go to court and the wife states a number of charges against the husband and asks for a divorce. After her charges are presented, the husband stands up and admits that what she said is true but then makes a number of charges against her. In almost all cases, the divorce would not be granted because the husband has engaged in *recrimination*. "The doctrine of recrimination is grounded on the old equity theory that one who asks relief must come into court with clean hands and that divorce laws are made to give relief to the innocent and not to the guilty party."[29] When recrimination is used, then there is no longer an innocent and guilty party but rather two guilty parties, and the general rule is no divorce granted to either party.

Two other legal factors are important in the contest for divorce. Suppose that the wife is asking for a divorce on the grounds that her husband committed adultery. But when the charge of adultery is brought out, the wife states that it really was not her husband's fault, that he was the victim of an immoral, unscrupulous woman and she, the wife, forgives him. Legally this is known as *condonation*, the forgiveness of a marital offense constituting a ground for divorce. In a situation of this type, a divorce would not usually be granted because a person can use an act for divorce only so long as he has not forgiven the act.[30]

Suppose that the wife is suing her husband for divorce on the grounds of adultery but it comes out in the testimony that the wife had little sexual interest and that she both knew and consented to her husband having

---

[27] Clarke, *Social Legislation*, p. 128.
[28] Ibid., p. 129.
[29] Ibid., p. 132.
[30] Ibid., p. 131.

sexual relations with another woman. This is legally an illustration of *connivance,* the consenting by one married person to the marital offenses and acts of the other. The legal theory is that if an individual consented to an act or a wrong, he cannot be injured by it and therefore it cannot be used as a ground for divorce.[31]

Usually the plaintiff must be present in person at the divorce trial, but in most divorce actions the defendant does not put in an appearance. Because the defendant is not present, it is assumed that he is guilty. He has been notified as to the time and place of the hearing, and therefore his absence creates the legal fiction that he must be guilty as charged or he would be there to defend himself. Because the defendant wants the divorce, he has usually been told to stay away from the court. As a result, over three quarters of all applications for divorce decrees are granted.

The legal procedure is clear. The plaintiff must go into court as the wronged party in the marriage and the defendant must be the villain. Any variation from these clearly defined legal roles leads to difficulty in obtaining a divorce. The fact that the legal picture has little to do with the realities of the divorce situation is often beside the point so far as the courts are concerned.

The legal contradictions are obvious. With collusion or agreement making divorce legally unobtainable, the implication is that one partner wants the divorce and the other does not and that the one has been wronged by the other. Yet, if the involved parties are not in agreement and the defendant recriminates, the divorce will not usually be granted. Therefore, in many divorce cases collusion must in fact occur to eliminate the possibility of recrimination in order that the divorce be granted. In most divorce cases, the parties are probably guilty of some legal violation although it is generally ignored—as shown by the fact that divorce is granted.

Another factor indicative of the manipulation of divorce laws is that the wife is the plaintiff in over three out of every four divorce suits. There is no reason to believe that within the social and psychological context of marriage wives should be the wronged party three times as often as husbands. The probability of the wife being the plaintiff in divorce cases has increased over the past 100 years in the United States. In the 1860s, when the first divorce statistics were gathered, the Census Bureau figures show that the husband was the plaintiff in about one third of the cases.[32] Kephart also points out that there are variations from state to state, "56 percent being wife-plaintiff cases in Georgia, as compared to a figure of 82 percent in Wisconsin."[33] But in general the wife is the plaintiff more often

---

[31] Ibid., p. 130.
[32] Ibid., p. 956.
[33] Ibid., p. 957.

than the husband for three important reasons: (1) More legal grounds for divorce are available to the wife than the husband; (2) out-of-state divorces are easier for the wife to obtain because the husband's occupation ties him closer to home; and (3) less social criticism is directed at the woman if she sues for divorce than if she is sued for divorce. However, there are some grounds for divorce *not* available to the wife. For example, an Alabama statute is typical. It provides that a divorce may be granted "in favor of the husband, when the wife was pregnant at the time of marriage, without his knowledge or agency." There are similar statutes found in many states. However, in no state is a woman allowed to divorce her husband, if, prior to marriage, he had caused another woman, not his wife, to become pregnant.[34]

There have been some recent changes in divorce laws by some states. The most significant legal changes were taken in 1969 in California. The new law abolished fault grounds and even did away with the term "divorce" and replaced it with "dissolution of marriage." Under the new law the court can end a marriage only after a finding of "irreconcilable differences" or of incurable insanity, the one ground retained from the old law. Also the new law prohibits proof of specific acts of marital misconduct unless they bear on the issue of child custody or where the court finds them necessary to establish the existence of irreconcilable differences. To guard the state against becoming a "divorce mill" the law retains the old residence requirement "—one of the parties must have resided in California for six months and in the county for three months immediately before filing the petition."[35]

Legal Grounds

Over the past 100 years, cruelty has been steadily increasing in relative importance as a ground for divorce. At the same time that cruelty has been increasingly used as a grounds for divorce, its meaning has been changing and cruelty has come more and more to be a catchall legal category. It is probably safe to assume that about two thirds of the divorce suits in this country at the present time use cruelty as the legal grounds.[36]

Adultery is the only ground recognized in all legal jurisdictions. The number of grounds that may be used varies among different states. Nearly a third of all legal jurisdictions grant divorces on ten or more different

[34] Leo Kanowitz, *Women and the Law* (Albuquerque: University of New Mexico, 1969), p. 96.

[35] Aiden R. Gough, "Divorce without Squalor: California Shows How," in Given B. Carr, *Marriage and Family in a Decade of Change* (California: Addison-Wesley Pub. Co., 1972), pp. 90–91.

[36] Ibid., p. 953.

legal grounds. However, legal grounds that sound the same may be defined very differently in the various legal jurisdictions. For example, desertion as a legal period for divorce ranges from six months in Hawaii to five years in Rhode Island.

That the legal grounds used for divorce bear little relation to the 'actual causes underlying marital breakdown is generally accepted. The lawyer often has to ignore what appears to be the actual reason for the couple's seeking a divorce and look for the available legal grounds that he may advise them to use. One study asked a sample of Idaho lawyers to classify the "real" causes, as opposed to the legal causes, actually used in 282 divorce cases. The major "real" causes were, in declining order: "Financial problems (including support), infidelity, drunkenness, and basic incompatibility."[37] But in most cases these were not the causes the lawyers could advise their clients to use in the divorce procedures.

New York is a state where significant changes in legal grounds for divorce have occurred. Up until 1968 the only legal ground available for divorce was that of adultery. That meant that the divorce rate was low in New York because many persons left the state for divorce. However, in the two years since the laws were liberalized the divorce rate has more than tripled. From an annual average of fewer than 4,000 divorces granted because of adultery the state courts were in 1970 processing more than 18,000 divorces. The state added five grounds for divorce: cruel and inhuman treatment, desertion, the imprisonment of the spouse for three or more consecutive years, and two types of legal separation each for a minimum two-year period.[38]

Cited on the positive side by legal authorities in New York on the changes in the divorce law has been a sharp reduction of fraud and collusion. Some have also argued that the law has largely ended discrimination against the poor who seek divorce. But on the negative side, the new law has, in the view of many, largely failed in its attempts at compulsory reconciliation. For example, of the 19,223 cases that came to the bureaus in the first year of the law, 563 or less than 3 percent are listed as resulting in reconciliations.[39] The main reason for the failure is that probably most people who are ready for a divorce are beyond any counseling help.

Kephart, in his extensive study of marital disruption, came to the conclusion that "while in most of the divorce suits, but, in no means all, the relationship between real and alleged cause is nebulous, specific incidents as a rule are not fabricated. They are usually exaggerated, both in frequency and intensity, and are sometimes distorted beyond reasonable rec-

---

[37] Harry C. Harmsworth and Mhyra S. Minnis, "Non-Statutory Causes of Divorce: The Lawyer's Point of View," *Marriage and Family Living*, vol. 17 (1955), pp. 316–21.

[38] *New York Times*, January 4, 1970.

[39] Ibid.

ognition."[40] He found that in general, the incidents reported by the plaintiff were not made up and did seem to have some basis in fact. "The inflation and distortion that exist appear to be in degree rather than kind."[41] For example, some cruelty may have occurred, but not to the extent presented at the divorce hearings.

Alimony

Alimony generally refers to the continued support of the wife by the husband after divorce. It is possible in 12 states for the husband to receive alimony from the wife, but such awards are rare. On the other hand, it is not unusual for alimony to be granted to the wife in cases in which the husband petitions for and obtains the divorce. In theory, the amount of alimony is to be determined by the standard of living that existed during the marriage, but usually the woman actually receives only a small amount of alimony.

Because of the great publicity given to large cash settlements in a few divorce cases, the impression often is that large amounts of money are involved in many cases. Cash settlements at the time of divorce may result from two different situations. One, the husband may make a total settlement rather than pay alimony over time. Second, a form of blackmail may be involved. A cash settlement may be a payoff for agreeing not to protest the divorce. This second situation sometimes leads to large cash settlements which receive a great deal of publicity, leading people to believe they are much more common than they are.

The amount of alimony and child support is determined by negotiations between the parties, and the courts simply confirm the agreement. Sometimes child support payments are camouflaged as alimony because of income tax laws. That is, taxes on alimony payments to an ex-wife are payable by her and not by the ex-husband. The total amount of alimony is subtracted from the ex-husband's income. The person who contributes more than half the support of the child can take the $600 dependency exemption for the child. In most cases the wife's income is less than the husband's and she therefore pays taxes at a lower rate. "As a result of lumping child-support payments together with alimony and designating the total sum as alimony, the husband has a tax advantage and the wife may be able to negotiate a larger total payment."[42]

Alimony payments should not be confused with child support. With

---

[40] William M. Kephart, "Drinking and Marital Disruption," *Quarterly Journal of Studies on Alcohol*, March, 1954, p. 65.

[41] Ibid., p. 65.

[42] "Report of the Task Force on Family Law and Policy to the Citizen's Advisory Council on the Status of Women," (Washington, D.C., April 1968) in Nancy Reeves, *Womankind: Beyond the Stereotype* (Chicago: Aldine, 1971), p. 230.

rare exceptions, the father is responsible for the economic support of his children after a divorce. This paternal responsibility usually continues until the father is no longer legally responsible for the youngsters, either because the children have grown up or, as in some cases, he has given up legal responsibility to an adopting father. Even when the father pays for the support of his children, the amount may not realistically meet the economic costs of rearing the child.

Migratory Divorces

As with large alimony payments, the amount of mass media attention given migratory divorces leads to a belief that they are more common than they actually are. Migratory divorce probably accounts for less than 5 percent of the total divorces granted annually. There seems little evidence that people seek migratory divorces because of easier grounds; rather, they seek it for personally favorable grounds and speed in having the divorce granted. (An illustration of seeking more favorable grounds for divorce through migration would be in the case of New Yorkers who had only adultery as a ground for divorce.)

The popularity of some states for migratory divorces is due to the speed in which divorces are processed in them and the short length of time needed to acquire legal residency within the state. The migratory divorce is valid in the United States because of reciprocity agreements between the states, meaning that the laws of one state are recognized by the other states. However, if it can be proved that the individual went to the other state to gain advantage from more liberal divorce laws but had no intention of establishing permanent residence in that state, the divorce may be declared invalid. In reality, almost always the individual does go to another state to gain advantage of the law; however, no legal action will be taken in the home state unless someone brings suit, and this rarely occurs.

There has also been the use of foreign divorces by many Americans. If the law of the books were enforced in a traditional way almost all of those divorces would be worthless. In fact, under the law, the parties might be sent to jail for bigamy. "But apart from, perhaps, New Jersey, the risk of a public prosecutor starting trouble is practically nonexistent. Only when someone tries to renege, or where a third party seeks to invoke the law of the books, is there any reason for a court to look into the matter."[43]

THE SOCIAL NATURE OF DIVORCE

The findings clearly show that divorce is a characteristic of the relatively young with a short marital duration. In recent years the median age at first divorce was about 31 for men and 28 years for women. Divorce is

---

[43] Rheinstein, *Marriage Stability*, p. 89.

occurring at younger ages. For example, the median age at divorce for women born in 1920 to 1924 was 29.6 years. That was three to four years younger than that for women born in 1910 to 1914 with a median divorce age of 33.3 years.[44] In general, the frequency of divorce rises rapidly after the first few months of marriage, reaches a maximum during the first three years of marriage, and then declines with increasing length of marriage. By the late 1960s there were more older people entering the divorce category. For example, half of all divorced persons and almost half of all separated persons were between their mid-30s and their mid-50s. Almost 40 percent of all broken marriages lasted ten years or more before ending and 13 percent lasted more than 20 years.[45] The pattern may be of more divorces occuring when the children grow up and leave home. Marriage becomes no longer acceptable when it is not supplemented by the parental role.

There is also a relationship between legal causes used for divorce and the length of marriage. For example, the marriages with the greatest duration by legal cause is 9.5 years for desertion, followed next by 7.2 years for nonsupport, and then 6.8 years for cruelty.[46]

As was mentioned, a marriage ends in a social sense in many cases well before it is legally ended through divorce. Kephart, in his study of the duration of marriage, found that "the recorded time period between marriage and divorce is, in good part, a legal fiction." He found in his sample of 1,434 divorce cases a difference in medians of 4.6 years between the legal duration of marriage and the actual duration.[47] More than 40 percent of the couples in our sample had separated within the first three years of married life! Within the same period divorces had been granted to but 16 percent of the couples."[48] The peak year for separations lies within the *first* year of marriage, and with each succeeding year the percentage decreases. "Using the divorce rate, the peak period lies within the second and fourth year, with a subsequent yearly decline."[49] Kephart's study indicates that for many couples who end their marriages with divorce, the process of alienation leading to separation and ultimate divorce begins shortly after the marriage takes place.

Premarital Factors

Chapter 13 discussed factors of dating and courtship related to success in marriage. In this section, the concern is with several social variables

---

[44] U.S. Bureau of the Census, "Marriage, Divorce, Remarriage," p. 6.

[45] Morton M. Hunt, *The World of the Formerly Married* (New York: McGraw-Hill Book Co., 1966), p. 19.

[46] U.S. Department of Health, Education, and Welfare, "Divorce," p. 11.

[47] William M. Kephart, "The Duration of Marriage," *American Sociological Review,* June 1954, p. 290.

[48] Ibid., p. 290.

[49] Ibid., p. 290.

rooted in the premarital stage which show some statistical relationship to divorce. There is evidence that a very young age at marriage is related to divorce for both men and women. In general, men who marry in their teens have high probabilities of divorce, while men who marry in their late 20s have a low probability of divorce. For women, those who marry before age 20 have substantially higher rates of marital disruption than women who marry at older ages. Women marrying for the first time at ages 30 and above have very low rates of marital disruption.[50]

Christensen found a relationship between premarital pregnancy and divorce. He found that of all the women who gave birth to their first child in less than 139 days after their marriage, 19.7 percent had divorces. For those who gave birth between 140 and 265 days after marriage, the divorce percentage was 14.1. The first group and many in the second group indicate premarital pregnancy. By contrast, of those women who gave birth to their first child between 266 and 391 days after marriage, 9.1 percent had been divorced.[51] This indicates that marriage brought about because of pregnancy has a greater probability of ending in divorce than does marriage in which pregnancy was not involved.

With all the problems that may be associated with divorce it is still better in the minds of many than other alternatives—particularly that of never marrying. Hunt found in his study that divorce was coming to be regarded as more normal than not marrying at all. "Especially in large cities, many a girl in her early 30s or bachelor in his 40s would rather have been married and divorced than never married."[52] Basically, people who never marry are often viewed as having some inadequacy or problem that led to that condition. The divorced have been able to try marriage even though they did leave it.

Religion

No religious groups encourage divorce, although they differ in tolerance and acceptance of divorce. In their study of divorce and desertion in Philadelphia, Monahan and Kephart found that "Jews account for about their expected share of divorces (but no more than that); that the Catholics account for one half to two thirds the number of divorces which one might expect from their proportion in the population; and conversely, that the Protestants account for a relatively greater part of Philadelphia's divorces."[53]

---

[50] Hugh Carter and Paul C. Glick, *Marriage and Divorce: A Social and Economic Study* (Cambridge, Mass.: Harvard University Press, 1970), pp. 311–12.

[51] Harold T. Christensen, *Marriage Analysis* (New York: The Ronald Press Co., 1958), p. 207.

[52] Hunt, *Formerly Married*, pp. 58–59.

[53] Monahan and Kephart, "Divorce and Dissertion," p. 460.

A study in Providence, Rhode Island found a lower rate of divorce for Jews. Both males and females, when compared with census data for the total population, showed a higher proportion of the Jewish population as married and a lower proportion as divorced or separated. "Almost three quarters of the total Jewish population over 14 years of age were married, as compared to two thirds of the total white males."[54] Religious intensity also influences the divorce rate. "Reform Jews have a higher proportion of divorce and separation, and a larger proportion marry more than once when compared to those who identify either as Conservative or Orthodox, controlling for age and generation."[55]

Separation and divorce are higher among mixed marriages and couples with no religion than for any of the three religious groups when the partners are of the same religion. This too may be a reflection of less conventional behavior, as reflected by the mixed marriage or no religion, that would make the couple more apt to turn to divorce. One recent study raises some interesting questions about mixed religious marriages. It was found in Iowa and Indiana that previous divorce lead to intermarriage.[56] It may be that people who get a divorce are by definition less restrictive in their views and as a result may be more willing to try mixed marriages. In other words, both divorce and marrying outside one's religion are mild forms of social deviancy that may go together.

There is some evidence that interdenominational marriages are less stable than marriages between spouses of the same denomination. In fact, some of the differences are as large or larger than those found for Protestant-Catholic marriages. "For example, outmarriages involving fundamentalists are over ten percentage points more unstable than marriages between fundamentalists."[57]

The impact of divorce on children causes a great amount of the social concern directed at American divorce. The implication is that when the disruption of the parental roles is added to those of the marriage roles, divorce becomes a greater problem. The impact of divorce on the child will be discussed in Chapter 22. The interest here involves some of the social characteristics with respect to children and the divorce of their parents.

The length of marriage prior to divorce is related to whether or not children are involved. For example, in 1961, "the median duration of marriages with no children under 18 years of age was 4.7 years, those with one

---

[54] Calvin Goldscheider and Sidney Goldstein, "Generational Changes in Jewish Family Structure," *Journal of Marriage and the Family*, May 1967, p. 269.

[55] Ibid., p. 275.

[56] Erich Rosenthal, "Divorce and Religious Intermarriage: The Effect of Previous Marital Status upon Subsequent Marital Behavior," *Journal of Marriage and the Family*, August 1970, p. 440.

[57] Larry L. Bumpass and James A. Sweet, "Differentials in Marital Instability: 1970," *American Sociological Review*, December 1972, pp. 764–65.

child 5.9 years, those with two children 8.9 years, and those with three children or more 12.1 years."[58] The fact that a majority of divorces do not involve children is due to the heavy concentration of divorces in the early years of marriage. It is also probable that many couples, who would get a divorce if they did not have children, remain married because of the children. Finally, some couples may get a divorce because they do not have children and their childlessness is an important reason for defining their marriages as a failure.

In recent years, an upswing in the proportion of divorce decrees involving children has occurred. In 1953 less than half (45.5 percent) of all divorce decrees involved children, but by 1957 the rate was 50.9 percent and by 1961 the rate had reached the level of three fifths (60.3 percent) of all divorce decrees.[59] This means that the number of children affected by divorce has increased more rapidly than has the number of divorces and may reflect some changes in attitudes about divorce and children. While social criticism continues to be directed at the couple getting a divorce when children are involved, it is probably less severe than it was in the past.

Because divorce tends to occur early in marriage, it means that when children are involved they are often very young. The indications are that about two thirds of the children affected by divorce are under ten years of age. It is clear that the presence of children is not necessarily a deterrent to divorce, although some couples do stay together "for the sake of the children" and as a result some unhappy or unsuccessful marriages are not ended until after the children grow up. It seems probable that when couples postpone divorce for the sake of the children, or for other reasons, they will be less apt to actually get a divorce when the time of postponement ends. This may be because they have worked out their problems or it may be that after putting up with their marriage until the children grew up, many reach a point of accommodation where they no longer feel divorce is necessary.

Custody of Children

In the great majority of divorce cases (about 90 percent) which involve minor children, the mother is given custody.[60] Custody of the child is almost universal for the mother when she is the plaintiff in the divorce action and also in about half the cases when the husband is the plaintiff.[61] It might seem logical to assume that in a divorce case—with an innocent

---

[58] U.S. Department of Health, Education, and Welfare, "Divorce," p. 11.

[59] Ibid., p. 14.

[60] Morris Ploscowe, *The Truth About Divorce* (New York: Hawthorne Books, 1955), p. 219.

[61] Ibid., p. 220.

party and a guilty party—the innocent party would almost always be given the custody of the children. This is almost always true when the mother initiates the action for divorce (when she is the innocent party). On the other hand, when the father is the plaintiff, the children are as likely to be assigned to the mother as to the father. Basically, this reflects the attitude that the children should be reared by the mother. Even if she is guilty of certain indiscretions that lead to the divorce, it is still assumed that she is better able than the husband to rear the children. Most divorced fathers, whether plaintiff or defendant, probably accept the notion that the mother is best able to care for the child.

The custody of the child and questions of child support are often handled by the courts in an offhand and—some would say—irresponsible fashion. "Usually the judge merely ratifies the separation agreement that has been drawn up by the lawyers representing the husband and wife. Yet those documents are rarely the products of sensible thinking, usually they are merely treaties with provision determined by the relative bargaining power of the two sides."[62]

Over the years, a great deal of criticism has been directed at divorce laws in the United States. One common complaint has been that there is a need for uniform, federal divorce laws. Yet there seems little reason to expect any significant change in divorce laws or the emergence of federal divorce laws in the near future. In all probability, the legal system of divorce will continue to have little connection with reality, and it will continue to be true that any couple desiring a divorce and having the time and the money to get it will be able to do so. While many Americans become righteously indignant about some social aspects of divorce, few are bothered by the hypocrisy of divorce laws. Given the desire for divorce, individuals will probably continue to use the divorce laws in the most beneficial personal manner, and the fact that the laws are being distorted and circumvented will continue for the most part to be socially and legally ignored.

SELECTED BIBLIOGRAPHY

Bumpass, Larry L., and Sweet, James A. "Differentials in Marital Instability, 1970." *American Sociological Review*, December 1972, pp. 754–66.

Carter, Hugh, and Glick, Paul C. *Marriage and Divorce: A Social and Economic Study*. Cambridge, Mass.: Harvard University Press, 1970.

Clarke, Helen I. *Social Legislation*. New York: Appleton-Century-Crofts, Inc., 1957.

Farley, Reynolds, and Hermalin, Albert I. "Family Stability: A Comparison

---

[62] Nelson M. Blake, *The Road to Reno* (New York: The Macmillan Company, 1962), p. 237.

of Trends Between Blacks and Whites." *American Sociological Review,* February 1971, pp. 1–17.

Fenilon, Bill   "State Variations in United States Divorce Rates." *Journal of Marriage and the Family,* May 1971, pp. 320–29.

Goldscheider, Calvin, and **Goldstein, Sidney**   "Generational Changes in Jewish Family Structure." *Journal of Marriage and the Family,* May 1967, pp. 267–76.

Kanowitz, Leo   *Women and the Law.* Albuquerque: University of New Mexico Press, 1969.

O'Brien, John E.   "Violence in Divorce Prone Families." *Journal of Marriage and the Family,* November 1971, pp. 694–99.

Reeves, Nancy   *Womankind: Beyond the Stereotype.* Chicago: Aldine Publishing Co., 1971.

Rheinstein, Max   *Marriage Stability, Divorce and the Law.* Chicago: University of Chicago Press, 1972.

Chapter *22*

Widowhood and Divorce

In chapter 21, some of the social and legal aspects of ending a marriage were discussed. This chapter focuses on the social and personal setting of marriages that end through the death of one of the marriage partners and through divorce. Some factors leading to divorce are treated in this chapter because of their relationship to both divorce roles and remarriage. Remarriage of the divorced and the widowed is discussed in Chapter 21.

BEREAVEMENT

All cultures have recognized the inevitability of death and all have developed various social procedures and rituals for dealing with it. While the death of any individual in any family role may alter the family configuration, only the impact of the spouse's death and its significance for the surviving partner is considered here. In the broadest sense, death of the spouse means that the surviving partner is immediately provided with a new social role that conveys to other members of society the person's new social position. The new role definitions of widow for the surviving wife and widower for the surviving husband provide fairly clear social prescriptions to guide behavior.

In the United States the changing nature of the family has brought about new problems in adjustment for the bereaved spouse. That is, the developing structure of the American family with its pattern of residential settlement has made the death of the spouse more and more disorganizing for the surviving partner. "In comparison to familistic groups of rural areas and past centuries, modern urban, and especially middle-class, wives are usually left alone when the husband dies."[1] Lopata goes on to point out that American widowhood is made even more difficult by the fact that society is increasingly couple-companionate in the expanding non-work sphere of action. "Single persons, and especially single women, are simply out of place in the system, while they simultaneously lack automatic membership in a close sex-segregated network. Those who never marry build over the years their own patterns of companionship and aloneness, but the widow is suddenly removed from a familiar world in which she had a comfortable position."[2]

The new roles of widow and widower are in some respects different because of sex differences. For several reasons, the new role of widow may be more socially and psychologically difficult to adjust to than the role of widower. First, because marriage is usually more important for the woman than for the man in American society, the ending of marriage means the ending of a role more basic to the wife than may be the case for a surviving husband. Second, the widow is given less personal and social encouragement to remarry and, therefore, she is more apt than the widower never to remarry. Third, related to the second point, are the widow's problems in taking on financial responsibility for herself and her children, because her financial potential will usually be less than that of the widower. Fourth, because the woman must be less socially aggressive, she often finds her social life more restricted than does the widower. Finally, because there are far more widows than widowers, the chances for changing status through remarriage is much more difficult for the widow than for the widower. This last point is shown by the fact that, in 1954, in the distribution of the American population 14 years of age and over, only 3.2 percent of the males were classified as widowers, while 9.8 percent of the females were widows,[3] a statistic that reflects both the greater proportion of widows than widowers at times of bereavement and their lower rate of remarriage.

As was pointed out in Chapter 13, widows outnumber widowers past age 65 by about five to one. When the spouse dies the surviving partner has a number of years of life ahead of him (her). The length of life is

---

[1] Helena Z. Lopata, "Loneliness: Forms and Components," *Social Problems,* Fall 1969, p. 249.

[2] Ibid., pp. 249–50.

[3] Paul C. Glick, *American Families* (New York: John Wiley & Sons, Inc., 1957), p. 104.

greater when the surviving spouse is the wife. The mean length of life for the widow is about 18.5 years and the mean length for the widower 13.5 years.[4]

Widowhood occurs for a number of women who are still relatively young. The average age at which women become widows is in their middle 50s. The significance of the years after widowhood is illustrated by the fact that for women 45 years of age, 48 percent can expect 25 more years of life.[5] The younger the age of the widow with years of life expectancy ahead, the more often she changes her status of widow through remarriage. This remarriage probability also reflects less interest and less chance for the older widow to remarry.

While a woman may be widowed at a young age, the greater numerical concentration is within the older population. This is an important part of the overall change related to an aging population in the United States. "Persons 65 and older in the United States quadrupled between 1900 and 1950. It is anticipated that nine percent of the population will soon be over 65 and that the percentage will level off at about ten percent by 1975."[6] One important consequence of an aging population is the large number of older women who have the status of widow (see Chapter 13). While the number of widowers has remained fairly constant from 1930 until the present, female survivors have shown a significant increase during that period. In 1940 there were twice as many widows as there were widowers. By 1960 the ratio of widows to widowers had risen to more than three and a half to one and climbed by the late 1960s to a ratio of more than four to one.[7]

The greater proportion of women to men also reflects the greater life expectancy of women over men at all ages. For example, between the ages of 40 to 45, the male has an average life expectancy of 31.5 years and the female of 36.9 years. In the 70 to 75 age range the male has 10.5 years while the female has 12.6 years of life expectancy.[8] The differences are also reflected in the ratios of widowed to married women in the population by age. "One of every eight American women 14 years old or older is a widow; one in every twelve is a widow between the ages of 45–54;

---

[4] Hugh Carter and Paul C. Glick, *Marriage and Divorce: A Social and Economic Study* (Cambridge, Mass.: Harvard University Press, 1970), p. 404.

[5] *Statistical Bulletin*, vol. 39 (Metropolitan Life Insurance Company, November 1958), p. 2.

[6] Quoted in Paul H. Glasser and Lois N. Glasser, "Role Reversal and Conflict Between Aged Parents and Their Children," *Marriage and Family Living*, February 1962, p. 46.

[7] Felix M. Berardo, "Widowhood Status in the United States: Perspective on a Neglected Aspect of the Family-Life Cycle," *The Family Coordinator*, July 1968, p. 191.

[8] "Life Tables," *Vital Statistics of the United States, 1961*, vol. 11, sec. 2 (United States Department of Health, Education, and Welfare, Public Health Service, National Office of Vital Statistics), p. 7.

one fifth of all women 55–64 are widowed; over two fifths at ages 64–74; and seven tenths past 75."[9]

With an aging population disproportionately represented with widows, one further family impact may be on their children's families. Because the marriage has been ended, the survivor may both need and desire to live with the adult children. Because there are more widows, and because there is a somewhat greater tendency for the widow than the widower to turn to the children, important effects on the way of life for the widow and her adult children may follow. A greater financial dependency on adult children is one implied effect. The extent of the dependency on the children is related to the age of the widow. This is because a majority of all widows are unemployed and the rate increases with their age. Consequently, they are partly or entirely dependent on the assistance of children or other relatives or are dependent on public or private funds. Frequent need for family financial aid during the older years is due to the low financial benefits available to older people. However, the programs of aid for the aged are improving and the economic independency of the widow may become better in the future. Medicare and other social programs may make it possible for a higher proportion of widows who now share the homes of children to become more self-sustaining by moving into their own apartments or entering a nursing home.[10]

Because many widows do live with their children does not mean that it is their first choice of a living arrangement. Lopata found that most widows prefer living alone to moving into the homes of their married children. The explanations given were that the women wanted their independence and believed that each woman should be the head of her own household. And the generation gap makes a difference in attitudes toward life and particularly toward childrearing as a source of strain when the older widow lives with her married children.[11]

The desire to live alone is reflected in the fact that the ratio of people living alone has been increasing. For example, the proportion of all occupied dwelling units in which people lived alone was 7.7 percent in 1940 but by 1965 made up 15.0 percent of all household units. "The rate is accelerated at about 50 years of age. In the age group 75–79 a peak is reached. In 1960, 21.7 percent of all people at this age lived alone.[12] Over a third of all widows in the United States live alone, as do 21 percent of all those who are separated and 29 percent of those who are

[9] Ethel P. Gould, "Special Report: The Single-Parent Family Benefits in Parents without Partners, Inc.," *Journal of Marriage and the Family,* November 1968, p. 669.

[10] Robert J. Parke and Paul C. Glick, "Prospective Changes in Marriage and the Family," *Journal of Marriage and the Family,* May 1967, p. 255.

[11] Lopata, "Loneliness," p. 259.

[12] John C. Belcher, "The One-Person Household: A Consequence of the Isolated Nuclear Family," *Journal of Marriage and the Family,* August 1967, p. 535.

divorced. "In other words, the probability is great that when a marriage has been broken for any reason, the individual will live alone."[13] And almost two thirds of all those living alone are female.

THE SOCIAL-PSYCHOLOGICAL SETTING
OF WIDOWHOOD

In a patriarchal society, becoming a widow meant a continued reliance on the social position given by the deceased husband and, possibly, the attainment of a new social position through remarriage. In modern American society, the continued influence of the deceased husband is probably of less importance. The widow is less apt to live in the community today as the "Widow Jones," but rather as Mrs. Jones with the responsibility of caring for herself and her children and attaining social recognition primarily on her own or through remarriage.

Important crises in the life of the individual call for a process of adjustment, with the initial adjustment to the loss of a significant role often more difficult than adjustment to a new role. However, society provides the bereaved individual with the means of easing some of the problems of adjustment. As Waller and Hill point out, bereavement is a personal crisis for which society "provides the individuals with models of every phase of the process: It tells him how he shall react to death, how he shall arrange for burial, and what he shall say and think, and it provides hints as to how long he shall mourn."[14] The social patterns often help the individual to adjust but, because of the strong ego-involvement in the death of the spouse, many highly personal adjustments must also be made.

When a marriage ends with the death of one partner, the general assumption is that without the death the marriage would have continued. Therefore, the surviving partner is seen as an individual not only having lost a loved one, but also having had a successful marital relationship ended. Often with death, no gradual transition from having a marriage partner to not having one occurs—in contrast to divorce, which often involves an extended period of alienation before the marriage is dissolved. The bereaved person is often a husband or wife one day, with a satisfactory marital role relationship, and a widower or a widow the next day, with the marital relationship completely ended. The marriage may have been an unhappy one in reality; but so long as this was not generally known, the death of the spouse is assumed to have ended a satisfactory marriage, thereby providing the survivor with sympathy for

---

[13] Ibid., pp. 537–38.

[14] Willard Waller and Reuben Hill, *The Family* (New York: The Dryden Press, 1951), p. 489.

the loss of a loved spouse. Thus, for some, bereavement may lead to an image of marriage (sometimes even for the surviving partner) quite different from what the marriage was in reality.

One of the important initial adjustments the surviving partner must make is that of being without a spouse in a world of paired relationships. One common tendency for older people is to seek out others like themselves as, for example, the interacting groups of elderly widows who all have the same marital status and live in a specialized "single" world. This world is different from that of the unmarried or divorced because, being widows, they can interact on many occasions in reference to their late husbands. In addition, they are recognized as not being a part of the "paired world" for reasons beyond their control. The widowed, like the divorced, must reorganize their friendship groups on a single basis, but for the former there are no estrangements nor is their status rendered ambiguous.

When it is the husband who survives the death of the spouse the problems of adjustment for him are greater than when the wife is the survivor. There are a number of social factors that aid the adjustment of widows but that may create problems for the adjustment of the widower. The widow has a greater chance for role continuity—"housekeeping, interacting with relatives, going to church, and participating in various other kinds of formal and informal relationships." Loss of spouse in the older ages, especially for men, is often characterized by unhappiness, low morale, mental disorders, high death rates, and high suicide rates.[15]

The extent to which widows socially interact is in part related to their age. One study found that widowhood had no detrimental effects on the social participation of people 70 and over, but that it did have detrimental effects on the friendships of those still in their 60s. Widowhood seems to have an adverse effect on social involvement only when it places a person in a position different from that of most of his age and sex peers. "People tend to form friendships with others in their own age group, and to the extent that this occurs, the widowed person under seventy is likely to be an 'odd' person at social gatherings, since most of his associates are probably still married and participate with their spouse in social activities."[16]

The above study also found some variation in the effects of widowhood by social class. In the lower class widowhood had consistently adverse effects on friendships. One reason was that in the middle class the mar-

---

[15] E. Wilbur Bock and Irving L. Webber, "Suicide among the Elderly: Isolating Widowhood and Mitigating Alternatives," *Journal of Marriage and the Family,* February 1972, p. 24.

[16] Zena Smith Blau, "Structural Constraints on Friendships in Old Age," in Rose Coser, *Life Cycle and Achievement in America* (New York: Harpers, 1969), p. 205.

ried woman, in contrast to the working-class woman, had more often been engaged in a pattern of shared activity with her husband. Those previously established social ties constituted a reservoir of social opportunities in widowhood that were less available to the working-class woman.[17] A second reason was that widowhood for the working-class woman imposes severe economic limitations which drastically limit her social activities.[18]

Becoming a widow has traditionally been associated with a number of problems. It has been related to adult and child dependency, poverty, unemployment, illness, "and the more significant facts of family disorganization and of women's insecure industrial status."[19] But the most common problem for the widow is loneliness. Lopata found in her sample of urban widows that half reported loneliness as the major problem they had encountered in widowhood and "an additional 22 percent refer to it in conjunction with other problems such as finances."[20]

Other highly negative factors of widowhood are related to life expectancy. Widows have a significantly higher mortality rate than do married persons of the same age. It is quite probable that many widows lose the will to live after the death of their spouse of many years. This is probably most true in those marriages that have been based on a high level of dependency by the surviving partner. With the death of the spouse there may be an inability to cope with life and a severe loss of motivation to do so.

The fact that many widows find life difficult to handle after the death of their spouse is also reflected in the higher suicide rates in any given age group for widows as compared to married persons. "The evidence is quite consistent that the widowed experience a substantially higher rate of mental disorders than the still married, particularly among the older populations."[21]

Those who are younger may have more difficulty accepting the new "single" world of the widowed because they are not willing to live simply with memories of the ended marriage relationship. Even holding constant the decreasing marriage market available to the older widow, the younger widow probably has a greater personal motivation to remarry. The very fact that many older widows find that many of their age-sex peers have the same marital status probably makes it easier for them than for the younger widow, most of whose peers are still married. Some of these factors will be further developed later in this chapter when some factors of remarriage for the widowed are discussed.

---

[17] Ibid., p. 221.

[18] Ibid., p. 221.

[19] Berardo, "Widowhood," p. 192.

[20] Lopata, "Loneliness," p. 250.

[21] Berardo, "Widowhood," p. 196.

DIVORCE

Unlike bereavement, divorce does not just suddenly happen. It is the termination of a process that may have developed over a long period of time. The background leading to the ending of marriage through divorce is very different from that of ending a marriage through bereavement. This difference in prior experience makes the new roles of the divorced and the widowed different.

The decision to end a marriage through divorce results from a vast variety of experiences when related to the range of differences among the involved couples. It may be assumed that most marriages start out with a high degree of personal satisfaction and that the extent to which the marital satisfaction becomes altered varies greatly with different marriages. The marriage that is defined as successful by its members is often one in which the couple accept the changing nature of their marriage relationship and are basically satisfied. In other marriages, the couple may feel with time that the marriage is becoming an unpleasant relationship and, as a result of experiences defined as unpleasant by the individuals, the process of marital alienation occurs. Each new crisis of unpleasantness in the marriage may more negatively define the marital relationship. One consequence may be even greater alienation and greater instability in the relationship, ultimately leading to the belief that the marriage relationship is no longer tolerable. However, this is not an inevitable process, because the degree of alienation may stop at any point. That is, the couple may not continue to be driven further apart or may with time return to a greater marital closeness. Furthermore, there is no set degree of alienation that means that the marriage is finished. Divorce is not a simple, inevitable consequence of extreme maladjustment. There may be maladjustment without divorce, and persons may walk out an open door without extreme maladjustment.

It would seem that, in a society in which the woman has a greater commitment and investment in marriage than the man, she would be less willing to see her marriage ended through divorce. The fact that three quarters of all plaintiffs in divorce suits are wives says little about the initial desire to end a marriage.

Considering the strong middle-class stress on ego-need satisfaction in marriage, any knowledge that the partner "wants out" may lead the individual to feel he has no choice but to end the marriage. The very fact that one partner wants to end the marriage means that the other is often seen as no longer satisfying his ego-needs. For the person to say he will continue the marriage when the partner wants to end it, often indicates he is willing to do without that which most middle-class Americans have accepted as a basic reason for marriage, being the love object. For example, the woman who says she will stay married for the sake of the children, even though her husband no longer loves her, may be commended for her sacrifice for the children but at the same time be viewed with some contempt for staying with a husband who no longer loves her.

In American society, it may be ironically true that the woman with the greater commitment to marriage finds herself in a position of being forced to end the marriage if the husband so desires. Behavior indicating rejection by her husband is often so disturbing to her ego that she may feel compelled to end the marriage as soon as possible. The husband feels less compulsion to formally end the marriage when the wife suggests it, perhaps reflecting less commitment to marriage on his part and therefore less feeling of personal threat when his wife no longer wants to continue the marriage.

The reactions of individuals to divorce are to a great extent determined by existing cultural values. All family systems have some kinds of escape mechanisms built into them to permit individuals to survive the pressures of the system, and one of these is divorce. In some societies divorce has been viewed with a very casual social interest, while in others it is viewed with great concern. In the American society, the social values in regard to divorce are in a stage of transition from the restrictive to a more permissive social acceptance. The very fact of transition in social attitudes toward divorce leads to confusion and contradiction in American middle-class response and behavior.

Divorce Prejudice

With very few exceptions, any discussion of divorce in this country, either of a professional or nonprofessional nature, states or implies that divorce is bad or undesirable. Divorce prejudice, like other prejudices, shows itself in the unconsidered parts of one's speech; for example, such common expressions as "alarming rise in the tide of divorce," "divorce evil," and "the unhappy children of the divorced." Implied in a great deal of the thinking about divorce is that it is a personal and social problem and should be alleviated or eliminated for the betterment of the individual and society.

Sometimes the concern is the fear that divorce is destroying the American marriage and family system. Yet, this fear is hard to support in reference to marriage when it is realized that the United States marriage rate is at a near record high and, even more important, that the remarriage rate of those who get divorces is very high. Very often divorce implies disillusionment with a specific marriage, but not marriage in general. Divorced persons have not emerged as a statistically significant new marital group when the remarriage factors are considered. For example, the marital distribution of persons 14 years of age and over show that in 1890, 0.2 percent of the men and 0.4 percent of the women were classified as divorced (and not remarried), and, by 1954, this had increased to only 1.8 and 2.2, respectively.[22]

Many of the contemporary values against divorce reflect traditional family values that have limited application to modern middle-class marriage. Often implied in negative attitudes toward divorce is the assumption that marriage is secondary to the greater family unit and functions. However, middle-class marriage is based to a great extent on the ego-needs of the individual, and the individual may feel that his marriage is not successful unless these needs are satisfied. The attitude many have today about divorce is that if the needs, expectations, and values cannot be met, realized, and adjusted, there seems—for those who can accept the idea of divorce—little reason to continue the marriage. The ego-need factor related to divorce is logically consistent with the ego-need factor that leads to marriage.

One point about divorce in the American middle class which needs to be emphasized is that divorce is causally related to the social framework of mate selection. The whole complex of romantic love, idealization, and ego-need satisfaction places a high premium on the personal nature of marriage; when these expectations are not achieved or are frustrated, marriage has not met the expectations held by the individual or society. Interestingly, the great bulk of social criticism is directed at divorce as if it were a decision made by the couple without a causal background related to social values. It would be socially naive to expect that with the system of courtship and marital expectations that prevail in today's American society a low divorce rate would prevail.

Some people also hold the view that divorce is due to some kind of "mental sickness" and that something is psychologically wrong with those who get divorces. The "sickness" approach to divorce suggests that those who remain married are mentally healthy, and thereby has the convenient supportive facility of negatively defining those who deviate from the traditional norms of marital stability. It also ignores the fact that divorces are a part of the American folkways and mores and, therefore, cannot be regarded as socially abnormal. In theory one might argue just the opposite—that in today's American society, many individuals who are unhappy in their marriage and do not get a divorce are resistant to the social means available for at least partially resolving their marital difficulty and regaining some degree of personal happiness.

Finally, some professional and lay people believe that when a couple want a divorce they should be given counseling which will help resolve their marital problems so that divorce will no longer be necessary. Those who believe that the incidence of divorce can be greatly reduced through the counseling of couples after they have already sought divorce are

---

[22] Glick, *American Families*, p. 104.

probably mistaken. By that time marital discord has usually grown too deep to be banished by verbal discussion. Marriage counseling probably has its greatest potential in the early stages of alienation before the marriage has reached a point of no return. The very fact that a couple have reached a stage in their relationship where divorce has been discussed and seen as a means of resolving their difficulty means that even if they remain married their marriage will often have been altered. Certainly some marriages return from the brink of divorce and become reasonably satisfactory to the individuals, but it is questionable that this happens in a large number of cases. Some couples are probably misled into maintaining their marriages when they might in the long run be better off divorced.

The overall picture appears to be that divorce in the United States is not yet institutionally accepted, but is in a process of becoming so.

THE ROLE OF THE DIVORCED

Social confusion prevails in the treatment of the divorced person. The general social view of divorce tends to reflect the legal one, that there is a guilty and an innocent party involved. To be the guilty party often means to be viewed with social criticism and so, frequently, both parties attempt to place the blame for the divorce on the partner. Waller and Hill write that "he [the divorced] can set himself right only by putting the divorced mate in the wrong, and by so doing he incurs at least a minimum amount of shame for having placed his heart so badly."[23] The point of personal error in mate selection is an important one because, with mate selection being for the most part the province of the individual, he must assume the responsibility of error when his choice proves to be so poor that divorce occurs.

Another aspect of the social confusion, the reaction to the divorced person, is illustrated by the problem faced by many when they come into contact with someone recently divorced—they don't know whether to extend condolences or congratulations. To say to a person recently divorced, "It's too bad," or "I'm sorry to hear it," may imply to the divorced person that he shouldn't have gotten the divorce. On the other hand, to congratulate the divorced person does not seem appropriate either, in light of the personal trauma usually found in divorce.

The Personal Setting

One realization with which all divorced persons are faced is that they have failed in their marriage and in their role as husband or wife. What

---

[23] Waller and Hill, *Family,* p. 555.

may make this particularly difficult for some to accept is that the majority of people do not end their marriage through divorce; therefore, the divorced person may feel that he has not been able to make a success of what has been achieved by the majority. Many divorced persons probably do not view their divorce as a basic personal failure, but honestly feel that they made a mistake in the selection of a mate. Others may attempt to rationalize their failure by arguing that most marriages that remain intact are really unhappy and unsatisfactory. Because of the high American divorce rate, the sizable minority of divorced persons will probably provide an increasingly significant reference group of self-justification for those entering divorce. Both the increasing number of divorces and the related changing attitudes may make the role of the divorced person somewhat easier and subject to less social stigma in the future.

Even with more liberal divorce attitudes, the individual divorcee tends to see his marriage in a highly personal way: The sense of failure in not having a successful marriage can only be partially eased by the fact that many others are also divorced. The trauma of divorce is not so overwhelming for the individual as to lead to personality disorganization. In part, this may be so because of the process nature of divorce: by the time the actual divorce occurs, the individual has psychologically accepted it. The greatest personal disturbance appeared at the time of the final separation rather than at the time of formal divorce. Therefore, the period leading to divorce may demand greater readjustment for the individual than entering the new divorced or remarriage roles.

Divorce is often related to personal and social problems for those who are involved. Yet, problems may be greater for those who are unhappy and stay married than for those who are unhappy and get a divorce. One study found that those who complained about their marriages were more likely than those who did not to report disabilities or chronic illness, or both, "and these unhappily married people also tended to be less healthy than the separated and divorced. In fact, of all marriages that had unhappiness in the past the divorced were the healthiest. It is possible that people who are healthier are more apt to dissolve their marriages. A person who is disabled or chronically ill might prefer an unhappy marriage to life without a partner."[24]

The same study found that people who turned to divorce appeared to be less neurotic than the unhappily married. The costs of remaining in an unhappy marriage can sometimes be great. It was found that unhappily married people not only *felt* more lonely than others, they also tended to *be* more isolated socially. The relatively low rates of depression and isolation among the still divorced, and very low rates among the happily

---

[24] Karen S. Renne, "Health and Marital Experience in an Urban Population," *Journal of Marriage and the Family*, May 1971, p. 341.

remarried, suggest that depression and isolation are consequences of unhappy marriage. "In other words, we can infer that a person who was depressed during an unhappy first marriage is less apt to be so during a subsequent period of divorce, and much less apt to be depressed during a satisfactory second marriage."[25]

Children

Probably the greatest area of social concern about divorce is its effects on children. While children are not involved in a majority of divorces, they are involved in a large enough number to justify the interest. The basic question often raised but never empirically answered is: Is it better for the child when the parents remain together in an unsuccessful marriage or when they end the marriage and alter their personal marital frustrations? A variety of attitudes prevail in the United States in regard to divorce and children. One common belief is that the couple should put aside their marriage role problems for the maintenance of parental roles. Implied in this belief is that the marriage roles are secondary to the parental roles. Yet in a society that places great emphasis on personal ego-need satisfaction in marriage, the placing of marriage in a secondary position may be difficult for the married person to accept. The crucial question again is whether children "gain" by having their parents remain married. A couple who are unhappy in their husband and wife roles are usually going to reflect their feelings for each other in ways which will influence their relationship to the children. One may also question whether a person dissatisfied with one basic role can stop that from negatively influencing another of his basic roles. Can an unhappy wife be a good mother? These role questions are only beginning to be adequately researched. While studies indicate the many problems that children face when their parents get a divorce, few studies have dealt specifically with the children in marriages when the parents have stayed together "for the children's sake."

There are a large number of children in the United States affected by divorce. In recent years, about 9 children out of each 1,000—representing over 1.5 million children—have been involved each year in divorces. The number of children involved is now six times larger than it was in 1922 and has doubled since 1950.[26] In 1922, only 34 percent of all divorces involved children, but by 1965 60 percent of all divorces involved children. There are about 1 million children under the age of 18 living in one-parent homes after the divorce of their parents. In part this is be-

---

[25] Ibid., p. 346.

[26] U.S. Department of Health, Education, and Welfare, series 21, no. 18, "Children of Divorced Couples: United States, Selected Years" (Washington, D.C., 1970), p. 1.

cause more than three times as many divorced women as divorced men are family heads.[27]

By contrast, there are about 3.4 million orphans in the United States and they represent almost 5 percent of all children under age 18. And almost three quarters of these are "paternal orphans," that is, children who have lost their fathers through death.[28] So whether it be through divorce or death, the chances are that the children will be reared by the mother.

The existing evidence suggests that the chances of psychological damage to children resulting from the divorce of their parents is no greater than that for children in unbroken homes marked by continual marital tension.[29] The evidence further suggests that the causes for ending marital relationships are not related to significant differences in problems for their children. For example, one study found that homes broken by parents' divorce, desertion, or separation seem to involve about the same mental health risks as homes broken by the death of one parent.[30] In a study of adolescents in the 7th and 11th grades in a metropolitan area, Burchinal states that "inimical effects associated with divorce or separation and, for some youth, with the remarriage of their parents with whom they were living, were almost uniformly absent in the populations studied. Acceptance of this conclusion requires the revision of widely held beliefs about the detrimental effects of divorce upon children."[31]

One study found that the values of a lot of education and working hard in school were values universally held by both husbandless and married mothers. In fact, it was found that husbandless mothers were actually more likely than married mothers to make high demands on their children.[32] "Lacking some of the indirect and informal supports and influences upon their children and also lacking the secure base for future support and encouragement, husbandless mothers try to push hard where they can. This pressure may sometimes be excessive."[33] It may be that some women when rearing the children by themselves are so anxious to succeed that they overreact in what they do.

---

[27] Carter and Glick, *Marriage and Divorce*, p. 402.

[28] Berardo, "Widowhood," pp. 194–95.

[29] See Judson T. Landis, "The Trauma of Children When Parents Divorce," *Marriage and Family Living*, February 1960, pp. 7–13; and F. Ivan Nye, "Child Adjustment in Broken and In Unhappy Unbroken Homes," *Marriage and Family Living*, November 1957, pp. 356–61.

[30] Thomas S. Langner and Stanley T. Michael, *Life Stress and Mental Health* (New York: The Free Press of Glencoe, 1963), p. 169.

[31] Lee G. Burchinal, "Characteristics of Adolescents from Unbroken, Broken, and Reconstituted Families," *Journal of Marriage and the Family*, February 1964, p. 50.

[32] Louis Kriesberg, "Rearing Children for Educational Achievement in Fatherless Families," *Journal of Marriage and the Family*, May 1967, p. 300.

[33] Ibid., p. 300.

Another recent study examined the impact of the absent-father family on sons and daughters. Thomes found that the assumption that boys would be more affected than girls by the absence of a father was not supported. "On the contrary, the differences that were found between the two groups of children tended to differentiate between girls whose fathers were absent and those whose fathers lived in the home."[34] It may be that fathers are believed to be more important by their daughters than by their sons.

Obviously the child must make important adjustments to the loss of a parent—usually the father—in his day-to-day life. In some ways, this is more difficult after divorce than after the death of a parent, because with the death of a parent the relationship is cleanly broken, whereas after divorce the relationship, particularly with the father, is greatly altered but not ended. The child may see his father for one day each week or month; thus, a new type of parent-child interaction emerges in which the child interacts with his parents one at a time in different settings for different periods of time. Because the parents are divorced, the child may also be caught in the middle of parental conflict and suffer a strong conflict of loyalty and emotional commitment to them. This may be particularly true if one of the divorced parents criticizes the other and the child feels it necessary either to argue or disagree with one parent's position.

However, the usual tendency is to see the parent-child relationship as either one where the parents are both present or where one parent is absent. This tendency often results in a failure to recognize that while a marriage may remain legally and sometimes even socially intact, the two parents may not both be actively functioning as parents. Generally the actual presence of a father is believed to be of crucial importance, even though he may have very little significant involvement in his parental role. It seems reasonable to suggest that there are many legally intact paired-parent families where the father has little more significant influence on his children than does the father who is divorced from his wife and not living with her and their children. In reality, there are several family types where the father as an influential parent for his children may fall somewhere between the ideal paired-parent family and the one-parent family. To illustrate, several categories are suggested, although they have not been examined through research.

1. *Altered Families—External.*   There are some families that for periods of time must function as one-parent families due to causes outside the family unit. For example, the occupation of the husband-father may call for long separations from his family. Or alterations may be due

---

[34] Mary M. Thomes, "Children with Absent Fathers," *Journal of Marriage and the Family,* February 1968, p. 96.

to one of the parents being institutionalized. These kinds of families would be legally intact, but socially nonintact for various periods of time.

2. *Altered Families—Internal Voluntary.* Some families may remain legally intact but function for varying lengths of time as one-parent families because one parent has voluntarily left his family roles. A common type would be the husband-father who deserts his family. This kind of family would be legally intact but socially one-parent as long as the father stays away.

3. *Altered Family—Internal Involuntary.* Some families may remain both legally and socially intact, but one of the adult members suffers a drastic loss in his family role functioning. Included here would be families where restrictive illness occurs, where the father is unable to work, where there is family role impairment due to alcoholism, and so forth. Here the parent would be physically present but would not be able to meet the minimal requirements of his parental role.

A final distinction should be made between the divorced man and woman when children are involved. While divorce means the ending of the specific marriage roles, it usually means the maintenance of the mother role for the wife, but a drastic alteration of the father role for the husband. In fact, in many cases, the divorced father loses most of the social functions of being a father. As the children grow older, and if the mother remarries, the father may find his contact with his children increasingly limited. In this respect, divorce may have more long-range trauma for the man in his role of father than for the woman in her role as mother.

Personal Feelings about Divorce

Not only does social confusion exist in regard to divorce, but also in many cases there may be a personal ambiguity of feelings. The fact that both the loss of the marriage partner and the ending of the marriage relationship are essentially personal means that the individual after divorce is often confused in reference to his divorce. As a result the individual may be affected by both the social confusion in regard to divorce and his own mixed feelings.

The feelings that the individual has in regard to his divorced status will often have a strong influence on how he will fill his new role of divorcee. For example, if the woman is extremely bitter toward her ex-husband, this may influence her attitudes and relationships with other males and thereby restrict or inhibit her heterosexual relationships. On the other hand, defining one's divorced status as better than the past marital status may have a positive influence on adjustment to the new divorce role.

The feelings in regard to the ex-husband are often influenced by the woman's ability to adjust to her divorced status. If she is unhappy and frustrated, she is apt to have strong negative attitudes about the ex-husband. The development of new relationships with men is of great importance because it is in this way that the divorced woman can reenter marriage, which is often seen as the best way of regaining that which was lost. By regaining "face" through remarriage, the hostility directed at the first spouse will often be reduced because the failure of the first marriage becomes less important.

SELECTED BIBLIOGRAPHY

Belcher, John C.   "The One-Person Household: A Consequence of the Isolated Nuclear Family." *Journal of Marriage and the Family,* August 1967, pp. 534–40.

Berardo, Felix M.   "Widowhood Status in the United States: Perspective on a Neglected Aspect of the Family Life-Cycle." *The Family Coordinator,* July 1968, pp. 191–203.

Bock, E. Wilbur, and Webber, Irving L.   "Suicide among the Elderly: Isolating Widowhood and Mitigating Alternatives." *Journal of Marriage and the Family,* February 1972, pp. 24–31.

Carter, Hugh, and Glick, Paul C.   *Marriage and Divorce: A Social and Economic Study.* Cambridge, Mass.: Harvard University Press, 1970.

Kriesberg, Louis   "Rearing Children for Educational Achievement in Fatherless Families." *Journal of Marriage and the Family,* May 1967, pp. 288–301.

Lopata, Helena Z.   "Loneliness: Forms and Components." *Social Problems,* Fall 1969, pp. 248–62.

Renne, Karen S.   "Health and Marital Experience in an Urban Population." *Journal of Marriage and the Family,* May 1971, pp. 338–50.

Rheinstein, Max   *Marriage Stability, Divorce, and the Law.* Chicago: University of Chicago Press, 1972.

Thomes, Mary M.   "Children with Absent Fathers." *Journal of Marriage and the Family,* February 1968, pp. 89–96.

Chapter 23

Remarriage

For many widows and widowers and for most divorced persons a second marriage occurs after the end of the first. Remarriage has different meanings for those who had marriages ended through death as against divorce. This chapter focuses on some of the social factors related to remarriage and the success possibilities of remarriage.

Before discussing some of the factors related to remarriage of the divorced, it is of value to look at those divorced persons who do not choose or are not selected for remarriage. Some suggestions of psychological types who remain in the divorced status follow.

The first may be called *the bitter*. The bitter would include persons who have defined their relationship with their first spouse as so unsatisfactory that they believe the past type of relationship would prevail in any marriage. It is also possible that the hostility of the ex-spouse is so great that it is projected to all in reference to that marriage role. For this group, then, marriage is a rejected relationship based on hostility to the opposite sex in the marriage role. The second group may be called *the frightened*. The important point here is the individual's fear about himself in marriage. The failure of his first marriage may make him feel he will not be able to make a success of marriage with another partner; or, if the breakup of the first marriage was very unpleasant, he may not want to face the possibility of going through the same experience again.

Therefore, the remarriage has risks the individual is not willing to take. Third might be *the overdemanding*. The person may feel he has learned from the first experience of marriage and before entering a second marriage will make sure that the mate selected will have qualities ensuring its success. As a result, the demands for the second mate may be so great the individual never finds a person who can meet them.

The fourth group may be called *the rejected*. They may never have an opportunity to enter a second marriage because of social or psychological factors which make them undesirable as a marriage mate. The fact that they were successful in finding a first mate is no guarantee that they will be successful in being chosen a second time. This has particular relevance for the woman because the older her age bracket, the greater her competition in the decreasingly available male market. One final group may be called *the adjusted*. These are individuals who accept the role of the divorced person and are satisfied to remain in it. Individuals in this group have generally rejected remarriage. The difference between them and the others is that they accept the divorce status, while the individuals in the other groups are more or less forced into it.

None of the suggested groups is autonomous and the influences probably overlap in the failure of many to remarry. As with those who never marry those who do not remarry may not choose to or are not chosen.

The best possible adjustment that many can make to divorce is remarriage. This provides the individual with an opportunity personally and socially to "right the wrong" of the previous marriage failure. The same strong remarriage desire does not usually exist for the widowed because their first marriage was not a failure. About one quarter of all brides and grooms are persons marrying for at least the second time. It may also be noted that almost three out of every four marrying for the second time had their first marriage end through divorce. Therefore, the divorced are involved in the majority of remarriages.

Social Factors

Before looking at some of the social psychological factors related to remarriage for the widowed and the divorced, some of the general social characteristics of remarriage will be considered. One obvious fact is that those who enter remarriage are older than those entering first marriage. In the United States in 1959, the median age at first marriage was 20.3 for brides and 22.8 for grooms; at second marriage, 34.0 for brides and 38.3 for grooms; and at third or later marriage, 41.4 for brides and 46.9 for grooms.[1] The vast majority of remarriages refer to second marriages as

---

[1] "Marriage and Divorce Statistics," *Vital Statistics of the United States, 1959*, sec. 2 (United States Department of Health, Education, and Welfare, Public Health Service, National Office of Vital Statistics), p. 9.

on 3 percent of the brides or grooms were marrying for the third time, and 0.5 percent entering a fourth or later marriage in 1959.[2] There is no evidence that in recent years the percentage of marriages involving a partner with a previous marriage has increased or decreased.[3] As a general statement, it may be useful to keep in mind that "one in four marriages ends in divorce; two out of three divorced persons remarry; more than nine out of ten of the remarried stay married."[4]

Not only are those who remarry older than those entering first marriage, but the age difference between the spouses is also greater. In 1959, the median ages of all first marriage brides and grooms was 20.3 and 22.8 years, with an age difference of 2.5 years.[5] For the same year for all remarriages, the median age of the bride was 35.4 years and the groom 39.8 years, with an age difference of 4.4 years.[6] Spouses are about two years further apart in age if either or both are remarrying than if neither partner was previously married. The divorced remarry at younger ages than do the widowed. The median age of remarriage of women born in 1920 to 1924 whose first marriage ended in divorce was 32.1 years. For those whose first marriage ended in widowhood, the median age at remarriage was about six years older (38.2 years).[7]

Remarriage occurs rapidly for most persons who get divorces. One fourth remarry within one year, one half within three years, and three fourths within nine years. Women tend to wait longer than men after divorce before they remarry. When the divorced are compared with the widowed there are differences in remarriage rates. The probability that a man will remarry within a given number of years after he has become widowed is about one half as large as remarriage after divorce. For women, the corresponding ratio is only about one fifth. "These comparisons reflect the older average age of persons at widowhood than at divorce as well as lower age-specific marriage rates for widowed than divorced persons."[8]

The divorced tend to enter remarriage after a shorter lapse of time from the end of their first marriage than do the widowed. "During the

---

[2] Ibid., p. 9.

[3] "Marriages," *Vital Statistics of the United States, 1961*, vol. III, secs. 1, 2, and 7 (United States Department of Health, Education, and Welfare, Public Health Service, National Office of Vital Statistics), p. 3.

[4] Ben J. Wattenberg and Richard M. Scammon, *This U.S.A.* (Garden City, N.Y.: Doubleday & Co., Inc., 1965), p. 36.

[5] "Marriages," *Vital Statistics of the United States*, p. 7.

[6] Ibid., p. 7.

[7] U.S. Bureau of the Census, Current Population Reports, series P-20, no. 239, "Marriage, Divorce and Remarriage by Year of Birth: June 1971," (Washington, D.C.: U.S. Government Printing Office, 1972), p. 6.

[8] Paul C. Glick and Arthur J. Norton, "Frequency, Duration, and Probability of Marriage and Divorce," *Journal of Marriage and the Family*, May 1971, pp. 313.

early 1950s, among those who had remarried the median length of time which had elapsed since their previous marriage had been dissolved was 2.7 years for those who had been divorced and 3.5 years for those who had been widowed."[9] Several reasons exist for this difference. First, the widowed have a longer period of "mourning" over the loss of the first spouse. Second, the widowed are less strongly motivated to rectify the ending of the first marriage by entering a second one. Third, the basic reason some attained a divorce was the involvement with the person who is to be the next spouse, so that courtship had begun before the divorce actually occurred. Fourth, the divorced are younger and have a greater and earlier chance for remarriage than the widowed. In point of fact, a large number of the divorced have a short period of time in the divorce role. Furthermore, whether the woman has children or not does not appear to significantly influence her probabilities of remarriage. When standardized by age, a woman with three or more children has about the same chance of remarriage as a childless woman.

In marriage choice the individual may select a mate from one of the three general marital categories—single, widowed, or divorced. About nine out of every ten individuals entering a first marriage selects a mate who is also entering a first marriage. About one half of all divorced women marry divorced men and about four in ten marry a single man. The pattern for the divorced man is essentially the same as for the divorced woman. Among the widowed population, there is a slightly greater tendency for the widower to select a widow, but for the widow to select a single or a divorced man. Taking the largest categories of choice for each of the three groups, like tend to select like—the single, widowed, and divorced marry each other.

In a given year about four out of every five people who marry are single. Of those who remarry, about two out of three are divorced. In 1963, of those marriages where the bride and groom were single, the median age of the bride was 20 years and that of the groom 22 years. Where both were divorced, the corresponding ages were 34 and 38; and where both were widowed, 57 and 63 years old.[10]

Morton Hunt, in his research, examined the attraction that the divorced had for the divorced when they reentered the courtship process. He found that to one divorced person another divorced individual was knowable and familiar and in a sense, dependable. The broken previous marriage is taken as an earnest intent on their part to try and have an unbroken marriage and the wreckage of love is taken as proof that love existed and can be rebuilt. "The customs and social mechanisms of the

---

[9] "Marriages," *Vital Statistics of the United States,* p. 138.

[10] Hugh Carter and Paul C. Glick, *Marriage and Divorce: A Social and Economic Study* (Cambridge, Mass.: Harvard University Press, 1970), p. 290.

world of the formerly married not only maximize the exposure of the divorced to other divorced people, but help them ready themselves to try to make good those hopes and promises."[11]

Bowerman's research into remarriage found several general social patterns. First, single persons selected as mates were younger than were those selected mates who had been previously married. And the median age of selected mates who had been previously widowed was higher than for those mates previously divorced. Second, as men grew older, they married women increasingly younger than themselves and the age differences were the greatest for men who married single women and the least for men who married widows. Third, as women increased in age, they tended to marry men closer to their own age. Fourth, there was a greater range in the ages of mates selected by older people than by younger ones. Finally, the variability in age differences between spouses was greater for males than for females.[12]

Because a single marriage relationship is the generally assumed pattern in American society, people who experience more than one marriage are sometimes viewed as having psychological problems. While we will discuss later in the chapter the divorce-prone—who often do suggest some particular psychological problems that make marriage difficult— it cannot be assumed that most of those who divorce and remarry have any special psychological problems that separate them from the once-married population. One national study of mental health found little difference in the mental health risk of men and women who have remarried, and "among neither men nor women is remarriage associated with a great increase in mental health risk."[13]

Hunt found several variables related to the speed of remarriage in the divorce sample he studied. As true in other studies, he found that generally the younger divorced persons married the quickest. He also found that those persons who had wanted the divorce also tend to remarry sooner than those who had not. Furthermore, people of substantial incomes are likely to remarry more quickly than those with more limited means. "Finally, though women are more highly motivated to remarry than men, they are at an economic and social disadvantage in the marketplace, where, furthermore, they already outnumbered men three to two."[14]

By age 30 for both men and women, the divorced and widowed have

---

[11] Morton M. Hunt, *The World of the Formerly Married* (New York: McGraw-Hill Book Co., 1966), p. 269.

[12] Charles E. Bowerman, "Age Relationships at Marriage, By Marital Status, and Age at Marriage," *Marriage and Family Living*, vol. 18 (1956), pp. 231–33.

[13] Thomas S. Langner and Stanley T. Michael, *Life Stress and Mental Health* (New York: The Free Press of Glencoe, 1963), p. 333.

[14] Hunt, *Formerly Married*, p. 233.

a better chance for remarriage than the single person has for making a first marriage. It may be recalled that roughly 7 or 8 percent of the population will never marry. In the younger age groups, the group that will never marry constitutes a small percentage of the total; but as age increases and more have entered marriage, the number of "marital rejects" accounts for an increasingly greater percentage of the "never married." By contrast, the widowed and divorced have shown their success on the marriage market by their previous marriage.

SOME SOCIAL-PSYCHOLOGICAL FACTORS IN REMARRIAGE

Widowed

The widowed person contemplating remarriage must reconcile his feelings for his first spouse in relationship to a second spouse. In a first marriage the individual of course has no other marriage experience with which to compare the spouse. In remarriage after divorce, the second spouse may be favorably compared with the first mate who was not successful as a marriage partner; but the widowed person contemplating a second marriage may feel a sense of personal conflict between the first and the second mate. If the widowed person felt close to his first mate, the idea of a second marriage partner may lead him to some confusion and conflict about his feelings. If he feels he really loved the first mate, he may wonder how he can also love the second one; or loving the second mate may suggest he really did not love the first, resulting in feelings of guilt. This ambiguity is often a reflection of the romantic notion of one and only one true love during a lifetime. In such cases, the widow and others sometimes rationalize by stating that the second love is different—more mature and rational—thereby minimizing conflict and leaving the romantic image of the first marriage intact. The belief in a single great love is probably becoming less important in the middle class; increasingly, people who remarry may feel less personal conflict in having loved two spouses.

It sometimes happens that the widowed person recalls his first mate in an idealized way. This idealization may even stop some from remarrying because no second mate could come close to the first mate's image. If such a person does remarry, the idealized image may create problems in the remarriage because of an unrealistic comparison of the two spouses. In successful remarriage of the widowed, the recollections of the first spouse are probably favorable, but realistic.

When at least one partner in a remarriage is a widowed person, there are several important areas of potential difficulty in which the couple must adjust. First is the tendency of the widowed spouse to idealize the deceased mate. Second, the knowledge that the partner's first marriage was not terminated voluntarily may imply to the second spouse that if the first partner were still alive, the mate would still be with him and that he is thus a second choice. Third, friends and relatives may feel that the new spouse is an intruder. Patterns of behavior were established in the past with the deceased person in the role of spouse. The second marriage partner is not only bound to be at least somewhat different, but is also moving into already established relationships; hence, the new spouse may feel or be treated as an intruder. Friends and relatives may also compare the second spouse to the first, leading to problems for the second mate. Fourth, an expansion of the family relationships often occurs with the addition of a new set of in-laws resulting from remarriage. A remarried widow not only must adjust to her new in-laws but may have to appease her old ones as well. The family of the deceased partner usually has a strong emotional commitment to his memory; remarriage of his spouse may lead to a feeling on their part that he is not being adequately respected. If children are involved, they may also fear that their relationship will be replaced by the new in-laws established through the remarriage.

Finally, a variety of problems may exist when children are involved. The children must adjust to a stepparent, and the mother or father must adjust to someone new in the counter parental role. The latter may be a problem for some individuals who first shared the parent role with their first spouse, then played a combined parental role when widowed, and finally, through remarriage, moved back into sharing the parental roles with a new marriage partner. The widowed person with young children may be faced with a dilemma in contemplating remarriage. On the one hand, he may feel that remarriage will once again provide the children with someone in the needed parental role. On the other hand, someone new in the parental role may be seen as disturbing to the memory and influence of the natural parent. Sometimes after remarriage, the children are faced with two persons in the same parental role, the memory of the first and the reality of the second. With or without remarriage, the influence of the deceased parent may continue to be strong for the children. The surviving parent may attribute to the deceased parent a variety of expectations for the children. The children may be told "your father would have wanted you to do this or that" and the attributing of expectations to the respected and idealized departed sometimes makes honest disagreement seem like an attack on the deceased parent's memory. The surviving parent functions in the role of interpreter and spokesman of the departed and what he attributes to the departed may or may not be true. In some cases, a deceased parent may actually become more of a force dead than he was when alive.

In the American society, the role of the widowed person is generally a respectable one. Little stigma is attached to the widowed and there is no strong taboo against remarriage. Remarriage for the widowed is often the respectable and even expected course, and if it is a widower with children, the social pressures for remarriage are often very great. This reflects the common belief that children need a woman in the role of mother. The widow is not subject to the same social pressures to find a new father for her children, because the father role is viewed as less important in its significance for children. It may also be that the widow is expected a little more than the widower to "treasure" the memory of the departed spouse by not remarrying.

The success of remarriages of the widowed seems to be reasonably good. Because the widowed enter second marriages at older ages than do the divorced or the single, they probably enter with less romantic expectations. Their successful first marriage may have provided the satisfaction of their romantic needs, and the second marriage may be entered for more rational reasons. Older persons may have less exacting standards; they may be willing to settle for less than when they were younger. The contrast between the loneliness of life without a spouse and the companionship and security of married status may tip the scales in favor of marriage, even if it is not a success by any other measure.

A study of 100 remarriages where the bride and groom were past age 60 and where they had been remarried at least five years gives some information about older remarriages. This study found that over half the individuals had known their spouse for a long time before being widowed, and the new spouse often resembled the first wife or husband. Factors related to success in remarriage were as follows: (1) success was more likely if they knew each other well before their marriage; (2) those with approval of friends and relatives had the greatest success; (3) those who had been able to adjust satisfactorily to the role changes of aging had the most success; and (4) those with insufficient incomes were the least successful in their remarriages.[15]

Divorced

As previously suggested, the role of the divorced in the United States continues to be somewhat ambiguous, but the high remarriage rates of the divorced indicate both the desire and ability to enter a second marriage. Because the divorced are younger than the widowed, they probably face less difficulty moving back into the dating-courtship process necessary for finding a second mate. The fact that they are *divorced* in many cases makes their courtship experience prior to a second marriage different than it was prior to their first marriage.

---

[15] Walter C. McKain, "A New Look at Older Marriages," *The Family Coordinator,* January 1972, p. 67.

Hunt found a number of forces in operation to lead many divorced persons into remarriage. He points out that loneliness may have many different meanings for different people. But to a divorced person it is "an amputation, a dismemberment, an incompleteness where once there was something whole."[16] They had been a part of a functioning paired relationship that no longer exists. So many of them want to fall in love again and remarry. But as Hunt points out, while most divorced persons are desperately eager to love again, they are often afraid of it. They are often "persistent in their drives toward a complete and binding love relationship but just as persistent in their stopping off at intermediate way stations to allay their own fears."[17]

Hunt also found that falling in love for the divorced is further complicated by the past love. The new love may be fragile while at the same time the old love appears to be a hardy plant; "even though crushed and broken, it lingers on and refuses to die."[18] Hunt says it is surprising how the old love endures even among those who wanted to escape. "Those of whom this is true try to hide the remnants of the old love not only from most other people but even from themselves, for to continue loving the former mate is to cast doubt on the validity of one's separation or divorce."[19]

The fact that a high percentage of divorcees remarry indicates that courtship opportunities are adequate. Yet we have no way of knowing if the choice of the second mate was "forced"; given the strong motivation for remarriage, the individual may make a quick decision within a limited set of choices. Women with fewer options may be more motivated to remarry. One study found that divorced women were better educated and less likely to be in low-status jobs than remarried women: "Remarriage, evidently 'selected' the less well educated and less well trained among them. Many of those who remarried, then, may have done so partly because they were not well equipped to support themselves."[20]

In the discussion of mate selection in Chapter 6, it was pointed out that the middle-class family today plays a rather insignificant part in helping the young person meet potential marriage mates. The same may also be true for the divorcee meeting potential marriage partners. The peer group is more effective than the family in producing men with whom the divorcee would consider marriage. This is due to the greater circle of acquaintanceships with eligible age peers of divorcees and their friends. Many divorcees are helped in finding a new mate by friends

---

[16] Hunt, *Formerly Married*, p. 49.

[17] Ibid., p. 174.

[18] Ibid., p. 206.

[19] Ibid., p. 207.

[20] Karen S. Renne, "Health and Marital Experience in an Urban Population," *Journal of Marriage and the Family*, May 1971, p. 347.

who have emotional identifications with the divorced person and desire to help them rectify the failure of the first marriage through a successful second one.

Courtship and Sexual Activity

Because some individuals view the divorced woman as "sinful," she is sometime faced with special sex problems. The divorcee, like the widow, had extensive personal sexual experience in her marriage, and some males view the ex-married woman as an experienced sex object who must desire sexual activity because of her marital experiences. She is older and sexually experienced, and the male may view her as a possible sexual partner with whom a minimum of commitment is called for on his part. Another attitude that sometimes enters the male's thinking is that if a woman divorced her husband, he may have been sexually inadequate in meeting her needs and she is therefore interested in a new sex partner. The most persistent sexual aggression often comes not from single or divorced men, but from married men. As one divorcee put it, "The minute a married man says, 'My wife doesn't understand me,' get ready for a proposition." Possibly, the married man perceives the divorced woman as one who will make few demands on him because he is already married.

A number of divorced women are probably faced with a personal conflict over the desire for sexual relationships and their lack of marital status. The divorced woman is probably much less inhibited in satisfying her sexual needs than a younger, less experienced, and never-married female. Furthermore, divorced persons are much more apt to be sexually active than a generation ago. In a 1973 study, Morton Hunt found that divorced males had a median of eight different sexual partners per year. He found that only 9 percent of the divorced women were sexually inactive. Of all these women who were sexually active they had a median of 3.5 sexual partners per year.[21]

Sexual attitudes and behavior during courtship are bound to be different for the divorced than for the single woman. First, since the divorcee is not a virgin, she does not have to concern herself with conveying the notion of virginity. Second, the divorcee's sexual activity will probably be more influenced by her personal interest in sex than by general social values. Third, the male may be less apt to define the divorcee as "bad" and unworthy of marriage because of premarital sexual activity.

Implied in society's general sexual values, as related to those persons in postmarital roles (those after the death of the spouse or because of

---

[21] Morton Hunt, "Sexual Behavior in the 1970s," *Playboy*, October 1973, p. 204.

divorce), is that they are assumed to behave within the same framework as they were expected to in their premarital days—that is, they must abstain from sexual activity. But of course the values, as well as the controls over the sexual behavior of the young and the inexperienced, cannot realistically function in the same way for those who are older and sexually experienced. Rarely in studies or textbooks about the American family is there a discussion of the sexual adaptations of the postmarital. It seems to be assumed that most postmarital persons, especially the women, will give up all sexual behavior once their marriage relationship has ended. Yet the available evidence indicates that postmarital women do not return to their premarital levels of sexual abstinence. Kinsey wrote that "the most notable aspect of the histories of these previously married females was the fact that their frequencies of activity had not dropped to the levels which they had known as single females, before they had ever married."[22] For example, Kinsey found that for women in the age range of 41–45, of those single (never married), 68 percent had some sexual outlet as compared to 93 percent of the married and 84 percent of the previously married.[23]

Masters and Johnson provide some data on the use of masturbation as a sexual outlet among unmarried women. They found that for women over 50 years of age there was an increased masturbatory rate. That is, the pattern of masturbatory release of sexual tensions increases after the menopause. Unmarried women who had followed this pattern in their younger years continue into the older ages. In addition, there are women married to men in poor health, and those who are widowed, divorced, or socially isolated who turn to masturbation. Masters and Johnson suggest that "the psychological freedom to enjoy masturbatory relief of unresolved sexual tensions has more and more become an acceptable behavior pattern for those women so handicapped by limited partner availability in this age group."[24]

One recent study indicates that an important factor in the desire of women to continue coitus after their marriage has ended was their capacity to achieve orgasm. Christenson and Gagnon point out that once the capacity for sexual orgasm is achieved by women, they are likely to have coitus after the end of their marriages.[25] As to types of sexual outlet, obviously married women have a higher frequency of heterosexual contact than do previously married women. However, the previ-

---

[22] Alfred C. Kinsey et al., *Sexual Behavior in the Human Female* (Philadelphia: W. B. Saunders, 1953), p. 533.

[23] Ibid., p. 549.

[24] William H. Masters and Virginia E. Johnson, *Human Sexual Inadequacy* (Boston: Little, Brown & Co., 1970), p. 342.

[25] Cornelia Christenson and John H. Gagnon, "Sexual Behavior in a Group of Older Women," *Journal of Gerontology,* July 1965, p. 356.

ously married women are more apt to turn to other sexual outlets. For example, the Kinsey data shows that for women in the age range 41 to 45, only 13 percent of the married as contrasted to 32 percent of the previously married women were using solitary sexual outlets. And while none of the married women were using homosexual outlets, 6 percent of the previously married women were.[26]

The evidence clearly indicates that sexual involvement of some type is a common experience for many postmarried men and women. For most of them the decision is an individual one and they must cope with any guilt feelings by themselves. However, for some postmarried, particularly the divorced, there emerges a subculture that helps them in their adjustment to their deviant status. Morton Hunt has provided a picture of the subcultural world of the divorced and how it helps provide a setting for many decisions and activities with regard to sexual behavior. Hunt suggests that divorced people, while they are a part of the overall American culture and interact with it, "elsewhere have a private and special set of norms that guide them in their interactions with each other, and from which they derive their own customs, moral values, rules of fair play, and devices for coping with the problems special to their condition."[27] Hunt also suggests that many of their life patterns are quite different from those of the inhabitants of the wider culture.

The subculture of the divorced is not highly restrictive; in fact, in most respects it is quite permissive. The individual can arrange the details of his new dating life to suit his personal needs. "No one need consent to any suggestion he or she dislikes, but it is not impossible for the other to have made it."[28]

The divorced people that Hunt studied were predominantly urban and highly educated. Therefore, their behavior was no doubt different from many other divorced persons in the United States. This limitation should be kept in mind. In his sample he found that almost none of the men and only about 20 percent of the women had no sexual experiences since their marriages had ended. Hunt found that about 80 percent of the "formerly married" started having sexual intercourse during the first year after their divorces and most of them with more than one partner. Nearly all of the men and a fairly large number of the women found their sex lives more intense, less inhibited, and more satisfying than they had been during their marriages.[29] Hunt suggests that those divorced persons who did not have sexual relations typically had problems. He writes that a common type of divorced woman without sexual

---

[26] Kinsey et al., *Female*, p. 562.

[27] Hunt, *Sexual Attitudes*, p. 4.

[28] Ibid., pp. 112–13.

[29] Ibid., p. 144.

experience had been characterized by a limited amount of sexual excitement in the past in what was an unhappy marriage. Her innate negative feelings about sex gradually gained the upper hand and anesthetized her sexual feeling or even caused her to find the act somewhat repellent. Hunt goes on to point out that the common male abstainer was generally of normal sexuality, "who lost potency or desire in the course of a deteriorating marriage and voids sex afterward out of fear of failure."[30]

Many of the divorced enter into their first sexual encounters with a great deal of fear and anxiety. They are faced not only with the general moral restrictions but with the fact that their previous sexual experience had been in a relationship that had failed. Therefore the anxiety is often both sexual and interpersonal. As would be expected, the anxiety about entering a sexual affair was greater for the woman than the man and greater for those married a long while than those married only briefly.[31] But, except for those with real neurotic problems about sex, the great majority did have successful sexual experiences—most only after some initial failures; the fortunate few, at once.[32]

The subcultural world of the divorced is like other areas of deviance in that many members often feel it necessary to hide some of their subcultural activities from the broader society. Even when the divorced are able to successfully adjust to their extramarital activities, they often feel it necessary to hide from their friends, parents, and especially their children. If they have older children, they usually say in effect that there is one set of values to govern their nonmarital sexual behavior and different values for their unmarried children. Hunt says they are caught between two cultures, "while they permit themselves their present conduct and justify it, they also have a nagging residual feeling that it is not really proper, and do not want their children to emulate them."[33]

Also, as has been pointed out for other patterns of sexual behavior, the higher-educated postmarital females have a greater frequency of involvement. Gebhard found that almost three quarters of the previously married women studied had some postmarital coitus.[34] By levels of education, the coital rates for females were 56 percent for those with 8 years or less education, 76 percent for those with 9 to 12 years, and 73 percent for those with 13 to 16 years of education.[35] Gebhard further found that the highest educated (postgraduate) white women had had

---

[30] Ibid., pp. 146–47.

[31] Ibid., p. 154.

[32] Ibid., p. 155.

[33] Ibid., p. 163.

[34] Paul H. Gebhard et al., *Pregnancy, Birth, and Abortion* (New York: Harper & Brothers, 1958), p. 144.

[35] Ibid., p. 145.

longer periods of time involved in postmarital coitus as well as greater frequency.[36]

The divorced and the widowed find themselves in a position of having functioned for various lengths of time in the paired world with their past spouse and then being required to function in it without the necessary partner. This is particularly difficult in the middle class in which the number and importance of social relations is often great. The unmarried often find that if they do not have a "social" partner, their hostesses will go to great lengths to provide one. This pairing may have a positive function for the unmarried person in that it provides him with the opportunity for meeting members of the opposite sex and the possibility of finding a new mate. It is probably more important for the female than for the male because she has less opportunity to seek out and meet members of the opposite sex. Another reason for pairing off the divorcee may be the desire to remove a "threat" to married couples. The divorced possess some degree of glamour in the eyes of many; in addition, they are often felt to be seeking a new mate. Thus, it is feared that they might even steal someone's spouse if given the chance —and it is therefore good sense to render them harmless by providing a partner for them.

Children

When age is held constant, the fact of having or not having children does not seem to have any significant influence on the chances of remarriage. This point is often ignored in the criticism directed at divorce which involves children and implies that after divorce the child will live in a personal world of separated parents. The fact is that a large number of the mothers, who usually have custody of the children, remarry not long after the divorce. Therefore, the child usually comes into a new relationship with the second husband as a stepfather. This relationship may be one of conflict and insecurity for the child, but in many cases it means that with time the divorce is compensated for at least in part by a new set of family relationships.

The fact that the family situation in a remarriage after divorce is more likely to involve a new father than a new mother is significant. The role of the mother is generally the most significant one in an involvement with the children; therefore, the individual as mother is constant in the relationship with the children in the first marriage, during divorce, and in remarriage. While the children have many adjustments to make, they almost always have available to them the parent of greatest significance and emotional involvement.

---

[36] Ibid., p. 147.

It may also be argued that over the long run, children may be better off when an unsuccessful marriage has been ended and replaced by one that is successful. The two important roles of marriage partner and parent are interrelated, and dissatisfaction and frustration in one role often influences the other. Couples who keep an unsuccessful marriage intact for the sake of the children may often function as inefficient and unsuccessful parents, because the frustration and unhappiness of the marriage role may rub off on the parental role. The parents may also, consciously or unconsciously, blame the children for their remaining in a marriage that is unsuccessful, with this having an effect on their relationship with their children. By contrast, if the remarriage is successful, the parent is satisfied with the marital role, and this may positively influence him in his role as parent.

There is some evidence as to a possible relationship between parent's remarriage and the mental health consequences for their children. Langner found that the mental health risk was greater for those children whose parent remarried than for those children with a remaining parent who did not remarry.[37] This would suggest that some children found their emotional involvement with their remaining parent threatened by the entrance of their parent's new spouse.

Stepparents. Persons with children contemplating remarriage must usually consider the implications for their two interrelated roles of marriage partner and of parent. Until recently there had been little research into the possible impact of remarriage on parental roles. Some recent research, especially that of Bowerman and Irish, is starting to fill in the research gap in this area of family relationships.[38]

The impact of remarriage on children appears to be related to the age of the child. The general consensus among remarried parents seems to be that very young or quite grown-up children tend to assimilate a new parent more easily than do adolescents. There may also be a social class difference related to children and their getting along with stepparents. For example, one study found a larger proportion of low social class respondents (31 percent) than high social class respondents (20 percent) not getting along with their stepparents.[39]

Remarriage of the parent the child lives with of course places the child in new parental relationships. If his parents' marriage ended through divorce, he may find himself with a father he has little contact with and a stepfather with whom he has day-to-day interaction. If his parent's marriage ended through the death of a parent (most often the father), and his mother remarries, he finds himself with memories of a

---

[37] Langner and Michael, *Life Stress,* p. 169.

[38] Charles E. Bowerman and Donald P. Irish, "Some Relationships of Stepchildren to Their Parents," *Marriage and Family Living,* May 1962, pp. 113–21.

[39] Langner and Michael, *Life Stress,* p. 174.

father and day-to-day interaction with a stepfather. Bowerman and Irish found that a greater proportion of children of divorce adjusted to stepparents than did the children of bereavement.[40] They suggest that this difference may be because the child of a divorce acquires a stepparent "more promptly after the event, at an earlier age, and in fewer numbers (per family) than do those who have experienced the death of a mother or father."[41]

When the child has a live natural parent and a stepparent of the parent's own sex, the adjustment is poorer toward the stepparent. But in most of the "parent-child and age-sex combinations the stepfather appears to fare better in comparison with the real father than do stepmothers in contrast with mothers in normal homes."[42] The level of affection by children toward stepfathers is usually much lower than toward real fathers,[43] but the lowest level of affection was found to be by children to their natural father and a stepmother.[44]

Often a child with both natural parents alive and caring for him does not and cannot state a choice of preference for one parent over the other. However, a child living with a natural parent and stepparent is more likely to express a preference for one parent to the other. Bowerman and Irish found that "girls and adolescents are more apt to express a preference than are the boys and our younger respondents. Stepchildren more often prefer the real parent over the stepparent."[45]

The difficulties that may be created because of a new marital partner as a stepparent may also contribute to some problems in the remarriage. That is, strains in the parental roles are often related to strains in the marital roles. Bowerman and Irish found this to be true in that level of marital discord was higher in stepparent homes than in first marriages.[46]

One study investigated a number of factors related to the relationship of stepparents and stepchildren. It found that the age of the stepfather was not an influence in his relationship with his stepchildren. However, age was meaningful for the stepmothers. "Seventy percent of those women who were 40 or less had excellent relations with their stepchildren, compared to 52 percent of those who were over 40."[47] This study also found that of those families who had children together, 78 percent rated as excellent their relationships between stepchildren and

---

[40] Bowerman, "Some Relationships of Stepchildren," p. 117.

[41] Ibid., p. 118.

[42] Ibid., p. 117.

[43] Ibid., p. 116.

[44] Ibid., p. 117.

[45] Ibid., p. 119.

[46] Ibid., p. 117.

[47] Lucile Duberman, "Step-Kin Relationships," *Journal of Marriage and the Family,* May 1973, p. 286.

stepparents, compared to 53 percent of those who did not have children together. "It can be inferred from this that the presence of natural children in a reconstituted family enhances the relationships between stepchildren and stepparents."[48]

Remarriage Success

Monahan, after careful study of divorce and remarriage, found that

with respect to remarriage the evidence is quite consistent and strong. Not only do second marriages ending in divorce show a shorter duration than first marriages, the duration also diminished with each successive remarriage. When the data are arranged to show the factors of divorce versus widowhood, it becomes apparent that it is the divorce group which exerts a major influence on the result. With each prior experience with divorce, the duration of the remarriage ending in divorce becomes shorter.[49]

Using divorce as a means of comparing the success of first and second marriage is very crude. First, the length of remarriage is bound to be shorter than in a first marriage because the person is older when he enters a second marriage. Second, the divorced person who remarries has been selected out of the total first married population as one who *has shown* he will turn to divorce. As divorces occur, the continued first-married population proportionately increases in being composed of individuals who would probably *not* turn to divorce under any conditions. While the remarried-divorce population clearly has a higher divorce rate than the first-married population, this indicates a greater tendency for the once-divorced to divorce again, but says little about the relative marital adjustment of the two groups.

The evidence for both divorce rate and ratings of marital success suggest a somewhat lower success rate in remarriage than in first marriage. However, it may also be argued that most remarriages of divorced persons are successful if they are compared with the individual's first marriage. All of their first marriages were failures (in that they ended in divorce), whereas the majority of divorcees who remarry have entered a new marriage that lasts. Therefore, when compared with their first marriage, most of the second marriages are successful.

There is some evidence of a slight decline in the proportion of remarriages ending in divorce. In 1958, for six reporting states, 31 percent of the divorcing husbands and 32 percent of the wives were ending a re-

---

[48] Ibid., p. 288.

[49] Thomas P. Monahan, "The Duration of Marriage to Divorce: Second Marriages and Migratory Types," *Marriage and Family Living*, May 1959, p. 136.

marriage. By 1961, as indicated from 18 reporting states, the percentages were 26 for husbands and 27 for wives.[50]

When we look at all divorcees and see that 97 percent of the men and 96 percent of the women have been divorced only once, it becomes clear that divorce is not an experience that any one person has very often. As one observer points out, "Divorce is working best not for those who marry promiscuously but for those who have made a mistake and are not inclined to repeat it."[51]

The Divorce-Prone

Divorce-proneness may result from a variety of social and psychological factors. The concept of divorce-proneness is supported by the fact that the divorce rate increases with each subsequent divorce. As an example, the writer once talked to an attractive and intelligent woman in her middle 30s who had been divorced from three husbands. She stated that her three husbands were essentially alike in personality and that their personalities in relationship with hers made a successful marriage impossible. Furthermore, she had enough insight into herself to say that if she married again, she would probably marry a man like the first three, implying that a fourth marriage would also end with divorce.

It is very probable that some persons who do not, for any number of reasons, have much chance of making a go of marriage are selected out of the remarriage market. Divorce may weed out of the once-married population a good many of the marital misfits; the exigencies of finding a second mate may select them out of the remarried population also. The result, so far as the unremarried widowed and divorced are concerned, is a population with adverse social characteristics; so far as remarried widowed and divorced are concerned, it may be a population with superior social characteristics. If Bernard's suggestion is true, it indicates that the rate of successful remarriage would be much less if all who were eligible for remarriage had an equal chance of finding a second mate. While it seems clear that some of the obvious marital misfits are weeded out, it is also evident that a number who will prove with future marriages to be divorce-prone are not.

It may also be suggested that the divorce-prone constitute an internal bias in the comparison of both the divorce frequency and marital adjustment of first marriages with remarriages. Here is a hypothetical illustra-

---

[50] "Divorces," *Vital Statistics of the United States, 1961*, vol. III, secs. 3, 4, and 7 (U.S. Department of Health, Education, and Welfare, Public Health Service, National Office of Vital Statistics), p. 9.

[51] Ben J. Wattenberg and Richard M. Scammons, *This U.S.A.* (Garden City, N.Y.: Doubleday and Company, Inc., 1965), p. 36.

tion: If we take all first marriages that occur in any given year, we know that out of that group at least one partner in a number of the marriages will prove with time to be divorce-prone. For the sake of illustration, it is suggested that such will prove to be the case in 5 percent of the first marriages. Suppose that for the same year, we take all second marriages in which at least one of the partners has been previously married and divorced. The very fact that all of these remarriages involve at least one divorced person means that the percentage of marriages with a divorce-prone partner will have greatly increased. Once again for the sake of illustration, suppose that 25 percent of the second marriages involve at least one partner who is divorce-prone. The illustration may be continued by taking for that same year all third marriages in which at least one of the partners is entering his third marriage after two prior divorces. It is now suggested that 50 percent of all third marriages have a partner who is divorce-prone. This might be projected to sixth or seventh marriages in which close to 100 percent would include a divorce-prone person. Thus, the probability of these marriages also ending in divorce would be very high.

Using the above illustration, it may be argued that if some way were found to control the divorce-prone group and then compare the "non-prone" in first marriages and remarriages, the divorce frequency and adjustment differences would no longer exist. Of course at the present time no such controls are available, but the divorce-prone bias should be recognized. One further point of bias is that, because the divorced tend to marry divorced persons, their remarriage relationship has a greater probability of having at least one divorce-prone partner than when the divorced marries the single or widowed, or when the widowed marries the single or widowed.

However, it must be stressed that many who divorce several times do not exhibit any evidence of being neurotic. Hunt suggests that many who divorce for a second time are acting on the basis of what they have learned. That is, that divorce is not as dreadful as they once thought. Furthermore, that the life of the formerly married is not necessarily unhappy or unrewarding. "That even the distressing aspects of divorce are less destructive of the personality than remaining in a bad marriage. Their second divorces do not show an inability ever to make a successful marriage, they do show an increased readiness to give up an unsuccessful one."[52]

The questions raised about the "success" of the divorced in remarriage are emphasized for this reason: Given the high divorce rate in the United States today and the great social concern directed at it, more careful analysis of what happens to the divorced is greatly needed. This

---

[52] Hunt, *Formerly Married*, pp. 278–79.

is important both sociologically and psychologically, because there is no indication that divorce is going to decrease significantly in the foreseeable future. The vast bulk of research is directed at the predivorce and divorce states, rather than the extended area of postdivorce adjustment to the divorced or remarried roles. Greater attention also needs to be directed at remarriage as a social force reducing some of the conditions often assumed to be problems of divorce. Increasingly, remarriage may emerge as a force of equilibrium in relationship to what is often called the divorce "problem."

SELECTED BIBLIOGRAPHY

Bowerman, Charles, and Irish, Donald P. "Some Relationships of Stepchildren to Their Parents." *Marriage and Family Living,* May 1962, pp. 113–21.

Burchinal, Lee G. "Characteristics of Adolescents from Unbroken, Broken, and Reconstituted Families." *Journal of Marriage and Family,* February 1964, pp. 44–51.

Carter, Hugh, and Glick, Paul C. *Marriage and Divorce: A Social and Economic Study.* Cambridge, Mass.: Harvard University Press, 1970.

Duberman, Lucile "Step-Kin Relationships." *Journal of Marriage and the Family,* May 1973, pp. 283–92.

Glick, Paul C., and Norton, Arthur J. "Frequency, Duration, and Probability of Marriage and Divorce." *Journal of Marriage and the Family,* May 1971, pp. 307–17.

Hunt, Morton M. *The World of The Formerly Married.* New York: McGraw-Hill Co., 1966.

McKain, Walter C. "A New Look at Older Marriages." *The Family Coordinator,* January 1972, pp. 61–69.

Chapter 24

The Future of Marriage and the Family

In Chapter 1 we discussed the traditional Western world family. It was an extended family with strong patterns of dependency between two and often three generations. While the small conjugal family unit of parents and children had existed for some time, it was often within the context of the more extended family. But in the United States the 20th-century family has overwhelmingly become two generational, with common patterns for its operations and maintenance. Mate selection came to rest primarily in the hands of those seeking mates, and growing up to get married was of major importance. Those who never married were pitied for not being able to fulfill their adult destiny. Marriage also implied set sex roles—the husband was the breadwinner, and the wife stayed home and took care of the children. Sexual expression was restricted to marriage and a part of the exclusive sexual, emotional relationship of the husband and wife. This general description illustrates an "ideal type," and there have often been some variations from it. However, these variations have not been great nor have they been common to large numbers of persons, although in recent years they have increased significantly.

First we examine some alternative patterns that existed in the past in the United States and second, some recent and present changes that are occurring. Finally, on the basis of the trends we will speculate about changes that may occur in the future.

Clearly implied in the approach to be taken here is that there is nothing that is absolute or indispensable to society. Too often the assumption is made that because something appears always to have been the case in the past it must necessarily be true in the future. This is an assumption often made by family sociologists who tend to treat the family as something that *must* continue to be important in the future. The family *may* continue to be important in the future or it *may not*. In part the bias is a reflection of the fact that it is easy to get carried away emotionally by pronouncements about marriage and the family because both words have been romanticized and sentimentalized. As Churchill points out, all of us tend to "fetishize the institutions that have left the greatest impression upon our minds during childhood and that, during childhood, appeared to be far different from what they may have been in reality."[1]

The worship of marriage and the family as social institutions tends to lead to distorted images of the past and therefore significance for the future. The traditional Judeo-Christian family has not been the source of *all* good things and, in fact, has been one major source of a great many social and moral evils. If all the applauded virtues are learned in the bosom of the family—virtues such as veracity, respect for authority and property, reverence, cleanliness, thrift, and industriousness—"it should also be remembered that many of the more contemptible vices have often been learned in the family: Complacency, jealousy, bigotry, narrow-mindedness, envy, selfishness, rivalry, avarice, prejudice, vanity, and greed are readily acquired in the special psychological circumstances that prevail in the family arrangement peculiar to our culture."[2]

Past Marriage and Family Variations

Before examining the changes occurring at the present time in marriage and family it is useful to look at the past. The patterns since first colonization in the United States have tended to be remarkably alike. And yet there have been isolated attempts to develop quite different patterns from the ones that prevailed at the time. Most of the attempts in the past were communal groups organized around some unifying religious belief such as the Hutterites, Mennonites, Shakers, Mormons, and Bruderhofs. Given the strong religious values, the family was often seen as secondary. Participation in the family inevitably detracts to some degree from participation in communal affairs by generating par-

---

[1] Wainwright Churchill, *Homosexual Behavior Among Males* (New York: Hawthorne Books, 1967), pp. 301–2.

[2] Ibid., p. 304.

ticularistic loyalties which are in competition with complete devotion to the communal aims. Most communes, whether religious or political, have tried either to abolish the institution of the family altogether or to delimit severely the influence of the family by relegating the responsibility to an institution less likely to threaten the exclusive allegiance of their members.[3] In this section we look briefly at two such religious communes of the past and some of the ways they treated traditional family functions.

The Moravian Experiment. This was one of the earliest experimental attempts and occurred during the colonial period in Bethlehem, Pennsylvania. It existed for a number of years and reached a peak population of over 1,000 members. Religious duties were so important to this group that means were developed for subordinating the Moravian family, and they developed family surrogates in the form of "choirs." The choirs were special living arrangement groups and they, rather than the family, took on the functions of socialization and social control. The choirs made it absolutely clear that children belonged more to the community than to parents. As a result, for a number of decades parental authority was almost nonexistent.[4]

Infants, children, the unmarried, the married, and the widowed lived in quarters where the sexes were kept apart. The children were usually taken from the parents and placed under institutional care at the age of one or one and a half. At age 5 or 6 the children were segregated by sex, and at age 17 they were initiated into the "'unmarried choirs." The young newcomer was given membership in a ready-made primary group in which a variety of religious and social activities went along with the heavy work load he was expected to perform. This left a person very little time for developing àny feelings of loneliness. When they married, the "brother" or "sister" continued their work in the "married people's choir." "Provisions were made to give this choir a home of its own, and couples, especially in the early years, did not generally live together. Arrangements were made to set aside a time and place for each couple to meet in privacy once a week."[5] Ultimately this commune failed because while they produced children, they failed to convert their children to the goals of the settlement. The inability to maintain commitment to a movement from one generation to another is probably the most common reason for the ultimate demise of most communes that last for more than one generation.

The Oneida Community. This community was founded in 1848 in

---

[3] Gillian Lindt Gollin, "Family Surrogates in Colonial America: The Moravian Experiment," in Michael Gordon, *The Nuclear Family in Crisis* (New York: Harper and Row, 1972), p. 46.

[4] Ibid., p. 51.

[5] Ibid., p. 50.

New York by a religious leader·named John Noyes and lasted until 1880. It was based on the belief that all persons were to love and share equally and was a so-called bible communism. Over the years the Oneida community has come to be associated with group marriage. However Noyes did not believe in romantic love nor in monogamous marriage. He saw such manifestations as selfish and smacking of possessiveness. "He taught that all men should love all women and that all women should love all men, but there was no attempt to impose this on the world."[6]

Sexual relations within the community were reportedly easy to arrange because the men and women all lived in the Mansion House. If a man wanted sexual intercourse with a particular woman, he was supposed to make his wish known to a central committee, who would convey his desire to the woman in question. If the latter consented, the man would go to her room at bedtime and spend an hour or so with her before returning to his own room. No woman was forced to submit to a sexual relationship which was distasteful to her.[7] The available evidence suggests that sexual activity was not openly discussed within the community, "and it is doubtful whether the subject of "Who was having relations with Whom?" ever became common knowledge.[8]

The community was not permissible in all social activities. For example, while dancing and card playing were permitted, since they were regarded as social activities, coffee drinking and smoking were condemned on the grounds that they were individualistic and appetitive in nature.[9] So the religious principles were against self-indulgence and not a puritanical restriction against all things that were pleasurable. Those things which were social in nature were generally acceptable.

The Oneida community and John Noyes are also often remembered in history for their beliefs about family planning. Noyes believed that not all adults should have children. Rather he believed that specially chosen adults should be used for selective breeding. This program was called "sterpiculture," and the birth-control values were so strong that for the first 20 years after the community was founded there were no children born. The method of birth control was *coitus reservatus,* where the male performed coitus up to the time of ejaculation and then withdrew so that no sperm would enter the vagina. The young men were taught this technique, and, until they learned, they were allowed to have sexual relations only with women who were past their menopause.

---

[6] William M. Kephart, "Experimental Family Organization: An Historico-Cultural Report on the Oneida Community," in Gordon, *Nuclear Family,* pp. 66–67.

[7] Ibid., p. 67.

[8] Ibid., p. 70.

[9] Ibid., p. 63.

While there was a great deal of skepticism about this method of birth control the evidence seems to indicate that it did work.

Because of the highly radical life patterns of the Oneida community many broader community pressures operated against them. But the community seemed to have thrived under the strong leadership of John Noyes. When he retired there was no effective leader to take over from him, and the community soon broke up by dropping many of the old patterns of life.

Modern Alternative Family Forms

It is useful to look briefly at the Kibbutz in Israel because the kibbutz has received a great deal of publicity in this country and has had a strong influence on many modern, American attempts to develop altered marriage and family patterns.

The Kibbutz. The Kibbutz grew out of the desire of a group of young, eastern European Jewish intellectuals at the beginning of the 20th century to found a new and democratic society in what was then Palestine. The founders were very concerned not to duplicate the old double standards, and they therefore introduced dramatic new patterns. They based their marriage relationship on consent rather than on legal contract. They developed living arrangements with communal kitchens, dining rooms, and laundries to free the women from household tasks and to give them full roles in the economic and social life of the Kibbutz.[10] When a woman gave birth she was relieved of work for about six weeks and then allowed to visit whenever necessary to feed her baby. By the time the baby was about nine months of age the mother usually made only short visits during the day.

In the Kibbutz, marriage does not affect the responsibilities of either the man or the woman. Both continue to work in whatever part of the economy they had been in before their marriage. The legal and social status of the two remain the same, and the woman keeps her maiden name. Given the unstructured nature of marriage, there has been some questioning of why couples get married. Spiro has argued that the motivation is the desire to satisfy the needs for intimacy, using that term in both its physical and psychological meanings. Often the young man, after a period of sexual experimentation, wants to establish a relatively permanent relationship with one person. "But in addition to the physical intimacy of sex, the union also provides a psychological intimacy that may be expressed by notions such as comradeship, secur-

---

[10] Leslie Rabkin and Karen Rabkin, "Children of the Kibbutz," in Gordon, *Nuclear Family*, p. 94.

ity, dependency, succorance, etc. And it is this psychological intimacy primarily that distinguishes couples from lovers."[11]

There has been some argument that marriage doesn't really exist on the Kibbutz. This has been argued when marriage was seen as a relationship between adults of opposite sex, characterized by sexual *and* economic activities. On the Kibbutz the relationship does *not* involve economic cooperation, just the sexual relationship. However, this criticism doesn't seem very relevant because whatever the nature and type of involvement between the couple, both they and the rest of the Kibbutz membership define them as married and they are treated as such.

On the Kibbutz, children are very important. Children are valued both for their own sake and as new members to further strengthen the Kibbutz. Yet, even with the great importance attached to children the natural parents do not provide directly for their care. In fact, the parents have no responsibility in this regard. The Kibbutz as a whole assumes the responsibility for all children. However, many observers have noted that Kibbutz children are very devoted to their parents. One study found that Kibbutz infants at 1, 6, and 12 months showed higher overall achievement than a U.S. sample. "Even when they were compared with infants of highly educated parents in private Israeli homes, Kibbutz babies consistently performed better. At the least, this should quiet pessimists who claim that collective childrearing retards the intellectual development of infants."[12] The person who grows up in the Kibbutz is described as a healthy, intelligent, generous, somewhat shy but warm human being, rooted in his community and in the larger Israeli society. "He shows no sign of the emotional disturbance we would expect from a violation of our ideal mother-child relationship."[13]

In Chapter 13 the family roles of the elderly in American society were discussed. It was pointed out that increasingly the American pattern has been one of agencies outside the family system providing care for elderly persons. In the Kibbutz the care of the elderly is quite different. In the first place, retirement does not occur at an arbitrary age when the person completely leaves his occupation. In the Kibbutz, retirement from work is gradual and does not call for the sharp break. Furthermore, parents are able to maintain close and constant relations with their children without losing their independence. Elderly and old people are thus spared much of the insecurity and isolation common in the United States. However, even though some problems are solved for the elderly on the Kibbutz there are still others. With equality an important value,

---

[11] Melford E. Spiro, "Is the Family Universal?—The Israeli Case," in Gordon, *Nuclear Family,* pp. 84–85.

[12] Rabkin and Rabkin, "Kibbutz," p. 99.

[13] Ibid., p. 94.

the aging members have no claim to special positions. Their contributions in the past do not entitle them to special consideration. Thus the
gradual withdrawal from the work area increases the importance of the
family to the older person. "Curtailment of outside activities brings about
a concomitant decline in the number and intensity of outside contacts,
but they may seek solace and emotional security in their relationships
with their children. Grandchildren thus become a major preoccupation,
especially with aging women."[14]

Contemporary American Family Forms.   As pointed out earlier in
the chapter the earlier alternative family forms in the United States
were almost all organized around religious beliefs and developed an
economic pattern of life compatible with the broader society. The recent
attempts have tended to reject the materialism of American culture and
have extolled the values of love and giving. "The older utopias attempted
to create a full-scale village or community with an elaborate division of
labor. The modern aim is rather to simplify."[15] Therefore, the assumption
of most communal living attempts has been that there was something
wrong with the basic structure of society and that there must be experimentation with new ways of dealing with the usual problems of marriage and the family. Many young people became involved in communal
living experiments not as a means of withdrawing from civilization but
as a way of becoming more involved in it.

The modern attempts differed from the older ones in another important way—they were sometimes antiintellectual. For example, some
turned to primitive techniques of childbirth and stated that natural childbirth was the centerpiece of their philosophy and that to create life was
the very essence of life itself. Some of the communes in southern California in the late 1960s believed that childbirth was the supreme experience to be shared with their mates. As a result many couples disregarded
the formal marital institution even though they remained monogamous
for a number of years. They often saw the birth certificate as a method
of accounting for an individual by putting him "in line for military
conscription, social security, taxation, and indoctrination through compulsory public education."[16]

Probably the most important value behind most of the communes
experimenting with alternative family forms during the late 1960s and
early 1970s was to get the individual further involved in his own
destiny. Communal life represented to many people an attempt to in-

---

[14] Yonina Talmon, "Aging in Israel, A Planned Society," in Gordon, *Nuclear Family*, p. 106.

[15] William Goode, *World Revolution and Family Patterns* (New York: The Free
Press of Glencoe, 1963), p. 49.

[16] David E. Smith and James L. Sternfield, "Natural Child Birth and Cooperative
Child Rearing in Psychadelic Communes," in Gordon, *Nuclear Family*, p. 199.

volve the individual in the broader community and to destroy the belief that the world outside the family is hostile, with love and safety to be found only in the bosom of the family. This meant some people turned away from the nuclear family and joined group or multilateral marriages. For others it meant continuing the nuclear family but within a communal context where group participation was a necessary and desired part of life. "Whatever shape family life takes, and there are many intermediary forms between complete monogamy and complete group marriage, the central idea is always the same: Break down the barrier between people and permit freedom and growth."[17]

In recent years people have tried a number of different living arrangements related to variations in family types. In the cities there have been several types of communal structures. There have been *crash pads* which were usually apartments or houses rented by a person or group where friends and strangers "crashed" the pad. They would come and go, stay as long as they liked, and may or may not have contributed to expenses. By contrast, the *cooperatives* have been more organized living arrangements, and their motive has been practicality. It was cheaper to live together rather than alone, and the people often shared political or social values.

Ald, in his study of rural communes, came up with four general types. First was the *collective settlement,* which is well ordered and work oriented. With few exceptions it is an agrarian, conservative, no-nonsense Kibbutz. Sex is generally open and spontaneous, although monogamous attachments tend to be the rule. Second is the *commune,* the most common form of societal living. It is characterized by open sexuality and unprogrammed, or even a deliberately anarchistic, structure. Third is the *expanded* or *extended family,* which may take two different forms: one where married or unmarried males and females enter into open, spontaneous relationships; and the second made up of only married couples. Fourth is the *tribal* group, which has a powerful mystical orientation rooted in unquestioned dominance of an individual or "nuclear personality."[18] Of course, over time individuals moved in and out of the above types.

Communes have not always been successful in their efforts towards sexual equality. Very often women found themselves doing the same secondary tasks they were doing under the traditional system. Whitehurst has pointed out that frequently male chauvinism creeps in seemingly because no one wants to do the dirty work of daily living. As a result men in the commune often left the menial tasks to the women, and the women too often accepted them. As Whitehurst points out,

---

[17] Gordon, *Nuclear Family,* p. 22.

[18] Ray Ald, *The Youth Communes* (New York: Tower Publications, 1970), p. 10.

"there is little evidence that either typical marriages or communal arrangements have been able to make equality in the division of labor really efficient."[19] There have been some communes where equality appears to have been achieved. Rose Moss Kanter says that at Twin Oaks there is no distinction between men and women, "the work of each sex, or their status or privileges. Men are just as likely to work in the kitchen, and women in the woodshop or the fields."[20]

Marriage. The traditional influences with regard to marriage have been seen in most communes in recent years. While many young people have tried to break the traditional monogamous love bond which has been the basis of the modern nuclear family, they nevertheless often show jealousy, bruised egos, and attempts to assert claims as a result of intimacies that last any length of time. Or they have sometimes attempted to separate completely sexuality from reproduction, but still the strongly maternal female was found in many of the communes.[21] Yet, although there were many similarities to the broader society, the communes attempted to make very different kinds of relationships based on different value assumptions. For example, the requirement of marriage was often removed from the having of children. Ald quotes one young woman who was annoyed with her parents' disapproval of her having a child out of wedlock as saying, "We're all married—married to each other from the day we're born." "She was expressing the new breed's awareness of the common bond of humanity and the conviction that the time for the ultimate decision has arrived. Oblivion or utopia."[22]

Although a number of young people have been experimenting with alternative styles of marriage, it has not represented any real, wholesale rejection of traditional marriage. For some young people, in and out of communes, the pattern has been an extension of the courtship process into what might be called experimental marriage. While this experimental form may delay marriage temporarily for some, the vast majority still adapt a more or less conventional conjugal marriage. "There is only a small percentage of couples who actually attempt to develop and permanently maintain a more conventional marriage from the traditional monogamous conjugal type."[23]

There has been a great deal of interest about the sexual patterns found in the alternative family styles. In the past some of the attempts

---

[19] Robert Whitehurst, "Some Comparisons of Conventional and Contracultural Families," *The Family Coordinator,* October 1972, p. 397.

[20] Rosebeth Moss Kanter, *Commitment and Community* (Cambridge, Mass.: Harvard University Press, 1972), p. 2.

[21] Ald, *Communes,* p. 89.

[22] Ibid., p. 96.

[23] David H. Olsen, "Marriage of the Future: Revolutionary or Evolutionary Change?" *The Family Coordinator,* October 1972, p. 389.

at different marriage forms placed importance on celibacy. Given the moral tone of the 19th century and the need for birth control, celibacy was more acceptable than free love. By contrast, the recent attempts have found group sex as the overwhelming preference.[24] The public image, as developed through the mass media, is that many people living on communes are having one continuous orgy. But there is no evidence that this is true, although the values with regard to sex are quite different from those of the broader society. Often the communal ideal value has been extrasexual, that is, seeking a communion of persons more intimate than the sexual connection on a physical plane. "The body is not only an end-purpose but a vehicle for a profounder, all-enveloping force."[25] This describes an ideal value about sex, and actual sexual practices are obviously generally engaged in for the pleasure of the act and are often spontaneous to the occasion. In this respect sex is not practiced with ritual but is more a happening. Because many of the values against sex common to American society are removed, sex is simply a part of the scene. This is generally true only if the person is a part of the subculture, because the sex setting is not one of free love.

Children. Many communes have a special interest in the rearing of children. It is clear that children are dependent on others for survival, and yet the common commune philosophy of doing one's own thing severely undercuts dependency. In some cases the adults have been so concerned with seeking and finding their own identity that the children have been abandoned for long periods of time. Yablonsky found that the children in the communes he visited were treated as playthings. "They were adored and adorned with affection and trinkets; however, in the communities I observed they are not cared for with the basic necessities of food, clothes, and adequate health facilities."[26] Ald, in his study, found the child to be better off the nearer his commune environment was to the family patterns of the broader society. He found that from necessity the commune child develops a surprising steadfastness in the face of much adult behavior which is ideosyncratic and offensive.[27] "I cannot say that communitarian children are inferior to those raised in the dominant culture. From what I could see, the communal youngster, in spite of the apparent neglect, is healthier or certainly as healthy."[28]

It appears that often children reared in communes are less often so restricted in their development as in the traditional family. They are more apt to be treated as autonomous persons at a much earlier age and kept in positions of dependency for a shorter period of time. Whitehurst

---

[24] Kantor, *Commitment,* p. 87.

[25] Ald, *Communes,* p. 87.

[26] Lewis Yablonsky, *The Hippie Trip* (New York: Pegasus, 1968), p. 146.

[27] Ald, *Communes,* p. 91.

[28] Ibid., pp. 93–94.

suggests that as both men and women take responsibility for contraception, both marriage and the children will continue to be redefined in terms of ecological and economic strategies felt to be appropriate for the coming world. "Clearly the meaning of having and rearing children is not the same as in times past."[29]

Older Persons. When one thinks of the various attempts at alternative family forms in recent years it is almost always as something by and involving young adults and children. Often the family type that develops in the commune provides a more complete and, in many ways, more humane solution for the problems of the elderly. But the current communal movement in this country has yet to show any real interest in older people. If specific communes are able to survive, then they will have to deal with the issue of old age. At the present time neither the communes nor the normal family system is in much of a position to claim it does a very good job in caring for the needs of the elderly and integrating them into social structures. What has often happened, as discussed in Chapter 13, is that many older people develop their own kinds of communes in the sense that they move into retirement apartments or villages and live in a very homogeneous world. This is rarely experimental but rather an extension of the kind of family life they led in their younger years, but modified by their being older and their children gone.

The Future of Marriage and the Family

It appears that even though the family continues to exert a strong and sentimental hold, its social significance is much less than it used to be. "All of us ideally are still born in intact families, but not all of us need to establish families to survive."[30] In the past a great deal of what seemed significant to the individual was obtained within the family setting, but this is no longer true. The important social frontiers today are outside the family in such areas as science, politics, and the arts. As Keller points out this must affect the attractiveness of family life for both men and women. "For men, because they will see less and less reason to assume full economic and social responsibility for four or five human beings in addition to themselves as it becomes more difficult and less necessary to do so. For women, the household may soon prove too small for the scope of their ambitions and power drives."[31] The greatest break away from the family is occurring for women, primarily because they had a far greater involvement in it. As women have increasingly

---

[29] Whitehurst, "Some Comparisons," p. 317.

[30] Suzanne Keller, "Does the Family Have a Future?" *A Warner Modular Publication,* reprint 64 (1973), p. 7.

[31] Ibid., p. 8.

moved outside the home into occupational roles it has been predicted that society would suffer. Yet this has not been the case, and, in fact, a strong argument can be made that society has benefited, to say nothing of the gains for women themselves. All the evidence clearly indicates that the woman-in-the-home dimension of the family is not nearly as significant as it previously was.

It seems reasonable to suggest that the changes in marriage and the family for the future will not be radical. It is highly unlikely that the present conjugal system will be thrown out and something significantly different put in its place. Rather, it appears that the middle-class, con-jugal marriage-and-family model will undergo some alterations.

In the past, marriage was seen as an unquestioned role for men and women in their adult years. As earlier suggested, persons who never married were to be pitied, but this is changing. To some utopians and other idealists, monogamous marriage has come to represent a barrier on the road to true brotherhood. Marriage has been seen as exclusive possession, a kind of slavery, as well as a source of jealousy and tension.[32] So there are a wide range of ideological attacks on marriage.

In the past it was commonly assumed that marriage was based on love and that love provided the reason for its continuation. But very often the institution of marriage is not based on love, sentiment, or compati-bility, but rather on economic necessity. This has often created problems because the ego-needs of the person are not met in this kind of marriage. The changes in the economic and ego-need aspects of marriage indicate that many more couples will attempt to work out their own set of ground rules governing their relationships. Whitehurst suggests that in the ab-sence of older and more conventional guidelines and of social control agencies, marriage in the immediate future is bound to become more difficult and problematic than ever before.[33]

One of the most important points, with reference to marriage, that has been suggested several times in this book is that recent evidence indicates that marriage may be decreasing in importance. The marriage rate which had been going up since the early 1960s began to falter at the end of the decade, and by the early 1970s it was leveling off and begin-ning to decline. There were proportionately more single young men and women in 1970 than in 1960, the decline being especially notable among 20-year-olds. This suggests that while fewer young people get married, many of them do establish ego-need relationships with other persons and live with them for varying lengths of time. As a result there may be important changes occurring in the marriage institution. First, there may be more young people involved in *ad hoc* kinds of arrangements which

[32] Kantor, *Commitment*, p. 44.
[33] Whitehurst, "Some Comparisons," p. 311.

specifically avoid legal entanglements. Second, there appears to be an increasing interest in the possibility of developing a limited, legalized marital form, for example, a marriage contract for five years. Third, it is likely that emotional and sexual permissiveness will be more openly acceptable in marriage relationships in the future.[34]

Not only has getting married become of decreasing importance but also the having of children. The major concern of society with marriage has always rested on its concern for children. Where there are no children, marriage becomes a totally different relationship, one that calls for little if any public surveillance. "To the extent that childlessness becomes common in the future, marriage will be increasingly private and personal and, for many husbands and wives, also more satisfactory."[35]

There are also strong social forces against having children. These did not exist in the past. They center primarily around the fear of population explosion, and there is increasingly a strong acceptance by many young people to limit the number of children they have or, in some cases, to have no children. The time may not be far off when no woman will be allowed to have more than two children. In any case we can predict that fewer marriages will involve children; and childlessness, which has long been on the decline, will increase in the future. Some women who delay birth will acquire nonfamilial roles which may be incompatible with having a child in the future. So in some cases when postponement eventually ends, the woman may have children or she may not because she has become absorbed in other roles.[36]

The following speculations about the future are suggested. First, the traditional conjugal, monogamous, legal marriage pattern will prevail for the majority, but there will be greater numbers involved in more variations from that model. Second, marriage will be less exclusive in the future. This means adults will have more close relationships during their adult years, and, as a result, marriage will become less emotionally possessive. Third, there will be a greater variety of sexual experiences both in and out of marriage. Fourth, there will be less concern with the importance of gender differences, and people will be human beings first and men and women second. Fifth, marriage will become less important to the total, adult, life cycle of the individual. This may mean that people will be married only during certain adult stages or married only to certain persons at stages of their lives. Sixth, people will have children

[34] Merven White and Carolyn Wells, "Student Attitudes Toward Alternative Marriage Forms," in Roger Libby and Robert Whitehurst, *Renovating Marriage* (California: Consensus Publishers, 1973), pp. 292–93.

[35] Jessie Bernard, *The Future of Marriage* (New York: World Publishing, 1972), p. 58.

[36] Jeanne Clare Ridley, "The Effects of Population Change on the Roles and Status of Women: Perspective and Speculation," in Constantina Sofilias-Rothschild, *Toward a Sociology of Women* (Lexington, Mass.: Xerox College Publishing, 1972), p. 380.

because they went them so there will be fewer children born. This will mean that marriage will have less dependency on the parental roles.

SELECTED BIBLIOGRAPHY

Ald, Roy *The Youth Communes.* New York: Tower Publications, 1970.

Bernard, Jessie *The Future of Marriage.* New York: World Publishing, 1972.

Gordon, Michael *The Nuclear Family in Crisis: The Search for an Alternative.* New York: Harper and Row, 1972.

Kanter, Rosabeth Moss *Commitment and Community.* Cambridge, Mass.: Harvard University Press, 1972.

Keller, Suzanne "Does the Family Have a Future?" *A Warner Modular Publication,* reprint 64 (1973), pp. 1–14.

Olson, David H. "Marriage of the Future: Revolutionary or Evolutionary Change?" *The Family Coordinator,* October 1972, pp. 383–93.

Whitehurst, Robert N. "Some Comparisons of Conventional and Counterculture Families." *The Family Coordinator,* October 1972, pp. 395–401.

Indexes

Name Index

Subject Index

603

This book has been set in 10 and 9 point Caledonia, leaded 2 points. Part numbers are 30 point Bell No. 402 italic. Chapter numbers are 24 point Bell No. 402 italic and 36 point Bodoni No. 175 italic. Part and chapter titles are 24 point Bell No. 402 italic. The size of the type page is 27 x 45½ picas.